Knowledge and Skills for Life

FIRST RESULTS FROM THE OECD PROGRAMME
FOR INTERNATIONAL STUDENT ASSESSMENT (PISA) 2000

OECD

ORGANISATION FOR ECONOMIC CO-OPERATION AND DEVELOPMENT

ORGANISATION FOR ECONOMIC CO-OPERATION AND DEVELOPMENT

Pursuant to Article 1 of the Convention signed in Paris on 14th December 1960, and which came into force on 30th September 1961, the Organisation for Economic Co-operation and Development (OECD) shall promote policies designed:

- to achieve the highest sustainable economic growth and employment and a rising standard of living in Member countries, while maintaining financial stability, and thus to contribute to the development of the world economy;
- to contribute to sound economic expansion in Member as well as non-member countries in the process of economic development; and
- to contribute to the expansion of world trade on a multilateral, non-discriminatory basis in accordance with international obligations.

The original Member countries of the OECD are Austria, Belgium, Canada, Denmark, France, Germany, Greece, Iceland, Ireland, Italy, Luxembourg, the Netherlands, Norway, Portugal, Spain, Sweden, Switzerland, Turkey, the United Kingdom and the United States. The following countries became Members subsequently through accession at the dates indicated hereafter: Japan (28th April 1964), Finland (28th January 1969), Australia (7th June 1971), New Zealand (29th May 1973), Mexico (18th May 1994), the Czech Republic (21st December 1995), Hungary (7th May 1996), Poland (22nd November 1996), Korea (12th December 1996) and the Slovak Republic (14th December 2000). The Commission of the European Communities takes part in the work of the OECD (Article 13 of the OECD Convention).

Publié en français sous le titre :

CONNAISSSANCES ET COMPÉTENCES : DES ATOUTS POUR LA VIE
PREMIERS RÉSULTATS DE PISA 2000

FOREWORD

Are students well prepared to meet the challenges of the future? Are they able to analyse, reason and communicate their ideas effectively? Do they have the capacity to continue learning throughout life? Parents, students, the public and those who run education systems need to know the answers to these questions.

Many education systems monitor student learning in order to provide some answers to these questions. Comparative international analyses can extend and enrich the national picture by providing a larger context within which to interpret national results. They can show countries their areas of relative strength and weakness and help them to monitor progress and raise aspirations. They can also provide directions for national policy, for schools' curriculum and instructional efforts and for students' learning. Coupled with appropriate incentives, they can motivate students to learn better, teachers to teach better and schools to be more effective.

In response to the need for internationally comparable evidence on student performance, the OECD has launched the Programme for International Student Assessment (PISA). PISA represents a new commitment by the governments of OECD countries to monitor the outcomes of education systems in terms of student achievement on a regular basis and within a common framework that is internationally agreed upon. PISA aims at providing a new basis for policy dialogue and for collaboration in defining and operationalising educational goals – in innovative ways that reflect judgements about the skills that are relevant to adult life. It provides inputs for standard-setting and evaluation; insights into the factors that contribute to the development of competencies and into how these factors operate in different countries, and it should lead to a better understanding of the causes and consequences of observed skill shortages. By supporting a shift in policy focus from educational inputs to learning outcomes, PISA can assist countries in seeking to bring about improvements in schooling and better preparation for young people as they enter an adult life of rapid change and deepening global interdependence.

PISA is a collaborative effort, bringing together scientific expertise from the participating countries, steered jointly by their governments on the basis of shared, policy-driven interests. Participating countries take responsibility for the project at the policy level through a Board of Participating Countries. Experts from participating countries serve on working groups that are charged with linking the PISA policy objectives with the best available substantive and technical expertise in the field of international comparative assessment of educational outcomes. Through participating in these expert groups, countries ensure that the PISA assessment instruments are internationally valid and take into account the cultural and curricular contexts of OECD Member countries, that they provide a realistic basis for measurement, and that they place an emphasis on authenticity and educational validity. The frameworks and assessment instruments for PISA 2000 are the product of a multi-year development process and were adopted by OECD Member countries in December 1999.

Knowledge and Skills for Life presents the initial results of PISA 2000. It contains evidence on the performance in reading, mathematical and scientific literacy of students, schools and countries, provides insights into the factors that influence the development of these skills at home and at school, and examines how these factors interact and what the implications are for policy development.

PISA reveals considerable variation in levels of performance between students, schools and countries. It shows that the socio-economic background of students and schools exerts an important influence on student performance, although this is much less marked in some countries than in others. More importantly, some of the countries which have been most successful in mitigating the effect of social disadvantage are among those with the highest levels of overall student performance. These countries demonstrate that it is possible to achieve high quality while minimising inequality. They define an important challenge for other countries by showing what it is possible to achieve in terms of better student performance.

PISA suggests that schools can make an important difference. However, it will require further analysis to identify precisely how school resources, policies and practices interact with home background and influence student performance. A series of more detailed thematic reports will be published in 2002 and 2003 in pursuit of a deeper understanding of how countries and schools can respond. In the meantime, the mere fact that high-quality learning outcomes are already a reality for most students in some countries is, in itself, an encouraging result that suggests that the challenges ahead can be tackled successfully.

This report is the product of a collaborative effort between the countries participating in PISA, the experts and institutions working within the framework of the PISA Consortium, and the OECD. The report was prepared by the OECD Directorate for Education, Employment, Labour and Social Affairs, principally by Andreas Schleicher in co-operation with Aletta Grisay, Barry McGaw, Claudia Tamassia, Richard J. Tobin and J. Douglas Willms (who played a leading role in the development of Chapter 8). The data underlying the report were prepared by the PISA Consortium, under the direction of Raymond Adams and Christian Monseur at the Australian Council for Educational Research. The development of the report was steered by the Board of Participating Countries, chaired by Eugene Owen of the National Center for Education Statistics in the United States. Annex C of the report lists the members of the various PISA bodies as well as the individual experts and consultants who have contributed to this report and to PISA in general.

The report is published on the responsibility of the Secretary-General of the OECD.

John P. Martin
Director for Education, Employment,
Labour and Social Affairs, OECD

Eugene Owen
Chair of the PISA Board of
Participating Countries

TABLE OF CONTENTS

LIST OF FIGURES

LIST OF BOXES

LIST OF TABLES

THE OECD PROGRAMME FOR INTERNATIONAL STUDENT ASSESSMENT

An overview of PISA

PISA seeks to assess how well 15-year-olds are prepared for life's challenges.

The OECD's Programme for International Student Assessment (PISA) is a collaborative effort among the Member countries of the OECD to measure how well young adults, at age 15 and therefore approaching the end of compulsory schooling, are prepared to meet the challenges of today's knowledge societies.[1] The assessment is forward-looking, focusing on young people's ability to use their knowledge and skills to meet real-life challenges, rather than on the extent to which they have mastered a specific school curriculum. This orientation reflects a change in the goals and objectives of curricula themselves, which are increasingly concerned with what students can do with what they learn at school, and not merely with whether they have learned it.

With the world's leading experts, participating countries and the OECD have created valid cross-country assessments…

PISA is the most comprehensive and rigorous international effort to date to assess student performance and to collect data on the student, family and institutional factors that can help to explain differences in performance. Decisions about the scope and nature of the assessments and the background information to be collected were made by leading experts in participating countries, and steered jointly by their governments on the basis of shared, policy-driven interests. Substantial efforts and resources were devoted to achieving cultural and linguistic breadth in the assessment materials. Stringent quality assurance mechanisms were applied in translation, sampling and data collection. As a consequence, the results of PISA have a high degree of validity and reliability, and can significantly improve our understanding of the outcomes of education in the world's most developed countries.

…of how students can use what they have learned in reading, mathematics and science.

PISA is based on a dynamic model of lifelong learning in which new knowledge and skills necessary for successful adaptation to a changing world are continuously acquired throughout life. PISA focuses on things that 15-year-olds will need in their future lives and seeks to assess what they can do with what they have learned. The assessment is informed – but not constrained – by the common denominator of national curricula. PISA does assess students' knowledge, but it also examines their ability to reflect on the knowledge and experience, and to apply that knowledge and experience to real world issues. For example, in order to understand and evaluate scientific advice on food safety, an adult would need not only to know some basic facts about the composition of nutrients, but also to be able to apply that information. The term "literacy" is used to encapsulate this broader conception of knowledge and skills.

PISA 2000 examined reading literacy in greatest detail. In a continuing cycle, PISA 2003 will focus on mathematical literacy, PISA 2006 on scientific literacy, and so on.

The first PISA survey was conducted in 2000 in 32 countries (including 28 OECD Member countries), using written tasks answered in schools under independently supervised test conditions. Another 13 countries will complete the same assessment in 2002 (see Figure 1.1). PISA 2000 surveyed reading literacy, mathematical literacy and scientific literacy, with a primary focus on reading. Measures of attitudes to learning, and information on how students manage their own learning, were also obtained in 25 countries as part of an international option. The survey will be repeated every three years, with the primary focus shifting to mathematics in 2003, science in 2006 and back to reading in 2009.

Figure 1.1

Countries participating in PISA

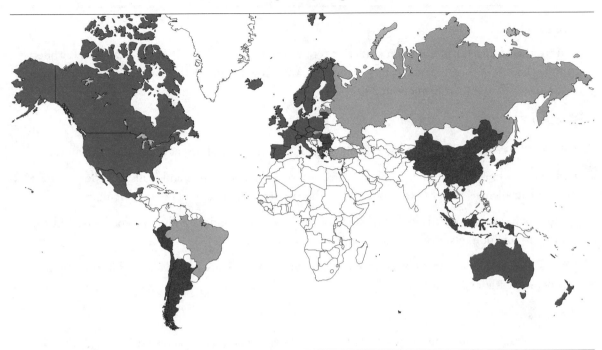

■ OECD countries participating in PISA2000

Australia
Austria
Belgium
Canada
Czech Republic
Denmark
Finland
France
Germany
Greece
Hungary
Iceland
Ireland
Italy
Japan
Korea
Luxembourg
Mexico
Netherlands
New Zealand
Norway
Poland
Portugal
Spain
Sweden
Switzerland
United Kingdom
United States

■ Non-OECD countries participating in PISA 2000

Brazil
Latvia
Liechtenstein
Russian Federation

■ Countries where the assessment will be completed in 2002

Albania
Argentina
Bulgaria
Chile
China
Special Administrative Region of Hong-Kong
Indonesia
Israel
Lithuania
Macedonia
Peru
Romania
Thailand

■ OECD countries participating in PISA from 2003 onwards

Slovak Republic
Turkey

Box 1.1 **PISA 2000 – an internationally standardised assessment of 15-year-olds**

Sample size

• More than a quarter of a million students, representing almost 17 million 15-year-olds enrolled in the schools of the 32 participating countries, were assessed in 2000. Another 13 countries will administer the same assessment in 2002.

Content

• PISA 2000 covered three domains: reading literacy, mathematical literacy and scientific literacy.

• PISA 2000 looked at young people's ability to use their knowledge and skills in order to meet real-life challenges rather than how well they had mastered a specific school curriculum.

• The emphasis was placed on the mastery of processes, the understanding of concepts, and the ability to function in various situations within each domain.

• As part of an international option taken up in 25 countries, PISA 2000 collected information on students' attitudes to learning.

Methods

• PISA 2000 used pencil-and-paper assessments, lasting two hours for each student.

• PISA 2000 used both multiple-choice items and questions requiring students to construct their own answers. Items were typically organised in units based on a passage describing a real-life situation.

• A total of seven hours of assessment items was included, with different students taking different combinations of the assessment items.

• Students answered a background questionnaire that took about 30 minutes to complete and, as part of an international option, completed questionnaires on learning and study practices as well as familiarity with computers.

• School principals completed a questionnaire about their school.

Outcomes

• A profile of knowledge and skills among 15-year-olds.

• Contextual indicators relating results to student and school characteristics.

• A knowledge base for policy analysis and research.

• Trend indicators showing how results change over time, once data become available from subsequent cycles of PISA.

Future assessments

• PISA will continue in three-year cycles. In 2003, the focus will be on mathematics and in 2006 on science. The assessment of cross-curricular competencies is being progressively integrated into PISA, beginning with an assessment of problem-solving skills in 2003.

This report summarises the performance of students and uses PISA to analyse what factors promote success in education. It presents the distributions of performance in each country, not only average scores. In addition, it uses background information on students, their schools and their education systems to examine a range of factors associated with different levels of performance. By revealing patterns of student proficiency in different countries alongside information about the characteristics and experiences of students, PISA provides a powerful tool to improve understanding of what promotes success in education. The remainder of this chapter looks in turn at:

This report summarises the performance of students in PISA 2000.

– the PISA approach;

– what PISA measures, overall and within each literacy domain, and the methods that were employed;

– how the results can be interpreted and how PISA can add to the understanding of education and lifelong learning, in ways relevant to policy-makers in each country;

– how PISA was developed; and

– how the report is organised.

The PISA approach

PISA assesses the levels of a wide range of knowledge and skills attained by 15-year-olds in the principal industrialised countries. The main features driving the development of PISA have been:

PISA is a major collaborative effort among countries to improve education policy...

– its policy orientation, with design and reporting methods determined by the need of governments to draw policy lessons;

– its innovative approach to literacy, not only in reading but also in science and mathematics;

– its focus on the demonstration of knowledge and skills in a form that is relevant to everyday life;

– its breadth of geographical coverage, with 45 countries participating, representing one third of the world population;

– its regularity, with a commitment to repeat the survey every three years;

– its collaborative nature, with governments from the participating countries jointly steering the project, and a consortium of the world's leading institutions in the field of assessment applying cutting-edge scientific know-how.

Through PISA, OECD Member countries are collaborating to improve comparative indicators on the performance of education systems. The OECD publishes a range of indicators annually in *Education at a Glance* (*e.g.*, OECD, 2001). These indicators provide information on the human and financial resources invested in education, on how education and learning systems operate and evolve, and on the individual, social and economic returns from educational

...by adding a strong, ongoing focus on outcomes to the OECD's work on international education indicators.

investment. In the past, the absence of regular and reliable indicators of educational *outcomes* across countries, especially indicators of knowledge and skills, has been a significant gap in the available data. Without such indicators, policy-makers, taxpayers, educators and parents lack a means of judging the comparative effectiveness of their education systems.

In response, the OECD has been working with Member countries to measure skills directly, through international comparative surveys. The International Adult Literacy Survey (IALS), jointly conducted between 1994 and 1998 by Statistics Canada and the OECD, provided a comparative assessment for adults. PISA is now adding measures of skills for life among school-age students.

The population surveyed is 15-year-olds enrolled in education, full-time or part-time...

In order to ensure the comparability of the results, PISA needs to assess comparable target populations. Differences between countries in the nature and extent of pre-primary education and care, in the age of entry to formal schooling, and in the structure of the education system, do not allow school grades to be defined so that they are internationally comparable. Valid international comparisons of educational performance must, therefore, define their populations with reference to a target age. PISA covers students who are aged between 15 years 3 months and 16 years 2 months at the time of the assessment, regardless of the grade or type of institution in which they are enrolled and of whether they are in full-time or part-time education. PISA excludes 15-year-olds not enrolled in educational institutions. In the remainder of this report "15-year-olds" is used as a shorthand to denote this population. With the exception of Brazil, Luxembourg and Poland, at least 95 per cent of this target population was covered in PISA 2000 by the actual samples, and more than 97 per cent in the majority of countries (for further information on the definition of the PISA population and the coverage of samples see Annex A3). This high level of coverage contributes to the comparability of the assessment results.

...enabling cross-country comparisons of the impact of differing educational experiences.

As a result, this report is able to make statements about the knowledge and skills of individuals born in the same year and still at school at 15 years of age, but having differing educational experiences, both within and outside school. The number of school grades in which these students are to be found depends on a country's policies on school entry and promotion. Furthermore, in some countries, students in the PISA target population represent different education systems, tracks or streams.

What PISA measures

PISA measures reading, mathematical and scientific literacy on continuous scales, rather than simply dividing people into those who are "literate" and those who are not.

International experts from OECD Member countries defined each of the three literacy domains examined in PISA 2000 – reading, science and mathematics – and drew up a framework for assessing it (OECD, 1999*a*). The concept of literacy used in PISA is much broader than the historical notion of the ability to read and write. Literacy is measured on a continuum, not as something that an individual either does or does not have. It may be necessary or desirable for some purposes to define a point on a literacy continuum below which levels of competence are considered inadequate, but the underlying variability is important. A literate person has a range of competencies. There is no precise dividing line between a person who is fully literate and one who is not.

The acquisition of literacy is a lifelong process – taking place not just at school or through formal learning but also through interactions with peers, colleagues and wider communities. Fifteen-year-olds cannot be expected to have learned everything they will need to know as adults, but they must have a solid foundation of knowledge in areas such as reading, mathematics and science. In order to continue learning in these domains and to apply their learning to the real world, they also need to understand elementary processes and principles and to use these flexibly in different situations. It is for this reason that PISA assesses the ability to complete tasks relating to real life, depending on a broad understanding of key concepts, rather than assessing the possession of specific knowledge.

Literacy acquisition is a lifelong process: PISA therefore assesses students' capacity to continue learning...

As well as assessing competencies in the three core domains, PISA aims progressively to examine competencies across disciplinary boundaries. PISA 2000 assessed student motivation, other aspects of students' attitudes towards learning, familiarity with computers and, under the heading "self-regulated learning", aspects of students' strategies for managing and monitoring their own learning. In subsequent PISA surveys, further "cross-curricular competencies", such as problem-solving and skills in information technologies, will play a growing role.

...and their ability to use knowledge in real life.

To what extent does PISA succeed in measuring "skills for life"? The answer will be based not only on subjective judgements about what is important in life, but also on evidence of whether people with the high levels of skills of the type which PISA measures are actually likely to succeed in life. Although the future outcomes for the students participating in PISA cannot yet be known, the International Adult Literacy Survey (IALS) shows that adults' reading and mathematical literacy skills are closely related to their labour-market success and earnings, and have an effect that is independent of their educational attainment (see Box 1.2).

The domains covered by PISA are defined in terms of:

- the **content** or **structure** of knowledge that students need to acquire in each domain (*e.g.,* familiarity with scientific concepts or various text types);

Knowledge is assessed in terms of content, processes and contexts.

- the **processes** that need to be performed (*e.g.,* retrieving written information from a text); and

- the **contexts** in which knowledge and skills are applied (*e.g.,* making decisions in relation to one's personal life, or understanding world affairs).

Box 1.2 **Does higher reading literacy improve the prospects for employment?**

The International Adult Literacy Survey (IALS) found that people with higher levels of reading literacy are more likely to be employed and to have higher average salaries than those with lower levels (OECD and Statistics Canada, 2000). Is this simply because they have better educational qualifications? If it is, then IALS (and PISA) would, at best, be measuring competencies that help people to gain a better education and, through it, better jobs. In IALS, adults who had completed some form of tertiary education scored, on average, between one and two reading literacy levels higher than those who did not complete secondary education, but there were significant numbers of adults in the 22 participating countries with a high level of reading literacy and a low level of education, or vice versa. Most importantly, reading literacy levels can help to predict how well people will do in the labour market *over and above* what can be predicted from their educational qualifications alone.

Figure 1.2 illustrates this by showing the likelihood of young people with different combinations of reading literacy and education having a white-collar, highly skilled job. The gaps between

Figure 1.2

Education, literacy and the probability of having a white-collar highly-skilled job
Probability of employment in the white-collar highly-skilled business sector, by level of education and increasing literacy score, all countries combined, IALS prose scale, population aged 26-35, 1994-1998

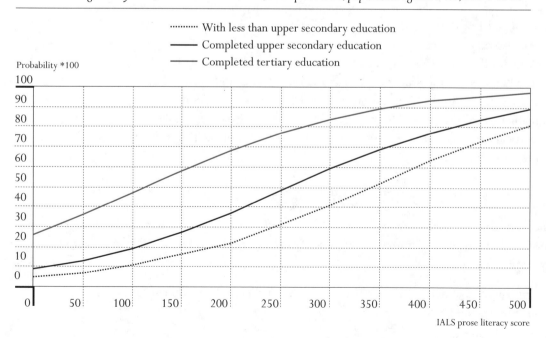

Source: OECD and Statistics Canada (2000).

the lines show the effects of increasing levels of education; the slopes of the lines show the effect of higher reading literacy at a given level of education. For a person who is between 26 and 35 years of age and working in the business sector, the probability of working in a white-collar, highly skilled job rises rapidly with an increase in reading literacy skills. The independent effect of reading literacy on labour-market outcomes is comparable to the independent effect of educational qualifications. Someone with medium qualifications (upper secondary only) has a two-in-five chance of being in a high-level job if their reading literacy level is 200 (at the low end of the scale) and a four-in-five chance if it is 400 (a high score). Conversely, someone with a medium level of reading literacy (a score of 300), has a two-in-five chance of getting such as job with a low level of education (lower secondary education only) and more than a four-in-five chance with a high level of education (a tertiary qualification).

Source: OECD and Statistics Canada (2000).

Materials in PISA are designed to assess students in each of the three domains. In order to obtain a deeper understanding of each domain over time, however, each cycle of PISA emphasises one domain. PISA 2000 concentrated on reading literacy, to which two-thirds of assessment time were devoted. Consequently, most of this report discusses the results of PISA 2000 in the field of reading literacy. In the other two domains, the report provides a summary profile of skills. In 2003, PISA will look more closely at mathematical literacy, and in 2006, at scientific literacy.

Reading literacy in PISA

Reading literacy is defined in PISA as the ability to understand, use and reflect on written texts in order to achieve one's goals, to develop one's knowledge and potential, and to participate effectively in society. This definition goes beyond the notion that reading literacy means decoding written material and literal comprehension. Reading incorporates understanding and reflecting on texts. Literacy involves the ability of individuals to use written information to fulfil their goals, and the consequent ability of complex modern societies to use written information to function effectively. PISA 2000 employed about 140 items representing the kinds of reading literacy that 15-year-olds would require in the future. Examples of the assessment items used in PISA to assess reading literacy can be found in Chapter 2 and the PISA Web site *www.pisa.oecd.org*.

PISA defines reading literacy as the ability to understand, use and reflect on written texts in order to participate effectively in life.

Readers respond to a given text in a variety of ways as they seek to use and understand what they are reading. This dynamic process has many dimensions, three of which were used to construct the PISA assessments:

PISA reading literacy tasks…

...are based on a variety of text forms, not just prose.

— The ***form of reading material***, or text. Many past assessments of reading literacy have focused on prose organised in sentences and paragraphs, or "continuous texts". PISA includes continuous *prose* passages and distinguishes between different types of prose, such as *narration*, *exposition* and *argumentation*. In addition, PISA includes "non-continuous texts", which present information in other ways, including *lists, forms, graphs* and *diagrams*. This variety is based on the principle that individuals encounter a range of written texts at school and in adult life that require different information-processing techniques. Flexibility, or the skill to match the type of text to the techniques that are appropriate for locating relevant information in the text, characterises efficient reading.

Students are expected to retrieve information from a text, to understand it and to reflect on it...

— The ***type of reading task***. This is determined, at one level, by the cognitive skills that are needed to be an effective reader and, at another, by the characteristics of the questions in PISA. The focus of PISA is on "reading to learn", rather than "learning to read". Students are thus not assessed on the most basic reading skills; it is assumed that most 15-year-olds have already acquired these. Rather, they are expected to demonstrate their proficiency in *retrieving* information, *understanding* texts at a general level, *interpreting* them, *reflecting* on the content and form of texts in relation to their own knowledge of the world, and *evaluating* and *arguing* their own point of view.

... and to relate it to a variety of situations in which written materials are encountered.

— The ***use for which the text was constructed*** - its context or situation. For example, a novel, personal letter or biography is written for people's "*private*" use. Official documents or announcements are for "*public*" use. A manual or report may be for "*occupational*" use and a textbook or worksheet for "*educational*" use.

Mathematical literacy in PISA

PISA defines mathematical literacy as the ability to formulate and solve mathematical problems in situations encountered in life.

Mathematical literacy is defined in PISA as the capacity to identify, understand and engage in mathematics, and to make well-founded judgements about the role that mathematics plays in an individual's current and future private life, occupational life, social life with peers and relatives, and life as a constructive, concerned and reflective citizen. As with reading, the definition revolves around the wider uses of mathematics in people's lives rather than being limited to mechanical operations. "Mathematical literacy" is used here to indicate the ability to put mathematical knowledge and skills to functional use rather than just mastering them within a school curriculum. To "engage in" mathematics covers not simply physical or social actions (such as deciding how much change to give someone in a shop) but also wider uses, including taking a point of view and appreciating things expressed mathematically (such as having an opinion about a government's spending plans). Mathematical literacy also implies the ability to pose and solve mathematical problems in a variety of situations, as well as the inclination to do so, which often relies on personal traits such as self-confidence and curiosity.

In order to transform this definition into an assessment of mathematical literacy, three broad dimensions were identified for use in PISA 2000:

— The **content of mathematics.** Content is defined primarily in terms of clusters of relevant, connected mathematical concepts that appear in real situations and contexts. These include quantity, space and shape, change and relationships, and uncertainty. The choice of these topics does not mean that more specific strands of the school curriculum, such as numbers, algebra and geometry, have been ignored. PISA 2000 established tasks that required students to have mastered a balanced mathematical curriculum. However, due to the fact that mathematics was only a minor domain in PISA 2000, the scope of the assessment in this area was more limited, with an emphasis on *change and relationships* and *space and shape*. These concepts were selected to allow a wide range of curriculum strands to be represented, without giving undue weight to number skills.

— The **process of mathematics.** Questions in PISA are structured around different types of skills needed for mathematics. Such skills are organised into three "competency clusters": the first cluster – *reproduction* – consists of simple computations or definitions of the type most familiar in conventional assessments of mathematics; the second – *connections* – requires the bringing together of mathematical ideas and procedures to solve straightforward and somewhat familiar problems; and the third cluster – *reflection* – consists of mathematical thinking, generalisation and insight, and requires students to engage in analysis, to identify the mathematical elements in a situation, and to pose their own problems.

— The **situations in which mathematics is used.** Mathematical literacy is assessed by giving students "authentic" tasks – based on situations which, while sometimes fictional, represent the kinds of problem encountered in real life. The situations vary in terms of "distance" from individuals – from those affecting people directly (*e.g.,* deciding whether a purchase offers value for money) to scientific problems of more general interest. In order of closeness to the student, the situations are classified as *private life/personal, school life, work and sports, local community and society,* and *scientific.*

Scientific literacy in PISA

Scientific literacy relates to the ability to think scientifically in a world in which science and technology shape lives. Such literacy requires an understanding of scientific concepts as well as an ability to apply a scientific perspective. PISA defines scientific literacy as the capacity to use scientific knowledge, to identify questions, and to draw evidence-based conclusions in order to understand and help make decisions about the natural world and the changes made to it through human activity.

Scientific literacy is considered a key outcome of education by age 15 for all students, whether or not they continue to learn science thereafter. Scientific

PISA mathematical literacy tasks…

…require students to be familiar with key mathematical concepts,…

… to reproduce standard mathematical operations, to make connections and to engage in wider mathematical thinking,…

…in various real-life situations.

PISA defines scientific literacy as the ability to think scientifically…

…in the belief that such thinking is needed by the many, not the few.

thinking is required by citizens, not just scientists. The inclusion of scientific literacy as a general competency for life reflects the growing centrality of scientific and technological questions. The definition used in PISA does not imply that tomorrow's adults will need large reserves of scientific knowledge. The key is to be able to think scientifically about the evidence that they will encounter. PISA 2000 was developed around three dimensions of scientific literacy:

PISA scientific literacy tasks require students to understand certain key scientific concepts,...

— **Scientific concepts**. Students need to grasp a number of key concepts in order to understand certain phenomena of the natural world and the changes made to it through human activity. These are the broad integrating ideas that help to explain aspects of the physical environment. PISA asks questions that bring together concepts drawn from physics, chemistry, the biological sciences, and earth and space sciences. More specifically, concepts are drawn from a number of themes including biodiversity, forces and movement, and physiological change.

...and to show that they can acquire, interpret and act on evidence,...

— **Scientific processes**. PISA assesses the ability to *use* scientific knowledge and understanding, namely students' ability to acquire, interpret and act on evidence. PISA examines five such processes: the recognition of scientific *questions*; the identification of *evidence*; the drawing of *conclusions*; the *communication* of these conclusions; and the demonstration of *understanding* of scientific concepts.

... in situations where science can be applied.

— **Scientific situations** and areas of application. The context of scientific literacy in PISA is principally everyday life rather than the classroom or laboratory. As with the other forms of literacy, the context thus includes issues that have a bearing on life in general as well as matters of direct personal concern. Questions in PISA 2000 were grouped in three areas in which science is applied: science in life and health; science in earth and the environment; and science in technology.

How PISA assesses students and collects information

Students were assessed for two hours in PISA and filled out a questionnaire, as did their principals.

PISA 2000 was carefully designed by an international network of leading institutions and experts to serve the purposes described above. Each student participated, in his/her own school, in a written assessment session of two hours, and spent about half an hour responding to a questionnaire about himself or herself. School principals were asked to give further information on school characteristics in another 30-minute questionnaire.

The assessment contained many different kinds of tasks...

The student assessments followed the same principles in each of the three domains and will do so from one survey to the next, although the amount of assessment material in each domain will differ in each three-year cycle. In PISA 2000, where the main focus was reading literacy, PISA was implemented in the following ways (for details, see the *PISA 2000 Technical Report*):

— *A wide range of assessment items*. PISA 2000 assessments were in printed form, with questions taking a range of formats. Students were required to consider written passages and diagrams, and to answer a series of questions on each. Much of the material was designed to determine whether students could reflect and think actively about the domain. Examples of items are given in Chapters 2 and 3.

— *Broad coverage of the domain*. Each student was assessed for two hours, but not all students were given the same assessment items. A range of items, equivalent to seven hours of assessment time, was drawn up in order to cover all the areas. Different combinations of items were grouped in nine different assessment booklets. Each item appeared in several booklets, which ensured that each was answered by a representative sample of students. Each student received one booklet.

…with widely varied content.

— *Co-operation between all participating countries in the development of internationally valid assessments*. On the basis of the internationally agreed assessment frameworks and test specifications, countries developed assessment items that were reviewed by subject-matter specialists and assessment experts. Additional items were developed to ensure that all areas of the frameworks were covered adequately. Items were pilot tested, the results were reviewed, and the revised set of items was then validated in a field trial. Finally, in order to ensure that the items were valid across countries, languages and cultures, items were rated by participating countries for cultural appropriateness, curricular and non-curricular relevance, and appropriate level of difficulty.

Thorough procedures ensured that tasks were valid across countries…

— *Standardised procedures for the preparation and implementation of the assessment*. PISA represents an unprecedented effort to achieve comparability of results across countries, cultures and languages. In addition to comprehensive coverage of 15-year-old students in each country, these efforts have included co-operation with a wide range of experts in all participating countries, the development of standardised procedures for the preparation and implementation of the assessment, and rigorous attention to quality control throughout. The assessment instruments were prepared in both English and French, and then translated into the languages of participating countries using procedures that ensured the linguistic integrity and equivalence of the instruments. For non-English and non-French speaking countries, two independent translations of the assessment instruments were prepared and then consolidated, drawing, in most cases, on both source versions. For further information on the PISA standards and procedures see Annexes A3-A7.

…and rigorous efforts were made to deliver the test in equivalent ways in different countries.

Reading literacy was assessed using a series of texts, students being set a number of tasks on each text. Forty-five per cent of the tasks required students to construct their own responses, either by providing a brief answer from a wide range of possible answers or by constructing a longer response, allowing for the possibility of divergent, individual responses and opposing viewpoints. The

About half of the reading literacy questions required students to construct their own responses…

latter items usually asked students to relate information or ideas in the stimulus text to their own experience or opinions, the acceptability of their answer depending less on the position taken by the student than on the ability to use what they had read when justifying or explaining that position. Partial credit was provided for partially correct or less sophisticated answers, and all of these items were marked by hand. A further 45 per cent of the items were asked in multiple-choice format, in which students either made one choice from among four or five given alternatives or a series of choices by circling a word or short phrase (for example "yes" or "no") for each point. The remaining 10 per cent of the items required students to construct their response from among a limited range of acceptable answers.

...while the majority of mathematical literacy tasks ...

Mathematical literacy was assessed through a combination of question types. As with reading literacy, there were a number of units, each presenting a situation or problem on which students were set several questions or tasks. Different combinations of diagrams and written information introduced each unit. About two-thirds of the items were in a form that could be marked unambiguously as correct or incorrect. Students demonstrated their proficiency by answering problems correctly and showing whether they understood the underlying mathematical principles involved in the task. For more complex items, students could gain full or partial credit.

...and scientific literacy tasks had unambiguously right and wrong answers.

Scientific literacy was assessed in a manner similar to that of mathematical literacy, using a series of units, each of which presented a real scientific situation, followed by questions about it. Some two-thirds of the items were in a form that could be marked unambiguously as correct or incorrect. For more complex items, students could gain full or partial credit.

Student questionnaires gathered information on students' background and activities; in many countries, students also reported on how they learned.

The PISA context questionnaires collected information that was important for the interpretation and analysis of the results. The questionnaires asked about students' characteristics, such as gender, economic and social background, and activities at home and school. As part of an international option, many students also reported on their attitudes towards learning, familiarity with computers and, under the heading "self-regulated learning", strategies for managing and monitoring their own learning. School principals in the schools in which students were assessed were asked about the characteristics of their school (such as size and resources) and how they organised learning.

Interpreting the results of PISA

PISA results are outcomes not only of schooling but also of learning more generally...

If one country's PISA scores are higher than those of another country, it cannot automatically be inferred that the schools in the former are more effective, since learning starts well before school and occurs in a range of institutional and out-of-school settings. Nonetheless, if a country's PISA scores are higher, one can legitimately conclude that the cumulative impact of all the learning experiences in that country, from early childhood up to the age of 15, in and out of school, has resulted in more desirable outcomes in the domains that PISA assesses.

As readers of this report will notice, the results of PISA 2000 often confirm and complement the findings of previous international assessments, such as the Third International Mathematics and Science Study (TIMSS), which was conducted in 1995 by the International Association for the Evaluation of Educational Achievement (IEA) among students in grades 3-4, 7-8 and the final year of secondary school, and repeated in 1999 among students in the 8th grade. However, some PISA findings differ from the results of TIMSS. Such differences are not unexpected, given the differences between the two studies. The assessment materials in TIMSS were constructed on the basis of an analysis of the intended curriculum in each participating country, so as to cover the core material common to the curriculum in the majority of participating countries. The assessment materials in PISA 2000, as described above, covered the range of skills and competencies that were, in the respective assessment domains, considered to be crucial to an individual's capacity to fully participate in, and contribute meaningfully to, a successful modern society. Finally, it needs to be borne in mind that the age-based PISA target population of 15-year-olds differs from the grade-based population employed in TIMSS.

...and therefore differ in some respects from the results of assessments focusing on the school curriculum.

How PISA can inform policy

PISA provides a broad assessment of comparative learning outcomes towards the end of compulsory schooling, which can both guide policy decisions and resource allocations, and provide insights into the factors that contribute to the development of knowledge and skills, and the extent to which these factors are common to different countries.

PISA provides insights into what contributes to learning outcomes.

PISA provides international comparisons of the performance of education systems, with strong, cross-culturally valid measures of competencies that are relevant to everyday, adult life. Assessments that test only mastery of the school curriculum can offer a measure of the *internal* efficiency of school systems. They do not reveal how effectively schools prepare students for life after they have completed their formal education.

It seeks to compare how well different school systems prepare students for life.

The information yielded by PISA allows policy-makers to look closely at the factors associated with educational success, not just to make comparisons between results in isolation. PISA can tell them, for example, how wide the performance gap is between students from richer and poorer homes in their own country, in comparison with those in other countries. PISA also offers insights into the characteristics of schools – such as the way in which learning is organised – and how these characteristics are associated with levels of student proficiency. Data from PISA can be used to look at which aspects of student attitudes seem to make the greatest contribution to learning. In these and many other ways, PISA offers a new approach to considering school outcomes, using as its evidence base the experiences of students across the world rather than in the specific cultural context of a single country. The international context allows policy-makers to question assumptions about the quality of their own country's educational outcomes.

It identifies and compares the relationships of individual, home and school characteristics with student performance...

...and thus allows countries to look at their own education system in the light of other countries' performance.

The international perspective of PISA offers policy-makers a lens through which to recognise the strengths and weaknesses of their own systems. The fact that some countries can achieve a high average level of student performance with only a modest gap between the highest and lowest level of student performance, as shown in Chapter 2, suggests that large disparities in outcomes do not have to be the price for high average performance. Similarly, the fact that the strength of the relationship between social background and learning outcomes varies widely between countries, as shown in Chapter 8, demonstrates that schools and education systems can succeed in moderating this relationship. Low levels of performance by students from lower social backgrounds is not inevitable. There are things that schools – and policy-makers – can do about poor performance.

The ongoing PISA cycle will allow countries to monitor changes in performance over time.

Finally, by reporting on student competencies to a preset timetable, PISA will enable governments regularly to monitor the progress of their education systems in terms of student outcomes and to evaluate national policies in the light of other countries' performances. The results of PISA 2000 reported here provide a baseline. In 2003, 2006, 2009 and so on, countries will be able to see what progress they have made.

In parallel with this first international report, most participating countries are publishing national reports that examine the findings from PISA and their policy implications in the national economic, social and educational context. Further, more detailed international, thematic reports are being prepared, using the outcomes from PISA 2000 to explore specific issues and their implications for policy. These thematic reports will give particular attention to issues of equity: gender differences in student performance, attitudes and motivation; the needs of both the most vulnerable and the exceptionally well-performing students; the role of engagement and motivation as prerequisites for adequate performance and future destinations; the nature, development and impact of literacy skills; and aspects of learning strategies and self-concept.

Developing PISA – a collaborative effort

PISA is the result of effective co-operation between national organisations, subject-matter experts, and school authorities...

PISA is a substantial, collaborative effort by the Member countries of the OECD to provide a new kind of assessment of student performance on a recurring basis. The assessments were developed co-operatively, agreed by participating countries, and implemented by national organisations. The constructive co-operation by teachers and principals in participating schools has been a crucial factor contributing to the success of PISA during all stages of the development and implementation.

...and is steered jointly by governments on the basis of shared, policy-driven interests...

A Board of Participating Countries, representing all countries at senior policy levels, laid down policy priorities and standards for the development of indicators, the establishment of the assessment instruments, and the reporting of results. Experts from participating countries served on working groups linking the programme's policy objectives with the best internationally available technical expertise in the three assessment domains. By participating in these expert groups, countries ensured that the instruments were internationally valid and took into account the cultural and educational contexts of the different OECD Member countries, that the assessment materials had strong measurement potential, and that the instruments emphasised authenticity and educational validity.

Participating countries implemented PISA at the national level through National Project Managers, subject to technical and administrative procedures common to all participating countries. These managers played a vital role in the development and validation of the international assessment instruments and ensured that the implementation of PISA was of high quality. They also contributed to the verification and evaluation of the survey results, analyses and reports.

The design and implementation of PISA 2000, within the framework established by the Board of Participating Countries, was the responsibility of an international consortium led by the Australian Council for Educational Research (ACER). The other partners in this consortium were the National Institute for Educational Measurement (CITO) in the Netherlands, Westat and the Education Testing Service (ETS) in the United States, and the National Institute for Educational Policy Research (NIER) in Japan.

The OECD Secretariat had overall managerial responsibility for the programme, monitored its implementation on a day-to-day basis, served as the secretariat for the Board of Participating Countries, fostered the building of a consensus between the countries involved, and served as the interlocutor between the Board of Participating Countries and the international consortium.

...through the OECD.

PISA is jointly financed by all participating countries.

Organisation of this report

Chapters 2 and **3** describe student performance in the three PISA literacy domains, and **Chapter 4** extends this with a profile of what students are like as learners at age 15 – in terms of their motivation, their engagement, their learning strategies and their beliefs in their own capacities. It also includes a description of students' familiarity with computers.

This report looks in turn at students' performance,...

Chapter 5 examines gender differences in student performance in the three literacy domains, for students overall and for specific sub-groups of students.

...at gender differences,...

Chapters 6 and **7** then situate student performance in the context of students' backgrounds and the broader learning environment. Chapter 6 focuses on a description of the family backgrounds of students, including aspects of the economic, cultural and social background, followed by Chapter 7 which then examines how the learning environment and the organisation of schools varies between countries. Chapter 7 also looks at the human and financial resources that countries invest in education, and at selected characteristics of national education systems.

...at the performance of students with different backgrounds and learning experiences...

...and at what these differences tell policy-makers about which factors are important.

Finally, **Chapter 8** seeks to expand upon these findings and addresses questions about the nature of the relationship between school performance and social background. Through an analysis of the simultaneous relationships between several different variables in a wide range of settings and a number of countries, including both family and school factors, it is possible to estimate the separate and overlapping influences of these factors, and to gauge the relative importance of school resources and school policy and practices in different types of school system. This can provide indications of what educational policy can do both to improve average performance and to moderate the impact of family background on student performance.

Note

1. In most OECD countries, the age at which compulsory schooling ends is 15 or 16 years, but in the United States it is 17 years and in Belgium, Germany and the Netherlands it is 18 years (OECD, 2001).

READERS' GUIDE

Data underlying the figures

The data referred to in Chapters 2 to 8 of this report are presented in Annex B1 and, with additional detail, on the web site *www.pisa.oecd.org*. Four symbols are used to denote missing data:

a The category does not apply in the country concerned. Data are therefore missing.

c There are too few observations to provide reliable estimates (*i.e.,* there are fewer than five schools or fewer than 30 students with valid data for this cell).

m Data are not available. Unless otherwise noted, these data were collected but subsequently removed from the publication for technical or other reasons at the request of the country concerned.

x Data are included in another category or column of the table.

Calculation of international averages

An OECD average was calculated for most indicators presented in this report. In the case of some indicators, a total representing the OECD area as a whole was also calculated:

– The **OECD average**, sometimes also referred to as the **country average**, is the mean of the data values for all OECD countries for which data are available or can be estimated. The OECD average can be used to see how a country compares on a given indicator with a typical OECD country. The OECD average does not take into account the absolute size of the student population in each country, *i.e.,* each country contributes equally to the average.

– The **OECD total** takes the OECD countries as a single entity, to which each country contributes in proportion to the number of 15-year-olds enrolled in its schools (see Annex A3 for data). It illustrates how a country compares with the OECD area as a whole.

Three OECD countries are excluded from the calculation of averages or other aggregate estimates: the Netherlands, the Slovak Republic (which became a Member of the OECD in 2000) and Turkey. The Netherlands are excluded because low response rates preclude reliable estimates of mean scores (see Annex A3). The Slovak Republic and Turkey will join PISA from the 2003 survey cycle onwards.

In the case of other countries, data may not be available for specific indicators, or specific data categories may not apply. Readers should, therefore, keep in mind that the terms *OECD average* and *OECD total* refer to the OECD countries included in the respective comparisons.

Reporting of student data

The report usually uses "15-year-olds" as shorthand for the PISA target population. In practice, this refers to students who were aged between 15 years and 3 (complete) months and 16 years and 2 (complete) months at the beginning of the assessment period and who were enrolled in an educational institution, regardless of the grade level or type of institution, and of whether they were attending full-time or part-time (for details see Annex A3).

Reporting of school data

The principals of the schools in which students were assessed provided information on their school's characteristics by completing a school questionnaire. Where responses from school principals are presented in this publication, they are weighted so that they are proportionate to the number of 15-year-olds enrolled in the school.

Rounding of figures

Because of rounding, some figures in tables may not exactly add up to the totals. Totals, differences and averages are always calculated on the basis of exact numbers and are rounded only after calculation.

Abbreviations used in this report

GDP   Gross Domestic Product
ISCED   International Standard Classification of Education
PPP   Purchasing Power Parity
RP   Response probability
SD   Standard deviation
SE   Standard error

Further documentation

For further information on the PISA assessment instruments and the methods used in PISA, see the *PISA 2000 Technical Report* (available in February 2002) and the PISA Web site (*www.pisa.oecd.org*).

WHAT PISA SHOWS THAT
15–YEAR–OLDS CAN DO:
A PROFILE OF STUDENT PERFORMANCE
IN READING LITERACY

Introduction

This chapter describes how PISA measures reading literacy, how many students are proficient at different levels of reading literacy, and how performance scores are distributed across countries.

This chapter provides a profile of student performance in reading literacy:

– First, the chapter explains how proficiency in reading literacy is scored in PISA, using three scales on which students are assigned *scores* according to their performance in tasks of varying difficulty.

– Second, the chapter describes proficiency in each country in terms of the range of performance of its students. To facilitate this description, each scale is divided into five levels of increasing proficiency, and each country's distribution is reported in terms of the percentages of students at each level. The levels are illustrated with examples of the tasks that a student must complete satisfactorily in order to reach each successive level.

– Third, the chapter summarises performance in each country in terms of the *mean* scores achieved by students and the *distribution* of scores across student populations.

Chapters 3 and 4 look at mathematical and scientific literacy and at how students learn.

Chapter 3 complements this with an analysis of student performance in mathematical and scientific literacy, and an examination of how performance in these domains differs from performance in reading literacy. Chapter 4 broadens the profile of PISA results further with students' reports on their familiarity with computers, their learning strategies and non-cognitive outcomes of schooling that are important for lifelong learning: their motivation, their engagement, and their belief in their own capacities.

How reading literacy is measured in PISA

PISA 2000 presented students with a range of reading tasks using different text forms and contexts...

The concept of reading literacy in PISA has three dimensions, which have guided the development of the assessment: the type of reading task, the form and structure of the reading material, and the use for which the text was constructed. Personal competence is best understood in terms of the first of these. The other two are properties of the task materials that were helpful in ensuring that a range of diverse tasks were included in the tests.

...and reported their skills in retrieving information, interpreting texts, and reflection and evaluation...

The "type of reading task" dimension is measured on three scales. A "retrieving information" scale reports on students' ability to locate information in a text. An "interpreting texts" scale reports on the ability to construct meaning and draw inferences from written information. A "reflection and evaluation" scale reports on students' ability to relate text to their knowledge, ideas and experiences. In addition, a combined reading literacy scale summarises the results from the three reading literacy scales.

...on scales in which two-thirds of students scored within 100 points of a 500-point average.

To facilitate the interpretation of the scores assigned to students, the combined reading literacy scale was designed to have an average score of 500 points, with about two-thirds of students across OECD countries scoring between 400 and 600 points. [1] These reference points provide an "anchor" for the measurement of student performance. The mean scores for the three scales that contribute to the combined reading scale differ slightly from 500.

The scores on each scale represent degrees of proficiency in a particular aspect of reading literacy. For example, a low score on the interpreting scale indicates that a student has limited skills in understanding relationships, constructing meaning or drawing inferences from one or more parts of a text. By contrast, a high score on the interpreting scale indicates that a student has advanced skills in this area.

Results are summarised by five levels of proficiency...

There are easier and harder tasks for each of the three reading literacy scales and there is no hierarchical relationship between the three scales. Each of the three reading literacy scales is divided into five levels of knowledge and skills. Level 5 corresponds to a score of more than 625, Level 4 to scores in the range 553 to 625, Level 3 to scores from 481 to 552, Level 2 to scores from 408 to 480, and Level 1 to scores from 335 to 407.

Students at a particular level not only demonstrate the knowledge and skills associated with that level but also the proficiencies required at lower levels. Thus all students proficient at Level 3 are also proficient at Levels 1 and 2. All students at a given level are expected to answer at least half of the items at that level correctly.

... students being assigned to the highest level at which they can be expected to do most of the tasks.

Students scoring below 335 points, *i.e.,* those who do not reach Level 1, are not able routinely to show the most basic skills that PISA seeks to measure. While such performance should not be interpreted to mean that those students have no literacy skills at all,[2] performance below Level 1 does signal serious deficiencies in students' ability to use reading literacy as a tool for the acquisition of knowledge and skills in other areas.

The division of the scales into levels of difficulty and of performance makes it possible not only to rank students' performance but also to describe what they can do (see Figure 2.1). Each successive reading level is associated with tasks of ascending difficulty. The tasks at each level of reading literacy were judged by panels of experts to share many features and requirements and to differ consistently from tasks at either higher or lower levels. The assumed difficulty of tasks was then validated empirically on the basis of student performance in participating countries.

Each level can be described in terms of what students at that level can do.

The reading literacy tasks used in PISA 2000 vary widely in terms of text type, situation and task requirements (see Chapter 1) as well as difficulty. Figure 2.2 shows sample items from three of the 36 units containing tasks that were used in PISA 2000, together with the associated reading literacy skills demonstrated by students at the various levels of the three reading literacy scales. The descriptions reflect the skills assessed by each item. These descriptions provide some insight into the range of processes required of students and the proficiencies which they need to demonstrate at various points along the reading literacy scales. A more complete set of sample tasks can be found at *www.pisa.oecd.org*.

Figure 2.1
What the proficiency levels measure

Retrieving information	Interpreting texts	Reflection and evaluation
What is being assessed on each of the reading literacy scales:		
Retrieving information is defined as locating one or more pieces of information in a text.	Interpreting texts is defined as constructing meaning and drawing inferences from one or more parts of a text.	Reflecting and evaluation is defined as relating a text to one's experience, knowledge and ideas.
Characteristics of the tasks associated with increasing difficulty on each of the reading literacy scales:		
Task difficulty depends on the number of pieces of information that need to be located. Difficulty also depends on the number of conditions that must be met to locate the requested information, and on whether what is retrieved needs to be sequenced in a particular way. Difficulty also depends on the prominence of information, and the familiarity of the context. Other relevant characteristics are the complexity of the text, and the presence and strength of competing information.	Task difficulty depends on the type of interpretation required, with the easiest tasks requiring identifying the main idea in a text, more difficult tasks requiring understanding relationships that are part of the text, and the most difficult requiring either an understanding of the meaning of language in context, or analogical reasoning. Difficulty also depends on how explicitly the text provides the ideas or information the reader needs in order to complete the task; on how prominent the required information is; and on how much competing information is present. Finally, the length and complexity of the text and the familiarity of its content affect difficulty.	Task difficulty depends on the type of reflection required, with the easiest tasks requiring simple connections or explanations relating the text to external experience, and the more difficult requiring an hypothesis or evaluation. Difficulty also depends on the familiarity of the knowledge that must be drawn on from outside the text; on the complexity of the text; on the level of textual understanding demanded; and on how explicitly the reader is directed to relevant factors in both the task and the text.

Level

	Retrieving information	Interpreting texts	Reflection and evaluation
5	Locate and possibly sequence or combine multiple pieces of deeply embedded information, some of which may be outside the main body of the text. Infer which information in the text is relevant to the task. Deal with highly plausible and/or extensive competing information.	Either construe the meaning of nuanced language or demonstrate a full and detailed understanding of a text.	Critically evaluate or hypothesise, drawing on specialised knowledge. Deal with concepts that are contrary to expectations and draw on a deep understanding of long or complex texts.
4	Locate and possibly sequence or combine multiple pieces of embedded information, each of which may need to meet multiple criteria, in a text with unfamiliar context or form. Infer which information in the text is relevant to the task.	Use a high level of text-based inference to understand and apply categories in an unfamiliar context, and to construe the meaning of a section of text by taking into account the text as a whole. Deal with ambiguities, ideas that are contrary to expectation and ideas that are negatively worded.	Use formal or public knowledge to hypothesise about or critically evaluate a text. Show accurate understanding of long or complex texts.
3	Locate, and in some cases recognise, the relationship between pieces of information, each of which may need to meet multiple criteria. Deal with prominent competing information.	Integrate several parts of a text in order to identify a main idea, understand a relationship or construe the meaning of a word or phrase. Compare, contrast or categorise taking many criteria into account. Deal with competing information.	Make connections or comparisons, give explanations, or evaluate a feature of text. Demonstrate a detailed understanding of the text in relation to familiar, everyday knowledge, or draw on less common knowledge.
2	Locate one or more pieces of information, each of which may be required to meet multiple criteria. Deal with competing information.	Identify the main idea in a text, understand relationships, form or apply simple categories, or construe meaning within a limited part of the text when the information is not prominent and low-level inferences are required.	Make a comparison or connections between the text and outside knowledge, or explain a feature of the text by drawing on personal experience and attitudes.
1	Take account of a single criterion to locate one or more independent pieces of explicitly stated information.	Recognise the main theme or author's purpose in a text about a familiar topic, when the required information in the text is prominent.	Make a simple connection between information in the text and common, everyday knowledge.

Source: OECD PISA, 2001.

Even a cursory glance at Figure 2.2 will reveal that, as might be expected, tasks at the lower end of each scale require very different skills from those at the higher end. A more careful analysis of the range of tasks along each reading literacy scale provides some indication of an ordered set of knowledge-construction skills and strategies. For example, all tasks on the retrieving information scale require students to locate information in prose texts or other forms of writing. The easiest tasks on this scale require students to locate explicitly stated information according to a single criterion where there is little, if any, competing information in the text.

Tasks at the lower end of each of the three reading scales require direct and straightforward use of text.

By contrast, tasks at the high end of this scale require students to locate and sequence multiple pieces of deeply embedded information, sometimes in accordance with multiple criteria. Often there is competing information in the text that shares some features with the information required for the answer. Similarly, on the interpreting scale and the reflection and evaluation scale, tasks at the lower end differ from those at the higher end in terms of the process needed to answer them correctly, the degree to which the reading strategies required for a correct answer are signalled in the question or the instructions, the level of complexity and familiarity of the text, and the quantity of competing or distracting information present in the text.

Difficult tasks at the top ends require more complex use of text and of the ideas expressed in it.

A description of the conceptual framework underlying the PISA assessment of reading literacy is provided in *Measuring Student Knowledge and Skills — A New Framework for Assessment* (OECD, 1999a).

Percentage of students proficient at each level of reading literacy

If students' proficiency is described in terms of five levels of reading literacy, it is possible either to indicate what proportion of them are proficient at a particular level or to identify the percentage that are proficient *at most* at that level (as presented in Tables 2.1a-d) — meaning that it is their highest level of proficiency. However, knowing that 10 per cent of students in one country and 20 per cent in another are exactly at, say, Level 3 is not especially meaningful without also knowing the percentages at the other levels. It is therefore generally more useful to know the

The results for a population can be expressed as the percentage of students within a particular level or as the percentage reaching at least a particular level (that is, at that level or above).

Box 2.1 **How to read Figure 2.2**

In the same way that students are allocated a performance score on each PISA scale, the level of difficulty of the tasks set can also be expressed in terms of these scales. While students receive scale scores according to their performance in the assessment tasks, the difficulty of a task is derived from the average performance in that task of students in all countries.

For example, Question 13 from the Reading Unit *Graffiti*, shown in Figure 2.2, requires students to compare claims made in two short texts with their own views and attitudes, and has a notional level of difficulty of 471 points. A student with a score of 471 is expected to be capable of dealing with tasks up to this level of difficulty. That does not mean that every student receiving a score of 471 or above will have answered this item correctly or that all students receiving scores below 471 will have answered it incorrectly. Nor does it mean that students with a score of 471 will answer correctly all items with a notional level of difficulty below this point and will answer incorrectly all items with a level of difficulty above it. The difficulty of a task is established in such as way that students with a score equal to that of a given item will have a known [3] probability of answering it correctly. Students with scores above/below 471 points will have a greater/smaller likelihood of answering the item taken as an example here (and others like it) correctly.

Students' answers to some open-ended questions may be partially correct, in which case they receive a partial credit, corresponding to a lower score on the proficiency scale than that of a fully correct answer.

Figure 2.2

Samples of the reading tasks used in PISA

GRAFFITI

I'm simmering with anger as the school wall is cleaned and repainted for the fourth time to get rid of graffiti. Creativity is admirable but people should find ways to express themselves that do not inflict extra costs upon society.

Why do you spoil the reputation of young people by painting graffiti where it's forbidden? Professional artists do not hang their paintings in the streets, do they? Instead they seek funding and gain fame through legal exhibitions.

In my opinion buildings, fences and park benches are works of art in themselves. It's really pathetic to spoil this architecture with graffiti and what's more, the method destroys the ozone layer. Really, I can't understand why these criminal artists bother as their "artistic works" are just removed from sight over and over again.

Helga

There is no accounting for taste. Society is full of communication and advertising. Company logos, shop names. Large intrusive posters on the streets. Are they acceptable? Yes, mostly. Is graffiti acceptable? Some people say yes, some no.

Who pays the price for graffiti? Who is ultimately paying the price for advertisements? Correct. The consumer.

Have the people who put up billboards asked your permission? No. Should graffiti painters do so then? Isn't it all just a question of communication – your own name, the names of gangs and large works of art in the street?

Think about the striped and chequered clothes that appeared in the stores a few years ago. And ski wear. The patterns and colours were stolen directly from the flowery concrete walls. It's quite amusing that these patterns and colours are accepted and admired but that graffiti in the same style is considered dreadful.

Times are hard for art.

Sophia

These two letters come from the Internet and are about graffiti. Graffiti is illegal painting and writing on walls and elsewhere. Refer to the letters to answer the questions.

Retrieving information	**Interpreting texts**	**Reflection and evaluation**
LEVEL	LEVEL	LEVEL

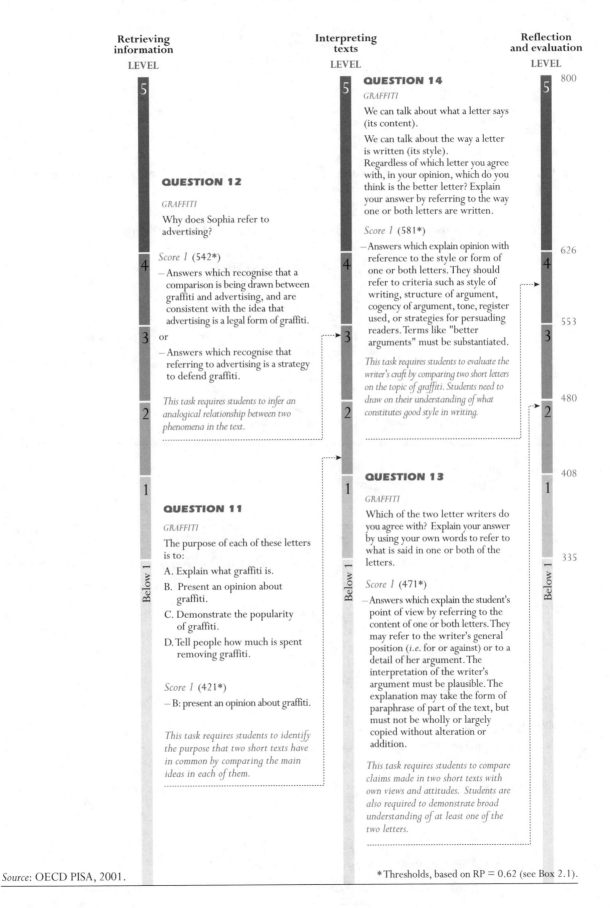

Interpreting texts

QUESTION 14

GRAFFITI

We can talk about what a letter says (its content).

We can talk about the way a letter is written (its style).
Regardless of which letter you agree with, in your opinion, which do you think is the better letter? Explain your answer by referring to the way one or both letters are written.

Score 1 (581)*

—Answers which explain opinion with reference to the style or form of one or both letters. They should refer to criteria such as style of writing, structure of argument, cogency of argument, tone, register used, or strategies for persuading readers. Terms like "better arguments" must be substantiated.

This task requires students to evaluate the writer's craft by comparing two short letters on the topic of graffiti. Students need to draw on their understanding of what constitutes good style in writing.

Retrieving information

QUESTION 12

GRAFFITI

Why does Sophia refer to advertising?

Score 1 (542)*

—Answers which recognise that a comparison is being drawn between graffiti and advertising, and are consistent with the idea that advertising is a legal form of graffiti.

or

—Answers which recognise that referring to advertising is a strategy to defend graffiti.

This task requires students to infer an analogical relationship between two phenomena in the text.

QUESTION 11

GRAFFITI

The purpose of each of these letters is to:

A. Explain what graffiti is.

B. Present an opinion about graffiti.

C. Demonstrate the popularity of graffiti.

D. Tell people how much is spent removing graffiti.

Score 1 (421)*

—B: present an opinion about graffiti.

This task requires students to identify the purpose that two short texts have in common by comparing the main ideas in each of them.

QUESTION 13

GRAFFITI

Which of the two letter writers do you agree with? Explain your answer by using your own words to refer to what is said in one or both of the letters.

Score 1 (471)*

—Answers which explain the student's point of view by referring to the content of one or both letters. They may refer to the writer's general position (*i.e.* for or against) or to a detail of her argument. The interpretation of the writer's argument must be plausible. The explanation may take the form of paraphrase of part of the text, but must not be wholly or largely copied without alteration or addition.

This task requires students to compare claims made in two short texts with own views and attitudes. Students are also required to demonstrate broad understanding of at least one of the two letters.

Reflection and evaluation scale values: 800, 626, 553, 480, 408, 335

Source: OECD PISA, 2001.

*Thresholds, based on RP = 0.62 (see Box 2.1).

Figure 2.2   (continued)
Samples of the reading tasks used in PISA

LABOUR

The tree diagram below shows the structure of a country's labour force or "working-age population". The total population of the country in 1995 was about 3.4 million.

The labour force structure year ended 31 March 1995 (000s)[1]

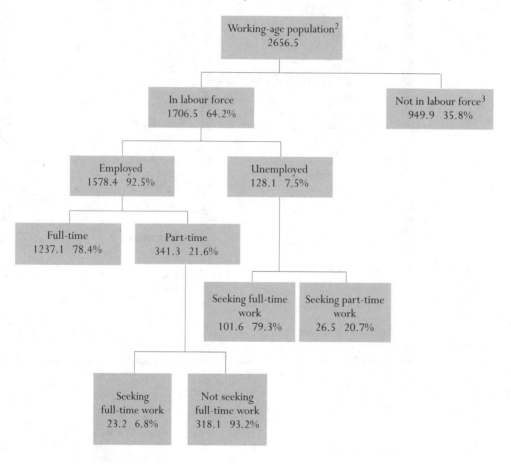

1. Numbers of people are given in thousands (000s).

2. The working-age population is defined as people between the ages of 15 and 65.

3. People "Not in labour force" are those not actively seeking work and/or not available for work.

Source: D. Miller, *Form 6 Economics*, ESA Publications, Box 9453, Newmarket, Auckland, NZ, p. 64.

Use the information about a country's labour force to answer the questions.

Retrieving information	Interpreting texts	Reflection and evaluation
LEVEL	LEVEL	LEVEL

800

QUESTION 16

LABOUR

How many people of working age were not in the labour force? (Write the number of people, not the percentage.)

Score 2 (631*)

– Answers which indicate that the number in the tree diagram AND the "000s" in the title/footnote have been integrated: 949 900. Allow approximations between 949 000 and 950 000 in figures or words. Also accept 900 000 or one million (in words or figures) with qualifier.

This task requires students to locate correct numerical information in a tree diagram and combine it with conditional information given in a footnote.

Score 1 (485*)

– Answers which indicate that the number in the tree diagram has been located, but that the "000s" in the title/footnote has not been correctly integrated. Answers stating 949.9 in words or figures. Allow approximations comparable to those for Score 2.

This task requires students to locate correct numerical information in the tree diagram. At this level, conditional information is not used.

QUESTION 17

LABOUR

In which part of the tree diagram, if any, would each of the people listed in the table below be included? Show your answer by placing a cross in the correct box in the table. The first one has been done for you (red box).

	"In labour force: employed"	"In labour force: unemployed"	"Not in labour force"	Not included in any category
A part-time waiter, aged 35	☒	☐	☐	☐
A business woman, aged 43, who works a sixty-hour week	☒	☐	☐	☐
A full-time student, aged 21	☐	☐	☒	☐
A man, aged 28, who recently sold his shop and is looking for work	☐	☒	☐	☐
A woman, aged 55, who has never worked or wanted to work outside the home	☐	☐	☒	☐
A grandmother, aged 80, who still works a few hours a day at the family's market stall	☐	☐	☐	☒

Score 2 (727*)

– 5 answers correct (checked boxes).

This task requires students to analyse and match several described cases to labour force status categories where some of the relevant information is in footnotes and therefore not prominent.

Score 1 (473*)

– 3 or 4 answers correct.

This task requires students to analyse and match some described cases to labour force status categories where some of the relevant information is in footnotes and therefore not prominent.

QUESTION 15

LABOUR

What are the two main groups into which the working-age population is divided?

A. Employed and unemployed.

B. Of working age and not of working age.

C. Full-time workers and part-time workers.

D. In the labour force and not in the labour force.

Score 1 (477*)

– D: In the labour force and not in the labour force.

This task requires students to understand the relationship of information presented in a tree diagram.

QUESTION 19

LABOUR

The information about the labour force structure is presented as a tree diagram, but it could have been presented in a number of other ways, such as a written description, a pie chart, a graph or a table.

The tree diagram was probably chosen because it is especially useful for showing:

A. Changes over time.

B. The size of the country's total population.

C. Categories within each group.

D. The size of each group.

Score 1 (486*)

– C: categories within each group.

This task requires students to evaluate the formal features of a tree diagram in order to recognise the appropriateness of its structure for showing categories within groups.

QUESTION 18

LABOUR

Suppose that information about the labour force was presented in a tree diagram like this every year.

Listed below are four features of the tree diagram. Show whether or not you would expect these features to change from year to year, by circling either "Change" or "No change".

Features of tree diagram	Answer
The labels in each box (*e.g.* "In labour force")	No change
The percentages (*e.g.* "64.2%")	Change
The numbers (*e.g.* "2656.5")	Change
The footnotes under the tree diagram	No change

Score 1 (445*)

– 3 answers correct.

This task requires students to draw on knowledge of the form and content of a tree diagram about the labour force to distinguish between variables and structural features.

626
553
480
408
335

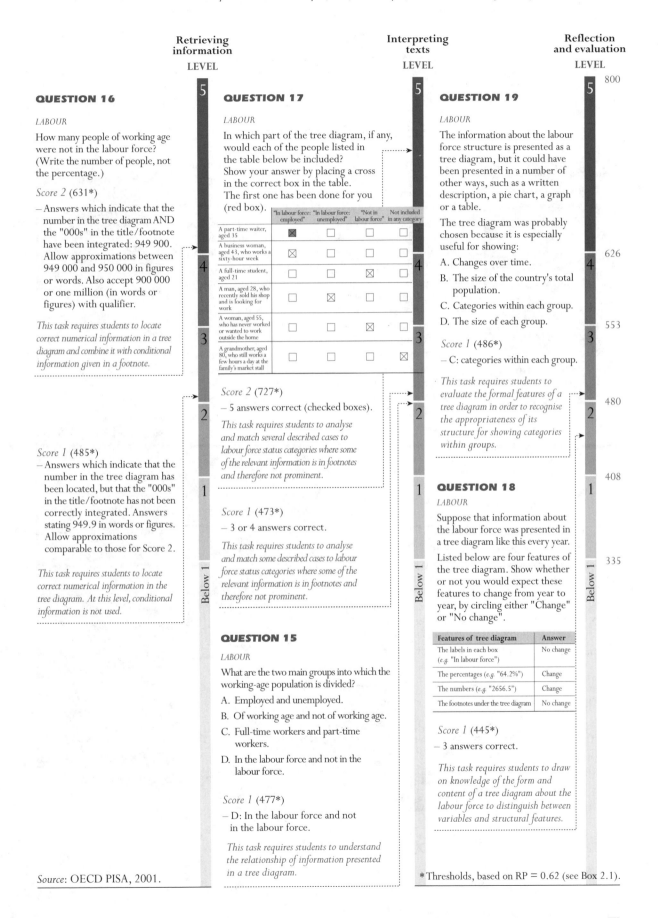

Figure 2.2 (continued)
Samples of the reading tasks used in PISA

Scientific Police Weapons

A murder has been committed but the suspect denies everything. He claims not to know the victim. He says he never knew him, never went near him, never touched him…

The police and the judge are convinced that he is not telling the truth. But how to prove it?

At the crime scene, investigators have gathered every possible shred of evidence imaginable: fibres from fabrics, hairs, finger marks, cigarette ends…The few hairs found on the victim's jacket are red. And they look strangely like the suspect's. If it could be proved that these hairs are indeed his, this would be evidence that he had in fact met the victim.

Every individual is unique

Specialists set to work. They examine some cells at the root of these hairs and some of the suspect's blood cells. In the nucleus of each cell in our bodies there is DNA. What is it? DNA is like a necklace made of two twisted strings of pearls. Imagine that these pearls come in four different colours and that thousands of coloured pearls (which make up a gene) are strung in a very specific order. In each individual this order is exactly the same in all the cells in the body: those of the hair roots as well as those of the big toe, those of the liver and those of the stomach or blood. But the order of the pearls varies from one person to another. Given the number of pearls strung in this way, there is very little chance of two people having the same DNA, with the exception of identical twins. Unique to each individual, DNA is thus a sort of genetic identity card.

Geneticists are therefore able to compare the suspect's genetic identity card (determined from his blood) with that of the person with the red hair. If the genetic card is the same, they will know that the suspect did in fact go near the victim he said he'd never met.

Just one piece of evidence

More and more often in cases of sexual assault, murder, theft or other crimes, the police are having genetic analyses done. Why? To try to find evidence of contact between two people, two objects or a person and an object. Proving such contact is often very useful to the investigation. But it does not necessarily provide proof of a crime. It is just one piece of evidence amongst many others.

Anne Versailles

We are made up of billions of cells

Every living thing is made up of lots of cells. A cell is very small indeed. It can also be said to be microscopic because it can only be seen using a microscope which magnifies it many times. Each cell has an outer membrane and a nucleus in which the DNA is found.

Genetic what?

DNA is made up of a number of genes, each consisting of thousands of "pearls". Together these genes form the genetic identity card of a person.

How is the genetic identity card revealed?

The geneticist takes the few cells from the base of the hairs found on the victim, or from the saliva left on a cigarette end. He puts them into a product which destroys everything around the DNA of the cells. He then does the same thing with some cells from the suspect's blood. The DNA is then specially prepared for analysis. After this, it is placed in a special gel and an electric current is passed through the gel. After a few hours, this produces stripes similar to a bar code (like the ones on things we buy) which are visible under a special lamp. The bar code of the suspect's DNA is then compared with that of the hairs found on the victim.

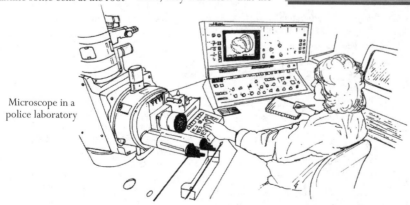

Microscope in a police laboratory

Refer to the magazine article to answer the questions.

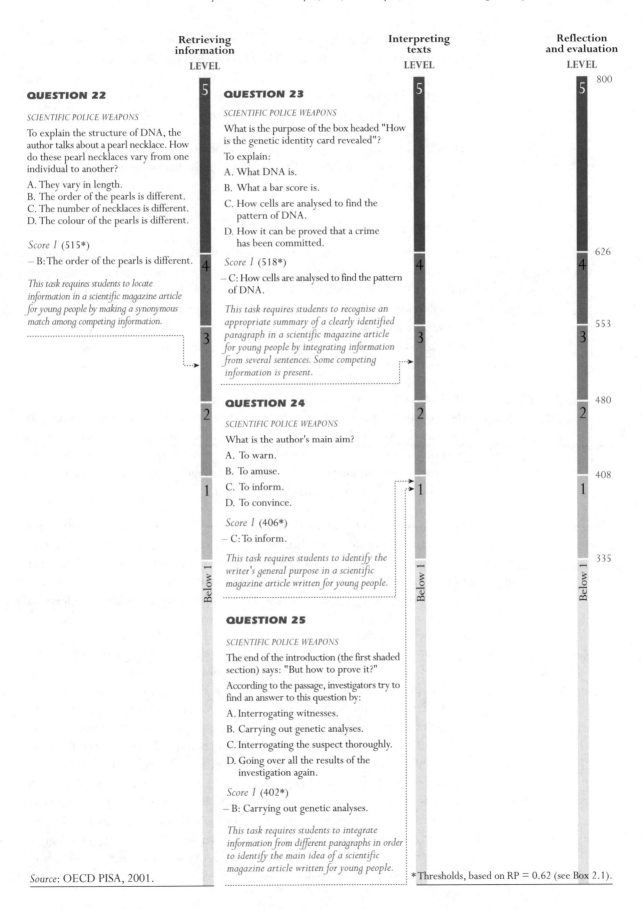

Retrieving information	Interpreting texts	Reflection and evaluation
LEVEL	LEVEL	LEVEL

QUESTION 22

SCIENTIFIC POLICE WEAPONS

To explain the structure of DNA, the author talks about a pearl necklace. How do these pearl necklaces vary from one individual to another?

A. They vary in length.
B. The order of the pearls is different.
C. The number of necklaces is different.
D. The colour of the pearls is different.

Score 1 (515)*

– B: The order of the pearls is different.

This task requires students to locate information in a scientific magazine article for young people by making a synonymous match among competing information.

QUESTION 23

SCIENTIFIC POLICE WEAPONS

What is the purpose of the box headed "How is the genetic identity card revealed"?

To explain:

A. What DNA is.

B. What a bar score is.

C. How cells are analysed to find the pattern of DNA.

D. How it can be proved that a crime has been committed.

Score 1 (518)*

– C: How cells are analysed to find the pattern of DNA.

This task requires students to recognise an appropriate summary of a clearly identified paragraph in a scientific magazine article for young people by integrating information from several sentences. Some competing information is present.

QUESTION 24

SCIENTIFIC POLICE WEAPONS

What is the author's main aim?

A. To warn.

B. To amuse.

C. To inform.

D. To convince.

Score 1 (406)*

– C: To inform.

This task requires students to identify the writer's general purpose in a scientific magazine article written for young people.

QUESTION 25

SCIENTIFIC POLICE WEAPONS

The end of the introduction (the first shaded section) says: "But how to prove it?"

According to the passage, investigators try to find an answer to this question by:

A. Interrogating witnesses.

B. Carrying out genetic analyses.

C. Interrogating the suspect thoroughly.

D. Going over all the results of the investigation again.

Score 1 (402)*

– B: Carrying out genetic analyses.

This task requires students to integrate information from different paragraphs in order to identify the main idea of a scientific magazine article written for young people.

Levels shown: 5, 4, 3, 2, 1, Below 1 (each column). Scale values: 800, 626, 553, 480, 408, 335.

Source: OECD PISA, 2001.

*Thresholds, based on RP = 0.62 (see Box 2.1).

percentage who are *at most* proficient at a given level since this information indicates what proportion of students are able to cope with certain demands of everyday life and work. For the purposes of analysis, later in this report and elsewhere, the attributes of groups of students who perform at a certain level may nevertheless be useful, in order to explore the limits of their proficiency.

Figure 2.3 presents an overall profile of proficiency on the combined reading literacy scale (see also Table 2.1a), the length of the bars showing the percentage of students proficient at each level.

Proficiency at Level 5 (above 625 points)

Students at Level 5 are capable of completing sophisticated reading tasks...

Students proficient at Level 5 on the combined reading literacy scale are capable of completing sophisticated reading tasks, such as managing information that is difficult to find in unfamiliar texts; showing detailed understanding of such texts and inferring which information in the text is relevant to the task; and being able to evaluate critically and build hypotheses, draw on specialised knowledge, and accommodate concepts that may be contrary to expectations. See Figure 2.1 for a more detailed description.

...with skills that are vital in knowledge-based economies.

Students performing at the highest PISA proficiency levels are likely to enhance their country's pool of talent. Today's proportion of students performing at these levels may also influence the contribution which that country will make to the pool of tomorrow's world-class knowledge workers in the global economy. Comparing the proportions of students reaching the highest level of reading proficiency is, therefore, of relevance in itself.

Level 5 accounts for over 15% of students in some countries and under 5% in others.

In the combined OECD area, 10 per cent of the students in PISA 2000 are proficient at Level 5. More than 15 per cent of students in Australia, Canada, Finland, New Zealand and the United Kingdom reach this level, and 12 per cent or more in Belgium, Ireland and the United States, but it is 5 per cent or less in Brazil, Greece, Latvia, Luxembourg, Mexico, Portugal, the Russian Federation and Spain (Table 2.1a).

Countries with many students at Level 5 are not always those with the smallest percentage of students performing poorly.

It is important to keep in mind that the proportion of students performing at Level 5 is influenced not only by the overall performance of countries in reading literacy but also by the variation that exists within countries between the students with the highest and the lowest levels of performance. While there is a general tendency for countries with a higher proportion of students scoring at Level 5 to have fewer students at Level 1 and below, this is not always the case. In Finland, for example, 18 per cent of students reach Level 5 while only 2 per cent are below Level 1, but Belgium and the United States, for example, which also have high percentages reaching Level 5, have relatively high proportions of students scoring below Level 1 as well (8 and 6 per cent, respectively). By contrast, in Korea, one of the countries that performs at a very high level in all three domains in PISA 2000, less than 6 per cent of students reach Level 5 and less than 1 per cent score below Level 1.

Figure 2.3

Percentage of students performing at each of the proficiency levels
on the combined reading literacy scale

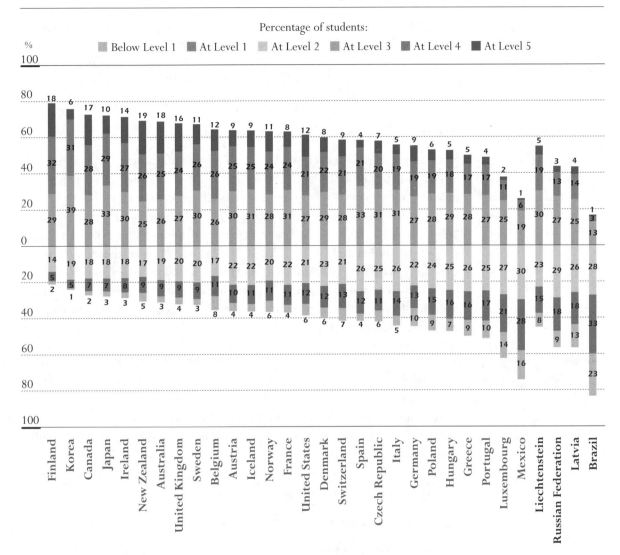

Source: OECD PISA database, 2001. Table 2.1a.

Examining the three components of the combined reading literacy scale shows even more variation, particularly in those countries with an above-average percentage of students performing at Level 5 on the combined reading literacy scale. In Finland, for example, 26 per cent of students reach Level 5 on the retrieving information scale (Table 2.1b), but only 14 per cent reach Level 5 on the reflection and evaluation scale (OECD average 11 per cent) (Table 2.1d). A similar picture, though less pronounced, can be observed in Australia, Belgium and Sweden. By contrast, Canada and the United Kingdom show higher percentages on the reflection and evaluation scale than on the retrieving information and interpreting scales, suggesting that high overall performance in

The percentage of students at Level 5 varies in the different aspects of reading.

these countries is achieved, in part, by strong performance in tasks that require students to engage in critical evaluation, to use hypotheses, and to relate texts to their own experience, knowledge and ideas (Tables 2.1b, c and d).[4]

Among the countries with the lowest percentage of students reaching Level 5 on the combined reading literacy scale, only 4 per cent of students in Greece reach Level 5 on the retrieving information and interpreting scales but three times that proportion, 12 per cent (OECD average is 11 per cent) reach Level 5 on the reflection and evaluation scale (Tables 2.1b and 2.1d).

Proficiency at Level 4 (from 553 to 625 points)

Tasks at Level 4 are still complex and difficult, and can be correctly answered by about a third of all students...

Students proficient at Level 4 on the combined reading literacy scale are capable of difficult reading tasks, such as locating embedded information, construing meaning from nuances of language and critically evaluating a text (see Figure 2.1 for a detailed description). In the combined OECD area, 31 per cent of students are proficient at Level 4 and beyond (that is, at Levels 4 and 5) (Table 2.1a). Half of the students in Finland and 40 per cent or more of those in Australia, Canada, Ireland, New Zealand and the United Kingdom attain at least Level 4. With the exception of Luxembourg and Mexico, at least one in five students in each OECD country reaches at least Level 4. In Brazil, the country with the lowest performance in reading literacy overall, only 4 per cent of students score at Level 4 or above.

...with fewer differences between performance on the three aspects of reading.

At Level 4, the differences in performance between the three reading literacy scales tend to be smaller than at Level 5. In Brazil, however, the proportion of students at least at Level 4 on the reflection and evaluation scale is more than twice the proportion of students at that level on the retrieving information scale: 7 per cent and 3 per cent respectively (Tables 2.1b-d). In Greece, Mexico, Portugal and Spain, the gap is 6 percentage points or more. The reverse is true in Belgium, Finland, France and Liechtenstein.

Proficiency at Level 3 (from 481 to 552 points)

Three in five students can perform reading tasks of moderate complexity; in Finland up to four in five...

Students proficient at Level 3 on the combined reading literacy scale are capable of reading tasks of moderate complexity, such as locating multiple pieces of information, making links between different parts of a text, and relating it to familiar everyday knowledge (see Figure 2.1 for a detailed description). In the combined OECD area, 60 per cent of students are proficient at least at Level 3 (that is, at Levels 3, 4 or 5) on the combined reading literacy scale (Table 2.1a). In nine out of 27 OECD countries, between two-thirds and 80 per cent of 15-year-old students are proficient at least at Level 3.

...but countries where most students are at least at Level 3 differ in other respects.

To what extent is the pattern of proficiency similar across countries? To examine this, consider the nine countries that have between two-thirds and just over three-quarters of students at Level 3 or above. These are, in order, Finland, Korea, Canada, Japan, Ireland, New Zealand, Australia, the United Kingdom and Sweden. How do these countries do in other respects? In one country,

Finland, relatively large proportions of students are also highly literate (18 per cent performing at Level 5, compared with the OECD average of 10 per cent), *and* a relatively large number are above the most basic level (only 7 per cent in Finland are at Level 1 or below). Finland thus shows strong results on the combined reading literacy scale.

In a further five countries, Australia, Canada, Ireland, New Zealand and the United Kingdom, there are large numbers at the highest level (between 14 and 19 per cent), but the percentage with performance at or below Level 1 is higher than in Finland, between 10 and 14 per cent (OECD average is 18 per cent). These countries perform well in getting students to the highest level of proficiency but succeed less well in reducing the proportion with low skills. In New Zealand, more students than in any other country are proficient at Level 5 (19 per cent), but a relatively high number (14 per cent) perform only at or below Level 1.

Some countries with many strong readers also have quite a few weak ones...

The results for Korea show that low disparities in literacy skills at a relatively high level are an attainable goal: three-quarters of its students are proficient at least at Level 3 and only 6 per cent are at or below Level 1. Like Korea, Japan has large numbers of students with at least Level 3 literacy but relatively few at either the highest or lowest levels. Finally, in Sweden, two-thirds of students are at least at Level 3, but the numbers with high and low levels of literacy are closer to the average.

...while in others the great majority are more homogeneous.

Proficiency at Level 2 (from 408 to 480 points)

Students proficient at Level 2 are capable of basic reading tasks, such as locating straightforward information, making low-level inferences of various types, working out what a well-defined part of a text means, and using some outside knowledge to understand it (see Figure 2.1 for a detailed description). In the combined OECD area, 82 per cent of students are proficient at Level 2 or above on the combined reading literacy scale. In every OECD country, at least half of all students are at Level 2 or above (Table 2.1a).

More than four in five students overall, and nowhere fewer than half, can perform basic reading tasks.

In Spain, only 4 per cent of students reach Level 5, but an above-average 84 per cent reach at least Level 2 (Table 2.1a). It is interesting to contrast Spain's performance with New Zealand's: similar proportions of students are at least at Level 2 (84 and 86 per cent, respectively) but the proportion in New Zealand at Level 5 is almost five times higher than that in Spain. By contrast, in Spain, a particularly large proportion of students, 42 per cent, have Level 2 as their highest proficiency level.

Proficiency at Level 1 (from 335 to 407 points)
or below (less than 335 points)

Reading literacy, as defined in PISA, focuses on the knowledge and skills required to apply "reading for learning" rather than on the technical skills acquired in "learning to read". Since comparatively few young adults in OECD countries have not acquired technical reading skills, PISA does not therefore seek to measure

The simplest tasks in PISA require students to do more than just read words fluently...

such things as the extent to which 15-year-old students are fluent readers or how well they spell or recognise words. In line with most contemporary views about reading literacy, PISA focuses on measuring the extent to which individuals are able to construct, expand and reflect on the meaning of what they have read in a wide range of texts common both within and beyond school. The simplest reading tasks that can still be associated with this notion of reading literacy are those at Level 1. Students proficient at this level are capable of completing only the least complex reading tasks developed for PISA, such as locating a single piece of information, identifying the main theme of a text or making a simple connection with everyday knowledge (see Figure 2.1 for a detailed description).

...so that students below Level 1 may have the technical capacity to read, though they may face serious difficulties in future life...

Students performing below 335 points, *i.e.* below Level 1, are not capable of the most basic type of reading that PISA seeks to measure. This does not mean that they have no literacy skills. In fact, most of these students can probably read in a technical sense, and the majority of them (54 per cent on average across OECD countries[5]) are able to solve successfully at least 10 per cent of the non-multiple choice[6] reading tasks in PISA 2000 (and 6 per cent a quarter of them). Nonetheless, their pattern of answers in the assessment is such that they would be expected to solve fewer than half of the tasks in a test made up of items drawn solely from Level 1, and therefore perform below Level 1. Such students have serious difficulties in using reading literacy as an effective tool to advance and extend their knowledge and skills in other areas. Students with literacy skills below Level 1 may, therefore, be at risk not only of difficulties in their initial transition from education to work but also of failure to benefit from further education and learning opportunities throughout life.

...and, along with those at Level 1, may not acquire the necessary literacy skills to sufficiently benefit from educational opportunities.

Education systems with large proportions of students performing below, or even at, Level 1 should be concerned that significant numbers of their students may not be acquiring the necessary literacy knowledge and skills to benefit sufficiently from their educational opportunities. This situation is even more troublesome in light of the extensive evidence suggesting that it is difficult in later life to compensate for learning gaps in initial education. OECD data suggest indeed that job-related continuing education and training often reinforce the skill differences with which individuals leave initial education (OECD, 2001). Adult literacy skills and participation in continuing education and training are strongly related, even after controlling for other characteristics affecting participation in training. Literacy skills and continuing education and training appear to be mutually reinforcing, with the result that training is least commonly pursued by those adults who need it most.

The percentage of students at or below Level 1 varies widely, from a few per cent to nearly half...

In the combined OECD area, 12 per cent of students perform at Level 1, and 6 per cent below Level 1, but there are wide differences between countries. In Finland and Korea, only around 5 per cent of students perform at Level 1, and less than 2 per cent below it, but these countries are exceptions. In all other OECD countries, between 10 and 44 per cent of students perform at or below Level 1 (Table 2.1a). Over 2 per cent and, in half of the OECD countries over 5 per cent, perform below Level 1.

The countries with 20 per cent or more of students at Level 1 or below are, in order, Brazil, Mexico, Luxembourg, Latvia, the Russian Federation, Portugal, Greece, Poland, Hungary, Germany, Liechtenstein and Switzerland. In Brazil, Mexico, Luxembourg, Latvia, Portugal and Germany, between close to 10 and 23 per cent of students do not reach Level 1, i.e. are unable routinely to show the most basic skills that PISA seeks to measure. This is most remarkable in the case of Germany, which has the relatively high figure of 9 per cent of its students performing at Level 5.

...and, in some countries, a considerable minority do not even reach Level 1.

Students at Level 1 and below are not a random group. Although the specific characteristics of these students can best be examined in the national context, some commonalities are apparent: in virtually all countries, the majority of these students are male (see Table 5.2a), and many of them come from disadvantaged backgrounds In addition, in many countries, a comparatively high proportion of students at Level 1 or below are foreign-born or have foreign-born parents. In Germany and Luxembourg, two of the four countries with the highest proportion of students performing at or below Level 1, more than 26 and 34 per cent of these students, respectively, are foreign-born, whereas among the students performing above Level 1, the corresponding figure is only 8 and 11 per cent respectively.[7] A more systematic analysis of gender differences among the students with the lowest level of performance follows in Chapter 5; the background characteristics of students with particularly low or high levels of performance are analysed in Chapters 6 and 7.

The majority of the students at Level 1 are males, from disadvantaged backgrounds or with foreign-born parents, especially in some countries with many weak performers.

As at the higher end of the proficiency scale, student performance at or below Level 1 shows substantial differences between the three reading literacy scales. In Greece, Mexico, Portugal and Spain, the weaknesses in student performance are greatest on the retrieving information scale, the proportion of students at or below Level 1 being between 5 and 15 percentage points higher than on the reflection and evaluation scale. Conversely, in France, Germany and Switzerland, the proportion of students at or below Level 1 is at least 2 percentage points lower on the retrieving information scale than on the reflection and evaluation scale. In Brazil, more than half of the students do not reach beyond Level 1 on the combined reading literacy scale. On the retrieving information scale, more than two-thirds of students in Brazil fail to go beyond Level 1, but only 46 per cent on the reflection and evaluation scale (Tables 2.1b-d).

Expectations of student performance

In any comparison of such data between countries, it must be borne in mind that education systems operate under a variety of economic conditions and that teachers, schools and society in general may have differing expectations of the performance of their students. School reports are a common means of informing students and parents about the extent to which students are meeting the expectations of their teachers and schools. Although assessment practices vary widely between countries, the scales that teachers use often include a "pass/fail" threshold that indicates whether the performance that students demonstrate in various school subjects is considered acceptable. How

Education systems vary in the expectations they have of their students...

this is expressed in terms of marks may be common to all schools in a country, or established by the school, or by individual teachers for each class. Similarly, the nature and difficulty of the tasks that 15-year-olds are required to perform successfully in order to obtain a given mark may vary, depending on the demands of the school, the class or the study programme.

...as is shown in students' reports of their school marks.

In PISA 2000, students were asked to report the marks they had received in their last school report in subjects related to the language used in the PISA reading literacy assessment (for details see the *PISA 2000 Technical Report*). These marks were then translated into three categories indicating whether they were above, at, or below the school's or the class teacher's pass/fail threshold. Particularly in countries with automatic promotion policies, the fact that a student does not reach the pass/fail threshold may not have any consequences for the student's educational pathway. However, it does signal that the student has not met expectations in a given subject area at the class or school level. A comparison between this information and students' performance on the PISA reading literacy scale can provide an additional frame of reference for interpreting PISA scores within the national context, despite the fact that school marks in language-related subjects relate to a much wider spread of knowledge and skills than reading literacy.

In countries with high average performance in PISA, teachers do not necessarily give pass marks to all students...

The results reveal that comparatively high performance in the PISA assessments does not necessarily translate into a high proportion of students meeting the expectations of their teachers. Conversely, in countries with comparatively low mean performance, the vast majority of students may still live up to what is expected of them.

France, for example, is one of the countries with a comparatively high proportion of students reporting not reaching the pass/fail threshold (31 per cent). Nevertheless, these students scored an average of 492 points, well within Level 3 (Table 2.5) and close to the OECD average.

...while, in some countries with low average performance in PISA, most students meet their teachers' expectations.

In Mexico, the percentage of students at Level 1 or below is 44 per cent. Despite this percentage, the average score of the 96 per cent of students reporting that they had reached or exceeded the pass mark in subjects related to the language of assessment in their last school report was only 424 points (Table 2.5). Consequently, even though these students may perform poorly by international standards, 96 per cent report that they meet or exceed the performance expectations of their teachers. Other countries in which students reported not reaching the pass/fail threshold score at comparatively low levels (around 400 points) include Greece, Poland, Sweden and the United Kingdom. In these countries, however, the percentage of such students is only 3 per cent or less.

The mean performances of countries

Average scores can usefully summarise country performances....

The discussion above has focused on comparisons of the distribution of student performance between countries. Another way to summarise student performance and to compare the relative standing of countries in reading literacy is by way of their mean scores. To the extent that high average performance at age 15 is predictive of a highly skilled future workforce, countries with high average performance will have a considerable economic and social advantage.

It should be appreciated, however, that average performance figures mask significant variation in performance within countries, reflecting different levels of performance among many different student groups. As in previous international studies of student performance, such as the IEA Third International Mathematics and Science Study (TIMSS), only around one tenth of the total variation in student performance in PISA lies between countries and can, therefore, be captured through a comparison of country averages (see Table 8.3). The remaining variation in student performance occurs within countries, that is, between education systems and programmes, between schools and between students within schools.

…but mask the widest differences in student performance, which are found within countries.

Figure 2.4 summarises the performance of participating countries on the combined reading literacy scale, and Tables 2.2a, b and c show the corresponding information for the three component scales. Figure 2.4 also shows which countries perform above, below, or at the OECD average.

Figure 2.4 shows country means…

Box 2.2 **Interpreting sample statistics**

Standard errors and confidence intervals. The statistics in this report represent *estimates* of national performance based on samples of students rather than the values that could be calculated if every student in every country had answered every question. Consequently, it is important to know the degree of uncertainty inherent in the estimates. In PISA 2000, each estimate has an associated degree of uncertainty, which is expressed through a standard error. The use of confidence intervals provides a means of making inferences about the population means and proportions in a manner that reflects the uncertainty associated with sample estimates. It can be inferred that the observed statistical result for a given population would lie within the confidence interval in 95 out of 100 replications of the measurement, using different samples drawn from the same population.

Judging whether populations differ. This report tests the statistical significance of differences between the national samples in percentages and in average performance scores in order to judge whether there are differences between the populations whom the samples represent. Each separate test follows the convention that, if in fact there is no real difference between two populations, there is no more than a 5 per cent probability that an observed difference between the two samples will erroneously suggest that the populations are different as the result of sampling and measurement error. In the figures and tables showing multiple comparisons of countries' mean scores, the significance tests are based on a procedure for multiple comparisons that limits to 5 per cent the probability that the mean of a given country will erroneously be declared to be different from that of any other country, in cases where there is in fact no difference (for details see Annex A4).

...with Finland clearly ahead of the other countries...

Finland's performance on the combined reading literacy scale is higher than that of any other OECD country (Figure 2.4). Its country mean, 546 points, is almost two-thirds of a proficiency level above the OECD average of 500 (or in statistical terms almost half the international standard deviation above the mean). Countries with mean performances significantly above the OECD average include Australia, Austria, Belgium, Canada, Finland, Iceland, Ireland, Japan, Korea, New Zealand, Sweden and the United Kingdom. Five countries perform around the OECD average (Denmark, France, Norway, Switzerland and the United States) and 14 significantly below the OECD average (Brazil, the Czech Republic, Germany, Greece, Hungary, Italy, Latvia, Liechtenstein, Luxembourg, Mexico, Poland, Portugal, the Russian Federation and Spain).[8]

...but not all of the differences shown are statistically significant.

As discussed in Box 2.2, when interpreting mean performance, only those differences between countries which are statistically significant should be taken into account. Accordingly, a country's ranking in Figure 2.4 should be read in the light of whether countries ranked close to it are significantly different from it. Figure 2.4 shows those pairs of countries where the difference in their mean scores is sufficient to say with confidence that the higher performance by sampled students in one country holds for the entire population of enrolled 15-year-olds. Read across the row for a country to compare its performance with the countries listed along the top of the figure. The symbols indicate whether the average performance of the country in the row is significantly lower than that of the comparison country, not statistically different, or significantly higher. For example, New Zealand is shown in Figure 2.4 to be significantly lower than Finland, not significantly different from Australia, Canada, Ireland, Japan, Korea and the United Kingdom, and significantly higher than all of the others. Finland is significantly ahead of all other countries.

In countries with low average performance, where poorly performing students often repeat grades, those in the usual grade for their age do much better in international comparisons.

Brazil and Mexico have performances significantly lower than those of all other countries and more than a full proficiency level below the OECD average. When their mean scores are interpreted, however, it needs to be borne in mind that 15-year-old students in both countries are spread across a wide range of grade levels. Fifteen-year-olds in these countries who are enrolled in grade 10 (the modal grade of 15-year-olds in OECD countries) score on average 463 and 466 points, respectively, *i.e.*, between the average scores of the Russian Federation and Portugal (for data see *www.pisa.oecd.org*).

In some countries, students perform better on one of the literacy scales than the others – but only in a minority are such differences important.

Tables 2.2a, b and c provide information on mean performance on the three separate scales in the way that Figure 2.4 does for the combined reading literacy scale. It is not appropriate to compare numerical scale scores directly between the different aspects of reading. Nevertheless, it is possible to determine the relative strengths of countries in the different aspects of reading literacy, on the basis of their relative rank-order positions on the respective scales[9] (values in parenthesis represent mean scores for the retrieving and for the reflection and evaluation scales respectively).

Figure 2.4

Multiple comparisons of mean performance on the combined reading literacy scale

Countries (top, left to right): Finland, Canada, New Zealand, Australia, Ireland, Korea, United Kingdom, Japan, Sweden, Austria, Belgium, Iceland, Norway, France, United States, Denmark, Switzerland, Spain, Czech Republic, Italy, Germany, Liechtenstein, Hungary, Poland, Greece, Portugal, Russian Fed., Latvia, Luxembourg, Mexico, Brazil

Country	Mean	S.E.
Finland	546	(2.6)
Canada	534	(1.6)
New Zealand	529	(2.8)
Australia	528	(3.5)
Ireland	527	(3.2)
Korea	525	(2.4)
United Kingdom	523	(2.6)
Japan	522	(5.2)
Sweden	516	(2.2)
Austria	507	(2.4)
Belgium	507	(3.6)
Iceland	507	(1.5)
Norway	505	(2.8)
France	505	(2.7)
United States	504	(7.0)
Denmark	497	(2.4)
Switzerland	494	(4.2)
Spain	493	(2.7)
Czech Republic	492	(2.4)
Italy	487	(2.9)
Germany	484	(2.5)
Liechtenstein	483	(4.1)
Hungary	480	(4.0)
Poland	479	(4.5)
Greece	474	(5.0)
Portugal	470	(4.5)
Russian Fed.	462	(4.2)
Latvia	458	(5.3)
Luxembourg	441	(1.6)
Mexico	422	(3.3)
Brazil	396	(3.1)

	Fin	Can	NZ	Aus	Ire	Kor	UK	Jpn	Swe	Aut	Bel	Ice	Nor	Fra	USA	Den	Swi	Spa	Cze	Ita	Ger	Lie	Hun	Pol	Gre	Por	Rus	Lat	Lux	Mex	Bra
Upper rank*	1	2	2	2	3	4	5	3	9	11	11	11	11	11	10	16	16	17	17	19	21	20	21	21	23	24	27	27	30	31	32
Lower rank*	1	4	8	9	9	9	9	10	11	16	16	15	16	16	20	19	21	21	21	24	25	26	26	27	28	28	29	29	30	31	32

*Note: Because data are based on samples, it is not possible to report exact rank order positions for countries. However, it is possible to report the range of rank order positions within which the country mean lies with 95 per cent likelihood.

Instructions

Read across the row for a country to compare performance with the countries listed along the top of the chart. The symbols indicate whether the mean performance of the country in the row is significantly lower than that of the comparison country, significantly higher than that of the comparison country, or if there is no statistically significant difference between the mean performance of the two countries.

▲ Mean performance statistically significantly higher than in comparison country.
○ No statistically significant difference from comparison country.
▽ Mean performance statistically significantly lower than in comparison country.

Statistically significantly above the OECD average
Not statistically significantly different from the OECD average
Statistically significantly below the OECD average

Source: OECD PISA database, 2001.

– On the basis of this comparison, Austria (502, 512), Canada (530, 542), Ireland (524, 533), Portugal (455, 480), Spain (483, 506) and the United Kingdom (523, 539) show stronger performance on the reflection and evaluation scale than on the retrieving information scale.

– Australia (536, 526), Belgium (515, 497), Finland (556, 533), France (515, 496), Germany (483, 478) and Switzerland (498, 488) show stronger performance on the retrieving information scale than on the reflection and evaluation scale.

– The relative strengths of the remaining countries cannot be determined with statistical significance.

The distribution of reading literacy within countries

High average scores are not enough: countries also want to raise the level of achievement of poor performers.

Mean performance scores are typically used to assess the quality of schools and education systems. However, it has been noted above that mean performance does not provide a full picture of student performance and can mask significant variation within an individual class, school or education system. Moreover, countries aim not only to encourage high performance but also to minimise internal disparities in performance. Both parents and the public at large are aware of the gravity of low performance and the fact that school-leavers who lack fundamental skills face poor prospects of employment. A high proportion of students at the lower end of the reading literacy scale may give rise to concern that a large proportion of tomorrow's workforce and voters will lack the skills required for the informed judgements that they must make.

The extent of variation in student performance indicates the magnitude of the task...

The analysis in this section needs to be distinguished from the examination of the distribution of student performance across the PISA proficiency levels discussed above. Whereas the distribution of students across proficiency levels indicates the proportion of students in each country that can demonstrate a specified level of knowledge and skills, and thus compares countries on the basis of *absolute* benchmarks of student performance, the analysis below focuses on the *relative* distribution of scores, *i.e.*, the *gap* that exists between students with the highest and the lowest levels of performance *within* each country. This is an important indicator of the equality of educational outcomes in the domain of reading literacy (see Box 2.3).

...and is shown in Figure 2.5...

Figure 2.5 shows the distribution of performance scores on the combined reading literacy scale (Table 2.3a). Since the results are relatively similar for each of the three component scales, these scales are not examined separately in this section. The data for the distribution of performance scores on the component scales can be found in Tables 2.3b, c and d.

...which identifies the scores of students at different points on each country's distribution.

The gradation bars in Figure 2.5 show the range of performance in each country between the 5th percentile (the point below which the lowest-performing 5 per cent of the students in a country score) and the 95th percentile (the point below which 95 per cent of students perform or, alternatively, above which the 5 per

Figure 2.5

Distribution of student performance on the combined reading literacy scale

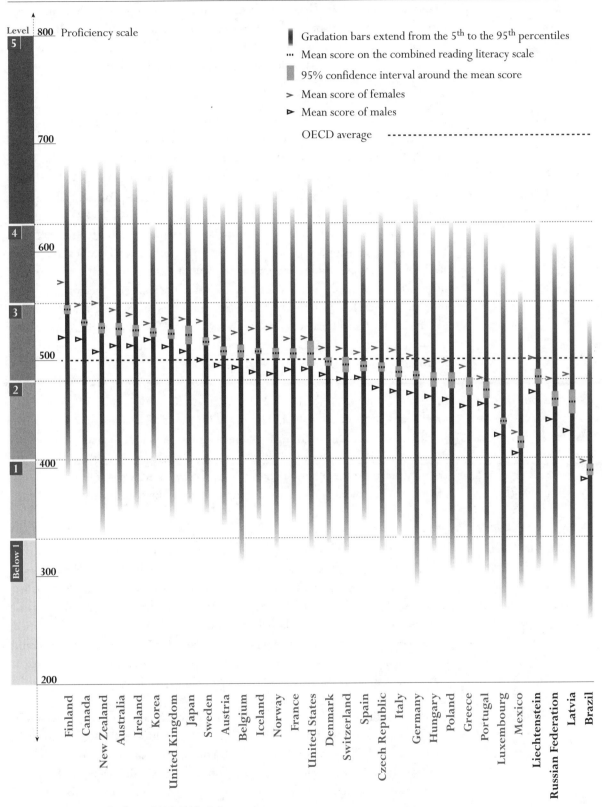

Source: OECD PISA database, 2001. Table 2.3a.

cent highest-performing students in a country score). The density of the bar represents the proportion of students performing at the corresponding scale points. In addition, Tables 2.3a-d indentify the 25th and 75th percentiles, *i.e.,* the scale points that mark the bottom and top quarters of performers in each country. The dotted, horizontal black line near the middle shows the mean score for each country (*i.e.,* the subject of the discussion in the preceding section) and is located inside a shaded box that shows its confidence interval.

Figure 2.5 shows that the range of student scores within countries exceeds the range of differences between national averages...

Figure 2.5 shows that there is wide variation in student performance on the combined reading literacy scale within countries. The middle 90 per cent of the population shown by the length of the bars exceeds by far the range between the mean scores of the highest and lowest performing countries. In almost all OECD countries, this group includes some students proficient at Level 5 and others not proficient above Level 1. In all but five OECD countries, even among the middle half of the population (from the 25th to the 75th percentiles), performance varies by more than the difference between the mean score of the highest and lowest performing countries. In all countries, the range of performance in the middle half of the students exceeds the magnitude of one proficiency level and in Australia, Belgium, Germany and New Zealand it exceeds twice this difference (OECD average 1.8). This suggests that educational programmes, schools and teachers need to cope with a wide range of student knowledge and skills.

...and that every country has some students above the mean of the best-performing country, and below the mean of the worst.

In every country, at least 5 per cent of students do not reach the mean proficiency level in the OECD country with the lowest level of performance, Mexico (Table 2.3a). In Germany, Hungary, and Poland, a quarter of students do not reach the lowest mean country score, but a quarter exceed the highest country mean. At the other end of the scale, every country has at least 5 per cent of students performing above the mean in Finland, the country with the highest average performance.

Even where students in the bottom quarter do relatively well by international standards, wide disparity within a country may cause concern.

In some countries with high average performance, such as Australia, New Zealand and the United Kingdom, the 25th percentile on the combined reading literacy scale lies well within proficiency Level 2 (around 458 points), indicating that students at the 25th percentile are doing reasonably well in absolute terms. Nevertheless, the difference between student performance at the 25th and 75th percentiles of the national performance distribution in these countries could indicate that the students at the 25th percentile are substantially below what is expected of them within their national education system.

Are these observed disparities inevitable? That is hard to say...

To what extent are differences in student performance a reflection of the natural distribution of ability and, therefore, difficult to influence through changes in public policy? It is not easy to answer such a question with data from PISA alone, not least because differences between countries are influenced by the social and economic context in which education and learning take place. Nonetheless, several findings suggest that public policy can play a role:

Box 2.3 **Interpreting differences in PISA scores: how large a gap?**

What is meant by a difference of, say, 50 points between the scores of two different groups of students? A difference of 73 points on the PISA scale represents one proficiency level in reading literacy. A difference of one proficiency level can be considered a comparatively large difference in student performance in substantive terms. For example, on the interpreting scale, Level 3 distinguishes students who can typically integrate several parts of a text, understand a relationship or construe the meaning of a word or phrase, and can compare, contrast and categorise competing information according to a range of criteria, from those at Level 2 who can be expected only to identify the main idea in a text, to understand relationships, make and apply simple categories, and construe meaning within a limited part of a text where information is not prominent but only low-level inferences are required (see also Figure 2.1).

Another benchmark is that the difference in performance on the combined reading literacy scale between the OECD countries with the third highest and the third lowest mean performance is 59 points; and the difference between the fifth highest and the fifth lowest OECD countries is 48 points.

Differences in scores can also be viewed in terms of the differences in student performance demonstrated by different groups of students on the combined reading literacy scale:

• The difference in performance between the highest national quarters of students on the PISA international socio-economic index of occupational status and the bottom quarters equals, on average across OECD countries, 81 points (Table 6.1a). That is, on average across OECD countries, 81 points separate students who report that their parents are, for example, secondary school teachers or managers of a small business enterprise from those whose parents are bricklayers, carpenters or painters.

• The difference in student performance between students whose mothers have completed tertiary education and those who have not completed upper secondary education equals, on average across OECD countries, 67 points (Table 6.7).

• The difference in student performance between students who speak the language of the assessment most of the time and those who do not equals, on average across OECD countries, 68 points (Table 6.11).

— First, the within-country variation in performance in reading literacy varies widely between countries, the difference between the 75th and 25th percentiles ranging from 92 points in Korea to more than 140 points in Australia, Belgium, Germany, New Zealand, Switzerland and the United States (Table 2.3a). Belgium shows the widest differences, with 150 points separating the 75th and 25th percentiles. This difference can be explained, at least partially, by the difference in performance between the Flemish and French Communities in Belgium) (see Annex B2 for details).

…but some countries contain them within a far narrower range than others.

— Second, countries with similar levels of average performance show a considerable variation in disparity of student performance. For example, Korea and the United Kingdom both show above-average performance on the combined reading literacy scale at around 525 points. The difference between the 75th and 25th percentiles in Korea is 93 points, significantly below the

This is true even among countries with similar mean scores.

OECD average, but in the United Kingdom it is 137 points, significantly above the OECD average. The same can be observed in countries scoring below the average. Germany and Italy, two countries that perform at around 486 points, significantly below the OECD average, vary in their internal differences. In Italy the difference between the 75th and 25th percentiles is 124 points, but it is 146 points in Germany. Bringing the bottom quarter of students closer to their current mean would be one way for countries with wide internal disparities to raise the country's overall performance.

Most importantly, some countries achieve both high average performance and small disparities.

– Third, it is evident from a comparison between the range of performance within a country and its average performance that wide disparities in performance are not a necessary condition for a country to attain a high level of overall performance. As an illustration, the three countries with the smallest differences between the 75th and 25th percentiles, Finland, Japan and Korea, are also among the best-performing countries in reading literacy. By contrast, one of the three countries with the highest performance differences, Germany, scores significantly below the OECD average.

Countries with the greatest differences overall also have large differences among the least able students.

Examining the range from the 25th to the 5th percentiles provides an indication of performance by the least successful students relative to the overall performance of the respective country. Does the range of performance become wider at the bottom end of the distribution? Generally, countries with a narrow range between the 75th and 25th percentiles, such as Finland, Japan, Korea and Spain, also show a narrow range of distribution at the bottom end, between the 25th and 5th percentiles. The three countries with the widest variation between the 75th and 25th percentiles, Belgium, Germany and New Zealand, also show the widest range at the bottom end of the performance distribution, the difference between the 25th and 5th percentile points amounting to more than 122 points.

The lowest-performing countries have a small minority who just manage to outperform the average student elsewhere...

In the four OECD countries with the lowest performance on the combined reading literacy scale, Greece, Luxembourg, Mexico and Portugal, less than a quarter of students score above the mean of the highest-performing country and in one of these, Mexico, less than 10 per cent of students reach this level. In Brazil, over 75 per cent of students score below the OECD average. The top 10 per cent of Brazilian students score just above the OECD average, and the top 5 per cent significantly above.

...but in some other below-average countries, the top 5% do extremely well, even compared with the top students elsewhere.

In some countries with below-average performance, the students who perform best nevertheless do extremely well. For example, 5 per cent of students in Germany score above 650 points, while the top 5 per cent of students in Korea only score above 629 points – even though the mean score of Germany is significantly below, and that of Korea significantly above, the OECD average. Conversely, the least proficient students can do poorly in countries with good average performance. In one of the countries with the highest average reading performance, New Zealand, 5 per cent of the population are below the comparatively low score of 337: a higher proportion of low scores than in several countries with only moderate average performance.

These results point further to the need for teachers, schools and education systems to address the differences in performance that exist within classes, schools and countries.

Differences between students must therefore be addressed.

How student performance varies between schools

Fifteen-year-olds in OECD countries attend schools in a variety of educational and institutional settings. In certain countries, some students enrol in vocationally oriented schools while others attend schools primarily designed to prepare students for entry into university-level education. Similarly, in countries where the transition from lower to upper secondary education occurs around the age of 15, some students surveyed by PISA may still be attending school at the lower secondary level while other students have already progressed to the upper secondary level. Furthermore, while the majority of students in all but two OECD countries attend public schools, a significant minority of students in several OECD countries attend schools that are privately managed and, in some cases, privately financed.

The 15-year-olds in PISA are in many different types of school...

The preceding analysis has shown that, in most countries, there are considerable differences in performance within each education system. This variation may result from the socio-economic backgrounds of students and schools, from the human and financial resources available to schools, from curricular differences, from selection policies and practices and from the way in which teaching is organised and delivered (see also Chapters 6 and 8). Some countries have non-selective school systems that seek to provide all students with the same opportunities for learning and that allow each school to cater for the full range of student performance. Other countries respond to diversity explicitly by forming groups of students of similar performance levels through selection either within or between schools, with the aim of serving students according to their specific needs. And in yet other countries, combinations of the two approaches occur. Even in comprehensive school systems, there may be significant variation between schools due to the socio-economic and cultural characteristics of the communities that the schools serve or to geographical differences (such as differences between regions, provinces or states in federal systems, or differences between rural and urban areas). Finally, there may be significant variation between individual schools that cannot be easily quantified or otherwise described, part of which could result from differences in the quality or effectiveness of the teaching that those schools provide.

...and are sometimes organised according to ability.

However, might within-country differences be attributable to other identifiable factors, besides variation in performance between schools or social groups? How do the policies and historical patterns that shape each country's school system affect and relate to the overall variation in student performance? Do countries with explicit tracking and streaming policies show a higher degree of overall disparity in student performance than countries that have non-selective education systems? Such questions occur particularly in countries where one observes comparably large variation in overall student performance, such as Belgium, Germany, New Zealand, Norway and the United States.

Are school differences important to PISA disparities?

Figure 2.6 compares the extent of the variation within countries...

Figure 2.6 shows the extent of variation attributable to different factors in each country. The length of the bars indicates the total observed variation in student performance on the combined reading literacy scale (Column 2 in Table 2.4).[10] Note that the values in Figure 2.6 and Table 2.4 are expressed as percentages of the average variation between OECD countries in student performance on the combined reading literacy scale, which is equal to 9 277 units.[11] A value in Column 2 larger than 100 indicates that variation in student performance is greater in the corresponding country than in a typical OECD country. Similarly, a value smaller than 100 indicates below-average variation in student performance.

...and breaks it down into between-school and within-school differences...

The bar for each country is aligned in Figure 2.6 so that variation between schools is represented by the length of the bar to the left of the vertical line down the centre of the figure, and variation within schools is represented by the length of the bar to the right of that vertical line. Longer segments to the left of the vertical line indicate greater variation in the mean performance of schools. Longer segments to the right of the vertical line indicate greater variation among students within schools.

...showing that over half the variation in performance is attributable to differences between schools in more selective systems.

As shown in Figure 2.6, in most countries a considerable portion of the variation in student performance lies between schools. On average, across the 26 OECD countries included in this comparison, differences between schools account for 36 per cent of the OECD average between-student variation. In Austria, Belgium, the Czech Republic, Germany, Greece, Hungary, Italy and Poland, more than 50 per cent of the OECD average between-student variation is between schools (Column 3 in Table 2.4). Where there is substantial variation between schools and less variation between students within schools, students will generally be in schools in which other students perform at levels similar to their own. This selectivity may reflect family choice of school or residential location, or policies on school enrolment, allocation of students or the curriculum.

Some countries have low variation between schools and within schools...

In Korea, overall variation in student performance on the combined reading literacy scale is about half the OECD average variation, and only 20 per cent of the OECD average variation in student performance is attributable to differences between schools. Korea thus not only achieves high average performance in reading and low overall disparity between students, but does so with relatively little variation in mean performance between schools. Spain also shows low overall variation (around three-quarters of the OECD average) and low between-school variation (16 per cent of the OECD average variation in student performance) but, unlike Korea, has a mean score significantly below the OECD average (Figure 2.4).

...particularly those with the lowest overall variation.

The smallest variation in reading performance among schools occurs in Finland, Iceland and Sweden, where differences between schools account for only between 7 and 11 per cent of the average between-student variation in OECD countries. In these countries performance is largely unrelated to the schools in which students are enrolled. They are thus likely to encounter a similar

Figure 2.6

Variation in student performance between schools and within schools on the combined reading literacy scale
Expressed as a percentage of the average variation in student performance in OECD countries

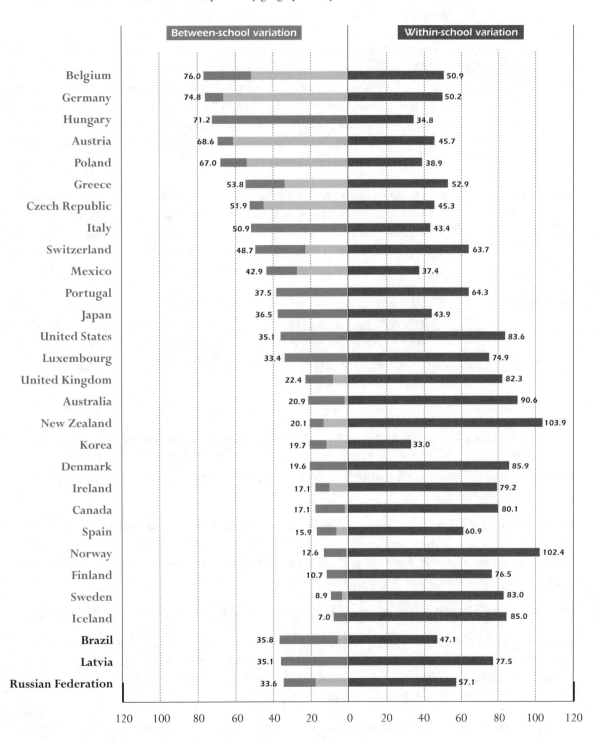

■ Variance explained by geographical, systemic and institutional factors

	Between-school variation	Within-school variation
Belgium	76.0	50.9
Germany	74.8	50.2
Hungary	71.2	34.8
Austria	68.6	45.7
Poland	67.0	38.9
Greece	53.8	52.9
Czech Republic	51.9	45.3
Italy	50.9	43.4
Switzerland	48.7	63.7
Mexico	42.9	37.4
Portugal	37.5	64.3
Japan	36.5	43.9
United States	35.1	83.6
Luxembourg	33.4	74.9
United Kingdom	22.4	82.3
Australia	20.9	90.6
New Zealand	20.1	103.9
Korea	19.7	33.0
Denmark	19.6	85.9
Ireland	17.1	79.2
Canada	17.1	80.1
Spain	15.9	60.9
Norway	12.6	102.4
Finland	10.7	76.5
Sweden	8.9	83.0
Iceland	7.0	85.0
Brazil	35.8	47.1
Latvia	35.1	77.5
Russian Federation	33.6	57.1

Source: OECD PISA database, 2001. Table 2.4.

learning environment in terms of the ability distribution of students. It is noteworthy that overall variation in student performance in these countries is below the OECD average and that very few students perform below the pass/ fail thresholds established by their schools or classroom teachers. These education systems succeed both in minimising differences between schools and in containing the overall variation in student performance in reading literacy.

High overall variation can result from high within-school differences...

Australia, New Zealand and Norway (with 112, 126 and 116 per cent of the OECD average between-student variation, respectively) are among the countries with the highest overall variation in reading performance, but only a comparatively small proportion (21, 20 and 13 per cent of the OECD average of student performance) results from differences between schools. In these countries, most variation occurs within schools, suggesting that individual schools need to cater for a more diverse client base.

...high between-school differences...

Belgium, Germany and Switzerland (124, 133 and 112 per cent of the average between-student variation in OECD countries) are also countries with comparatively high overall variation in student performance, but a large proportion of this variation (76, 75 and 49 per cent of the OECD average variation in student performance) results from differences in performance between schools.

...or a combination of the two.

The United States, another country with comparatively large overall variation in student performance (118 per cent of the average variation between students in OECD countries), is somewhere in the middle, 35 per cent of the average OECD variation in student performance being found between schools.

Box 2.4 **Factors associated with between-school variation in student performance**

Many factors contribute to the variation in average student performance between schools. Some of these are as follows:

• **Sub-national differences**: In several countries school systems operate under sub-national jurisdictions (such as the communities in Belgium, the provinces in Canada, the Länder in Germany, or the states in Australia and the United States) or vary between a combination of sub-national jurisdictions and linguistic communities (as in Switzerland).

• **Rural and urban areas**: Schooling and curricula often differ between urban and rural settings.

• **Publicly and privately managed schools**: In many countries, publicly and privately managed schools compete. In some countries, private schools usually have more selective enrolment policies. In addition, schools that are privately financed may hinder participation by students from disadvantaged socio-economic backgrounds.

• **Programme type**: Some systems distinguish between types of school, which can differ substantially in the curriculum offered (*e.g.,* preparing students either for university education or for direct entry into the labour market). Even in systems in which differentiation occurs within schools, there may be distinct vocational and general tracks.

• **Level of education**: In a few countries, some 15-years-old students attend upper secondary schools while others attend lower secondary, depending either on their month of birth or on the promotion practices used. In other countries, the same school may host more than one level of education. This means that the variation in student performance attributable to the difference in curriculum between lower and upper secondary education is included in the between-school variation in the former case, and in the within-school between-student variation in the latter.

• **Socio-economic intake**: The socio-economic characteristics of the communities served by schools often vary, although the size of this variation differs greatly between countries. The variation in school intake can affect the performance of the students enrolled.

Where does this variation in student performance on the combined reading literacy scale originate? The answer will vary between countries (see also Box 2.4). Participating countries provided an indication of those geographical, systemic or institutional aspects of their education systems captured by PISA that they considered most likely to account for differences in performance between schools. The variation in student performance accounted for by these variables is indicated in Figure 2.6 on the left-hand side of the bar:

Some of the variation between schools is attributable to geography, institutional factors or selection of students by ability…

— In Australia, discounting differences between states and territories reduces the between-school variation in student performance from 21 to 19 per cent of the OECD average between-student variation (see Table 2.4).

— In Austria, discounting the differences between the various tracks to which students are allocated across six school types reduces the between-school variation from 68 to 8 per cent. In Belgium, discounting differences between the linguistic communities and between school type reduces the between-school variation from 76 to 25 per cent. Discounting differences between school and programme types reduces the between-school variation in Germany from 75 to 10 per cent, in Hungary from 71 to 19, in Poland from 67 to 14 and in Korea from 20 to 9 per cent over the OECD average between-student variation.

— Discounting differences between general and vocational schools, and between upper secondary and lower secondary programmes, reduces the between-school variation from 52 to 7 per cent in the Czech Republic, and in Greece from 54 to 21 per cent.

— In Ireland, discounting differences between school types, between regular and special schools, and between rural and urban areas, reduces between-school variation from 17 to 7 per cent.

– Discounting level of education and programme type reduces the between-school variation in Italy (Licei versus vocational and technical schools) from 51 to 23 per cent, and in Mexico from 43 to 16 per cent.

– In Canada, discounting differences between provinces reduces between-school variation in student performance from 17 to 16 per cent.

– In Iceland, discounting school size and level of urbanisation reduces between-school variation from 7 to 6 per cent.

– In New Zealand, discounting school intake (including average socio-economic status and the proportion of Maori and Pacific students) reduces variation between schools from 20 to 7 per cent.

– Discounting immigrant students reduces variation between schools in Norway from 13 to 12 per cent and in Sweden from 9 to 6 per cent.

– In Spain, discounting differences between publicly and privately managed schools reduces between-school variation from 16 to 10 per cent.

– In Switzerland, discounting differences between programme types and levels of education, and between the linguistic communities in which schools are located, reduces the between-school variation from 49 to 27 per cent.

– In the United Kingdom, discounting differences between schools managed by local authorities versus other bodies such as self-governing trusts and church foundations, between co-educational and single-gender schools, and between regions, reduces the between-school variation from 22 to 15 per cent.

...which can be compounded by the bunching of socially privileged students, particularly in countries with different types of secondary school....

Broadly, the data also suggest that, in school systems with differentiated school types, the clustering of students with particular socio-economic characteristics in certain schools is greater than in systems where the curriculum does not vary significantly between schools. In Austria, Belgium, the Czech Republic, Germany, Italy and the Netherlands, for example, the between-school variation associated with the fact that students attend different types of school is considerably compounded by differences in social and family background. This may be a consequence of selection or self-selection: when the school market provides some differentiation, students from lower social backgrounds may tend to be directed to, or choose for themselves, less demanding study programmes, or may opt not to participate in the selection procedures of the education system.

...since students' results are associated not only with their own individual backgrounds but – to a greater extent – with the backgrounds of others at their school.

The fuller analysis in Chapter 8 suggests that the overall social background of a school's intake on student performance tends to be greater than the impact of the individual student's social background. Students from a lower socio-economic background attending schools in which the average socio-economic background is high tend to perform much better than when they are enrolled in a school with a below-average socio-economic intake – and the reverse is true for more advantaged students in less advantaged schools. This is not surprising, but the *magnitude* of the difference is striking. As shown in Chapter 8, the difference in the expected results for a given student in two alternative schools separated by, say, 10 points in the average socio-economic status of their students (as defined by the PISA index) would be greater than the expected difference between two students separated by 10 points attending the same school. This suggests that institutional differentiation in education systems, often compounded by the social background of a school's intake and self-selection by students and/or their parents, can have a major impact on an individual student's success at school.

Conclusions

The results of PISA 2000 show wide differences between countries in the knowledge and skills of 15-year-olds in reading literacy. One hundred and twenty-four points – 1.7 proficiency levels – separate the highest and lowest average performances by OECD countries on the combined reading literacy scale. Differences *between* countries represent, however, only a fraction of overall variation in student performance, differences in performance within countries being on average about ten times as great as the variation between country means. Catering for such a diverse client base and narrowing the gaps in student performance represent formidable challenges for all countries.

Differences between countries in reading literacy are substantial, though differences within countries ones are greater.

An average of 10 per cent of 15-year-olds reach the highest proficiency level in PISA, demonstrating the ability to complete sophisticated reading tasks, to show detailed understanding of texts and the relevance of their components, and to evaluate information critically and build hypotheses drawing on specialised knowledge. At the other end of the scale, an average of 6 per cent of students do not reach proficiency Level 1. They fail to demonstrate routinely the most basic knowledge and skills that PISA seeks to measure. These students may still be able to read in a technical sense, but they show serious difficulties in applying reading literacy as a tool to advance and extend their knowledge and skills in other areas. Although the proportion of these students is as low as 2 per cent in three countries and exceeds 14 per cent in only two OECD countries, the existence of a small but significant minority of students who, near the end of compulsory schooling, lack the foundation of literacy skills needed for further learning, must be of concern to policy-makers seeking to make lifelong learning a reality for all. This is so, in particular, in the face of mounting evidence that continuing education and training beyond school tend to reinforce rather than to mitigate skill differences resulting from unequal success in initial education.

PISA reveals a huge gap between the 10% of students capable of sophisticated reading tasks and the 6% incapable of simple tasks...

Adding to this proportion of students not reaching Level 1, those who perform only at Level 1, namely those who are capable only of completing the most basic of reading tasks, such as locating a simple piece of information, identifying the main theme of a text or making a simple connection with everyday knowledge, brings the proportion of low performers to an average of 18 per cent across OECD countries. Parents, educators, and policy-makers in systems with large proportions of students performing at or below Level 1 need to recognise that

...as well as the 12% capable only of simple tasks, who also pose a serious challenge, especially in countries where they are most numerous.

significant numbers of students are not benefiting sufficiently from available educational opportunities and are not acquiring the necessary knowledge and skills to do so effectively in their further school careers and beyond. In countries such as Brazil and Mexico, which have comparatively low levels of national income and where spending on educational institutions per student up to age 15 is only around one fourth of the OECD average (Table 3.6), fostering the education of those most in need represents a considerable challenge, and specific policies to that end have often only been recently introduced.

Even where relatively few students underperform internationally, a large number may be below national benchmarks.

Wide variation in student performance does not, however, always mean that a large part of the student population will have a low level of reading literacy. In fact, in some countries with high average performance, such as Australia, New Zealand and the United Kingdom, the 25th percentile on the combined reading literacy scale lies well within proficiency Level 2 (around 458 points), indicating that students at the 25th percentile are doing reasonably well by international comparative standards. Nevertheless, the variation in the distribution of student performance in these countries suggests that the students at the 25th percentile may be performing substantially below expected benchmarks of good performance in the countries in question.

The countries that achieve both high average performance and relatively low variation between students provide a challenge for others...

To what extent is the observed variation in student performance on the PISA 2000 assessments a reflection of the innate distribution of students' abilities and thus a challenge for education systems that cannot be influenced directly by education policy? The analysis in this chapter has shown not only that the magnitude of within-country disparities in reading literacy varies widely between countries but also that wide disparities in performance are not a necessary condition for a country to attain a high level of overall performance. Although more general contextual factors need to be considered when such disparities are compared between countries, public policy may therefore have the potential to make an important contribution to providing equal opportunities and equitable learning outcomes for all students. Showing that countries differ not just in their mean performance, but also in the extent to which they are able to close the gap between the students with the lowest and the highest levels of performance and to reduce some of the barriers to equitable distribution of learning outcomes is an important finding which has direct relevance to policy making.

...particularly those that have systems allowing wide differences between schools...

Many factors contribute to variation in student performance. Disparities can result from the socio-economic backgrounds of students and schools, from the human and financial resources available to schools, from curricular differences, and from the way in which teaching is organised and delivered. As the causes of variation in student performance differ, so too do the approaches chosen by different countries to address the challenge. Some countries have non-selective school systems that seek to provide all students with the same opportunities for learning and require each school to cater for the full range of student performance. Other countries respond to diversity by forming groups of students of similar levels of performance through selection either within or between schools, with the aim of serving students according to their specific needs.

How do such policies and practices affect actual student performance? It is hard to give a clear answer since such policies and practices are often applied informally within schools and difficult to compare transnationally. Nonetheless, the data from PISA 2000 suggest that both overall variation in student performance, and the relative proportion of that variation that is found between schools, tend to be greater in those countries with explicit differentiation at an early age between types of programme and school. The data also suggest that the effects of social clustering are larger in school systems with differentiated types of school than in systems in which the curriculum does not vary significantly between schools. These findings are examined more closely in Chapter 8, together with some policy levers that appear, in some countries, to moderate the relationship between social background and performance and thus to help to foster equal learning opportunities for all students.

...since PISA suggests, so far tentatively, that overall variation is greater where students are channelled into different kinds of school from an early age.

In countries such as Australia, New Zealand and Norway, where there is considerable variation in student performance on the combined reading literacy scale within schools, reforms within schools that aim to bolster the performance of less successful students are more likely to be effective in improving overall student performance than reforms targeted at improving particular schools. Conversely, in countries where schools vary substantially in performance, such as Austria, Belgium, Germany, Hungary and Poland, reforms aimed at improving the performance of the schools with the lowest levels of performance are likely to be effective in improving overall performance.

For some countries the task is to reduce differences between schools, for others, to reduce differences within schools, and in some cases, both.

Notes

1. Technically, the mean score for student performance across OECD countries was set at 500 points and the standard deviation at 100 points, with the data weighted so that each OECD country contributed equally.

2. The concept of literacy used in PISA is much broader than the historical notion of the ability to read and write. In particular, the PISA definition goes beyond the notion that reading literacy means decoding written material and literal comprehension, so that the PISA tests did not seek to measure that kind of technical literacy. Those who fail to reach Level 1 may well be literate in the technical sense.

3. As a result of the fact that all students within a proficiency level, including those at the lower end of the level, are expected to answer at least half of the items at that level correctly, and given the established width of the proficiency levels, a student with a particular score will be expected to have a 62 per cent chance of success in an item that has the same notional level of difficulty as their score. This is sometimes referred to as the RP (response probability) value 0.62.

4. In order to confirm that these differences are statistically significant, the relative probability of each country assuming each rank-order position on each reading scale was determined from the country's mean scores, their standard errors and the covariance between the performance scales. This reveals whether, with a likelihood of 95 per cent, a country would rank statistically significantly higher, at the same level, or statistically significantly lower in one reading scale than in the other reading scale. For details on the methods employed see the *PISA 2000 Technical Report*.

5. For data see the *PISA 2000 Technical Report*.

6. Multiple-choice items were excluded from this comparison because students might answer these correctly simply by guessing at random.

7. In Germany, 11.3 per cent of students are foreign-born (standard error 0.59); 5.1 per cent of students are foreign-born and score at Level 1 or below (standard error 0.51); 88.7 per cent of students were born in Germany (standard error 0.59); 14.4 per cent of students were born in Germany and score at Level 1 or below (standard error 0.82). In Luxembourg, 18.6 per cent of students are foreign-born (standard error 0.64); 11.5 per cent of students are foreign-born and score at Level 1 or below (standard error 0.55); 81.5 per cent of students were born in Luxembourg (standard error 0.64); 22.3 per cent of students were born in Luxembourg and score at Level 1 or below (standard error 0.62).

8. Poland's performance may be slightly overestimated, because of the exclusion of the 6.7 per cent of 15-year-olds enrolled in primary schools. This may imply that the performance of Poland on the combined reading literacy scale is overestimated by up to two rank-order positions. The performance of the Netherlands cannot be estimated accurately because the response rate of schools was too low. It can, however, be said with confidence that the Netherlands would lie between the 2nd and 14th position among OECD countries on the combined reading literacy scale (for details see Annex A3).

9. The relative probability of a country's assuming each rank-order position on each scale is determined from the country mean scores, their standard errors and the covariance between the performance scales of two domains. From this it can be concluded whether, with a likelihood of 95 per cent, a country would rank statistically significantly higher, not statistically differently, or statistically significantly lower in one domain than in the other domain. For details on the methods employed see the *PISA 2000 Technical Report*.

10. Owing to the sampling methods used in Japan, the between-school variation in Japan includes variation between classes within schools.

11. Variation in Figure 2.6 and Table 2.4 is expressed by statistical variance. This is obtained by squaring the standard deviation referred to earlier in this chapter. The statistical variance rather than the standard deviation is used for this comparison to allow for the decomposition of the components of variation in student performance. For reasons explained in the *PISA 2000 Technical Report*, the sum of the between-school and within-school variance components may, in the case of some countries, differ slightly from the square of the standard deviation shown in Table 2.3. The average is calculated over the OECD countries included in Table 2.4.

Chapter

3

WHAT PISA SHOWS
THAT 15-YEAR-OLDS CAN DO:
A PROFILE OF STUDENT PERFORMANCE IN
MATHEMATICAL AND SCIENTIFIC LITERACY

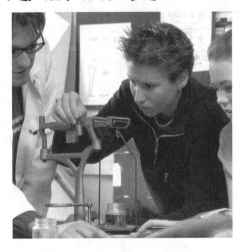

Introduction

Mathematics and science today need to be used by the many, not just the few...

For much of the last century, the content of school mathematics and science curricula was dominated by the need to provide the foundations for the professional training of a small number of mathematicians, scientists and engineers. With the growing role of science, mathematics and technology in modern life, however, the objectives of personal fulfilment, employment and full participation in society increasingly require that all adults, not just those aspiring to a scientific career, should be mathematically, scientifically and technologically literate.

...if people are to understand and participate in the modern world.

Mathematical and scientific literacy are important for understanding environmental, medical, economic and other issues that confront modern societies, which rely heavily on technological and scientific advances. Further, the performance of a country's best students in mathematics and scientific subjects may have implications for the part which that country will play in tomorrow's advanced technology sector, and for its general international competitiveness. Conversely, deficiencies in mathematical and scientific literacy can have negative consequences for individuals' labour-market and earnings prospects and for their capacity to participate fully in society.

PISA looks at students' mathematical and scientific knowledge and skills in ways pertinent to their futures as adults.

Consequently, policy-makers and educators alike attach great importance to mathematics and science education. Addressing the increasing demand for mathematical and scientific skills requires excellence throughout education systems, and it is important to monitor how well countries provide young adults with fundamental skills in this area. Mathematical and scientific knowledge and skills therefore form an integral part of the PISA literacy concept. Moreover, the definition of mathematical and scientific literacy used in PISA, which is described in Chapter 1, makes the results more relevant to advanced industrial societies than assessments that focus solely on the common denominators to be found in national curricula.

This chapter reviews the results of PISA in mathematical and scientific literacy, and examines the degree to which these coincide with or differ from the results in reading presented in Chapter 2. The chapter:

– describes the criteria for rating performance in mathematical and scientific literacy and gives examples of easier, medium and harder tasks used in PISA 2000;

– summarises performance in each country in terms of the mean scores achieved by students and the distribution of scores across student populations;

– examines how performance varies between reading, mathematical and scientific literacy.

Chapter 4 broadens this discussion further by analysing the non-cognitive aspects of learning outcomes, such as the motivation of 15-year-olds, their engagement, their learning strategies, and their belief in their own capacities.

PISA 2000 devoted most attention to reading literacy. For this reason, the assessment of mathematical and scientific literacy was more limited and the analysis of the results is not as detailed as in the case of reading. This analysis will be deepened in PISA 2003, when most attention will be given to mathematics, and in PISA 2006, when most attention will be given to science. Descriptions of the conceptual frameworks underlying the PISA assessments of mathematical and scientific literacy are provided in *Measuring Student Knowledge and Skills — A New Framework for Assessment* (OECD, 1999*a*).

Student performance in mathematical literacy

How mathematical literacy is measured in PISA

Performance in mathematical literacy is marked in PISA 2000 on a single scale which, as in the case of reading literacy, was constructed with an average score of 500 points and a standard deviation of 100 points, and with about two-thirds of students across OECD countries scoring between 400 and 600 points.[1] The scale measures the ability of students to recognise and interpret mathematical problems encountered in their world, to translate these problems into a mathematical context, to use mathematical knowledge and procedures to solve the problems within their mathematical context, to interpret the results in terms of the original problem, to reflect upon the methods applied, and to formulate and communicate the outcomes.

Mathematical literacy is rated on a single scale...

The criteria that define the level of difficulty of tasks involve:

— *The number and complexity of processing or computational steps involved in the tasks.* Tasks range from single-step problems requiring students to recall and reproduce basic mathematical facts or to complete simple computations, to multi-step problems calling for advanced mathematical knowledge and complex decision-making, information processing, and problem-solving and modelling skills.

...in which the difficulty of tasks is determined by the complexity of the processing steps involved...

— *The requirement to connect and integrate material.* The simplest tasks typically require students to apply a single representation or technique to a single piece of infor- mation. More complicated tasks require students to make connections between and to integrate more than one piece of information, using different representa- tions, or different mathematical tools or knowledge in a sequence of steps.

...the need to combine different information...

— *The requirement to represent and interpret material and reflect on situations and methods.* This ranges from recognising and using a familiar formula to the formulation, translation or creation of an appropriate model within an unfamiliar context, and the use of insight, reasoning, argumentation and generalisation.

...and the extent to which students have to think mathematically in order to formulate and solve problems.

Since the assessment of mathematical and scientific literacy was more limited than that of reading literacy in PISA 2000, no attempt was made to define levels of proficiency, as was done in reading. It is nonetheless possible to provide a broad description of performance in mathematics and science in terms of the knowledge and skills that students need to demonstrate at various points on the relevant scales.

Figure 3.1
Samples of the mathematics tasks used in PISA

APPLES

A farmer plants apple trees in a square pattern. In order to protect the trees against the wind he plants conifers all around the orchard.

Here you see a diagram of this situation where you can see the pattern of apple trees and conifers for any number (n) of rows of apple trees:

✕ = conifer

● = apple tree

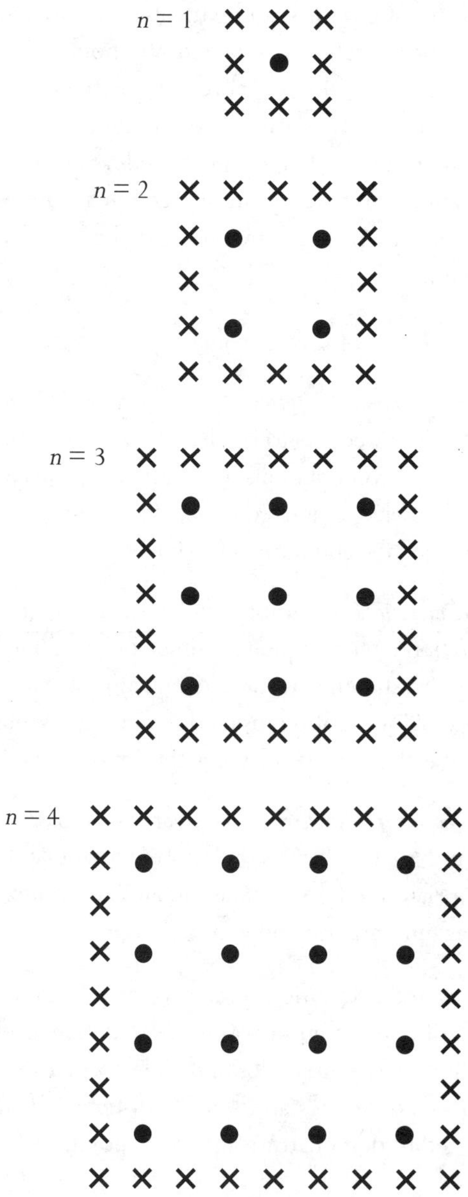

```
n = 1   ✕ ✕ ✕
        ✕ ● ✕
        ✕ ✕ ✕

n = 2   ✕ ✕ ✕ ✕ ✕
        ✕ ●     ● ✕
        ✕         ✕
        ✕ ●     ● ✕
        ✕ ✕ ✕ ✕ ✕

n = 3   ✕ ✕ ✕ ✕ ✕ ✕ ✕
        ✕ ●   ●   ● ✕
        ✕           ✕
        ✕ ●   ●   ● ✕
        ✕           ✕
        ✕ ●   ●   ● ✕
        ✕ ✕ ✕ ✕ ✕ ✕ ✕

n = 4   ✕ ✕ ✕ ✕ ✕ ✕ ✕ ✕ ✕
        ✕ ●   ●   ●   ● ✕
        ✕               ✕
        ✕ ●   ●   ●   ● ✕
        ✕               ✕
        ✕ ●   ●   ●   ● ✕
        ✕               ✕
        ✕ ●   ●   ●   ● ✕
        ✕ ✕ ✕ ✕ ✕ ✕ ✕ ✕ ✕
```

**TASK
DIFFICULTY**

QUESTION 3

APPLES

Suppose the farmer wants to make a much larger orchard with many rows of trees. As the farmer makes the orchard bigger, which will increase more quickly: the number of apple trees or the number of conifers?

Explain how you found your answer.

Score 2 (723*)

— Answers which are correct (apple trees) AND which give some algebraic explanations based on the formulae n^2 and $8n$.

Score 1

— Answers which are correct (apple trees) AND are based on specific examples or on extending the table.

— Answers which are correct (apple trees) and show SOME evidence that the relationship between n^2 and $8n$ is understood, but not so clearly expressed as in Score 2.

highest

► 750

This task requires students to show insight into mathematical functions by comparing the growth of a linear function with that of a quadratic function. Students are required to construct a verbal description of a generalised pattern, and to create an argument using algebra. Students need to understand both the algebraic expressions used to describe the pattern and the underlying functional relationships, in such a way that they can see and explain the generalisation of these relationships in an unfamiliar context. A chain of reasoning is required, and communication of this in a written explanation.

This task requires students to interpret expressions containing words and symbols, and to link different representations (pictorial, verbal and algebraic) of two relationships (one quadratic and one linear). Students have to find a strategy for determining when the two functions will have the same solution (for example, by trial and error, or by algebraic means), and to communicate the result by explaining the reasoning and calculation steps involved.

middle

QUESTION 2

APPLES

There are two formulae you can use to calculate the number of apple trees and the number of conifers for the pattern described above:

• number of apple trees = n^2

• number of conifers = $8n$

• where *n* is the number of rows of apple trees.

There is a value of *n* for which the number of apple trees equals the number of conifers. Find the value of n and show your method of calculating this.

Score 2 (655*)

— Answers which give n=8, with the algebraic method explicitly shown.

— Answers which give n=8, but no clear algebra is presented, or no work shown.

— Answers which give n=8 using other methods, *e.g.*, using pattern expansion or drawing.

► 570

Students are given a hypothetical scenario involving planting an orchard of apple trees in a square pattern, with a row of protective conifer trees around the square. They are asked to complete a table of values generated by the functions that describe the number of trees as the size of the orchard is increased. This question requires students to interpret a written description of a problem situation, to link this to a tabular representation of some of the information, to recognise a pattern and then to extend this pattern. Students need to work with given models and to relate two different representations (pictorial and tabular) of two relationships (one quadratic and one linear) in order to extend the pattern.

lowest

QUESTION 1

APPLES

Complete the table:

Score 2 (548*)

— Answers which show all 7 entries correct.

n	Number of apple trees	Number of conifers
1	1	8
2	4	16
3	9	24
4	16	32
5	25	40

► 380

Source: OECD PISA, 2001.

*Thresholds, based on RP = 0.62 (see Box 2.1).

In the case of the mathematical literacy scale, this description is as follows:

The most difficult tasks require creative mathematical thinking and insight...

— Towards the top end, around 750 points, students typically take a creative and active role in their approach to mathematical problems. They interpret and formulate problems in terms of mathematics, can handle more complex information, and can negotiate a number of processing steps. Students at this level identify and apply relevant tools and knowledge (frequently in an unfamiliar problem context), use insight to identify a suitable way of finding a solution, and display other higher-order cognitive processes such as generalisation, reasoning and argumentation to explain and communicate results.

Figure 3.1 (continued)

Samples of the mathematics tasks used in PISA

SPEED OF A RACING CAR

This graph shows how the speed of a racing car varies along a flat 3 kilometre track during its second lap.

Speed of a racing car along a 3 km track (second lap)

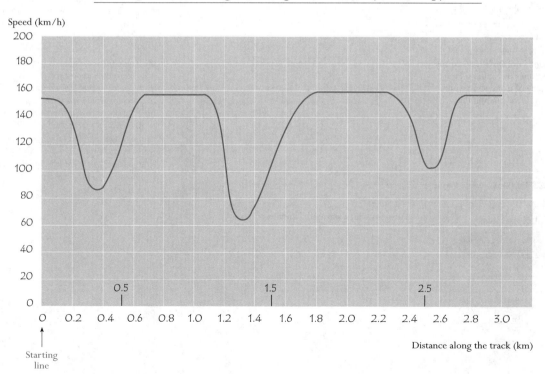

TASK DIFFICULTY

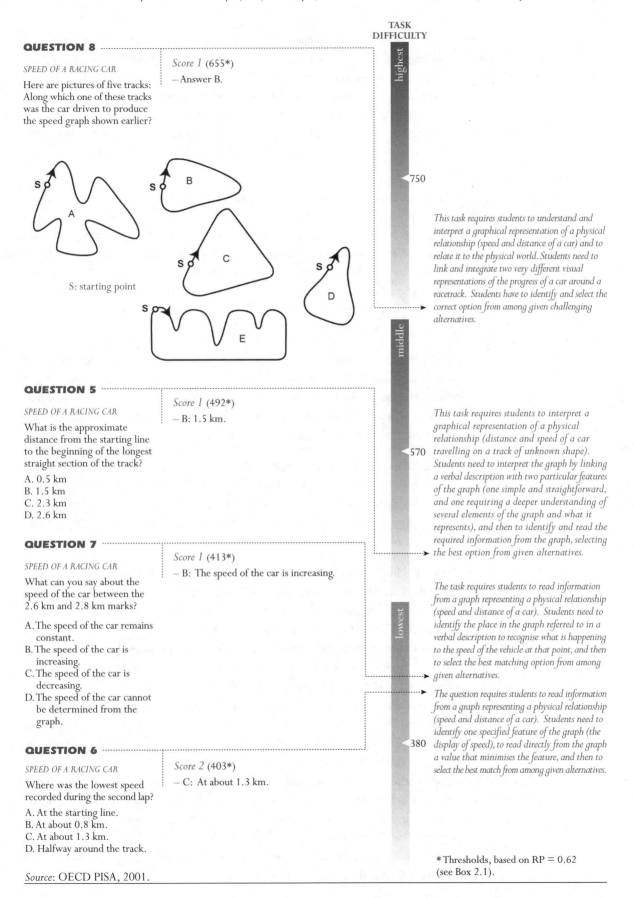

QUESTION 8

SPEED OF A RACING CAR

Here are pictures of five tracks: Along which one of these tracks was the car driven to produce the speed graph shown earlier?

S: starting point

Score 1 (655*)
– Answer B.

highest

750

This task requires students to understand and interpret a graphical representation of a physical relationship (speed and distance of a car) and to relate it to the physical world. Students need to link and integrate two very different visual representations of the progress of a car around a racetrack. Students have to identify and select the correct option from among given challenging alternatives.

middle

QUESTION 5

SPEED OF A RACING CAR

What is the approximate distance from the starting line to the beginning of the longest straight section of the track?

A. 0.5 km
B. 1.5 km
C. 2.3 km
D. 2.6 km

Score 1 (492*)
– B: 1.5 km.

570

This task requires students to interpret a graphical representation of a physical relationship (distance and speed of a car travelling on a track of unknown shape). Students need to interpret the graph by linking a verbal description with two particular features of the graph (one simple and straightforward, and one requiring a deeper understanding of several elements of the graph and what it represents), and then to identify and read the required information from the graph, selecting the best option from given alternatives.

QUESTION 7

SPEED OF A RACING CAR

What can you say about the speed of the car between the 2.6 km and 2.8 km marks?

A. The speed of the car remains constant.
B. The speed of the car is increasing.
C. The speed of the car is decreasing.
D. The speed of the car cannot be determined from the graph.

Score 1 (413*)
– B: The speed of the car is increasing.

lowest

The task requires students to read information from a graph representing a physical relationship (speed and distance of a car). Students need to identify the place in the graph referred to in a verbal description to recognise what is happening to the speed of the vehicle at that point, and then to select the best matching option from among given alternatives.

The question requires students to read information from a graph representing a physical relationship (speed and distance of a car). Students need to identify one specified feature of the graph (the display of speed), to read directly from the graph a value that minimises the feature, and then to select the best match from among given alternatives.

QUESTION 6

SPEED OF A RACING CAR

Where was the lowest speed recorded during the second lap?

A. At the starting line.
B. At about 0.8 km.
C. At about 1.3 km.
D. Halfway around the track.

Score 2 (403*)
– C: At about 1.3 km.

380

*Thresholds, based on RP = 0.62 (see Box 2.1).

Source: OECD PISA, 2001.

...less difficult tasks require students to bring together and process information...

— At around 570 points on the scale, students are typically able to interpret, link and integrate different representations of a problem or different pieces of information; and/or to use and manipulate a given model, often involving algebra or other symbolic representations; and/or to verify or check given propositions or models. Students typically work with given strategies, models or propositions (*e.g.*, by recognising and extrapolating from a pattern), and they select and apply relevant mathematical knowledge in order to solve a problem that may involve a small number of processing steps.

...while the easiest tasks require only a single processing step in a familiar context.

— At the lower end of the scale, around 380 points, students are usually able to complete only a single processing step consisting of reproducing basic mathematical facts or processes, or applying simple computational skills. Students typically recognise information from diagrammatic or text material that is familiar and straightforward and in which a mathematical formulation is provided or readily apparent. Any interpretation or reasoning typically involves recognition of a single familiar element of a problem. The solution calls for application of a routine procedure in a single processing step.

In the PISA assessment, the best 5 per cent of students achieved 655 points on average across OECD countries, 10 per cent reached 625 points and 25 per cent, 571 points. At the lower end of the scale, more than three-quarters achieved at least 435 points, more than 90 per cent reached 367 points and more than 95 per cent, 326 points (Table 3.1).

Mathematics questions vary widely in difficulty:...

The tasks used for the assessment of mathematical literacy in PISA vary widely in difficulty. Figure 3.1 shows the tasks from two of the 16 units used for the assessment of mathematical literacy, along with a description of the criteria used to mark students' answers (a more complete set of sample tasks can be found at *www.pisa.oecd.org*).

... only a few students can solve tasks requiring them to show insight into mathematical functions...

Question 3 in the unit *Apples* was the most difficult of the sample questions shown in Figure 3.1. Students were given a hypothetical scenario involving planting apple trees in a square pattern, with a "row" of protective conifer trees around the square. The scenario required students to show insight into mathematical functions by comparing the growth of a linear function with that of a quadratic function. Students were asked to construct a verbal description of a generalised pattern and to develop an argument using algebra. In order to answer correctly, students had to understand both the algebraic expressions used to describe the pattern and the underlying functional relationships, in such a way that they could see and explain the generalisation of these relationships in an unfamiliar context. To receive full credit for Question 3, which corresponds to a score of 723 points on the mathematical literacy scale, students had to provide the correct answer as well as a valid explanation. Students with a score of 723 points should theoretically be able to answer questions of this level of difficulty correctly 62 out of 100 times (see also Box 2.1). On average across OECD countries, 8 per cent of students received full credit for this open-ended question. A further 10 per cent received partial credit (for data, see *www.pisa.oecd.org*).

In Question 2 in the same unit – a slightly less difficult question with a difficulty of 655 points on the PISA mathematical literacy scale – students were given two algebraic expressions describing the growth in the number of trees as the orchard increased in size. Students were asked to find a value for which the two expressions coincide. This question required students to interpret expressions containing words and symbols and to link different representations (pictorial, verbal and algebraic) of two relationships (one quadratic and one linear). Students had to find a strategy for determining when the two functions had the same solution and then to communicate the result by explaining the reasoning and calculation steps involved. On average across OECD countries 25 per cent of students received full credit for this open-ended question.

...a quarter can solve less difficult tasks requiring them to interpret expressions, to link different representations and to compare solutions...

The easiest question in the unit *Apples* asked students to complete a table of values generated by the functions describing the number of trees as the size of the orchard increased. The question required students to interpret a written description of a situation, to link this to a tabular representation of some of the information, to recognise a pattern, and then to extend this pattern. Students had to work with given models and to relate two different representations (pictorial and tabular) of two relationships (one quadratic and one linear) in order to extrapolate from the pattern. On average across OECD countries, 50 per cent of students received full credit for this open-ended question, and a further 13 per cent received partial credit.

...half are able to translate a description into a table that they had to complete...

The second sample unit shown in Figure 3.1, *Racing Car,* provides questions illustrating the middle and the lower end of the mathematical literacy scale. In Question 5, which is located at 492 points on the mathematical literacy scale, students were given a graph showing the speed of a car as it moves around a racetrack. Students were asked to interpret the graph to find a distance that satisfies a given condition. Students needed to interpret the graph by linking a verbal description with two particular features of the graph (one simple and straightforward, and one requiring a deeper understanding of several elements of the graph and what it represents), and then to identify and read the required information from the graph, selecting the best option from among a number of given alternatives. On average across OECD countries, 67 per cent of students answered this multiple-choice question correctly.

...two-thirds are able to interpret a graph by linking two features...

At the lower end of the mathematical literacy scale, Question 7 (with a level of difficulty of 413 points) asked students to interpret the speed of the car at a particular point in the graph. The question required students to read information from a graph representing a physical relationship (speed and distance of a car). Students had to identify the place in the graph referred to in a verbal description, to recognise what happens to the speed of a vehicle at that point, and then to select the best option from among a number of given alternatives. On average across OECD countries, 83 per cent answered this multiple-choice question correctly (for data, see *www.pisa.oecd.org*).

...and the great majority of students are able to read and understand straightforward information on a graph.

The mean performances of countries in mathematical literacy

Countries vary widely in their average level of mathematical literacy...

For policy-makers in OECD countries, international comparisons of student performance have become an essential tool for assessing the performance of their countries' education systems. Such comparisons offer an external point of reference for the objective evaluation of the effectiveness of education systems. The first question that is often asked is how nations compare in their mean performance. As with reading, performance in mathematical literacy can be summarised by countries' mean scores.

Figure 3.2 orders countries by the mean performance of their students on the mathematical literacy scale. The figure also shows which countries have a level of performance above, below, or about the same as the OECD average.

As in the case of reading literacy, only those differences between countries that are statistically significant should be taken as valid. Figure 3.2 shows the pairs of countries where the difference in their mean scores is large enough to say with confidence that the higher performance by sampled students in one country would hold for the entire student population in both countries. Read across the row for a country to compare its mean performance with those of the countries listed along the top of the figure. The symbols indicate whether the average performance of the country in the row is statistically significantly lower than that of the comparison country, not statistically different from it, or significantly higher.[2]

Students in Japan display the highest mean scores in mathematical literacy but Japan's mean performance cannot be distinguished with statistical significance from that in Korea and New Zealand. The other countries that also score above the OECD average are Australia, Austria, Belgium, Canada, Denmark, Finland, France, Iceland, Liechtenstein, the Netherlands,[3] Sweden, Switzerland and the United Kingdom.

Although the tasks for the PISA assessment of mathematical literacy were designed so that students not using calculators would not be disadvantaged, students were allowed to use their own calculators or those provided by test administrators. There is no indication that the use of calculators provided an advantage to students in terms of their performance in PISA.[4]

The distribution of mathematical literacy within countries

...but variation in performance within countries is several times larger...

While there are large differences in mean performance between countries, the variation in performance between students within each country is, as in the case of reading literacy, many times larger. Mean performance does not therefore provide a full picture of student performance and can mask significant variation within an individual class, school or education system. One of the major challenges faced by education systems is to encourage high performance while at the same time minimising internal disparities.

Figure 3.2

Multiple comparisons of mean performance on the mathematical literacy scale

	Mean	S.E.	Japan	Korea	New Zealand	Finland	Australia	Canada	Switzerland	United Kingdom	Belgium	France	Austria	Denmark	Iceland	**Liechtenstein**	Sweden	Ireland	Norway	Czech Republic	United States	Germany	Hungary	**Russian Fed.**	Spain	Poland	**Latvia**	Italy	Portugal	Greece	Luxembourg	Mexico	**Brazil**
Mean			557	547	537	536	533	533	529	529	520	517	515	514	514	**514**	510	503	499	498	493	490	488	**478**	476	470	**463**	457	454	447	446	387	**334**
S.E.			(5.5)	(2.8)	(3.1)	(2.1)	(3.5)	(1.4)	(4.4)	(2.5)	(3.9)	(2.7)	(2.5)	(2.4)	(2.3)	**(7.0)**	(2.5)	(2.7)	(2.8)	(2.8)	(7.6)	(2.5)	(4.0)	**(5.5)**	(3.1)	(5.5)	**(4.5)**	(2.9)	(4.1)	(5.6)	(2.0)	(3.4)	**(3.7)**
Japan	557	(5.5)		○	○	▲	▲	▲	▲	▲	▲	▲	▲	▲	▲	▲	▲	▲	▲	▲	▲	▲	▲	▲	▲	▲	▲	▲	▲	▲	▲	▲	▲
Korea	547	(2.8)	○		○	○	○	▲	▲	▲	▲	▲	▲	▲	▲	▲	▲	▲	▲	▲	▲	▲	▲	▲	▲	▲	▲	▲	▲	▲	▲	▲	▲
New Zealand	537	(3.1)	○	○		○	○	○	○	○	▲	▲	▲	▲	▲	▲	▲	▲	▲	▲	▲	▲	▲	▲	▲	▲	▲	▲	▲	▲	▲	▲	▲
Finland	536	(2.1)	▽	○	○		○	○	○	○	▲	▲	▲	▲	▲	○	▲	▲	▲	▲	▲	▲	▲	▲	▲	▲	▲	▲	▲	▲	▲	▲	▲
Australia	533	(3.5)	▽	○	○	○		○	○	○	○	▲	▲	▲	▲	○	▲	▲	▲	▲	▲	▲	▲	▲	▲	▲	▲	▲	▲	▲	▲	▲	▲
Canada	533	(1.4)	▽	▽	○	○	○		○	○	▲	▲	▲	▲	▲	○	▲	▲	▲	▲	▲	▲	▲	▲	▲	▲	▲	▲	▲	▲	▲	▲	▲
Switzerland	529	(4.4)	▽	▽	○	○	○	○		○	○	○	○	○	○	○	▲	▲	▲	▲	▲	▲	▲	▲	▲	▲	▲	▲	▲	▲	▲	▲	▲
United Kingdom	529	(2.5)	▽	▽	○	○	○	○	○		○	▲	▲	▲	▲	○	▲	▲	▲	▲	▲	▲	▲	▲	▲	▲	▲	▲	▲	▲	▲	▲	▲
Belgium	520	(3.9)	▽	▽	▽	▽	○	▽	○	○		○	○	○	○	○	○	▲	▲	▲	▲	▲	▲	▲	▲	▲	▲	▲	▲	▲	▲	▲	▲
France	517	(2.7)	▽	▽	▽	▽	▽	▽	○	▽	○		○	○	○	○	○	▲	▲	▲	○	▲	▲	▲	▲	▲	▲	▲	▲	▲	▲	▲	▲
Austria	515	(2.5)	▽	▽	▽	▽	▽	▽	○	▽	○	○		○	○	○	○	▲	▲	▲	○	▲	▲	▲	▲	▲	▲	▲	▲	▲	▲	▲	▲
Denmark	514	(2.4)	▽	▽	▽	▽	▽	▽	○	▽	○	○	○		○	○	○	▲	▲	▲	○	▲	▲	▲	▲	▲	▲	▲	▲	▲	▲	▲	▲
Iceland	514	(2.3)	▽	▽	▽	▽	▽	▽	○	▽	○	○	○	○		○	○	▲	▲	▲	○	▲	▲	▲	▲	▲	▲	▲	▲	▲	▲	▲	▲
Liechtenstein	**514**	**(7.0)**	▽	▽	○	○	○	○	○	○	○	○	○	○	○		○	○	○	○	○	▲	▲	▲	▲	▲	▲	▲	▲	▲	▲	▲	▲
Sweden	510	(2.5)	▽	▽	▽	▽	▽	▽	▽	▽	○	○	○	○	○	○		○	○	▲	○	▲	▲	▲	▲	▲	▲	▲	▲	▲	▲	▲	▲
Ireland	503	(2.7)	▽	▽	▽	▽	▽	▽	▽	▽	▽	▽	▽	▽	▽	○	○		○	○	○	▲	○	▲	▲	▲	▲	▲	▲	▲	▲	▲	▲
Norway	499	(2.8)	▽	▽	▽	▽	▽	▽	▽	▽	▽	▽	▽	▽	▽	○	○	○		○	○	○	○	▲	▲	▲	▲	▲	▲	▲	▲	▲	▲
Czech Republic	498	(2.8)	▽	▽	▽	▽	▽	▽	▽	▽	▽	▽	▽	▽	▽	○	▽	○	○		○	○	○	○	▲	▲	▲	▲	▲	▲	▲	▲	▲
United States	493	(7.6)	▽	▽	▽	▽	▽	▽	▽	▽	○	○	○	○	○	○	○	○	○	○		○	○	○	○	○	▲	▲	▲	▲	▲	▲	▲
Germany	490	(2.5)	▽	▽	▽	▽	▽	▽	▽	▽	▽	▽	▽	▽	▽	▽	▽	▽	○	○	○		○	○	▲	▲	▲	▲	▲	▲	▲	▲	▲
Hungary	488	(4.0)	▽	▽	▽	▽	▽	▽	▽	▽	▽	▽	▽	▽	▽	▽	▽	○	○	○	○	○		○	○	○	▲	▲	▲	▲	▲	▲	▲
Russian Fed.	**478**	**(5.5)**	▽	▽	▽	▽	▽	▽	▽	▽	▽	▽	▽	▽	▽	▽	▽	▽	▽	○	○	○	○		○	○	○	▲	▲	▲	▲	▲	▲
Spain	476	(3.1)	▽	▽	▽	▽	▽	▽	▽	▽	▽	▽	▽	▽	▽	▽	▽	▽	▽	▽	○	▽	○	○		○	○	▲	▲	▲	▲	▲	▲
Poland	470	(5.5)	▽	▽	▽	▽	▽	▽	▽	▽	▽	▽	▽	▽	▽	▽	▽	▽	▽	▽	○	▽	○	○	○		○	○	○	○	▲	▲	▲
Latvia	**463**	**(4.5)**	▽	▽	▽	▽	▽	▽	▽	▽	▽	▽	▽	▽	▽	▽	▽	▽	▽	▽	▽	▽	▽	○	○	○		○	○	○	▲	▲	▲
Italy	457	(2.9)	▽	▽	▽	▽	▽	▽	▽	▽	▽	▽	▽	▽	▽	▽	▽	▽	▽	▽	▽	▽	▽	▽	▽	○	○		○	○	▲	▲	▲
Portugal	454	(4.1)	▽	▽	▽	▽	▽	▽	▽	▽	▽	▽	▽	▽	▽	▽	▽	▽	▽	▽	▽	▽	▽	▽	▽	○	○	○		○	○	▲	▲
Greece	447	(5.6)	▽	▽	▽	▽	▽	▽	▽	▽	▽	▽	▽	▽	▽	▽	▽	▽	▽	▽	▽	▽	▽	▽	▽	○	○	○	○		○	▲	▲
Luxembourg	446	(2.0)	▽	▽	▽	▽	▽	▽	▽	▽	▽	▽	▽	▽	▽	▽	▽	▽	▽	▽	▽	▽	▽	▽	▽	▽	▽	▽	○	○		▲	▲
Mexico	387	(3.4)	▽	▽	▽	▽	▽	▽	▽	▽	▽	▽	▽	▽	▽	▽	▽	▽	▽	▽	▽	▽	▽	▽	▽	▽	▽	▽	▽	▽	▽		▲
Brazil	**334**	**(3.7)**	▽	▽	▽	▽	▽	▽	▽	▽	▽	▽	▽	▽	▽	▽	▽	▽	▽	▽	▽	▽	▽	▽	▽	▽	▽	▽	▽	▽	▽	▽	
Upper rank*			1	2	4	4	4	5	4	6	9	10	10	10	11	9	13	16	17	17	16	20	20	21	23	23	25	26	26	27	29	31	32
Lower rank*			3	3	8	7	9	8	10	10	15	15	16	16	16	18	17	19	20	20	23	22	23	25	25	26	28	28	29	30	30	31	32

**Note*: Because data are based on samples, it is not possible to report exact rank order positions for countries. However, it is possible to report the range of rank order positions within which the country mean lies with 95 per cent likelihood.

Instructions

Read across the row for a country to compare performance with the countries listed along the top of the chart. The symbols indicate whether the mean performance of the country in the row is significantly lower than that of the comparison country, significantly higher than that of the comparison country, or if there is no statistically significant difference between the mean performance of the two countries.

▲ Mean performance statistically significantly higher than in comparison country.
○ No statistically significant difference from comparison country.
▽ Mean performance statistically significantly lower than in comparison country.

Statistically significantly above the OECD average
Not statistically significantly different from the OECD average
Statistically significantly below the OECD average

Source: OECD PISA database, 2001.

Figure 3.3 shows the distribution of performance scores on the mathematical literacy scale.[5] The gradation bars show the range of performance in each country between the 5th and 95th percentiles. The density of the bar represents the proportion of students performing at the corresponding scale points. In addition, Table 3.1 shows the 25th and 75th percentiles, *i.e.*, the scale points that mark the bottom and top quarters of performers in each country. The middle of each bar shows the mean country score, which was the subject of the discussion in the preceding section, together with its confidence interval.

...with a significant minority of students in many countries having difficulty applying simple computational skills...

In every country, education systems, educational programmes, schools and teachers are called to serve students with a wide range of knowledge and skills, and to enhance these effectively. In about half of the countries, more than 10 per cent of students do not reach the mean score of the OECD country with the lowest level of performance (Table 3.1). Figure 3.1 shows that these students will typically find it difficult to complete simple tasks consisting of reproducing basic mathematical facts or processes, or applying simple computational skills. Furthermore, tasks requiring interpretation or reasoning skills that go beyond recognition of a single familiar element of the problem, and solution processes more complex than the application of a routine procedure in a single processing step, will normally be beyond the level of knowledge and skills of these students. In fact, all of the sample questions shown in Figure 3.1 are typically beyond the ability of students performing below the mean performance level of Mexico (387 points).

...though at least 10% of the students in all but two countries reach the mean of the best-performing country.

At the other end of the scale, all countries but two have at least 10 per cent of students performing above the mean of the country with the best performance, Japan (557 points).

These findings suggest that education systems in many countries need to address a wide range of student needs, both those with the greatest difficulties and those who perform exceptionally well.

Strikingly, the smallest disparities tend to be in well-performing countries...

It is evident from a comparison between the range of performance within a country and its average performance that wide disparities in performance are not a necessary condition for a country to attain a high level of overall performance. On the contrary, it is striking to see that mean performance in six out of the eight countries with the smallest differences between the 75th and 25th percentiles (which covers the middle half of the national performance distribution), namely Canada, Denmark, Finland, Iceland, Japan and Korea, all perform statistically significantly above the OECD average (Table 3.1). Furthermore, four of them, Canada, Finland, Japan and Korea, are among the six countries with the best performance in mathematical literacy in the OECD.

...while some countries with low mean performance show wide disparities.

On the other hand, four of the five countries with the most unequal distribution of mathematical literacy skills (as measured by the difference between the 75th and 25th percentiles) – Germany, Greece, Hungary and Poland – perform statistically significantly below the OECD average (Belgium is the exception, having a very unequal distribution of scores but a mean above the OECD average).

Figure 3.3

Distribution of student performance on the mathematical literacy scale

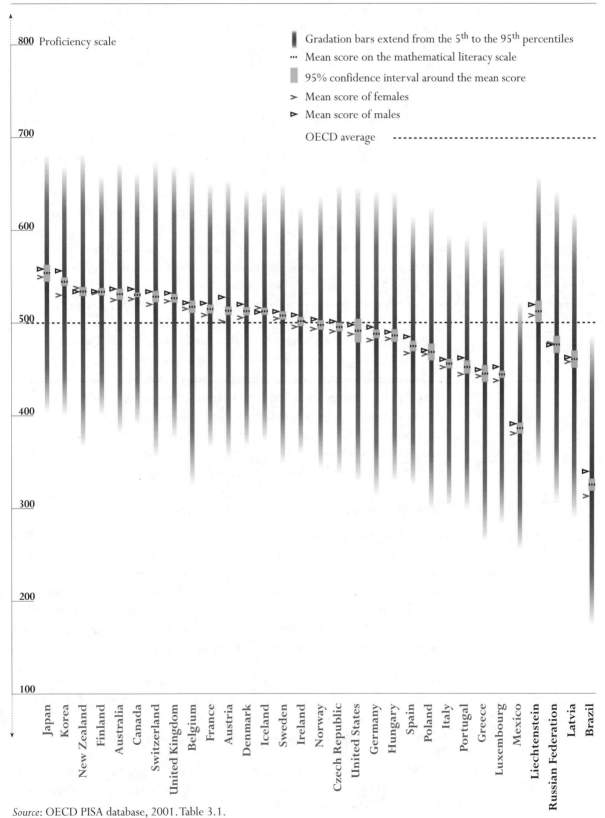

Source: OECD PISA database, 2001. Table 3.1.

The pattern in the distribution of student performance on the mathematical literacy scale tends to be similar to that in reading literacy, with Belgium, Germany, Greece, Hungary, New Zealand, Poland, Switzerland and the United States showing a relatively large gap between the 75th and 25th percentiles — between 135 and 149 points on the mathematical literacy scale (Table 3.1). On the other hand, Finland, Iceland, Ireland, Japan and Korea show comparatively small disparities, less than 113 points separating their 75th and 25th percentiles. There are exceptions, though: for example, Australia shows comparatively large disparities on the combined reading literacy scale while its difference between the 75th and 25th percentiles in mathematical literacy, 121 points, is below the OECD average interquartile range.

Students in countries with low mathematical performance are not necessarily less likely, on average, to meet their teachers' expectations.

As explained in Chapter 2, students participating in PISA were asked to report the marks that they had received in mathematics in their last school report and to indicate how their marks were interpreted by the school. From this information, it was determined whether the students' school marks were above, at, or below the school's or class teacher's pass/fail threshold. Comparing this information with student performance on the PISA mathematical literacy scale can provide a frame of reference for interpreting PISA scores within the national context (Table 3.2). The data show that countries with comparatively high performance on the PISA assessments do not necessarily have a comparatively low proportion of students meeting the expectations of their teachers. By contrast, in countries with comparatively low mean performance, the vast majority of students still report that they live up to what is expected of them by their teachers. The international evidence that there are substantial differences between countries in mean levels of performance suggests that countries setting low expectations and achieving low mean performance levels could raise both.

Mathematical and reading literacy performance

Countries have strengths and weaknesses in different domains...

It is not appropriate to compare numerical scale scores directly between the reading and mathematical literacy scales (the mean scores for reading and mathematical literacy provided in brackets below are for reference only). Nevertheless, it is possible to determine the relative strengths of countries in the two domains, on the basis of their relative rank-order positions on the reading and mathematical literacy scales.[6] Note that this comparison does not compare performance between countries, but rather between the domains within countries.

...with some countries performing better in mathematical than in reading literacy...

– On the basis of this comparison, Denmark (497, 514), Hungary (480, 488), Latvia (458, 463), Liechtenstein (483, 514), Japan (522, 557), Korea (525, 547), the Russian Federation (462, 478) and Switzerland (494, 529) show better performance in mathematical literacy than in reading literacy.

– Canada (534, 533), Finland (546, 536), Greece (474, 447), Ireland (527, 503), Italy (487, 457), Norway (505, 499), Spain (493, 476), Sweden (516, 510) and the United States (504, 493) perform better in reading.

– The relative strengths of the remaining countries are essentially the same on both scales.

Student performance in scientific literacy

How scientific literacy is measured in PISA

Like performance in mathematical literacy, performance in scientific literacy is marked in PISA 2000 on a single scale with an average score of 500 points and a standard deviation of 100 points, and with about two-thirds of students across OECD countries scoring between 400 and 600 points. The scale measures students' ability to use scientific knowledge (understanding of scientific concepts), to recognise scientific questions and to identify what is involved in scientific investigations (understanding of the nature of scientific investigation), to relate scientific data to claims and conclusions (use of scientific evidence), and to communicate these aspects of science.

Scientific literacy measures students' ability to use scientific knowledge and approach problems scientifically...

The criteria defining the increasing difficulty of tasks along the scale involve: the complexity of the concepts used, the amount of data given, the chain of reasoning required and the precision required in communication. In addition, the level of difficulty is influenced by the context of the information, the format, and the presentation of the question. The tasks in PISA require scientific knowledge involving (in ascending order of difficulty): recall of simple scientific knowledge or common scientific knowledge or data; the application of scientific concepts or questions and a basic knowledge of investigation; the use of more highly developed scientific concepts or a chain of reasoning; and knowledge of simple conceptual models or analysis of evidence in order to try out alternative approaches.

...the difficulty of tasks being determined by the complexity of concepts, the amount of data given, and the chain of reasoning required.

– Towards the top end of the scientific literacy scale (around 690 points) students are generally able to create or use conceptual models to make predictions or give explanations; to analyse scientific investigations in order to grasp, for example, the design of an experiment or to identify an idea being tested; to compare data in order to evaluate alternative viewpoints or differing perspectives; and to communicate scientific arguments and/or descriptions in detail and with precision.

The most difficult tasks require complex conceptual skills...

– At around 550 points, students are typically able to use scientific concepts to make predictions or provide explanations; to recognise questions that can be answered by scientific investigation and/or identify details of what is involved in a scientific investigation; and to select relevant information from competing data or chains of reasoning in drawing or evaluating conclusions.

...less difficult tasks still require sound scientific thinking...

– Towards the lower end of the scale (around 400 points), students are able to recall simple factual scientific knowledge (*e.g.* names, facts, terminology, simple rules); and to use common scientific knowledge in drawing or evaluating conclusions.

...and the easiest tasks only require recall and use of simple scientific knowledge.

Figure 3.4
A sample of the science tasks used in PISA

SEMMELWEIS' DIARY – TEXT 1

'July 1846. Next week I will take up a position as "Herr Doktor" at the First Ward of the maternity clinic of the Vienna General Hospital. I was frightened when I heard about the percentage of patients who die in this clinic. This month not less than 36 of the 208 mothers died there, all from puerperal fever. Giving birth to a child is as dangerous as first-degree pneumonia.'

Number of deaths per 100 deliveries from puerperal fever

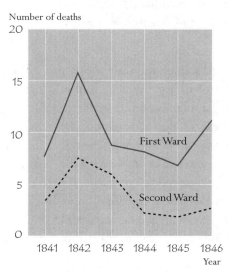

These lines from the diary of Ignaz Semmelweis (1818-1865) illustrate the devastating effects of puerperal fever, a contagious disease that killed many women after childbirth. Semmelweis collected data about the number of deaths from puerperal fever in both the First and the Second Wards (see diagram).

Physicians, among them Semmelweis, were completely in the dark about the cause of puerperal fever. Semmelweis' diary again:

'December 1846. Why do so many women die from this fever after giving birth without any problems? For centuries science has told us that it is an invisible epidemic that kills mothers. Causes may be changes in the air or some extraterrestrial influence or a movement of the earth itself, an earthquake.'

Nowadays not many people would consider extraterrestrial influence or an earthquake as possible causes of fever. We now know it has to do with hygienic conditions. But in the time Semmelweis lived, many people, even scientists, did! However, Semmelweis knew that it was unlikely that fever could be caused by extraterrestrial influence or an earthquake. He pointed at the data he collected (see diagram) and used this to try to persuade his colleagues.

SEMMELWEIS' DIARY – TEXT 2

Part of the research in the hospital was dissection. The body of a deceased person was cut open to find a cause of death. Semmelweis recorded that the students working on the First ward usually took part in dissections on women who died the previous day, before they examined women who had just given birth. They did not pay much attention to cleaning themselves after the dissections. Some were even proud of the fact that you could tell by their smell that they had been working in the mortuary, as this showed how industrious they were!

One of Semmelweis' friends died after having cut himself during such a dissection. Dissection of his body showed he had the same symptoms as mothers who died from puerperal fever. This gave Semmelweis a new idea.

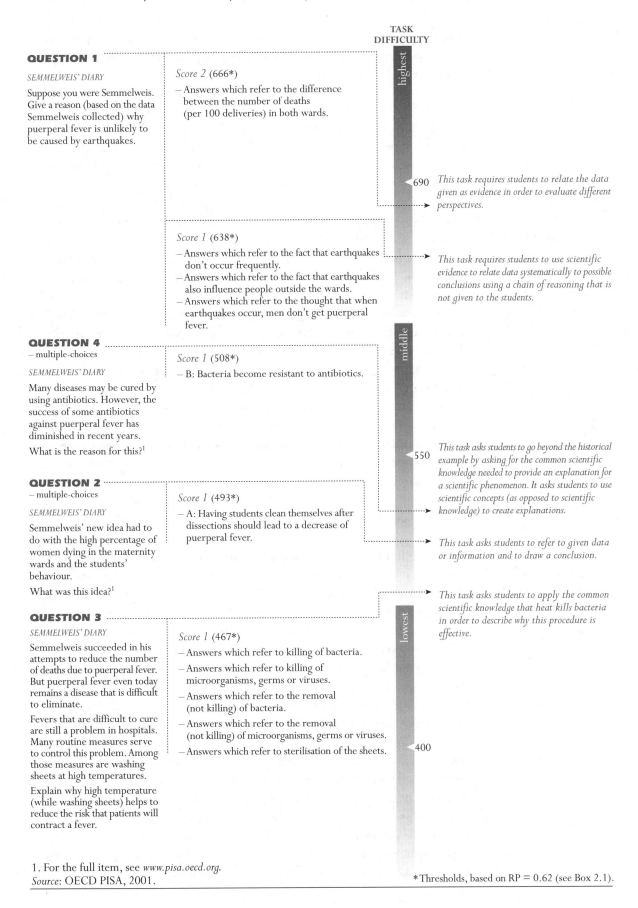

TASK DIFFICULTY

QUESTION 1

SEMMELWEIS' DIARY

Suppose you were Semmelweis. Give a reason (based on the data Semmelweis collected) why puerperal fever is unlikely to be caused by earthquakes.

Score 2 (666*)

— Answers which refer to the difference between the number of deaths (per 100 deliveries) in both wards.

highest

690

This task requires students to relate the data given as evidence in order to evaluate different perspectives.

Score 1 (638*)

— Answers which refer to the fact that earthquakes don't occur frequently.
— Answers which refer to the fact that earthquakes also influence people outside the wards.
— Answers which refer to the thought that when earthquakes occur, men don't get puerperal fever.

This task requires students to use scientific evidence to relate data systematically to possible conclusions using a chain of reasoning that is not given to the students.

QUESTION 4
— multiple-choices

SEMMELWEIS' DIARY

Many diseases may be cured by using antibiotics. However, the success of some antibiotics against puerperal fever has diminished in recent years.

What is the reason for this?[1]

Score 1 (508*)

— B: Bacteria become resistant to antibiotics.

middle

550

This task asks students to go beyond the historical example by asking for the common scientific knowledge needed to provide an explanation for a scientific phenomenon. It asks students to use scientific concepts (as opposed to scientific knowledge) to create explanations.

QUESTION 2
— multiple-choices

SEMMELWEIS' DIARY

Semmelweis' new idea had to do with the high percentage of women dying in the maternity wards and the students' behaviour.

What was this idea?[1]

Score 1 (493*)

— A: Having students clean themselves after dissections should lead to a decrease of puerperal fever.

This task asks students to refer to given data or information and to draw a conclusion.

This task asks students to apply the common scientific knowledge that heat kills bacteria in order to describe why this procedure is effective.

QUESTION 3

SEMMELWEIS' DIARY

Semmelweis succeeded in his attempts to reduce the number of deaths due to puerperal fever. But puerperal fever even today remains a disease that is difficult to eliminate.

Fevers that are difficult to cure are still a problem in hospitals. Many routine measures serve to control this problem. Among those measures are washing sheets at high temperatures.

Explain why high temperature (while washing sheets) helps to reduce the risk that patients will contract a fever.

lowest

Score 1 (467*)

— Answers which refer to killing of bacteria.

— Answers which refer to killing of microorganisms, germs or viruses.

— Answers which refer to the removal (not killing) of bacteria.

— Answers which refer to the removal (not killing) of microorganisms, germs or viruses.

— Answers which refer to sterilisation of the sheets.

400

1. For the full item, see *www.pisa.oecd.org.*
Source: OECD PISA, 2001.

* Thresholds, based on RP = 0.62 (see Box 2.1).

A description of the conceptual framework underlying the PISA assessment of scientific literacy is provided in *Measuring Student Knowledge and Skills – A New Framework for Assessment* (OECD, 1999a).

In the PISA assessment, the best 5 per cent of students achieved 657 points on average across OECD countries, 10 per cent reached 627 points and 25 per cent, 572 points. At the lower end of the scale, more than three-quarters achieved at least 431 points, more than 90 per cent reached 368 points and more than 95 per cent, 332 points (Table 3.3).

Students were, for example, presented with an experimental problem facing a 19th century scientist...

The tasks used for the assessment of scientific literacy in PISA vary widely. Figure 3.4 shows the tasks from one of the 13 units used in PISA 2000, along with a description of the criteria used to mark students' answers (a more complete set of sample tasks can be found at *www.pisa.oecd.org*). The sample unit refers to Semmelweis's research on the causes of puerperal fever. Semmelweis was puzzled by a remarkably high death rate due to puerperal fever in a maternity ward. The students are presented with this finding by way of graphs and then confronted with the suggestion that puerperal fever may be caused by extraterrestrial influences or natural disasters, not an uncommon thought in Semmelweis's time. Semmelweis tried to convince his colleagues to consider more rational explanations. Students are invited to imagine themselves in Semmelweis's position and to use the data that Semmelweis collected to defend the idea that earthquakes are an unlikely cause of the disease. The graphs show a similar variation in death rate over time, the first ward consistently having a higher death rate than the second ward. If earthquakes were the cause, the death rates in both wards should be about the same. The graphs suggest that something about the wards explains the difference. Figure 3.4 shows an extract of the criteria used to mark students' answers.

...with the hardest task, answered correctly by only a minority, requiring them to assess evidence and draw inferences...

To receive full credit for Question 1 in this sample unit, students needed to refer to the idea that death rates in both wards should have been similar over time if earthquakes were the cause. Full credit for this question corresponds to a score of 666 points on the scientific literacy scale. Students with a score of 666 points should theoretically be able to answer questions of this level of difficulty correctly 62 out of 100 times (see also Box 2.2). On average across OECD countries, 22 per cent of students answered this question correctly (for data, see *www.pisa.oecd.org*). Some students provided answers that did not refer to Semmelweis's findings, but to a characteristic of earthquakes that made it unlikely that they were the cause, such as their infrequent occurrence, while the fever was present all the time. Other students provided original and justifiable statements, such as "if it were earthquakes, why do only women get the disease, and not men?" or "if so, women outside the wards would also get that fever". Although it can be argued that these students did not consider the data that Semmelweis collected, as the question asks, they received a partial score because their answers demonstrated an ability to use scientific facts to reach a conclusion. On average across OECD countries, 28 per cent of students received at least partial credit for this question (for data, see *www.pisa.oecd.org*).

Question 2 in the same sample unit asked students to identify Semmelweis's idea that was most relevant to reducing the incidence of puerperal fever. Students needed to put two pieces of relevant information from the text together: the behaviour of a medical student and the death of Semmelweis's friend of puerperal fever after the student had dissected a cadaver. This question exemplifies average performance, at a level of difficulty of 493 points. The question required students to refer to given data or information in order to draw a conclusion and assessed their understanding of the nature of scientific investigation. On average across OECD countries, 64 per cent of students answered this question correctly, by choosing the response option stating that having students clean themselves after dissection should lead to a decrease in puerperal fever.

...and easier questions requiring them to link information from the text...

Most people are now aware that bacteria cause many diseases, and that heat can kill these bacteria. However, many people may not realise that routine procedures in hospitals use this observation to reduce the risks of fevers and other diseases. Question 3 in the sample unit asked students to apply the common scientific knowledge that heat kills bacteria to explain why these procedures are effective. This is another example of a question of low to moderate difficulty, with a value of 467 points on the scientific literacy scale. On average across OECD countries, 68 per cent of students received full credit for answering this open-ended question correctly.

...to draw on common scientific knowledge...

Finally, Question 4 went beyond the historical example, asking students to provide an explanation for a scientific phenomenon. Students were required to explain why antibiotics have become less effective over time. In order to answer correctly, they needed to know that the frequent and extended use of antibiotics creates strains of bacteria resistant to the initially lethal effects. This question is located at a moderate level on the scientific literacy scale, 508 points, because it asks students to use scientific concepts (as opposed to common scientific knowledge, which is at a lower level) to find explanations. On average across OECD countries, 60 per cent of students answered this question correctly, by choosing the multiple-choice option that bacteria become resistant to antibiotics.

...and to use scientific concepts to provide an explanation.

The mean performances of countries in scientific literacy

As with mathematical literacy, performance in scientific literacy can be summarised by way of countries' mean scores (Figure 3.5). Japan and Korea show the highest performance on the scientific literacy scale. Other countries that score statistically significantly above the OECD average are Australia, Austria, Canada, the Czech Republic, Finland, Ireland, New Zealand, Sweden and the United Kingdom. Mean scores in Belgium, France, Hungary, Iceland, Norway, Switzerland and the United States are not significantly different from the OECD average.[7]

Mean scores for country performance in scientific literacy are summarised in Figure 3.5...

Some countries have mean scores significantly above the OECD average in all three domains: Australia, Austria, Canada, Finland, Japan, Korea, New Zealand, Sweden and the United Kingdom.

Figure 3.5

Multiple comparisons of mean performance on the scientific literacy scale

			Korea	Japan	Finland	United Kingdom	Canada	New Zealand	Australia	Austria	Ireland	Sweden	Czech Republic	France	Norway	United States	Hungary	Iceland	Belgium	Switzerland	Spain	Germany	Poland	Denmark	Italy	Liechtenstein	Greece	Russian Fed.	Latvia	Portugal	Luxembourg	Mexico	Brazil
	Mean		552	550	538	532	529	528	528	519	513	512	511	500	500	499	496	496	496	496	491	487	483	481	478	476	461	460	460	459	443	422	375
		S.E.	(2.7)	(5.5)	(2.5)	(2.7)	(1.6)	(2.4)	(3.5)	(2.5)	(3.2)	(2.5)	(2.4)	(3.2)	(2.7)	(7.3)	(4.2)	(2.2)	(4.3)	(4.4)	(3.0)	(2.4)	(5.1)	(2.8)	(3.1)	(7.1)	(4.9)	(4.7)	(5.6)	(4.0)	(2.3)	(3.2)	(3.3)
Korea	552	(2.7)		○	▲	▲	▲	▲	▲	▲	▲	▲	▲	▲	▲	▲	▲	▲	▲	▲	▲	▲	▲	▲	▲	▲	▲	▲	▲	▲	▲	▲	▲
Japan	550	(5.5)	○		○	○	▲	▲	▲	▲	▲	▲	▲	▲	▲	▲	▲	▲	▲	▲	▲	▲	▲	▲	▲	▲	▲	▲	▲	▲	▲	▲	▲
Finland	538	(2.5)	▽	○		○	○	○	○	▲	▲	▲	▲	▲	▲	▲	▲	▲	▲	▲	▲	▲	▲	▲	▲	▲	▲	▲	▲	▲	▲	▲	▲
United Kingdom	532	(2.7)	▽	○	○		○	○	○	▲	▲	▲	▲	▲	▲	▲	▲	▲	▲	▲	▲	▲	▲	▲	▲	▲	▲	▲	▲	▲	▲	▲	▲
Canada	529	(1.6)	▽	▽	○	○		○	○	▲	▲	▲	▲	▲	▲	▲	▲	▲	▲	▲	▲	▲	▲	▲	▲	▲	▲	▲	▲	▲	▲	▲	▲
New Zealand	528	(2.4)	▽	▽	○	○	○		○	○	▲	▲	▲	▲	▲	▲	▲	▲	▲	▲	▲	▲	▲	▲	▲	▲	▲	▲	▲	▲	▲	▲	▲
Australia	528	(3.5)	▽	▽	○	○	○	○		○	○	▲	▲	▲	▲	▲	▲	▲	▲	▲	▲	▲	▲	▲	▲	▲	▲	▲	▲	▲	▲	▲	▲
Austria	519	(2.5)	▽	▽	▽	▽	▽	○	○		○	○	○	▲	▲	○	▲	▲	▲	▲	▲	▲	▲	▲	▲	▲	▲	▲	▲	▲	▲	▲	▲
Ireland	513	(3.2)	▽	▽	▽	▽	▽	▽	○	○		○	○	○	○	○	▲	▲	▲	▲	▲	▲	▲	▲	▲	▲	▲	▲	▲	▲	▲	▲	▲
Sweden	512	(2.5)	▽	▽	▽	▽	▽	▽	▽	○	○		○	○	▲	○	▲	▲	▲	▲	▲	▲	▲	▲	▲	▲	▲	▲	▲	▲	▲	▲	▲
Czech Republic	511	(2.4)	▽	▽	▽	▽	▽	▽	▽	○	○	○		○	○	○	▲	▲	▲	○	▲	▲	▲	▲	▲	▲	▲	▲	▲	▲	▲	▲	▲
France	500	(3.2)	▽	▽	▽	▽	▽	▽	▽	▽	○	○	○		○	○	○	○	○	○	○	▲	○	▲	▲	○	▲	▲	▲	▲	▲	▲	▲
Norway	500	(2.7)	▽	▽	▽	▽	▽	▽	▽	▽	○	▽	○	○		○	○	○	○	○	○	▲	○	▲	▲	▲	▲	▲	▲	▲	▲	▲	▲
United States	499	(7.3)	▽	▽	▽	▽	▽	▽	▽	○	○	○	○	○	○		○	○	○	○	○	○	○	○	○	○	▲	▲	▲	▲	▲	▲	▲
Hungary	496	(4.2)	▽	▽	▽	▽	▽	▽	▽	▽	▽	▽	▽	○	○	○		○	○	○	○	○	○	○	▲	○	▲	▲	▲	▲	▲	▲	▲
Iceland	496	(2.2)	▽	▽	▽	▽	▽	▽	▽	▽	▽	▽	▽	○	○	○	○		○	○	○	○	○	▲	▲	○	▲	▲	▲	▲	▲	▲	▲
Belgium	496	(4.3)	▽	▽	▽	▽	▽	▽	▽	▽	▽	▽	▽	○	○	○	○	○		○	○	○	○	○	▲	○	▲	▲	▲	▲	▲	▲	▲
Switzerland	496	(4.4)	▽	▽	▽	▽	▽	▽	▽	▽	▽	▽	○	○	○	○	○	○	○		○	○	○	○	▲	○	▲	▲	▲	▲	▲	▲	▲
Spain	491	(3.0)	▽	▽	▽	▽	▽	▽	▽	▽	▽	▽	▽	○	○	○	○	○	○	○		○	○	○	○	○	▲	▲	▲	▲	▲	▲	▲
Germany	487	(2.4)	▽	▽	▽	▽	▽	▽	▽	▽	▽	▽	▽	▽	▽	○	○	○	○	○	○		○	○	○	○	▲	▲	▲	▲	▲	▲	▲
Poland	483	(5.1)	▽	▽	▽	▽	▽	▽	▽	▽	▽	▽	▽	○	○	○	○	○	○	○	○	○		○	○	○	▲	▲	○	▲	▲	▲	▲
Denmark	481	(2.8)	▽	▽	▽	▽	▽	▽	▽	▽	▽	▽	▽	▽	▽	○	○	▽	○	○	○	○	○		○	○	▲	▲	▲	▲	▲	▲	▲
Italy	478	(3.1)	▽	▽	▽	▽	▽	▽	▽	▽	▽	▽	▽	▽	▽	○	▽	▽	▽	▽	○	○	○	○		○	○	○	○	▲	▲	▲	▲
Liechtenstein	476	(7.1)	▽	▽	▽	▽	▽	▽	▽	▽	▽	▽	▽	○	▽	○	○	○	○	○	○	○	○	○	○		○	○	○	○	▲	▲	▲
Greece	461	(4.9)	▽	▽	▽	▽	▽	▽	▽	▽	▽	▽	▽	▽	▽	▽	▽	▽	▽	▽	▽	▽	▽	▽	○	○		○	○	○	▲	▲	▲
Russian Fed.	460	(4.7)	▽	▽	▽	▽	▽	▽	▽	▽	▽	▽	▽	▽	▽	▽	▽	▽	▽	▽	▽	▽	▽	▽	○	○	○		○	○	▲	▲	▲
Latvia	460	(5.6)	▽	▽	▽	▽	▽	▽	▽	▽	▽	▽	▽	▽	▽	▽	▽	▽	▽	▽	▽	▽	○	▽	○	○	○	○		○	○	▲	▲
Portugal	459	(4.0)	▽	▽	▽	▽	▽	▽	▽	▽	▽	▽	▽	▽	▽	▽	▽	▽	▽	▽	▽	▽	▽	▽	▽	○	○	○	○		▲	▲	▲
Luxembourg	443	(2.3)	▽	▽	▽	▽	▽	▽	▽	▽	▽	▽	▽	▽	▽	▽	▽	▽	▽	▽	▽	▽	▽	▽	▽	▽	▽	▽	○	▽		▲	▲
Mexico	422	(3.2)	▽	▽	▽	▽	▽	▽	▽	▽	▽	▽	▽	▽	▽	▽	▽	▽	▽	▽	▽	▽	▽	▽	▽	▽	▽	▽	▽	▽	▽		▲
Brazil	375	(3.3)	▽	▽	▽	▽	▽	▽	▽	▽	▽	▽	▽	▽	▽	▽	▽	▽	▽	▽	▽	▽	▽	▽	▽	▽	▽	▽	▽	▽	▽	▽	
	Upper rank*		1	1	3	3	4	4	4	8	9	9	10	13	13	11	13	14	13	13	16	19	19	21	22	20	25	26	25	26	30	31	32
	Lower rank*		2	2	4	7	8	8	8	10	12	13	13	18	18	21	21	20	21	21	22	23	25	25	25	26	29	29	29	29	30	31	32

**Note*: Because data are based on samples, it is not possible to report exact rank order positions for countries. However, it is possible to report the range of rank order positions within which the country mean lies with 95 per cent likelihood.

Instructions

Read across the row for a country to compare performance with the countries listed along the top of the chart. The symbols indicate whether the mean performance of the country in the row is significantly lower than that of the comparison country, significantly higher than that of the comparison country, or if there is no statistically significant difference between the mean performance of the two countries.

▲ Mean performance statistically significantly higher than in comparison country.
○ No statistically significant difference from comparison country.
▽ Mean performance statistically significantly lower than in comparison country.

Statistically significantly above the OECD average
Not statistically significantly different from the OECD average
Statistically significantly below the OECD average

Source: OECD PISA database, 2001.

Figure 3.6

Distribution of student performance on the scientific literacy scale

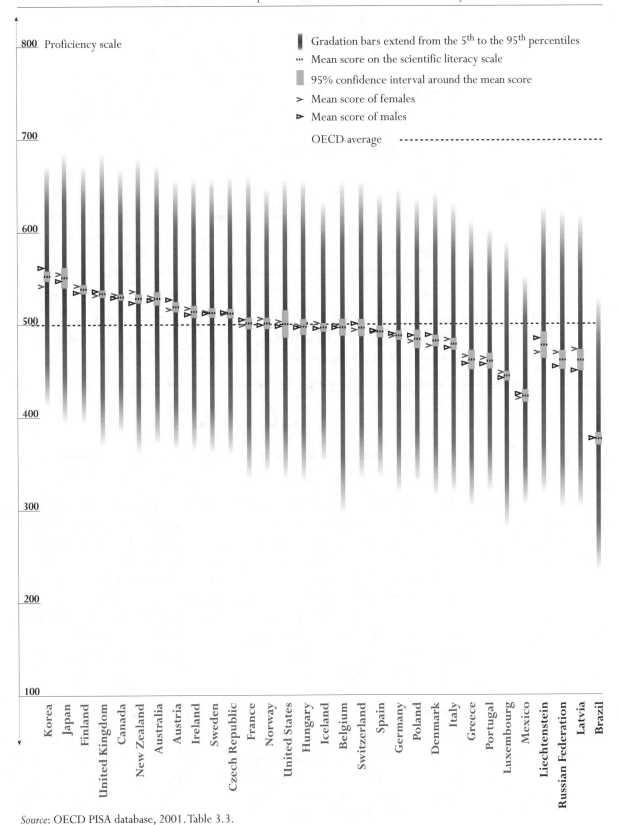

Source: OECD PISA database, 2001. Table 3.3.

The distribution of scientific literacy within countries

Some countries combine high levels of scientific literacy with low disparities.

Figure 3.6 shows the distribution of performance scores on the scientific literacy scale in a format similar to that of Figure 3.3. In addition, Table 3.5 provides an indication of the proportion of this variation that lies between schools. For the interpretation of these data refer to Chapter 2. As in the case of reading literacy and mathematical literacy, three main conclusions apply: variation in student performance within countries is much greater than variation in mean performance between countries; the extent of variation within countries varies considerably; and the size of the variation within countries is not related to the level of their overall mean performance (Table 3.3).

Performance in reading and scientific literacy

Many countries have similar rank orders in reading, mathematical and scientific literacy...

Most countries rank about the same in scientific as in reading literacy; but these are exceptions. A comparison of the relative rank order of countries reveals the following concerning the performance of students in reading and scientific literacy. Values in parenthesis indicate mean scores for reading and scientific literacy respectively:

...but there are exceptions.

– Austria (507, 519), the Czech Republic (492, 511), Hungary (480, 496), Japan (522, 550) and Korea (525, 552) and the United Kingdom (523, 532) show better performance in scientific literacy than in reading literacy.

– Belgium (507, 496), Canada (534, 529), Denmark (497, 481), Finland (546, 538), Iceland (507, 496), Ireland (527, 513) and Italy (487, 478) perform better in reading literacy than in scientific literacy.

– The relative rank order positions of the remaining countries are essentially the same on both scales.

Mathematical literacy scores vary more between countries than reading scores, possibly because they are more closely linked to schooling.

The performances of countries differ widely, especially on the mathematical literacy scale: 169 points (more than one and a half international standard deviations) separate the two countries with the highest and lowest mean scores on the mathematical literacy scale, and 101 points separate the two countries with the second highest and the second lowest mean scores (Table 3.1). Variation in mean performance between countries is somewhat smaller in scientific literacy, and smallest in reading literacy.[8] A possible reason might be that learning in mathematics and science is more closely related to schooling, so that differences between education systems in these domains appear to be more pronounced than in reading.

Investment in education and student performance

The performance of countries needs to be interpreted in the economic context.

In any comparison of the outcomes of education systems it is necessary to take into account countries' economic circumstances and the resources that they can devote to education. The relative prosperity of some countries allows them to spend more on education, while other countries find themselves constrained by a relative lack of national income.

Figure 3.7a

Student performance and national income

Relationship between average performance across the combined reading, mathematical and scientific literacy scales and GDP per capita, in US$, converted using purchasing power parities (PPPs)

■ OECD countries   □ Non-OECD countries

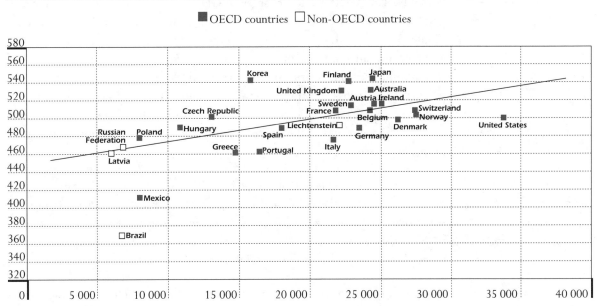

GDP per capita (US$ converted using PPPs)

Figure 3.7b

Student performance and spending per student

Relationship between average performance across the combined reading, mathematical and scientific literacy scales and cumulative expenditure on educational institutions up to age 15 in US$, converted using purchasing power parities (PPPs)

■ OECD countries   □ Non-OECD countries

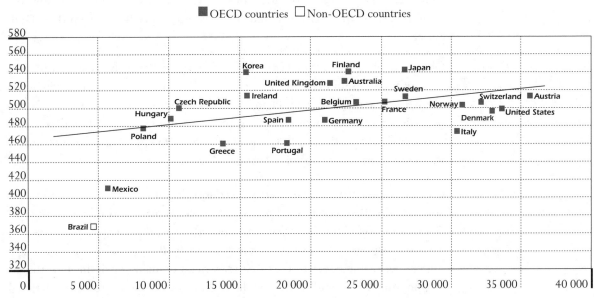

Cumulative expenditure (US$ converted using PPPs)

Note: Trend line does not take non-OECD countries into account.
Source: OECD PISA database, 2001. Table 3.6.

Figure 3.7a displays the relationship between adjusted national income (GDP) per capita and the average performance of students in the PISA assessment in each country. For this comparison, the mean performance of countries has been averaged across the reading, mathematical and scientific literacy domains. The GDP values represent GDP per capita in 2000 at current prices, adjusted for differences in purchasing power between OECD countries (Table 3.6). For the 23 OECD countries for which comparable data are available for all columns in Table 3.6.[9] the figure also shows a trend line that summarises the relationship between GDP per capita and mean student performance across the three literacy domains. It should be borne in mind, however, that the number of countries involved in this comparison is small and that the trend line is therefore strongly affected by the countries included in this comparison.

Countries with higher income per capita tend to perform better, on average...

The scatter plot suggests that countries with higher national income tend to perform better on the combined reading, mathematical and scientific literacy scale than countries with lower national income. In fact, the relationship suggests that 27 per cent of the variation between countries' mean scores can be predicted on the basis of their GDP per capita.[10]

...but some countries do better or worse than their income would predict...

Countries close to the trend line are where the predictor GDP per capita suggests that they would be; examples include Austria, Belgium, France, Ireland and Spain. For example, Ireland outperforms Spain in all three assessment domains to an extent that one would predict from the difference in their GDP per capita, as shown in Figure 3.7a. Countries above the trend line have higher average scores on the PISA assessments than would be predicted on the basis of their GDP per capita (and on the basis of the specific set of countries used for the estimation of the relationship). Countries below the trend line show lower performance than would be predicted from their GDP per capita.

...so national income relates to but does not determine performance.

Obviously, the existence of a correlation does not necessarily mean that there is a causal relationship between the two variables; there are, indeed, likely to be many other factors involved. Figure 3.7a does suggest, however, that countries with higher national income are at a relative advantage. This should be taken into account, in particular, in the interpretation of the performance of countries with comparatively low levels of national income.

Another factor is spending per student...

GDP per capita provides a measure of a country's ability to pay for education but does not directly measure the financial resources actually invested in education. Figure 3.7b compares the money that countries spend per student, on average, from the beginning of primary education up to the age of 15, with average student performance across the three assessment domains. Spending per student is approximated by multiplying public and private expenditure on educational institutions per student in 1998 at each level of education by the theoretical duration of education at the respective level, up to the age of 15.[11] The results are expressed in U.S. dollars using purchasing power parities (OECD, 2001).

The figure shows a positive relationship between spending per student and mean country performance, when averaged across the three assessment domains (Table 3.6). As expenditure per student on educational institutions increases, so also does a country's mean performance, expenditure per student explaining 17 per cent of the variation between countries in mean performance.[12]

...which explains a sixth of country variations.

Deviations from the trend line suggest that moderate spending per student cannot automatically be equated with poor performance by education systems. Korea and Japan perform similarly well, on average across the three assessment domains, but Korea spends only PPP US$ 30 844 per student, compared with PPP US$ 53 255 in Japan. Similarly, Ireland performs statistically significantly better than Germany in all three domains but spends about a quarter less per student than Germany.

Money matters...

The figures also suggest that, as much as spending on educational institutions is a necessary prerequisite for the provision of high-quality education, spending alone is not sufficient to achieve high levels of outcomes. There are a number of countries for which the trend line would predict higher performance than what they achieve, including Denmark, Greece, Italy, Mexico, Portugal and the United States.

...but it is not the only important factor.

Conclusions

In an increasingly technological world, all adults, not just those aspiring to a scientific career, need to be mathematically and scientifically literate. The wide disparities in student performance on the mathematical and scientific literacy scales that emerge from the analysis in this chapter suggest, however, that this remains still a remote goal and that countries need to serve a wide range of student abilities, including those who perform exceptionally well but also those most in need.

The goal that everyone should be mathematically and scientifically literate is still remote...

At the same time, the analysis has shown that, as with performance on the reading literacy assessment, wide disparities in performance are not a necessary condition for a country to attain a high level of overall performance. It is striking to note that the six out of the eight countries with the smallest internal variation on the mathematical literacy scale all perform statistically significantly above the OECD average.

...but there are countries that succeed with high average performance and low disparities.

Although the variation in student performance within countries is many times larger than the variation between countries, significant differences between countries in the average performance of students should not be overlooked. To the extent that these are predictive of student career paths, these differences may, particularly in subject areas such as mathematics and science, raise questions about countries' future competitiveness. In addition, differences in countries' relative performance across the three subject areas may point to significant systemic factors influencing student performance.

Differences between countries could affect future competitiveness.

Higher spending is associated with higher performance, but does not guarantee it.

The comparison between spending per student and mean student performance across countries cannot be interpreted in a causal way. Nevertheless, the data reveal a positive association between the two. At the same time, as much as spending on educational institutions is a necessary prerequisite for the provision of high-quality education, the comparison also suggests that spending alone is not sufficient to achieve high levels of outcomes and that other factors, including the effectiveness with which resources are invested, play a crucial role.

Notes

1. Technically, the mean score for student performance across OECD countries was set at 500 points and the standard deviation at 100 points, with the data weighted so that each OECD country contributed equally.

2. Polands's performance may be overestimated slightly, due to the exclusion of the 6.7 per cent of 15-year-olds enrolled in primary schools. This exclusion is unlikely to affect its rank-order position on the mathematical literacy scale (for details see Annex A3).

3. The performance of students in the Netherlands cannot be estimated accurately because the response rate of its schools was too low. It can, however, be said with confidence that the Netherlands would lie between the 1st and 4th position among OECD countries on the mathematical literacy scale. Therefore, the Netherlands does not appear in Figure 3.2 (for details, see Annex A3).

4. In Australia, Austria, Canada, the Czech Republic, Denmark, Finland, Germany, Greece, Iceland, Liechtenstein, Mexico, the Netherlands, New Zealand, Norway, Portugal, Sweden, Switzerland, the United Kingdom and the United States, between one half and three quarters of students used calculators during the PISA assessment. In Belgium, France, Hungary, Italy, Latvia, the Russian Federation and Spain, between one third and one half of students used calculators. Lower rates of calculator use were reported in Poland (31 per cent), Ireland (27 per cent), Luxembourg (7 per cent) and Brazil (6 per cent). Students did not use calculators in Japan. No information was available for Korea. With the exception of Brazil and Greece, scores on the mathematical literacy scale for students who used calculators in the PISA assessment tended to be higher than for students who did not use them. However, the differences between the scores of students on the mathematical literacy scale who used calculators and those who did not are very closely mirrored by the differences in scores on the reading literacy scale between these two groups (which did not involve numerical calculations). There is therefore no indication that the use of calculators provided an advantage to students in terms of their performance in PISA.

5. In addition, Table 3.5 provides an indication of the proportion of this variation that lies between schools. For the interpretation of these data refer to Chapter 2.

6. The relative probability of each country assuming each rank-order position on each scale can be determined from the country's mean scores, their standard errors and the covariance between the performance scales of two domains. This reveals whether, with a likelihood of 95 per cent, a country would rank statistically significantly higher, at the same level, or statistically significantly lower in one domain than in the other domain. For details on the methods employed see the *PISA 2000 Technical Report*.

7. Poland's performance may be overestimated slightly, due to the exclusion of the 6.7 per cent of 15-year-olds enrolled in primary schools. As a result of this, Poland's performance on the scientific literacy scale may be overestimated by two rank-order positions. The performance of students in the Netherlands cannot be estimated accurately because the response rate of its schools was too low. It can, however, be said with confidence that the Netherlands would lie between the 3rd and 14th position among OECD countries on the scientific literacy scale (for details see Annex A3).

8. Differences in performance between countries can also be summarised in terms of the overall variation in performance of the combined OECD student population that is accounted for by differences between countries. This amounts to 14 per cent on the mathematical literacy scale, 8 per cent on the combined reading literacy scale and 9 per cent on the scientific literacy scale.

9. Canada, Iceland, Luxembourg and New Zealand are not included in this comparison because expenditure per student cannot be estimated on a comparable basis.

10. For the 23 countries included in this comparison, the correlation between mean student performance across the three assessment domains and GDP per capita is 0.52. The explained variation is obtained as the square of the correlation. The correlation between student performance and GDP per capita can also be calculated separately for the three assessment domains. In reading literacy it amounts to 0.59, in mathematical literacy to 0.55 and in scientific literacy to 0.39.

11. Cumulative expenditure for a given country is approximated as follows: let $n(0)$, $n(1)$ and $n(2)$ be the typical number of years spent by a student from the beginning of primary education up to the age of 15 years in primary, lower secondary and upper secondary education. Let $E(0)$, $E(1)$ and $E(2)$ be the annual expenditure per student in U.S dollars converted using purchasing power parities in primary, lower secondary and upper secondary education, respectively. The cumulative expenditure is then calculated by multiplying current annual expenditure E by the typical duration of study n for each level of education i using the following formula:

$$CE = \sum_{i=0}^{2} n(i) * E(i)$$

Estimates for $n(i)$ are based on the International Standard Classification of Education (ISCED) (OECD, 1997).

12. The correlation for the overall relationship is 0.42. Taken separately, the correlation is 0.44 for the combined reading literacy scale, 0.47 for the mathematical literacy scale and 0.29 for the scientific literacy scale.

Chapter 4

GENERAL OUTCOMES
OF LEARNING

Introduction

Students need to leave school not only with sound subject-matter knowledge, but also ready to continue learning...

Most children come to school ready and willing to learn. How can schools foster and strengthen this predisposition and ensure that young adults leave school with the capacity to continue learning throughout life? Students will need to be able to use the knowledge and skills acquired in reading, mathematics and science in their future lives. Without this knowledge and these skills and the ability to add to them, individuals will not be well prepared to acquire the new knowledge and skills necessary for successful adaptation to changing circumstances.

...and able to manage their own learning.

In schools, much of the learning is managed for students by teachers. However, learning is enhanced if students have a positive disposition towards learning and can manage their own learning, and once they leave school, people have to manage most of their learning for themselves. To do this they must be able to establish goals, to persevere, to monitor their progress, to adjust their learning strategies as necessary and to overcome difficulties in learning.

PISA 2000 surveyed students' interest and engagement in learning as well as their ability to organise the learning process...

A comprehensive assessment of "how well a country is doing" in education must look at such general outcomes as well as at performance in traditional school subjects. To this end, PISA 2000 surveyed 15-year-old students' attitudes towards reading and mathematics, and their more general engagement in learning and schooling. In addition, 25 of the 32 countries participating in PISA 2000 took up an option to surveying students' approaches to learning and beliefs in their own abilities.[1] This chapter presents the results, and seeks to expand on the PISA profile of what young people are like as learners at age 15. The chapter looks first at the motivation and engagement of students, with the focus on identifying patterns of interest in reading and mathematics and of general engagement in schooling. It then examines how students manage the learning process and the learning strategies which they use.

...and examined the relationship between these characteristics and performance in the PISA literacy domains.

While effective lifelong learning strategies are an important outcome of schooling and therefore warrant examination in themselves, questions naturally arise about the extent to which effective learning strategies are also prerequisites for success at school. To address these questions, this chapter reviews not only the nature and distribution of students' attitudes towards learning and their use of particular learning strategies, but also tries to establish the relationship between these factors and the results of the PISA assessments.

The relationships between performance, attitudes and approaches to learning may be mutually reinforcing, not simply causal in one direction.

This in turn leads to questions about the direction of such relationships and causality. But, pertinent as these questions are, they remain difficult to answer. It may be, for example, that good performance and attitudes towards learning are mutually reinforcing or that students with higher natural ability both perform well and use particular learning strategies. There may also be third factors, such as home background or differences in the schooling environment to which students are exposed. In what follows, readers are therefore cautioned that the exact nature and strength of cause-and-effect relationships are uncertain, and indeed beyond the scope of this first report on PISA. Demonstration of the fact that such relationships exist, however, may stimulate policy discourse and future research.

The important question of how attitudes, motivation and self-concept differ between the genders is deferred to Chapter 5.

This report presents only a small selection of the PISA data on students' approaches to learning and their beliefs in their own abilities, namely those for which cross-national comparability has been verified (see Box 4.1). A wider range of measures will be presented in a thematic report in 2002.

Motivation and engagement with school

Motivation and engagement are the "energy base" of learning. Students who leave school with the autonomy to set their own learning goals and with a sense that they can reach those goals are potential learners throughout life. Motivation

Motivation and engagement are central to lifelong learning...

Box 4.1 **Interpreting students' self-reports**

Most of the measures presented in this chapter are based on self-reported behaviours and preferences, and on students' assessments of their own abilities. These measures rely on reports from the students themselves rather than on external observations, and they may be influenced by cross-cultural differences in response behaviour or the social desirability of certain responses. Comparisons must be undertaken with care, even though the instruments used to assess students' approaches to learning and their beliefs in their own abilities are based on well-established research and were tested extensively before their use in PISA 2000.

Several of the measures are presented as indices that summarise student responses to a series of related questions. The questions were selected from larger constructs on the basis of established theoretical considerations and previous research (see also Annex A1). Structural equation modelling was used to confirm the theoretically expected results of the indices and to validate their comparability across countries. For this purpose, a model was estimated separately for each country and, collectively, for all OECD countries.

The indices were constructed in such a way that two-thirds of the OECD student population are between the values of -1 and 1, with an average score of 0 (*i.e.,* the mean for the combined student population from participating OECD countries is set to 0 and the standard deviation is set to 1). It is important to note that negative values on an index do not necessarily imply that students responded negatively to the underlying questions. A negative value merely indicates that a group of students (or all students, collectively, in a single country) responded less positively than all students did, on average, across OECD countries. Likewise, a positive value on an index indicates that a group of students responded more favourably, or more positively, than all students did, on average, across OECD countries. For detailed information on the construction of the indices, see Annex A1.

and engagement can also affect students' quality of life during their adolescence and can influence whether they will successfully pursue further educational or labour market opportunities.

...and learning autonomy can be nurtured at school.

Autonomous learning requires both a critical, realistic judgement of the difficulty of a task and the ability to invest enough energy to accomplish it. These skills are the product of learning habits developed and shaped, among other things, by regular exposure to school tasks and teachers' evaluation of schoolwork. Both enjoyment of learning and activities that promote learning also enhance motivation.

Subject interest in reading and mathematics

Subject interest can affect learning engagement.

Interest in particular subjects affects both the degree and continuity of engagement in learning and the depth of understanding reached. This effect is largely independent of students' general motivation to learn. For example, a student who is interested in mathematics and therefore tends to study diligently may or may not show a high level of general learning motivation, and vice versa. Hence, an analysis of the pattern of students' interest in various subjects is of importance. Such an analysis can reveal significant strengths and weaknesses in attempts by education systems to promote motivation to learn in various subjects among differing sub-groups of students.

Positive attitudes to reading vary widely between countries...

About half of the 15-year-olds surveyed in PISA are generally positive about reading. On average across OECD countries, about 21 per cent of students agree that reading is fun and that they would not want to give it up.[2] Another 27 per cent of students agree "somewhat" with this statement. Twenty-eight per cent of students also indicate that they become totally absorbed when reading, and another 29 per cent agree somewhat with this statement. There is substantial variation between countries in the responses to each of these questions. For example, while fewer than one-third of students in Belgium (Flemish Community) and Korea agree fully or somewhat that reading is fun and that they would not want to give it up, at least 60 per cent of students in Denmark, Mexico and Portugal share these feelings about reading (for data, see *www.pisa.oecd.org*).

Figure 4.1 compares countries on an index that summarises interest in reading. The index is constructed with the average score across countries set at 0 and two-thirds scoring between 1 and -1. A positive value on the index indicates that students report an interest in reading higher than the OECD average, and a negative value an interest lower than the OECD average (for the definition of the index and references to its conceptual underpinning see Annex A1). The upper part of Figure 4.1 shows the distribution on the interest-in-reading index. Half of a standard deviation on this index separates Denmark, Finland and Portugal, countries in which students report a high interest in reading, from Belgium (Flemish Community) and Korea, the countries with the lowest levels of interest.

Figure 4.1
Interest in reading and mathematics, and student performance

A

Index of interest in reading: ○ Top quarter ▫ Third quarter ▫ Second quarter △ Bottom quarter

Index of interest in mathematics: ● Top quarter ▬ Third quarter ■ Second quarter ▲ Bottom quarter

B

Performance on the combined reading literacy scale: ■ Top quarter – Third quarter – Second quarter ▲ Bottom quarter

Performance on the mathematical literacy scale: ▪ Top quarter – Third quarter ▭ Second quarter △ Bottom quarter

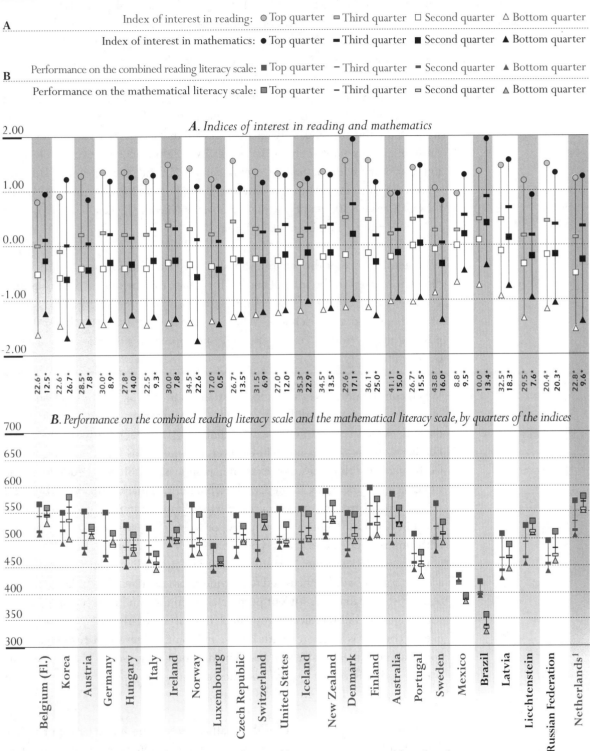

A. Indices of interest in reading and mathematics

B. Performance on the combined reading literacy scale and the mathematical literacy scale, by quarters of the indices

* Change in the combined reading literacy score/mathematical literacy score per unit of the index of interest in reading and the index of interest in mathematics.

1. Response rate is too low to ensure comparability (see Annex A3).

Note: For the definitions of the indices, see Annex A1.

Source: OECD PISA database, 2001. Tables 4.1 and 4.2.

...and positive attitudes are associated with higher reading performance within countries.

Figure 4.1 also compares the reading performance of the quarter of students in each country who have the greatest interest in reading with the quarter of students with the least interest. What the results do *not* show is that countries with keener readers achieve, on average, better reading results. In fact, some countries with above-average performance in reading, such as Austria and Korea, show comparatively low interest in reading. What the results *do* show, however, is that *within* countries students with a greater interest in reading tend to achieve better results than those with less interest.[3] On average, the difference in performance on the combined reading literacy scale between the students in the top and bottom quarters of the interest-in-reading index is substantial, 75 points or about the size of a whole proficiency level (Table 4.1). In the country with the highest overall values, Finland, the quarter of students who report the lowest level of interest in reading perform at the level of the OECD average (502 points) while the quarter with the highest level of interest score 599 points, a difference of 97 points.

The causal nature of this relationship may well be complex and is difficult to discern. Interest in the subject and performance may be mutually reinforcing. They may also be affected by other factors, such as the social backgrounds of students and their schools. Whatever the nature of this relationship, a positive disposition to reading remains an important educational goal in its own right.

When comparing the performance by students in the top and bottom quarters of the index between different countries, the reader should bear in mind that the overall level of interest in reading may vary itself between countries. Furthermore, as will be shown in Chapter 5, some of this variation is accounted for by gender differences. For example, as shown in Table 4.1, students in the top quarter of the index in the Czech Republic, Denmark, Finland and Ireland report a much greater interest in reading than students in the top quarter of the index in Belgium (Flemish Community) or Korea. Similarly, the range of values of the interest index also varies substantially between countries. In Ireland there is much wider variation in students' interest in reading than in Mexico. To account for these differences and to provide an assessment of the relative impact of interest in reading on student performance on the combined reading literacy scale, Figure 4.1 also indicates how much improvement in reading performance in each country is associated with a single unit on the interest-in-reading index.[4] For example, in Australia and Sweden, one unit increase on the interest-in-reading index is associated with an increase in reading performance of more than 40 points (OECD average 28 points).

Only a minority of students sees mathematics as important for their futures.

About half of 15-year-olds consider mathematics to be important, but rather fewer think this a reason for pursuing it further. On average across OECD countries, 20 per cent of students report that mathematics is important for them personally.[5] Another 32 per cent declare that it is somewhat important for them. By contrast, only 14 per cent, on average across OECD countries, agree that because doing mathematics is fun, they would not want to give it up; another 26 per cent declare this to be somewhat the case. Twenty-six per cent disagree that mathematics is fun, and another 29 per cent disagree somewhat (for data, see *www.pisa.oecd.org*).

In addition to examining interest in reading, Figure 4.1 also provides a summary of interest in mathematics (for the definition of the index and references to its conceptual underpinning see Annex A1). Towards the higher end of the index, more students report that they become totally absorbed when they do mathematics, that mathematics is important to them personally, and that because doing mathematics is fun, they would not want to give it up.

Country means vary more on the interest-in-mathematics index than they do on the interest-in-reading index – although the variation within countries is still much larger than that between countries (Table 4.2). Since more learning takes place in school in the case of mathematics than in that of reading, such differences between countries may suggest that education systems have an impact on the attitudes of young people towards mathematics. This, if confirmed by further research, will be an important finding for education policy. Given the increasing importance of mathematics for students' future lives, it is of great importance for education systems to ensure that students have both the interest and the motivation to continue learning in this area beyond school.

Interest in mathematics varies more strongly between countries than interest in reading.

As in reading, the country-level relationship between interest in mathematics and performance on the mathematical literacy scale is mixed. The examples of Denmark, and to a lesser extent Iceland and New Zealand, show that a relatively high average level of students' interest in mathematics can be combined with strong country performance in mathematics (Table 4.2). At the same time, students in Austria, Korea and Sweden perform above the OECD average on the mathematical literacy scale, but they display low or average levels of interest in mathematics.

As with reading, low average interest does not always mean poor country performance…

While the pattern varies between countries, within countries the relationship between interest in mathematics and performance in mathematical literacy is positive, albeit less pronounced than in reading.[6] On average across OECD countries, 35 points on the mathematical literacy scale separate the top and bottom quarters of students on the interest-in-mathematics index, compared with 75 points in reading literacy.

…although within countries, interest in mathematics and performance are positively associated.

The fact that, in some countries at least, student interest varies between subject domains may be another indication that interest is related to the way in which learning and teaching occur. The difference is largest in Denmark, where students show a much stronger interest in mathematics than in reading – a pattern that is mirrored in above-average performance in mathematical literacy compared with only average performance in reading literacy. The

The fact that interest can vary by subject suggests that it may be related to how learning occurs.

three countries with the next largest differences are Finland, Norway and Sweden. These countries show a much greater interest in reading than in mathematics.

Reading activities and engagement in reading

Reading activities and engagement in reading are decisive factors in developing and maintaining literacy skills...

In addition to subject motivation, reading activities and engagement in reading are decisive factors in the maintenance and further development of reading skills. The International Adult Literacy Survey finding that reading skills can deteriorate after the completion of initial education if they are not used (OECD and Statistics Canada, 1995) points to the importance of the maintenance of literacy skills. Positive reading activities and engagement in reading are, therefore, important outcomes of initial education as well as predictors of learning success throughout life.

Students' reports on the frequency with which, for example, they read for pleasure, enjoy talking about books or visit bookstores and libraries, and the general importance they attach to reading, can indicate the degree to which they will read in the future (for the definition of the index and references to its conceptual underpinning see Annex A1).

...but many students read only if they have to, or consider reading a waste of time.

Among OECD countries, the results of PISA 2000 suggest that much more needs to be done to foster the positive engagement of students in reading. On average across OECD countries, 44 per cent of students report reading only to obtain the information that they need,[7] more than one-third report that they read only if they have to, and 21 per cent agree or strongly agree with the statement that reading is a waste of time[8] (for data, see *www.pisa.oecd.org*).

Figure 4.2 compares countries on an index that summarises the various questions in PISA 2000 about student engagement in reading. This index extends the index shown in Figure 4.1 by incorporating a broader range of attitudes towards reading. A positive value on the index indicates that students in the country concerned report *more frequently* than students at the OECD average level that reading is one of their favourite hobbies, that they like talking about books with other people, that they feel happy if they receive a book as a present and that they enjoy going to a bookstore or a library. A positive value also indicates that students report *less frequently* that they read only if they have to, that they find it hard to finish books, that reading is a waste of time, that they read only to get the information that they need and that they cannot sit still and read for more than a few minutes.

Engagement in reading differs widely between countries...

Figure 4.2 shows the mean values for countries on the engagement-in-reading index. The gap between countries that report high levels of engagement in reading (such as the Czech Republic, Finland, Mexico and Portugal) and those with low levels of engagement (Belgium, the Netherlands and Norway) is approximately half a standard deviation on the index (Table 4.3).

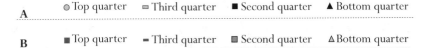

Engagement in reading and student performance

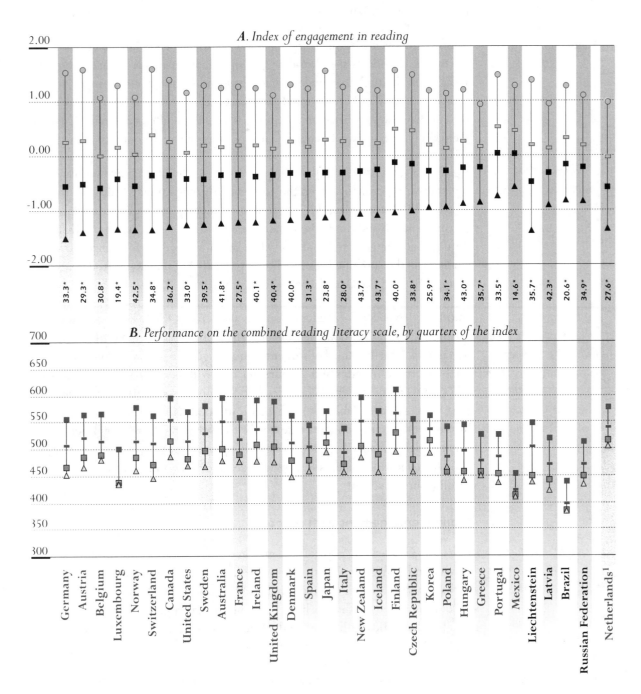

* Change in the combined reading literacy score per unit of the index of engagement in reading.
1. Response rate is too low to ensure comparability (see Annex A3).
Note: For the definition of the index, see Annex A1.
Source: OECD PISA database, 2001. Table 4.3.

...but in every country keen readers perform much better than those reporting low levels of engagement.

Figure 4.2 also compares performance on the combined reading literacy scale between students in the bottom and top quarters of the engagement-in-reading index, and the increase in performance per unit change in the index. In virtually every country, there is a close association between engagement in reading and student performance which, in 12 out of 28 countries, exceeds 100 points, *i.e.,* one international standard deviation and, in all but seven countries, one proficiency level (Table 4.3).[9]

A substantial minority of students...

Another important factor in the equation of student engagement in reading is the time that students spend reading for enjoyment. In interpreting the observed variation in the time that students actually spend reading for enjoyment, it is of course necessary to keep in mind that the time students *can* actually devote to reading may also vary between countries, as a result of differences in the length of the school day, homework requirements, or other out-of-school activities.

...do not spend time reading for enjoyment.

Figure 4.3 shows the time that students spend reading for enjoyment each day together with performance on the combined reading literacy scale. On average across OECD countries, 32 per cent of students, and in Austria, Belgium, Germany, Japan and the United States more than 40 per cent, report that they do not read for enjoyment at all.[10] The mean average performance for these students on the combined reading literacy scale – 474 points – is well below the average for the OECD as a whole (Table 4.4).

Education systems should strive for a learning environment that encourages reading beyond schools.

Another 31 per cent of students, on average across OECD countries, read for 30 minutes or less per day. Their mean performance is above the OECD average, 513 points. A further third of students, on average across OECD countries, read for between 30 minutes and 2 hours per day, with performance levels around 527 points. Students who report reading for longer score 506 points, close to the OECD average (Table 4.4) and their lower performance might be explained by the fact that these students take longer to read materials than high achievers. The low performance by students who do not read for enjoyment points to the need for education systems to provide a learning environment that encourages reading outside school.

Broader engagement with school

Positive relationships with school are important...

Disruptive behaviour, poor attendance and negative attitudes towards school may often be associated with low academic performance and the decision to withdraw from school. On the other hand, research has shown that if students become involved in their school curricula or extra-curricular activities and develop strong ties with other students and teachers, they are more likely to do well in their studies and to complete secondary school.

...but in many countries large numbers of students feel negative about school...

In PISA 2000, 15-year-old students were asked to report their attitudes towards school. In 20 of the 28 OECD countries, more than one-quarter of students agree or strongly agree that school is a place where they do not want to go. In Belgium, Canada, France, Hungary, Italy and the United States, this proportion

Figure 4.3
Time spent reading for enjoyment and student performance

A. *Percentage of students who report that they…*

■ read more than 2 hours each day for enjoyment
■ read between 1 and 2 hours each day for enjoyment
■ read between 30 and 60 minutes each day for enjoyment
■ read 30 minutes or less each day for enjoyment
■ do not read for enjoyment

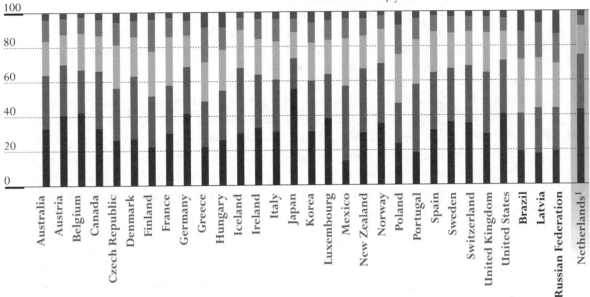

B. *Performance on the combined reading literacy scale of students who report that they…*

■ read more than 2 hours each day for enjoyment
▬ read between 1 and 2 hours each day for enjoyment
− read between 30 and 60 minutes each day for enjoyment
▬ read 30 minutes or less each day for enjoyment
▲ do not read for enjoyment

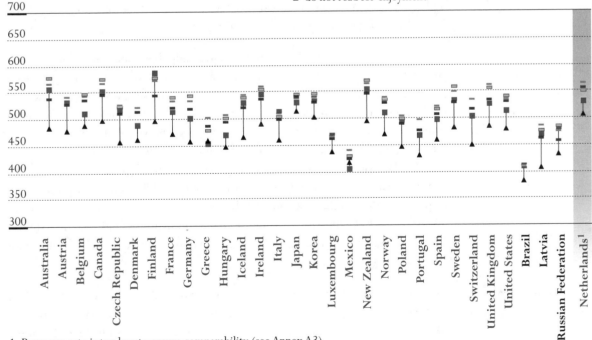

1. Response rate is too low to ensure comparability (see Annex A3).
Source: OECD PISA database, 2001. Table 4.4.

ranges, in order, from 35 to 42 per cent (for data, see *www.pisa.oecd.org*). Even in some of the countries with the best performance in PISA, such as Australia, Canada and Korea, between 30 and 37 per cent of students agree or strongly agree that school is a place where they do not want to go. By contrast, this figure is less than 20 per cent in Denmark, Mexico, Portugal and Sweden. In almost half of the OECD countries, the majority of students also agree or strongly agree that school is a place in which they feel bored,[11] and in Greece, Ireland and Spain these feelings are held by around two-thirds of students. But again, student responses vary considerably between countries (for data, see *www.pisa.oecd.org*), which suggests that disaffection with school at this age is, although common, not inevitable.

...and on average perform worse than those with more positive views.

Does it matter that many students do not like being at school? Perhaps young people need not like all the things that are good for them. The evidence is, however, that those who do like school perform better than those who do not. In almost all countries, students who report that school is a place to which they want to go perform better, on average, on the combined reading literacy scale than students who say that school is a place where they do not want to go (for data, see *www.pisa.oecd.org*).

Figure 4.4 shows that, across the OECD, an average of 87 per cent of students report that school is a place where they make friends easily, and three-quarters say that school is a place where they feel they belong,[12] the proportion ranging from around half or less in France and Spain to 88 per cent in Hungary and Mexico (for data, see *www.pisa.oecd.org*). By contrast, there is a small but significant group of students for whom school is a difficult social environment. On average, across the OECD, 13 per cent of students report that school is a place where they feel awkward and out of place though, in Sweden and the United Kingdom, this figure is less than 9 per cent.

Negative attitudes to school do not necessarily cause low achievement, but they are undesirable...

The data do not establish a causal relationship between these factors and student performance. In addition, there are other factors that influence both performance and attitudes towards school or, conversely, doing well at school might cause students to like it, rather than vice versa. In view of the substantial investment that all countries make in education, however, it is unsatisfactory that a significant minority of students, and in some cases even a majority, display a lack of engagement and negative attitudes towards school. It is hard to imagine that schools can achieve optimal results unless students are positively disposed. Although this is a considerable challenge in the case of the age group assessed in PISA, the results suggest that school policy and practice should devote sufficient attention to creating an engaging learning environment for all students.

...and can deter future learning.

Moreover, not only is this lack of engagement associated negatively with student performance, but students who are disaffected with school may also be less likely to engage in learning activities, either inside or outside educational institutions, in later life.

Figure 4.4

Broader engagement with school

Distribution of mean percentages of students who agree or strongly agree that "School is a place where...

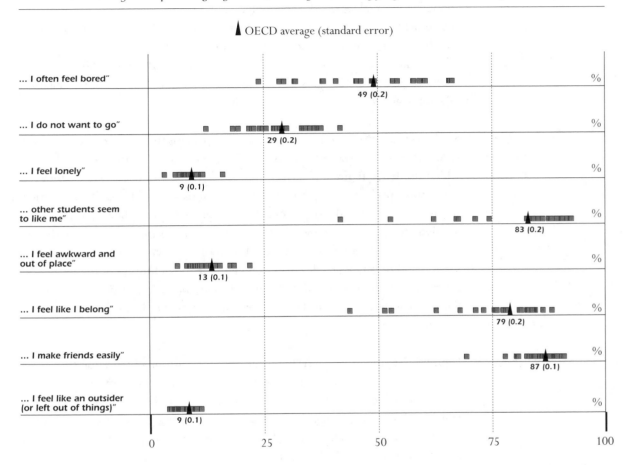

▲ OECD average (standard error)

Note: Countries are represented by the square symbols.
Source: OECD PISA database, 2001. For data, see *www.pisa.oecd.org.*

Learning strategies

Controlling the learning process

Students do not passively receive and process information. They are active participants in the learning process, constructing meaning in ways shaped by their own prior knowledge and new experiences. Students with a well-developed ability to manage their own learning are able to choose appropriate learning goals, to use their existing knowledge and skills to direct their learning, and to select learning strategies appropriate to the task in hand. While the development of these skills and attitudes has not always been an explicit focus of teaching in schools, they are increasingly being identified explicitly as major goals of schooling and should, therefore, also be regarded as significant outcomes of the learning process.

Students need to participate actively in managing learning...

...and to develop appropriate strategies for each learning task.

An effective learner processes information efficiently. This requires more than the capacity to memorise new information. It calls for the ability to relate new material to existing knowledge and to determine how knowledge can be applied in the real world. A good understanding of learning strategies strengthens students' capacity to organise their own learning. Good learners can apply an effective arsenal of learning strategies in a suitably flexible manner. On the other hand, students who have problems learning on their own often have no access to effective strategies to facilitate and monitor their learning, or fail to select a strategy appropriate to the task in hand.

PISA asked students about the learning process itself...

Students were also asked about the learning process itself. An index of control strategies was derived from responses to questions about the frequency with which students figure out what they need to learn, work out as they go what concepts they have not understood, look for additional information when they do not understand, check whether they remember what they have learned, and make sure they have remembered the most important things. The composite index was constructed with the average score across countries set at 0 and the standard deviation set at 1 (for the definition of the index and references to its conceptual underpinning see Annex A1). A positive value on the index indicates use of these control strategies that is more frequent than the OECD average.

Figure 4.5 compares countries on the basis of 15-year-olds' reports on their use of control strategies in the learning process. The mean score on the index of control strategies varies, students in Austria, the Czech Republic, Germany, Hungary, Italy and Portugal reporting the most frequent use of self-regulating control strategies. Students in Finland, Iceland, Korea and Norway report using them least frequently (Table 4.5).

...and found that the use of strategies to manage personal learning is positively related to performance.

Using control strategies effectively is positively related to student performance. Within each country, students who use them more frequently tend to perform better on the combined PISA reading literacy scale than those who do not (although whether the learning strategies *cause* the better results cannot be established). The association is most marked in Australia, New Zealand and Portugal, where the quarter of students who use these strategies for learning the most are, on average, a full proficiency level ahead of the quarter who use them least. At the OECD average level, the difference between the top and bottom quarters is 52 points. In relative terms, a difference of one unit on the index corresponds to 16 points, on average across OECD countries.[13] The strategies are essential for effective self-regulation of learning because they help students to adapt their learning to the particular features of the task on which they are working. Schools may need to give more explicit attention to allowing students to manage and control their learning in order to help them all to develop effective strategies, not only to support their learning at school but also to provide them with the tools to manage their learning later in life.

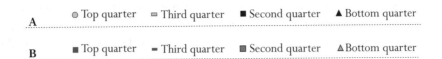

Figure 4.5

Controlling the learning process and student performance

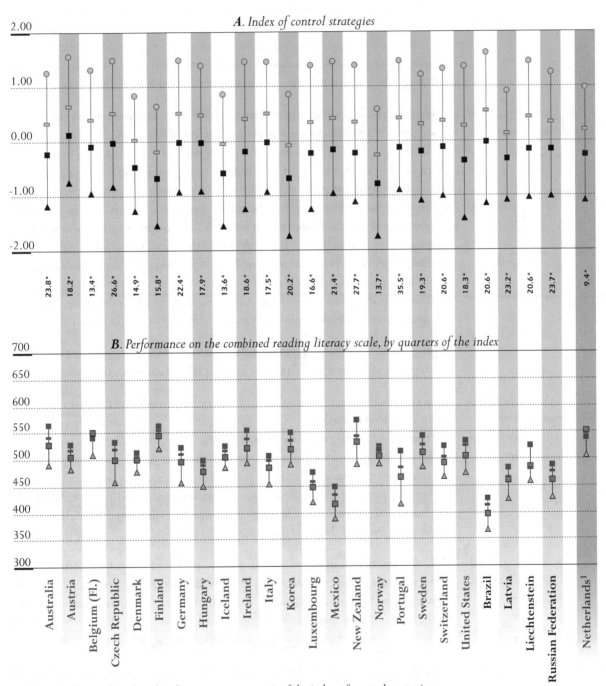

* Change in the combined reading literacy score per unit of the index of control strategies.
1. Response rate is too low to ensure comparability (see Annex A3).
Note: For the definition of the index, see Annex A1.
Source: OECD PISA database, 2001. Table 4.5.

Memorisation and elaboration

Students need both to memorise new information and to understand how it relates to their prior knowledge.

Memorisation strategies (*e.g.*, reading material aloud several times and learning key terms) are important in many tasks, but they commonly only lead to verbatim representations of knowledge, new information being stored in the memory with little further processing. Where the learner's goal is to be able to retrieve the information as presented, memorisation is an appropriate strategy but such "learning by rote" rarely leads to deep understanding. In order to achieve understanding, new information must be integrated into a learner's prior knowledge base. Elaboration strategies (*e.g.*, exploring how the material relates to things one has learned in other contexts, or asking how the information might be applied in other contexts) can be used to reach this goal.

Memorisation and elaboration strategies are complementary.

Students were asked separate questions on their use of memorisation and elaboration strategies. On the basis of their responses, an index was created for each of these learning strategies. The memorisation index is derived from responses to questions about the frequency with which the student tries to memorise everything covered, aims to memorise new material in order to be able to recite it, and practises by saying the material over and over again. The elaboration index is derived from responses to questions about the frequency with which the student tries to understand the material better by relating it to things already known, tries to relate the new material to things learned in other subjects, or figures out how the information might be useful in the real world (for the definition of the indices and references to their conceptual underpinning see Annex A1). The indices are constructed with the average score across countries set at 0 and the standard deviation set at 1.

Figure 4.6 uses the memorisation and elaboration indices to compare countries on the basis of 15-year-olds' reported use of these two types of strategies.

The use of elaboration strategies is associated with good performance...

Frequent use of elaboration strategies tends to be positively associated with performance on the combined reading literacy scale, the difference in performance between the top and bottom national quarters on the index being 32 points, on average across OECD countries. The apparent advantage of using these strategies varies greatly, however, the top quarter of students being 61 points ahead (almost one proficiency level) of the bottom quarter in Portugal, 60 points ahead in Korea and 51 points in Germany, but less than 25 points ahead in Belgium (Flemish Community), Ireland, Italy, the Netherlands, New Zealand and the United States (Table 4.7).[14]

...while memorisation strategies play a less obvious role.

Use of memorisation strategies shows a mixed relationship with student performance on the combined reading literacy scale. Eleven countries show higher performance by students in the top quarter of the index than by those in the bottom quarter, five countries show the reverse, and the remaining countries show no statistically significant differences (Table 4.6).

Schools should help students to understand and develop strategies for managing their own learning.

Overall, the data suggest that elaboration strategies are more strongly related to student performance. They may thus be more important than straightforward memorisation strategies, which students might use more intuitively. As with control strategies, it is clear that schools should help students to understand and develop the

Figure 4.6

Memorisation and elaboration strategies, and student performance

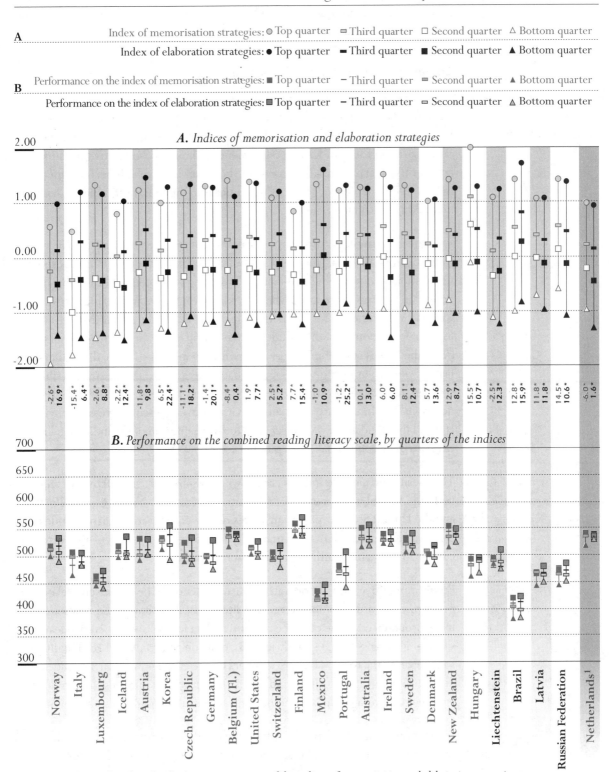

A Index of memorisation strategies: ◐ Top quarter ⊟ Third quarter □ Second quarter △ Bottom quarter

Index of elaboration strategies: ● Top quarter ▬ Third quarter ■ Second quarter ▲ Bottom quarter

B Performance on the index of memorisation strategies: ■ Top quarter – Third quarter ▬ Second quarter ▲ Bottom quarter

Performance on the index of elaboration strategies: ■ Top quarter – Third quarter ▬ Second quarter △ Bottom quarter

A. Indices of memorisation and elaboration strategies

B. Performance on the combined reading literacy scale, by quarters of the indices

* Change in the combined reading literacy score per unit of the indices of memorisation and elaboration strategies.

1. Response rate is too low to ensure comparability (see Annex A3).

Note: For the definitions of the indices, see Annex A1.

Source: OECD PISA database, 2001. Tables 4.6 and 4.7.

strategies that will best enhance their learning. There will be a benefit while they are at school but potentially an even larger benefit when they learn with less support in adult life. As ever, any conclusions need to be drawn, however, in close connection with the cultural and educational context of the country concerned.

Co-operative and competitive learning

Co-operative and competitive learning can complement each other.

Learning in adult life occurs most frequently in circumstances in which people work together and depend on one another. In formal education, particularly at the secondary and tertiary levels, learning often occurs in isolation, in a context of preparation for competitive assessment. Although co-operative learning and competitive learning can be in conflict, both can lead to high performance. The results of PISA 2000 suggest that, if acquired in tandem, both types of learning may add to learning efficiency.

Separate PISA indices for co-operative and competitive learning were created from students' reports. The co-operative learning index is derived from responses to questions about whether students like working with others, like helping others do well in a group, learn most when working with others and perform best when working with others. The competitive learning index is derived from responses to questions about whether students like trying to do better than others, like being the best at something, work well when trying to be better than others and learn faster when trying to be better than others. Note that it was possible for students to provide positive or negative answers independently to either set of questions. The indices are constructed with the average score across countries set at 0 and the standard deviation set at 1 (for the definition of the indices and references to their conceptual underpinning see Annex A1).

In several countries, students report the use of both co-operative and competitive learning practices...

The mean scores of the indices are shown in Figure 4.7, and further details can be found in Tables 4.8 and 4.9. Students in Denmark, New Zealand, Portugal and the United States report high scores on the co-operative learning index. By contrast, Korean students are markedly negative about both co-operative and competitive learning, although less so about the latter.

... both types being positively related to performance...

Both competitive and co-operative learning tend to be positively related to performance on the combined reading literacy scale although the relationship is more pronounced in the case of competitive than in that of co-operative learning. On average across OECD countries, 23 points on the combined reading literacy scale separate the top and bottom quarters on the co-operative learning index, the difference being statistically significant in 20 out of 25 countries. In competitive learning, the average gap is 33 points (and statistically significant in 20 countries).

...which suggests that active learners use both strategies, as appropriate.

Students who like co-operative learning tend to perform better than those who do not. Those who like competitive learning also tend to perform better than those who do not. Behind this is a general tendency for those who like co-operative learning also to like competitive learning – and perhaps they have a positive disposition towards learning in general. This evidence suggests that

Figure 4.7

Co-operative and competitive learning

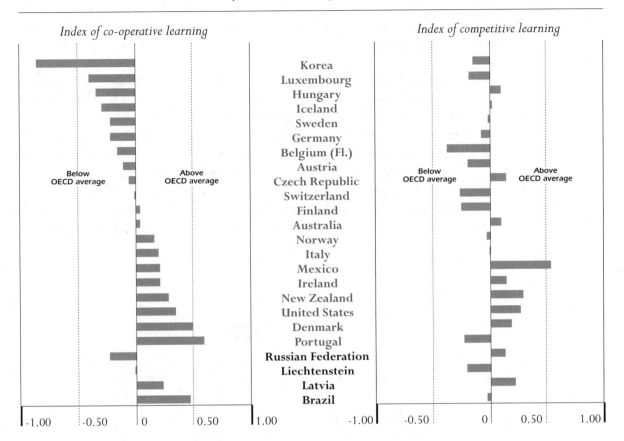

Note: For the definitions of the indices, see Annex A1.
Source: OECD PISA database, 2001. Tables 4.8 and 4.9.

active learners use both strategies on different occasions, rather than limiting themselves to a single strategy that may not be the best in a particular situation. Further research is needed to explore these aspects in more detail.

Computers as a tool for learning

OECD economies are increasingly dependent on technological knowledge and skills in the labour force. Students with little or no exposure to computers and information technology may face difficulties in making a smooth transition to the modern labour market.

Computer skills are now essential.

PISA 2000 explored three aspects of familiarity with computers among 15-year-olds: interest in computers, self-assessment of students' attitudes and ability to work with computers, and use of and experience with computers. This survey was an international option, in which 20 of the 32 countries participating in PISA took part.[15]

The majority of students are interested in using computers...

On average across the 16 OECD countries surveyed, 65 per cent of students state that they use a computer because they are very interested in doing so, and in no country is this figure less than 50 per cent (for data, see *www.pisa.oecd.org*). An average of 60 per cent of the students consider it very important to work with a computer.

Figure 4.8 compares countries on an index that summarises the various questions on interest in computers. The index is constructed with the average score across all countries set at 0 and the standard deviation set at 1 (for the definition of the index and references to its conceptual underpinning see Annex A1). A positive value on the index indicates that students frequently report that it is very important to them to work with a computer, that playing or working with a computer is fun, that they use a computer because they are very interested, and that they forget the time when they are working with a computer. The figure shows the mean scores on the interest-in-computers index.

Figure 4.8

Interest in computers

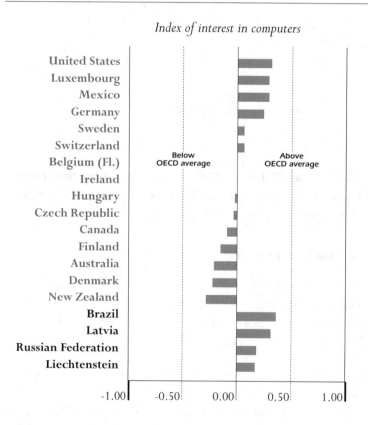

Index of interest in computers

Note: For the definition of the index, see Annex A1.
Source: OECD PISA database, 2001. Table 4.10.

Students in Germany, Luxembourg, Mexico and the United States report the greatest level of interest in computers, well over half a standard deviation above the values in Denmark and New Zealand, the countries with the lowest level of interest in computers (Table 4.10).

...but there are differences between countries...

In most countries, males show much stronger interest in computers than females, but the United States is an exception to this, with both males and females showing an equally strong interest in computers (Table 4.10).

...and between the genders.

An interest in computers may be a prerequisite for their effective use, but familiarity is also needed. On average across OECD countries, 69 per cent of students say they are comfortable or very comfortable with using a computer to write a paper, and 55 per cent are comfortable or very comfortable taking a test on a computer (for data, see *www.pisa.oecd.org*).

The majority of students are also comfortable with computers.

Figure 4.9 compares countries on an index that summarises the various questions on comfort with and perceived ability to use computers. The index is constructed with the average score across countries set at 0 and the standard deviation set at 1

Figure 4.9

Comfort with and perceived ability to use computers

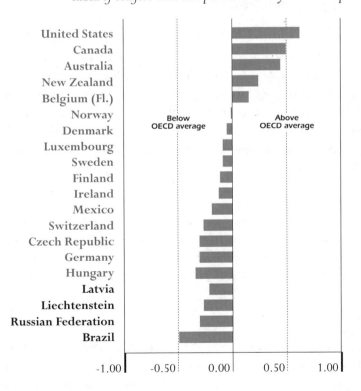

Index of comfort with and perceived ability to use computers

Note: For the definition of the index, see Annex A1.
Source: OECD PISA database, 2001. Table 4.11.

(for the definition of the index and references to its conceptual underpinning see Annex A1). A positive value on the index indicates that students frequently report that it is very important to them to work with a computer, that they are comfortable with using a computer, that they are comfortable with using a computer to write a paper, that they are comfortable with taking a test on a computer, and that they rate their ability to use a computer as higher than that of other 15-year-olds (Table 4.11).

Interest in computers is associated with higher reading literacy, but the relationship is complicated.

Students with higher values on the index of interest in computers tend to perform better on the combined reading literacy scale. This relationship needs, however, to be interpreted with great caution since not only information on the direction of this relationship is absent but there may also be third factors in operation, such as that students in more affluent families or with more educational resources at home or at school also have better access to computers, and therefore greater interest in them.

The majority of students use computers regularly at home and school...

To what extent is working with a computer related to school? On average across OECD countries, 60 per cent of 15-year-olds use a computer at home almost every day or at least a few times per week but this ranges from 21 per cent in Mexico, 42 and 45 per cent in Hungary and the Czech Republic to more than 70 per cent in Australia, Canada, Norway and Sweden (for data, see *www.pisa.oecd.org*). The percentage of students who use a computer at school almost every day or at least a few times per week is much lower, at 36 per cent at the OECD average level, with proportions ranging from 15 per cent in Germany to 55 per cent or more in Denmark, Hungary and the United Kingdom.

...and, in some countries, nearly half use the Internet almost daily.

On average across OECD countries, one-quarter of students use a computer to access the Internet every day and another quarter at least a few times each week.[16] The most frequent use of the Internet is made in Canada and Sweden, where 46 and 48 per cent of students respectively use a computer to access the Internet almost every day. An average of 42 per cent of students use a computer for electronic communication almost every day or at least a few times per week, and 30 per cent use one to learn school material (for data, see *www.pisa.oecd.org*).

The incorporation of computers into teaching and learning is a gradual process, but they are already a key tool for today's 15-year-olds.

Although progress with incorporating computers into teaching and learning is gradual (Pelgrum and Anderson, 1999), the results of PISA 2000 suggest that computers are already a tool that captures the interest of 15-year-olds, and that many of them are comfortable with using computers for everyday purposes.

Conclusions

Students who leave school able to set their own learning goals and with a sense that they can achieve them are potential learners for life...

Lifelong learning is a well-recognised need for individuals that contemporary education policy increasingly seeks to address. The need raises important questions of opportunities and access beyond formal education but also important questions about how to develop the capacities of individuals to benefit from those opportunities.

Developing the predisposition of students to engage with learning and the capacity to do so effectively is an important goal of school education, and is increasingly explicit in national education policies, especially with an eye to fostering lifelong learning. Students who leave school with the autonomy to set their own learning goals and with a sense that they can reach those goals are potential learners for life. Motivation and engagement can also affect students' quality of life during the adolescence, and can influence whether they will successfully pursue further educational or labour market opportunities.

The results of PISA show that those most likely to memorise information do not always achieve the best results, but those who process or elaborate what they learn do well. Finally, PISA does not indicate that co-operative learning is superior to competitive learning, or *vice versa*. The evidence suggests, rather, that the two strategies can be used in a complementary fashion to promote higher performance. Since the use of co-operative learning in particular is closely dependent on the way in which learning opportunities are organised in schools, this conclusion is relevant for both education policy and educational practice.

...and PISA points to some of the learning strategies that can help students reach these goals.

Given the substantial investment that all countries make in education, it is unsatisfactory that a significant minority of students in all countries display negative attitudes towards learning and a lack of engagement with school, even if this may to some extent be determined by the age of the population assessed. Not only do negative attitudes seem to be associated with poor student performance, but students who are disaffected with learning at school will also be less likely to engage in learning activities, either inside or outside of school, in later life.

More needs to be done to foster positive engagement by students with learning...

Of course, the links between attitudes, motivation and performance are complex and the analysis in this chapter does not pretend to have established causal links. Indeed, for performance and attitudes, the relationship may well be reciprocal, students liking what they do well at, and doing well at what they like. Schools and education systems need to aim at both performance and satisfaction, and should not take the risk of addressing one in the belief that the other will follow. If both are achieved, a more secure foundation for productive engagement with lifelong learning will have been established.

...so that strong performance and satisfaction with school reinforce one another.

Notes

1. The 25 countries participating in the international option on students' approaches to learning and their beliefs in their own abilities included 20 OECD countries. The OECD average refers to these countries only. Data for Belgium refer to the Flemish Community only.

2. The scale had the response categories "disagree", "disagree somewhat", "agree somewhat" and "agree".

3. In all countries except Mexico, the difference in reading performance between students in the top and bottom quarters of the interest-in-reading index is statistically significant. However, the relationship between successive quarters is less clear, some countries even showing reversals between successive quarters.

4. This is estimated by the unstandardised regression coefficient of performance on the combined reading literacy scale on the PISA index of interest in reading. These coefficients indicate the difference in reading performance associated with one unit increase (i.e. one standard deviation) on the PISA interest-in-reading index. In all countries the relationship is statistically significant. On average across OECD countries, the relationship explains 10 per cent of the overall variation in student performance (see Annex A2).

5. This and the remaining scales in this section had the response categories "disagree", "disagree somewhat", "agree somewhat" and "agree".

6. In all countries except Liechtenstein, Luxembourg, Mexico and Switzerland the difference in performance on the mathematical literacy scale between students in the top and bottom quarters of the interest-in-mathematics index is statistically significant. However, the relationship between successive quarters is less clear, some countries even showing reversals between successive quarters.

7. These students agreed or strongly agreed with the statement "I read only to get the information I need" on a scale with the response categories "strongly disagree", "disagree", "agree" and "strongly agree".

8. The scale had the response categories "strongly disagree", "disagree", "agree" and "strongly agree".

9. In all countries, the difference in performance on the combined reading literacy scale between students on the top and bottom quarters of the engagement-in-reading index is statistically significant. However, the relationship between successive quarters is less clear, some countries even showing reversals between successive quarters. The unstandardised regression coefficients are also statistically significant in all countries.

10. The scale had the response categories "I do not read for enjoyment", "30 minutes or less each day", "more than 30 minutes to less than 60 minutes each day", "1 to 2 hours each day" and "more than 2 hours each day".

11. The scale had the response categories "strongly disagree", "disagree", "agree" and "strongly agree".

12. The scale had the response categories "strongly disagree", "disagree", "agree" and "strongly agree".

13. On average across OECD countries, the relationship explains 4.6 per cent of the overall variation in student performance.

14. Differences between the two quarters in Belgium (Flemish Community), the Netherlands and the United States are not statistically significant.

15. The 20 countries participating in the international option on familiarity with computers included 16 OECD countries. The OECD average refers to these countries only.

16. The scales referred to in this section had the response categories "almost every day", "a few times each week", "between once a week and once a month", "less than once a month" and "never".

Chapter 5

GENDER DIFFERENCES

Introduction

*All countries seek to
reduce gender
differences...*

Recognising the impact that education has on participation in labour markets, occupational mobility and the quality of life, all countries emphasise the importance of reducing educational disparities between men and women.

*...and have generally
done so successfully in
respect of educational
attainment...*

Significant progress has been achieved in reducing the gender gap in educational attainment. Younger women today are far more likely to have completed a tertiary qualification than women 30 years ago: in 18 of the 29 OECD countries with comparable data, more than twice as many women aged 25 to 34 have completed tertiary education as women aged 55 to 64 years. Furthermore, university-level graduation rates for women now equal or exceed those for men in 17 of the 25 OECD countries for which comparable data are available (OECD, 2001).

*...although women
remain under-
represented in some
university subjects.*

Nevertheless, in certain fields of study, gender differences in tertiary qualifications remain persistently high. The proportion of women among university graduates in mathematics and computer science is below 31 per cent, on average, among OECD countries. In Austria, the Czech Republic, Hungary, Iceland, the Netherlands, Norway and Switzerland, the proportion is between 12 and 19 per cent. Though much smaller in scale, a gender gap in university-level graduation rates is also evident in the life sciences and physical sciences (OECD, 2001). In this context, it is noteworthy that past international assessments indicate that relatively small gender differences in favour of males in mathematics and science performance in the early grades become more pronounced and pervasive in many countries at higher grade levels (see Box 5.1).

*Females now perform so
well in some areas that
there is growing concern
about the
underachievement of
males.*

In the past, concern about gender differences has therefore almost universally addressed the underachievement of females. However, as females have first closed the gap and then surpassed males in many aspects of education, there are now many instances in which there is concern about the underachievement of males. Gender differences in student performance need to receive close attention from policy-makers.

*This chapter looks at
gender gaps in
performance, as well as
in wider aspects of
learning.*

This chapter concludes the profile of student performance begun in the preceding chapters by examining gender differences in student performance in the three literacy domains and describing gender differences in the interest shown by students in various subject areas, in motivation and in "self-concept". The remaining chapters of this report situate students' performance in the context of their backgrounds and the broader learning environment, look at the human and financial resources that countries invest in education and at selected characteristics of national education systems, and explore the nature of the relationship between school performance and family background.

Gender differences in reading, mathematical and scientific literacy

Figure 5.1 shows differences in mean performance in the three PISA assessment domains. The scale used for comparing the performance of males and females is the same as that used in Chapters 2 and 3 for comparing the performance

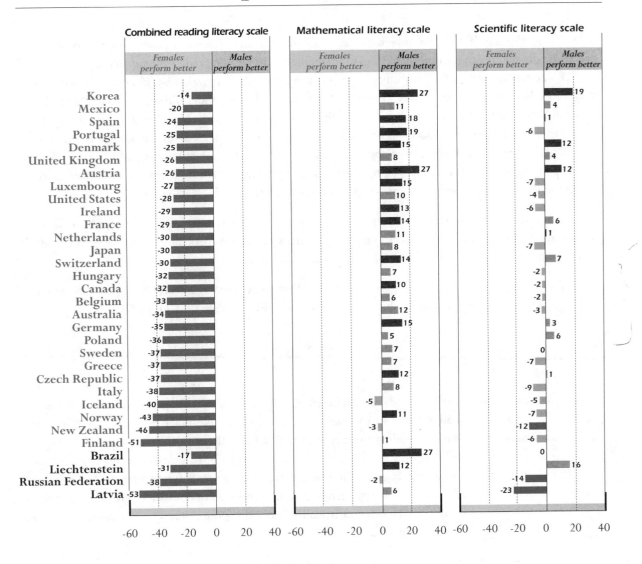

Figure 5.1

Gender differences in student performance
Differences in PISA scale scores

Note: Statistically significant differences are marked in black and red.
Source: OECD PISA database, 2001. Table 5.1a.

of countries. On that scale, about two-thirds of 15-year-olds in the OECD are within 100 points of the mean score, roughly 50 points separate the countries with the fifth highest and the fifth lowest performance on the combined reading literacy scale, and one proficiency level is equal to just over 70 points. As in Chapters 2 and 3, it also needs to be taken into account that the mean score differences between males and females in this chapter may mask significant variation in gender differences between different educational programmes, schools or types of students.

Box 5.1 **Changes in gender differences in mathematics and science performance as students get older**

In 1994/95, the IEA Third International Mathematics and Science Study (TIMSS) revealed statistically significant gender differences in mathematics among 4th-grade students in only three out of the 16 participating OECD countries (Japan, Korea and the Netherlands), in favour of males in all cases. However, the same study showed statistically significant gender differences in mathematics at the 8th-grade level in six of the same 16 OECD countries, all in favour of males. And finally, in the last year of upper secondary schooling, gender differences in mathematics literacy performance in the TIMSS assessment were large and statistically significant in all participating OECD countries, except Hungary and the United States (again, all in favour of males). A similar and even more pronounced picture emerged in science (Beaton *et al.*, 1996; Mullis *et al.*, 1998).

Although the groups of students assessed at the two grade levels were not made up of the same individuals, the results suggest that gender differences in mathematics and science become more pronounced and pervasive in many OECD countries at higher grade levels.

Despite this general tendency, TIMSS also showed that some countries were managing to contain the growth in gender disparities at higher grade levels (OECD, 1996; OECD, 1997).

Females have higher levels of reading literacy everywhere; males have higher mathematical literacy in half the countries.

PISA 2000 shows a pattern of gender differences that is fairly consistent across countries: in every country, on average, females reach higher levels of performance in reading literacy than males. In mathematical literacy, there are statistically significant differences in about half the countries, in all of which males do better. In scientific literacy, there are fewer differences between males and females, and the pattern of the differences is not consistent. Twenty-four OECD countries show no statistically significant gender differences in science performance (Table 5.1a).

The advantage of females in reading literacy performance is large...

The better performance of females in reading is not only universal but also large. On average it is 32 points, almost half of one proficiency level, and generally greater than the typical difference in mean scores between countries. The average gap in mathematics is around one third of this value, 11 points in favour of males. In science, gender differences average out across countries (Table 5.1a).

...but in some countries much larger than in others...

The significant advantage of females in reading literacy in all countries, and the advantage of males in mathematical literacy in many countries, may be the result of the broader societal and cultural context or of educational policies and practices. Whatever the cause, they suggest that countries are having differing success at eliminating gender gaps, and that females typically remain better at reading and males better at mathematics.

However, the wide variation between countries in gender differences (in reading literacy, from 25 points or less in Denmark, Korea, Mexico, Portugal and Spain to about twice that amount in Finland and Latvia, and in mathematical literacy from not statistically significant differences in 15 OECD countries to 27 points in Austria, Brazil and Korea) suggests that the current differences are not the inevitable outcomes of differences between young males and females in learning styles. These gaps can be closed.

…suggesting that gender differences are not inevitable.

Some countries do appear to provide a learning environment that benefits both genders equally, either as a direct result of a educational efforts or because of a more favourable societal context. In reading literacy, Korea, and to a lesser extent Ireland, Japan and the United Kingdom, achieve both high mean scores and limited gender differences. In mathematical literacy, Belgium, Finland, Japan, New Zealand and the United Kingdom achieve both high mean performance and small gender differences (Table 5.1a).

Several countries combine low gender inequality with high performance…

At the same time, some of the countries with the largest gender gaps have high mean performances. In Finland, for example, it is not that males do poorly in reading literacy – their scores are well above the average for all students in PISA and there is no other country where males do better – but rather that females score exceptionally well: 18 points ahead of the country with the next highest-scoring females, New Zealand.

…but some of the widest gender gaps occur also in high-performing countries.

Differences in reading performance between males and females tend to be larger on the reflection and evaluation scale, that is, on tasks requiring critical evaluation and the relating of text to personal experience, knowledge and ideas. On average, gender differences are 45 points on the reflection and evaluation scale in favour of females, compared with 29 points on the interpretation scale and 24 points on the retrieving information scale (Table 5.1b). In Finland, the country with the greatest gender differences, females have an exceptionally high mean on the reflection and evaluation scale, 564 points, while males score only at the OECD average, 501 points. These findings may be associated with the types of reading material to which young men and women are exposed or which they tend to favour (see below).

Females tend to be furthest ahead in the reflection and evaluation aspects of reading.

Future PISA surveys will allow for assessment of the extent to which gender differences in performance change over time. In the meantime, a comparison of gender differences in the International Adult Literacy Survey (IALS) between different age groups suggests that women have been pulling ahead. Among 56 to 64-year-olds, as an illustration, men out-performed women on the IALS document scale in 17 out of 21 countries. However, this difference was counter-balanced among 16 to 25-year-olds. Similarly, on the IALS prose scale, men were at an advantage among 56 to 64-year-olds in the majority of countries but women had the advantage in all but two IALS countries among 16 to 25-year-olds (OECD and Statistics Canada, 2000).

Among adults, women seem already to be pulling ahead in reading.

Females are less far behind males in mathematics and science than was the case in TIMSS...

Gender differences in mathematical and scientific literacy, in which males have often been more proficient in the past, tend to be much smaller than the difference in favour of females in reading. In science, there is no clear pattern of gender differences, females performing better than males in Latvia, New Zealand and the Russian Federation, and males performing better in Austria, Denmark and Korea. In the remaining countries, the differences are not statistically significant (Table 5.1a). These results are quite different from those of the IEA Third International Mathematics and Science Study (TIMSS), where gender differences in science performance among 8th-grade students were much larger, almost always favouring males.

...which may be because of PISA's emphasis on application and differences in subject-matter focus.

The differences in results between PISA and TIMSS may be explained in part by the fact that the PISA assessment of scientific literacy placed greater emphasis than TIMSS on life sciences. This was an area in which females tended to perform well also in TIMSS, which placed greater emphasis than PISA on physics, in which males generally tend to perform well. In addition, PISA placed greater emphasis on scientific processes and the application of knowledge. Finally, the fact that PISA had a higher proportion of open-ended and contextualised items, in which females tend to do better, rather than multiple-choice items in which males tend to do better, may also have contributed to the higher performance by females.

In some countries, gender differences vary between subjects, suggesting that differences may result from learning experiences.

In all countries, gender differences tend to be similar in the three content areas of reading, mathematical and scientific literacy, suggesting that there are underlying features of education systems and/or societies and cultures that affect gender differences in performance throughout school careers. Nonetheless, some important differences do exist. Finland, for example, shows the highest gender differences on the combined reading literacy scale (51 points in favour of females) while its gender differences on the mathematical and scientific literacy scales are small. Conversely, Korea shows the lowest gender differences in reading literacy (14 points in favour of females) while gender differences in mathematical literacy (27 points in favour of males) and scientific literacy (19 points in favour of males) are among the largest in the OECD. Such variation across the domains suggests that these differences are the result of students' learning experiences and thus amenable to changes in policy.

In all countries more males than females are among the weakest readers...

The large gender differences among the students with the lowest levels of performance is of concern to policy-makers (Figure 5.2). In all OECD countries, males are more likely than females to be among the lowest-performing students, *i.e.*, to perform at Level 1 and below on the combined reading literacy scale, with the ratio of males to females at this level ranging from 1.3 to 3.5 in OECD countries. In Canada, Finland, Japan and Korea, 6 per cent or less of females perform at Level 1 or below, compared with between 7 and 14 per cent of males (Table 5.2a). Even in the country with the best performance, Finland, only 3 per cent of females are at Level 1 or below, compared with 11 per cent of males.

On the mathematical literacy scale, males tend to perform better than females, overall. However, much of this difference is attributable to larger differences in favour of males among the better students, not a relative absence

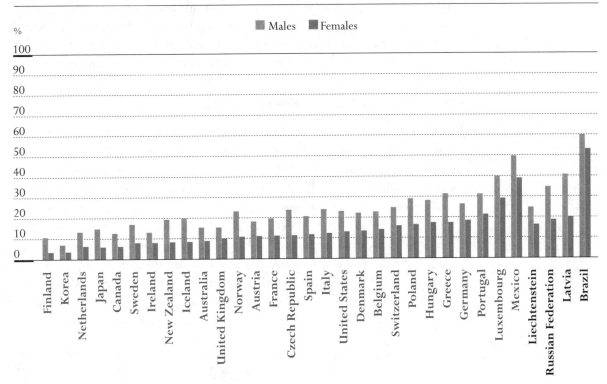

Figure 5.2

Proportions of males and females among the lowest performers on the combined reading literacy scale
Percentage of males and females at or below Level 1

■ Males ■ Females

Source: OECD PISA database, 2001. Table 5.2a.

of males among the poorer performers. Among students who perform at least 100 points below the international average on the mathematical literacy scale (*i.e.*, those students typically able to complete only a single processing step consisting of reproducing basic mathematical facts or processes or applying simple computational skills), the proportion of females and males is roughly equal (Table 5.2b). By contrast, in 15 of the participating OECD countries men are more likely to be among the best-performing students, scoring more than one standard deviation above the OECD average, while in no country is the reverse the case.

...and in mathematical literacy, males' average advantage is heavily influenced by some males doing very well.

These findings suggest that the underachievement of young men is a significant challenge for education policy that will need particular attention if the gender gap is to be closed and the proportion of students at the lowest levels of proficiency is to be reduced.

Underachievement among 15-year-old males is therefore an important concern.

One factor contributing to gender differences may be selection and self-selection practices in differentiated education systems. With the exception of Korea, girls are over-represented in the more demanding upper secondary programmes preparing for entry to university.[1] On average across the 16 countries with tracked education systems that report student participation by type of

Selection and self-selection practices in differentiated education systems may contribute to gender differences.

programme, the proportion of girls in programmes oriented towards university-level education is 8 percentage points higher than that of boys and in Poland it is more than 20 percentage points higher (for data, see *www.pisa.oecd.org*). Among those enrolled in programmes preparing for entry to university, gender differences in reading literacy tend to be smaller (in favour of females) while they tend to be twice as large, on average, in mathematical literacy (in favour of males) when compared with the overall population of 15-year-old students.

Gender differences in subject interest

Males and females also differ in their interest in different subject domains.

Figure 5.3a compares students' interest in reading (horizontal axis) with performance on the combined reading literacy scale (vertical axis). The index of interest in reading is described in Chapter 4. Each country is represented by two symbols in this diagram: the symbols in grey show the mean index of interest in reading for males and their mean performance on the combined reading literacy scale. The corresponding country positions for females are shown in red. The top of the vertical axis represents high average performance in reading literacy. The right-hand end of the horizontal axis indicates that, on average, students more frequently report that they often read in their spare time, that reading is important to them personally, that they would not want to give up reading because it is fun, and that they sometimes become totally absorbed in reading.

Figure 5.3a

Relationship between interest in reading and performance on the combined reading literacy scale for males and females

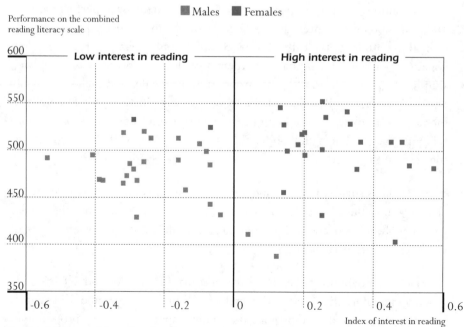

For the definition of the index, see Annex A1.
Note: Countries are represented by the square symbols.
Source: OECD PISA database, 2001. Table 4.1.

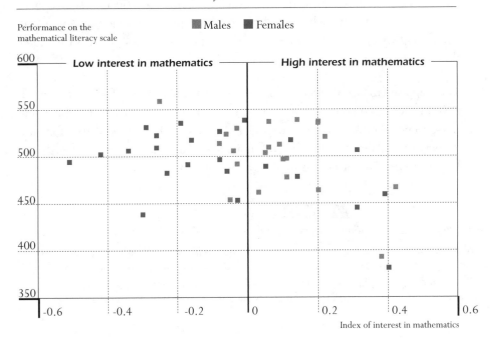

Figure 5.3b

Relationship between interest in mathematics and performance on the
mathematical literacy scale for males and females

For the definition of the index, see Annex A1.
Note: Countries are represented by the square symbols.
Source: OECD PISA database, 2001. Table 4.2.

Figure 5.3b shows the pattern of interest in mathematics and performance on
the mathematical literacy scale.

Figures 5.3a and b show clearly that females tend to express greater interest
in reading than males, while the reverse is the case in mathematics. Gender
differences in performance in reading and mathematical literacy are thus closely
mirrored in student interest in the respective subject areas. This overall relationship can be said to hold true in all countries (Tables 4.1 and 4.2) in the case of
reading, and in the majority of countries in that of mathematics, Portugal being
the only country where females report a higher level of interest in mathematics
than males.

Gender differences in subject-matter interest closely mirror those in performance...

The causal nature of this relationship cannot be concluded from these data and
may well be complex in that interest and performance probably reinforce one
another. Nonetheless, the fact that subject interest differs consistently between
the genders and that it is so closely interrelated with learning outcomes in the
respective domains is, in itself, of relevance for policy development. It reveals
inequalities between the genders in the effectiveness with which schools and
societies promote motivation and interest in the different subject areas. The
findings also point to the potential consequences of these inequalities in terms
of educational outcomes.

...suggesting that schools and societies do not motivate males and females equally.

Gender differences in engagement in reading

Females are more closely engaged in reading...

Gender differences in favour of females are also reflected in the broader engagement of students in reading activities, which PISA measures through self-reports on the frequency with which students read for pleasure, enjoy talking about books, and visit bookstores and libraries, and on the general importance which they attach to reading.

...with males tending to read only if they have to...

There appears to be only limited engagement in reading among 15-year-old males beyond what is required of them (Figure 5.4). On average across the OECD countries, 46 per cent of males read only if they have to, whereas this is true for only 26 per cent of females (for data on individual countries, see *www.pisa.oecd.org*). Furthermore, 58 per cent of males (as against 33 per cent of females) report

Figure 5.4

Gender differences in engagement in reading – attitudes towards reading

Distribution of mean percentages of males and females who agree or strongly agree with the following statements

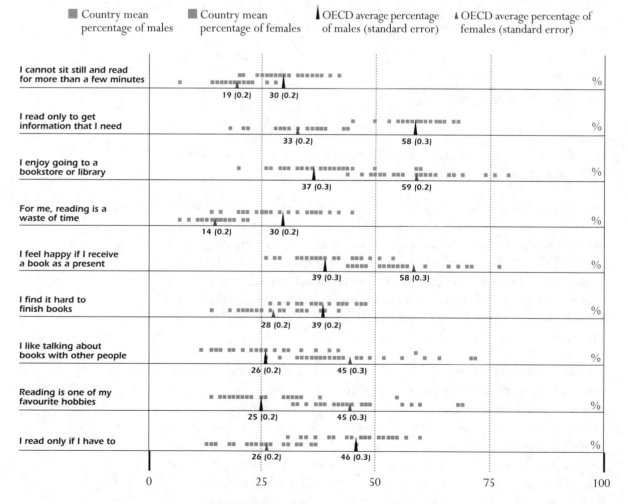

Note: Countries are represented by the square symbols.
Source: OECD PISA database, 2001. For data, see *www.pisa.oecd.org*.

that they read only to get the information they need; and this figure rises to more than two-thirds of males in the Czech Republic, Germany, Ireland and Mexico. Similarly, 45 per cent of females report that reading is one of their favourite hobbies, and 45 per cent say that they like talking about books with other people, compared with only 25 per cent of males (for data on individual countries, see *www.pisa.oecd.org*).

Males also tend to spend much less time reading for enjoyment than females. On average across OECD countries, 45 per cent of females report that they read for enjoyment for more than 30 minutes each day (the proportion ranging from 27 per cent of females in Japan to more than twice that figure in the Czech Republic, Finland, Poland and Portugal). The comparable figure for males is 30 per cent, the proportion ranging from 20 per cent or less in Austria, the Netherlands and Switzerland to over 40 per cent in Greece, Korea and Poland (Figure 5.5 and Table 5.3).

...and girls more likely to read for enjoyment.

Although these findings do not permit the establishment of causal links, they suggest that the differing reading habits of females and males may have far-reaching consequences for learning that need to be addressed if gender equality is to be achieved within school systems.

The differing reading habits of males and females may have far-reaching consequences.

Figure 5.5

Gender differences in engagement in reading – time spent reading for enjoyment

Percentages of males and females who read for more than 30 minutes per day for enjoyment

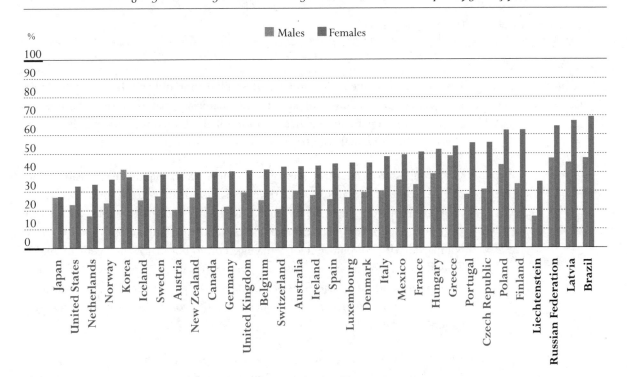

Source: OECD PISA database, 2001. Table 5.3.

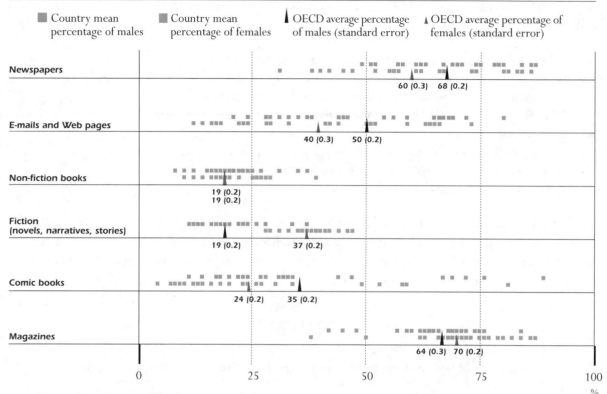

Figure 5.6

Gender differences in engagement in reading – diversity of reading materials

Distribution of mean percentages of males and females who report reading the following materials several times a month or several times per week

Note: Countries are represented by the square symbols.
Source: OECD PISA database, 2001. For data, see *www.pisa.oecd.org*.

Males and females also like reading different things...

Finally, 15-year-old males and females differ not only with regard to their engagement in reading, but also in the materials that they read voluntarily (Figure 5.6). In general, females are more likely to read more demanding texts (for data on individual countries, see *www.pisa.oecd.org*).

...with females reading more fiction, and males more newspapers, comics, e-mails and Web pages.

On average across countries, females are more likely than males to read fiction (37 per cent of females several times per month or several times per week compared with 19 per cent of males). Males are more likely than females to read newspapers (68 per cent of males several times per month or per week compared with 60 per cent of females), comic books (35 per cent of males several times per month or per week, compared with 24 per cent of females) and e-mails and Web pages (50 per cent of males several times per month or per week, and 40 per cent of females). For data on individual countries, see *www.pisa.oecd.org*.

Females and males are, on average across countries, equally likely to read magazines (around two-thirds of both females and males several times per week) and non-fiction (19 per cent of both females and males several times per month or per week).

Gender differences in learning strategies and self-concept

Chapter 4 provides a profile of the student learning strategies reported by students in PISA 2000. It is noteworthy that the strategies reported by students differ consistently between males and females.

Learning strategies also differ by gender…

In the majority of countries, 15-year-old females report emphasising memorisation strategies more than males, only three countries showing a statistically significant difference in the other direction (Table 4.6). Conversely, males report using elaboration strategies more often than females, there being only one country in which a statistically significant proportion of females report more frequent use of elaboration strategies (Table 4.7).

…with females emphasising memorisation and males elaboration strategies.

However, in almost all countries with statistically significant gender differences, females report using control strategies more often than males (Table 4.5). This suggests that females are more likely to adopt a self-evaluating perspective during the learning process though, in most countries, they could benefit from training in the use of elaboration strategies. Males, on the other hand, could benefit from more general assistance in planning, organising and structuring learning activities.

Females are more likely to evaluate their own learning.

Finally, there is abundant evidence that individuals' beliefs about themselves are strongly related to successful learning. Successful learners are confident of their abilities and believe that investment in learning can make a difference. By contrast, students who lack confidence in their ability to learn what they judge to be important are exposed to failure, not only at school, but also in their adult lives. For this reason, PISA 2000 examined students' "self-concept" in reading and mathematics. This is shown in two indices that summarise student responses to a series of related questions on self-concept which, in turn, were selected from constructs used in previous research (see also Annex A1). The scale used in the indices places two-thirds of the OECD student population between the values of -1 and 1, with an average score of zero.

More confident students tend to do better…

Figure 5.7a shows the relationship between self-concept in reading and performance on the combined reading literacy scale. Dots represent the average position of males and females in participating countries. In all countries except Korea, females state more frequently that they receive good marks in language-related subjects and that they learn things quickly. The differences are especially pronounced in Finland, Germany, Italy and the United States (Table 5.4a). In mathematics (Figure 5.7b), males tend to express a higher self-concept than females, particularly in Germany, Norway and Switzerland (Table 5.4b). These gender differences have a close relationship with gender differences in student performance in reading and mathematics. Self-concept is positively related to student performance, more so in mathematics than in reading.

…and the self-confidence of males and females in reading and mathematics corresponds to their performance…

Many of these issues will need to be further explored, and this will be subject of a thematic report that is currently being prepared. However, it is already clear that gender differences in student performance need to be reviewed and

… raising issues for further analysis.

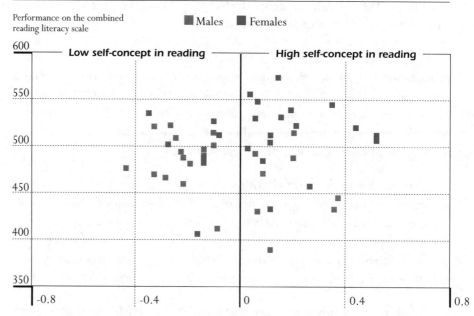

Figure 5.7a

Relationship between self-concept in reading and performance on the combined reading literacy scale for males and females

For the definition of the index, see Annex A1.
Note: Countries are represented by the square symbols.
Source: OECD PISA database, 2001. Table 5.4a.

Figure 5.7b

Relationship between self-concept in mathematics and performance on the mathematical literacy scale for males and females

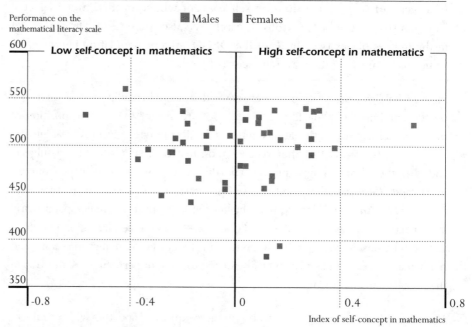

For the definition of the index, see Annex A1.
Note: Countries are represented by the square symbols.
Source: OECD PISA database, 2001. Table 5.4b.

analysed in close relationship with the habits, attitudes and self-concepts of young males and females.

Conclusions

Policy-makers have given considerable priority to issues of gender equality, with particular attention being paid to the disadvantages faced by females. The results of PISA point to successful efforts in many countries but also to a growing problem for males, particularly in reading literacy and at the lower tail of the performance distribution. In mathematics, females remain at a disadvantage in many countries, on average, but the advantage of males, in those countries where this persists, is mainly due to high levels of performance of a comparatively small number of males.

While some disadvantages remain for females, males' underperformance is a growing problem...

At the same time, there is significant variation between countries in the size of gender differences. The evidence from those countries where females are no longer at a disadvantage is that effective policies and practices can overcome what were long taken to be the inevitable outcomes of differences between males and females in learning style and, even, in underlying capacities. Indeed, the results of PISA 2000 make clear that some countries provide a learning environment or broader context that benefits both genders equally. The enduring differences in other countries, and the widespread disadvantage now faced by young males in reading literacy, require serious policy attention.

...though some countries have demonstrated that gender differences can be successfully addressed.

The analysis also reveals inequalities between the genders in the effectiveness with which schools and societies promote motivation and interest in different subject areas. The close interrelationship between subject interest and learning outcomes also suggests that the differing habits and interests of young females and males have far-reaching consequences for learning, and that education policy needs to address these.

Gender inequalities remain in the promotion of motivation and interest in different subjects.

Education systems have made significant strides towards closing the gender gap in educational attainment in recent decades (OECD, 2001), but much remains to be done. At age 15, many students are about to face the transition from education to work. Their performance at school, and their motivation and attitudes in different subject areas, can have a significant influence on their further educational and occupational pathways. These, in turn, will have an impact not only on individual career and salary prospects, but also on the broader effectiveness with which human capital is developed and utilised in OECD economies and societies. Improving the level of engagement of males in reading activities, and stimulating interest and self-concept among females in mathematics, need to be major policy objectives if greater gender equality in educational outcomes is to be achieved.

Improving males' engagement in reading and females' interest and self-concept in mathematics remains essential in order to ensure that all students realise their potential.

Note

1. These are programmes classified at Level 3A in the International Standard Classification of Education (ISCED).

FAMILY BACKGROUND AND STUDENT PERFORMANCE

Introduction

Schools need to cater for children from all backgrounds...

Students come from a variety of family, socio-economic and cultural backgrounds. As a result, schools need to provide appropriate and equitable opportunities for a very diverse student body. The learning environment can be enhanced by the variety of students' backgrounds and interests. However, heterogeneous levels of ability and differences in school preparedness increase the challenges that schools face in meeting the needs of students from widely varying socio-economic backgrounds.

...and looking at links between background and performance can help them to do so more effectively.

Identifying the characteristics of the students most likely to perform poorly can help educators and policy-makers to locate areas requiring action. Similarly, identifying the characteristics of students who may flourish academically can assist policy-makers to promote high levels of performance. If it can be shown that some countries find it easier than others to accommodate both groups, this would suggest that it is feasible to foster both equity and quality.

This chapter examines the relationship between students' performance in reading, mathematical and scientific literacy and various aspects of their home backgrounds, such as their parents' levels of education and occupations, their exposure to various levels of cultural and economic capital, their country of birth, and the language that they speak at home (see Box 6.1).

Box 6.1 **Interpreting the PISA indices**

The PISA 2000 indices are based on students' and school principals' accounts of the learning environment and organisation of schools, and of the social and economic contexts in which learning takes place. The indices rely on self-reports rather than on external observations and may be influenced by cross-cultural differences in response behaviour or the social desirability of certain responses.

Several of the indices summarise the responses of students or school principals to a series of related questions. The questions were selected from larger constructs on the basis of theoretical considerations and previous research.[1]

Unless otherwise noted, comparisons of student performance in this chapter refer to the performance of students on the combined reading literacy scale.

Structural equation modelling was used to confirm the theoretically expected dimensions of the indices and to validate their comparability across countries. For this purpose, a model was estimated separately for each country and, collectively, for all OECD countries.

Occupational status

Higher parental occupational status can influence students' occupational aspirations and expectations and, in turn, their commitment to learning as the means of satisfying those aspirations. High parental occupational status can also increase the range of options of which children are aware.

Parental occupation is a measure of socio-economic status and can influence students' aspirations and attitudes.

PISA captures this aspect of students' home backgrounds through information on parents' occupations and the activities associated with those occupations in a way that is internationally comparable. The resulting *socio-economic index of occupational status* (Ganzeboom *et al.*, 1992), which has values ranging from 0 to 90, measures the attributes of occupation that convert a person's education into income. The higher the value on the index, the higher the occupational status of a student's parents. On average across OECD countries, the value of the index is 49 and its standard deviation is 16 (see Box 6.2).

As can be seen in Figure 6.1, differences in the socio-economic index of occupational status are associated with large differences in student performance within countries (Table 6.1a). Among those in the top national quarters of students on the socio-economic index, the mean score of OECD countries on the combined reading literacy scale is 545 points, or 45 points above the OECD average. By contrast, the average score among the bottom national quarters of students on the socio-economic index is only 463 points. The average gap between the two groups is more than the magnitude of an entire proficiency level in reading.[2] On average across OECD countries, the index explains 11 per cent of the total variation in student performance on the combined reading literacy scale (see Annex A2). Similar results are evident in mathematical and scientific literacy (Tables 6.1b-c).

Students whose parents have higher-status jobs show higher literacy performance on average…

Figure 6.1 also shows that the gap in performance on the combined reading literacy scale between students in each country's top and bottom quarters of the socio-economic index differs considerably between countries. The smallest gap is found in Korea (33 points), where students whose parents have lower levels of occupational status perform well both in relative terms (*i.e.* when compared with those Korean students whose parents have high occupational status) and in absolute terms, *i.e.* when compared with students whose parents have similar occupational status in other countries. Finland and Iceland are the two European countries in the OECD with the smallest differences between the two extreme quarters (52 and 53 points respectively). These three countries also have the smallest gaps between students in the top and bottom quarters of the index in terms of performance on the mathematical and scientific literacy scales.

…but in some countries the advantage is much greater than in others…

The largest differences, of 100 points or more in all three literacy domains, are found in Belgium, Germany and Switzerland. In Germany, the difference is particularly striking. Students whose parents have the best jobs (the top quarter on the occupational index) score on average about as well as the average student in Finland, the best-performing country in PISA; those whose parents have

Box 6.2 **How to read Figure 6.1**

The PISA international socio-economic index of occupational status groups students according to their parents' occupations, ranked by the direct role that occupation plays in maximising income. In each country, the population is divided into quarters, ranked by the national values on the index. The skills required to perform the requirements of an occupation serve as the primary criterion for distinguishing different levels of occupational status.

Figure 6.1 compares the average performances of students in the top and bottom quarters of the index in each country. Thus, the length of the different lines demonstrates the gap in each country between people in its highest and lowest national occupational groups. Note that the average occupational status of each quarter differs between OECD countries, although the mean of the bottom quarter varies no more than 5 points, on a 90-point index, for all but four OECD countries. In the top quarter there is somewhat more variation.

Typical occupations among parents of 15-year-olds with between 16 and 35 points on the index include small-scale farming, metalworking, motor mechanics, taxi and lorry-driving, and waiting. Between 35 and 53 index points, the most common occupations are book-keeping, sales, small business management and nursing. As the required skills increase, so also does the status of the occupation. Between 54 and 70 index points, typical occupations are marketing management, teaching, civil engineering and accountancy. Finally, between 71 and 90 points, the top international quarter of the index, occupations include medicine, university teaching and law.

the lowest-status jobs score about the same as students in Mexico, the OECD country with the lowest performance.

Also, the Czech Republic, Hungary, the United Kingdom and the United States have differences of more than 90 points for students in the top and bottom quarters of the socio-economic index in all three domains, well above the equivalent of one proficiency level. As in Belgium, Germany and Switzerland, students in these countries who are in the bottom quarter of the occupational index are more than twice as likely as other students also to be among the bottom 25 per cent of their country's performers on the PISA literacy scales (Table 6.1a).

...and many factors contribute to this relationship. It cannot be assumed, however, that all of these differences are a direct result of the home advantages and higher expectations conferred by parents in higher occupations. Many factors affect students' performance in the three domains. For example, socio-economic status may be related to where students live and the quality of the schools to which they have access (this would be important in school systems that are dependent on local taxes), to the likelihood that they are enrolled in private schools, to the level of parental support and involvement, etc.

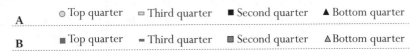

Figure 6.1

Occupational status of parents and student performance

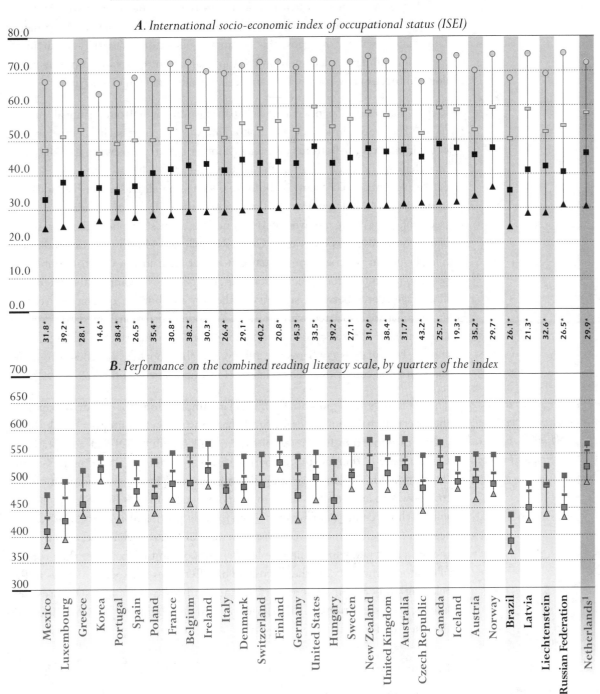

* Change in the combined reading literacy score per 16.3 units (1 standard deviation)
of the international socio-economic index of occupational status.
1. Response rate is too low to ensure comparability (see Annex A3).
Note: For the definition of the index, see Annex A1.
Source: OECD PISA database, 2001. Table 6.1a.

In some countries, students with parents in lower-status jobs perform better than the average OECD student.

It is important to note that although students in the bottom national quarter have lower mean scores than their peers in a given country, they do not necessarily fare poorly in absolute terms. For example, students in the bottom quarter of the socio-economic index in Finland and Korea have mean scores statistically significantly above the OECD average of 500 in each domain *and* have higher average scores than students in the top quarter in two countries. In other words, while higher socio-economic status provides a performance "advantage" within countries, this advantage does not necessarily occur in all countries. Similarly, placement in the top quarter on the socio-economic index does not necessarily convey the same relative advantage in every country.

It should also be recognised that being in the top (or bottom) national quarter on the socio-economic index in one country is not necessarily comparable to being in the top (or bottom) quarter in another country. Likewise, the "distance" or difference between those in the bottom and top quarters varies considerably between countries. For example, both the Czech Republic and France have identical mean values (48 index points) on the socio-economic index of occupational status (see Table 6.1a), but the average difference between students in the lowest and highest quarters is 35 points in the Czech Republic and 44 in France, thus indicating a larger gap in socio-economic status in France than in the Czech Republic. In order to take into account such differences, it is possible to compare the differences in average scores between students in the top and bottom quarters in reading literacy that are associated with a difference of one international standard deviation (16 units) on the socio-economic index of occupational status (Tables 6.1a, b and c). This analysis confirms the relatively high importance of socio-economic status in some countries and its relatively low importance in others.

Differences in performance hinder economic and social mobility from one generation to the next.

These findings have potentially important implications for policy-makers. As the International Adult Literacy Study has shown, reading literacy is a skill that enhances opportunities for employment and earnings (OECD and Statistics Canada, 2000). Furthermore, performance in reading is also an important foundation for lifelong learning. In consequence, intergenerational mobility from lower to higher levels of socio-economic status may be limited in countries with high percentages of weaker or marginally proficient readers. The weaker readers (as well as those weak in mathematical and scientific literacy) may be the ones least likely to obtain employment opportunities that offer the promise of economic mobility. As the discussion of differences between countries in the relationship between student performance and socio-economic status reveals, however, these disparities differ widely between countries. This may indicate that they are not inevitable.

Family wealth

While family wealth should not affect educational opportunities in public education systems...

Relative wealth, typically closely related to occupation, is generally an advantage. By definition, wealthier people have access to more resources. They also tend to have more discretionary income than do the less wealthy, and find it easier to acquire what they want, including goods and services of high quality.

However, in publicly supported education systems committed to equality of opportunity, the wealth of a student's family should not influence access to educational quality.

To assess the relationship between wealth and outcomes, reports were obtained from students on the availability of various items in their homes. A composite index of family wealth was constructed from the responses. For the OECD countries this index has an average of zero and a standard deviation of one.

As Table 6.2 shows, the relationship between wealth and performance in PISA is mixed but generally positive. Students from wealthier families typically do better than students from the least wealthy families in each domain. Wealthier students do tend to have higher average scores than less wealthy students within countries. On average, students in OECD countries in the top quarter of the wealth index score about 34 points higher on the reading literacy scale than students in the bottom quarter (the differences are statistically significant in all but three OECD countries).[3]

...in practice, students from wealthier families tend to do better, although the pattern is less pronounced than in the case of parental occupational status.

Among the participating countries, the United States shows the largest differences, the gap in reading performance between students in the top and bottom quarters of wealth being 85 points (OECD average difference 34 points). Expressed differently, students in the United States are at least twice as likely to be among the 25 per cent lowest performers in reading literacy if they are in the bottom quarter of the PISA index of wealth as if they are in the top quarter. Brazil, Mexico and Portugal have the next largest gaps, averaging about 70 points for the three domains (see Table 6.2 for reading literacy and *www.pisa.oecd.org* for mathematical and scientific literacy).

In some countries the relationship is much more pronounced than in others...

The relationship between family wealth and student performance is comparatively weak in the Nordic countries, in Austria, Belgium, Italy, Japan, Latvia and Poland.[4] Furthermore, in several OECD countries a relative lack of wealth is not a barrier to performance above the international average. Indeed, students in the bottom national quarter of wealth have mean scores at or above the OECD average literacy scores in about a third of countries. Among students in the bottom quarter for wealth, high scores are found in Finland (in reading literacy) and in Japan (in all three domains) (see Table 6.2 for reading literacy and *www.pisa.oecd.org* for mathematical and scientific literacy). Students in the bottom quarter of wealth in these countries have higher mean scores than those of students in the top quarter of wealth in many other OECD countries.

...where a relative lack of wealth is not a barrier to performance above the international average.

Possessions and activities related to "classical" culture

In addition to family wealth, students may also have access to possessions related to classical culture that research has frequently shown to be related to educational success. Unlike family wealth, which typically depends on parents' success in the marketplace, cultural possessions are more readily available, in principle at least, to whoever seeks them. To assess the relationship between cultural possessions and performance in the three domains, the PISA survey

PISA also asked students about possessions in their home related to classical culture, such as literature and art.

asked students to indicate whether they had classic literature, books of poetry, and works of art (such as paintings) in their homes. The responses were combined to create a summary index of cultural possessions in the family home; it was set to have an average of zero and a standard deviation of one for the OECD countries.

The highest levels of possessions related to classical culture are found in Iceland, Latvia and the Russian Federation (Table 6.3). In Iceland, for example, 75 per cent or more of students indicate that their homes contain classic literature, books of poetry or works of art (for data, see *www.pisa.oecd.org*). In the Russian Federation, nearly 90 per cent of students report that they have classic literature and books of poetry at home. These percentages contrast with countries such as Mexico and New Zealand, where less than one-third of students report having classic literature at home, and Brazil, France and Mexico, where one-third or less students have works of art in their homes.

Within countries, cultural possessions are associated more closely with performance than is family wealth...

The possession of items related to classical culture is closely related to differences in performance, as can be seen in Figure 6.2,[5] and generally more closely than family wealth. Moreover, the differences in performance between students in the bottom and top national quarters of the index of cultural possessions in the family home are consistently high, ranging on average across OECD countries from 55 points in mathematical literacy to 68 points in reading literacy (see Table 6.3 for reading literacy and *www.pisa.oecd.org* for mathematical and scientific literacy).[6] This relationship is, naturally, closely intertwined with other background factors, such as socio-economic status and wealth.

...although students who lack cultural possessions do not everywhere perform poorly in international terms.

The lack of possessions related to classical culture is, of course, relative. Students in some countries may have few such possessions and perform poorly in comparison with their fellow students. At the same time, however, such students may perform well when compared with students at the bottom quarter of the index in other countries. A relative lack of possessions related to classical culture, therefore, does not seem to prevent students in several countries from exceeding the OECD average performance in each domain.

The quarter of students with the most cultural possessions have very high scores in many countries...

Students with the highest values on the index of cultural possessions typically do exceptionally well. Eight OECD countries have average scores of 550 points or more in each domain among such students. In reading, this would place these students around the boundary between proficiency Levels 3 and 4. In Australia and the United Kingdom, average scores for students in the top quarter exceed 560 points in reading, mathematical and scientific literacy, and are well within Level 4 in reading literacy. On average in OECD countries, performance increases by 27 points in reading for each increase of one unit on the index of cultural possessions (Table 6.3).

...and much of the difference is between the bottom quarter and the rest.

It is also possible to examine how PISA literacy scores progressively increase among students with successively higher levels of cultural possessions. Even more pronounced than in the case of family wealth, an average of 40 per cent of

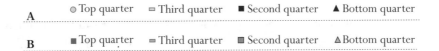

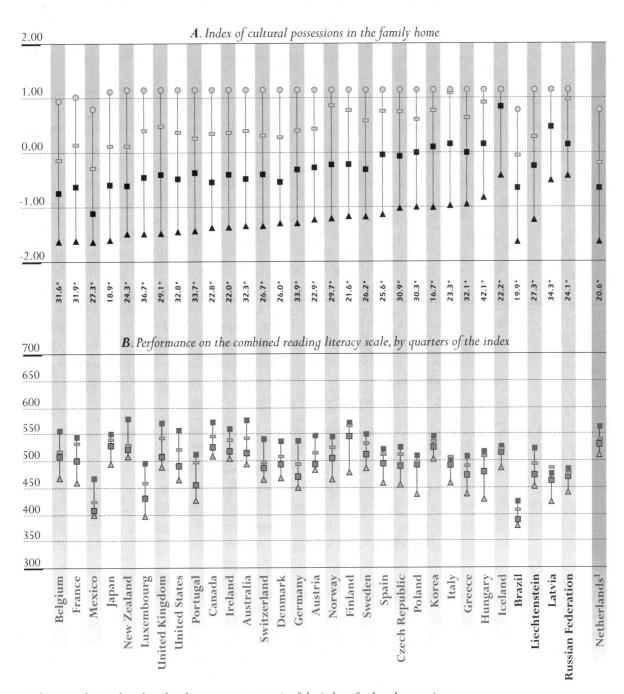

A. Index of cultural possessions in the family home

B. Performance on the combined reading literacy scale, by quarters of the index

* Change in the combined reading literacy score per unit of the index of cultural possessions.
1. Response rate is too low to ensure comparability (see Annex A3).
Note: For the definition of the index, see Annex A1.
Source: OECD PISA database, 2001. Table 6.3.

this difference lies between the bottom and the second quarters on the index of cultural possessions. In Iceland, Italy, Japan, Latvia, Poland, the Russian Federation and Spain, the proportion is more than 60 per cent.

Although cultural possessions are closely interrelated with other factors, it does seem that the kind of cultural capital on which school curricula often build and which examinations and tests assess makes a difference. The fact that the effects are even higher in reading than in mathematical and scientific literacy (for data on these subjects *www.pisa.oecd.org*) emphasises that there is educational benefit in home-based access to literature and other cultural possessions.

PISA also asked about activities related to classical culture...

PISA 2000 also asked students to indicate the frequency with which they participated in activities related to classical culture, such as visiting a museum or art gallery, watching live theatre, or attending an opera, ballet or classical symphony concert. A composite index of cultural activities was created from the responses. Index values above zero indicate that students participate in cultural activities more frequently than the average of students across all OECD countries; values below zero indicate that students participate less frequently than the typical or average 15-year-old in the OECD countries.

...which students from different countries undertook with varying frequency...

Countries with the highest frequencies of participation in cultural activities include the Czech Republic, Hungary and Latvia (Table 6.4). Nearly 30 per cent of students in the Czech Republic and Hungary said that they had watched live theatre three or more times in the past year (compared with an international average of only 12 per cent) (for data, see *www.pisa.oecd.org*). Similarly, one-third of Hungarian students had visited a museum or art gallery three or more times in the past year (compared with the international average of 14 per cent). On the other hand, an average of 43 per cent of the students reported that they had never visited a museum or art gallery.

...and it was found virtually everywhere that those involved in such activities more frequently had higher literacy scores on average.

The frequency of participation in cultural activities as measured by the index explains, on average across OECD countries, 5.7 per cent of the variation in student performance on the combined reading literacy scale (see Annex A2). In every country except Brazil, there is a statistically significant difference between the average performances of students in the bottom national quarter of the index of participation in cultural activities and those in the top quarter, with particularly large differences, of 70 scale points or more, in Belgium, Germany, Spain, the United Kingdom and the United States (Table 6.4).

Communication on social issues and aspects of culture

Parental involvement is widely seen as essential for success at school...

Parents' support for their children's education is widely deemed to be an essential element of success at school. When parents interact and communicate well with their children, they can offer encouragement, demonstrate their interest in their children's progress, and otherwise convey their concern for how their children are doing, both in and out of school. Indeed, considerable previous research has demonstrated the important relationship between parental involvement and children's academic success.

PISA asked students to indicate how often their parents interacted or communicated with them in six areas: discussing political or social issues; discussing books, films or television programmes; listening to music together; discussing how well the student was doing in school; eating the main meal with the student; and spending time just talking. Research confirms that these indicators operate in many countries as good proxies for social and cultural communication.

...and PISA therefore asked students how frequently they communicated with their parents...

Responses to the first three questions were combined to create an index of cultural communication; responses to the last three questions were combined to create an index of social communication. On both indices, values above the OECD average, which was set at zero, reflect comparatively high levels of communication between students and their parents. Note that values below the average do not signify the absence of communication but rather that students report that communication and interaction occur less frequently than on average across OECD countries.

...in cultural and social contexts.

According to students' reports, Italian parents, followed by those in Hungary and the Russian Federation, display the highest levels of communication on social issues with their children (Table 6.5 and Figure 6.3). In these three countries, for example, more than 70 per cent of students indicate that their parents discuss how well they are doing at school or "spend time just talking" with them several times a week (for data, see *www.pisa.oecd.org*). Students in Italy, again, report having the highest levels of communication on aspects of culture, followed, in order, by students in Hungary, France and Latvia (Table 6.6 and Figure 6.3). In Brazil, Hungary, Italy and the Russian Federation, more than 40 per cent of students indicate that their parents discuss books, films or television programmes with them several times a week. This percentage contrasts with the situation in several other countries, where 40 per cent or more of students never discuss books or films with their parents or do so only a few times a year (for data, see *www.pisa.oecd.org*).

On both indices, the more frequent the reported communication and interaction, the higher the average mean scores in every country on the combined reading literacy scale.[7] On average, cultural communication shows a stronger relationship with reading scores than does social communication. By way of illustration, the OECD average score in reading rises from 471 points for the bottom quarter on the index of cultural communication to 530 for the top quarter (a difference of almost 60 points), and from 481 points to 511 (a difference of 30 points) on the index of social communication (Tables 6.5 and 6.6).[8]

Results are better for those communicating more, especially on cultural matters.

Again, the impact of parental communication needs to be evaluated in the context of other background factors (see also Chapter 8). Nonetheless, this simple analysis indicates that educational success may be related to positive synergies between the home and school environments, and that communication between parents and children can be of educational benefit to children. An important objective for public policy may therefore be to work with parents,

Figure 6.3

Social and cultural communication with parents and student performance

Index of social communication and index of cultural communication

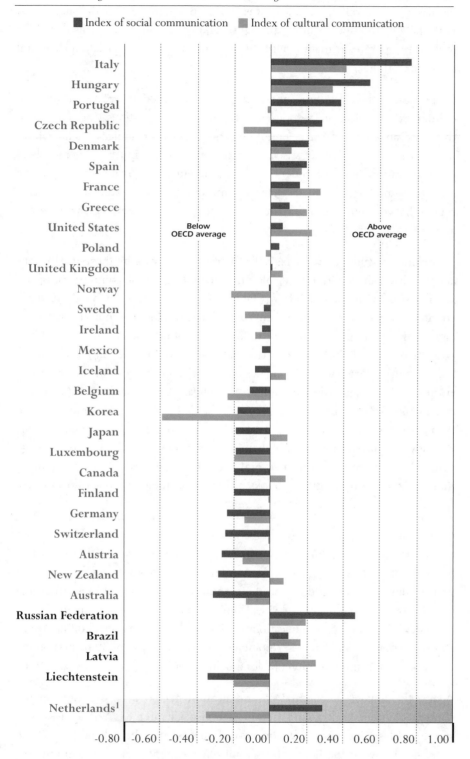

■ Index of social communication   ■ Index of cultural communication

Note: For the definition of the indices, see Annex A1.
1. Response rate is too low to ensure comparability (see Annex A3).
Source: OECD PISA database, 2001. Tables 6.5 and 6.6.

particularly those whose own educational attainment is more limited, in order to facilitate their interaction with their children and their children's schools in ways that enhance their children's learning. This is no easy task but it is important that support in parenting is seen as a key adjunct to the education of children.

Parental education

Research shows consistently that the parental level of education continues to be a significant source of disparities in student performance, notwithstanding the considerable efforts undertaken to guarantee equal educational opportunities for all. A highly supportive learning environment at home, to which a high level of parental educational attainment can contribute, is likely to be reflected in higher educational performance by their children. A supportive environment can be equated not only with the financial capital to support children's education – including higher education – and hence higher occupational status, but also with day-to-day interaction between parents and children that is of greater value for the type of education with which schools are concerned.

Parental level of education can also contribute to a supportive home environment.

Figure 6.4 uses three categories of educational attainment (completion of primary or lower secondary education, completion of upper secondary education, and completion of tertiary education) for students' mothers and provides mean performance scores in reading for each country. These categories are defined in such a way that they are internationally comparable, on the basis of the International Standard Classification of Education (ISCED). The mother's education was chosen because the literature often identifies this as a stronger predictor for student performance than the father's education.

Students whose mothers have completed upper secondary education achieve higher levels of performance in reading than other students, in all countries, and in most countries the mother's completion of tertiary education gives a further advantage (Table 6.7).

Mothers' education is positively associated with student performance...

Students whose mothers have not completed upper secondary education are particularly vulnerable. In all OECD countries, mean reading scores for students with mothers in this category are, on average, lower by about 45 points in reading, mathematical and scientific literacy than for students whose mothers have completed upper secondary education (Table 6.7).[9] The largest differences between the middle and lowest categories of attainment in reading are in Germany (99 points), Mexico (75 points), Belgium and Switzerland (73 points each) and the Czech Republic (71 points). In these countries, students whose mothers have not completed upper secondary education are between 2.1 and 3 times as likely to perform in the bottom quarter of the national student population than students whose mothers have completed upper secondary education. The extent of the disadvantage suffered by those whose mothers have not completed upper secondary education is summarised in Figure 6.4 (second panel), where it is shown as the increased likelihood of children of mothers without upper secondary education being in the bottom quarter of the national

...with particularly low performance among students whose mothers have not completed upper secondary education...

Figure 6.4

Mothers' education and student performance

Percentage of mothers who have completed various levels of education

■ Mothers with tertiary education (ISCED Levels 5 or 6)
■ Mothers with completed upper secondary education (highest level is ISCED Level 3)
■ Mothers with completed primary or lower secondary education (highest level is ISCED Levels 1 or 2)

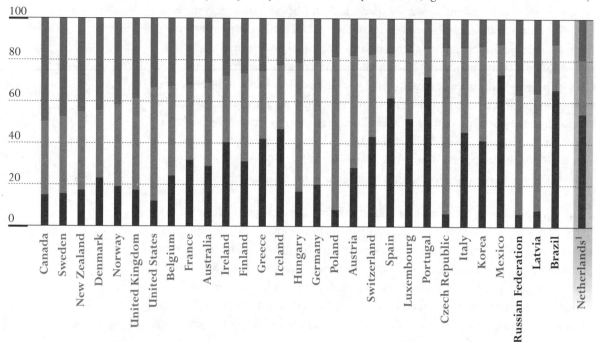

Increased likelihood of students whose mothers have not completed upper secondary education scoring in the bottom quarter of the national reading literacy performance distribution[2]

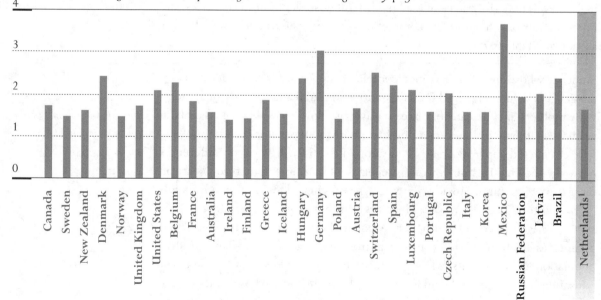

1. Response rate is too low to ensure comparability (see Annex A3).
2. For all countries, the ratio is statistically significantly greater than 1.
Source: OECD PISA database, 2001. Table 6.7.

distribution in reading performance. Despite these findings, the expected relationship between the mother's education and student performance is not universal – and may therefore not be automatic or inevitable.

A mother's completion of tertiary-level education provides little or no additional boost in some countries in the mean score of her child beyond that associated with the completion of upper secondary education. In others, it makes a big difference.

…whereas tertiary education is less consistently associated with student performance.

Although the data indicate that students with the least educated mothers often have the lowest mean scores, "low" scores should be placed in perspective. In Australia, Finland and Korea, mean performance scores for these students are above the OECD average in all three domains. In Ireland in reading, and in Canada, Iceland and New Zealand in mathematical literacy, students with the least educated mothers are above the OECD average (see Chapter 2 and Table 6.7). This also suggests that other educational and societal factors can compensate for deficiencies in parental education.

In some countries, even students with less educated mothers do well in international terms…

In societies that aim for equality of opportunity, the association between students' educational performance and their mothers' educational attainment seems high. Although PISA data are not suitable for direct predictions about differences in educational performance beyond the age of 15, data from the International Adult Literacy Survey (IALS) provide evidence of the probability of obtaining a tertiary qualification for groups whose parents have reached different levels of attainment. Table 6.8 shows the ratio of the chance of obtaining a tertiary qualification if at least one parent reached that level, to the chance of doing so if neither parent has completed secondary school.

…which suggests that other educational and societal factors can compensate for deficiencies in parental education…

In the 12 countries surveyed in IALS, the intergenerational mobility ranges from 2.0 in Australia to 5.8 in Poland: that is, having well-educated parents makes one twice as likely in Australia and nearly six times as likely in Poland to complete tertiary education than if one has poorly educated parents. These findings suggest that in many OECD countries, but in some more than in others, barriers to educational mobility persist which, in turn, can create problems in terms of equity and in raising the overall level of the stock of human capital.

…and perhaps reduce the remaining and substantial barriers to educational mobility.

Family structure

The family environment may also promote academic performance. Parents may read to young learners, assist them with homework and, in some countries, volunteer to help in schools. For older students, a supportive family environment can also be helpful with respect to homework, encouragement, and attendance at meetings with teachers or school administrators. Providing and maintaining such an environment may be difficult when students live in a single-parent family, where parents often find themselves having to cope with the double responsibility of work and education.

Single parents may find it harder than couples to give students sufficient support.

Students from a single-parent family perform less well than others in some countries...

The PISA context questionnaires asked students who usually lived at home with them. From the responses, it was possible to compare the performance of students in different types of family structure.[10] Among all OECD countries, approximately 15 per cent of PISA students report that they live in single-parent families (Table 6.9). Latvia, New Zealand, the United Kingdom and the United States have the highest proportions, slightly over 20 per cent, while Greece, Korea and Poland have the lowest proportions, all less than 10 per cent. In the majority of OECD countries, the findings of PISA show that students in single-parent families do less well than their peers in other types of family environment.[11]

...and where single-parent families are more common, the gap is greatest...

Overall, there is a 12-point difference in performance on the combined reading literacy scale, to the disadvantage of those in single-parent families. The largest differences, exceeding 28 points or more, are found in the Netherlands, the United Kingdom and the United States (Table 6.9). That is, two out of the three countries with the highest proportion of students in single-parent families also have the largest differences in mean scores in reading. That is, not only is living in a single-parent family more common in the United Kingdom and the United States, but the association with student performance is also more pronounced.[12] Other countries with comparatively large differences include Belgium, Finland, France, Denmark, Ireland, Korea, New Zealand, Norway and Sweden.

...but the relationship is complex and many factors are involved.

However, other social background factors, including wealth, often reinforce this relationship (see also Chapter 8), although to different degrees, given that the social profile of single parents varies considerably.

Issues of family structure are sensitive as well as important. Evidence that children in families with two parents perform better might seem to offer only a counsel of despair to those for whom an arrangement with one parent is preferable on non-educational grounds and, in any case, already exists. On the other hand, if there is evidence of disadvantage it needs to be addressed. The issue is how to facilitate productive home support for children's learning in ways that do not demand more time than single parents can provide. Strategic allocation of time to activities with the greatest potential yield will increase efficiency where time is limited. The policy question for education systems and individual schools interacting with parents is what kinds of parental engagement should be encouraged.

Place of birth and language spoken at home

Increased migration can cause educational difficulties...

Migration from one country to another is increasingly common as international trade expands, as employment opportunities attract people to better or different livelihoods, and as countries find themselves assisting refugees from political and economic turmoil. Whatever the reasons for which people migrate from one country to another, their children of school age often find themselves in a new environment in which they are different in some ways or in which the language of instruction is unfamiliar to them. Although it is very difficult to compare the context of migration between countries, cross-national analysis may provide some insight into the characteristics that help certain countries to succeed better than others in accommodating these disparities.

In order to examine the effects of immigrant and language status on performance in the three domains, the PISA context questionnaire asked students to indicate whether they themselves and each of their parents were born in the country in which they were living, or in another country. Students were also asked what language they spoke at home most of the time.

...and PISA therefore asked students about their migration status and home language.

It is important to recognise the limitations of the data available. PISA did not ask students how long they had lived in the country where the assessment took place. While many of them were children of immigrant parents and probably fluent in the language of instruction, others were doubtless recent arrivals and only in their second year of schooling in their "new" country.[13] Likewise, there is no information about how similar or different a student's first language might be to the language of instruction. One might reasonably expect, for example, that having parents born, say, in New Zealand would have less impact on the score of a student now living in Australia or the United States than having parents born, say, in a country speaking a language other than English. However accommodating schools in the "new" countries might be, the differences in language might reduce performance in reading in the second language (or in mathematical or scientific literacy), especially among recent arrivals.

These questions did not take full account of the varied situation of children in immigrant families.

To assess the effect of place of birth on performance, three categories of students were compared, as shown in Figure 6.5:

The analysis compares:

— those students who were born in the country where the assessment took place and who had at least one parent born in that country (referred to below as "*native students*");

..."native" students...

— those born in the country where the assessment took place but whose parents were born in another country (referred to below as "*first-generation*" students); and

..."first-generation" students...

— those born outside the country where the assessment took place and whose parents were also born in another country (referred to below as "*non-native*" students).

...and "non-native" students.

For many of the non-native students, the language of the test will have been a second language, and some of these students will not have had many years of experience in the educational system of the country in which they were tested. First-generation students are also in families in which the first language, or the language spoken at home, may not be the language of instruction. Regardless of their place of birth, students in the second and third categories need to acquire the same knowledge and skills that native-born students are expected to have as they move towards the completion of their formal education.

Language is a key issue for many students born abroad or with immigrant parents.

Figure 6.5

Place of birth, home language and student performance

Percentage of non-native and first-generation students (left scale) and performance of non-native, first-generation and native students on the combined reading literacy scale (right scale)

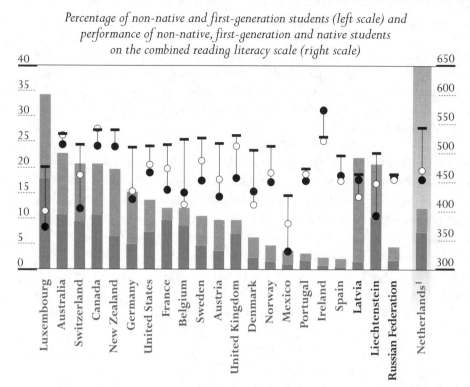

Left scale

■ Percentage of students who were foreign-born and whose parents were also foreign-born ("non-native students")

■ Percentage of students who were born in the country of assessment but whose parents were foreign-born ("first-generation students")

Right scale

— Mean performance on the combined reading literacy scale of students who were born in the country of assessment with at least one of their parents born in the same country ("native students")

○ Mean performance on the combined reading literacy scale of students who were born in the country of assessment but whose parents were foreign-born ("first-generation students")

● Mean performance on the combined reading literacy scale of students who were foreign-born and whose parents were also foreign-born ("non-native students")

Percentage of students who speak a language at home most of the time that is different from the language of assessment, from other official languages or from other national dialects (left scale) and performance of students on the combined reading literacy scale by language group (right scale)

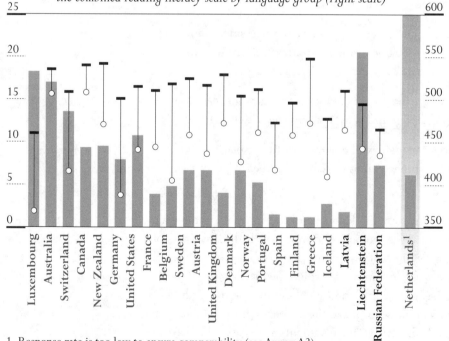

Left scale

■ Percentage of students who speak a language at home most of the time that is different from the language of assessment, from other official languages or from other national dialects

Right scale

— Mean performance on the combined reading literacy scale of students who speak a language at home most of the time that is the **same as** the language of assessment, other official languages or another national dialects

○ Mean performance on the combined reading literacy scale of students who speak a language at home most of the time that is **different from** the language of assessment, from other official languages or from other national dialects

1. Response rate is too low to ensure comparability (see Annex A3).
Source: OECD PISA database, 2001. Table 6.10.

A comparison of the performance in reading literacy of first-generation students with that of native students in the 14 countries in which first-generation students represent at least 3 per cent of students assessed in PISA 2000, reveals comparatively large and statistically significant differences – in favour of native students – in ten countries. The differences in performance on the combined reading literacy scale range from 31 to 41 points in France, New Zealand, Sweden and the United States, from about 53 to 62 points in Austria, Liechtenstein and Switzerland, exceed 70 points, or approximately a full proficiency level, in Germany, Luxembourg and the Netherlands, and rise to 112 points in Belgium (Table 6.10). A similar pattern exists for the relationship between place of birth and performance on the mathematical and scientific literacy scales.

In most countries with significant immigrant populations, first-generation students read well below the level of native students...

These are troubling differences because both groups of students were born in the country where the assessment took place and, presumably, had experienced the same curriculum that the national education system offers to all students. Despite whatever similarities there might be in their educational "histories", something about being a first-generation student puts them at a relative disadvantage in these countries. Concern about such differences is especially justified in those countries with significant performance gaps and comparatively large percentages of first-generation students, including Belgium (8 per cent), France (10 per cent), Luxembourg (18 per cent) and Switzerland (9 per cent).

...even though they were themselves born in the country – which is disturbing.

As one would expect, non-native students tend to lag even further behind native students than do first-generation students. On average, in 10 out of the 16 countries included in this comparison, native students outscore their non-native peers in reading literacy by at least 71 points, or a full proficiency level. The differences range from 103 to 112 points in Liechtenstein, Luxembourg and Switzerland, and from 60 to 100 points in Austria, Belgium, Denmark, Germany, Greece, the Netherlands, Norway and Sweden. The smallest but still statistically significant differences are in Canada (27 points), New Zealand (30 points) and the United Stated (45 points). In the case of New Zealand, this is about the same difference as between non-native and first-generation students in that country.

Students born abroad lag behind even more, although to widely varying degrees in different countries.

Australia and Canada provide interesting exceptions to the general pattern. In Australia, neither a student's place of birth nor the birthplace of his or her parents seems, on average, to influence performance in reading, mathematical and scientific literacy. Australia achieves these results in the face of high propor-tions of non-native students (12 per cent of all students) and first-generation students (11 per cent). Similar patterns of success are also found in Canada as the three groups of Canadian students score statistically above the OECD average in two out of the three domains.

A few countries stand out because they appear to avoid these differences.

One can hypothesise that students who speak the language of assessment or another national language or dialect at home most of the time ("majority-language students") will perform better in PISA than students who routinely converse with their parents and siblings in another language ("minority-language" students).[14] On the whole, the data support this hypothesis. Among

Not surprisingly, students not speaking the majority language at home perform much less well than those who do...

the OECD countries, the average difference between the two groups is 66 points in reading and in scientific literacy, and 49 points in mathematical literacy (Table 6.11).

...and are much more likely to score among the lowest quarter of students in each country...

One implication of these differences is that the 15-year-old-students in Belgium, Denmark, Germany, Luxembourg and Switzerland who do not speak the language of assessment or another national language or national dialect at home are at least two and a half times more likely to be among the 25 per cent lowest performers in reading literacy than those students who speak the language of assessment most of the time. In Austria, France, Greece, the Netherlands, New Zealand, Sweden and the United States, minority-language students are more than twice as likely as majority-language students to be in the bottom quarter of performance in each domain.

...which can affect a country's average reading score significantly.

The differences in mean reading scores between majority and minority-language students clearly affect countries' overall performance in reading. As an illustration, if Germany were able to raise the mean scores of minority-language speakers to the same level as that of majority-language speakers, the national mean score in Germany would be above the OECD average of 500 points in mathematical literacy, rather than 10 points below it.

Conclusions

Differences between countries in the impact of home background on student performance give some hope that it can be reduced.

The goal of public policy in education must be to provide equal opportunities for all students to achieve their full potential. While reaching this goal can be frustrated by the strong impact of home background factors on student performance, the fact that the impact differs greatly between countries gives rise to optimism that greater equality in educational opportunities is attainable.

The aspects of home background investigated in this chapter are related, and their effects are not independent. Nevertheless, implications for policy arise from each one considered separately:

Parental occupation is strongly associated with performance...

— Parental occupational status has a particularly strong association with student performance in reading, mathematical and scientific literacy. Having parents in more prestigious jobs can influence students' own job expectations, and raise their commitment to learning as the means of satisfying high occupational aspirations. High parental occupational status can also widen the range of options of which children are aware. Education systems need to widen occupational knowledge and aspirations as well as tackling more immediate issues of educational performance.

...as are possessions and activities related to "classical" culture.

— The role of possessions and activities related to "classical" culture is complex, but the possession of the kind of cultural capital on which school curricula tend to build and which examinations and tests assess appears to be related to student performance. While possession of such advantages is related to the other home background characteristics, its effects in isolation are generally strong. The fact that the effects are even higher in reading literacy than in mathematical and scientific literacy emphasises the educational benefit of home-based access to literature and other cultural possessions.

— Parental education and patterns of social and cultural communication between parents and children, particularly communications related to school and learning, are interconnected and, together, may be of significant educational benefit for children. The results of PISA suggest that educational success may be related to patterns of communication between parents and children. An important objective for public policy may therefore be to support parents, particularly those whose own educational attainment is limited, to facilitate their interaction with their children and their children's schools in ways that enhance their children's learning.

Parents' education and quality of communication with children show a positive association as well...

— Family wealth, interrelated with parental occupations, is also associated with higher levels of performance, although the relationship appears to be weaker than that of the other factors examined in this chapter.

...while family wealth tends to be less strongly associated with student performance.
The disadvantages of migrants are complex and varied, but need to be addressed.

— Finally, all OECD countries are experiencing increased migration, much of it of people whose home language is not the language of instruction in the schools that their children attend. The nature of the educational disadvantage that students with ethnic minority background and/or the children of migrants suffer is substantially influenced by the circumstances from which they have come. Educational disadvantage in their country of origin can be magnified in their country of adoption even though, in absolute terms, their educational performance might have been raised. Concentrated help in the language of instruction could be one policy option for such students. These students may be academically disadvantaged either because they are immigrants entering a new education system or because they need to learn a new language in a home environment that may not facilitate this learning. In either case, they may be in need of special or extra attention.

Together, the findings have potentially important implications for policy-makers. Literacy skills are an important foundation for lifelong learning and enhance future opportunities for employment and earnings. In consequence, intergenerational mobility from lower to higher socio-economic status may be limited in countries with high percentages of weaker or marginally proficient readers. The weaker students may be the ones least likely to obtain employment opportunities that offer the promise of economic mobility. Chapter 8 takes the analysis further by considering how the different background factors interact, and explores what policy levers exist in different countries both to improve average performance and to moderate the impact of family background on student performance.

Family disadvantage will remain from generation to generation unless education systems take steps to mitigate its effect.

Notes

1. For detailed information on the construction of the indices, see Annex A1.

2. In all countries the differences are statistically significant.

3. In standardised terms, the equivalent increases per unit on the wealth index are 20 points on the combined reading literacy scale (see Table 6.2), 24 points for mathematical literacy and 18 points for scientific literacy (for data, see *www.pisa.oecd.org*).

4. On average across OECD countries, the index explains 2.6 per cent of the variation in student performance on the combined reading literacy scale.

5. On average across OECD countries, the index explains 8.2 per cent of the variation in student performance on the combined reading literacy scale.

6. The differences are statistically significant in all OECD countries and in all three assessment domains.

7. In the case of cultural communication, the differences are statistically significant in all countries. In that of social communication, they are statistically significant in all countries except Italy. The index of cultural communication explains 5.8 per cent of the variation in student performance on the combined reading literacy scale. The index of social communication explains 2.2 per cent of the variation in student performance on the combined reading literacy scale.

8. Another way to assess the importance of social and cultural communication is to consider their relative contribution to differences in performance on the combined reading literacy scale. In all OECD countries, an increase of one unit on the index of cultural communication adds about 21 points to the average reading score, compared with a difference of only 10 points in reading for each additional unit on the index of social communication.

9. These differences are statistically significant in all countries and all three assessment domains, except for Portugal and Poland in mathematical literacy.

10. In the discussion that follows, students in single-parent families are compared with students in all other types of family environment, including nuclear families (*i.e.*, a traditional family with a mother and a father), mixed families (a family with a mother and a male guardian, a father and a female guardian, or two guardians), and other possible family environments (*e.g.*, living with grandparents or siblings).

11. The differences are statistically significant in 14 countries.

12. Although students in single-parent families in the United Kingdom do less well than their peers in other family structures, the scores of both groups of students are close to or exceed the OECD average on the combined reading literacy scale. This is not the case in the United States.

13. Students who were unable to read or speak the language of the test because they had received less than one year of teaching in the language of the assessment were excluded from the assessment (see Annex A3).

14. In response to the question, "what language do you speak at home most of the time", students could indicate that they spoke the language in which the assessment was undertaken, an "other official national language", "other national dialects or languages", or "other languages". The data presented here compare students in the last group (*i.e.*, "other languages") with students in the first three groups in the countries in which at least 3 per cent of students indicated that the language spoken in their home most of the time was an "other language".

THE LEARNING ENVIRONMENT AND THE ORGANISATION OF SCHOOLING

Introduction

This chapter considers how the school environment is associated with student success.

The amount of knowledge and skills acquired depends greatly on the extent to which students have access to effective learning opportunities both at home and at school. This chapter takes the search for factors contributing to educational success further by turning attention to the learning environment that schools and families provide for 15-year-old students and by comparing aspects of school management and financing.

Box 7.1 **Interpreting the PISA indices**

Several of the indices summarise the responses of students or school principals to a series of related questions. The questions were selected from larger constructs on the basis of theoretical considerations and previous research.[1] For detailed information on the construction of the indices, see Annex A1.

The PISA 2000 indices are based on students' and school principals' accounts of the learning environment and organisation of schools, and of the social and economic contexts in which learning takes place. The indices rely on self-reports rather than on external observations and may be influenced by cross-cultural differences in response behaviour or the social desirability of certain responses.

Several limitations of the information collected from principals should be taken into account in the interpretation of the data. In most countries, no more than 150 principals were surveyed. In addition, although principals are best suited to provide information about their schools, generalising from a single source of information for each school (and then "matching" that information with students' reports) is not straightforward. Most importantly, students' performance in each of the domains depends on many factors, including all the education that they have received in earlier years, not just the period in which they have interacted with their current teachers. Nevertheless, the information from the school questionnaire can be instructive as it provides unique insights into the ways in which national and sub-national authorities implement their educational objectives.

Where information based on reports from school principals is presented in this report, it has been weighted so that it reflects the number of 15-year-olds enrolled in each school.

Unless otherwise noted, comparisons of student performance in this chapter refer to the performance of students on the combined reading literacy scale.

School and classroom climate

Teacher support

Research suggests that students benefit from clear expectations on their performance and do better if teachers are interested in their progress and willing to help them meet the expectations.

The literature on school effectiveness suggests that students (particularly those with a low level of performance) benefit from teaching practices that demonstrate teachers' interest in the progress of their students, give the clear message that all students are expected to attain reasonable performance standards, and show a willingness to help all students to meet these standards. In order to examine the extent to which such practices are common in different OECD countries, and the extent to which they promote higher levels of performance, students were asked to indicate the frequency with which teachers in the language of assessment show an interest in every student's learning, give students an opportunity to express opinions, help students with their work and continue to teach until students understand.

A summary index of teacher support was created from the responses to these and related questions. Values above the OECD average, which is set at 0, indicate higher than average student perceptions that teachers are supportive (at least in lessons of the language of assessment), while negative values indicate below-average student perceptions of teachers' supportiveness.[2]

Students in Australia, Brazil, Canada, New Zealand, Portugal, the United Kingdom and the United States have the most positive perceptions of their teachers' supportiveness. By contrast, students in Austria, Belgium, the Czech Republic, France, Germany, Italy, Japan, Korea, Latvia, Luxembourg and Poland report below-average support from their teachers of the language of assessment (Table 7.1).

The great majority of students feel well supported in some countries but only a minority in others.

For example, in Australia, Canada, Denmark, Iceland, New Zealand, Portugal, Sweden and the United Kingdom, between two-thirds and three-quarters of students report that their teachers of the language of assessment continue to teach until students understand, in most lessons or every lesson. Conversely, in the Czech Republic, Japan, Korea and Poland, less than half of students make such a report. Similarly, in Australia, Canada, Denmark, Hungary, Iceland, New Zealand, Portugal, Sweden and the United Kingdom, two-thirds or more of students report that their teachers of the language of assessment do a lot to help students in most lessons or every lesson, while less than half of students in France, Korea, Japan, Luxembourg and Poland make that report (for data, see *www.pisa.oecd.org*). From the data available, there is no way of assessing the extent to which these results reflect true differences in teachers' attitudes and practices – within and between countries – rather than differences in students' subjective reports, since students in each country applied only their own judgement. Despite this caveat, some of the differences between countries are so large that they merit attention.

To the extent that teachers typically use more "supportive" practices in classes attended by a majority of less able students, the correlation between support and performance would be expected to be negative. At the same time, to the extent that the encouragement offered is effective, one would expect that performance would be higher in classes that receive more support than in other classes.

The relationship between teacher support and performance is complex…

As might be anticipated from this, the relationship is mixed and generally weak.[3] However, in most countries with a value on the teacher support index *above* the OECD average, the correlation between teacher support and performance in reading literacy tends to be positive and statistically significant (Figure 7.1).

…but in most countries with high levels of teacher support the association with performance tends to be weakly positive.

Figure 7.1

Teacher support and student performance

Correlation between the index of teacher support and performance on the combined reading literacy scale

	Positive correlation between teacher support index and performance on the combined reading literacy scale	No statistically significant correlation	**Negative** correlation between teacher support index and performance on the combined reading literacy scale
Mean index of teacher support is **above** the OECD average (0.0)	Australia, Brazil, Canada, Denmark, Finland, Iceland, New Zealand, Russian Federation, Sweden, United Kindom, United States	Greece, Hungary, Ireland, Mexico, Portugal, Spain	Liechtenstein, Switzerland
Mean index of teacher support is **below** the OECD average (0.0)	Japan, Korea, **Latvia**, Norway, Poland	Austria, Czech Republic, France, Netherlands	Belgium, Germany, Italy, Luxembourg

Source: OECD PISA database, 2001.

In countries with less support overall, the picture is more mixed...

In countries where students report lower teacher support than the OECD average, the pattern of relationships is mixed. For example, Japan, Korea, Latvia and Poland are countries with below-average values on the index of teacher support, but those students who benefit from more supportive teachers show higher PISA scores than other students. By contrast, Belgium, the Czech Republic, Germany, Italy and Luxembourg are countries with below-average teacher support in which students who report more teacher support tend to achieve lower results. In these countries, at least 51 per cent of students say that their teachers of the language of assessment never show interest in every student's learning or do so only in some lessons (as opposed to most lessons or every lesson), at least 27 per cent of students say that their teachers never or only in some lessons provide an opportunity for students to express their opinions, and 58 per cent or more of students say that their teachers never or only in some lessons help them with their learning (for data, see *www.pisa.oecd.org*).

...perhaps because teacher support tends to be limited to the weak performers.

Many factors may contribute to this pattern, and further research is needed to explore these. In the countries with below-average levels of teacher support and a negative relationship with performance, "supportiveness" may be included in teachers' professional culture to a lesser extent than in other countries, and teachers may tend to limit their efforts to classes or individual students experiencing the most serious difficulties. Or perhaps it is only once a critical mass of teacher support is provided in a school that the effects on student performance become sufficiently beneficial to have a positive impact on student performance.

Student-related factors affecting the school climate

Both the school and student context questionnaires in PISA included questions that allow the identification and comparison of students' and principals' perceptions of factors that affect schools' climate for learning. Principals were asked to indicate the extent to which learning is hindered by such factors as student absenteeism, the use of alcohol or illegal drugs, and disruption of classes by students. Students, in turn, were asked how frequently certain disruptive situations occur in their classes of the language of assessment. For example, students indicated the frequency with which "students cannot work well", "there is noise and disorder", and "at the start of class, more than five minutes are spent doing nothing". Such data should be interpreted with some caution, though. Principals in different countries do not necessarily apply the same criteria when considering the learning climate. For example, principals in countries with generally low absenteeism may consider a modest level of absenteeism in their school to be a major cause of disciplinary problems, whereas principals in countries with higher levels of absenteeism may see things differently.

PISA looked at how far learning is hindered by inappropriate student behaviours – in the eyes of principals.

Figure 7.2

The climate for learning – the school principals' perspective

Distribution of mean percentages of students enrolled in schools where principals report that learning is hindered to some extent or a lot by the following factors

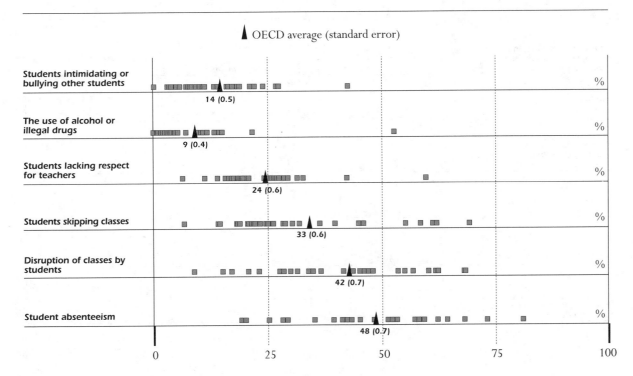

Note: Countries are represented by the square symbols.
Source: OECD PISA database, 2001. For data, see *www.pisa.oecd.org*.

Close to half of principals are concerned about the effects of absenteeism and disruption...

In all OECD countries, principals identify student absenteeism as the most frequent obstacle to learning, 48 per cent of them, on average, identifying this as hindering learning by 15-year-olds either to some extent or a lot (see Figure 7.2 and *www.pisa.oecd.org*). Disruptive behaviour is the next most frequently indicated cause, mentioned by 42 per cent, then students skipping classes, mentioned by 33 per cent, and students lacking respect for teachers, mentioned by 24 per cent. Fourteen per cent of principals indicate that students' intimidation or bullying of other students hinders learning to some extent or even a lot.

...while students are most concerned about delays in getting down to work.

From the students' perspective, wasting time at the beginning of lessons is the most frequently reported disciplinary problem. An average of 40 per cent of students report that, in most lessons or every lesson of the language of assessment, more than five minutes at the start of class is spent doing nothing, and a quarter of students report that students do not start working for a long time after lessons begin (see Figure 7.3 and *www.pisa.oecd.org*). On average across OECD countries, a third of students report that the teacher must wait a long

Figure 7.3

The climate for learning – the students' perspective

Distribution of mean percentages of students who report that the following statements are true for most lessons or every lesson

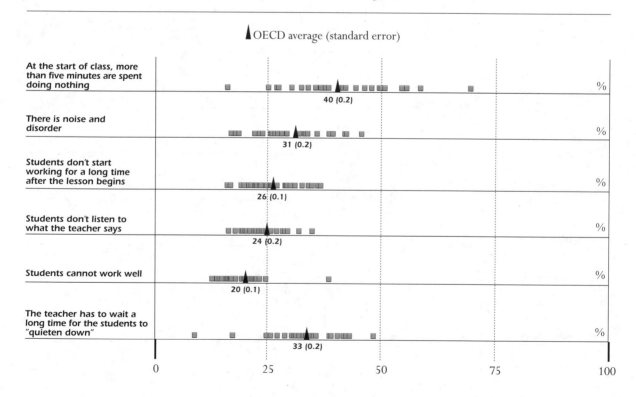

Note: Countries are represented by the square symbols.
Source: OECD PISA database, 2001. For data, see *www.pisa.oecd.org*.

time for students to quieten down in most lessons or every lesson and that there is noise and disorder in their lessons of the language of assessment. Less than one in five students in Denmark, Iceland, Japan, Mexico, Poland, Switzerland and the United Kingdom report that students tend not to listen to what the teacher says, while about a third of students in Korea and Italy do so.

These averages indicate a general pattern throughout the OECD, but it should be noted that the averages disguise considerable variation within and between OECD countries. To examine how countries differ, summary indices were constructed using data from both principals and students. In the case of the student-level index, the higher the score *above* zero, the more positive an education system's learning climate in the opinion of students. On the school-level index, values *above* zero reflect a positive perception on the part of school principals of the disciplinary climate, *i.e.,* the view that learning is hindered by the various factors mentioned in this index to less than the OECD average degree. By contrast, scores *below* zero reflect the opinion that the learning climate (on the school-level index) and discipline (on the student-level index) are worse than the average in each case.

But patterns vary by country, as shown on two indices, of students' and principals' views of the learning climate.

Among school principals, those in Greece and the Russian Federation believe that their schools have the greatest problems with such disciplinary issues as absenteeism, disruption by students, and students skipping classes. In the Russian Federation, for example, principals in schools representing 85 per cent of that country's 15-year-old students say that students' skipping classes hinders learning to some extent or a lot (for data see *www.pisa.oecd.org*).

Principals demonstrate most concern in Greece and the Russian Federation...

Countries deemed by their principals to have the fewest disciplinary problems include the Czech Republic, Denmark, Japan and Korea (Table 7.2). Even in these countries, however, which compare relatively well internationally with regard to their learning climate, responses from principals do not suggest the absence of problems.

...and least concern in the Czech Republic, Denmark, Japan and Korea...

Consider, for example, Japan and Korea, two of the three countries with the highest scores on the index that summarises principals' perceptions of student-related factors affecting school climate. In Japan, 39 per cent of principals nonetheless report that learning is hindered a lot or to some extent by student absenteeism (OECD average 48 per cent), 18 per cent report that it is similarly hindered by students skipping classes (OECD average 33 per cent), 29 per cent that it is similarly hindered by students lacking respect for teachers (OECD average 24 per cent), and 5 per cent that it is similarly hindered by students intimidating or bullying other students (OECD average 14 per cent) (see Figure 7.2 and *www.pisa.oecd.org*). Similarly, 20 per cent of principals in Korea identify student absenteeism, 17 per cent disruption of classes by students, 14 per cent students' skipping of classes and 29 per cent students lacking respect for teachers, as obstacles that hinder learning to some extent or a lot. This suggests that there is room for improvement even in the countries with the fewest problems.

... but there is much room for improvement even in the countries with the fewest problems.

Figure 7.4

The climate for learning – a summary picture

Index of disciplinary climate and index of student-related factors affecting school climate

■ Index of disciplinary climate, based on reports by students   ■ Index of student-related factors affecting school climate, based on reports by school principals

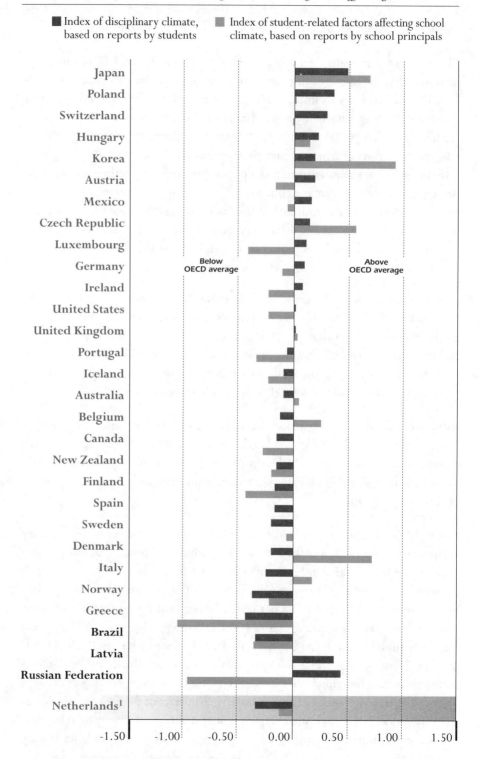

1. Response rate is too low to ensure comparability (see Annex A3).
Note: For the definitions of the indices, see Annex A1.
Source: OECD PISA database, 2001. Tables 7.2 and 7.3.

Students in Latvia, Liechtenstein, Japan, Poland, the Russian Federation and Switzerland are the most likely to indicate that they rarely or only infrequently encounter disruptive conditions in their classrooms (Table 7.3). By contrast, students in Brazil, Greece and Norway judge their classrooms to be disrupted by inappropriate behaviour relatively frequently.

How do the perceptions of students and principals compare? As noted above, although both questionnaires concerned the climate for learning, they adopted different approaches and asked different questions. Nonetheless, it is possible to compare their perspectives on the learning climate indirectly by comparing how the two groups responded to their respective sets of questions. In many countries, there is a relatively high level of agreement between the views of students and their principals on student-related aspects of disciplinary climate, but there are exceptions, as can be seen in Figure 7.4.

In many respects, principals and students express similar views about the school climate.

Most importantly, what is the relationship between perceptions of learning climate and student performance? Tables 7.2 and 7.3 show mean scores on the combined reading literacy scale for the top and bottom national quarters of the school climate indices (the top quarter being associated with more desirable learning climates). In many countries, school principals' perceptions of student-related factors affecting school climate are closely related to student performance. In particular, in Belgium, Germany, Hungary, Italy, Japan, Poland, the Netherlands and the United Kingdom, the school principals' index of student-related factors affecting school climate explains between 12 and 21 per cent of the variation in reading performance.[4] In these countries, between 80 and 114 points separate the performance of students in schools in which the principals' views fall in the top and bottom quarters of the indices on student-related factors affecting disciplinary climate. The relationship between students' perceptions of disciplinary climate and reading performance tends to be weaker but is clearly visible in many countries.[5]

Student performance is closely associated with climate, especially in the view of principals...

The questions of how these relationships operate, and what contextual and mediating factors may affect them, remain beyond the scope of this initial report and will require further research and analysis.

...although there may be many contextual and mediating factors contributing to this relationship.

Teacher-related factors affecting the school climate

Principals in PISA 2000 were also asked questions about their perceptions of teacher-related factors affecting school climate. In particular, principals were asked to indicate the extent to which they perceived learning in their schools to be hindered by such factors as the low expectations of teachers, poor student-teacher relations, absenteeism among teachers, staff resistance to change, teachers not meeting individual students' needs, and students not being encouraged to achieve their full potential. The responses were combined to create a composite index of teacher-related factors affecting school climate. Positive values reflect principals' perceptions that teacher-related factors affecting school climate hinder learning to a lesser extent, and negative values

PISA also looked at whether teacher behaviour and attitudes are perceived to hinder learning...

that school principals believe teachers' behaviour to hinder learning to a greater extent compared to the OECD average.

Compared with other countries, school principals in Greece, Luxembourg, Mexico, the Netherlands and the Russian Federation were most concerned about teacher-related factors posing an obstacle to learning. By contrast, school principals in the Czech Republic, Denmark, Hungary, Iceland, Korea and Latvia report the fewest problems with teacher-related factors affecting school climate (Table 7.4).

...and found a weak positive relationship with student performance.

As one would expect, in most countries the relationship between school principals' perceptions of teacher-related factors affecting school climate and reading performance tends to be positive, *i.e.* the higher the concern with teacher-related factors affecting school climate, the lower the student performance in reading. However, the relationship is, with few exceptions, not very strong (see Table 7.4).[6]

Principals were also asked about teacher morale and commitment...

In addition to questions on teacher-related factors affecting school climate, school principals were asked to provide their views on teachers' morale and commitment. To do so, they were asked to indicate how strongly they agreed or

Figure 7.5

Teacher-related factors affecting school climate

Distribution of mean percentages of students enrolled in schools where principals report that learning is hindered to some extent or a lot by the following factors

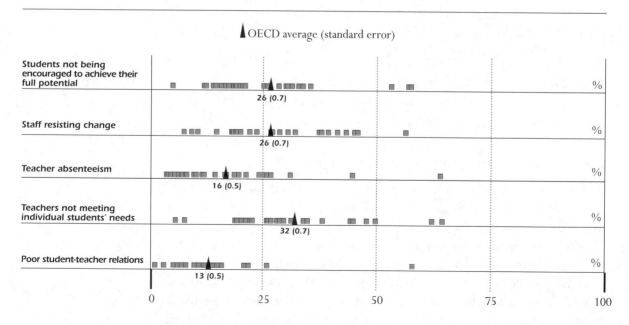

Note: Countries are represented by the square symbols.
Source: OECD PISA database, 2001. For data, see *www.pisa.oecd.org*.

disagreed with statements such as "teachers work with enthusiasm", "teachers take pride in this school", and "the morale of teachers in this school is high". From the responses, an index of teacher morale and commitment was created, with an OECD country average of zero. Higher index scores indicate greater perceived morale and commitment.

Austria has the highest positive value indicating, in the opinion of its principals, high morale and commitment among its teachers. By contrast, principals in Korea, Italy, Poland, and Portugal believe that their teachers have comparatively low levels of morale and commitment (Table 7.5).

The relationship between school principals' perceptions of teacher morale and commitment and their students' scores in reading literacy tends to be modest. However, there are countries where the association is stronger. For example, in Belgium, Japan, Luxembourg and Poland, the index of teacher morale and commitment explains between 4 and 8 per cent of the variation in reading performance, and in Australia, Hungary, Korea, the Russian Federation, Spain and the United Kingdom, it explains still more than 2 per cent.[7]

...and the association with performance appears to be modest, though stronger in some countries.

Learning outside school

Policy-makers looking to improve educational outcomes seek to increase or use more effectively the time for which students are engaged in learning activities. The instruction time, *i.e.*, the number of hours that each student spends in organised learning, is closely related to factors such as class size, teachers' working hours (teaching time) and ratios of students to teaching staff. The optimal balance between these factors may vary in different subject areas and at different levels of education.

Learning time needs to be deployed effectively.

Homework policies and practices are another element in this equation that can have a substantial influence on how much time students devote to learning. In many OECD countries, homework constitutes a major part of students' learning time. In PISA 2000, students were asked to specify how much time they spent each week on homework in the language of assessment, mathematics and science (Figure 7.6).

Homework and other out-of-school learning play an important part...

Adding these responses results in an average of 4.6 hours per week in the three subject areas alone, ranging from 3.3 hours or less in Japan and Sweden to 5.8 hours or more in Greece and Hungary (Figure 7.6).[8] This amount compares to an average of 12 hours per week of statutory instruction time in these subject areas (OECD, 2001). In addition, a substantial proportion of students report sometimes or regularly attending additional or remedial courses outside their school in order to improve their skills. For example, on average across OECD countries, 25 per cent of students report that, in the last three years, they sometimes or regularly attended courses in the language of assessment, courses in other subjects or additional courses outside their school. In the case of Japan and Korea, the figures are 71 and 64 per cent, respectively (Table 7.7).

...with close to the equivalent of a third of the instruction time at school in the PISA domains devoted to homework.

Figure 7.6

Time spent on homework

Index of time spent in homework for language, mathematics and science courses

Estimated mean number of hours spent on homework for language, mathematics and science courses

Country	Index	Hours
Greece		7.0
Hungary		5.8
United Kingdom		5.4
Spain		5.4
Poland		5.3
Mexico		5.2
Italy		5.2
Ireland		5.4
Portugal		5.0
France		4.9
Canada		5.0
New Zealand		4.7
Australia		4.7
Denmark		4.7
Iceland		4.7
Germany		4.5
United States		4.6
Norway		4.3
Belgium		4.3
Korea		4.4
Switzerland		3.9
Luxembourg		4.0
Finland		3.5
Czech Republic		3.6
Sweden		3.3
Austria		3.5
Japan		2.9
Russian Federation		m
Latvia		m
Brazil		4.4
Liechtenstein		m
Netherlands1		4.1

Below OECD average   Above OECD average

-1.00   -0.50   0.00   0.50   1.00

1. Response rate is too low to ensure comparability (see Annex A3).
Note: For the definition of the index, see Annex A1.
Source: OECD PISA database, 2001. Table 7.6.

Homework increases a student's opportunity to spend time in learning and should, therefore, be positively related to learning outcomes. However, several factors complicate this relationship. For example, teachers may tend to assign more (or more regular) homework to those students who need it most to improve their performance. Alternatively, slower learners may need more time to complete the same amount of homework. Conversely, students who report spending relatively little time on homework may either be able students who can complete their homework quickly or disengaged students who do not care to spend much time on school activities at home.

For various reasons, students spending more time on homework are not always the best performers...

Despite this multifaceted relationship, the association between the time spent on homework in the three subject areas and student performance tends to be consistently positive. In order to analyse this association, it is technically most appropriate to construct an index similar to those used earlier in this chapter, in this case combining students' reports on the time that they spend on homework in subjects related to the three PISA assessment domains. This index is shown in Table 7.6 and Figure 7.6.

...although they perform better on average...

The homework index explains between 7 and 15 per cent of variation in reading performance in Australia, Belgium, France, Greece, Hungary, Italy, Poland, Spain, the Russian Federation, the United Kingdom and the United States.[9] The association tends to be stronger in countries where the mean index is greater than 0.2, perhaps suggesting that a certain level of homework needs to be reached in an education system before the positive effects of homework become consistent or clearly visible.

...particularly in countries where the average homework load is comparatively high.

One consideration is that homework may reinforce disparities in student performance that result from home background factors. And in fact, in some countries such as Belgium, Greece, Hungary, Korea and the United Kingdom, the socio-economic index of occupational status explains 2 per cent or more of the variation in the homework index. However, in other countries, including Italy and Poland, the PISA homework index is positively associated with reading performance and there is almost no relationship with the PISA socio-economic index of occupational status. This suggests that homework can be given in ways that engage socio-economically disadvantaged students as well (see Table 7.6 and Annex A2).

In some countries, but not all, students from more advantaged homes do more homework on average.

Resources invested in education

Teacher shortage

The recruitment and retention of a highly qualified teaching force is a major policy concern in OECD countries. Ageing teacher populations and rising student participation rates continue to put pressure on the demand for teachers in many countries, but aspiring teachers in some countries find that teaching can be unduly stressful, that the profession is under-appreciated, and that salaries are low by comparison with salaries in professions with comparable qualifications (OECD, 2001).

Countries are worried about the supply of qualified teachers...

...and PISA therefore asked principals to what extent teacher shortages hinder learning.

The PISA school questionnaire provides an opportunity to assess school principals' perspectives of the adequacy of teacher supply as well as the impact of perceived shortages on student performance. Using responses to four questions about the extent to which the shortage or inadequacy of teachers in the language of assessment and in mathematics and science hinders learning by 15-year-olds, an index of teacher shortage was constructed, and its effect on student learning examined. This index has a mean value of zero for all OECD countries. The greater the value of the index above the average, the greater the perceived adequacy of teacher supply, at least in the opinion of principals. Values below zero indicate a perceived higher than average shortage or inadequacy of teachers, hindering learning among 15-year-old students.

Of all the countries participating in PISA, principals in Greece and the Russian Federation were the most likely to perceive that a shortage or inadequacy of teachers hindered learning in their schools. Principals also indicated comparatively high levels of concern about perceived shortages of teachers in Iceland, Mexico, the Netherlands and the United Kingdom. In Austria, the Czech Republic and Spain, principals were the least likely to believe that a shortage of teachers hindered learning (Table 7.8).

In the interpretation of these responses, it needs to be borne in mind that teacher shortage was not measured in terms of an internationally comparable unit of measurement, such as the number of students per teacher, but that the focus of PISA was on the extent to which school principals perceived that the inadequacy of teacher supply hindered learning. For example, some of the countries in which school principals expressed an above-average concern about the negative impact of teacher supply on student learning, such as Greece, Italy and Norway, have some of the smallest student/teaching staff ratios in OECD countries (OECD, 2001).

Overall, students perform somewhat worse in schools with greater shortages...

Overall, there appears to be a modest negative relationship between a shortage of teachers and student performance in reading.[10] As the shortages perceived by school principals increase, performance decreases, as might be expected. The highest reading scores are typically found among schools and students in the top quarter (where higher index values reflect little or no concern about a shortage or inadequacy of teachers).

...but this gap is larger in some countries and absent in others...

On average across all OECD countries, the overall difference in average reading scores between the top and bottom quarters of the index of teacher shortage is 22 points, but the range of scores among countries is considerable. In several countries, average reading scores drop by as much as 40 points or more in Austria, Belgium, the Czech Republic, Poland, the United Kingdom and, especially, Germany (98 points), between the top and bottom quarters on the index of teacher shortage (Table 7.8). By contrast, mean reading scores do not differ statistically significantly between the top and bottom quarters in Greece, Ireland, Italy, Luxembourg, Mexico, the Netherlands, Norway and the Russian Federation, although principals in those countries also believe that they do not have enough teachers.

While principals in Australia, Iceland, Ireland, Japan, New Zealand, Norway, Sweden and the United Kingdom all perceive above-average teacher shortages, in each of these countries the quarter of students whose schools report the greatest difficulties in this respect still score around or above the OECD average in reading.

...and shortages do not consistently prevent students from doing well internationally.

The quality of schools' physical infrastructure and educational resources

Ensuring the availability of a suitable physical infrastructure and an adequate supply of educational resources may not guarantee high performance, but the absence of such an environment will possibly affect learning. Buildings in good condition and adequate amounts of teaching space all contribute to a physical environment that is conducive to learning. Much the same can be said for schools with adequate educational resources, such as computers, library and teaching materials, including textbooks, and multimedia resources for learning.

Buildings, books and other resources contribute to the learning environment...

Using principals' responses to a series of questions about the perceived extent to which material and educational resources hinder learning among 15-year-old students, two composite indices were created – one for the perceived quality of

...and principals were asked whether lack of physical and educational resources hinders learning.

Figure 7.7

Principals' views on the quality of educational resources at school

Distribution of mean percentages of students enrolled in schools where principals report that learning is hindered to some extent or a lot by the following factors

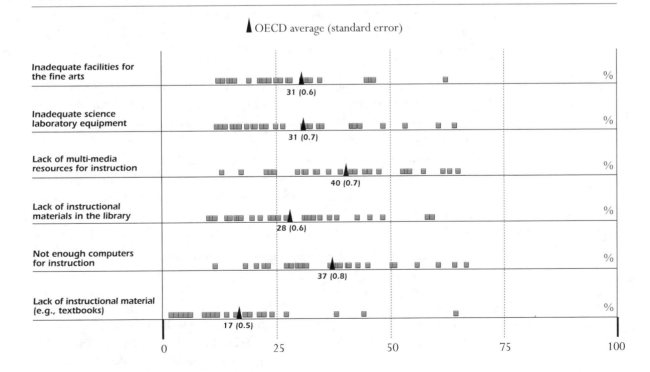

Note: Countries are represented by the square symbols.
Source: OECD PISA database, 2001. For data, see *www.pisa.oecd.org*.

the school's physical infrastructure and the other for the perceived quality of educational resources. Like the indices discussed earlier, these indices have an average of zero and a standard deviation of one across OECD countries. Positive values on the index reflect a below-average concern among school principals that the physical infrastructure and educational resources available in their schools hinder learning by 15-year-olds.

In the Czech Republic, Hungary and Switzerland, few principals report that the quality of the school's infrastructure hinders learning (Table 7.9). The other countries in which principals report less frequently that their school's physical infrastructure hinders learning are Belgium, Brazil, Canada and Iceland. By contrast, principals in Greece, Korea, Luxembourg, Mexico, Norway, the Russian Federation and the United Kingdom report being more concerned about the consequences for learning of what they deem to be inadequate physical facilities, at least relative to the OECD average (Figure 7.7).

Physical resources are at most weakly associated with performance...

In Belgium, Hungary, Switzerland and the United States, school principals report comparatively infrequently that the quality of educational resources hinders learning (Table 7.10). By contrast, principals in Greece, Latvia, Mexico, Norway, the Russian Federation and the United Kingdom are, by comparison with the OECD average, more concerned about the inadequacy of their schools' educational resources.

Do differences in schools' physical infrastructure affect student performance? Although there are some differences in students' scale scores in reading literacy between the top and bottom quarters on the index of schools' physical infrastructure, most of the differences are small and not statistically significant.[11]

...while the association with educational resources is somewhat stronger.

Educational resources appear to be more closely related to performance than physical infrastructure.[12] In 13 OECD countries plus Brazil, differences in educational resources are associated with differences of more than 22 points in reading performance, the largest differences being in Mexico (81 points), Luxembourg (63 points), Germany (55 points), Brazil (41 points) and the United Kingdom (39 points) between the bottom and the top quarters of the index of educational resources. The average difference for the OECD countries as a whole is about 23 points.[13]

Approaches to school management and financing
School autonomy and teacher participation

Principals reported in PISA on who has responsibility for various aspects of school policy and management in their school.

Placing more decision-making authority at lower levels has been a main aim of the restructuring and systemic reform of the education system in many countries since the early 1980s. School-based management is intended to increase creativity and responsiveness to community needs. This involves enhancing the decision-making responsibility and accountability of principals and, in some cases, the management responsibilities of teachers or department

Figure 7.8

School autonomy and student performance

Distribution of mean percentages of students enrolled in schools where principals report that the school has at least some responsibility for the following aspects of school policy and management

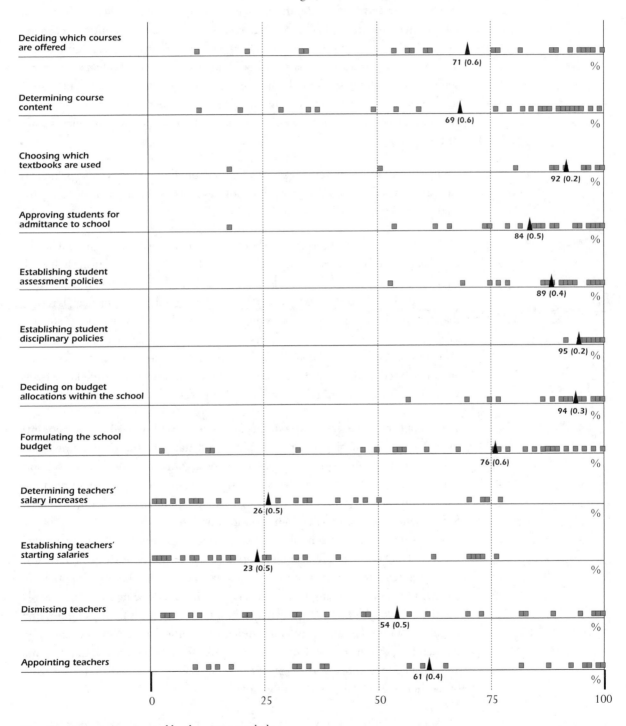

▲ OECD average (standard error)

Deciding which courses are offered — 71 (0.6) %

Determining course content — 69 (0.6) %

Choosing which textbooks are used — 92 (0.2) %

Approving students for admittance to school — 84 (0.5) %

Establishing student assessment policies — 89 (0.4) %

Establishing student disciplinary policies — 95 (0.2) %

Deciding on budget allocations within the school — 94 (0.3) %

Formulating the school budget — 76 (0.6) %

Determining teachers' salary increases — 26 (0.5) %

Establishing teachers' starting salaries — 23 (0.5) %

Dismissing teachers — 54 (0.5) %

Appointing teachers — 61 (0.4) %

0   25   50   75   100

Note: Countries are represented by the square symbols.
Source: OECD PISA database, 2001. For data, see *www.pisa.oecd.org*.

heads. Nonetheless, while school autonomy may stimulate responsiveness to local requirements, it is sometimes seen as creating mechanisms for choice that favour groups in society that are already advantaged.

In order to gauge the extent to which school staff have a say in decisions relating to school policy and management, principals were asked to report whether teachers, department heads, the principal, an appointed or elected board, or education authorities, had the main responsibility for: appointing teachers, dismissing teachers, establishing teachers' starting salaries, determining teachers' salary increases, formulating school budgets, allocating budgets within the school, establishing student disciplinary policies, establishing student assessment policies, approving students for admittance to school, choosing which textbooks to use, determining course content and deciding which courses were offered (Figure 7.8).

Table 7.11 shows the percentage of students enrolled in schools whose principals have at least some responsibility for various aspects of school management (for data on individual countries, see *www.pisa.oecd.org*).[14]

Most schools in most countries have no say in teachers' initial pay...

Unlike private sector enterprises, schools in most countries have little say in the establishment of teachers' starting salaries. In all countries other than the Czech Republic, Greece, the Netherlands, the United Kingdom and the United States, two-thirds or more of 15-year-olds are enrolled in schools whose principals report that schools have no responsibility for the establishment of teachers' starting salaries. The scope to reward teachers financially, once they have been hired, is also limited. Only in the Czech Republic, Greece, Sweden, the United Kingdom and the United States are more than two-thirds of the students enrolled in schools which have some responsibility for determining teachers' salary increases.

...while many do have a say in the appointment and dismissal of teachers.

There appears to be greater flexibility for schools with regard to the appointment and dismissal of teachers. Germany and Italy are the only countries in which about 90 per cent or more of 15-year-olds are enrolled in schools whose principals report that the school has no responsibility in these matters. Conversely, in Belgium, the Czech Republic, Denmark, Iceland, Sweden, Switzerland, the United Kingdom and the United States, between 93 and 99 per cent of students attend schools that have some responsibility for the appointment of teachers (OECD average 61 per cent). In the majority of countries, principals tend to report a more prominent role for the school in appointing teachers than in dismissing them, the largest differences being found in Canada and Denmark (21 and 40 percentage points, respectively). In Belgium, the Czech Republic, Hungary, Iceland, Latvia, the Netherlands, New Zealand, the Russian Federation and the United States, more than 95 per cent of the students are enrolled in schools whose principals report having some say in the dismissal of teachers (OECD average 54 per cent).

There is variation also with regard to the roles that schools play in the formulation of budgets, Austria and Germany reporting the least involvement of schools with this task. Schools in Australia, Belgium, Italy, Luxembourg, the Netherlands, New Zealand, the United Kingdom and the United States have a comparatively high degree of school autonomy with regard to budget formulation. In most countries, principals generally report a high degree of school involvement in decisions on how money is spent within schools (OECD average 94 per cent).

There is greater variation in whether schools formulate budgets and decide on how money is spent within schools.

In all OECD countries, the majority of 15-year-olds are enrolled in schools which have some responsibility for their own admissions (OECD average 84 per cent).

Most schools have some responsibility for admissions…

With the exception of Germany, Italy and Switzerland, the majority of 15-year-olds are also enrolled in schools that play a role in deciding on the courses offered (OECD average 71 per cent). Finally, most principals (OECD average around 90 per cent) report that disciplinary policies, assessment policies and choice of textbooks are school responsibilities.

…and decide on courses, discipline, assessment and textbooks.

Does the distribution of decision-making responsibilities affect student performance? In this field, the association between the different aspects of school autonomy and student performance within a given country is often weak. This is understandable because national legislation frequently specifies the distribution of decision-making responsibilities. Consequently, there is little variation within countries.

It is hard to link levels of autonomy with performance…

However, the data suggest that in those countries in which principals report, on average, a higher degree of school autonomy with regard to choice of courses, the average performance on the combined reading literacy scale tends to be higher (the correlation between country averages in student performance and the respective proportion of schools involved in decisions concerning choice of courses is 0.51). The picture is similar, though less pronounced, for other aspects of school autonomy, including the relationship between mean performance and the degree of school autonomy in budget allocation within the school (country-level correlation 0.37) (Table 7.11).

…but students tend to do better on average in countries with more autonomy, particularly in choice of courses and in budget allocation.

Table 7.12 shows the percentages of students enrolled in schools in which teachers have the main responsibility for the various decision-making areas. In most countries, the responsibilities of teachers in school management focus, among the questions covered, on the choice of textbooks (OECD average 70 per cent), course content (OECD average 55 per cent), assessment policies (OECD average 57 per cent) and disciplinary policies (OECD average 49 per cent). There are few schools in which teachers have the main responsibility for decisions concerning salary policies, the appointment and dismissal of teachers and budget formulation.

In most countries, teachers have the main responsibility for the choice of textbooks, course content, assessment policies and disciplinary policies.

Again, countries with a strong involvement of teachers in school management seem to perform better, on average, on the combined reading literacy scale. The country-level correlations between the proportions of schools in which

In countries where teachers have greater responsibility for teaching content, students tend to do better…

teachers have the main responsibility in decisions regarding course content and choice of courses, and mean performance on the combined reading literacy scale, are 0.46 and 0.55 respectively (Table 7.12).

...although it cannot be inferred that autonomy improves student performance.

As in other analyses of this kind, such correlations cannot be interpreted in a causal sense since many other factors may be at play. Nonetheless, the findings do suggest that school autonomy and teacher involvement in decision-making tend, at least at the cross-country level, to be positively associated with reading performance.

Public and private stakeholders

The private sector plays a small but growing role in schooling...

School education is mainly a public enterprise. In two-thirds of OECD countries, the private share of the funds invested in primary and secondary education is below 10 per cent, and in Italy, Norway, Portugal and Sweden, less than 2 per cent of school funding originates from private sources (see OECD, 2001). Nevertheless, the degree of private funding is growing, and with an increasing variety of educational opportunities, programmes and providers, governments are forging new partnerships to mobilise resources for education and to design new policies that allow the different stakeholders to participate more fully and to share costs and benefits more equitably.

...with, on average, 6% of students in schools that are predominantly privately funded and run ...

On average across the 24 OECD countries with available data, 6 per cent of 15-year-old students are enrolled in schools that are privately managed and predominantly privately financed (referred to as independent private schools) (Table 7.13). These are schools which principals report to be managed by non-governmental organisations such as churches, trade unions or business enterprises and/or to have governing boards consisting mostly of members not selected by a public agency. At least 50 per cent of their funds come from private sources, such as fees paid by parents, donations, sponsorships or parental fund-raising and other non-public sources.

...and around a third in two countries.

There are only a few countries in which such a model of private education is common. Only in Korea (34 per cent), Japan (30 per cent) and Mexico (15 per cent) is the percentage of students enrolled in independent private schools greater than 10 per cent (Table 7.13). By contrast, in many countries the financing of schools by students and their families is considered a potential barrier to student access. In 9 of the 24 countries with available data, for example, less than 1 per cent of 15-year-olds are enrolled in independent private schools.

But other forms of private schooling are more common in OECD countries...

Private education is not only a way of mobilising resources from a wider range of funding sources but is sometimes also regarded as a way of making education more cost-effective. Publicly financed schools do not necessarily have to be publicly managed. Instead, governments can transfer funds to public and private educational institutions according to various allocation mechanisms (OECD, 2001). By making the funding for educational institutions dependent on parents' choosing to enrol their children, governments sometimes seek to introduce incentives for institutions to organise programmes and teaching in ways that better meet diverse student requirements and interests, thus reducing the costs of failure and mismatches. Direct public funding of institutions based on student enrolments or student credit-hours is one model for this. Giving money to students and their families (through, for example, scholarships or vouchers) to spend in public or private educational institutions of their choice is another method.

Schools that are privately managed but predominantly financed through the public purse, defined here as government-dependent private schools, are a much more common model of private schooling in OECD countries than are privately financed schools. On average across the 24 OECD countries with comparable data, 10 per cent of 15-year-olds are enrolled in government-dependent private schools and in Ireland and the Netherlands, between 58 and 75 per cent are in such schools.

...particularly government-dependent private schools.

How do these institutional arrangements relate to student performance? On average across the 17 countries included in this comparison, students in independent private schools statistically significantly outperform students in reading literacy in public schools in ten countries. The difference in student performance between government-dependent private schools and public schools is about half this size in favour of private schools (Figure 7.9).

Students in both kinds of private school perform well...

In the interpretation of these figures, it is important to recognise that students are usually not distributed randomly between public and private schools. Insufficient family wealth can, for example, be an important impediment to students wanting to attend independent private schools with a high level of tuition fees. Even government-dependent private schools that charge no tuition fees can cater for a different clientele or apply more restrictive transfer or selection practices.

...but their students may note be representative...

One way to examine this is to compare the socio-economic backgrounds of students enrolled in different types of school. Table 7.13 shows the percentages of students enrolled in public and private schools and their mean scores, as well as the average positions on the international socio-economic index of occupational status of students enrolled in the various types of school.

...and an examination of their social backgrounds...

As can be seen, in most countries the mean international socio-economic index of occupational status differs little between government-dependent private schools and public schools, with larger differences found between public and independent private schools, in favour of independent private schools.

...shows that private schools in some countries tend to enrol more advantaged students, though this is less pronounced in government-dependent schools.

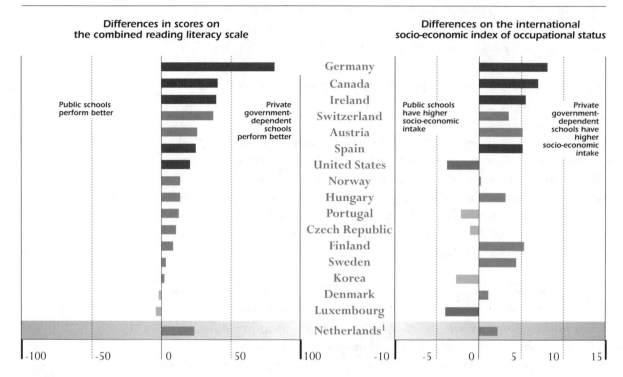

Figure 7.9

Student performance and public and private control

Differences between public and private government-dependent schools in student performance on the combined reading literacy scale and in the international socio-economic index of occupational status

Statistically significant differences are marked in black and red.
1. Response rate is too low to ensure comparability (see Annex A3).
Source: OECD PISA database, 2001. Table 7.13.

Conclusions

Students' performance is associated with the characteristics of their schools as well as their family background.

Important as socio-economic factors are in influencing student performance, school policies and practices can make an important difference, and effective learning depends on students having access to high-quality learning opportunities. School policies and practices can have both direct effects on outcomes and indirect effects that mitigate the influence of socio-economic factors (see Chapters 6 and 8).

Some school principals report inadequacies in school resources...

While all countries invest considerable resources in education, school principals in some countries perceive considerable deficiencies in the quality of the educational and human resources at the disposal of these schools. In many countries, these deficiencies appear to be associated with lower student performance.

...but the climate of the school and the classroom show a much stronger association with student performance ...

But not all obstacles that school principals perceive as hindering learning in their schools are of a material nature. Disciplinary climate is another factor, which PISA shows to be closely related to student performance. Student absenteeism, disruptive behaviour, students lacking respect for teachers, and bullying of students are the factors referred to most frequently by school principals as obstacles to effective learning. From the student perspective, wasting time at the beginning of lessons, noise and disorder, and students tending not to listen to what the teacher says, are the most frequently mentioned impediments to discipline. Addressing these issues is not an issue of money alone.

Learning does not begin with the school day and does not end with it. Homework, and in some countries extension or remedial courses outside school often account for a considerable portion of student learning time; and typically add up to more than one third of statutory instruction time in the three PISA domains. Given the amount of time involved, it is important to ensure that this time is spent effectively and that the corresponding learning opportunities are organised appropriately. One concern is that homework and learning outside school may reinforce the disparities in student performance that result from socio-economic factors or variation in educational resources or support at home. However, the experiences of some countries where homework is positively associated with student performance and where there appears to be no relationship between home background and performance suggest that learning can be extended outside school without putting disadvantaged students at risk.

...as does school work done outside school.

Finally, there may be more room for innovation in the management of schools. In most countries, few schools seem to have a say in the establishment of teachers' salaries or salary increases. There appears to be somewhat greater flexibility with regard to the appointment and dismissal of teachers and the establishment and implementation of school budgets. However, the degree of freedom for schools and teachers is once again limited in many countries. The tendency for countries with greater degrees of school autonomy to show higher average levels of student performance may suggest that there is a case for pursuing school autonomy as one route to school improvement.

School autonomy may be another important factor in this equation.

Since the factors examined in this chapter are interrelated, it is difficult to assess their relative importance. The next, concluding chapter seeks to gauge the relative importance of school resources and of school policy and practices in different types of school system. This may provide indications of what educational policy can do both to improve average performance and to moderate the impact of family background on student performance.

Chapter 8 gives a better idea of how these factors are interrelated.

Notes

1. Structural equation modelling was used to confirm the theoretically expected dimensions of the indices and to validate their comparability across countries. For this purpose, a model was estimated separately for each country and, collectively, for all OECD countries.

2. Note that students were asked to indicate their perceptions of a single group of teachers in a single year of learning. Consequently, results should not be interpreted as a characterisation of all teachers that 15-year-olds have encountered during their years as students.

3. On average across OECD countries, the index explains 0.5 per cent of the variation in student performance on the combined reading literacy scale and this exceeds 1 per cent only in 7 countries (see Annex A2).

4. On average across OECD countries, the school-level index of student-related factors affecting school climate explains 5.8 per cent of the variation in student performance on the combined reading literacy scale (see Annex A2).

5. On average across OECD countries, the student-level index of disciplinary climate explains 1.6 per cent of the variation in student performance on the combined reading literacy scale (see Annex A2).

6. On average across OECD countries, the index explains 1.2 per cent of the variation in student performance on the combined reading literacy scale (see Annex A2).

7. On average across OECD countries, the index explains 1.9 per cent of the variation in student performance on the combined reading literacy scale (see Annex A2).

8. For each of the three subject areas, students were asked to report whether they spent "no time", "less than 1 hour a week", "between 1 and 3 hours a week" or "3 hours or more a week" on homework. The total weekly homework time was estimated by adding these responses, "no time" being coded as 0, "less than 1 hour a week" as 0.5, "between 1 and 3 hours a week" as 2 and "3 hours or more a week" as 4. Students who had missing responses for any of the three subject areas were excluded from this comparison.

9. On average across OECD countries, the index explains 4.5 per cent of the variation in student performance on the combined reading literacy scale (see Annex A2).

10. On average across OECD countries, the index explains 1.7 per cent of the variation in student performance on the combined reading literacy scale (see Annex A2).

11. On average across OECD countries, the index explains 1.0 per cent of the variation in student performance on the combined reading literacy scale (see Annex A2).

12. On average across OECD countries, the index explains 1.3 per cent of the variation in student performance on the combined reading literacy scale (see Annex A2).

13. In 14 countries, these differences are statistically significant.

14. Technically, this percentage was derived by subtracting from 100 the weighted percentage of school principals who had checked the response category "*not a school responsibility*" for the relevant question.

WHAT MAKES A DIFFERENCE TO PISA RESULTS: SOME INDICATIONS FOR POLICY

Introduction: influences inside and outside school

Influences on performance from inside and outside school need to be considered together...

Performance in school is affected by more than what happens in school. Family, neighbourhood and the wider community in which students live are also important, although their influences are not entirely independent of those of the school itself. These influences need to be examined jointly in order to understand their separate and combined effects and to identify the possible causes and consequences of high and low student performance.

...and this chapter does so...

Chapters 2 to 5 of this report considered how well different countries educate their students, and Chapters 6 and 7 highlighted associations between student and school background characteristics and student performance. This chapter now expands upon those findings and addresses questions about the nature of the relationships between performance, family background and school. By examining the relationships between a range of variables, including both family and school factors, in a wide range of school settings in many different countries, the chapter seeks to gauge the relative importance of school resources and school policy and practice in different types of education systems. The aim is to provide indications of what education policy can do to improve both mean performance and equity in educational opportunities and outcomes.

...by looking first at individual students...

The chapter begins with an analysis of the relationship between *individual* student performance and family background. An understanding of this relationship is fundamental for policy development as it reveals how well students of differing backgrounds fare in their school performance.

...then at how student background affects whole schools...

The chapter then examines the extent to which differences in the performance of *schools* are associated with socio-economic factors. This information is important for gauging the impact of institutional settings on the distribution of educational outcomes, and for planning educational reforms.

...and lastly at how schools can make a difference.

Finally, the chapter seeks to identify *policy levers* and *school-level characteristics* that may help to raise levels of student performance and achieve a more equitable distribution of educational opportunities and outcomes.

The analysis in this chapter focuses on student performance on the combined reading literacy scale. Reference to performance on the mathematical and scientific literacy scales is made only where the analysis and conclusions drawn in this chapter differ significantly between the three subject domains.

The relationship between socio-economic background and student performance

A global perspective

This chapter uses a composite index of students' economic, cultural and social background...

As shown in Chapter 6, the performances of students on the PISA assessments of reading, mathematical and scientific literacy are closely related to the socio-economic backgrounds of their families. Students whose parents are working in less prestigious jobs and have lower levels of educational attainment, tend to perform less well at school than students whose parents have high levels of educational qualifications and are working in prestigious occupations. To facilitate the analysis, this chapter combines into a single index the different economic, social and cultural aspects of family background that were examined separately in Chapter 6. It is referred to as the PISA index of economic, social and cultural status, or at times, more loosely as students' socio-economic background.[1]

Figure 8.1 depicts the relationship between student performance and the index of students' economic, social and cultural status for the OECD area as a whole.[2] This relationship is called the socio-economic gradient. The figure describes how well students from differing socio-economic backgrounds perform on the combined reading literacy scale. This relationship is affected both by how well education systems are doing and by wider economic, social and cultural factors (see Box 8.1).

...and relates this to student performance.

Figure 8.1

Relationship between student performance and socio-economic background for the OECD area as a whole

Student performance on the combined reading literacy scale and index of economic, social and cultural status,* and socio-economic gradient for the OECD area as a whole

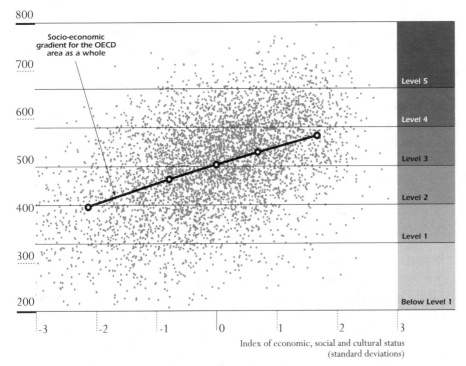

Performance on the combined reading literacy scale
(PISA scale score)

*Index of economic, social and cultural status
(standard deviations)*

*Each dot represents 2 000 students from the OECD area.
Source: OECD PISA database, 2001. Table 8.1.

Box 8.1 **How to read Figure 8.1**

Each dot on this graph represents 2000 15-year-old students in the combined OECD area. The graph plots their performance in reading literacy against their economic, social and cultural status.

The vertical axis shows student scores on the combined reading literacy scale, for which the mean is 500. Note that since the standard deviation was set at 100 when the PISA scale was constructed, two-thirds of the dots fall between 400 and 600. The different shaded areas show the five proficiency levels in reading.

The horizontal axis shows values on the PISA index of economic, social and cultural status. This has been constructed to have a mean of 0 and a standard deviation of 1, so that two-thirds of students are between +1 and −1.

The dark line represents the international socio-economic gradient, which is the best-fitting line showing the association between reading performance and socio-economic status across OECD countries. This line extends from the point below which are found the 5 per cent of most disadvantaged students to the point above which are the 5 per cent of students with the highest values on the index of economic, social and cultural status. The three points marked along the line show the locations of the 25th, 50th and 75th percentiles, *i.e.* the points below which 25 per cent, 50 per cent and 75 per cent of students are ranked, in terms of socio-economic status.

Since the focus in the figure is not on comparing education systems but on highlighting a relationship throughout the OECD area, each student in the OECD area contributes equally to this picture, *i.e.* larger countries, with more students in the PISA population, such as Japan, Mexico and the United States, influence the international gradient line more heavily than smaller countries, such as Iceland or Luxembourg.

Understanding this relationship is a starting point for examining the distribution of educational opportunities.

An understanding of this relationship is a useful starting point for analysing the distribution of educational opportunities. Raising student performance levels and softening the impact of socio-economic background on success in education are critical objectives for education systems in all OECD countries. From a school policy perspective, understanding the relationship is also important because it indicates how equitably the benefits of schooling are being shared among students from differing socio-economic backgrounds.

Figure 8.1 points to several findings:

Advantaged students perform better...

— Students from more advantaged socio-economic backgrounds in general perform better. This is shown by the upward slope of the gradient line.

...by similar amounts at different levels of advantage...

— A given difference in socio-economic status is associated with a gap in student reading performance that is roughly the same throughout the distribution — *i.e.* the marginal benefit of extra socio-economic advantage neither diminishes nor rises as this advantage grows. This is shown by the fact that the socio-economic gradient is nearly a straight line.[3]

— Differences in student performance vary slightly more for students with lower levels of socio-economic status than for those with higher levels. This is shown by the vertical dispersion of points to the right of the graph (the range of reading performances of those with socio-economic advantage) being less than the vertical dispersion of points to the left of the graph (the range of reading performances of those with socio-economic disadvantage).

– There is no one-to-one relationship between student performance and the index of economic, social and cultural status. Many disadvantaged students shown on the left of the figure score well above what is predicted by the international gradient line.[4]

…but socio-economic background does not determine performance.

The strength of the socio-economic effect in different countries

To what extent does the relationship between students' performance and their socio-economic background vary between countries? Socio-economic gradients at the country level provide a device to examine this. They also provide a useful starting point for understanding what factors contribute to the success of an education system in providing equal opportunities to all students. Usually the aim of national education policy is to increase overall levels of performance, while evening out variation in performance between jurisdictions, between socio-economic groups and between the genders. The key question in the present discussion is whether high average performance and low disparities in the performance levels of students from different socio-economic backgrounds can be achieved jointly.

The key question is whether high overall performance and low disparities can be achieved jointly.

Figure 8.2 displays the relationship in each country between student performance on the combined reading literacy scale and the index of economic, social and

Within each country, the impact of socio-economic background on performance can be examined…

Figure 8.2

Relationship between student performance and socio-economic background
for each country
Socio-economic gradients for each country

Performance on the combined reading literacy scale
(PISA scale score)

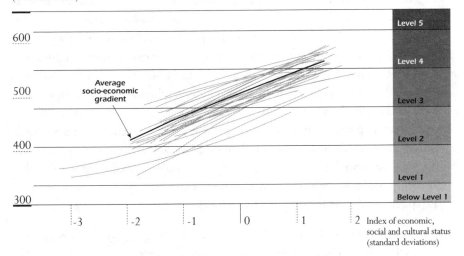

Note: For the identification of individual countries, see Table 8.1 and Figure 8.3a-c.
Source: OECD PISA database, 2001. Table 8.1.

cultural status. The gradient for each country is shown by a light grey line. The dark line is the gradient for all OECD countries combined, [5] repeated from Figure 8.1.

...in terms of four properties of "gradient lines":

The gradient lines summarising the relationship between student performance and the index of economic, social and cultural status in each country are characterised by their *level*, their *slope*, their *length* and the *strength* of the relationship that they describe. These are shown as follows in Figure 8.2 and in the corresponding Table 8.1. [6]

...overall performance: the average score, corrected for the country's socio-economic make-up...

— The *level* of the gradient lines in Figure 8.2 – their average height – is given in Column 2 of Table 8.1. This shows the average reading literacy score reached by those students in each country whose economic, social and cultural background is equal to the average socio-economic background across OECD countries. The level of a gradient for a country can be considered an indication of what would be the overall level of performance of the education system if the economic, social and cultural background of the student population were identical to the OECD average. The average gradient level across OECD countries is 505 points. [7]

...the difference between the scores of more and less advantaged groups of students...

— The *slope* of the gradient line is an indication of the extent of inequality in reading literacy attributable to socio-economic factors (Column 3 in Table 8.1). Steeper gradients indicate a greater impact of economic, social and cultural status on student performance, *i.e.* more inequality, whereas gentler gradients indicate a lower impact of socio-economic background on student performance, *i.e.* less inequality. On average across OECD countries, the slope of the gradient is 41, which means that students' scores on the combined reading literacy scale are, on average across OECD countries, 41 points higher for each extra unit on the index of economic, social and cultural status. [8] The unit on the index of economic, social and cultural status is one standard deviation and, in a normal population distribution, two-thirds of the population are within the range of plus and minus one standard deviation from the mean. In the case of Norway, for example, which has a gradient at the OECD average of 41 points, the average reading literacy score of students one unit below the socio-economic status mean is 464, 41 points below the overall mean of 505 points for Norway, and the average reading literacy score of students one unit above the socio-economic status mean is 546, 41 points above Norway's overall mean. Another way of expressing this is to say that, in Norway, students who are among the most disadvantaged one-sixth of the OECD population have mean reading literacy scores that differ by more than 82 points – equivalent to more than one proficiency level from those among the most advantaged one-sixth of students. In Germany, the country with the steepest gradient (60 points), the top and bottom sixths (internationally) in socio-economic status differ in average reading literacy scores by more than 120 points – equivalent to almost two proficiency levels.

...how widely students are dispersed by socio-economic background...

— The *length* of the gradient lines is determined by the range of socio-economic scores for the middle 90 per cent of students (between the 5th and 95th percentiles) in each country, as well as by the slope. Column 5 of Table 8.1

shows the range of the index of economic, social and cultural status spanned by the gradient line. This indicates how widely the student population is dispersed in terms of socio-economic background. Longer gradient lines represent a wider dispersion of socio-economic background in the student population within the country in question.

– The *strength* of the relationship between reading literacy performance and socio-economic background refers to how much individual student performance varies above and below the gradient line. This can be seen for all countries in Figure 8.1 by the dispersion of dots above and below the line, but is not shown in Figure 8.2. Rather, Column 4 in Table 8.1 gives the "explained variance", a statistical indicator that summarises the strength of the relationship by showing what proportion of the observed difference in student scores can be attributed to the relationship shown by the gradient line. If this number is low, relatively little of the variation in student performance is associated with students' socio-economic background; if it is high, the reverse is the case. In the OECD area, 20 per cent of the variation in student performance on the combined reading literacy scale is associated with scores on the index of economic, social and cultural status, but this ranges from a low of 5 per cent in Iceland to a high of 26 per cent in Hungary.

...and how closely background is related to performance.

Figure 8.2 and Table 8.1 point to several findings:

– First, countries vary in their socio-economic gradients. The figure not only shows countries with relatively high and low levels of performance on the combined reading literacy scale, but also countries which have greater or lesser degrees of inequality in performance among students from different socio-economic backgrounds. It is worth emphasising the considerable extent of this difference. Consider two students. One is from a less advantaged background, so that five sixths of students internationally have a higher score on the PISA index of economic, social and cultural status. The other is from a relatively privileged background, so that only one out of every six students has a higher score on the index. The performance gap between these two students varies between countries by a factor of nearly three. In Japan and Korea this gap is 42 points, or 0.6 proficiency levels, but in Germany it is 120 points, or 1.7 proficiency levels (in each case double the gradient score, which represents one standard deviation). The figure also shows clearly that high performance does not have to come at the expense of inequalities, as some of the countries with the best levels of performance have relatively gentle gradients.

The performance gap between more and less advantaged students varies between countries by a factor of three...

– Second, the range of the index of economic, social and cultural status spanned by the gradient lines varies widely between countries, with less than 2.7 index points separating the 5 per cent of students from the most advantaged socio-economic background from the 5 per cent of least advantaged students in Austria, the Czech Republic, Japan and Sweden, but 4 points or more separating them in Brazil and Mexico. The challenges that education systems

...but countries have differing social profiles.

face as a result of differences in the distribution of the economic and social background in the student population therefore differ widely. It will be much more demanding for the education systems of Brazil and Mexico to overcome inequities in educational opportunities than for the education systems of Japan and Sweden.

Extra socio-economic advantage yields similar returns all the way up the scale...

– Third, the gradients for most countries are roughly linear. Thus, in most countries each increment on the index of economic, social and cultural status is associated with a constant increase in performance on the combined reading literacy scale. One might have expected that the gradients would be steep at low levels of economic, social and cultural status, and then level off at higher status levels. [9] The gradients for performance on the combined reading literacy scale follow this pattern in several countries; however, the change in the slopes as economic, social and cultural status increases is slight, and barely discernible in Figure 8.2. Moreover, in the two countries with very low levels of economic, social and cultural status – Brazil and Mexico – the gradients display the opposite pattern – they are relatively gentle at very low levels of socio-economic status, and become steeper at higher levels. Since, in these two countries, comparatively large proportions of the population are well below the bottom 5 per cent of students in most OECD countries, in both reading performance and socio-economic background, this could indicate that there is a "take-off point" at a minimal level of socio-economic status below which socio-economic differences have little impact on the ability of students to tackle the kinds of task tested by PISA.

...so there is no single point of social disadvantage determining where intervention is most effective.

The finding that gradients tend to be linear across the range of economic, social and cultural status in all countries has an important policy implication. Many social policies are aimed at increasing resources for the most disadvantaged, either through taxation or by targeting benefits and social programmes to certain groups. The PISA results suggest that it is not easy to establish a "low economic, social and cultural status baseline", below which performance sharply declines. Moreover, if economic, social and cultural status is taken to be a surrogate for the decisions and actions of parents aimed at providing a richer environment for their children – such as reading to them or taking an interest in their school work – then these findings suggest that there is room for improvement at all levels on the socio-economic continuum. The fact that it is difficult to discern a baseline, however, does not imply that differentiated student support is not warranted. The success in many countries in closing gender gaps in student performance through differential provision is a good example of targeted efforts being very effective in reducing disparities.

Differences between countries are greater among disadvantaged than among advantaged students.

– Fourth, the gradients tend to converge at higher levels of economic, social and cultural status: the lines in Figure 8.2 are closer together on the right than on the left of the graph. This tendency, though moderate, [10] means that countries with high levels of performance on the combined reading literacy scale tend to have gentler gradients. Another implication is that students with high levels of economic, social and cultural status tend to vary somewhat less in their reading performance than do students with relatively low levels of economic, social and cultural status. The impact of different educational experiences on student performance may therefore be greatest for students from disadvantaged socio-economic backgrounds.

Figure 8.2 shows very broadly that there is wide variation between countries in both the nature and the strength of the relationship between socio-economic background and student performance. A closer examination reveals several patterns. Figures 8.3a to 8.3c group countries according to combinations of "average quality" (in terms of the overall mean performance of students in the country) and "equality" (as measured by the impact of economic, social and cultural status on student performance – the steepness of the gradient).

Countries can be grouped according to combinations of overall performance and equality:

Figure 8.3a shows the 12 countries that score above the average on the combined reading literacy scale. Among these countries, there are six – Canada, Finland, Iceland, Japan,[11] Korea and Sweden – in which relatively *high quality* of student performance is combined with relatively *high equality* between different socio-economic groups[12] (Table 8.1). The average score on the combined reading literacy scale for the countries in this category is about 525 – well above the OECD average of 500 – yet their average slope is 30, well below the average OECD country slope of 41. This shows that it is possible for a country to achieve relatively high performance while maintaining a relatively high degree of equality between advantaged and disadvantaged socio-economic groups. In three other countries – Australia, Belgium and the United Kingdom – high quality of performance is combined with above-average *inequality* in student performance between different socio-economic groups.[13] In the remaining countries shown in this figure – Austria, Ireland and New Zealand – mean performance is also above the OECD average but the gradients are not statistically significantly different from the OECD average gradient.

...countries doing well overall reveal differing degrees of equality between students...

Figure 8.3b shows the five countries whose score is not significantly different from the OECD average. Among these countries, France, Switzerland and the United States show *above-average inequality* between different socio-economic groups, while in Denmark and Norway, the socio-economic gradients are not significantly different from the OECD average gradient.

...countries with average performance may have wide differences between social groups...

Figure 8.3c shows the 13 countries with below-average performance on the combined reading literacy scale. Four of these countries – the Czech Republic, Germany, Hungary and Luxembourg – show *above-average inequality* combined with below-average performance. This suggests that these countries could lift their average performance significantly if they were to mitigate the impact of socio-economic background on student performance. Conversely, in Italy, Mexico, the Russian Federation and Spain, below-average performance combines with above-average equality in performance between different socio-economic groups. The remaining countries shown in this figure – Brazil, Greece,

...and some countries with below-average performance also show high levels of inequality.

Figure 8.3

Relationship between student performance and socio-economic background
for each country
Socio-economic gradients for each country

Below-average impact of
socio-economic background
on student performance

Impact of socio-economic
background not statistically
significantly different from
OECD average impact

Above-average impact of
socio-economic background
on student performance

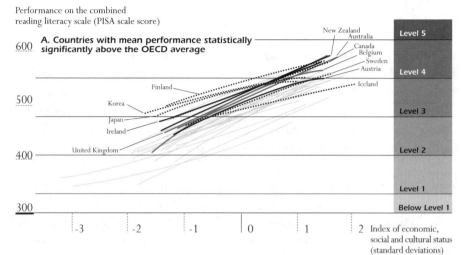

Performance on the combined
reading literacy scale (PISA scale score)

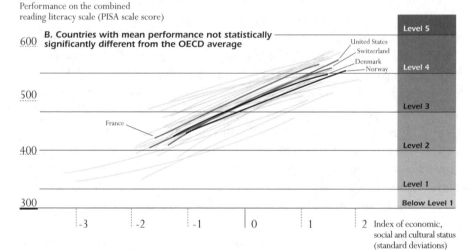

Performance on the combined
reading literacy scale (PISA scale score)

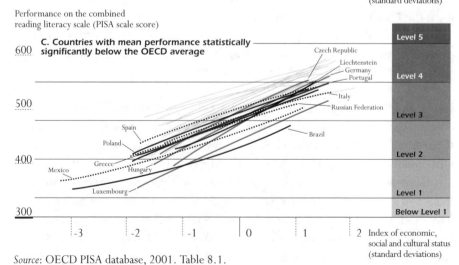

Performance on the combined
reading literacy scale (PISA scale score)

Source: OECD PISA database, 2001. Table 8.1.

Liechtenstein, Poland and Portugal – perform below the OECD average, but their socio-economic gradients are not significantly different from the OECD average gradient.

Obviously, the overall context in which education systems operate and, in particular, the distribution of economic and social variables within each country need to be taken into account in the interpretation of these relationships.

The components of socio-economic background

The analysis in this chapter so far has used a composite index of economic, social and cultural status. But it is also useful to look at the different impacts of specific features of a student's background in relation to PISA performance so as to assess more accurately why and how the relationship between socio-economic background and student performance differs between countries. The following analysis does so, looking both at the components of the index of economic, social and cultural status and at related variables such as family structure and whether or not the student was born outside the country.[14]

It is also possible to distinguish the individual impact of each aspect of a student's background...

The easiest way to consider the impact of these elements on a consistent basis across countries is to imagine a group of 1 000 students in each country with the same profile as a group sampled randomly across the OECD area[15] (drawing the same number of students from each participating country).

...by imagining first a group of students with a "typical" socio-economic profile in each country.

This group of 1000 would, on average, contain:

– 501 males and 499 females (for data, see *www.pisa.oecd.org*);

– 162 students from single-parent families (Table 6.9);

– 41 students born outside the country of testing (Table 6.10);

– 55 students whose language spoken at home most of the time is different from the language of assessment, from other official languages or from other national dialects (Table 6.11);

– between 1 and 2 brothers and sisters per student (for data, see *www.pisa.oecd.org*);

– students whose parents had completed on average 12.3 years of schooling (see Annex A1);

– an average score of 49 on the socio-economic index of occupational status for the parent with the higher such score (see Table 6.1a), and an average score of zero on the PISA index of cultural possessions in the family home (see Table 6.3) – because of the way these indices were constructed (see Annex A1).

In considering the predicted performance of such a sample in each country, the following analysis starts by adjusting PISA results for the *composition* of the student population as a factor that explains differences in performance. It then looks at the impact of specific characteristics on predicted student results. This discussion helps to distinguish where better or worse results are explained by differences in the relative performance of certain groups, rather than by the differences in the numbers of students who belong to such groups in each country.

The second column of Table 8.2 adjusts mean scores for socio-economic characteristics...

Table 8.2 summarises the results. The first column in Table 8.2 shows the actual performance of students on the combined reading literacy scale, as presented in Chapter 2. The second column of Table 8.2 provides an estimate of how well a representative group, as described above, would perform in each country. On average across OECD countries (shown in the bottom row of Table 8.2), the adjusted score on the combined reading literacy scale is 505 points. However, the adjusted scores vary substantially between OECD countries, from 450 (Mexico) to 543 (Finland). That is, even after adjusting for a range of background variables including home possessions, immigration, etc., mean performance still varies substantially between countries.

...and the remaining columns show the independent effects of each characteristic. Having a single parent has an independent impact in only a minority of countries...

The remainder of Table 8.2 indicates the difference made to the reading literacy score, in each country, by the individual features of socio-economic background.

Column 3 in Table 8.2 shows the difference in performance between students from single-parent families and those from other types of families (see also Table 6.9). Values in bold show relationships that are statistically significant. On average across OECD countries, the performance gap on the combined reading literacy scale is nearly 11 points, students from two-parent families (all other things being equal) performing better. In Finland, the United Kingdom and the United States, the gap is between 14 and 17 points, and in France, Ireland, Korea and Sweden between 11 and 12 points. Except in Italy (8 points), the differences in all other countries are not statistically significant.

...being born outside the country makes more of a difference, but not everywhere...

Students who were born outside the country (see also Table 6.10) tend to have lower scores than their native peers in most countries, even after accounting for all other factors. This is indicated in Column 5 of Table 8.2. On average across all OECD countries, the gap is about 26 points. However, the size of the gap varies substantially. In Austria, Liechtenstein, Mexico and Switzerland, the gap is more than 50 points, *i.e.*, more than half the standard deviation on the combined reading literacy score, whereas in the Czech Republic, Portugal, the Russian Federation and the United States, the gap is less than 10 points and not statistically significant.[16] How well non-native children perform is, of course, a function of many other factors besides the background characteristics measured in PISA and examined in this analysis. Their performance is clearly also affected by the circumstances of their relocation and their educational experience before moving, in addition to the effectiveness of the education system into which they have moved.

...having a parent of high occupational status matters hugely in some countries but much less so in others...

Column 6 in Table 8.2 indicates that, on average across OECD countries, an increase in the international socio-economic index of occupational status by one standard deviation[17] is associated with an increase of approximately 28 points[18] in performance on the combined reading literacy scale but, again, the impact varies widely. The increase ranges from a high of 67 in Germany, to small and statistically non-significant differences in Brazil, Denmark, Finland, Greece, Iceland, Ireland, Korea, Norway and Sweden.[19]

Each additional year of parental education (see Annex A1) is associated with an increase of about 5 points, on average across OECD countries, on the combined reading literacy scale. This average is statistically significant, as are the corresponding increases in almost all countries (Column 7 in Table 8.2). A one-point (*i.e.*, one standard deviation) increase on the PISA indices of home educational resources and cultural possessions in the family home (see Table 6.3) is, on average, associated with increases in reading literacy of 12 and 13 points, respectively (Columns 8 and 9 in Table 8.2). As with the other variables, the effects of each of these variables vary widely between the participating countries.

...having better-educated parents matters almost everywhere.

In sum, many of the socio-economic background factors measured in PISA have an important impact on student performance in OECD countries, but the nature and strength of this relationship varies between countries. The analysis demonstrates that the differences between the performances of students in the various PISA countries do not disappear when differences in students' family background are taken into account.

Background matters, but to greatly varying degrees...

While appropriate policy responses to such differences in student performance depend, of course, also on economic and social factors that are outside the control of educators, the analysis of gradients provides a means of characterising school performance, and providing guidance for education policy. A central aim of PISA is to enable countries to monitor their educational performance. Just as comparisons can be made between national means, distributions and socio-economic gradients, so they can be made within countries, between states or provinces or other groups of students. Countries will also be able to compare changes in index scores between the PISA 2000 assessment and future PISA survey cycles.

...and PISA provides tools for countries to explore this phenomenon further.

The role that schools can play in moderating the impact of socio-economic disadvantage

Many of the factors of socio-economic disadvantage are not directly amenable to education policy, at least not in the short term. For example, the educational attainment of parents can only gradually improve, and family wealth depends on the long-term economic and social development of a country as well as individual savings. This gives rise to a vital question for policy-makers: to what extent can schools and school policies moderate the impact of social disadvantage on student performance?

Student disadvantage is not easily removed. But can schools moderate its effect?

An understanding of which policies might increase overall student performance and moderate the impact of socio-economic background on student performance, *i.e.* raise and flatten a country's socio-economic gradient line, requires an examination of how performance is distributed within and between schools.

It is necessary to know whether differences are between schools or within them.

To this end, the gradient for a country can be decomposed into *within-school* gradients, which describe the relationship between individual student performance and family background for students who share a common school environment, and a *between-school* gradient, which describes the relationship between schools' average levels of performance and the average economic, social and cultural status of their intakes.

Countries with a high degree of social segregation between schools might consider resource allocation and selection practices in order to improve social gradients...

In some countries, students are highly segregated along socio-economic lines, in part because of residential segregation and economic factors, but also because of features of the education system. Such countries tend to have steep overall gradients. In these countries, it is possible that private schools, or selective schools or tracks within the public education system, contribute to socio-economic segregation. To increase quality and equality (*i.e.*, to raise and flatten the gradient) in such countries would require specific attention to between-school differences. Reducing the socio-economic segregation of schools would be one strategy but, regardless of whether it is employed, allocating resources differentially to schools and programmes, and seeking to provide students with differentiated and appropriate educational opportunities, are others. In these countries, it is important to understand how the allocation of school resources within a country is related to the socio-economic intake of its schools.

...whereas more mixed school systems might consider within-school improvements.

In other countries, there is relatively little socio-economic segregation between schools *i.e.*, schools tend to be similar in their average socio-economic intake. In these countries, quality (the level) and equality (the slope of the gradient) are affected mainly by the relationship between student performance and the socio-economic background of individual students within each school. To increase quality and equality in these countries will require action predominantly within schools. Reducing the segregation of students of differing economic, social and cultural status within schools would be one strategy, and might require a review of classroom streaming practices. More direct assistance for poorly performing students may also be needed. In these countries, it is important to understand how the allocation of resources within schools is related to the socio-economic characteristics of their students.

The following section examines more closely the role that school policy can play in this equation. The analysis builds on the consideration in Chapter 2 of the extent to which performances on the combined reading literacy scale vary between students within schools, or between schools (see Table 2.4). First, there is an examination of the degree to which these two forms of variation – between students and between schools – are attributable to the influence of gender or of economic, social and cultural factors. Finally, the section examines whether variation between schools that is *not* associated with students' characteristics and family background is related to the socio-economic background of the school, to factors describing features of the education system, and to school policy and practice.

Socio-economic background and variation in performance between schools

Chapter 2 shows that the performance of 15-year-olds varies considerably between schools in most countries. On average across OECD countries, 36 per cent of the total variation in student performance on the combined reading literacy scale is attributable to variation between schools (Table 2.4). Understanding why some schools, or separate education systems within a country, perform better than others is one key to school improvement. It requires an analysis which examines the effects of both student and school factors on student performance within schools and across schools in each country.

Just over a third of variation in student performance consists of differences between schools.

It is possible to estimate the proportion of the variation in student performance within and between schools that is attributable to students' family background, as measured by the background factors used in the analysis for Table 8.2. The results are shown in Table 8.3. For example, 16 per cent of the within-school variation and 64 per cent of the between-school variation in Australia is attributable to the family background factors shown in Columns 3 to 9 in Table 8.2. These percentages differ markedly from, say, those of Poland, where students' family background accounts for 2 per cent of the within-school variation, and 10 per cent of the between-school variation.

In comparing the extent to which the between-school differences are attributable in various countries to students' family backgrounds it is important also to take account of the size of the differences between schools (see Table 2.4). For example, family background factors account for more of the between-school differences in Sweden (73 per cent, see Table 8.3) than in any other country, but Sweden has less variation in performance between schools than all other countries but Iceland (9 per cent, see Table 2.4). Family background factors account for less of the between-school variation in Poland (10 per cent, see Table 8.3) than in any other country, but Poland has more variation in performance between schools than all but four other countries (Austria, Germany, Hungary and Switzerland, see Table 2.4). In general, the greater the differences between schools, the smaller the proportion that can be attributed to students' family backgrounds.

Differences in student background explain varying amounts of between-school and within-school variation…

There are also marked differences between countries in the percentage of within-school variation that can be attributed to differences in family background, though these percentages are considerably smaller than those for differences between schools. However, it is generally the case that the greater the within-school differences (Table 2.4), the greater the proportion that can be attributed to family background (Table 8.3). For example, family background factors account for around 20 per cent of within-school variation in Norway and New Zealand, the two countries with the greatest differences within schools. Only in Finland and Luxembourg does family background account for more of the within-school variation (around 20 per cent). Family background factors account for less of the within-school variation in Poland (2 per cent) than in

…but where within-school differences are high, this may be due to socio-economic differences.

any other country, but Poland has less within-school variation than all but three other countries (Hungary, Korea and Mexico).

How the social make-up of the school reinforces the effect of students' individual backgrounds

The effect of between-school social differences can be compounded by the collective advantages of better-off schools.

The previous section has shown that a substantial portion of the between-school variation in performance on the combined reading literacy scale is associated with differences in students' socio-economic backgrounds. This effect can operate in two ways. First, students' individual backgrounds may influence their performance. But in addition, the aggregate impact of the socio-economic backgrounds of all the students enrolled in a school can also influence students. Understanding this collective impact is of key importance for policy-makers wishing to provide all students with equal opportunities.

The manner in which students are allocated to schools within a district or region, or to classes and programmes within schools, has significant implications for the teaching and learning conditions in schools and, consequently, for educational outcomes. A number of studies have found that schools with a higher average level of socio-economic status among their intake tend to have several advantages. They are likely to have greater support from parents, fewer disciplinary problems, better teacher-student relations, higher teacher morale, and generally a school climate that is oriented towards higher performance.[20] There is often also a faster-paced curriculum. Talented and motivated teachers are more likely to be attracted to schools with higher socio-economic status, and less likely to transfer to another school or to leave the profession. Some of the "contextual effect" associated with high socio-economic status may also stem from peer interactions as talented students work with each other. Peer pressure, peer competition and the focus in some schools or school programmes on entry into tertiary education may also play a role.

In most countries there is a clear advantage in attending a school whose students are from more advantaged family backgrounds...

Figure 8.4 provides estimates of the effects on student reading literacy of the economic, social and cultural status and the other background variables included in Table 8.2, on the one hand of the individual student and on the other of all the students at a given school. These were estimated with a multilevel model that included economic, social and cultural status, gender, ethnicity, and family structure at the student level, and mean economic, social and cultural status at the school level. The bars in Figure 8.4 indicate the differences in scores on the combined reading literacy scale associated with a difference of half a standard deviation on the socio-economic index for the individual student and for the average for the student's school (for data, see Table 8.4).

In almost all countries, and for all students, there appears to be a clear advantage in attending a school whose students are, on average, from more advantaged family backgrounds. On average across OECD countries, the effect associated with an increase in the school's socio-economic composition by half a student-level standard deviation is about 32 points, *i.e.* close to half a proficiency level

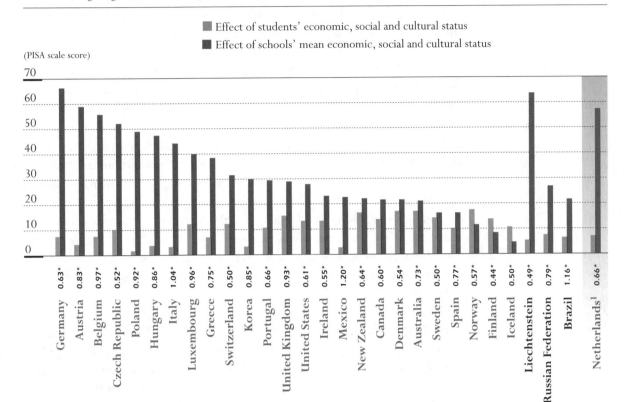

Figure 8.4

Effects of students' and schools' socio-economic background on student performance
on the combined reading literacy scale

*Differences in performance on the combined reading literacy scale associated with a change
of half a student-level standard deviation on the index of economic, social and cultural status*

■ Effect of students' economic, social and cultural status
■ Effect of schools' mean economic, social and cultural status

* Interquartile range of school mean index of economic, social and cultural status.
1. Response rate is too low to ensure comparability (see Annex A3).
Source: OECD PISA database, 2001. Table 8.4.

on the combined reading literacy scale. [21] The socio-economic intake of the
school thus has a considerable impact on student performance on the combined
reading literacy scale, over and above the student's individual home background. In fact, in the majority of OECD countries the effect of the average
economic, social and cultural status of students within schools far outweighs the
effects of the individual socio-economic background. Since no data on students'
earlier achievement are available from PISA, it is not possible to determine
whether and to what extent the school background relates directly or indirectly
to students' performance – by way of selection or self-selection, for example.
In the interpretation of these findings, it also needs to be borne in mind that
differences in the averages of schools' socio-economic backgrounds are naturally
much smaller than comparable differences between individual students, given
that every school's intake is mixed in terms of socio-economic variables. To aid
in the interpretation, the typical range of the average socio-economic status of
schools has been added to Figure 8.4. [22]

...and in many cases the impact of the school's socio-economic background on student performance is far stronger than that of individuals...

Austria and Germany are countries where the effect on student performance of a school's average economic, social and cultural status is appreciable. Consider two hypothetical students in Austria or Germany who have similar ability, and are living in families with average socio-economic background, as measured by the index of economic, social and cultural status. One student attends a school in a relatively affluent area, in which the mean index of economic, social and cultural status of the school's intake is a quarter of a (student-level) standard deviation above the OECD average. Most of this student's peers will therefore come from families that are more affluent than his or her own. The other student attends a school in a more disadvantaged area; the school's mean economic, social and cultural background is a quarter of a standard deviation below the OECD average, so that the student comes from a more affluent family than his or her peers. The data in Figure 8.4 indicate that the first student would be likely to have a much higher reading performance – 66 points on the combined reading literacy scale in Germany and 59 points in Austria – than the second student. On the other hand, two students living in families whose different economic, social and cultural status give them scores on the index a quarter of a student-level standard deviation above and a quarter below the mean, and who attend the same school with an average social profile, would have a much smaller gap in their predicted performance: 8 points in Germany and 4 points in Austria.

In reading, the effect associated with an increase in a school's socio-economic status of half a student-level standard deviation is, on average, about 2 points stronger for males than for females.[23] On the mathematical literacy scale this difference is about 4 points and in science 3 points. This suggests that males are especially advantaged or disadvantaged by the socio-economic segregation of schools. Conversely, the economic, social and cultural status intake of the school has a slightly weaker effect on the performance of females.

...a phenomenon which has complex causes, and may be partly associated with concentration of students by ability...

Some of this observed "contextual effect" might be due to aspects of school quality associated with the factors discussed above. For example, to the extent that schools differentiated by academic tracking are also differentiated by socio-economic status, the "contextual effect" of socio-economic status would be reinforced by systematic curriculum differences. Some of the "contextual effect" might also be due to peer effects. But some of it might be due to other factors which are not accounted for. For example, the parents of the student attending the more socio-economically advantaged school in the first example above may, on average, be more engaged in the student's learning at home, even though their socio-economic background is comparable to that of the student attending the less-privileged school. Also, and perhaps more importantly, the example assumes that the two hypothetical students are of comparable ability and motivation. However, in many education systems students are allocated to different types of school or programme on the basis of factors which include their ability. For example, in the two countries examined above, Austria and Germany, differences in performance between schools derive mainly from the allocation of students to general and vocational school programmes. Assignment to these tracks is influenced by student performance which, in turn, is intertwined with socio-economic background. Thus, important though the findings are for policy development, they should not lead to the conclusion that transferring a group of students from a school with a low socio-economic intake to a school with a high socio-economic intake would result automatically in the gains suggested by Figure 8.4. That is, the estimated contextual effects in Figure 8.4 are descriptive of the distribution of school performance, and should not be interpreted in a causal sense.

In any attempt to develop education policy in the light of the above findings, there needs to be some understanding of the nature of the formal and informal selection mechanisms that contribute to between-school socio-economic segregation, and its effect on students' performance. In some countries, socio-economic segregation may be firmly entrenched through residential segregation in major cities, or by a large urban/rural economic divide. In other countries, structural features of the education system stream or track students into programmes with different curricula and teaching practices. To the extent that the allocation of students to programmes in such systems is interlinked with students' socio-economic background, those from disadvantaged backgrounds may not achieve their full potential.

...and should be understood in the context of what mechanisms create socio-economic segregation.

PISA gives two different messages about the ways to increase both quality and equality. On the one hand, there is the message that social segregation brings benefits for the advantaged that will enhance the performance of the elite and, perhaps as a consequence, overall average performance. On the other hand, there is also the message that segregation of schools is likely to decrease equality. However, there is strong evidence that this dilemma can be resolved from countries that have achieved both high quality and high equality. Just how others might match this is the key question. Moving all students to schools with higher socio-economic status is a logical impossibility. Seeking either to remove socio-economic segregation or to mitigate its effects are the policy options. In either case, the central task will be to try to replicate the benefits for quality that social segregation can provide while gaining the benefits for equality that social heterogeneity can provide.

But the key challenge is to reduce inequalities associated with segregation without levelling down.

School factors that can raise performance levels and moderate the impact of socio-economic background

What can schools do to achieve the desired effect? Studies such as PISA can answer this question only up to a point, because many important contextual factors cannot be captured by international comparative surveys of student performance and because such surveys do not look closely enough at processes over time to allow cause and effect to be firmly established. However, PISA does make it possible to estimate the effects of some important characteristics of schools on student performance.

PISA reveals the estimated effects of some school characteristics on performance.

The analysis below provides estimates of the separate influences of school factors and family background factors, and of their combined influence. In each of the three subject domains, the impact of three groups of school factors on student performance is examined: school resources, school policies and practice, and classroom practice. The estimates are based on the combined impact of the variables at the student, school and country level. The results of this analysis, undertaken for the combined OECD student population (with countries given approximately equal weight), are shown in Table 8.5.

Several school resource factors are associated with performance...

Several of the school resource factors examined in this comparison emerge as having a statistically significant impact on student performance when OECD countries are examined jointly: the extent to which students make use of school resources, the student-teaching staff ratio, the size of the school and the proportion of teachers with a university-level qualification[24] in the relevant subject domain.

...such as how much students use school libraries, computers, calculators and laboratories.

Although PISA does not permit strong causal inferences, student performance in reading literacy is, on average across OECD countries, higher in schools where students use school resources more frequently, as indicated by the frequency with which students report using their school's library, computers, calculators, laboratories and the Internet. An increase on the PISA index of students' use of school resources (for a definition of the index see Annex A1) of one unit (which corresponds to one international standard deviation on this index) is associated with an average difference in student performance on the combined reading literacy scale of 18 points. The quality of the school's physical infrastructure (see Table 7.9), based on school principals' reports on the extent to which learning at age 15 is hampered by various resource factors, does not appear to have a statistically significant effect on reading performance, nor does the percentage of computers in the school available to students (after taking into account other variables such as the reported use of those computers).

The ratio of students to teachers matters as well...

Figure 8.5 displays the average effect of the student-teaching staff ratio on student performance on the combined reading literacy scale.[25] The student-teaching staff ratio is estimated from the reports of school principals on the number of students enrolled and the number of full-time equivalent teachers employed at the school (for data, see *www.pisa.oecd.org*). As can be seen, the effects associated with the student-teaching staff ratio are non-linear, that is, the impact of the student-teaching staff ratio on performance changes as one moves from small to large student-teaching staff ratios.

Schools with student-teaching staff ratios below 10, on average, score about 5 to 10 points below the OECD average. This may be because such schools serve students with special needs or are relatively small rural schools.

...but it is only at ratios above 25 that performance drops steadily with each extra student per teacher.

Differences in student-teaching staff ratios ranging from 10 to 25 are associated with relatively small effects. However, as the student-teaching staff ratio rises above 25, there is a continuous decline in school performance in all PISA subject domains, when OECD countries are considered jointly. Note that these

Figure 8.5

Average effect of student-teaching staff ratio on student performance
on the combined reading literacy scale, for all OECD countries combined

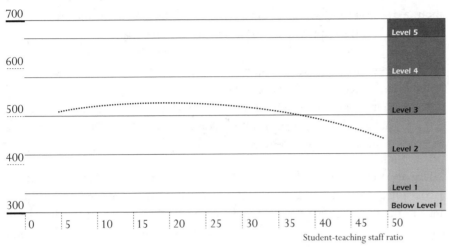

Source: OECD PISA database, 2001. For data, see *www.pisa.oecd.org*.

results, and other results in Table 8.5, pertain to the *average* within-country effect. Therefore, although the relationship between student performance and the student-teaching staff ratio varies between countries, the results in Figure 8.5 are not the artefact of some very poorly performing schools in only a few countries.[26]

Note also that the concept of student-teaching staff ratio is different from that of class size. As indicated above, the student-teaching staff ratio is based on the number of students in a school, and the number of equivalent full-time teaching staff in that school. In many countries, the teaching staff includes the school administrator, as well as other staff such as librarians and special education teachers. The student-teaching staff ratio is important as it indicates the amount of teaching resources used, directly and indirectly, in educating each student. It is also closely related to the overall costs of educating a student in the system. Class size refers to the actual number of students being taught in a class. This is difficult to measure at the secondary level in national and international studies, because students attend different classes for different subjects, and the size of each class varies with student attendance on a particular day.

The relationship between reading performance and school size across OECD countries is also non-linear. An increase of 100 students is associated with gains in performance of about 3 to 4 points for schools of up to 1 000 students. Thereafter, at school sizes above 1 000 students, the relationship is very weak.

Students perform better in larger schools with up to 1 000 students...

...and where more teachers have better and specialised initial training.

Student performance in all PISA domains is higher in schools where a higher proportion of teachers have specialised training in the subjects that they teach (on the basis of school principals' reports on the number of teachers with a university-level qualification in the relevant subject domain). For example, in reading, a 10 percentage point increase in the proportion of teachers with a university-level qualification in the relevant subject domain is associated with about a 3.7 point difference in performance on the combined reading literacy scale.[27] By contrast, principals' reports on teachers' participation in formal programmes designed to enhance teaching skills or pedagogical practices during the last three months, does not show a major impact on student performance. It needs to be recognised, however, that the rate of participation in professional development programmes in a three-month period is a weaker indicator of in-service teacher education than is possession of a full tertiary qualification as a measure of substantive preparation.

School policies and practice also have an impact, but are more difficult to discern.

There are three aspects of school policy and practice which have, on average across OECD countries, a statistically significant impact on student performance in the three subject domains: principals' perceptions of *i)* teacher-related factors affecting school climate (see also Table 7.4); *ii)* teacher morale and commitment (see also Table 7.5); and *iii)* school autonomy (see also Table 7.11). An increase of one unit on these indices (corresponding to one international standard deviation) is associated with gains on the combined reading literacy scale of about 6, 2 and 5 points, respectively. Note that these effects are small relative to the 18-point difference associated with a one-unit improvement in the use of school resources. School principals' reports on teacher autonomy and the use of formal assessments (see Annex A1) do not show statistically significant effects, when OECD countries are considered together.

Good classroom practices, including positive relations between teachers and students, and good discipline, make a clear difference.

Similarly, there are three aspects of classroom practice that have statistically significant, positive relationships with student performance in the PISA domains: students' perceptions of *i)* teacher-student relations; *ii)* disciplinary climate of the classroom (see also Table 7.3), and *iii)* "achievement press".[28] Teacher-student relations and classroom disciplinary climate have the strongest relationships – a one-point difference on these indices, equivalent to one international standard deviation, is associated with a difference on the combined reading literacy scale of about 18 and 10 points, respectively. "Achievement press", which was measured by students' perceptions of the extent to which teachers emphasise academic performance and place high demands on students, is only moderately related to performance, and the effect on performance, on average across OECD countries, on the mathematical and scientific literacy scales is not statistically significant.

The above factors help to explain differences between schools...

Overall, across the three subject domains, the combined influence of this set of school-level variables explains about 31 per cent of the variation between schools within countries, and 21 per cent of the variation between countries (Table 8.5). While this is a respectable performance for such a large-scale international study, it means that there is a large proportion of variation in student performance that remains unexplained by the school-level factors examined by PISA.

The preceding analysis suggests that family background and the mean socio-economic status of the school also help to explain differences in student performance. On average across countries, students' individual family backgrounds, together with the mean socio-economic status of the school, explain about 11 to 12 per cent of the differences between students within schools, across the three subject domains. On the other hand, they account for 66 per cent of the differences in performance between schools in reading literacy and 62 and 63 per cent, respectively, of the between-school variation in mathematical and scientific literacy (see second set of columns in Table 8.5). They also account for about one-third of the differences between countries in reading and mathematics performance.

…but a greater part is explained by socio-economic background.

Box 8.2 provides an indication of the comparative magnitude of the effect of some of the key factors influencing student performance in PISA, as described above.

Box 8.2 **Comparing the impact of different factors**

It is not easy to compare the impact of different factors associated with better student performance, since factors are measured in a variety of ways. However, the model used here does compare some of them in an essentially "like-with-like" fashion. This box applies to the combined reading literacy scale, but results for the mathematical literacy and scientific literacy scales are very similar.

It is possible to compare the effects of three important variables which can be measured consistently across countries: the number of students per member of teaching staff, the number of students per school, and the percentage of teachers in the school with a university-level qualification in the relevant subject. It can be predicted from calculations that a student score which is 10 points higher in one school than another is associated with an average of:

— *3.3 less students per teacher*

— *207 more students in the school*

— *27 per cent more of the teaching force* having a university tertiary-level qualification with a major in their subject.

This allows some comparison of how much change in each factor is associated with a given difference in student performance.

PISA has also looked at a range of factors that are less easy to measure, especially at an international level. Its approach here has been to construct indices related not to the intrinsic features of what is measured but to the distribution of each characteristic in schools across OECD countries. Specifically, it has set a mean of 0 and a standard deviation of 1. On this basis, a *single unit of difference* (one standard deviation) is, on average across OECD countries, associated with higher student scores of:

— *18 points* where students use school resources more frequently;

— *6 points* where school principals report a better school climate with regard to teacher-related factors;

— *5 points* where school principals report a greater level of school autonomy;

— *18 points* where students report better teacher-student relations;

— *10 points* where students report a better disciplinary climate; and

— *67 points* where the average economic, social and cultural index of students is higher.

For data, see Tables 8.5 and 8.5a.

Background and school factors between them explain most differences in performance between schools. In addition, school and socio-economic background factors do, of course, interact. Differences in performance between schools are the combined result of how the schools and their educational processes differ and how their intakes differ in home background. It can be estimated that around 70 per cent of observed variation between schools within countries is accounted for by the combination of the school-level and student background factors identified (see third set of columns in Table 8.5). This is true in all three PISA domains. These factors can also explain some of the differences in student performance between countries. At the country level, the percentages of variation in reading literacy, mathematical literacy and scientific literacy jointly explained by school and background factors are 43 per cent, 32 per cent, and 16 per cent, respectively.[29]

Part of the advantage of socio-economic background is attributable to more privileged students attending schools with successful characteristics...

As can be seen, the combined influence of school and background factors on differences in school performance is not simply the sum of the influence of school factors and that of background factors. This is because many characteristics of schools are closely associated with the characteristics of the families of their students. This means that some of the effect of family background on school results is *mediated* by the school characteristics. Consider, for example, the predicted difference between PISA reading literacy scores in two schools whose students have different backgrounds – with a gap of one unit in their average scores on the index of economic, social and cultural status. In total, students at the better-off school are expected to score 67 points more, on average, across OECD countries. Some of this difference arises because, on average, better-off students attend schools with features associated with better performance – this is the *mediated* portion. It accounts for about 10 of the 67 points' difference. The remaining effect of student background – that which is not associated with school variables – accounts for 57 points. This 10-point difference can be taken as a measure of the extent to which school systems tend, on average, to reinforce the advantage of those students who already come from advantaged backgrounds.

...while conversely, schools with these characteristics get better results partly because of their more advantaged intake.

Conversely, it is possible to examine the extent to which the association between individual school factors (such as more resources) and higher performance can be accounted for by the more advantaged background of students who attend schools with better features. In most cases, the separate impact of the school factors becomes smaller once family background is taken into account, because many of the factors related to school quality are correlated with the school's economic, social and cultural status. For example, on average across OECD countries, half the reported effect of differences in school resources, and two-thirds of the effect of school size and student-teaching staff ratios, are associated with family background. In the case of variables describing school policy and practice, there is an even greater association. On the other hand, most of the impact of teacher-student relations and disciplinary climate is independent of family background.

It should be emphasised that these findings do not imply that school factors are less important – simply that it is impossible to disentangle them fully from background factors. This can be illustrated by imagining a hypothetical extreme case, in which only students from better-off families attend schools with desirable characteristics, and these schools perform better than others. Some of the better performance may occur regardless of the quality of the school – directly as a result of students' home background. But some could be attributed to the better quality of the school. The greater the overlap between these two types of advantage, the harder it is to determine the contribution of each to better performance.

Two conclusions follow from the above analysis:

– First, important school factors which affect school and country performance are interrelated with the socio-economic status of the school, as estimated by the average index of economic, social and cultural status of the PISA population enrolled in the school. This means that some of the *inequality of outcomes* observed in the analysis of socio-economic gradients is associated with *inequality of opportunity*.

Social disadvantage is reinforced by unequal educational opportunities…

– Second, among those factors that were examined in PISA, there is no single factor that explains why some schools or some countries have better results than others. Rather, successful performance is attributable to a constellation of factors that includes school resources, school policy and practices, and classroom practices.

…but in heterogeneous ways.

The above analysis has focused on the impact of certain factors on student performance overall, *i.e.* across OECD countries. The following section now seeks to discern how these factors are distributed between countries, *i.e.* once it is known which factors matter across all countries together, it will be helpful to know what factors prevail in which national education systems. In this context, it is not only necessary to consider whether and to what extent schools in a given country have certain positive characteristics, but also the degree to which these characteristics are concentrated in schools with more privileged intakes. Table 8.6 provides estimates of both. For each of 10 school variables, it gives each country a score on a scale of 0 to 10, and also quantifies the degree to which each is correlated with the socio-economic profile of schools (see Box 8.3).

In individual countries, the presence of the identified success factors can be categorised on a 10-point scale…

For example, consider the United States. It has a value of 10 for the impact of the student-teaching staff ratio on reading literacy performance, indicating that its schools have, on average, student-teaching staff ratios below 25. Its value for school size is 3.6, which indicates that there are some very small schools. Given the findings for all OECD countries combined, these schools may be less successful than other schools of moderate size. Its value on the index for teacher qualifications is 7.5. On average, schools in the United States have a higher percentage of teachers with the relevant subject qualifications than OECD countries as a whole. On the remaining seven indicators, with the exception of teacher morale, the values for the United States are all above the OECD average of 5.0.

…10 indicating favourable conditions and 0 indicating unfavourable conditions…

Box 8.3 **How to read Table 8.6**

For each school variable, the table shows an **index value** on a scale of 0 to 10. Higher scores are positive, *i.e.* at the international level associated with higher student performance in PISA. The following values have been assigned:

Variable	Value	Index value
Student-teaching staff ratio	Below 25	10 [30]
	25 to 27.5	9
	27.5 to 30	8
	…	…
	Greater than 47.5	0
School size	1 000 to 2 500	10
	900 to 999	9
	800 to 899	8
	…	…
	below 100	10
Percentage of teachers with a university tertiary-level qualification with a major in the subject assessed	90 to 100	10
	80 to 90	9
	…	…
	0 to 10	0
Other variables (with scales based on international standard deviations)	Re-scaled so that mean equals 5, standard deviation equals 2, and outliers are given values of zero and 10	

The index score for each country represents the average for schools in that country. The values for the correlations for each country in Table 8.6 indicate the degree to which variations in each factor within the country are associated positively with differences in student intake – *e.g.*, the degree to which more favourable student-teaching staff ratios are found in schools with students from more advantaged socio-economic backgrounds. A negative correlation means that the relationship is in the other direction. A correlation of zero would indicate that students from different backgrounds have equal chances of going to schools with favourable conditions. The size of this effect can be compared with the OECD average to give some indication of its relative importance.

…but note that the averages may mask considerable variation between countries in the significance of the various factors.

It should be noted that the analysis above does not examine the effects of these variables on performance within each country. However, Table 8.5a provides results for a similar model fitted separately to the data for each country, and a statistical summary (meta-effects) of the results across the OECD countries. The summary of these country-by-country analyses yields findings broadly similar to those reported in Table 8.5;[31] however, it also shows that the effects of many variables vary considerably between countries, and in many cases differ from the global relationships[32]. For example, Greece, Italy and the Netherlands have relatively low values on the 10-point index for disciplinary climate, yet the effect of disciplinary climate on student performance appears to be substantial in Italy, but negligible in Greece and the Netherlands. It is possible that other factors are at work in these countries, so that schools with relatively poor classroom discipline fare relatively well, and do not follow the general pattern. These findings emphasise the need for further analysis within each country.

Next to the index values, Table 8.6 shows the school-level correlation of each variable with the mean index of economic, social and cultural status. A positive correlation indicates that schools enrolling students with advantaged backgrounds tend to do better in terms of the policy variables considered than schools enrolling students from less advantaged backgrounds (see Box 8.3 for details).

Several results stand out from this table:

– For all OECD countries taken together, the results show that the majority of schools have student-teaching staff ratios at or below 25. The PISA results do not predict substantial improvements in student performance at ratios below this level. On the other hand, the mean value on the 10-point index for school size is 4.3, well below the level that would predict maximum student performance, and the results indicate that average school size tends to vary substantially in all participating countries. Differences in student-teaching staff ratios are not usually closely associated with the socio-economic background of students within individual countries.

Student-teacher ratios are mainly below the level at which they make a difference.

– The mean value on the 10-point index for teacher qualifications is 7.1, which indicates that about two-thirds of teachers have a university-level qualification in the relevant subject. The correlation between the proportion of teachers who have a university tertiary-level qualification with a major in the relevant subject domain and the school mean socio-economic status is highest (between 0.47 and 0.58) in Belgium, Germany and Luxembourg, suggesting that specialist teachers in these countries tend to be employed in schools or school types with a more advantaged socio-economic background.

In some countries, well-qualified teachers are concentrated in schools with privileged intakes.

– The level of resources provided to schools is not in most cases closely associated with students' backgrounds. However, the reverse is true when it comes to students' use of them. The PISA index of students' use of school resources is more strongly associated with students' economic, social and cultural status than any other school variable. This suggests that less advantaged students do not tend to use school resources as regularly as students of higher economic, social and cultural status.

Socially advantaged students do not get more resources, but use them more.

– In some countries, principals' perceptions of teacher-related factors affecting school climate are positively associated with the school's socio-economic status, particularly in Korea, Spain and the United Kingdom (correlations between 0.41 and 0.58). There are a few countries in which perceived teacher morale and commitment are positively related to the socio-economic status of the school, but Poland stands out in that morale and commitment are

Teacher morale is in some cases lower in schools with less advantaged students.

generally rated by principals as low (3.8), but particularly in schools with low socio-economic status (correlation 0.51).

Disciplinary climate can be strongly associated with socio-economic background.

– Schools with a higher socio-economic intake also tend to have a better disciplinary climate (as reported by students), especially in Italy, Japan, Spain, the United Kingdom and the United States. Among these countries, Italy stands out in that students generally rate the disciplinary climate poorly, particularly in schools with a low socio-economic intake. There are some counter-examples, however, where the disciplinary climate is rated more positively by students in less well-off schools – in the case of Mexico and New Zealand, the correlations are -0.33 and -0.36, respectively.

Conclusions

PISA shows the powerful influence of home background...

Home background influences educational success, and socio-economic status may reinforce its effects. Although PISA shows that poor performance in school does not automatically follow from a disadvantaged socio-economic back-ground, it appears to be one of the most powerful factors influencing perform-ance on the PISA reading, mathematical and scientific literacy scales.

...but while there are limits to how far schools can compensate...

This represents a significant challenge for public policy, which strives to provide learning opportunities for all students irrespective of their home backgrounds. National research evidence from various countries has generally been discouraging. Schools have appeared to make little difference. Either because privileged families are better able to reinforce and enhance the effect of schools, or because schools are better able to nurture and develop young people from privileged backgrounds, it has often been apparent that schools reproduce existing patterns of privilege rather than delivering equal opportunities in a way that can distribute outcomes more equitably.

...some countries combine more equal outcomes with high quality.

The international evidence of PISA is more encouraging. While all countries show a clear positive relationship between home background and educational outcomes, some countries demonstrate that high average quality and equality of educational outcomes can go together: Canada, Finland, Iceland, Japan, Korea and Sweden all display above-average levels of student performance on the combined reading literacy scale and, at the same time, a below-average impact of economic, social and cultural status on student performance. Conversely, average performance in reading literacy in the Czech Republic, Germany, Hungary and Luxembourg is significantly below the OECD average while, at the same time, there are above-average disparities between students from advantaged and disadvantaged socio-economic backgrounds.

The challenge is made greater by the combined impact of a school's intake...

One of the most important findings of PISA is that the student's own home back-ground is only part of the story of socio-economic disparities in education – and in most countries the smaller part. The combined impact of the school's socio-economic intake can have an appreciable effect on the student's performance, and generally has a greater effect on predicted student scores than the student's own family characteristics.

A second key finding from the analysis of PISA results is that beneficial school effects are reinforced by socio-economic background. Schools with more resources and policies and practices associated with better student performance tend, to varying degrees, to have more advantaged students. In Belgium, Germany and Luxembourg, larger numbers of specialist teachers tend to be employed in schools with a more advantaged socio-economic background. Students report that schools with a higher socio-economic intake also have a better disciplinary climate, particularly in Italy, Japan, Spain, the United Kingdom and the United States. And finally, students in schools with low socio-economic status also tend not to use school resources as regularly as students in better-off schools.

...and by the fact that more advantaged students tend to go to schools with other advantages...

The net result of this effect is that in countries where there is a high degree of segregation along socio-economic lines, students from disadvantaged socio-economic backgrounds do worse. This, in turn, means that some of the *inequality of outcomes* observed in the analysis of socio-economic gradients is associated with *inequality of opportunity*. In such circumstances, talent remains unused and human resources are wasted.

...resulting in more unequal opportunities.

In some countries, students are highly segregated along socio-economic lines, in part because of residential segregation and economic factors, but also because of features of the education system. Education policy in such countries might attempt to moderate the impact of socio-economic background on student performance by reducing the extent of segregation along socio-economic lines, or by allocating resources to schools differentially. In these countries, it may be necessary to examine how the allocation of school resources within a country relates to the socio-economic intake of its schools. In other countries, there is relatively little socio-economic segregation, *i.e.*, schools tend to be similar in their socio-economic intake. Education policy in these countries might aim at moderating the impact of socio-economic background through measures aimed at improving school resources and reducing within-school segregation according to students' economic, social and cultural status. In the end, of course, what matters most is how effectively resources are used. Approaches might include, for example, eliminating classroom streaming or providing more assistance for students with a poor level of performance.

Policy responses depend partly on whether and how schools are segregated by socio-economic background...

In countries where the impact of socio-economic background on student performance is moderate, not all successes can be credited to the education system and, in countries where gradients are steep, not all of the problems should be attributed to schools either. The analysis has shown that the challenges which education systems face as a result of the differences in the distribution of home background factors in the student population differ widely. For example, the unequal distribution of family wealth, as measured by PISA, in Brazil, Mexico, Poland, Portugal and the United States (see Chapter 6), makes it far more difficult to provide equitable learning opportunities in those countries than in Finland, Japan or Korea, where wealth is distributed more equally. Many

...and on countries' overall socio-economic profiles.

of the factors of socio-economic disadvantage are also not directly amenable to education policy, at least not in the short term. For example, the educational attainment of parents can only gradually improve, and family wealth will depend on long-term national economic development.

PISA has identified some factors within schools that can make a difference.

But PISA results suggest that school policy and schools themselves can play a crucial role in moderating the impact of social disadvantage on student performance. The results reveal some school resource factors, school policies and classroom practices that appear to make a significant difference to student performance. The extent to which students make use of school resources, and the extent to which specialist teachers are available, can both have an impact on student performance. According to principals' perceptions of teacher-related factors affecting school climate, teacher morale and commitment, and school autonomy, also appear to make a difference. Finally, there are aspects of classroom practice that show a positive relationship with student performance, such as teacher-student relations and the disciplinary climate in the classroom.

While no single factor provides the key…

PISA results suggest that there is no single factor that explains why some schools or some countries have better results than others. Successful performance is attributable to a constellation of factors, including school resources, school policy and practice, and classroom practice. It will require much further research and analysis to identify how these factors operate, interact with home background, and influence student performance.

… deeper analysis, to follow, will aim to produce better understanding of causes.

In pursuit of this deeper understanding, the intention is to publish a series of thematic PISA reports in 2002 and 2003 that will analyse the impact of school and system-level factors on student performance more extensively, and will seek to understand in more detail *why* some countries achieve better and more equitable learning outcomes than others. In the meantime, the mere fact that high-quality learning outcomes are already a reality for most students in some countries is, in itself, an encouraging result that shows that the challenges ahead can be tackled successfully.

Notes

1. For the definition of the index, see Annex A1.

2. This includes all OECD countries participating in PISA except the Netherlands (see Annex A3).

3. There is a statistically significant curvilinear effect, but it is relatively small, and not discernible to the eye in Figure 8.1.

4. In statistical terms, the variation explained by the PISA index of economic, social and cultural status for the combined OECD area, 20 per cent, is much lower than if there were a perfect relationship (100 per cent).

5. The overall OECD gradient shown in Figure 8.1 is very similar to the average "within-country" gradient.

6. For the treatment of missing data, see Annex A1. The percentage of cases with missing data on the resulting index of economic, social and cultural status is shown in Table 8.1.

7. The main reason why the value is greater than 500, the OECD average of performance on the combined reading literacy scale, is that the larger countries, which influence the weighted average more heavily, tend to perform above the OECD average. Missing values on the socio-economic data also contribute to this difference.

8. The analysis also included the squared index of economic, social and cultural status (X) to test for any non-linear effects in the relationship. The resulting coefficient is relatively small: -1.21. The socio-economic gradients for mathematics and science differ slightly from that shown for reading literacy: $Y = 506.42 + 40.58 X - 4.14 X^2$ for mathematics, and $Y = 507.66 + 38.50 X - 1.37 X^2$ for science.

9. This is the case for income gradients associated with many health outcomes, including longevity (House *et al.*, 1990; Mirowsky and Hu, 1996; Wolfson *et al.,* 1993): once people have their basic needs met, further increases in income contribute only marginally to their health.

10. In statistical terms, the correlation between levels and slopes, at an average level of economic, social and cultural status, is -0.38.

11. More than 50 per cent of the data on parental occupation and parental years of schooling were missing in the case of Japan. For students with missing data values, the index of economic, social and cultural status was imputed from data available on the PISA index of family wealth, the PISA index of cultural possessions in the family home and the PISA index of home educational resources. The slope of the gradient for those students with imputed indices is nearly identical to the slope for those with indices based on all five variables, suggesting that the imputation procedure did not introduce a substantial bias in the estimates.

12. In these countries, student performance is statistically significantly higher than the OECD average, and the socio-economic gradient is statistically significantly gentler than the OECD average gradient.

13. In these countries, student performance is statistically significantly higher than the OECD average, and the socio-economic gradient is statistically significantly steeper than the OECD average gradient.

14. These analyses were based on an ordinary least squares regression of performance on the combined reading literacy scale on: *i)* the international socio-economic index of occupational status (Table 6.1) and the square of this index, *ii)* parental years of schooling (see Annex A1), *iii)* the PISA index of home educational resources (see *www.pisa.oecd.org*), *iv)* the PISA index of cultural possessions in the family home (Table 6.3), *v)* a dummy variable denoting the student's gender, *vi)* two dummy variables denoting whether the student lived in a single or two-parent family, or was living in other types of families (see Table 6.9), *vii)* the number of siblings (see *www.pisa.oecd.org*) , *viii)* a dummy variable denoting whether the student was born in the country (Table 6.10), and *ix)* three dummy variables denoting the presence of missing data for the international socio-economic index of occupational status, parental years of schooling, and the number of siblings. In preliminary analyses, the PISA index of family wealth (Table 6.2) was also included, but in most countries this variable turned out to be collinear with the other factors comprising the index of economic, social and cultural status, and was therefore dropped from the analysis. The results pertaining to the differences between males and females were similar to those reported in Chapter 6, and are therefore not reported in Table 8.2. The coefficients for "other types of families" were in most cases statistically significant, but as this is a relatively small category, these findings are not shown in Table 8.2.

15. This includes all OECD countries participating in PISA except the Netherlands.

16. The small size of the non-native student populations makes it very difficult to detect statistically significant differences in some countries, given the sample sizes employed in PISA.

17. One standard deviation on the PISA socio-economic index of occupational status is, on average across OECD countries, equal to 16.3 index points.

18. Note that this value differs from the figures shown in Table 6.1a. The reason for this difference is that Table 8.2 presents the unique contribution of the impact of the index of economic, social and cultural status on student performance, assuming all other factors shown in the table to be equally distributed across OECD countries. By contrast, Table 6.1a shows the impact of the index of economic, social and cultural status on student performance without accounting for differences in other factors.

19. Other countries where the effects are not statistically significant are Hungary, Poland, the United Kingdom and the United States.

20. See Brookover *et al.*, 1978; Henderson *et al.*, 1978; Rumberger *et al.*, 1992; Shavit *et al.*, 1985; Summers *et al.*, 1977; and Willms, 1986.

21. Half of a student-level standard deviation was chosen for the following comparisons because this value describes realistic differences between schools in terms of their socio-economic composition. On average across OECD countries, the difference between the 75th and 25th quartiles of the school mean index of economic, social and cultural status is 0.72 of a student-level standard deviation and, in all but one OECD country, this difference is greater than half a student-level standard deviation on the socio-economic index.

22. The typical range is represented by the difference between the 75th and 25th percentiles of the school mean values for the PISA index of economic, social and cultural status.

23. The effects associated with an increase in the school mean index of economic, social and cultural status by half a student-level standard deviation are: reading literacy 34.1 for males and 31.8 for females; mathematical literacy 34.8 for males and 30.5 for females; scientific literacy 33.7 for males and 30.7 for females.

24. This covers all qualifications at Level 5A of the International Standard Classification of Education (ISCED).

25. In order to allow for a possible non-linear relationship between student-teaching staff ratios and performance, linear and quadratic terms were used in the model. Also, there were a number of schools with very large student-teaching staff ratios, which unduly affected the relationships. To capture the effect of student-teaching staff ratios in these schools, a separate term was introduced in the model.

26. In some countries there were schools with student-teaching staff ratios above 50. These schools were treated separately in the analysis by modelling them with a separate dummy variable. The results indicate that the average scores on the combined reading literacy scale in these schools were also substantially below the OECD average.

27. It needs to be taken into account that, in many countries, there is little variation in teacher qualifications so that the relationship would be expected to be weak.

28. The variables for achievement press and teacher-student relations had non-linear relationships with student performance. To overcome this, the measures of achievement press used in this analysis indicate extreme cases where students reported "never" to items such as "The teacher tells students that they can do better". Similarly, the measure of teacher-student relations used in this chapter indicates the proportion of responses where students indicated "strongly diagree" to statements indicating a positive student-teacher relationship.

29. The between-country variation in student performance on the scientific literacy scale that is explained jointly by school factors and socio-economic factors is less than that explained by school factors alone. In these models, the effects of the school mean index of economic, social and cultural status were allowed to vary between countries. The variance components were calculated for a student with average values on the index of economic, social and cultural status, in a school with a school mean index of economic, social and cultural status of zero (*i.e* the average for all OECD students). The reduction in variance when the mean index of economic, social and cultural status is added to the model suggests that there may be significant interactions between school resources and school mean economic, social and cultural status.

30. At the international level, the impact of the student-teaching staff ratio on student performance levels off after 25. This value was therefore chosen as the highest category on this index.

31. The analysis fitted a two-level hierarchical model within each country. The model is the same as the three-level model used for Table 8.5, except that the two measures for the student-teaching staff ratio were replaced by separate dummy variables indicating the effects of student-teaching staff ratios of 20 to 25, 25 to 30, and above 30, compared with student-teaching staff ratios below 20. This allowed for a more direct comparison of the non-linear effect within each country. Also, the model did not include school size, as the effects varied substantially between countries, and in most cases were not statistically significant. The results of the meta-analysis yielded findings similar to those derived from the three-level model, except that the effect of achievement press was smaller and not statistically significant.

32. The coefficients for the within-country analyses vary considerable, as indicated by the size of their standard errors. Coefficients can vary from country to country because of "true" variation in their effects for each country, but also because of measurement error and sampling error. In these analyses, sampling error plays a significant role because the accuracy of the coefficients for school-level variables depends mainly on the number of schools sampled within each country, rather than the number of students. The number of schools in this analysis varied from 24 schools in Luxembourg to 1 111 schools in Canada, with an average of about 214 schools in OECD countries. This problem especially affects the coefficients for student-staff ratios, as in some cases these are based on the results for a very small number of schools.

REFERENCES

Audas, R. and **Willms, J. D.** (2000), *Engagement and Dropping out of School: A life-course perspective,* Report prepared for Human Resources Development, Canada.

Baumert, J., **Heyn. S.** and **Köller, O.** (1994), *Das Kieler Lernstrategien-Inventar (KSI),* Institut für die Pädagogik der Naturwissenschaften an der Universität Kiel, Kiel.

Baumert, J., **Gruehn, S.**, **Heyn, S.**, **Köller, O.** and **Schnabel, K.U.** (1997), *Bildungsverläufe und Psychosoziale Entwicklung im Jugendalter (BIJU): Dokumentation - Band 1,* Max-Planck-Institut für Bildungsforschung, Berlin.

Beaton, A.E., **Mullis, I.V.**, **Martin, M.O.**, **Gonzalez, E.J.**, **Kelly, D.L.** and **Smith, T.A.** (1996), *Mathematics Achievement in the Middle School Years,* Center for the Study of Testing, Evaluation and Educational Policy, Boston College.

Brookover, W.B., **Schweitzer, J.H.**, **Schneider, J.M.**, **Beady, C.H.**, **Flood, P.K.** and **Wisenbaker, J.M.** (1978), "Elementary school social climate and school achievement", *American Educational Research Journal,* Vol. 15, pp. 301-318.

Eignor, D., **Taylor, C.**, **Kirsch, I.** and **Jamieson, J.** (1998), *Development of a Scale for Assessing the Level of Computer Familiarity of TOEFL Students,* TOEFL Research Report No. 60, Educational Testing Service, Princeton, NJ.

Ganzeboom, H.B.G., **De Graaf, P.** and **Treiman, D.J.** (with De Leeuw, J.). (1992), "A standard international socio-economic index of occupational status", *Social Science Research,* Vol. 21(1), pp. 1-56.

Ganzeboom, H.B.G., **Treiman, D.J.** and **Donald, J.** (1996), "Internationally comparable measures of occupational status for the 1988 International Standard Classification of Occupations", *Social Science Research,* Vol. 25, pp. 201-239.

Henderson, V., **Mieszkowski, P.** and **Sauvageau, Y.** (1978), "Peer group effects and educational production functions", *Journal of Public Economics,* Vol. 10, pp. 97-106.

House, J., **Kessler**, **R.**, **Herzog**, **R.**, **Mero**, **R.P.**, **Kinney, A.M.** and **Breslow, M.J.** (1990), "Age, socioeconomic status, and health", *The Millbank Quarterly,* Vol. 68, pp. 383-411.

INSEE-DPD (1999), *Etude de la fiabilité des déclarations des élèves de 15 ans dans le cadre de l'opération PISA 2000,* document interne, DPD-INSEE, France.

Marsh, H.W. Shavelson, R.J. and **Byrne, B.M.** (1992), "A multidimensional, hierarchical self-concept", in R. P. Lipka and T. M. Brinthaupt (Eds.), *Studying the Self: Self-perspectives across the life-span,* State University of New York Press, Albany.

Mirowsky, J. and **Hu, P.** (1996), "Physical impairment and the diminishing effects of income", *Social Forces,* Vol. 74(3), pp. 1073-1096.

Mullis, I.V. Martin, M.O., **Beaton, A.E.**, **Gonzalez, E.J.**, **Kelly, D.L.** and **Smith, T.A.** (1998), *Mathematics and Science Achievement in the Final Year of Secondary School,* Center for the Study of Testing, Evaluation and Educational Policy, Boston College.

OECD (1996), *Education at a Glance - OECD Indicators,* Paris.

OECD (1997), *Education at a Glance - OECD Indicators,* Paris.

OECD (1999a), *Measuring Student Knowledge and Skills – A New Framework for Assessment,* Paris.

OECD (1999b), *Classifying Educational Programmes. Manual for ISCED-97 Implementation in OECD Countries,* Paris.

OECD (2001), *Education at a Glance - OECD Indicators,* Paris.

OECD and **Statistics Canada** (1995), *Literacy, Economy and Society: Results of the First International Adult Literacy Survey,* Paris and Ottawa.

OECD and **Statistics Canada** (2000), *Literacy in the Information Age,* Paris and Ottawa

Owens, L. and **Barnes, J.** (1992), *Learning Preferences Scales,* ACER, Victoria, Australia.

Pelgrum, W.J. and **Anderson, R.E.** (1999), *ICT and the Emerging Paradigm for Lifelong Learning: a worldwide educational assessment of infrastructure, goals, and practices,* International Association for the Evaluation of Educational Achievement (IEA), Amsterdam.

Pintrich, P.R., **Smith, D.A.F.**, **Garcia, T.** and **McKeachie, W.J.** (1993), "Reliability and predictive validity of the motivated strategies for learning questionnaire (MLSQ)", *Educational and Psychological Measurement,* Vol. 53, pp. 801-813.

Rumberger, R. and **Willms, J.D.** (1992), "The impact of racial and ethnic segregation on the achievement gap in California high schools", *Educational Evaluation and Policy Analysis*, Vol. 14(4), pp. 377-396.

Shavit, Y. and **Williams, R.A.** (1985), "Ability grouping and contextual determinants of educational expectations in Israel", *American Sociological Review*, Vol. 50, pp. 62-73.

Summers, A.A. and **Wolfe, B.L.** (1977), "Do schools make a difference?", *American Economic Review,* Vol. 67, pp. 639-652.

Warm, T.A. (1985), "Weighted maximum likelihood estimation of ability in Item Response Theory with tests of finite length", *Technical Report CGI-TR-85-08,* U.S. Coast Guard Institute, Oklahoma City.

Willms, J.D. (1986), "Social class segregation and its relationship to pupils' examination results in Scotland", *American Sociological Review,* Vol. 51, pp. 224-241.

Willms, J.D. and **Chen, M.** (1989), "The effects of ability grouping on the ethnic achievement gap in Israeli elementary schools", *American Journal of Education*, Vol. 97(3), pp. 237-257.

Wolfson, M., **Rowe, G.**, **Gentleman, J.F.** and **Tomiak, M.** (1993), "Career earnings and death: A longitudinal analysis of older Canadian men", *Journal of Gerontology*, Vol. 48(4), pp. S167-S179.

ANNEX

TECHNICAL BACKGROUND

Annex A1: Construction of indices and other derived measures from the student and school context questionnaires

Several of PISA's measures reflect indices that summarise responses from students or school representatives (typically principals) to a series of related questions. The questions were selected from larger constructs on the basis of theoretical considerations and previous research. Structural equation modelling was used to confirm the theoretically expected behaviour of the indices and to validate their comparability across countries. For this purpose, a model was estimated separately for each country and, collectively, for all OECD countries.

This section explains the indices derived from the student and school context questionnaires that are used in this report. For a description of other PISA indices and details on the methods see the *PISA 2000 Technical Report* which will be available on the Internet at the end of 2001.

Unless otherwise indicated, where an index involves multiple questions and student responses, the index was scaled using a weighted maximum likelihood estimate, using a one-parameter item response model (referred to as a WARM estimator; see Warm, 1985) with three stages:

- The question parameters were estimated from equal-sized sub-samples of students from each OECD country.
- The estimates were computed for all students and all schools by anchoring the question parameters obtained in the preceding step.
- The indices were then standardised so that the mean of the index value for the OECD student population was zero and the standard deviation was one (countries being given equal weight in the standardisation process).

It is important to note that negative values in an index do not necessarily imply that students responded negatively to the underlying questions. A negative value merely indicates that a group of students (or all students, collectively, in a single country) or principals responded less positively than all students or principals did on average across OECD countries. Likewise, a positive value on an index indicates that a group of students or principals responded more favourably, or more positively, than students or principals did, on average, in OECD countries.

Terms enclosed in brackets < > in the following descriptions were replaced in the national versions of the student and school questionnaires by the appropriate national equivalent. For example, the term <qualification at ISCED level 5A> was translated in the United States into "Bachelor's Degree, post-graduate certificate program, Master's degree program or first professional degree program". Similarly the term <classes in the language of assessment> in Luxembourg was translated into "German classes" or "French classes" depending on whether students received the German or French version of the assessment instruments.

For the reliabilities of the indices, see the *PISA 2000 Technical Report.*

Student characteristics and family background

Family structure

Students were asked to report who usually lived at home with them. The response categories were then grouped into four categories: *i) single-parent family* (students who reported living with one of the following: mother, father, female guardian or male guardian); *ii) nuclear family* (students who reported living with a mother and a father); *iii) mixed family* (students who reported living with a mother and a male guardian, a father and a female guardian, or two guardians); and *iv) other response combinations.*

Number of siblings

Students were asked to indicate the number of siblings older than themselves, younger than themselves, or of the same age. For the analyses in Chapter 8, the numbers in each category were added together.

Country of birth

Students were asked if they, their mother and their father were born in the country of assessment or in another country. The response categories were then grouped into three categories: *i) "native"* students (those students born in the country of assessment and who had at least one parent born in that country); *ii) "first-generation"* students (those born in the country of assessment but whose parents were born in another country); and *iii)* "**non-native**" students (those born outside the country of assessment and whose parents were also born in another country).

Language spoken at home

Students were asked if the language spoken at home most of the time is the language of assessment, another official national language, another national dialect or language, or another language. The responses were then grouped into two categories: *i)* the language spoken at home most of the time is different from the language of assessment, from other official national languages, and from other national dialects or languages, and *ii)* the language spoken at home most of the time is the language of assessment, other official national languages, or other national dialects or languages.

Economic, social and cultural status

Students were asked to report their mothers' and fathers' occupations, and to state whether each parent was: in full-time paid work; part-time paid work; not working but looking for a paid job; or "other". The open-ended responses were then coded in accordance with the International Standard Classification of Occupations (ISCO 1988).

The PISA *International Socio-Economic Index of Occupational Status* (ISEI) was derived from students' responses on parental occupation. The index captures the attributes of occupations that convert parents' education into income. The index was derived by the optimal scaling of occupation groups to maximise the indirect effect of education on income through occupation and to minimise the direct effect of education on income, net of occupation (both effects being net of age). For more information on the methodology, see Ganzeboom *et al.* (1992). The PISA International Socio-Economic Index of Occupational Status is based on either the father's or mother's occupations, whichever is the higher.

Values on the index range from 0 to 90; low values represent low socio-economic status and high values represent high socio-economic status.

To capture wider aspects of a student's family and home background in addition to occupational status, the PISA *index of economic, social and cultural status* was created on the basis of the following variables: the International Socio-Economic Index of Occupational Status (ISEI) (see Table 6.1); the highest level of education of the student's parents, converted into years of schooling (for data on parental levels of education see Table 6.7, for the conversion coefficients see Table A1.1); the PISA index of family wealth (see Table 6.2); the PISA index of home educational resources; and the PISA index of possessions related to "classical" culture in the family home (see Table 6.3). The ISEI represents the first principle component of the factors described above. The index has been constructed such that its mean is 0 and its standard deviation is 1.

Among these components, the data most commonly missing relate to the International Socio-Economic Index of Occupational Status (ISEI), parental education, or both. Separate factor analyses were therefore undertaken for all students with valid data for: *i)* the socio-economic index of occupational status, the index of family wealth, the index of home educational resources and the index of possessions related to "classical" culture in the family home; *ii)* years of parental education, the index of family wealth, the index of home educational resources and the index of possessions related to "classical" culture in the family home; and *iii)* the index of family wealth, the index of home educational resources and the index of possessions related to "classical" culture in the family home. Students were then assigned a factor score based on the amount of data available. For this to be done, students had to have data on at least three variables. In the case of France, questions remain about the reliability of students' responses regarding parental occupation and education (see INSEE, 1999).

Parental education

Students were asked to classify the highest level of education of their mother and father on the basis of national qualifications, which were then coded in accordance with the International Standard Classification of Education (ISCED 1997) in order to obtain internationally comparable categories of educational attainment. The resulting categories were: did not go to school; completed <ISCED Level 1 (primary education)>; completed <ISCED Level 2 (lower secondary education)>; completed <ISCED Level 3B or 3C (upper secondary education, aimed in most countries at providing direct entry into the labour market)>; completed <ISCED Level 3A (upper secondary education, aimed in most countries at gaining entry into tertiary education)>; and completed <ISCED Level 5A, 5B or 6 (tertiary education)>.

For a list of the national institutional categories used in the brackets < > above, see the *PISA 2000 Technical Report*.

For the analyses in Chapter 8, the highest level of educational attainment of the parents was converted into an estimate of *years of schooling* based on the coefficients shown in Table A1.1.

Parental interest

The PISA index of *cultural communication* was derived from students' reports on the frequency with which their parents (or guardians) engaged with them in the following activities: discussing political or social issues; discussing books, films or television programmes; and listening to classical music.

The PISA index of *social communication* was derived from students' reports on the frequency with which their parents (or guardians) engaged with them in the following activities: discussing how well they are doing at school; eating <the main meal> with them around a table; and spending time simply talking with them.

Students responded to each statement on a five-point scale with the response categories: 'never or hardly ever', 'a few times a year', 'about once a month', 'several times a month' and 'several times a week'. Both indices were derived using the WARM estimator described above.

Table A.1.1
Levels of parental education converted into years of schooling

		Did not go to school	Completed <ISCED Level 1 (primary education)>	Completed <ISCED Level 2 secondary education)>	Completed <ISCED Levels 3B or 3C (upper secondary education aimed at direct entry into the labour market)>	Completed <ISCED Level 3A (upper secondary education aimed at entry into tertiary education)>	Completed <ISCED Level 5A, 5B or 6 (tertiary education)>
OECD COUNTRIES	Australia	0.0	7.5	11.0	13.0	13.0	16.5
	Austria	0.0	4.0	8.0	11.0	13.0	15.5
	Belgium (Fl.)	0.0	6.0	8.0	12.0	12.0	16.5
	Belgium (Fr.)	0.0	6.0	8.5	12.0	12.0	16.5
	Canada	0.0	6.0	9.0	12.0	12.0	14.5
	Czech Republic	0.0	5.0	9.0	12.0	13.0	16.0
	Denmark	0.0	6.0	9.5	12.0	12.0	15.0
	Finland	0.0	6.0	9.0	12.0	12.0	15.0
	France	0.0	5.0	9.0	12.0	12.0	15.0
	Germany	0.0	4.0	9.5	12.5	13.0	18.0
	Greece	0.0	6.0	9.0	11.5	12.0	16.0
	Hungary	0.0	4.0	9.0	11.5	12.5	15.0
	Iceland	0.0	7.0	11.0	13.5	14.0	18.0
	Ireland	0.0	8.0	11.0	12.0	13.5	15.5
	Italy	0.0	5.0	8.0	12.0	13.0	16.5
	Japan	0.0	6.0	9.0	12.0	12.0	15.5
	Korea	0.0	5.0	9.0	12.0	12.0	16.0
	Luxembourg	0.0	6.0	8.5	13.0	13.0	15.5
	Mexico	0.0	6.0	9.5	12.0	12.0	15.0
	New Zealand	0.0	6.0	10.0	12.0	13.0	16.0
	Norway	0.0	7.0	10.0	13.0	13.0	16.5
	Poland	0.0	8.0	11.0	12.5	16.0	16.0
	Portugal	0.0	6.5	9.0	12.0	12.0	16.0
	Spain	0.0	6.0	9.5	11.5	11.5	15.0
	Sweden	0.0	9.0	11.0	12.0	12.0	15.5
	Switzerland	0.0	6.0	9.5	11.5	12.5	16.0
	United Kingdom	0.0	6.0	9.0	11.0	12.5	14.5
	United States	0.0	6.0	9.0	12.0	12.0	14.5
NON-OECD COUNTRIES	Brazil	0.0	6.0	9.0	12.0	12.0	15.5
	Liechtenstein	0.0	5.0	9.0	13.0	13.0	16.0
	Russian Federation	0.0	4.0	8.0	11.0	11.0	16.0
	Netherlands[1]	0.0	6.0	9.5	12.0	12.0	16.5

1. Response rate is too low to ensure comparability (see Annex A3).

Participation in additional courses

Students were asked if they had sometimes or regularly *attended any special courses* outside school during the previous three years in order to improve results. The response categories were then grouped into two categories: *i)* students who attended additional courses in the <language of assessment>, courses in other subjects or extension or other additional courses outside school; and *ii)* students who attended remedial courses in the <language of assessment>, remedial courses in other subjects outside school or other training to improve study skills or private tutoring.

Cultural activities

The PISA index of *activities related to "classical" culture* was derived from students' reports on how often they had participated in the following activities during the preceding year: visited a museum or art gallery; attended an opera, ballet or classical symphony concert; and watched live theatre. Students responded to each statement on a four-point scale with the following categories: 'never or hardly ever', 'once or twice a year', '3 or 4 times a year', and 'more than 4 times a year'. The index was derived using the WARM estimator described above.

Family possessions

The PISA index of *family wealth* was derived from students' reports on: *i)* the availability, in their home, of a dishwasher, a room of their own, educational software, and a link to the Internet; and *ii)* the number of cellular phones, television sets, computers, motor cars and bathrooms at home.

The PISA index of *home educational resources* was derived from students' reports on the availability and number of the following items in their home: a dictionary, a quiet place to study, a desk for study, textbooks and calculators.

The PISA index of *possessions related to "classical" culture in the family home* was derived from students' reports on the availability of the following items in their home: classical literature (examples were given), books of poetry and works of art (examples were given).

These indices were derived using the WARM estimator (Warm, 1985) described above.

Learning strategies and attitudes

Engagement in reading

The PISA index of *engagement in reading* was derived from students' level of agreement with the following statements: I read only if I have to; reading is one of my favourite hobbies; I like talking about books with other people; I find it hard to finish books; I feel happy if I receive a book as a present; for me reading is a waste of time; I enjoy going to a bookstore or a library; I read only to get information that I need; and, I cannot sit still and read for more than a few minutes. A four-point scale with the response categories 'strongly disagree', 'disagree', 'agree' and 'strongly agree' was used. The indices were derived using the WARM estimator described above.

Student interest in reading

The PISA index of *interest in reading* was derived from students' level of agreement with the following statements: because reading is fun, I wouldn't want to give it up; I read in my spare time; and, when I read, I sometimes get totally absorbed. A four-point scale with the response categories 'disagree', 'disagree somewhat', 'agree somewhat' and 'agree' was used. The indices were derived using the WARM estimator described above. For information on the conceptual underpinning of the index see Baumert *et al.* (1997).

Student interest in mathematics

The PISA index of *interest in mathematics* was derived from students' level of agreement with the following statements: when I do mathematics, I sometimes get totally absorbed; mathematics is important to me personally; and because doing mathematics is fun, I wouldn't want to give it up. A four-point scale with the response categories 'disagree', 'disagree somewhat', 'agree somewhat' and 'agree' was used. The indices were derived using the WARM estimator described above. For information on the conceptual underpinning of the index see Baumert *et al.* (1997).

Control strategies

The PISA index of **control strategies** was derived from the frequency with which students used the following strategies when studying: I start by figuring out what exactly I need to learn; I force myself to check to see if I remember what I have learned; I try to figure out which concepts I still haven't really understood; I make sure that I remember the most important things; and, when I study and I don't understand something, I look for additional information to clarify this. A four-point scale with the response categories 'almost never', 'sometimes', 'often' and 'almost always' was used. The indices were derived using the WARM estimator described above. For information on the conceptual underpinning of the index see Baumert *et al.* (1994).

Memorising

The PISA index of **memorisation strategies** was derived from the frequency with which students used the following strategies when studying: I try to memorise everything that might be covered; I memorise as much as possible; I memorise all new material so that I can recite it; and I practice by saying the material to myself over and over. A four-point scale with the response categories 'almost never', 'sometimes', 'often' and 'almost always' was used. The indices were derived using the WARM estimator described above. For information on the conceptual underpinning of the index see Baumert (1994) and Pintrich *et al.* (1993).

Elaboration

The PISA index of **elaboration strategies** was derived from the frequency with which students used the following strategies when studying: I try to relate new material to things I have learned in other subjects; I figure out how the information might be useful in the real world; I try to understand the material better by relating it to things I already know; and, I figure out how the material fits in with what I have already learned. A four-point scale with the response categories 'almost never', 'sometimes', 'often' and 'almost always' was used. The indices were derived using the WARM estimator described above. For information on the conceptual underpinning of the index see Baumert *et al.* (1994).

Co-operative and competitive learning

The PISA index of **co-operative learning** was derived from students' level of agreement with the following statements: I like to work with other students; I learn the most when I work with other students; I do my best work when I work with other students; I like to help other people do well in a group; and, it is helpful to put together everyone's ideas when working on a project. A four-point scale with the response categories 'disagree', 'disagree somewhat', 'agree somewhat' and 'agree' was used. The indices were derived using the WARM estimator described above. For information on the conceptual underpinning of the index, see Owens and Barnes (1992).

The PISA index of **competitive learning** was derived from the students' level of agreement with the following statements: I like to try to be better than other students; trying to be better than others makes me work well; I would like to be the best at something; and, I learn things faster if I'm trying to do better than the others. A four-point scale with the response categories 'disagree', 'disagree somewhat', 'agree somewhat' and 'agree' was used. The indices were derived using the WARM estimator described above. For information on the conceptual underpinning of the index see Owens and Barnes (1992).

Student self-concept in reading

The PISA index of **self-concept in reading** was derived from students' level of agreement with the following statements: I'm hopeless in <classes of the language of assessment>; I learn things quickly in the <classes of the language of assessment>; and, I get good marks in the <language of assessment>. A four-point scale with the response categories 'disagree', 'disagree somewhat', 'agree somewhat' and 'agree' was used. The indices were derived using the WARM estimator described above. For information on the conceptual underpinning of the index see Marsh *et al.* (1992).

Student self-concept in mathematics

The PISA index of **self-concept in mathematics** was derived from students' level of agreement with the following statements: I get good marks in mathematics; mathematics is one of my best subjects; and, I have always done well in mathematics. A four-point scale with the response categories 'disagree', 'disagree somewhat', 'agree somewhat' and 'agree' was used. The indices were derived using the WARM estimator described above. For information on the conceptual underpinning of the index see Marsh *et al.* (1992).

Interest in computers

The PISA index of *interest in computers* was derived from the students' responses to the following statements: it is very important to me to work with a computer; to play or work with a computer is really fun; I use a computer because I am very interested in this; and, I forget the time, when I am working with the computer. A two-point scale with the response categories 'yes' and 'no' was used. The indices were derived using the WARM estimator described above. For information on the conceptual underpinning of the index see Eignor *et al.* (1998).

Comfort with and perceived ability to use computers

The PISA index of *comfort with and perceived ability to use computers* was derived from students' responses to the following questions: How comfortable are you with using a computer?; How comfortable are you with using a computer to write a paper?; How comfortable are you with taking a test on a computer?; and, If you compare yourself with other 15-year-olds, how would you rate your ability to use a computer? For the first three questions, a four-point scale was used with the response categories 'very comfortable', 'comfortable', 'somewhat comfortable' and 'not at all comfortable'. For the last questions, a four-point scale was used with the response categories 'excellent', 'good', 'fair' and 'poor'. The indices were derived using the WARM estimator described above. For information on the conceptual underpinning of the index see Eignor *et al.* (1998).

Time spent on homework

The PISA index of *time spent on homework* was derived from students' reports on the amount of time they devote to homework per week in the <language of assessment>, mathematics and science. Students rated the amount on a four-point scale with response categories 'no time', 'less than 1 hour per week', 'between 1 and 3 hours per week', '3 hours or more per week'. The indices were derived using the WARM estimator described above.

School policies and practices

Use of student assessments

School principals reported on the frequency with which 15-year-olds in their school are assessed using: standardised tests; tests developed by teachers; teachers' judgmental ratings; student <portfolios>; and student assignments/projects/homework. School principals rated each form of assessment on a five-point scale with the response categories: 'never', 'yearly', '2 times a year', '3 times a year', and '4 or more times a year'. School principals also provided information on whether the assessment of 15-year-old students was used to: compare a school's performance with <district or national> performance; monitor the school's progress from year to year; and make judgements about teachers' effectiveness.

The PISA index of the *use of formal assessments* was derived from school principals' reports on the frequency with which standardised tests were used, and on their reports on how those assessments were used. The indices were derived using the WARM estimator described above. High values on the index identify schools where standardised assessment played an important role as a monitoring tool.

The PISA index of the *use of informal assessments* was derived from principals' reports on the frequency with which tests developed by teachers, teachers' judgmental ratings, student <portfolios> and student assignments/projects/homework were used, and on their reports on the uses made of those assessments. The indices were derived using the WARM estimator described above. High positive values on the index identify schools where informal assessment plays an important role as a monitoring tool.

School and teacher autonomy

School principals were asked to report whether teachers, department heads, the school principal, an appointed or elected board or an education authorities at a higher level had the main responsibility for: appointing teachers; dismissing teachers; establishing teachers' starting salaries; determining teachers' salary increases; formulating school budgets; allocating budgets within the school; establishing student disciplinary policies; establishing student assessment policies; approving students for admittance to school; choosing which textbooks to use; determining course content; and deciding which courses were offered.

The PISA index of *school autonomy* used in Chapter 8 was derived from the number of categories that principals classified as not being a school responsibility. The scale was then inverted so that high values indicate a high degree of autonomy.

The PISA index of *teacher autonomy* used in Chapter 8 was derived from the number of categories that principals identified as being mainly the responsibility of teachers.

The indices were derived using the WARM estimator described above.

Staff professional development

School principals reported the percentage of teachers involved in *professional development programmes*. Professional development included formal programmes designed to enhance teaching skills or pedagogical practices. Such programmes might or might not lead to a recognised qualification. For the purpose of this question, a programme had to be at least one full day in length and to focus on teaching and education.

School principals' perceptions of teacher-related factors affecting school climate

The PISA index of the *principals' perceptions of teacher-related factors affecting school climate* was derived from principals' reports on the extent to which the learning by 15-year-olds was hindered by: low expectations of teachers; poor student-teacher relations; teachers not meeting individual students' needs; teacher absenteeism; staff resisting change; teachers being too strict with students; and students not being encouraged to achieve their full potential. A four-point scale with the response categories 'not at all', 'very little', 'to some extent' and 'a lot' was used. The indices were derived using the WARM estimator described above. This index was inverted so that lower values indicate a poorer disciplinary climate.

School principals' perceptions of teachers' morale and commitment

The PISA index of the *principals' perceptions of teachers' morale and commitment* was derived from the extent to which school principals agreed with the following statements: the morale of the teachers in this school is high; teachers work with enthusiasm; teachers take pride in this school; and teachers value academic achievement. A four-point scale with the response categories 'strongly disagree', 'disagree', 'agree' and 'strongly agree' was used. The indices were derived using the WARM estimator described above.

Shortage of teachers

The PISA index of the *teacher shortage* was derived from the principals' view on how much learning by 15-year-old students was hindered by the shortage or inadequacy of teachers in general, teachers in the <language of assessment>, mathematics or science. The index was derived using the WARM estimator described above. This index was inverted so that low values indicate problems with teacher shortage.

Classroom practices

Teacher support

The PISA index of *teacher support* was derived from students' reports on the frequency with which: the teacher shows an interest in every student's learning; the teacher gives students an opportunity to express opinions; the teacher helps students with their work; the teacher continues teaching until the students understand; the teacher does a lot to help students; and, the teacher helps students with their learning. A four-point scale with the response categories 'never', 'some lessons', 'most lessons' and 'every lesson' was used. The index was derived using the WARM estimator (Warm, 1985) described above.

Disciplinary climate

The PISA index of *disciplinary climate* summarises students' reports on the frequency with which, in their <class of the language of assessment>: the teacher has to wait a long time for students to <quieten down>; students cannot work well; students don't listen to what the teacher says; students don't start working for a long time after the lesson begins; there is noise and disorder; and, at the start of class, more than five minutes are spent doing nothing. A four-point scale with the response categories 'never', 'some lessons', 'most lessons' and 'every lesson' was used. This index was inverted so that low values indicate a poor disciplinary climate.

The PISA index of the *principals' perceptions of student-related factors affecting school climate* was derived from principals' reports on the extent to which learning by 15-year-olds in their school was hindered by: student absenteeism; disruption of classes by students; students skipping classes; students lacking respect for teachers; the use of alcohol or illegal drugs; and students intimidating or bullying other students. A four-point scale with the response categories 'not at all', 'very little', 'to some extent' and 'a lot' was used. This index was inverted so that low values indicate a poor disciplinary climate. The indices were derived using the WARM estimator described above.

Pressure to achieve

The PISA index of **achievement press** was derived from students' reports on the frequency with which, in their <class of the language of assessment>: the teacher wants students to work hard; the teacher tells students that they can do better; the teacher does not like it when students deliver <careless> work; and, students have to learn a lot. A four-point scale with the response categories 'never', 'some lessons', 'most lessons' and 'every lesson' was used. The indices were derived using the WARM estimator described above with 'never' coded as 1 and all other response categories coded as 0.

Teacher-student relations

The PISA index of **teacher-student relations** was derived from students' reports on their level of agreement with the following statements: students get along well with most teachers; most teachers are interested in students' well-being; most of my teachers really listen to what I have to say; if I need extra help, I will receive it from my teachers; and most of my teachers treat me fairly. A four-point scale with the response categories 'strongly disagree', 'disagree', 'agree' and 'strongly agree' was used. The indices were derived using the WARM estimator described above with 'strongly agree' coded as 1 and all other response categories coded as 0.

School resources and type of school

Quality of the schools' physical infrastructure

The PISA index of the **quality of the schools' physical infrastructure** was derived from principals' reports on the extent to which learning by 15-year-olds in their school was hindered by: poor condition of buildings; poor heating and cooling and/or lighting systems; and lack of instructional space (*e.g.*, in classrooms).

A four-point scale with the response categories 'not at all', 'very little', 'to some extent' and 'a lot' was used. The index was derived using the WARM estimator described above. This index was inverted so that low values indicate a low quality of physical infrastructure.

Quality of the schools' educational resources

The PISA index of the **quality of the schools' educational resources** was derived based on the school principals' reports on the extent to which learning by 15-year-olds was hindered by: not enough computers for instruction; lack of instructional materials in the library; lack of multi-media resources for instruction; inadequate science laboratory equipment; and inadequate facilities for the fine arts.

A four-point scale with the response categories 'not at all', 'very little', 'to some extent' and 'a lot' was used. The index was derived using the WARM estimator described above. This index was inverted so that low values indicate a low quality of educational resources.

Availability of computers

School principals provided information on the total number of computers available in their schools and, more specifically, on the number of computers: available to 15-year-olds; available only to teachers; available only to administrative staff; connected to the Internet; and connected to a local area network. The PISA index of the **availability of computers** was derived by dividing the total number of computers available to 15-year-olds by the total number of computers in the school.

Student-teaching staff ratio and class size

School principals indicated the number of full-time and part-time teachers employed in their schools. Principals also specified: the numbers of teachers that were <language of assessment> teachers, mathematics teachers and science teachers; the number of teachers fully certified as teachers by the <appropriate national authority>; and the numbers of teachers with a qualification at <ISCED level 5A> in <pedagogy>, at <ISCED level 5A> in the <language of assessment>, at <ISCED level 5A> in

<mathematics>, and at <ISCED level 5A> in <science>. The proportions of teachers in the respective categories are used in Chapter 8.

The **student-teaching staff ratio** was defined as the number of full-time equivalent teachers divided by the number of students in the school. In order to convert head-counts into full-time equivalents, a full-time teacher, defined as a teacher employed for at least 90 per cent of the statutory time as a classroom teacher, received a weight of 1 and a part-time teacher, defined as a teacher employed for less than 90 per cent of the time as a classroom teacher, received a weight of 0.5.

An estimate of **class size** was obtained from students' reports on the number of students in their respective <language of assessment>, mathematics and science classes.

Use of school resources

The PISA index of the **use of school resources** was derived from the frequency with which students reported using the following resources in their school: the school library; calculators; the Internet; and <science> laboratories. Students responded on a five-point scale with the following categories: 'never or hardly ever', 'a few times a year', 'about once a month', 'several times a month' and 'several times a week'. The index was derived using the WARM estimator described above.

Hours of schooling

The PISA index of **hours of schooling per year** was derived from the information which principals provided on: the number of weeks in the school year for which the school operates; the number of <class periods> in the school week; and the number of teaching minutes in a single <class period>. The index was derived from the product of these three factors, divided by 60.

School type

A school was classified as either public or private according to whether a public agency or a private entity had the ultimate power to make decisions concerning its affairs. A school was classified as **public** if the school principal reported that it was: controlled and managed directly by a public education authority or agency; or controlled and managed either by a government agency directly or by a governing body (council, committee, etc.), most of whose members were either appointed by a public authority or elected by public franchise. A school was classified as **private** if the school principal reported that it was controlled and managed by a non-governmental organisation (*e.g.*, a church, a trade union or a business enterprise) or if its governing board consisted mostly of members not selected by a public agency.

A distinction was made between "government-dependent" and "independent" private schools according to the degree of a private school's dependence on funding from government sources. School principals were asked to specify the percentage of the school's total funding received in a typical school year from: government sources; student fees or school charges paid by parents; donations, sponsorships or parental fund-raising; and other sources. Schools were classified as **government-dependent private** if they received 50 per cent or more of their core funding from government agencies. Schools were classified as **government-independent private** if they received less than 50 per cent of their core funding from government agencies.

Annex A2: Explained variation in student performance

In several tables of Chapters 4, 6 and 7, the change in student performance associated with one unit change on a given measure has been estimated by means of regression methods. The variation in student performance that is explained by this regression is shown in Table A2.1 and conventionally referred to as R^2. For the definitions of the indices, see Annex A1.

Table A2.1
Explained variation in student performance (R^2)
Results are expressed as percentages

	Index of comfort with and and perceived ability to use computers	Index of competitive learning	Index of control strategies	Index of co-operative learning	Index of activities related to "classical" culture	Index of cultural communication	Index of possessions related to "classical" culture in the family home	Index of disciplinary climate
OECD COUNTRIES								
Australia	2.9	3.2	5.7	0.2	7.1	9.7	10.3	2.3
Austria	a	1.0	3.4	1.5	7.0	6.6	5.7	0.4
Belgium	0.6	0.1	1.6	0.1	11.8	1.9	8.8	0.1
Canada	2.1	a	a	a	7.0	5.0	5.9	1.7
Czech Republic	2.9	3.2	8.4	1.8	7.3	5.4	9.2	2.2
Denmark	1.1	3.1	1.7	0.3	5.5	11.4	6.9	0.6
Finland	0.2	3.6	2.4	1.4	2.9	6.1	5.8	1.0
France	a	a	a	a	7.2	5.4	12.1	0.0
Germany	0.0	2.1	4.8	0.8	9.0	5.1	8.9	1.1
Greece	a	a	a	a	0.8	4.0	8.4	0.1
Hungary	1.3	3.6	3.1	0.0	6.7	2.9	15.3	2.9
Iceland	a	5.0	2.0	1.3	5.1	4.5	3.4	0.7
Ireland	2.0	2.8	4.8	0.0	2.6	3.8	5.6	3.5
Italy	a	0.3	3.3	0.2	3.8	3.8	5.4	2.3
Japan	a	a	a	a	3.9	5.9	5.1	4.7
Korea	a	7.1	8.9	1.5	1.1	3.6	4.8	1.0
Luxembourg	0.1	0.1	3.8	0.1	5.6	3.0	14.6	0.1
Mexico	4.8	1.6	5.7	0.8	9.4	6.6	10.1	0.0
New Zealand	2.3	3.4	6.9	0.3	2.0	2.4	5.1	1.2
Norway	0.0	7.3	1.7	3.6	3.6	8.2	8.6	0.4
Poland	a	a	a	a	5.4	2.8	7.6	5.2
Portugal	a	0.3	11.7	1.9	5.1	12.4	11.9	0.8
Spain	a	a	a	a	10.5	11.0	8.5	2.0
Sweden	0.2	1.6	3.8	0.0	2.6	6.1	7.7	1.3
Switzerland	1.3	0.1	3.6	1.3	5.6	7.1	6.7	0.9
United Kingdom	a	a	a	a	8.7	6.6	9.5	4.3
United States	4.5	6.5	4.0	2.5	7.1	4.7	10.4	1.8
OECD average	*1.6*	*2.8*	*4.6*	*1.0*	*5.7*	*5.8*	*8.2*	*1.6*
NON-OECD COUNTRIES								
Brazil	4.5	0.0	7.2	0.6	0.2	6.8	4.8	0.3
Latvia	0.4	6.2	3.3	3.0	1.7	2.5	7.5	0.8
Liechtenstein	0.9	0.0	4.7	0.1	7.1	4.7	7.2	0.1
Russian Federation	1.5	4.0	5.4	1.7	3.7	2.8	3.9	1.3
Netherlands[1]	a	0.0	0.8	0.7	10.0	7.5	4.7	0.1

	Index of elaboration strategies	Index of engagement in reading	Index of family wealth	Index of home educational resources	Index of interest in computers	Index of interest in mathematics	Index of interest in reading	Index of memorisation strategies
OECD COUNTRIES								
Australia	1.5	17.2	2.0	5.4	0.1	0.1	11.7	0.8
Austria	1.3	14.4	0.8	4.0	a	0.4	10.9	1.7
Belgium	0.0	8.8	0.5	11.2	0.0	0.1	5.3	0.9
Canada	a	17.2	1.7	3.1	a	a	a	a
Czech Republic	4.3	15.4	1.1	9.8	0.0	0.2	12.0	1.6
Denmark	1.7	16.8	0.9	4.8	0.1	2.0	10.6	0.2
Finland	2.5	22.2	1.0	1.8	1.0	3.5	17.9	0.5
France	a	9.2	4.7	7.6	a	a	a	a
Germany	4.0	15.7	3.8	7.9	0.1	0.0	10.7	0.0
Greece	a	7.4	1.8	6.8	a	a	a	a
Hungary	1.2	15.6	4.4	9.5	0.2	0.6	10.6	2.1
Iceland	2.0	20.2	0.2	1.1	a	4.0	12.9	0.0
Ireland	0.5	18.1	1.2	6.7	0.1	0.2	13.1	0.4
Italy	0.6	9.1	0.7	2.7	a	0.1	6.4	2.4
Japan	a	9.1	0.1	3.8	a	a	a	a
Korea	11.6	11.0	2.1	3.2	a	6.9	9.4	0.8
Luxembourg	1.0	5.0	5.2	11.2	0.1	0.6	3.6	0.1
Mexico	1.5	1.7	10.8	13.5	4.3	0.3	0.5	0.0
New Zealand	0.6	15.3	3.3	9.8	0.3	0.0	10.8	1.3
Norway	2.7	16.5	0.1	9.4	a	1.8	13.8	0.1
Poland	a	9.4	0.8	8.3	a	a	a	a
Portugal	5.1	10.0	9.1	8.0	a	0.7	6.9	0.0
Spain	a	13.0	2.9	4.6	a	a	a	a
Sweden	1.8	19.1	0.5	2.1	0.2	0.1	13.7	0.6
Switzerland	1.9	16.2	1.3	5.7	0.1	0.3	10.1	0.0
United Kingdom	a	14.7	1.6	6.5	a	a	a	a
United States	0.7	10.5	8.6	11.2	4.1	0.5	6.9	0.0
OECD average	*2.3*	*13.3*	*2.6*	*6.7*	*0.8*	*1.1*	*9.9*	*0.7*
NON-OECD COUNTRIES								
Brazil	3.7	4.5	10.0	10.8	1.5	1.0	0.9	2.2
Latvia	0.9	10.6	0.4	3.7	0.7	1.3	8.8	0.7
Liechtenstein	1.7	16.5	1.6	7.5	a	1.3	9.4	0.1
Russian Federation	1.3	8.8	1.4	5.9	5.8	1.4	5.3	1.6
Netherlands[1]	0.0	8.4	0.1	8.4	a	0.3	7.7	0.3

1. Response rate is too low to ensure comparability (see Annex A3).

Table A2.1 *(continued)*

Explained variation in student performance (R²)

Results are expressed as percentages

	Index of the principals' perceptions of teachers' morale and commitment	Index of school autonomy	Index of school selectivity	Index of self-concept in mathematics	Index of self-concept in reading	Index of social communication	Index of the principals' perceptions of student-related factors affecting school climate	Index of teacher autonomy
OECD COUNTRIES								
Australia	2.7	2.5	0.0	2.5	1.1	2.9	4.9	0.7
Austria	0.5	0.2	13.4	0.9	2.3	1.3	1.8	3.6
Belgium	8.0	0.7	0.5	0.0	0.0	0.9	18.4	0.0
Canada	0.3	0.2	0.1	a	a	2.0	1.1	0.1
Czech Republic	0.2	0.0	1.3	2.3	1.9	1.2	8.5	0.6
Denmark	0.6	0.0	0.0	7.1	1.8	4.0	1.7	0.5
Finland	0.3	0.0	0.1	8.9	5.5	0.4	0.1	0.0
France	m	m	m	a	a	1.6	m	m
Germany	1.1	0.0	4.6	0.6	1.7	0.5	12.3	2.9
Greece	0.9	0.1	3.9	a	a	0.9	0.0	0.1
Hungary	2.7	0.4	3.6	2.7	2.3	1.7	13.5	0.1
Iceland	0.1	0.0	0.0	11.1	4.4	1.5	0.4	0.0
Ireland	0.6	1.9	0.1	2.7	0.2	1.1	3.3	0.0
Italy	0.1	0.1	a	2.2	1.5	0.5	13.3	0.2
Japan	7.5	0.0	4.9	a	a	6.3	16.0	1.3
Korea	2.4	0.0	1.0	4.2	4.5	9.0	10.2	0.1
Luxembourg	4.0	a	6.9	0.0	1.3	1.3	0.6	a
Mexico	0.5	8.2	6.8	0.3	0.1	3.4	0.3	0.1
New Zealand	1.1	0.3	0.3	4.3	0.2	1.7	3.5	0.3
Norway	0.0	a	0.0	9.1	5.1	2.4	0.1	a
Poland	6.5	a	0.1	a	a	2.4	16.7	a
Portugal	0.8	1.0	2.0	1.7	1.0	4.6	1.3	0.1
Spain	2.9	4.1	0.2	a	a	1.7	4.8	1.8
Sweden	0.4	0.0	0.1	5.3	1.9	0.3	1.4	0.3
Switzerland	0.2	0.0	2.4	0.0	0.0	1.6	2.4	0.1
United Kingdom	2.8	0.5	4.5	a	a	1.9	11.8	0.2
United States	1.4	0.4	0.1	3.6	2.0	1.8	1.3	0.5
OECD average	*1.9*	*0.9*	*2.3*	*3.5*	*1.9*	*2.2*	*5.8*	*0.6*
NON-OECD COUNTRIES								
Brazil	0.7	10.4	4.3	1.0	0.3	2.9	2.9	0.1
Latvia	0.3	0.2	4.5	0.8	1.5	0.8	0.6	0.1
Liechtenstein	0.0	1.3	9.7	0.1	0.1	1.6	1.9	13.0
Russian Federation	3.5	1.1	0.0	4.8	4.4	1.8	1.1	0.1
Netherlands[1]	0.8	0.1	0.0	0.2	0.0	7.1	21.3	1.6

	Index of teacher shortage	Index of teacher support	Index of the principals' perceptions of teacher-related factors affecting school climate	Index of teacher-student relations	Index of the quality of the schools' educational resources	Index of the quality of the schools' physical infrastructure	Index of time spent on homework	International socio-economic index of occupational status (ISEI)
OECD COUNTRIES								
Australia	1.8	0.5	2.1	2.6	0.9	0.0	7.0	10.2
Austria	3.5	0.0	1.5	0.1	0.1	0.1	0.1	11.0
Belgium	3.8	0.2	5.1	0.0	0.7	1.3	8.6	14.0
Canada	0.1	0.2	0.2	2.1	0.2	0.0	4.5	7.4
Czech Republic	7.2	0.0	0.0	0.3	0.0	0.2	2.0	15.0
Denmark	0.4	1.1	0.3	3.0	0.3	0.1	0.4	9.3
Finland	0.0	0.3	0.1	1.4	0.2	0.1	1.5	5.5
France	m	m	m	0.1	m	m	9.0	12.8
Germany	11.9	1.5	1.2	0.1	4.1	1.2	0.9	15.8
Greece	0.2	0.0	0.1	0.0	0.7	1.2	15.2	10.3
Hungary	1.5	0.1	1.3	1.0	1.0	0.9	7.8	16.8
Iceland	0.3	0.8	0.4	3.4	0.3	0.0	0.2	4.7
Ireland	0.1	0.0	0.0	1.4	0.0	0.2	2.2	9.9
Italy	0.1	1.2	0.8	0.2	1.6	0.5	7.0	8.1
Japan	2.1	0.6	4.0	3.8	1.9	0.2	6.5	0.7
Korea	0.9	0.5	1.3	0.9	0.0	0.2	6.2	3.5
Luxembourg	0.2	0.3	0.5	0.1	2.5	6.3	0.1	16.2
Mexico	0.2	0.1	0.0	0.1	13.0	4.9	1.4	14.9
New Zealand	1.3	0.2	1.8	1.5	1.1	0.1	3.3	9.7
Norway	0.2	1.8	0.2	3.1	0.4	0.0	1.9	7.6
Poland	0.6	0.7	1.3	0.2	0.6	3.0	8.8	12.4
Portugal	0.0	0.0	0.4	0.3	0.3	2.4	1.6	15.4
Spain	0.1	0.1	1.3	0.6	1.6	1.3	8.8	10.2
Sweden	0.7	0.4	0.1	1.7	0.4	0.4	0.0	8.8
Switzerland	2.0	1.6	0.1	0.1	0.5	0.8	0.1	15.9
United Kingdom	3.8	0.4	4.9	2.9	2.8	0.8	7.9	14.7
United States	1.5	0.5	1.1	3.5	0.0	0.0	7.6	11.3
OECD average	*1.7*	*0.5*	*1.2*	*1.3*	*1.3*	*1.0*	*4.5*	*10.8*
NON-OECD COUNTRIES								
Brazil	0.5	0.3	0.8	0.1	3.1	1.2	2.6	10.4
Latvia	0.3	1.6	0.4	0.6	0.7	0.0	2.4	5.8
Liechtenstein	22.7	1.7	9.6	0.0	0.1	5.3	0.2	11.1
Russian Federation	0.0	0.4	0.5	0.1	1.0	2.5	9.9	9.2
Netherlands[1]	2.8	0.3	6.8	0.5	1.8	0.1	1.0	11.6

1. Response rate is too low to ensure comparability (see Annex A3).

Annex A3: The PISA target population and the PISA samples

The PISA concept of "yield" and the definition of the PISA target population

PISA 2000 provides an assessment of the cumulative yield of education and learning at a point at which most young adults are still enrolled in initial education.

A major challenge for an international survey is to operationalise such a concept in ways that guarantee the international comparability of national target populations.

Differences between countries in the nature and extent of pre-primary education and care, the age of entry to formal schooling, and the institutional structure of educational systems do not allow the definition of internationally comparable grade levels of schooling. Consequently, international comparisons of educational performance typically define their populations with reference to a target age. Some previous international assessments have defined their target population on the basis of the grade level that provide maximum coverage of a particular age cohort. A disadvantage of this approach is that slight variations in the age distribution of students across grade levels often lead to the selection of different target grades in different countries, or between education systems within countries, raising serious questions about the comparability of results across, and at times within, countries. In addition, because not all students of the desired age are usually represented in grade-based samples, there may be a more serious potential bias in the results if the unrepresented students are typically enrolled in the next higher grade in some countries and the next lower grade in others. This would exclude students with potentially higher levels of performance in the former countries and students with potentially lower levels of performance in the latter.

In order to address this problem, PISA uses an age-based definition for its target population, *i.e.* a definition that is not tied to the institutional structures of national education systems: PISA assessed students who were aged between 15 years and 3 (complete) months and 16 years and 2 (complete) months at the beginning of the assessment period and who were enrolled in an educational institution, regardless of the grade levels or type of institution in which they were enrolled, and regardless of whether they were in full-time or part-time education (15-year-olds enrolled in Grade 6 or lower were excluded from PISA but, among the countries participating in PISA 2000, such students only exist in significant numbers in Brazil). Educational institutions are generally referred to as **schools** in this publication, although some educational institutions (in particular some types of vocational education establishments) may not be termed schools in certain countries. As expected from this definition, the average age of students across OECD countries was 15 years and 8 months, a value which varied by less than 0.2 years between participating countries).

As a result of this population definition, PISA 2000 makes statements about the knowledge and skills of a group of individuals who were born within a comparable reference period, but who may have undergone different educational experiences both within and outside schools. In PISA, these knowledge and skills are referred to as the **yield** of education at an age that is common across countries. Depending on countries' policies on school entry and promotion, these students may be distributed over a narrower or a wider range of grades. Furthermore, in some countries, students in PISA's target population are split between different education systems, tracks or streams.

If a country's scale scores in reading, scientific or mathematical literacy are significantly higher than those in another country, it cannot automatically be inferred that the schools or particular parts of the education system in the first country are more effective than those in the second. However, one can legitimately conclude that the cumulative impact of learning experiences in the first country, starting in early childhood and up to the age of 15 and embracing experiences both in school and at home, have resulted in higher outcomes in the literacy domains that PISA measures.

The PISA target population did not include residents attending schools in a foreign country.

To accommodate countries that desired grade-based results for the purpose of national analyses, PISA 2000 provided an international option to supplement age-based sampling with grade-based sampling.

Population coverage

All countries attempted to maximise the coverage of 15-year-olds enrolled in education in their national samples, including students enrolled in special educational institutions. As a result, PISA 2000 reached standards of population coverage that are unprecedented in international surveys of this kind.

The sampling standards used in PISA permitted countries to exclude up to a total of 5 per cent of the relevant population either by excluding schools or by excluding students within schools. All but three countries achieved the required coverage of at least 95 per cent of the national desired target population, and half of the countries achieved 98 per cent or more. The ceiling for population exclusions of 5 per cent ensures that potential bias resulting from exclusions is likely to remain within one standard error of sampling.

Exclusions within the above limits include:

— *At the school level*: *i)* schools which were geographically inaccessible or where the administration of the PISA assessment was not considered feasible; and *ii)* schools that provided teaching only for students in the categories defined under "within-school exclusions", such as schools for the blind. The percentage of 15-year-olds enrolled in such schools had to be less than 2.5 per cent of the nationally desired target population. The magnitude, nature and justification of school-level exclusions is documented in the *PISA 2000 Technical Report*.

Table A3.1
PISA target populations and samples

		Population and sample information												Coverage indices	
		(1)	(2)	(3)	(4)	(5)	(6)	(7)	(8)	(9)	(10)	(11)	(12)	(13)	(14)
		Total population of 15-years old	Total enrolled population of 15-years old	Total in national desired target population	School-level exclusions	Total in national desired target population after school exclusions and before within-school exclusions	Percentage of school-level exclusions	Number of participating students	Weighted number of participating students	Number of excluded students	Weighted number of excluded students	Within-school exclusion rate (%)	Overall exclusion rate (%)	Coverage index 1: Coverage of national desired population	Coverage index 2: Coverage of national enrolled population
		SF 2(a)	SF 2(b)	SF 3(a)	SF 3(b)	SF 3(c)	3(b)/3(a)	P	P		E	E/(P+E)		P/(P+E)* (3[c]/3[a])	P/(P+E)* (3[c]/2[b])
OECD COUNTRIES	Australia	266 878	248 908	248 738	2 850	245 888	1.15	5 176	229 152	63	2 688	1.16	2.29	0.98	0.98
	Austria	95 041	90 354	90 354	32	90 322	0.04	4 745	71 547	41	500	0.69	0.73	0.99	0.99
	Belgium	121 121	119 055	118 972	1 091	117 881	0.92	6 670	110 095	100	1 596	1.43	2.33	0.98	0.98
	Canada	403 803	396 423	391 788	2 035	389 990	0.52	29 687	348 481	1 584	16 197	4.44	4.94	0.95	0.94
	Czech Republic	134 627	132 508	132 508	2 181	130 327	1.65	5 365	125 639	13	297	0.24	1.88	0.98	0.98
	Denmark	53 693	52 161	52 161	345	51 816	0.66	4 235	47 786	119	1 195	2.44	3.08	0.97	0.97
	Finland	66 571	66 561	66 319	550	65 769	0.83	4 864	62 826	58	673	1.06	1.88	0.98	0.98
	France	788 387	788 387	750 460	17 728	732 732	2.36	4 673	730 494	59	8 208	1.11	3.45	0.97	0.92
	Germany	927 473	924 549	924 549	5 423	919 126	0.59	5 073	826 816	60	9 163	1.10	1.68	0.98	0.98
	Greece	128 175	124 656	124 187	200	123 987	0.16	3 644	111 363	21	682	0.61	0.77	0.99	0.99
	Hungary	120 759	115 325	115 325	0	115 325	0.00	4 887	107 460	34	765	0.71	0.71	0.99	0.99
	Iceland	4 062	4 044	4 044	18	4 026	0.45	3 372	3 869	79	79	2.01	2.44	0.98	0.98
	Ireland	65 339	64 370	63 572	1 021	62 551	1.61	3 854	56 209	134	1 734	2.99	4.55	0.95	0.94
	Italy	584 417	574 864	574 864	775	574 089	0.13	4 984	510 792	117	12 247	2.34	2.47	0.98	0.98
	Japan	1 490 000	1 485 269	1 459 296	34 124	1 425 172	2.34	5 256	1 446 596	0	0	0.00	2.34	0.98	0.96
	Korea	712 812	602 605	602 605	1 820	600 785	0.30	4 982	579 109	6	826	0.14	0.44	1.00	1.00
	Luxembourg	4 556	4 556	4 556	416	4 140	9.13	3 528	4 138	0	0	0.00	9.13	0.91	0.91
	Mexico	2 127 504	1 098 605	1 073 317	0	1 073 317	0.00	4 600	960 011	2	564	0.06	0.06	1.00	0.98
	New Zealand	54 220	51 464	51 464	976	50 488	1.90	3 667	46 757	137	1 590	3.29	5.12	0.95	0.95
	Norway	52 165	51 587	51 474	420	51 054	0.82	4 147	49 579	93	944	1.87	2.67	0.97	0.97
	Poland	665 500	643 528	643 528	56 524	587 004	8.78	3 654	542 005	53	5 484	1.00	9.70	0.90	0.90
	Portugal	132 325	127 165	127 165	0	127 165	0.00	4 585	99 998	122	2 777	2.70	2.70	0.97	0.97
	Spain	462 082	451 685	451 685	2 180	449 505	0.48	6 214	399 055	153	8 998	2.21	2.68	0.97	0.97
	Sweden	100 940	100 940	100 940	1 360	99 580	1.35	4 416	94 338	174	3 349	3.43	4.73	0.95	0.95
	Switzerland	81 350	79 232	79 232	954	78 278	1.20	6 100	72 010	62	822	1.13	2.32	0.98	0.98
	United Kingdom	731 743	705 875	705 875	17 674	688 201	2.50	9 340	643 041	219	15 990	2.43	4.87	0.95	0.95
	United States	3 876 000	3 836 000	3 836 000	0	3 836 000	0.00	3 846	3 121 874	211	132 543	4.07	4.07	0.96	0.96
NON-OECD COUNTRIES	Brazil	3 464 330	1 841 843	1 837 236	6 633	1 830 603	0.36	4 893	2 402 280	14	7 842	0.33	0.69	0.99	0.99
	Latvia	38 000	35 981	35 981	886	35 095	2.46	3 920	30 063	62	402	1.32	3.75	0.96	0.96
	Liechtenstein	415	326	326	0	326	0.00	314	325	2	2	0.61	0.61	0.99	0.99
	Russian Federation	2 268 566	2 259 985	2 259 985	10 867	2 249 118	0.48	6 701	1 968 131	22	4 960	0.25	0.73	0.99	0.99
	Netherlands[1]	178 924	178 924	178 924	7 800	171 124	4.36	2 503	157 327	1	23	0.01	4.37	0.96	0.96

For details see the *PISA 2000 Technical Report*.
1. Response rate is too low to ensure comparability (see Annex A3).

— *At the student level*: i) students who were considered in the professional opinion of the school principal or of other qualified staff members, to be educable mentally retarded or who had been defined as such through psychological tests (including students who were emotionally or mentally unable to follow the general instructions given in PISA); ii) students who were permanently and physically disabled in such a way that they could not perform in the PISA assessment situation (functionally disabled students who could respond were to be included in the assessment); and iii) non-native language speakers with less than one year of instruction in the language of the assessment. Students could not be excluded solely because of normal discipline problems. The percentage of 15-year-olds excluded within schools had to be less than 2.5 per cent of the *nationally desired target population*.

Table A3.1 describes the target population of the countries participating in PISA 2000. Further information on the target population and the implementation of PISA sampling standards can be found in the *PISA 2000 Technical Report*.

— **Column 1** shows the total number of 15-year-olds according to 2000 national population registers.

— **Column 2** shows the number of 15-year-olds enrolled in schools (as defined above), which is referred to as the *eligible population*.

— **Column 3** shows the national desired target population. As part of the school-level exclusions, countries were allowed to exclude up to 0.5 per cent of students *a priori* from the eligible population, essentially for practical reasons. The following a priory exclusions exceed this limit but were agreed with the PISA Consortium: **Canada** excluded 1.17 per cent of the eligible population, of which 0.73 per cent accounted for schools on Federal Indian reservations and 0.43 per cent were in the Yukon, Northwest, and Nunuvuk territories. In the case of **France,** the eligible population included students in the Territoires d'Outre-Mer, but because countries were not required to assess students in outlying territories not subject to the national education systems, it was permissible to exclude these students. French students in outlying *départements* were, as required, included in PISA 2000. **Ireland** excluded 1.61 per cent of the eligible population. This covered 1.15 per cent of students enrolled in schools not aided by the Department of Education and Science, 0.36 per cent in very small schools, and 0.12 per cent in "designated disadvantaged schools". **Japan** excluded 4.0 per cent of the eligible population, of which 1.7 per cent were students educated by mail and students in "other small streams (Bekka, Koto-senmon-gakko)", and 2.3 per cent were in part-time education ('Teiji-sei"). **Mexico** excluded 2.3 per cent of its eligible population in geographically remote schools. Among the non-OECD countries, **Brazil** excluded 15-year-olds enrolled in grades 1 to 6 which accounted for 16 per cent of 15-year-olds enrolled in Brazil. This exclusion was legitimate because such students are not part of the PISA target population. Subtracting the students excluded *a priori* from the eligible population results in the national desired target population in Column 3.

— **Column 4** shows the number of students enrolled in schools that were excluded from the national desired target population.

— **Column 5** shows the size of the national desired target population after subtracting the students enrolled in excluded schools. This is obtained by subtracting Column 4 from Column 3.

— **Column 6** shows the percentage of students enrolled in excluded schools. This is obtained by dividing Column 4 by Column 3.

— **Column 7** shows the *number of students participating in PISA 2000*. Note that this number does not account for 15-year-olds assessed as part of additional national options. These national options account for an additional 82 105 15-year-old students across all countries.

— **Column 8** shows the *weighted number of participating students*, *i.e.*, the number of students in the nationally defined target population that the PISA sample represents.

— Each country attempted to maximise the coverage of PISA's target population within the sampled schools. In the case of each sampled school, all eligible students, namely those 15 years of age, regardless of grade, were first listed. Sampled students who were to be excluded had still to be included in the sampling documentation, and a list drawn up stating the reason for their exclusion. **Column 9** indicates the number of *excluded students, i.e.* students who fell into one of the categories specified above. **Column 10** indicates the *weighted number of excluded students*, *i.e.*, the overall number of students in the nationally defined target population represented by the number of students excluded from the sample.

— **Column 11** shows the *percentage of students excluded within schools.* This is calculated as the weighted number of excluded students (Column 10) divided by the weighted number of excluded and participating students (Column 8 plus Column 10).

– **Column 12** shows the *overall exclusion rate* which represents the weighted percentage of the national desired target population excluded from PISA either through school-level exclusions or through the exclusion of students within schools. It is obtained by multiplying the percentage of school-level exclusions (Column 6) by 100, minus the percentage of students excluded within schools (Column 11) and adding the percentage of students excluded within schools (Column 11) to the result.

– **Column 13** presents an *index of the extent to which the national desired target population is covered by the PISA sample*. The index is expressed in per cent of the national desired target population covered. Luxembourg, Poland and Brazil are the only countries in which less than 95 per cent of the population that PISA seeks to cover is represented by the PISA samples. In the case of **Poland**, the exclusion rate is 10 per cent. This includes the 6.7 per cent of 15-year-olds enrolled in primary schools. The performance of these students in the PISA assessments can be expected to be lower than the performance of 15-year-olds in secondary schools, and this exclusion may imply that the performance of Polish students on the combined reading literacy scale is overestimated by two rank-order positions and on the scientific literacy scale by about three rank-order positions. No rank-order shifts are expected on the mathematical literacy scale. **Luxembourg** has an exclusion rate of 9.1 per cent, due largely to students instructed in languages other than the languages of assessment in Luxembourg. Permissible exclusions included 28 students with special needs; 297 students attending the European School; 32 students attending the American International School; 45 students attending other schools not under the authority of the Ministry of Education; and 14 students attending small schools. It is not expected that the exclusions in Luxembourg overestimate its rank-order position on the PISA scales. Among non-OECD countries, in **Brazil**, the school-level exclusion rate is 18 per cent but much of this is explained by 15-year-olds enrolled in Grade 5 and 6 who do not belong to the PISA target population. No rank order shifts are expected of the exclusions in Brazil. For further information see the *PISA 2000 Technical Report*.

– **Column 14** presents an *index of the extent to which 15-year-olds enrolled in schools are covered by the PISA sample*. The index measures the overall proportion of the national enrolled population that is covered by the non-excluded portion of the student sample. The index takes into account both school-level and student-level exclusions. Values close to 100 indicate that the PISA sample represents the entire education system as defined for PISA 2000. The index is the weighted number of participating students (Column 9) divided by the weighted number of participating and excluded students (Columns 9 plus Column 11), times the nationally defined target population (Column 5) divided by the national desired target population (times 100).

Sampling procedures and response rates

The accuracy of any survey results depends on the quality of the information on which national samples are based as well as on the sampling procedures. Quality standards, procedures, instruments and verification mechanisms were developed for PISA that ensured that national samples yielded comparable data and that the results could be compared with confidence.

Most PISA samples were designed as two-stage stratified samples (where countries applied different sampling designs, these are documented in the *PISA 2000 Technical Report*). The first stage consisted of sampling individual schools in which 15-year-old students were enrolled. Schools were sampled systematically with probabilities proportional to size, the measure of size being a function of the estimated number of eligible (15-year-old) students enrolled. A minimum of 150 schools were selected in each country (where this number existed), although the requirements for national analyses often required a somewhat larger sample. As the schools were sampled, replacement schools were simultaneously identified, in case a sampled school chose not to participate in PISA 2000.

In the case of **Iceland**, **Liechtenstein** and **Luxembourg**, all schools and all eligible students within schools were included in the sample. However, since not all students in the PISA samples were assessed in mathematical and scientific literacy, these national samples represent a complete census only in respect of the assessment of reading literacy, and a partial census of the assessment of mathematical and scientific literacy.

Experts from the PISA Consortium monitored the sample selection process in each participating country.

The second stage of the selection process sampled students within sampled schools. Once schools were selected, a list of each sampled school's 15-year-old students was prepared. From this list, 35 students were then selected with equal probability (all 15-year-old students were selected if fewer than 35 were enrolled).

Data quality standards in PISA required minimum participation rates for schools as well as for students. These standards were established to minimise the potential for response biases. In the case of countries meeting these standards, it is likely that any bias resulting from non-response will be negligible, *i.e.* typically smaller than the sampling error.

A minimum response rate of 85 per cent was required for the schools initially selected. Where the initial response rate of schools was between 65 and 85 per cent, however, an acceptable school response rate could still be achieved through the use of replacement schools. This procedure brought with it a risk of increased response bias. Participating countries were, therefore, encouraged to persuade as many of the schools in the original sample as possible to participate. Schools with a student participation rate between 25 and 50 per cent were not regarded as participating schools, but data from these schools were included in the database and contributed to the various estimations. Data from schools with a student participation rate of less than 25 per cent were excluded from the database.

PISA 2000 also required a minimum participation rate of 80 per cent of students within participating schools (original sample and replacement). This minimum participation rate had to be met at the national level, not necessarily by each participating school. Make-up sessions were required in schools in which too few students had participated in the original assessment

Table A3.2
Response rates

	Initial sample – before school replacement			Final sample – after school replacement			Final sample – students within schools after school replacement				
	(1)	(2)	(3)	(4)	(5)	(6)	(7)	(8)	(9)	(10)	(11)
	Weighted school participation rate before replacement (%)	Number of responding schools (weighted) by enrolment)	Number of schools sampled (responding and non-responding) (weighted by enrolment)	Weighted school participation rate after replacement (%)	Number of responding schools (weighted) by enrolment)	Number of schools sampled (responding and non-responding) (weighted by enrolment)	Weighted student participation rate after replacement (%)	Number of students assessed (weighted)	Number of students sampled (assessed and absent) (weighted)	Number of students assessed (unweighted)	Number of students sampled (assessed and absent) (unweighted)
OECD COUNTRIES											
Australia	80.95	197 639	244 157	93.65	228 668	244 175	84.24	161 607	191 850	5 154	6 173
Austria	99.38	86 062	86 601	100.00	86 601	86 601	91.64	65 562	71 547	4 745	5 164
Belgium	69.12	81 453	117 836	85.52	100 833	117 911	93.30	88 816	95 189	6 648	7 103
Canada	87.91	335 100	381 165	93.31	355 644	381 161	84.89	276 233	325 386	29 461	33 736
Czech Republic	95.30	123 345	129 422	99.01	128 551	129 841	92.76	115 371	124 372	5 343	5 769
Denmark	83.66	42 027	50 236	94.86	47 689	50 271	91.64	37 171	40 564	4 212	4 592
Finland	96.82	63 783	65 875	100.00	65 875	65 875	92.80	58 303	62 826	4 864	5 237
France	94.66	704 971	744 754	95.23	709 454	744 982	91.19	634 276	695 523	4 657	5 115
Germany	94.71	885 792	935 222	94.71	885 792	935 222	85.65	666 794	778 516	4 983	5 788
Greece	83.91	92 824	110 622	99.77	130 555	130 851	96.83	136 919	141 404	4 672	4 819
Hungary	98.67	209 153	211 969	98.67	209 153	211 969	95.31	100 807	105 769	4 883	5 111
Iceland	99.88	4 015	4 020	99.88	4 015	4 020	87.09	3 372	3 872	3 372	3 872
Ireland	85.56	53 164	62 138	87.53	54 388	62 138	85.59	42 088	49 172	3 786	4 424
Italy	97.90	550 932	562 763	100.00	562 755	562 755	93.08	475 446	510 792	4 984	5 369
Japan	82.05	1 165 576	1 420 533	90.05	1 279 121	1 420 533	96.34	1 267 367	1 315 462	5 256	5 450
Korea	100.00	589 018	589 018	100.00	589 018	589 018	98.84	572 767	579 470	4 982	5 045
Luxembourg	93.04	3 852	4 140	93.04	3 852	4 140	89.19	3 434	3 850	3 434	3 850
Mexico	92.69	985 745	1 063 524	100.00	1 063 524	1 063 524	93.95	903 100	961 283	4 600	4 882
New Zealand	77.65	39 328	50 645	86.37	43 744	50 645	88.23	35 616	40 369	3 667	4 163
Norway	85.95	43 207	50 271	92.25	46 376	50 271	89.28	40 908	45 821	4 147	4 665
Poland	79.11	432 603	546 842	83.21	455 870	547 847	87.70	393 675	448 904	3 639	4 169
Portugal	95.27	120 521	126 505	95.27	120 521	126 505	86.28	82 395	95 493	4 517	5 232
Spain	95.41	423 900	444 288	100.00	444 288	444 288	91.78	366 301	399 100	6 214	6 764
Sweden	99.96	100 534	100 578	99.96	100 534	100 578	87.96	82 956	94 312	4 416	5 017
Switzerland	91.81	89 208	97 162	95.84	92 888	96 924	95.13	65 677	69 037	6 084	6 389
United Kingdom	61.27	400 737	654 095	82.14	537 219	654 022	80.97	419 713	518 358	9 250	11 300
United States	56.42	2 013 101	3 567 961	70.33	2 503 666	3 559 661	84.99	1 801 229	2 119 392	3 700	4 320
NON-OECD COUNTRIES											
Brazil	97.38	2 425 608	2 490 788	97.96	2 439 152	2 489 942	87.15	1 463 000	1 678 789	4 885	5 613
Latvia	82.39	29 354	35 628	88.51	31 560	35 656	90.73	24 403	26 895	3 915	4 305
Liechtenstein	100.00	327	327	100.00	327	327	96.62	314	325	314	325
Russian Federation	98.84	4 445 841	4 498 235	99.29	4 466 335	4 498 235	96.21	1 903 348	1 978 266	6 701	6 981
Netherlands[1]	27.13	49 019	180 697	55.50	100 283	180 697	84.03	72 656	86 462	2 503	2 958

1. Response rate is too low to ensure comparability (see above).

sessions. Student participation rates were calculated over all participating schools, whether original sample or replacement schools, and from the participation of students in both the original assessment and any make-up sessions. A student who did not participate in the first assessment session was not regarded as a participant but was included in the international database and contributed to the statistics presented in this publication if he or she participated in the second assessment session and provided at least a description of his or her father's or mother's occupation.

Table A3.2 shows the response rates for students and schools, before and after replacement.

– **Column 1** shows the *weighted participation rate of schools before replacement.* This is obtained by dividing Column 2 by Column 3. The Netherlands, the United Kingdom and the United States did not meet PISA's requirements for response rates before replacement. In the **United Kingdom,** the initial response rate fell short of the requirements by 3.7 per cent and in the **United States** by 8.6 per cent. Both countries provided extensive evidence to the PISA Consortium that permitted an assessment of the expected performance of non-participating schools. On the basis of this evidence, PISA's Technical Advisory Group determined that the impact of these deviations on the assessment results was negligible. The results from these countries were included in all analyses. The initial response rate for the **Netherlands** was only 27 per cent. As a result, the PISA Consortium initiated supplementary analyses that confirmed that the data from the Netherlands might be sufficiently reliable and could be used in some relational analyses. Despite this conclusion, the response rate was too low to give confidence that the sample results reflect those for the national population reliably, with the level of accuracy and precision required in PISA 2000. Assuming negligible to moderate levels of bias due to non-response, the rank-order position of the Netherlands may be expected, with 95 per cent confidence, to lie between 2nd and 14th among countries on the combined reading literacy scale, between 1st and 4th on the mathematical literacy scale, and between 3rd and 14th on the scientific literacy scale (for further details see the *PISA 2000 Technical Report*). Mean performance scores for the Netherlands can, therefore, not be compared with those from other countries. In tables where the focus is on the comparison of mean scores, the Netherlands has been excluded. Where the performance of sub-groups is shown, only the relative differences in performance between the relevant sub-groups within the Netherlands should be considered, and the sub-group means should not be compared with those from other countries.

– **Column 2** shows the *weighted number of responding schools before school replacement* (weighted by student enrolment)

– **Column 3** shows the *weighted number of sampled schools before school replacement* (including both responding and nonresponding schools).

– **Column 4** shows the *weighted participation rate of schools after replacement.* This is obtained by dividing Column 5 by Column 6.

– **Column 5** shows the *weighted number of responding schools after school replacement* (weighted by student enrolment).

– **Column 6** shows the *weighted number of schools sampled after school replacement* (including both responding and nonresponding schools).

– **Column 7** shows the *weighted student participation rate after replacement.* This is obtained by dividing Column 8 by Column 9.

– **Column 8** shows the *weighted number of students assessed.*

– **Column 9** shows the *weighted number of students sampled* (including both students that were assessed and students who were absent on the day of the assessment).

– **Column 10** shows the *unweighted number of students assessed.*

– **Column 11** shows the *unweighted number of students sampled* (including both students that were assessed and students who were absent on the day of the assessment).

Annex A4: Standard errors, significance tests and multiple comparisons

The statistics in this report represent *estimates* of national performance based on samples of students rather than values that could be calculated if every student in every country had answered every question. Consequently, it is important to have measures of the degree of uncertainty of the estimates. In PISA 2000, each estimate has an associated degree of uncertainty, which is expressed through a *standard error*. The use of *confidence intervals* provides a way to make inferences about the population means and proportions in a manner that reflects the uncertainty associated with the sample estimates. From an observed sample statistic it can, under the assumption of a normal distribution, be inferred that the corresponding population result would lie within the confidence interval in 95 out of 100 replications of the measurement on different samples drawn from the same population.

In many cases, readers are primarily interested in whether a given value in a particular country is different from a second value in the same or another country, *e.g.*, whether females in a country perform better than males in the same country. In the tables and charts used in this report, differences are labelled as *statistically significant* when a difference of that size, or larger, would be observed less than 5 per cent of the time, if there was actually no difference in corresponding population values. Similarly, the risk of reporting as significant if there is, in fact, no correlation between to measures is contained at 5 per cent.

Although the probability that a particular difference will falsely be declared to be statistically significant is low (5 per cent) in each single comparison, the probability of making such an error increases when several comparisons are made simultaneously.

It is possible to make an adjustment for this which reduces to 5 per cent the maximum probability that differences will be falsely declared as statistically significant at least once among all the comparisons that are made. Such an adjustment, based on the Bonferroni method, has been incorporated into the multiple comparison charts in Chapters 2 and 3 since the likely interest of readers in those contexts is to compare a country's performance with that of all other countries.

For all other tables and charts readers should note that, if there were no real differences on a given measure, then the *multiple comparison* in conjunction with a 5 per cent significance level, would erroneously identify differences on 0.05 times the number of comparisons made, occasions. For example, even though the significance tests applied in PISA for identifying gender differences ensure that, for each country, the likelihood of identifying a gender difference erroneously is less than 5 per cent, a comparison showing differences for 27 countries would, on average, identify 1.4 cases (0.05 times 27) with significant gender differences, even if there were no real gender difference in any of the countries. The same applies for other statistics for which significance tests have been undertaken in this publication, such as correlations and regression coefficients.

Annex A5: Quality assurance

Quality assurance procedures were implemented in all parts of PISA.

The consistent quality and linguistic equivalence of the PISA assessment instruments were facilitated by providing countries with equivalent source versions of the assessment instruments in English and French and requiring countries (other than those assessing students in English and French) to prepare and consolidate two independent translations using both source versions. Precise translation guidelines were also supplied, including a description of what each item was intended to measure as well as instructions for the selection and training of the translators. For each country, the translation and format of the assessment instruments were verified by experts from the PISA Consortium (whose mother tongue was the language of instruction in the country concerned and knowledgeable about education systems) before they were used in the PISA Field Trial and Main Study. Experts from participating countries were required to translate and submit the marking guidelines for verification. For further information on the PISA translation procedures see the *PISA 2000 Technical Report*.

The survey was implemented through standardised procedures. The PISA Consortium provided comprehensive manuals that explained the implementation of the survey, including precise instructions for the work of School Co-ordinators and scripts for Test Administrators for use during the assessment sessions. The PISA Consortium verified the national translation and adaptation of these manuals.

To establish the credibility of PISA as valid and as unbiased and to encourage uniformity in the administration of the assessment sessions, Test Administrators in participating countries were selected using the following criteria: It was *required* that the Test Administrator not be the reading, mathematics, or science instructor of any students in the sessions he or she would administer for PISA; it was *recommended* that the Test Administrator not be a member of the staff of any school where he or she would administer PISA, and it was considered *preferable* that the Test Administrator not be a member of the staff of any school in the PISA sample. Participating countries organised an in-person training session for Test Administrators.

Participating countries were not allowed to introduce modifications in the assessment session script and instructions described in the Test Administrator Manual without prior approval by the PISA Consortium. Participating countries were required to ensure that: Test Administrators worked with the School Co-ordinator to prepare the assessment session, including updating student tracking forms and identifying excluded students; no extra time was given for the cognitive items (while it was permissible to give extra time for the student questionnaire); no instrument was administered before the two 1-hour parts of the cognitive session; Test Administrators recorded the student participation status on the student tracking forms and filled in a Session Report Form; no cognitive instrument was photocopied or lent by the Test Administrator to any person before the assessment session; and that Test Administrators returned the material to the national centre immediately after the assessment sessions.

National Project Managers were encouraged to organise a follow-up session when more than 15 per cent of the PISA sample was not able to attend the original assessment session.

National Quality Monitors from the PISA Consortium visited all national centres to review data-collection procedures. Finally, School Quality Monitors from the PISA Consortium visited a sample of 25 per cent of the schools during the assessment. For further information on the field operations see the *PISA 2000 Technical Report*.

Software specially designed for PISA 2000 facilitated data entry, detected common errors during data entry, and facilitated the process of data cleaning. Training sessions familiarised National Project Managers with these procedures.

For a description of the quality assurance procedures applied in PISA and the results see the *PISA 2000 Technical Report*.

Annex A6: Development of the PISA assessment instruments

The development of the PISA 2000 assessment instruments was an interactive process between the PISA Consortium, the various expert committees, OECD governments and national experts. A panel of international experts led, in close consultation with participating countries, the identification of the range of skills and competencies that were, in the respective assessment domains, considered to be crucial for an individual's capacity to fully participate in and contribute to a successful modern society. A description of the assessment domains – the assessment framework – was then used by participating countries, and other test development professionals, as they contributed assessment materials. The development of this assessment framework involved the following steps:

- development of a working definition for the domain and description of the assumptions that underlay that definition;
- evaluation of how to organise the set of tasks constructed in order to report to policy-makers and researchers on performance in each assessment domain among 15-year-old students in participating countries;
- identification of a set of key characteristics to be taken into account when assessment tasks were constructed for international use;
- operationalisation of the set of key characteristics to be used in test construction, with definitions based on existing literature and the experience of other large-scale assessments;
- validation of the variables, and assessment of the contribution which each made to the understanding of task difficulty in participating countries; and
- preparation of an interpretative scheme for the results.

The frameworks were agreed at both scientific and policy levels and subsequently provided the basis for the development of the assessment instruments (OECD, 1999a). They provided a common language and a vehicle for participating countries to develop a consensus as to the measurement goals of PISA.

Assessment items were then developed to reflect the intentions of the frameworks and were piloted in a Field Trial in all participating countries before a final set of items was selected for the PISA 2000 Main Study. Tables A6.1-A6-3 show the distribution of PISA 2000 assessment items by the various dimensions of the PISA frameworks.

Table A6.1
Distribution of items by the dimensions of the PISA framework for the assessment of reading literacy

	Number of items[1]	Number of multiple-choice items	Number of complex multiple-choice items	Number of closed constructed-response items	Number of open constructed-response items	Number of short response items
Distribution of reading items by text structure						
Continuous	89	42	3	3	34	7
Non-continuous	52	14	4	12	9	13
Total	*141*	*56*	*7*	*15*	*43*	*20*
Distribution of reading items by type of task (process)						
Interpreting texts	70	43	3	5	14	5
Reflection and evaluation	29	3	2	–	23	1
Retrieving information	42	10	2	10	6	14
Total	*141*	*56*	*7*	*15*	*43*	*20*
Distribution of reading items by text type						
Advertisements	4	–	–	–	1	3
Argumentative and persuasive	18	7	1	2	8	–
Charts and graphs	16	8	–	2	3	3
Descriptive	13	7	1	–	4	1
Expository	31	17	1	–	9	4
Forms	8	1	1	4	1	1
Injunctive	9	3	–	1	5	–
Maps	4	1	–	–	1	2
Narrative	18	8	–	–	8	2
Schematics	5	2	2	–	–	1
Tables	15	2	1	6	3	3
Total	*141*	*56*	*7*	*15*	*43*	*20*
Distribution of reading items by context						
Educational	39	22	4	1	4	8
Occupational	22	4	1	4	9	4
Personal	26	10	–	3	10	3
Public	54	20	2	7	20	5
Total	*141*	*56*	*7*	*15*	*43*	*20*

1. Nine items were eliminated from subsequent analysis.

Table A6.2
Distribution of items by the dimensions of the PISA framework for the assessment of mathematical literacy

	Number of items[1]	Number of multiple-choice items	Number of closed constructed-response items	Number of open constructed-response items
Distribution of mathematics items by 'main mathematical theme'				
Growth and change	18	6	9	3
Space and shape	14	5	9	–
Total	32	11	18	3
Distribution of mathematics items by mathematical strands				
Algebra	5	–	4	1
Functions	5	4	–	1
Geometry	8	3	5	–
Measurement	7	3	4	–
Number	1	–	1	–
Statistics	6	1	4	1
Total	32	11	18	3
Distribution of mathematics items by competency class				
Class 1	10	4	6	–
Class 2	20	7	11	2
Class 3	2	–	1	1
Total	32	11	18	3
Distribution of mathematics items by context				
Community	4	–	2	2
Educational	6	2	3	1
Occupational	3	1	2	–
Personal	12	6	6	–
Scientific	7	2	5	–
Total	32	11	18	3

1. One item was eliminated from subsequent analysis.

Due attention was paid to reflecting the national, cultural and linguistic variety among OECD countries. As part of this effort the PISA Consortium included, in addition to the items that were developed by the PISA Consortium, assessment material contributed by participating countries that the Consortium's multi-national team of test developers deemed appropriate given the requirements laid out by the PISA assessment frameworks. As a result, the item pool included assessment items from Australia, Austria, Belgium, Czech Republic, Denmark, Finland, France, Germany, Greece, Ireland, Italy, Japan, Korea, New Zealand, Norway, the Russian Federation, Sweden Switzerland the United Kingdom and the United States. The share of items submitted by participating countries was slightly more than 50 per cent in both the Field Trial and the Main Study.

Approximately 290 units and 1 169 items were contributed or developed for the Field Trial, including about 150 Reading Units comprising some 781 Reading Items. After the first consultation process, the Field Trial included 69 Reading Units with 342 Reading Items. Of these Reading Units, the stimulus material for 24 came from national contributions, 26 originated with the PISA Consortium, and 19 units came from the International Adult Literacy Survey (IALS). Material was drawn from IALS because countries wanted to have the possibility of comparing results from it with PISA results.

Each item included in the assessment pool was then rated by each country: for potential cultural, gender or other bias; for relevance to 15-year-olds in school and non-school contexts; and for familiarity and level of interest. A first consultation of countries on the item pool was undertaken as part of the process of developing the Field Trial assessment instruments. A second consultation was undertaken after the Field Trial to assist in the final selection of items for the Main Study and completed by a review of the assessment material by an international cultural fairness panel.

Following the Field Trial, in which all items were tested in all participating countries, test developers and expert groups considered a variety of aspects in selecting the items for the Main Study: *i)* the results from the Field Trial, *ii)* the outcome of the item review from countries, and *iii)* queries received during the Field Trial marking process. The test developers and expert groups selected a final set of items in October 1999 which, following a period of negotiation, was adopted by participating countries at both scientific and policy levels.

Table A6.3
Distribution of items by the dimensions of the PISA framework for the assessment of scientific literacy

	Number of items[1]	Number of multiple-choice items	Number of complex multiple-choice items	Number of closed constructed-response items	Number of open constructed-response items	Number of short response items
Distribution of science items by science processes						
Communicating to other valid conclusions from evidence and data	3	–	–	–	3	–
Demonstrating understanding scientific knowledge	15	9	1	–	3	2
Drawing and evaluating conclusions	7	1	2	1	3	–
Identifying evidence and data	5	2	1	–	2	–
Recognising questions	5	1	3	–	1	–
Total	*35*	*13*	*7*	*1*	*12*	*2*
Distribution of science items by science area						
Earth and environment	13	3	2	1	6	1
Life and health	13	6	1	–	5	1
Technology	9	4	4	–	1	–
Total	*35*	*13*	*7*	*1*	*12*	*2*
Distribution of science items by science application						
Atmospheric change	5	–	1	1	3	–
Biodiversity	1	1	–	–	–	–
Chemical and physical change	1	–	–	–	1	–
Earth and universe	5	3	1	–	–	1
Ecosystems	3	2	–	–	1	–
Energy transfer	4	–	2	–	2	–
Form and function	3	1	–	–	2	–
Genetic control	2	1	1	–	–	–
Geological change	1	–	–	–	1	–
Human biology	3	1	–	–	2	–
Physiological change	1	–	–	–	–	1
Structure of matter	6	4	2	–	–	–
Total	*35*	*13*	*7*	*1*	*12*	*2*
Distribution of science items by context						
Global	16	4	3	1	7	1
Historical	4	2	–	–	2	–
Personal	8	4	2	–	2	–
Public	7	3	2	–	1	1
Total	*35*	*13*	*7*	*1*	*12*	*2*

1. One item was eliminated from subsequent analysis.

The Main Study included 37 Reading Units with 141 items (counting different parts of questions as separate items). The stimulus for 14 of these units came from national contributions, the PISA Consortium was the source of the stimulus material for 13 units, and 10 units came from the International Adult Literacy Survey. The Main Study instruments also included 16 Mathematics Units (32 Items) and 14 Science Units (35 Items).

Five item types were used in the PISA assessment instruments:

— *Multiple-choice items*: these items required students to circle a letter to indicate one choice among four or five alternatives, each of which might be a number, a word, a phrase or a sentence. They were scored dichotomously.

— *Complex multiple-choice items*: in these items, the student made a series of choices, usually binary. Students indicated their answer by circling a word or short phrase (for example *yes* or *no*) for each point. These items were scored dichotomously for each choice, yielding the possibility of full or partial credit for the whole item.

— *Closed constructed-response items*: these items required students to construct their own responses, there being a limited range of acceptable answers. Most of these items were scored dichotomously with a few items included in the marking process.

— *Short response items*: as in the closed constructed-response items, students were to provide a brief answer, but there was a wide range of possible answers. These items were hand-marked, thus allowing for dichotomous as well as partial credit.

— *Open constructed-response items*: in these items, students constructed a longer response, allowing for the possibility of a broad range of divergent, individual responses and differing viewpoints. These items usually asked students to relate information or ideas in the stimulus text to their own experience or opinions, with the acceptability depending less on the position taken by the student than on the ability to use what they had read when justifying or explaining that position. Partial credit was often permitted for partially correct or less sophisticated answers, and all of these items were marked by hand.

PISA 2000 was designed to yield group-level information in a broad range of content. The PISA assessment of reading included material allowing for a total of 270 minutes of assessment time, of which 45 per cent was devoted to items requiring open-ended responses. The mathematics and science assessments included 60 minutes of assessment time, of which 35 per cent was assessed through open-ended items. Each student, however, sat assessments lasting a total of 120 minutes.

In order to cover the intended broad range of content while meeting the limit of 120 minutes of individual assessment time, the assessment in each domain was divided into clusters, organised into nine booklets. There were nine 30-minute reading clusters, four 15-minute mathematics clusters and four 15-minute science clusters. In PISA 2000, every student answered reading items, and over half the students answered items on science and mathematics.

This assessment design had a number of particular features. First, the majority of the reading material was presented in a balanced way in order to avoid position effects and to ensure that each item had equal weight in the assessment. Second, seven of the nine booklets began with reading, and all booklets contained at least 60 minutes of reading. Five booklets also contained science items, and five contained mathematics items. Third, PISA 2000 included a link between PISA and IALS through two reading blocks containing only IALS items, which were presented in six of the nine booklets. Finally, the design ensured that a representative sample of students responded to each block of items.

For further information on the development of the PISA assessment instruments and the PISA assessment design, see the *PISA 2000 Technical Report*.

Annex A7: Reliability of the marking of open-ended items

The process of marking open-ended items was an important step in ensuring the quality and comparability of results from PISA.

Detailed guidelines contributed to a marking process that was accurate and consistent across countries. The marking guidelines consisted of: marking manuals, training materials for recruiting markers, and workshop materials used for the training of national markers. Before national training, the PISA Consortium organised training sessions to present the material and train the marking co-ordinators from the participating countries, who were later responsible for training their national markers.

For each assessment item, the relevant marking manual described the aim of the question and how to code students' responses to each item. This description included the credit labels – full credit, partial credit or no credit – attached to the possible categories of responses. PISA 2000 also included a system of double-digit coding for the mathematics and science items in which the first digit represented the score and the second digit represented different strategies or approaches that students used to solve the problem. The second digit generated national profiles of student strategies and misconceptions. By way of illustration, the marking manuals also included real examples of students' responses (drawn from the Field Trial) accompanied by a rationale for their classification.

In each country, a sub-sample of assessment booklets was marked independently by four markers and examined by the PISA Consortium. In order to examine the consistency of this marking process in more detail within each country and to estimate the magnitude of the variance components associated with the use of markers, the PISA Consortium conducted an inter-marker reliability study on a sub-sample of assessment booklets. Homogeneity analysis was applied to the national sets of multiple marking and compared with the results of the Field Trial. For details see the *PISA 2000 Technical Report*.

At the between-country level, an inter-country reliability study was carried out on a sub-set of items. The aim was to check whether the marking given by national markers was of equal severity in each country, both overall and for particular items. In this process, independent marking of the original booklets was undertaken by trained multilingual staff and compared to the ratings by the national markers in the various countries. The results showed that very consistent marks were achieved across countries. The average index of "agreement" in the inter-country reliability study was 92 per cent (out of 41 796 student responses that were independently scored by the international verifiers). "Agreement" meant both cases where the international verifier agreed with at least three of the national markers and cases where the verifier disagreed with the national markers, but the adjudication undertaken by the PISA Consortium's test developers concluded that the national markers had given the correct mark. Only 8 countries had rates of agreement lower than 90 per cent. On average, marking was too harsh in 1 per cent of cases (with a maximum of 2.5 per cent in Latvia), and too lenient in 2.5 per cent of cases (with a maximum of 9.4 per cent in Latvia). A full description of this process and the results can be found in the *PISA 2000 Technical Report*.

ANNEX

DATA TABLES

Annex B1: Data tables for the chapters

Annex B2: Performance differences between the Flemish and French Communities of Belgium and the different linguistic communities in Switzerland

Annex B1: Data tables for the chapters

Table 2.1*a*
Percentage of students at each level of proficiency on the combined reading literacy scale

		Below Level 1 (less than 335 score points)		Level 1 (from 335 to 407 score points)		Level 2 (from 408 to 480 score points)		Level 3 (from 481 to 552 score points)		Level 4 (from 553 to 625 score points)		Level 5 (above 625 score points)	
		%	S.E.	%	S.E.	%	S.E.	%	S.E.	%	S.E.	%	S.E.
OECD COUNTRIES	Australia	3.3	(0.5)	9.1	(0.8)	19.0	(1.1)	25.7	(1.1)	25.3	(0.9)	17.6	(1.2)
	Austria	4.4	(0.4)	10.2	(0.6)	21.7	(0.9)	29.9	(1.2)	24.9	(1.0)	8.8	(0.8)
	Belgium	7.7	(1.0)	11.3	(0.7)	16.8	(0.7)	25.8	(0.9)	26.3	(0.9)	12.0	(0.7)
	Canada	2.4	(0.3)	7.2	(0.3)	18.0	(0.4)	28.0	(0.5)	27.7	(0.6)	16.8	(0.5)
	Czech Republic	6.1	(0.6)	11.4	(0.7)	24.8	(1.2)	30.9	(1.1)	19.8	(0.8)	7.0	(0.6)
	Denmark	5.9	(0.6)	12.0	(0.7)	22.5	(0.9)	29.5	(1.0)	22.0	(0.9)	8.1	(0.5)
	Finland	1.7	(0.5)	5.2	(0.4)	14.3	(0.7)	28.7	(0.8)	31.6	(0.9)	18.5	(0.9)
	France	4.2	(0.6)	11.0	(0.8)	22.0	(0.8)	30.6	(1.0)	23.7	(0.9)	8.5	(0.6)
	Germany	9.9	(0.7)	12.7	(0.6)	22.3	(0.8)	26.8	(1.0)	19.4	(1.0)	8.8	(0.5)
	Greece	8.7	(1.2)	15.7	(1.4)	25.9	(1.4)	28.1	(1.7)	16.7	(1.4)	5.0	(0.7)
	Hungary	6.9	(0.7)	15.8	(1.2)	25.0	(1.1)	28.8	(1.3)	18.5	(1.1)	5.1	(0.8)
	Iceland	4.0	(0.3)	10.5	(0.6)	22.0	(0.8)	30.8	(0.9)	23.6	(1.1)	9.1	(0.7)
	Ireland	3.1	(0.5)	7.9	(0.8)	17.9	(0.9)	29.7	(1.1)	27.1	(1.1)	14.2	(0.8)
	Italy	5.4	(0.9)	13.5	(0.9)	25.6	(1.0)	30.6	(1.0)	19.5	(1.1)	5.3	(0.5)
	Japan	2.7	(0.6)	7.3	(1.1)	18.0	(1.3)	33.3	(1.3)	28.8	(1.7)	9.9	(1.1)
	Korea	0.9	(0.2)	4.8	(0.6)	18.6	(0.9)	38.8	(1.1)	31.1	(1.2)	5.7	(0.6)
	Luxembourg	14.2	(0.7)	20.9	(0.8)	27.5	(1.3)	24.6	(1.1)	11.2	(0.5)	1.7	(0.3)
	Mexico	16.1	(1.2)	28.1	(1.4)	30.3	(1.1)	18.8	(1.2)	6.0	(0.7)	0.9	(0.2)
	New Zealand	4.8	(0.5)	8.9	(0.5)	17.2	(0.9)	24.6	(1.1)	25.8	(1.1)	18.7	(1.0)
	Norway	6.3	(0.6)	11.2	(0.8)	19.5	(0.8)	28.1	(0.8)	23.7	(0.9)	11.2	(0.7)
	Poland	8.7	(1.0)	14.6	(1.0)	24.1	(1.4)	28.2	(1.3)	18.6	(1.3)	5.9	(1.0)
	Portugal	9.6	(1.0)	16.7	(1.2)	25.3	(1.0)	27.5	(1.2)	16.8	(1.1)	4.2	(0.5)
	Spain	4.1	(0.5)	12.2	(0.9)	25.7	(0.7)	32.8	(1.0)	21.1	(0.9)	4.2	(0.5)
	Sweden	3.3	(0.4)	9.3	(0.6)	20.3	(0.7)	30.4	(1.0)	25.6	(1.0)	11.2	(0.7)
	Switzerland	7.0	(0.7)	13.3	(0.9)	21.4	(1.0)	28.0	(1.0)	21.0	(1.0)	9.2	(1.0)
	United Kingdom	3.6	(0.4)	9.2	(0.5)	19.6	(0.7)	27.5	(0.9)	24.4	(0.9)	15.6	(1.0)
	United States	6.4	(1.2)	11.5	(1.2)	21.0	(1.2)	27.4	(1.3)	21.5	(1.4)	12.2	(1.4)
	OECD total	*6.2*	*(0.4)*	*12.1*	*(0.4)*	*21.8*	*(0.4)*	*28.6*	*(0.4)*	*21.8*	*(0.4)*	*9.4*	*(0.4)*
	OECD average	*6.0*	*(0.1)*	*11.9*	*(0.2)*	*21.7*	*(0.2)*	*28.7*	*(0.2)*	*22.3*	*(0.2)*	*9.5*	*(0.1)*
NON-OECD COUNTRIES	Brazil	23.3	(1.4)	32.5	(1.2)	27.7	(1.3)	12.9	(1.1)	3.1	(0.5)	0.6	(0.2)
	Latvia	12.7	(1.3)	17.9	(1.3)	26.3	(1.1)	25.2	(1.3)	13.8	(1.1)	4.1	(0.6)
	Liechtenstein	7.6	(1.5)	14.5	(2.1)	23.2	(2.9)	30.1	(3.4)	19.5	(2.2)	5.1	(1.6)
	Russian Federation	9.0	(1.0)	18.5	(1.1)	29.2	(0.8)	26.9	(1.1)	13.3	(1.0)	3.2	(0.5)

Table 2.1*b*

Percentage of students at each level of proficiency on the reading / retrieving information scale

		Proficiency levels										
		Below Level 1 (less than 335 score points)		Level 1 (from 335 to 407 score points)		Level 2 (from 408 to 480 score points)		Level 3 (from 481 to 552 score points)		Level 4 from 553 to 625 score points)		Level 5 (above 625 score points)	
		%	S.E.	%	S.E.	%	S.E.	%	S.E.	%	S.E.	%	S.E.
OECD COUNTRIES	Australia	3.7	(0.4)	8.8	(0.8)	17.2	(1.0)	24.7	(1.0)	24.7	(1.0)	20.9	(1.2)
	Austria	5.2	(0.5)	11.1	(0.7)	22.6	(0.9)	29.1	(1.0)	23.5	(0.9)	8.6	(0.7)
	Belgium	9.1	(1.0)	10.3	(0.6)	15.4	(0.7)	22.2	(0.8)	25.2	(0.9)	17.8	(0.7)
	Canada	3.4	(0.3)	8.4	(0.3)	18.5	(0.5)	26.8	(0.6)	25.5	(0.6)	17.4	(0.6)
	Czech Republic	9.0	(0.7)	13.8	(0.8)	24.5	(0.8)	27.1	(0.8)	17.6	(1.0)	8.0	(0.6)
	Denmark	6.9	(0.7)	12.4	(0.6)	21.0	(0.8)	27.8	(0.8)	21.7	(0.8)	10.2	(0.7)
	Finland	2.3	(0.5)	5.6	(0.4)	13.9	(0.9)	24.3	(1.2)	28.3	(0.8)	25.5	(0.9)
	France	4.9	(0.6)	10.5	(0.9)	19.2	(0.8)	27.0	(0.9)	25.2	(1.1)	13.2	(1.0)
	Germany	10.5	(0.8)	12.6	(0.7)	21.8	(0.9)	26.8	(1.1)	19.0	(1.0)	9.3	(0.5)
	Greece	15.1	(1.6)	17.9	(1.1)	25.3	(1.2)	24.1	(1.2)	13.5	(1.0)	4.1	(0.6)
	Hungary	10.2	(0.9)	15.7	(1.1)	23.0	(0.9)	25.3	(1.2)	18.1	(1.2)	7.8	(0.9)
	Iceland	6.5	(0.4)	12.0	(0.6)	21.6	(0.9)	28.4	(1.2)	21.0	(0.9)	10.6	(0.6)
	Ireland	4.0	(0.5)	8.7	(0.7)	18.2	(0.9)	28.1	(1.0)	25.8	(0.9)	15.2	(0.8)
	Italy	7.6	(0.8)	13.4	(0.8)	23.4	(0.9)	28.1	(0.9)	19.2	(0.9)	8.4	(0.6)
	Japan	3.8	(0.8)	7.8	(1.0)	17.3	(1.1)	29.8	(1.1)	26.7	(1.3)	14.5	(1.2)
	Korea	1.5	(0.3)	6.3	(0.6)	18.6	(0.9)	32.4	(1.0)	29.7	(1.0)	11.6	(0.8)
	Luxembourg	17.9	(0.7)	21.1	(0.9)	25.4	(0.8)	22.2	(0.9)	11.1	(0.8)	2.4	(0.4)
	Mexico	26.1	(1.4)	25.6	(1.3)	25.5	(1.0)	15.8	(1.1)	5.8	(0.8)	1.2	(0.3)
	New Zealand	5.6	(0.5)	8.6	(0.6)	15.7	(0.7)	22.7	(1.2)	25.2	(1.1)	22.2	(1.0)
	Norway	7.4	(0.6)	10.8	(0.6)	19.5	(0.9)	26.7	(1.3)	23.0	(1.2)	12.6	(0.8)
	Poland	11.5	(1.1)	15.1	(1.0)	22.7	(1.2)	24.5	(1.1)	18.2	(1.3)	8.0	(1.2)
	Portugal	13.9	(1.3)	18.2	(1.1)	24.3	(1.0)	24.5	(1.2)	14.8	(1.0)	4.4	(0.5)
	Spain	6.4	(0.6)	13.9	(1.0)	25.6	(0.8)	30.5	(1.0)	19.0	(0.9)	4.8	(0.4)
	Sweden	4.9	(0.4)	10.2	(0.8)	19.9	(0.9)	26.8	(0.9)	23.5	(0.9)	14.6	(0.8)
	Switzerland	8.8	(0.8)	12.5	(0.8)	19.3	(0.9)	25.9	(1.1)	21.6	(0.9)	12.1	(1.1)
	United Kingdom	4.4	(0.4)	9.4	(0.6)	18.6	(0.7)	26.9	(0.9)	24.1	(0.9)	16.5	(0.9)
	United States	8.3	(1.4)	12.2	(1.1)	20.7	(1.0)	25.6	(1.2)	20.8	(1.4)	12.6	(1.4)
	OECD total	*8.5*	*(0.4)*	*12.4*	*(0.3)*	*20.7*	*(0.3)*	*26.1*	*(0.4)*	*21.0*	*(0.4)*	*11.4*	*(0.4)*
	OECD average	*8.1*	*(0.2)*	*12.3*	*(0.2)*	*20.7*	*(0.2)*	*26.1*	*(0.2)*	*21.2*	*(0.2)*	*11.6*	*(0.2)*
NON-OECD COUNTRIES	Brazil	37.1	(1.6)	30.4	(1.3)	20.5	(1.2)	9.4	(0.6)	2.2	(0.5)	0.4	(0.2)
	Latvia	17.1	(1.6)	17.7	(1.2)	23.6	(1.1)	21.6	(1.0)	14.1	(1.1)	5.9	(0.7)
	Liechtenstein	8.6	(1.6)	12.6	(2.1)	19.9	(2.5)	28.3	(3.6)	21.8	(3.6)	8.8	(1.6)
	Russian Federation	14.4	(1.3)	19.4	(0.8)	26.0	(0.8)	22.9	(1.0)	12.4	(0.9)	4.9	(0.6)

Table 2.1c

Percentage of students at each level of proficiency on the reading / interpreting texts scale

		Proficiency levels										
		Below Level 1 (less than 335 score points)		Level 1 (from 335 to 407 score points)		Level 2 (from 408 to 480 score points)		Level 3 (from 481 to 552 score points)		Level 4 from 553 to 625 score points)		Level 5 (above 625 score points)	
		%	S.E.	%	S.E.	%	S.E.	%	S.E.	%	S.E.	%	S.E.
OECD COUNTRIES	Australia	3.7	(0.4)	9.7	(0.7)	19.3	(1.0)	25.6	(1.1)	24.0	(1.2)	17.7	(1.3)
	Austria	4.0	(0.4)	10.7	(0.6)	21.8	(1.0)	30.0	(1.1)	23.8	(1.0)	9.7	(0.8)
	Belgium	6.3	(0.7)	11.5	(0.8)	17.8	(0.7)	25.3	(0.9)	25.7	(0.9)	13.4	(0.7)
	Canada	2.4	(0.2)	7.8	(0.4)	18.4	(0.4)	28.6	(0.6)	26.4	(0.5)	16.4	(0.5)
	Czech Republic	5.4	(0.6)	10.7	(0.6)	23.2	(0.9)	30.3	(0.7)	21.7	(0.9)	8.7	(0.7)
	Denmark	6.2	(0.6)	12.6	(0.8)	23.5	(0.8)	28.7	(0.9)	20.8	(1.0)	8.2	(0.7)
	Finland	1.9	(0.5)	5.1	(0.4)	13.8	(0.8)	26.0	(0.9)	29.7	(0.9)	23.6	(0.9)
	France	4.0	(0.5)	11.5	(0.8)	21.8	(0.9)	30.3	(1.0)	23.4	(1.1)	9.0	(0.7)
	Germany	9.3	(0.8)	13.2	(0.9)	22.0	(1.0)	26.4	(1.0)	19.7	(0.7)	9.5	(0.5)
	Greece	6.6	(1.1)	16.0	(1.4)	27.3	(1.2)	30.1	(1.5)	16.2	(1.2)	3.7	(0.6)
	Hungary	6.0	(0.7)	15.9	(1.3)	26.0	(1.1)	29.9	(1.3)	17.9	(1.1)	4.3	(0.6)
	Iceland	3.6	(0.4)	10.1	(0.6)	21.1	(0.7)	29.2	(1.1)	24.4	(1.0)	11.7	(0.6)
	Ireland	3.5	(0.5)	8.3	(0.7)	18.2	(0.9)	28.8	(1.1)	26.1	(1.1)	15.2	(1.0)
	Italy	4.1	(0.7)	13.1	(0.8)	26.9	(1.2)	32.3	(1.3)	18.8	(0.9)	4.8	(0.4)
	Japan	2.4	(0.7)	7.9	(1.1)	19.7	(1.4)	34.2	(1.5)	27.5	(1.6)	8.3	(1.0)
	Korea	0.7	(0.2)	4.8	(0.6)	19.5	(1.0)	38.7	(1.4)	30.5	(1.2)	5.8	(0.6)
	Luxembourg	13.8	(0.6)	19.5	(0.9)	27.7	(1.0)	24.3	(0.9)	12.3	(0.6)	2.3	(0.4)
	Mexico	14.5	(0.9)	31.0	(1.5)	32.3	(1.3)	17.6	(1.2)	4.4	(0.6)	0.3	(0.1)
	New Zealand	5.2	(0.5)	9.9	(0.7)	17.7	(0.7)	23.9	(1.1)	23.9	(0.9)	19.5	(0.9)
	Norway	6.3	(0.5)	11.3	(0.8)	20.2	(0.7)	27.7	(0.8)	23.0	(0.9)	11.5	(0.7)
	Poland	7.5	(0.9)	14.6	(0.9)	24.5	(1.4)	28.7	(1.3)	18.7	(1.3)	6.0	(0.9)
	Portugal	7.8	(0.9)	16.9	(1.3)	26.9	(1.1)	27.9	(1.2)	16.6	(1.1)	4.0	(0.5)
	Spain	3.8	(0.5)	12.6	(0.9)	26.5	(0.8)	32.8	(1.1)	20.1	(0.8)	4.1	(0.4)
	Sweden	3.1	(0.3)	9.5	(0.6)	19.7	(0.8)	28.6	(1.0)	25.4	(1.0)	13.7	(0.8)
	Switzerland	6.7	(0.6)	12.9	(0.9)	22.3	(0.9)	27.4	(1.1)	21.4	(1.0)	9.3	(1.1)
	United Kingdom	4.4	(0.5)	11.0	(0.6)	21.1	(0.7)	26.6	(0.7)	22.9	(0.9)	14.0	(0.9)
	United States	6.3	(1.2)	11.6	(1.1)	21.7	(1.2)	26.5	(1.2)	21.2	(1.5)	12.7	(1.3)
	OECD total	*5.8*	*(0.4)*	*12.6*	*(0.4)*	*22.7*	*(0.4)*	*28.4*	*(0.4)*	*21.2*	*(0.4)*	*9.3*	*(0.4)*
	OECD average	*5.5*	*(0.1)*	*12.2*	*(0.2)*	*22.3*	*(0.2)*	*28.4*	*(0.3)*	*21.7*	*(0.2)*	*9.9*	*(0.1)*
NON-OECD COUNTRIES	Brazil	21.5	(1.3)	33.2	(1.4)	28.1	(1.5)	13.4	(1.0)	3.3	(0.5)	0.6	(0.2)
	Latvia	11.1	(1.2)	18.6	(1.4)	27.2	(1.3)	26.6	(1.2)	13.1	(1.2)	3.4	(0.6)
	Liechtenstein	6.6	(1.7)	15.2	(2.7)	23.9	(3.3)	29.7	(3.0)	19.8	(2.3)	4.9	(1.2)
	Russian Federation	8.0	(0.9)	18.0	(0.8)	28.3	(0.9)	27.8	(1.1)	14.2	(1.1)	3.8	(0.6)

Table 2.1*d*
Percentage of students at each level of proficiency on the reading / reflection and evaluation scale

		Proficiency levels											
		Below Level 1 (less than 335 score points)		Level 1 (from 335 to 407 score points)		Level 2 (from 408 to 480 score points)		Level 3 (from 481 to 552 score points)		Level 4 from 553 to 625 score points)		Level 5 (above 625 score points)	
		%	S.E.	%	S.E.	%	S.E.	%	S.E.	%	S.E.	%	S.E.
OECD COUNTRIES	Australia	3.4	(0.4)	9.1	(0.7)	19.0	(0.9)	26.9	(1.2)	25.6	(1.2)	15.9	(1.2)
	Austria	5.0	(0.5)	10.1	(0.5)	20.0	(0.9)	28.2	(1.1)	25.2	(1.3)	11.6	(1.0)
	Belgium	9.8	(1.2)	11.5	(0.8)	17.5	(0.7)	26.2	(1.0)	24.3	(0.8)	10.7	(0.6)
	Canada	2.1	(0.2)	6.6	(0.4)	16.2	(0.4)	27.5	(0.5)	28.3	(0.5)	19.4	(0.5)
	Czech Republic	7.5	(0.7)	13.2	(0.9)	24.9	(0.9)	28.3	(0.8)	19.0	(1.0)	7.2	(0.7)
	Denmark	6.2	(0.6)	11.7	(0.7)	21.3	(0.8)	29.0	(1.0)	21.9	(0.8)	9.9	(0.8)
	Finland	2.4	(0.5)	6.4	(0.5)	16.2	(0.7)	30.3	(0.9)	30.6	(0.9)	14.1	(0.7)
	France	5.9	(0.7)	12.5	(0.8)	23.4	(0.8)	28.7	(1.1)	21.0	(1.0)	8.6	(0.6)
	Germany	13.0	(0.8)	13.5	(0.7)	20.4	(1.1)	24.0	(0.9)	18.9	(0.8)	10.2	(0.6)
	Greece	8.9	(1.1)	13.3	(1.1)	21.6	(1.1)	23.8	(1.1)	19.8	(1.2)	12.5	(1.1)
	Hungary	8.2	(0.8)	15.2	(1.3)	23.6	(1.3)	27.9	(1.1)	18.8	(1.2)	6.3	(0.8)
	Iceland	4.8	(0.5)	11.0	(0.6)	23.1	(0.8)	30.9	(0.9)	22.1	(0.8)	8.1	(0.5)
	Ireland	2.4	(0.4)	6.6	(0.8)	16.8	(1.0)	30.3	(1.0)	29.5	(1.0)	14.5	(0.9)
	Italy	8.0	(0.9)	14.3	(1.1)	24.1	(1.3)	28.0	(1.0)	19.1	(0.8)	6.5	(0.6)
	Japan	3.9	(0.8)	7.9	(0.9)	16.6	(1.1)	28.2	(1.1)	27.3	(1.2)	16.2	(1.4)
	Korea	1.2	(0.3)	5.4	(0.5)	19.0	(1.0)	36.7	(1.2)	29.5	(1.2)	8.2	(0.7)
	Luxembourg	17.0	(0.7)	17.9	(0.8)	25.4	(1.1)	23.3	(0.8)	12.9	(0.5)	3.6	(0.4)
	Mexico	16.0	(0.9)	20.7	(1.0)	25.6	(0.9)	21.1	(0.8)	11.8	(0.9)	4.8	(0.6)
	New Zealand	4.5	(0.5)	8.5	(0.6)	17.5	(0.9)	25.4	(1.2)	25.6	(1.0)	18.5	(1.2)
	Norway	7.3	(0.7)	10.8	(0.7)	18.8	(0.8)	27.1	(0.9)	23.8	(1.0)	12.2	(0.8)
	Poland	11.0	(1.1)	14.4	(1.2)	22.6	(1.8)	26.2	(1.4)	18.1	(1.3)	7.7	(1.1)
	Portugal	9.1	(0.9)	15.0	(1.2)	24.4	(1.2)	26.2	(1.1)	19.0	(1.1)	6.4	(0.7)
	Spain	3.9	(0.4)	11.0	(0.7)	22.1	(1.1)	31.1	(1.2)	23.6	(0.9)	8.4	(0.6)
	Sweden	4.3	(0.4)	10.2	(0.6)	20.7	(0.7)	30.4	(0.8)	24.3	(0.9)	10.1	(0.7)
	Switzerland	9.9	(0.9)	13.6	(0.9)	21.6	(1.1)	25.2	(1.0)	19.1	(0.9)	10.5	(1.1)
	United Kingdom	2.6	(0.3)	7.2	(0.6)	17.4	(0.7)	26.7	(0.7)	26.5	(0.9)	19.6	(1.0)
	United States	6.2	(1.1)	11.2	(1.2)	20.6	(1.1)	27.3	(1.1)	22.2	(1.7)	12.5	(1.3)
	OECD total	*6.9*	*(0.3)*	*11.5*	*(0.3)*	*20.6*	*(0.3)*	*27.3*	*(0.4)*	*22.3*	*(0.5)*	*11.5*	*(0.4)*
	OECD average	*6.8*	*(0.1)*	*11.4*	*(0.2)*	*20.7*	*(0.2)*	*27.6*	*(0.2)*	*22.5*	*(0.2)*	*10.9*	*(0.2)*
NON-OECD COUNTRIES	Brazil	18.7	(1.2)	27.2	(1.1)	29.3	(1.1)	17.7	(1.0)	6.0	(0.7)	1.2	(0.2)
	Latvia	15.6	(1.5)	16.6	(1.1)	23.4	(1.6)	24.1	(1.6)	14.2	(1.2)	6.0	(0.9)
	Liechtenstein	11.9	(2.0)	16.1	(3.1)	24.4	(3.3)	24.8	(2.8)	17.0	(2.9)	5.8	(1.3)
	Russian Federation	11.7	(1.1)	19.3	(1.0)	28.1	(1.1)	24.9	(0.9)	12.3	(0.8)	3.7	(0.5)

Table 2.2a

Multiple comparisons of mean performance on the reading / retrieving information scale

Country	Mean	S.E.	Finland	Australia	New Zealand	Canada	Korea	Japan	Ireland	United Kingdom	Sweden	France	Belgium	Norway	Austria	Iceland	United States	Switzerland	Denmark	Liechtenstein	Italy	Spain	Germany	Czech Republic	Hungary	Poland	Portugal	Russian Fed.	Latvia	Greece	Luxembourg	Mexico	Brazil
			556	536	535	530	530	526	524	523	516	515	515	505	502	500	499	498	498	492	488	483	483	481	478	475	455	451	451	450	433	402	365
			(2.8)	(3.7)	(2.8)	(1.7)	(2.5)	(5.5)	(3.3)	(2.5)	(2.4)	(3.0)	(3.9)	(2.9)	(2.3)	(1.6)	(7.4)	(4.4)	(2.8)	(4.9)	(3.1)	(3.0)	(2.4)	(2.7)	(4.4)	(5.0)	(4.9)	(4.9)	(5.7)	(5.4)	(1.6)	(3.9)	(3.4)
Finland	556	(2.8)	□	▲	▲	▲	▲	▲	▲	▲	▲	▲	▲	▲	▲	▲	▲	▲	▲	▲	▲	▲	▲	▲	▲	▲	▲	▲	▲	▲	▲	▲	▲
Australia	536	(3.7)	▽	□	○	○	○	○	○	○	▲	▲	▲	▲	▲	▲	▲	▲	▲	▲	▲	▲	▲	▲	▲	▲	▲	▲	▲	▲	▲	▲	▲
New Zealand	535	(2.8)	▽	○	□	○	○	○	○	○	▲	▲	▲	▲	▲	▲	▲	▲	▲	▲	▲	▲	▲	▲	▲	▲	▲	▲	▲	▲	▲	▲	▲
Canada	530	(1.7)	▽	○	○	□	○	○	○	○	▲	▲	▲	▲	▲	▲	▲	▲	▲	▲	▲	▲	▲	▲	▲	▲	▲	▲	▲	▲	▲	▲	▲
Korea	530	(2.5)	▽	○	○	○	□	○	○	○	▲	▲	▲	▲	▲	▲	▲	▲	▲	▲	▲	▲	▲	▲	▲	▲	▲	▲	▲	▲	▲	▲	▲
Japan	526	(5.5)	▽	○	○	○	○	□	○	○	○	○	○	▲	▲	▲	○	▲	▲	▲	▲	▲	▲	▲	▲	▲	▲	▲	▲	▲	▲	▲	▲
Ireland	524	(3.3)	▽	○	○	○	○	○	□	○	○	○	○	▲	▲	▲	▲	▲	▲	▲	▲	▲	▲	▲	▲	▲	▲	▲	▲	▲	▲	▲	▲
United Kingdom	523	(2.5)	▽	○	○	○	○	○	○	□	○	○	○	▲	▲	▲	▲	▲	▲	▲	▲	▲	▲	▲	▲	▲	▲	▲	▲	▲	▲	▲	▲
Sweden	516	(2.4)	▽	▽	▽	▽	▽	○	○	○	□	○	○	○	▲	▲	○	▲	▲	▲	▲	▲	▲	▲	▲	▲	▲	▲	▲	▲	▲	▲	▲
France	515	(3.0)	▽	▽	▽	▽	▽	○	○	○	○	□	○	○	○	○	○	○	○	▲	▲	▲	▲	▲	▲	▲	▲	▲	▲	▲	▲	▲	▲
Belgium	515	(3.9)	▽	▽	▽	▽	▽	○	○	○	○	○	□	○	○	○	○	○	○	▲	▲	▲	▲	▲	▲	▲	▲	▲	▲	▲	▲	▲	▲
Norway	505	(2.9)	▽	▽	▽	▽	▽	▽	▽	▽	○	○	○	□	○	○	○	○	○	○	▲	▲	▲	▲	▲	▲	▲	▲	▲	▲	▲	▲	▲
Austria	502	(2.3)	▽	▽	▽	▽	▽	▽	▽	▽	▽	○	○	○	□	○	○	○	○	○	○	▲	▲	▲	▲	▲	▲	▲	▲	▲	▲	▲	▲
Iceland	500	(1.6)	▽	▽	▽	▽	▽	▽	▽	▽	▽	○	○	○	○	□	○	○	○	○	○	○	○	○	▲	▲	▲	▲	▲	▲	▲	▲	▲
United States	499	(7.4)	▽	▽	▽	▽	▽	○	▽	▽	○	○	○	○	○	○	□	○	○	○	○	○	○	○	○	○	▲	▲	▲	▲	▲	▲	▲
Switzerland	498	(4.4)	▽	▽	▽	▽	▽	▽	▽	▽	▽	○	○	○	○	○	○	□	○	○	○	○	○	○	▲	▲	▲	▲	▲	▲	▲	▲	▲
Denmark	498	(2.8)	▽	▽	▽	▽	▽	▽	▽	▽	▽	○	○	○	○	○	○	○	□	○	○	○	○	○	▲	▲	▲	▲	▲	▲	▲	▲	▲
Liechtenstein	492	(4.9)	▽	▽	▽	▽	▽	▽	▽	▽	▽	▽	▽	○	○	○	○	○	○	□	○	○	○	○	○	○	▲	▲	▲	▲	▲	▲	▲
Italy	488	(3.1)	▽	▽	▽	▽	▽	▽	▽	▽	▽	▽	▽	▽	○	○	○	○	○	○	□	○	○	○	○	○	▲	▲	▲	▲	▲	▲	▲
Spain	483	(3.0)	▽	▽	▽	▽	▽	▽	▽	▽	▽	▽	▽	▽	▽	○	○	○	○	○	○	□	○	○	○	○	▲	▲	▲	▲	▲	▲	▲
Germany	483	(2.4)	▽	▽	▽	▽	▽	▽	▽	▽	▽	▽	▽	▽	▽	○	○	○	○	○	○	○	□	○	○	○	▲	▲	▲	▲	▲	▲	▲
Czech Republic	481	(2.7)	▽	▽	▽	▽	▽	▽	▽	▽	▽	▽	▽	▽	▽	○	○	○	○	○	○	○	○	□	○	○	▲	▲	▲	▲	▲	▲	▲
Hungary	478	(4.4)	▽	▽	▽	▽	▽	▽	▽	▽	▽	▽	▽	▽	▽	▽	○	▽	▽	○	○	○	○	○	□	○	▲	▲	▲	▲	▲	▲	▲
Poland	475	(5.0)	▽	▽	▽	▽	▽	▽	▽	▽	▽	▽	▽	▽	▽	▽	○	▽	▽	○	○	○	○	○	○	□	▲	▲	▲	▲	▲	▲	▲
Portugal	455	(4.9)	▽	▽	▽	▽	▽	▽	▽	▽	▽	▽	▽	▽	▽	▽	▽	▽	▽	▽	▽	▽	▽	▽	▽	▽	□	○	○	○	▲	▲	▲
Russian Fed.	451	(4.9)	▽	▽	▽	▽	▽	▽	▽	▽	▽	▽	▽	▽	▽	▽	▽	▽	▽	▽	▽	▽	▽	▽	▽	▽	○	□	○	○	○	▲	▲
Latvia	451	(5.7)	▽	▽	▽	▽	▽	▽	▽	▽	▽	▽	▽	▽	▽	▽	▽	▽	▽	▽	▽	▽	▽	▽	▽	▽	○	○	□	○	○	▲	▲
Greece	450	(5.4)	▽	▽	▽	▽	▽	▽	▽	▽	▽	▽	▽	▽	▽	▽	▽	▽	▽	▽	▽	▽	▽	▽	▽	▽	○	○	○	□	○	▲	▲
Luxembourg	433	(1.6)	▽	▽	▽	▽	▽	▽	▽	▽	▽	▽	▽	▽	▽	▽	▽	▽	▽	▽	▽	▽	▽	▽	▽	▽	▽	○	○	○	□	▲	▲
Mexico	402	(3.9)	▽	▽	▽	▽	▽	▽	▽	▽	▽	▽	▽	▽	▽	▽	▽	▽	▽	▽	▽	▽	▽	▽	▽	▽	▽	▽	▽	▽	▽	□	▲
Brazil	365	(3.4)	▽	▽	▽	▽	▽	▽	▽	▽	▽	▽	▽	▽	▽	▽	▽	▽	▽	▽	▽	▽	▽	▽	▽	▽	▽	▽	▽	▽	▽	▽	□

Instructions

Read across the row for a country to compare performance with the countries listed along the top of the chart. The symbols indicate whether the mean performance of the country in the row is significantly lower than that of the comparison country, significantly higher than that of the comparison country, or if there is no statistically significant difference between the mean performance of the two countries.

▲ Mean performance statistically significantly higher than in comparison country.

○ No statistically significant difference from comparison country.

▽ Mean performance statistically significantly lower than in comparison country.

Statistically significantly above the OECD average
Not statistically significantly different from the OECD average
Statistically significantly below the OECD average

Table 2.2b
Multiple comparisons of mean performance on the reading / interpreting texts scale

Legend: ▲ = Mean performance statistically significantly higher than in comparison country. ○ = No statistically significant difference from comparison country. ▽ = Mean performance statistically significantly lower than in comparison country. □ = same country (diagonal).

Country	Mean	S.E.	Finland	Canada	Australia	Ireland	New Zealand	Korea	Sweden	Japan	Iceland	United Kingdom	Belgium	Austria	France	Norway	United States	Czech Republic	Switzerland	Denmark	Spain	Italy	Germany	Liechtenstein	Poland	Hungary	Greece	Portugal	Russian Fed.	Latvia	Luxembourg	Mexico	Brazil
(Mean)			555	532	527	526	526	525	522	518	514	514	512	508	506	505	505	500	496	494	491	489	488	484	482	480	475	473	468	459	446	419	400
(S.E.)			(2.9)	(1.6)	(3.5)	(3.3)	(2.7)	(2.3)	(2.1)	(5.0)	(1.4)	(2.5)	(3.2)	(2.4)	(2.7)	(2.8)	(7.1)	(2.4)	(4.2)	(2.4)	(2.6)	(2.6)	(2.5)	(4.5)	(4.3)	(3.8)	(4.5)	(4.3)	(4.0)	(4.9)	(1.6)	(2.9)	(3.0)
Finland	555	(2.9)	□	▲	▲	▲	▲	▲	▲	▲	▲	▲	▲	▲	▲	▲	▲	▲	▲	▲	▲	▲	▲	▲	▲	▲	▲	▲	▲	▲	▲	▲	▲
Canada	532	(1.6)	▽	□	○	○	○	▲	▲	▲	▲	▲	▲	▲	▲	▲	▲	▲	▲	▲	▲	▲	▲	▲	▲	▲	▲	▲	▲	▲	▲	▲	▲
Australia	527	(3.5)	▽	○	□	○	○	○	○	○	▲	▲	▲	▲	▲	▲	▲	▲	▲	▲	▲	▲	▲	▲	▲	▲	▲	▲	▲	▲	▲	▲	▲
Ireland	526	(3.3)	▽	○	○	□	○	○	○	○	▲	▲	▲	▲	▲	▲	▲	▲	▲	▲	▲	▲	▲	▲	▲	▲	▲	▲	▲	▲	▲	▲	▲
New Zealand	526	(2.7)	▽	○	○	○	□	○	○	○	▲	▲	▲	▲	▲	▲	▲	▲	▲	▲	▲	▲	▲	▲	▲	▲	▲	▲	▲	▲	▲	▲	▲
Korea	525	(2.3)	▽	▽	○	○	○	□	○	○	▲	▲	▲	▲	▲	▲	▲	▲	▲	▲	▲	▲	▲	▲	▲	▲	▲	▲	▲	▲	▲	▲	▲
Sweden	522	(2.1)	▽	▽	○	○	○	○	□	○	▲	▲	▲	▲	▲	▲	▲	▲	▲	▲	▲	▲	▲	▲	▲	▲	▲	▲	▲	▲	▲	▲	▲
Japan	518	(5.0)	▽	▽	○	○	○	○	○	□	○	○	○	○	○	▲	○	▲	▲	▲	▲	▲	▲	▲	▲	▲	▲	▲	▲	▲	▲	▲	▲
Iceland	514	(1.4)	▽	▽	▽	▽	▽	▽	▽	○	□	○	○	▲	▲	▲	○	▲	▲	▲	▲	▲	▲	▲	▲	▲	▲	▲	▲	▲	▲	▲	▲
United Kingdom	514	(2.5)	▽	▽	▽	▽	▽	▽	▽	○	○	□	○	○	▲	▲	○	▲	▲	▲	▲	▲	▲	▲	▲	▲	▲	▲	▲	▲	▲	▲	▲
Belgium	512	(3.2)	▽	▽	▽	▽	▽	▽	▽	○	○	○	□	○	○	○	○	▲	▲	▲	▲	▲	▲	▲	▲	▲	▲	▲	▲	▲	▲	▲	▲
Austria	508	(2.4)	▽	▽	▽	▽	▽	▽	▽	○	▽	○	○	□	○	○	○	▲	▲	▲	▲	▲	▲	▲	▲	▲	▲	▲	▲	▲	▲	▲	▲
France	506	(2.7)	▽	▽	▽	▽	▽	▽	▽	▽	▽	▽	○	○	□	○	○	○	▲	▲	▲	▲	▲	▲	▲	▲	▲	▲	▲	▲	▲	▲	▲
Norway	505	(2.8)	▽	▽	▽	▽	▽	▽	▽	▽	▽	▽	○	○	○	□	○	○	○	▲	▲	▲	▲	▲	▲	▲	▲	▲	▲	▲	▲	▲	▲
United States	505	(7.1)	▽	▽	▽	▽	▽	▽	▽	○	○	○	○	○	○	○	□	○	○	○	○	▲	▲	▲	▲	▲	▲	▲	▲	▲	▲	▲	▲
Czech Republic	500	(2.4)	▽	▽	▽	▽	▽	▽	▽	▽	▽	▽	▽	▽	○	○	○	□	○	○	▲	▲	▲	▲	▲	▲	▲	▲	▲	▲	▲	▲	▲
Switzerland	496	(4.2)	▽	▽	▽	▽	▽	▽	▽	▽	▽	▽	▽	▽	▽	○	○	○	□	○	○	○	○	○	▲	▲	▲	▲	▲	▲	▲	▲	▲
Denmark	494	(2.4)	▽	▽	▽	▽	▽	▽	▽	▽	▽	▽	▽	▽	▽	▽	○	○	○	□	○	○	○	○	▲	▲	▲	▲	▲	▲	▲	▲	▲
Spain	491	(2.6)	▽	▽	▽	▽	▽	▽	▽	▽	▽	▽	▽	▽	▽	▽	○	▽	○	○	□	○	○	○	○	▲	▲	▲	▲	▲	▲	▲	▲
Italy	489	(2.6)	▽	▽	▽	▽	▽	▽	▽	▽	▽	▽	▽	▽	▽	▽	▽	▽	○	○	○	□	○	○	○	○	▲	▲	▲	▲	▲	▲	▲
Germany	488	(2.5)	▽	▽	▽	▽	▽	▽	▽	▽	▽	▽	▽	▽	▽	▽	▽	▽	○	○	○	○	□	○	○	○	▲	▲	▲	▲	▲	▲	▲
Liechtenstein	484	(4.5)	▽	▽	▽	▽	▽	▽	▽	▽	▽	▽	▽	▽	▽	▽	▽	▽	○	○	○	○	○	□	○	○	○	○	▲	▲	▲	▲	▲
Poland	482	(4.3)	▽	▽	▽	▽	▽	▽	▽	▽	▽	▽	▽	▽	▽	▽	▽	▽	▽	▽	○	○	○	○	□	○	○	○	▲	▲	▲	▲	▲
Hungary	480	(3.8)	▽	▽	▽	▽	▽	▽	▽	▽	▽	▽	▽	▽	▽	▽	▽	▽	▽	▽	▽	○	○	○	○	□	○	○	▲	▲	▲	▲	▲
Greece	475	(4.5)	▽	▽	▽	▽	▽	▽	▽	▽	▽	▽	▽	▽	▽	▽	▽	▽	▽	▽	▽	▽	▽	○	○	○	□	○	○	▲	▲	▲	▲
Portugal	473	(4.3)	▽	▽	▽	▽	▽	▽	▽	▽	▽	▽	▽	▽	▽	▽	▽	▽	▽	▽	▽	▽	▽	○	○	○	○	□	○	▲	▲	▲	▲
Russian Fed.	468	(4.0)	▽	▽	▽	▽	▽	▽	▽	▽	▽	▽	▽	▽	▽	▽	▽	▽	▽	▽	▽	▽	▽	▽	▽	▽	○	○	□	○	▲	▲	▲
Latvia	459	(4.9)	▽	▽	▽	▽	▽	▽	▽	▽	▽	▽	▽	▽	▽	▽	▽	▽	▽	▽	▽	▽	▽	▽	▽	▽	▽	▽	○	□	▲	▲	▲
Luxembourg	446	(1.6)	▽	▽	▽	▽	▽	▽	▽	▽	▽	▽	▽	▽	▽	▽	▽	▽	▽	▽	▽	▽	▽	▽	▽	▽	▽	▽	▽	▽	□	▲	▲
Mexico	419	(2.9)	▽	▽	▽	▽	▽	▽	▽	▽	▽	▽	▽	▽	▽	▽	▽	▽	▽	▽	▽	▽	▽	▽	▽	▽	▽	▽	▽	▽	▽	□	▲
Brazil	400	(3.0)	▽	▽	▽	▽	▽	▽	▽	▽	▽	▽	▽	▽	▽	▽	▽	▽	▽	▽	▽	▽	▽	▽	▽	▽	▽	▽	▽	▽	▽	▽	□

Instructions

Read across the row for a country to compare performance with the countries listed along the top of the chart. The symbols indicate whether the mean performance of the country in the row is significantly lower than that of the comparison country, significantly higher than that of the comparison country, or if there is no statistically significant difference between the mean performance of the two countries.

▲ Mean performance statistically significantly higher than in comparison country.

○ No statistically significant difference from comparison country.

▽ Mean performance statistically significantly lower than in comparison country.

| Statistically significantly above the OECD average |
| Not statistically significantly different from the OECD average |
| Statistically significantly below the OECD average |

Table 2.2c

Multiple comparisons of mean performance on the reading / reflection and evaluation scale

Reading across each row, the symbols indicate the comparison of the row country against each column country: ▲ = row country significantly higher, ○ = no significant difference, ▽ = row country significantly lower, ◻ = same country.

	Mean	S.E.	Canada	United Kingdom	Ireland	Finland	Japan	New Zealand	Australia	Korea	Austria	Sweden	United States	Norway	Spain	Iceland	Denmark	Belgium	France	Greece	Switzerland	Czech Republic	Italy	Hungary	Portugal	Germany	Poland	Liechtenstein	Latvia	Russian Fed.	Mexico	Luxembourg	Brazil
			542	539	533	533	530	529	526	526	512	510	507	506	506	501	500	497	496	495	488	485	483	481	480	478	477	468	458	455	446	442	417
			(1.6)	(2.5)	(3.1)	(2.7)	(5.4)	(2.9)	(3.4)	(2.6)	(2.7)	(2.3)	(7.1)	(3.0)	(2.8)	(1.3)	(2.6)	(4.3)	(2.9)	(5.6)	(4.8)	(2.6)	(3.1)	(4.3)	(4.5)	(2.9)	(4.7)	(5.7)	(5.9)	(4.0)	(3.7)	(1.9)	(3.3)
Canada	542	(1.6)	◻	○	○	○	○	○	▲	▲	▲	▲	▲	▲	▲	▲	▲	▲	▲	▲	▲	▲	▲	▲	▲	▲	▲	▲	▲	▲	▲	▲	▲
United Kingdom	539	(2.5)	○	◻	○	○	○	○	○	○	▲	▲	▲	▲	▲	▲	▲	▲	▲	▲	▲	▲	▲	▲	▲	▲	▲	▲	▲	▲	▲	▲	▲
Ireland	533	(3.1)	○	○	◻	○	○	○	○	○	▲	▲	▲	▲	▲	▲	▲	▲	▲	▲	▲	▲	▲	▲	▲	▲	▲	▲	▲	▲	▲	▲	▲
Finland	533	(2.7)	○	○	○	◻	○	○	○	○	▲	▲	▲	▲	▲	▲	▲	▲	▲	▲	▲	▲	▲	▲	▲	▲	▲	▲	▲	▲	▲	▲	▲
Japan	530	(5.4)	○	○	○	○	◻	○	○	○	○	○	○	○	○	▲	▲	▲	▲	▲	▲	▲	▲	▲	▲	▲	▲	▲	▲	▲	▲	▲	▲
New Zealand	529	(2.9)	○	○	○	○	○	◻	○	○	▲	▲	▲	▲	▲	▲	▲	▲	▲	▲	▲	▲	▲	▲	▲	▲	▲	▲	▲	▲	▲	▲	▲
Australia	526	(3.4)	▽	○	○	○	○	○	◻	○	○	○	○	▲	▲	▲	▲	▲	▲	▲	▲	▲	▲	▲	▲	▲	▲	▲	▲	▲	▲	▲	▲
Korea	526	(2.6)	▽	○	○	○	○	○	○	◻	○	▲	○	▲	▲	▲	▲	▲	▲	▲	▲	▲	▲	▲	▲	▲	▲	▲	▲	▲	▲	▲	▲
Austria	512	(2.7)	▽	▽	▽	▽	○	▽	○	○	◻	○	○	○	○	○	○	○	○	○	▲	▲	▲	▲	▲	▲	▲	▲	▲	▲	▲	▲	▲
Sweden	510	(2.3)	▽	▽	▽	▽	○	▽	○	▽	○	◻	○	○	○	○	○	○	○	○	▲	▲	▲	▲	▲	▲	▲	▲	▲	▲	▲	▲	▲
United States	507	(7.1)	▽	▽	○	○	○	○	○	○	○	○	◻	○	○	○	○	○	○	○	○	○	○	○	○	○	○	▲	▲	▲	▲	▲	▲
Norway	506	(3.0)	▽	▽	▽	▽	○	▽	▽	▽	○	○	○	◻	○	○	○	○	○	○	○	▲	▲	▲	▲	▲	▲	▲	▲	▲	▲	▲	▲
Spain	506	(2.8)	▽	▽	▽	▽	○	▽	▽	▽	○	○	○	○	◻	○	○	○	○	○	○	▲	▲	▲	▲	▲	▲	▲	▲	▲	▲	▲	▲
Iceland	501	(1.3)	▽	▽	▽	▽	▽	▽	▽	▽	○	○	○	○	○	◻	○	○	○	○	○	▲	▲	▲	▲	▲	▲	▲	▲	▲	▲	▲	▲
Denmark	500	(2.6)	▽	▽	▽	▽	▽	▽	▽	▽	○	○	○	○	○	○	◻	○	○	○	○	○	▲	○	○	▲	▲	▲	▲	▲	▲	▲	▲
Belgium	497	(4.3)	▽	▽	▽	▽	▽	▽	▽	▽	○	○	○	○	○	○	○	◻	○	○	○	○	○	○	○	○	○	○	▲	▲	▲	▲	▲
France	496	(2.9)	▽	▽	▽	▽	▽	▽	▽	▽	○	○	○	○	○	○	○	○	◻	○	○	○	○	○	○	▲	○	▲	▲	▲	▲	▲	▲
Greece	495	(5.6)	▽	▽	▽	▽	▽	▽	▽	▽	○	○	○	○	○	○	○	○	○	◻	○	○	○	○	○	○	○	○	▲	▲	▲	▲	▲
Switzerland	488	(4.8)	▽	▽	▽	▽	▽	▽	▽	▽	▽	▽	○	○	○	○	○	○	○	○	◻	○	○	○	○	○	○	○	○	▲	▲	▲	▲
Czech Republic	485	(2.6)	▽	▽	▽	▽	▽	▽	▽	▽	▽	▽	○	▽	▽	▽	○	○	○	○	○	◻	○	○	○	○	○	○	▲	▲	▲	▲	▲
Italy	483	(3.1)	▽	▽	▽	▽	▽	▽	▽	▽	▽	▽	○	▽	▽	▽	▽	○	○	○	○	○	◻	○	○	○	○	○	○	▲	▲	▲	▲
Hungary	481	(4.3)	▽	▽	▽	▽	▽	▽	▽	▽	▽	▽	○	▽	▽	▽	○	○	○	○	○	○	○	◻	○	○	○	○	○	▲	▲	▲	▲
Portugal	480	(4.5)	▽	▽	▽	▽	▽	▽	▽	▽	▽	▽	○	▽	▽	▽	○	○	○	○	○	○	○	○	◻	○	○	○	○	▲	▲	▲	▲
Germany	478	(2.9)	▽	▽	▽	▽	▽	▽	▽	▽	▽	▽	○	▽	▽	▽	▽	○	▽	○	○	○	○	○	○	◻	○	○	○	▲	▲	▲	▲
Poland	477	(4.7)	▽	▽	▽	▽	▽	▽	▽	▽	▽	▽	○	▽	▽	▽	▽	○	○	○	○	○	○	○	○	○	◻	○	○	○	▲	▲	▲
Liechtenstein	468	(5.7)	▽	▽	▽	▽	▽	▽	▽	▽	▽	▽	▽	▽	▽	▽	▽	○	▽	○	○	○	○	○	○	○	○	◻	○	○	○	▲	▲
Latvia	458	(5.9)	▽	▽	▽	▽	▽	▽	▽	▽	▽	▽	▽	▽	▽	▽	▽	▽	▽	▽	○	▽	○	○	○	○	○	○	◻	○	○	○	▲
Russian Fed.	455	(4.0)	▽	▽	▽	▽	▽	▽	▽	▽	▽	▽	▽	▽	▽	▽	▽	▽	▽	▽	▽	▽	▽	▽	▽	▽	○	○	○	◻	○	○	▲
Mexico	446	(3.7)	▽	▽	▽	▽	▽	▽	▽	▽	▽	▽	▽	▽	▽	▽	▽	▽	▽	▽	▽	▽	▽	▽	▽	▽	▽	○	○	○	◻	○	▲
Luxembourg	442	(1.9)	▽	▽	▽	▽	▽	▽	▽	▽	▽	▽	▽	▽	▽	▽	▽	▽	▽	▽	▽	▽	▽	▽	▽	▽	▽	▽	○	○	○	◻	▲
Brazil	417	(3.3)	▽	▽	▽	▽	▽	▽	▽	▽	▽	▽	▽	▽	▽	▽	▽	▽	▽	▽	▽	▽	▽	▽	▽	▽	▽	▽	▽	▽	▽	▽	◻

Instructions

Read across the row for a country to compare performance with the countries listed along the top of the chart. The symbols indicate whether the mean performance of the country in the row is significantly lower than that of the comparison country, significantly higher than that of the comparison country, or if there is no statistically significant difference between the mean performance of the two countries.

▲ Mean performance statistically significantly higher than in comparison country.

○ No statistically significant difference from comparison country.

▽ Mean performance statistically significantly lower than in comparison country.

Statistically significantly above the OECD average

Not statistically significantly different from the OECD average

Statistically significantly below the OECD average

Table 2.3*a*

Variation in student performance on the combined reading literacy scale

			Standard deviation		Percentiles												
	Mean				5th		10th		25th		75th		90th		95th	
	Mean score	S.E.	S.D.	S.E.	Score	S.E.	Score	S.E.	Score	S.E.	Score	S.E.	Score	S.E.	Score	S.E.
Australia	528	(3.5)	102	(1.6)	354	(4.8)	394	(4.4)	458	(4.4)	602	(4.6)	656	(4.2)	685	(4.5)
Austria	507	(2.4)	93	(1.6)	341	(5.4)	383	(4.2)	447	(2.8)	573	(3.0)	621	(3.2)	648	(3.7)
Belgium	507	(3.6)	107	(2.4)	308	(10.3)	354	(8.9)	437	(6.6)	587	(2.3)	634	(2.5)	659	(2.4)
Canada	534	(1.6)	95	(1.1)	371	(3.8)	410	(2.4)	472	(2.0)	600	(1.5)	652	(1.9)	681	(2.7)
Czech Republic	492	(2.4)	96	(1.9)	320	(7.9)	368	(4.9)	433	(2.8)	557	(2.9)	610	(3.2)	638	(3.6)
Denmark	497	(2.4)	98	(1.8)	326	(6.2)	367	(5.0)	434	(3.3)	566	(2.7)	617	(2.9)	645	(3.6)
Finland	546	(2.6)	89	(2.6)	390	(5.8)	429	(5.1)	492	(2.9)	608	(2.6)	654	(2.8)	681	(3.4)
France	505	(2.7)	92	(1.7)	344	(6.2)	381	(5.2)	444	(4.5)	570	(2.4)	619	(2.9)	645	(3.7)
Germany	484	(2.5)	111	(1.9)	284	(9.4)	335	(6.3)	417	(4.6)	563	(3.1)	619	(2.8)	650	(3.2)
Greece	474	(5.0)	97	(2.7)	305	(8.2)	342	(8.4)	409	(7.4)	543	(4.5)	595	(5.1)	625	(6.0)
Hungary	480	(4.0)	94	(2.1)	320	(5.6)	354	(5.5)	414	(5.3)	549	(4.5)	598	(4.4)	626	(5.5)
Iceland	507	(1.5)	92	(1.4)	345	(5.0)	383	(3.6)	447	(3.1)	573	(2.2)	621	(3.5)	647	(3.7)
Ireland	527	(3.2)	94	(1.7)	360	(6.3)	401	(6.4)	468	(4.3)	593	(3.6)	641	(4.0)	669	(3.4)
Italy	487	(2.9)	91	(2.7)	331	(8.5)	368	(5.8)	429	(4.1)	552	(3.2)	601	(2.7)	627	(3.1)
Japan	522	(5.2)	86	(3.0)	366	(11.4)	407	(9.8)	471	(7.0)	582	(4.4)	625	(4.6)	650	(4.3)
Korea	525	(2.4)	70	(1.6)	402	(5.2)	433	(4.4)	481	(2.9)	574	(2.6)	608	(2.9)	629	(3.2)
Luxembourg	441	(1.6)	100	(1.5)	267	(5.1)	311	(4.4)	378	(2.8)	513	(2.0)	564	(2.8)	592	(3.5)
Mexico	422	(3.3)	86	(2.1)	284	(4.4)	311	(3.4)	360	(3.6)	482	(4.8)	535	(5.5)	565	(6.3)
New Zealand	529	(2.8)	108	(2.0)	337	(7.4)	382	(5.2)	459	(4.1)	606	(3.0)	661	(4.4)	693	(6.1)
Norway	505	(2.8)	104	(1.7)	320	(5.9)	364	(5.5)	440	(4.5)	579	(2.7)	631	(3.1)	660	(4.6)
Poland	479	(4.5)	100	(3.1)	304	(8.7)	343	(6.8)	414	(5.8)	551	(6.0)	603	(6.6)	631	(6.0)
Portugal	470	(4.5)	97	(1.8)	300	(6.2)	337	(6.2)	403	(6.4)	541	(4.5)	592	(4.2)	620	(3.9)
Spain	493	(2.7)	85	(1.2)	344	(5.8)	379	(5.0)	436	(4.6)	553	(2.6)	597	(2.6)	620	(2.9)
Sweden	516	(2.2)	92	(1.2)	354	(4.5)	392	(4.0)	456	(3.1)	581	(3.1)	630	(2.9)	658	(3.1)
Switzerland	494	(4.3)	102	(2.0)	316	(5.5)	355	(5.8)	426	(5.5)	567	(4.7)	621	(5.5)	651	(5.3)
United Kingdom	523	(2.6)	100	(1.5)	352	(4.9)	391	(4.1)	458	(2.8)	595	(3.5)	651	(4.3)	682	(4.9)
United States	504	(7.1)	105	(2.7)	320	(11.7)	363	(11.4)	436	(8.8)	577	(6.8)	636	(6.5)	669	(6.8)
OECD total	*499*	*(2.0)*	*100*	*(0.8)*	*322*	*(3.4)*	*363*	*(3.3)*	*433*	*(2.5)*	*569*	*(1.6)*	*622*	*(2.0)*	*653*	*(2.1)*
OECD average	*500*	*(0.6)*	*100*	*(0.4)*	*324*	*(1.3)*	*366*	*(1.1)*	*435*	*(1.0)*	*571*	*(0.7)*	*623*	*(0.8)*	*652*	*(0.8)*
Brazil	396	(3.1)	86	(1.9)	255	(5.0)	288	(4.5)	339	(3.4)	452	(3.4)	507	(4.2)	539	(5.5)
Latvia	458	(5.3)	102	(2.3)	283	(9.7)	322	(8.2)	390	(6.9)	530	(5.3)	586	(5.8)	617	(6.6)
Liechtenstein	483	(4.1)	96	(3.9)	310	(15.9)	350	(11.8)	419	(9.4)	551	(5.8)	601	(7.1)	626	(8.2)
Russian Federation	462	(4.2)	92	(1.8)	306	(6.9)	340	(5.4)	400	(5.1)	526	(4.5)	579	(4.4)	608	(5.3)

OECD COUNTRIES

NON-OECD COUNTRIES

Table 2.3b
Variation in student performance on the reading / retrieving information scale

		Mean		Standard deviation		Percentiles											
						5th		10th		25th		75th		90th		95th	
		Mean score	S.E.	S.D.	S.E.	Score	S.E.	Score	S.E.	Score	S.E.	Score	S.E.	Score	S.E.	Score	S.E.
OECD COUNTRIES	Australia	536	(3.7)	108	(1.6)	351	(5.3)	393	(4.7)	462	(5.0)	612	(3.7)	671	(5.0)	704	(5.5)
	Austria	502	(2.3)	96	(1.5)	332	(5.5)	374	(4.6)	440	(3.2)	571	(2.8)	619	(3.1)	648	(3.4)
	Belgium	515	(3.9)	120	(2.7)	293	(9.9)	343	(8.5)	437	(7.0)	603	(2.6)	656	(2.6)	685	(3.0)
	Canada	530	(1.7)	102	(1.2)	355	(4.1)	397	(2.9)	463	(2.3)	601	(1.8)	657	(2.4)	690	(2.8)
	Czech Republic	481	(2.7)	107	(1.9)	294	(8.4)	343	(5.6)	415	(3.1)	555	(3.4)	614	(3.9)	647	(3.5)
	Denmark	498	(2.8)	105	(1.9)	313	(7.5)	359	(5.9)	430	(3.7)	572	(2.9)	626	(3.3)	657	(4.1)
	Finland	556	(2.8)	102	(2.1)	377	(6.9)	423	(4.7)	492	(3.8)	627	(3.0)	682	(3.2)	713	(3.7)
	France	515	(3.0)	101	(2.1)	335	(7.8)	376	(6.4)	449	(4.8)	588	(2.8)	638	(4.0)	668	(3.8)
	Germany	483	(2.4)	114	(2.0)	274	(10.5)	331	(6.2)	415	(4.1)	563	(2.9)	621	(3.1)	652	(3.2)
	Greece	450	(5.4)	109	(3.0)	259	(11.6)	306	(9.2)	378	(8.0)	527	(4.4)	585	(5.0)	617	(6.2)
	Hungary	478	(4.4)	107	(2.2)	294	(7.3)	333	(6.2)	404	(5.8)	555	(4.8)	613	(4.9)	645	(5.8)
	Iceland	500	(1.6)	103	(1.3)	319	(4.6)	362	(4.2)	433	(2.8)	572	(2.7)	628	(2.9)	659	(3.6)
	Ireland	524	(3.3)	100	(1.7)	348	(7.2)	392	(6.5)	462	(4.4)	596	(3.2)	647	(3.3)	675	(3.9)
	Italy	488	(3.1)	104	(3.0)	309	(10.1)	352	(5.8)	422	(4.0)	560	(2.9)	617	(4.0)	649	(3.7)
	Japan	526	(5.5)	97	(3.1)	353	(12.2)	397	(10.2)	468	(7.7)	592	(4.5)	644	(4.7)	674	(5.2)
	Korea	530	(2.5)	82	(1.6)	386	(5.0)	421	(4.3)	476	(3.1)	588	(3.1)	631	(3.4)	655	(3.5)
	Luxembourg	433	(1.6)	109	(1.4)	244	(5.5)	290	(4.3)	364	(3.0)	513	(2.5)	567	(2.6)	599	(3.3)
	Mexico	402	(3.9)	101	(2.2)	239	(4.7)	270	(4.5)	331	(4.3)	472	(5.3)	533	(6.0)	570	(7.2)
	New Zealand	535	(2.8)	116	(2.1)	327	(6.6)	377	(6.3)	460	(4.1)	616	(3.9)	677	(3.9)	708	(6.9)
	Norway	505	(2.9)	110	(1.9)	307	(6.8)	356	(6.5)	437	(4.6)	583	(2.8)	637	(3.3)	667	(4.3)
	Poland	475	(5.0)	112	(3.3)	278	(9.6)	324	(8.6)	401	(6.0)	557	(6.2)	615	(7.1)	648	(8.6)
	Portugal	455	(4.9)	107	(2.2)	268	(8.1)	311	(7.9)	383	(6.2)	534	(4.9)	588	(4.3)	621	(4.7)
	Spain	483	(3.0)	92	(1.2)	320	(5.2)	361	(4.9)	424	(4.1)	549	(3.0)	597	(2.8)	623	(3.4)
	Sweden	516	(2.4)	104	(1.5)	335	(4.6)	378	(4.3)	448	(3.7)	591	(2.8)	645	(2.7)	676	(3.4)
	Switzerland	498	(4.4)	113	(2.1)	295	(7.3)	344	(6.4)	423	(5.5)	578	(4.9)	636	(5.2)	668	(5.8)
	United Kingdom	523	(2.5)	105	(1.5)	342	(5.9)	384	(4.5)	455	(3.3)	597	(3.0)	656	(4.3)	687	(4.5)
	United States	499	(7.4)	112	(2.7)	302	(13.0)	348	(12.0)	427	(9.3)	577	(6.4)	638	(6.0)	672	(7.3)
	OECD total	*496*	*(2.1)*	*111*	*(0.9)*	*300*	*(3.8)*	*346*	*(3.5)*	*425*	*(2.8)*	*574*	*(1.8)*	*632*	*(1.8)*	*665*	*(2.2)*
	OECD average	*498*	*(0.7)*	*111*	*(0.4)*	*303*	*(1.5)*	*349*	*(1.3)*	*426*	*(1.1)*	*576*	*(0.7)*	*634*	*(0.9)*	*667*	*(0.8)*
NON-OECD COUNTRIES	Brazil	365	(3.4)	97	(2.1)	203	(6.3)	239	(5.2)	300	(5.1)	428	(4.3)	489	(3.5)	524	(6.6)
	Latvia	451	(5.7)	117	(2.4)	250	(10.1)	296	(8.5)	373	(7.3)	535	(6.2)	599	(5.7)	633	(6.7)
	Liechtenstein	492	(4.9)	106	(4.7)	303	(18.6)	345	(13.9)	422	(10.8)	567	(7.8)	620	(7.7)	653	(14.0)
	Russian Federation	451	(4.9)	108	(2.1)	269	(7.1)	309	(7.1)	378	(6.0)	526	(5.2)	587	(5.6)	624	(6.5)

Table 2.3c
Variation in student performance on the reading / interpreting texts scale

		Mean		Standard deviation		Percentiles												
						5th		10th		25th		75th		90th		95th	
		Mean score	S.E.	S.D.	S.E.	Score	S.E.	Score	S.E.	Score	S.E.	Score	S.E.	Score	S.E.	Score	S.E.
OECD COUNTRIES	Australia	527	(3.5)	104	(1.5)	349	(5.0)	389	(4.9)	456	(3.9)	601	(4.5)	659	(4.8)	689	(4.9)
	Austria	508	(2.4)	93	(1.6)	347	(5.3)	384	(3.6)	447	(3.2)	575	(3.2)	624	(3.9)	650	(3.7)
	Belgium	512	(3.2)	105	(2.0)	322	(6.5)	363	(6.2)	440	(5.9)	591	(2.4)	638	(2.6)	665	(2.9)
	Canada	532	(1.6)	95	(1.0)	368	(3.8)	406	(2.8)	469	(2.1)	599	(1.5)	651	(2.1)	682	(2.3)
	Czech Republic	500	(2.4)	96	(1.6)	331	(7.8)	374	(4.9)	440	(3.4)	568	(3.0)	619	(3.3)	649	(4.0)
	Denmark	494	(2.4)	99	(1.7)	324	(6.9)	362	(4.5)	430	(4.1)	563	(2.6)	617	(3.7)	647	(3.7)
	Finland	555	(2.9)	97	(3.3)	390	(6.4)	429	(4.4)	496	(3.1)	622	(2.7)	671	(2.8)	701	(2.9)
	France	506	(2.7)	92	(1.7)	345	(5.4)	381	(5.0)	444	(4.2)	571	(2.8)	621	(3.3)	649	(4.2)
	Germany	488	(2.5)	109	(1.8)	294	(4.8)	340	(6.0)	417	(4.3)	564	(2.9)	623	(2.3)	654	(2.9)
	Greece	475	(4.5)	89	(2.4)	322	(7.4)	356	(7.3)	415	(6.8)	538	(4.4)	588	(4.3)	615	(4.9)
	Hungary	480	(3.8)	90	(1.9)	327	(6.2)	359	(4.6)	418	(5.1)	545	(4.2)	594	(4.5)	621	(4.9)
	Iceland	514	(1.4)	95	(1.4)	349	(4.5)	387	(3.8)	451	(2.2)	581	(2.2)	633	(3.1)	664	(4.2)
	Ireland	526	(3.3)	97	(1.7)	354	(6.7)	396	(5.8)	464	(4.7)	595	(3.4)	646	(3.3)	676	(3.8)
	Italy	489	(2.6)	86	(2.4)	343	(6.9)	376	(5.3)	432	(3.5)	549	(3.2)	598	(2.9)	625	(3.0)
	Japan	518	(5.0)	83	(2.9)	370	(9.5)	406	(9.4)	467	(6.5)	575	(4.3)	618	(4.6)	644	(4.5)
	Korea	525	(2.3)	69	(1.5)	404	(4.5)	434	(3.8)	480	(2.9)	574	(2.5)	609	(2.7)	630	(3.0)
	Luxembourg	446	(1.6)	101	(1.3)	271	(4.8)	314	(3.6)	381	(2.5)	519	(2.6)	571	(2.6)	600	(3.9)
	Mexico	419	(2.9)	78	(1.7)	294	(3.8)	319	(3.3)	363	(3.1)	472	(4.3)	521	(4.9)	550	(5.8)
	New Zealand	526	(2.7)	111	(2.0)	333	(6.3)	376	(4.3)	453	(3.8)	606	(3.4)	665	(4.4)	699	(6.7)
	Norway	505	(2.8)	104	(1.6)	322	(5.0)	364	(5.0)	438	(4.2)	579	(2.9)	633	(2.8)	662	(3.5)
	Poland	482	(4.3)	97	(2.7)	314	(7.1)	350	(6.4)	418	(4.9)	552	(5.5)	604	(6.2)	633	(6.5)
	Portugal	473	(4.3)	93	(1.6)	315	(5.9)	348	(5.9)	408	(5.8)	541	(4.6)	591	(4.4)	617	(4.5)
	Spain	491	(2.6)	84	(1.1)	347	(4.9)	380	(3.6)	435	(3.7)	551	(2.6)	595	(2.2)	620	(3.0)
	Sweden	522	(2.1)	96	(1.3)	355	(4.2)	393	(3.8)	458	(3.1)	590	(2.8)	641	(2.7)	669	(3.4)
	Switzerland	496	(4.2)	101	(2.0)	320	(4.7)	359	(5.9)	429	(5.6)	569	(4.6)	622	(5.5)	653	(5.9)
	United Kingdom	514	(2.5)	102	(1.4)	341	(5.0)	380	(4.0)	445	(3.3)	586	(3.1)	644	(4.1)	678	(4.8)
	United States	505	(7.1)	106	(2.6)	322	(11.2)	363	(10.5)	435	(8.3)	579	(6.8)	640	(6.6)	672	(7.5)
	OECD total	*498*	*(2.0)*	*99*	*(0.8)*	*327*	*(3.3)*	*365*	*(3.1)*	*432*	*(2.4)*	*568*	*(1.8)*	*622*	*(2.1)*	*654*	*(2.4)*
	OECD average	*501*	*(0.6)*	*100*	*(0.4)*	*330*	*(1.1)*	*368*	*(1.1)*	*435*	*(1.0)*	*571*	*(0.7)*	*625*	*(0.7)*	*656*	*(1.0)*
NON-OECD COUNTRIES	Brazil	400	(3.0)	84	(1.8)	264	(5.3)	295	(4.4)	345	(3.7)	455	(4.1)	511	(4.9)	543	(5.1)
	Latvia	459	(4.9)	95	(2.0)	294	(7.2)	332	(7.6)	395	(6.0)	528	(5.0)	580	(5.3)	611	(6.2)
	Liechtenstein	484	(4.5)	94	(3.6)	320	(18.2)	356	(12.1)	419	(9.5)	551	(7.5)	597	(8.8)	627	(11.1)
	Russian Federation	468	(4.0)	92	(1.8)	313	(5.9)	346	(5.6)	404	(4.7)	531	(3.9)	586	(4.4)	615	(4.5)

Table 2.3d
Variation in student performance on the reading / reflection and evaluation scale

		Mean		Standard deviation		Percentiles											
						5th		10th		25th		75th		90th		95th	
		Mean score	S.E.	S.D.	S.E.	Score	S.E.	Score	S.E.	Score	S.E.	Score	S.E.	Score	S.E.	Score	S.E.
OECD COUNTRIES	Australia	526	(3.5)	100	(1.5)	356	(5.6)	393	(5.3)	459	(4.0)	596	(3.9)	651	(4.7)	683	(5.5)
	Austria	512	(2.7)	100	(1.8)	335	(5.1)	379	(5.0)	449	(3.5)	582	(3.2)	633	(4.6)	663	(5.3)
	Belgium	497	(4.3)	114	(4.1)	283	(16.0)	336	(9.4)	426	(7.3)	579	(2.4)	629	(2.4)	656	(3.0)
	Canada	542	(1.6)	96	(1.0)	377	(3.9)	416	(3.1)	481	(2.0)	609	(1.6)	661	(1.8)	691	(2.4)
	Czech Republic	485	(2.6)	103	(1.8)	304	(7.9)	354	(5.0)	422	(3.4)	557	(3.1)	611	(3.9)	641	(4.7)
	Denmark	500	(2.6)	102	(2.1)	321	(6.8)	365	(5.5)	436	(3.7)	571	(2.9)	625	(4.0)	657	(3.6)
	Finland	533	(2.7)	91	(3.9)	374	(7.3)	415	(5.0)	480	(2.9)	595	(2.2)	640	(2.5)	665	(3.7)
	France	496	(2.9)	98	(1.8)	325	(7.3)	365	(6.1)	432	(4.4)	566	(2.7)	618	(3.5)	649	(3.4)
	Germany	478	(2.9)	124	(1.8)	254	(7.7)	311	(7.4)	401	(4.8)	566	(3.0)	627	(3.1)	662	(3.4)
	Greece	495	(5.6)	115	(3.1)	293	(10.4)	343	(9.3)	418	(7.7)	577	(5.8)	638	(5.8)	675	(6.5)
	Hungary	481	(4.3)	100	(2.2)	307	(8.2)	347	(5.6)	413	(6.3)	553	(4.4)	606	(4.5)	636	(5.1)
	Iceland	501	(1.3)	93	(1.3)	337	(5.6)	378	(3.8)	442	(2.7)	567	(2.2)	616	(2.5)	645	(4.1)
	Ireland	533	(3.1)	90	(1.7)	373	(7.1)	414	(6.3)	478	(4.3)	595	(3.2)	642	(3.3)	671	(3.3)
	Italy	483	(3.1)	101	(2.9)	307	(7.9)	348	(6.3)	418	(4.8)	555	(2.9)	607	(3.1)	636	(4.0)
	Japan	530	(5.5)	100	(3.3)	352	(12.6)	397	(9.1)	469	(7.2)	599	(4.7)	651	(4.7)	680	(5.8)
	Korea	526	(2.6)	76	(1.7)	395	(6.0)	428	(4.5)	479	(3.5)	577	(2.7)	619	(3.0)	642	(3.9)
	Luxembourg	442	(1.9)	115	(1.8)	243	(6.1)	293	(4.9)	371	(3.3)	523	(2.9)	581	(3.6)	613	(3.9)
	Mexico	446	(3.7)	109	(2.2)	267	(5.6)	303	(4.4)	370	(3.8)	521	(5.2)	586	(6.5)	624	(6.3)
	New Zealand	529	(2.9)	107	(1.8)	340	(5.9)	387	(5.1)	460	(3.8)	605	(3.7)	662	(4.7)	692	(5.6)
	Norway	506	(3.0)	108	(1.8)	313	(5.5)	357	(5.2)	439	(4.4)	582	(3.0)	636	(3.1)	667	(4.2)
	Poland	477	(4.7)	110	(3.2)	279	(9.7)	328	(8.0)	406	(6.4)	556	(6.2)	613	(6.4)	642	(7.0)
	Portugal	480	(4.5)	101	(1.7)	304	(5.1)	342	(6.8)	411	(6.5)	554	(4.2)	607	(3.8)	634	(4.5)
	Spain	506	(2.8)	91	(1.2)	346	(4.7)	383	(4.3)	446	(4.3)	570	(2.8)	618	(2.7)	646	(4.1)
	Sweden	510	(2.3)	95	(1.2)	343	(4.4)	382	(4.1)	449	(3.0)	576	(2.7)	626	(4.0)	654	(3.7)
	Switzerland	488	(4.8)	113	(2.2)	291	(7.2)	336	(6.5)	414	(6.1)	568	(5.4)	629	(6.0)	663	(6.7)
	United Kingdom	539	(2.5)	99	(1.6)	369	(5.7)	408	(4.5)	473	(3.4)	608	(3.1)	664	(3.5)	695	(4.8)
	United States	507	(7.1)	105	(2.7)	323	(11.5)	367	(11.9)	438	(8.5)	580	(6.3)	638	(6.3)	669	(7.6)
	OECD total	*503*	*(1.9)*	*107*	*(0.8)*	*314*	*(3.5)*	*361*	*(3.2)*	*435*	*(2.5)*	*577*	*(1.8)*	*633*	*(2.1)*	*665*	*(1.9)*
	OECD average	*502*	*(0.7)*	*106*	*(0.4)*	*315*	*(1.5)*	*361*	*(1.4)*	*435*	*(1.0)*	*576*	*(0.7)*	*630*	*(0.9)*	*661*	*(0.9)*
NON-OECD COUNTRIES	Brazil	417	(3.3)	93	(2.2)	264	(6.2)	298	(5.2)	355	(4.1)	480	(4.2)	536	(5.6)	569	(6.1)
	Latvia	458	(5.9)	113	(2.3)	261	(8.1)	305	(7.3)	381	(7.6)	538	(6.1)	598	(7.1)	634	(7.0)
	Liechtenstein	468	(5.7)	108	(4.3)	277	(18.3)	323	(12.9)	398	(8.9)	548	(8.8)	603	(9.6)	633	(13.0)
	Russian Federation	455	(4.0)	98	(1.7)	289	(5.3)	326	(6.2)	389	(5.1)	523	(4.0)	580	(4.2)	612	(4.8)

Table 2.4
Between-school and within-school variation in student performance on the combined reading literacy scale

Variation expressed as a percentage of the average variation
in student performance (SP) across OECD countries

	Total variation in SP[1]	Total variation in SP expressed as a percentage of the average variation in SP across OECD countries	Total variation in SP between schools	Total variation in SP within schools	Variation explained by the international socio-economic index of occupational status of students		Variation explained by the international socio-economic index of occupational status of students and schools	
					Between-school variation	Within-school variation	Between-school variation	Within-school variation
OECD COUNTRIES								
Australia	10 357	111.6	20.9	90.6	8.3	6.7	14.2	6.9
Austria	8 649	93.2	68.6	45.7	10.4	0.4	42.6	0.3
Belgium	11 455	123.5	76.0	50.9	11.0	1.8	44.2	1.9
Canada	8 955	96.5	17.1	80.1	4.6	5.0	7.8	5.1
Czech Republic	9 278	100.0	51.9	45.3	8.8	1.8	34.4	1.8
Denmark	9 614	103.6	19.6	85.9	10.2	8.0	11.6	8.1
Finland	7 994	86.2	10.7	76.5	1.5	4.6	1.7	4.6
France	m	m	m	m	m	m	m	m
Germany	12 368	133.3	74.8	50.2	11.7	2.3	51.5	2.3
Greece	9 436	101.7	53.8	52.9	7.0	1.1	25.0	1.1
Hungary	8 810	95.0	71.2	34.8	8.3	0.3	49.4	0.2
Iceland	8 529	91.9	7.0	85.0	1.6	5.0	1.7	5.0
Ireland	8 755	94.4	17.1	79.2	5.5	5.7	10.1	5.7
Italy	8 356	90.1	50.9	43.4	3.4	0.5	23.8	0.5
Japan[2]	7 358	79.3	36.5	43.9	m	m	m	m
Korea	4 833	52.1	19.7	33.0	1.0	0.2	7.1	0.2
Luxembourg	10 088	108.7	33.4	74.9	11.1	8.3	26.7	8.2
Mexico	7 370	79.4	42.9	37.4	5.2	0.1	25.7	0.1
New Zealand	11 701	126.1	20.1	103.9	7.3	10.9	11.6	11.0
Norway	10 743	115.8	12.6	102.4	3.7	8.7	4.9	8.7
Poland	9 958	107.3	67.0	38.9	6.3	1.1	42.4	1.1
Portugal	9 436	101.7	37.5	64.3	10.6	4.6	23.8	4.6
Spain	7 181	77.4	15.9	60.9	5.4	3.0	9.1	3.1
Sweden	8 495	91.6	8.9	83.0	4.5	6.9	5.8	6.9.
Switzerland	10 408	112.2	48.7	63.7	12.7	4.0	24.3	3.9
United Kingdom	10 098	108.9	22.4	82.3	9.6	8.4	16.0	8.7
United States	10 979	118.3	35.1	83.6	12.0	5.6	25.5	5.8
OECD average	*9 277*	*100*	*36.2*	*65.1*	*7.3*	*4.2*	*21.6*	*4.2*
NON-OECD COUNTRIES								
Brazil	7 427.0	80.1	35.8	47.1	6.5	1.9	19.7	2.1
Latvia	10 434.6	112.5	35.1	77.5	4.9	4.4	16.7	4.5
Liechtenstein	m	m	m	m	m	m	m	m
Russian Federation	8 465.8	91.3	33.6	57.1	4.8	2.4	15.4	2.3

Variation expressed as a percentage of the average variation in student performance (SP) across OECD countries

	Variation explained by geographical/systemic/institutional factors		Variation explained by geographical/systemic/institutional factors and the international socio-economic index of occupational status of students and schools		Total variation between schools expressed as a percentage of the total variation within the country[3]
	Between-school variation	Within-school variation	Between-school variation	Within-school variation	
OECD COUNTRIES					
Australia	1.8	0.1	15.0	7.0	18.8
Austria	60.4	0.0	61.6	0.5	60.0
Belgium	50.7	0.0	61.9	1.9	59.9
Canada	1.1	0.0	8.4	5.1	17.6
Czech Republic	44.5	0.0	46.8	1.8	53.4
Denmark	m	m	m	m	18.6
Finland	m	m	m	m	12.3
France	m	m	m	m	m
Germany	65.2	0.0	66.9	2.3	59.8
Greece	33.3	0.0	40.1	0.4	50.4
Hungary	52.5	0.0	58.7	0.1	67.2
Iceland	0.9	0.0	2.3	5.0	7.6
Ireland	9.7	0.0	12.7	5.5	17.8
Italy	27.6	0.0	30.1	0.5	54.0
Japan[2]	m	m	m	m	45.4
Korea	10.9	0.0	12.0	0.2	37.4
Luxembourg	m	m	m	m	30.8
Mexico	26.5	0.0	35.3	0.1	53.4
New Zealand	12.9	0.0	14.8	11.0	16.2
Norway	0.5	3.8	5.2	10.1	10.9
Poland	53.0	0.0	55.9	1.1	63.2
Portugal	m	m	m	m	36.8
Spain	6.2	0.0	10.9	3.1	20.7
Sweden	2.7	2.6	6.9	8.1	9.7
Switzerland	22.1	0.0	29.7	4.1	43.4
United Kingdom	7.3	0.0	17.1	6.7	21.4
United States	m	m	m	m	29.6
OECD average	*24.5*	*0.3*	*29.6*	*3.7*	
NON-OECD COUNTRIES					
Brazil	5.3	0.0	21.7	2.1	43.1
Latvia	m	m	m	m	31.2
Liechtenstein	m	m	m	m	43.9
Russian Federation	16.6	0.0	21.0	2.3	37.1

1. The total variation in student performance is obtained as the square of the standard deviation shown in Table 2.3a. The statistical variance in SP and not the standard deviation is used for this comparison to allow for the decomposition of the components of variation in student performance. For reasons explained in the *PISA 2000 Technical Report*, the sum of the between and within-school va-riance compo-nents may, for some countries, differ slightly from the square of the standard deviation shown in Table 2.3a.

2. Due to the sampling methods used in Japan, the between-school vari-ance in Japan includes variation between classes within schools.

3. This index is often referred to as the intra-class correlation (rho).

Table 2.5

School's or classroom teacher's pass/fail threshold and performance on the combined reading literacy scale

		Below school's or classroom teacher's pass/fail threshold				At or above school's or classroom teacher's pass/fail threshold			
		Percentage of students		Performance on the combined reading literacy scale		Percentage of students		Performance on the combined reading literacy scale	
		%	S.E.	Mean score	S.E.	%	S.E.	Mean score	S.E.
OECD COUNTRIES	Australia	6.4	(0.5)	474	(7.8)	93.6	(0.5)	534	(3.5)
	Austria	3.4	(0.3)	485	(8.6)	96.6	(0.3)	511	(2.4)
	Belgium	28.3	(1.6)	466	(10.2)	71.7	(1.6)	502	(5.7)
	Canada	10.4	(0.2)	488	(2.6)	89.6	(0.2)	542	(1.5)
	Czech Republic	0.9	(0.2)	454	(13.3)	99.1	(0.2)	502	(2.2)
	Denmark	0.6	(0.2)	c	c	99.4	(0.2)	505	(2.3)
	Finland	0.5	(0.1)	c	c	99.5	(0.1)	548	(2.6)
	France	31.2	(1.1)	492	(3.1)	68.8	(1.1)	531	(2.7)
	Germany	m	m	m	m	m	m	m	m
	Greece	1.0	(0.2)	401	(17.0)	99.0	(0.2)	479	(4.7)
	Hungary	0.0	(0.0)	a	a	100.0	(0.0)	482	(4.0)
	Iceland	9.2	(0.5)	424	(5.1)	90.8	(0.5)	521	(1.7)
	Ireland	m	m	m	m	m	m	m	m
	Italy	15.0	(0.8)	442	(6.2)	85.1	(0.8)	498	(2.7)
	Japan	m	m	m	m	m	m	m	m
	Korea	m	m	m	m	m	m	m	m
	Luxembourg	m	m	m	m	m	m	m	m
	Mexico	4.5	(0.4)	385	(8.5)	95.5	(0.4)	424	(3.3)
	New Zealand	22.4	(0.8)	479	(3.7)	77.6	(0.8)	549	(3.0)
	Norway	0.6	(0.1)	c	c	99.4	(0.1)	511	(2.7)
	Poland	3.0	(0.4)	414	(12.1)	97.0	(0.4)	487	(4.4)
	Portugal	m	m	m	m	m	m	m	m
	Spain	28.8	(1.2)	451	(3.3)	71.2	(1.2)	515	(2.6)
	Sweden	2.9	(0.3)	406	(9.2)	97.1	(0.3)	521	(2.1)
	Switzerland	3.9	(0.3)	439	(9.9)	96.1	(0.3)	503	(4.2)
	United Kingdom	3.0	(0.4)	391	(8.5)	97.0	(0.4)	530	(3.1)
	United States	m	m	m	m	m	m	m	m
	OECD total	*11.2*	*(0.2)*	*461*	*(1.8)*	*88.8*	*(0.2)*	*495*	*(1.1)*
	OECD average	*8.2*	*(0.1)*	*460*	*(1.6)*	*91.8*	*(0.1)*	*509*	*(0.7)*
NON-OECD COUNTRIES	Liechtenstein	m	m	m	m	m	m	m	m
	Brazil	m	m	m	m	m	m	m	m
	Latvia	4.6	(1.2)	c	c	95.4	(1.2)	494	(4.6)
	Russian Federation	m	m	m	m	m	m	m	m
	Netherlands[1]	8.3	(0.7)	523	(9.3)	91.7	(0.7)	539	(3.0)

1. Response rate is too low to ensure comparability (see Annex A3).

Table 3.1
Variation in student performance on the mathematical literacy scale

| | | Mean | | Standard deviation | | Percentiles | | | | | | | | | | | |
| | | | | | | 5th | | 10th | | 25th | | 75th | | 90th | | 95th | |
		Mean score	S.E.	S.D.	S.E.	Score	S.E.	Score	S.E.	Score	S.E.	Score	S.E.	Score	S.E.	Score	S.E.
OECD COUNTRIES	Australia	533	(3.5)	90	(1.6)	380	(6.4)	418	(6.4)	474	(4.4)	594	(4.5)	647	(5.7)	679	(5.8)
	Austria	515	(2.5)	92	(1.7)	355	(5.3)	392	(4.6)	455	(3.5)	581	(3.8)	631	(3.6)	661	(5.2)
	Belgium	520	(3.9)	106	(2.9)	322	(11.0)	367	(8.6)	453	(6.5)	597	(3.0)	646	(3.9)	672	(3.5)
	Canada	533	(1.4)	85	(1.1)	390	(3.2)	423	(2.5)	477	(2.0)	592	(1.7)	640	(1.9)	668	(2.6)
	Czech Republic	498	(2.8)	96	(1.9)	335	(5.4)	372	(4.2)	433	(4.1)	564	(3.9)	623	(4.8)	655	(5.6)
	Denmark	514	(2.4)	87	(1.7)	366	(6.1)	401	(5.1)	458	(3.1)	575	(3.1)	621	(3.7)	649	(4.6)
	Finland	536	(2.2)	80	(1.4)	400	(6.5)	433	(3.6)	484	(4.1)	592	(2.5)	637	(3.2)	664	(3.5)
	France	517	(2.7)	89	(1.9)	364	(6.4)	399	(5.4)	457	(4.7)	581	(3.1)	629	(3.2)	656	(4.6)
	Germany	490	(2.5)	103	(2.4)	311	(7.9)	349	(6.9)	423	(3.9)	563	(2.7)	619	(3.6)	649	(3.9)
	Greece	447	(5.6)	108	(2.9)	260	(9.0)	303	(8.1)	375	(8.1)	524	(6.7)	586	(7.8)	617	(8.6)
	Hungary	488	(4.0)	98	(2.4)	327	(7.1)	360	(5.7)	419	(4.8)	558	(5.2)	615	(6.4)	648	(6.9)
	Iceland	514	(2.3)	85	(1.4)	372	(5.7)	407	(4.7)	459	(3.5)	572	(3.0)	622	(3.1)	649	(5.5)
	Ireland	503	(2.7)	84	(1.8)	357	(6.4)	394	(4.7)	449	(4.1)	561	(3.6)	606	(4.3)	630	(5.0)
	Italy	457	(2.9)	90	(2.4)	301	(8.4)	338	(5.5)	398	(3.5)	520	(3.5)	570	(4.4)	600	(6.1)
	Japan	557	(5.5)	87	(3.1)	402	(11.2)	440	(9.1)	504	(7.4)	617	(5.2)	662	(4.9)	688	(6.1)
	Korea	547	(2.8)	84	(2.0)	400	(6.1)	438	(5.0)	493	(4.2)	606	(3.4)	650	(4.3)	676	(5.3)
	Luxembourg	446	(2.0)	93	(1.8)	281	(7.4)	328	(4.2)	390	(3.8)	509	(3.4)	559	(3.2)	588	(3.9)
	Mexico	387	(3.4)	83	(1.9)	254	(5.5)	281	(3.6)	329	(4.1)	445	(5.2)	496	(5.6)	527	(6.6)
	New Zealand	537	(3.1)	99	(1.9)	364	(6.1)	405	(5.4)	472	(3.9)	607	(4.0)	659	(4.2)	689	(5.2)
	Norway	499	(2.8)	92	(1.7)	340	(7.0)	379	(5.2)	439	(4.0)	565	(3.9)	613	(4.5)	643	(4.5)
	Poland	470	(5.5)	103	(3.8)	296	(12.2)	335	(9.2)	402	(7.0)	542	(6.8)	599	(7.7)	632	(8.5)
	Portugal	454	(4.1)	91	(1.8)	297	(7.3)	332	(6.1)	392	(5.7)	520	(4.3)	570	(4.3)	596	(5.0)
	Spain	476	(3.1)	91	(1.5)	323	(5.8)	358	(4.3)	416	(5.3)	540	(4.0)	592	(3.9)	621	(3.1)
	Sweden	510	(2.5)	93	(1.6)	347	(5.8)	386	(4.0)	450	(3.3)	574	(2.6)	626	(3.3)	656	(5.5)
	Switzerland	529	(4.4)	100	(2.2)	353	(9.1)	398	(6.0)	466	(4.8)	601	(5.2)	653	(5.8)	682	(4.8)
	United Kingdom	529	(2.5)	92	(1.6)	374	(5.9)	412	(3.6)	470	(3.2)	592	(3.2)	646	(4.3)	676	(5.9)
	United States	493	(7.6)	98	(2.4)	327	(11.7)	361	(9.6)	427	(9.7)	562	(7.5)	620	(7.7)	652	(7.9)
	OECD total	*498*	*(2.1)*	*103*	*(0.9)*	*318*	*(3.1)*	*358*	*(3.4)*	*429*	*(3.0)*	*572*	*(2.1)*	*628*	*(1.9)*	*658*	*(2.1)*
	OECD average	*500*	*(0.7)*	*100*	*(0.4)*	*326*	*(1.5)*	*367*	*(1.4)*	*435*	*(1.1)*	*571*	*(0.8)*	*625*	*(0.9)*	*655*	*(1.1)*
NON-OECD COUNTRIES	Brazil	334	(3.7)	97	(2.3)	179	(5.5)	212	(5.2)	266	(4.2)	399	(5.5)	464	(7.5)	499	(8.9)
	Latvia	463	(4.5)	103	(2.6)	288	(9.0)	328	(8.9)	393	(5.7)	536	(6.2)	593	(5.6)	625	(6.6)
	Liechtenstein	514	(7.0)	96	(6.0)	343	(19.7)	380	(18.9)	454	(15.5)	579	(7.5)	635	(16.9)	665	(15.0)
	Russian Federation	478	(5.5)	104	(2.5)	305	(9.0)	343	(7.4)	407	(6.6)	552	(6.6)	613	(6.8)	648	(7.8)

Table 3.2

School's or classroom teacher's pass/fail threshold and performance on the mathematical literacy scale

		Below school's or classroom teacher's pass/fail threshold				At or above school's or classroom teacher's pass/fail threshold			
		Percentage of students		Performance on the mathematical literacy scale		Percentage of students		Performance on the mathematical literacy scale	
		%	S.E.	Mean score	S.E.	%	S.E.	Mean score	S.E
OECD COUNTRIES	Australia	11.5	(0.7)	498	(5.6)	88.5	(0.7)	540	(3.7)
	Austria	7.5	(0.6)	506	(6.7)	92.5	(0.6)	519	(2.5)
	Belgium	21.3	(1.6)	491	(11.5)	78.7	(1.6)	513	(6.7)
	Canada	14.9	(0.4)	504	(2.3)	85.1	(0.4)	540	(1.4)
	Czech Republic	1.5	(0.3)	445	(17.9)	98.5	(0.3)	505	(2.8)
	Denmark	0.9	(0.2)	c	c	99.1	(0.2)	522	(2.3)
	Finland	1.2	(0.2)	456	(11.2)	98.8	(0.2)	539	(2.1)
	France	38.7	(1.3)	506	(3.2)	61.3	(1.3)	544	(3.1)
	Germany	m	m	m	m	m	m	m	m
	Greece	3.6	(0.7)	374	(16.7)	96.4	(0.7)	454	(5.4)
	Hungary	a	a	a	a	100.0	(0.0)	490	(4.0)
	Iceland	24.8	(1.0)	465	(3.7)	75.2	(1.0)	536	(2.4)
	Ireland	m	m	m	m	m	m	m	m
	Italy	29.1	(1.2)	433	(4.0)	70.9	(1.2)	469	(3.2)
	Japan	m	m	m	m	m	m	m	m
	Korea	m	m	m	m	m	m	m	m
	Luxembourg	m	m	m	m	m	m	m	m
	Mexico	9.1	(0.7)	370	(6.5)	90.9	(0.7)	390	(3.5)
	New Zealand	27.2	(1.2)	489	(4.0)	72.8	(1.2)	561	(3.3)
	Norway	1.4	(0.3)	401	(16.6)	98.6	(0.3)	505	(2.7)
	Poland	6.5	(0.8)	433	(11.2)	93.5	(0.8)	479	(5.5)
	Portugal	m	m	m	m	m	m	m	m
	Spain	37.7	(1.5)	442	(3.6)	62.3	(1.5)	501	(3.1)
	Sweden	4.3	(0.6)	388	(9.7)	95.7	(0.6)	516	(2.4)
	Switzerland	9.6	(0.7)	490	(7.4)	90.4	(0.7)	540	(4.6)
	United Kingdom	4.6	(0.5)	424	(10.2)	95.4	(0.5)	538	(3.1)
	United States	m	m	m	m	m	m	m	m
	OECD total	*16.7*	*(0.3)*	*459*	*(2.1)*	*83.3*	*(0.3)*	*485*	*(1.3)*
	OECD average	*12.5*	*(0.2)*	*465*	*(1.5)*	*87.5*	*(0.2)*	*508*	*(0.9)*
NON-OECD COUNTRIES	Brazil	m	m	m	m	m	m	m	m
	Latvia	m	m	m	m	m	m	m	m
	Liechtenstein	9.0	(2.2)	c	c	91.0	(2.2)	525	(7.8)
	Russian Federation	m	m	m	m	m	m	m	m
	Netherlands[1]	22.0	(1.4)	569	(8.0)	78.0	(1.4)	577	(4.0)

1. Response rate is too low to ensure comparability (see Annex A3).

Table 3.3
Variation in student performance on the scientific literacy scale

		Mean		Standard deviation		Percentiles											
						5th		10th		25th		75th		90th		95th	
		Mean score	S.E.	S.D.	S.E.	Score	S.E.	Score	S.E.	Score	S.E.	Score	S.E.	Score	S.E.	Score	S.E.
OECD COUNTRIES	Australia	528	(3.5)	94	(1.6)	368	(5.1)	402	(4.7)	463	(4.6)	596	(4.8)	646	(5.1)	675	(4.8)
	Austria	519	(2.6)	91	(1.7)	363	(5.7)	398	(4.0)	456	(3.8)	584	(3.5)	633	(4.1)	659	(4.3)
	Belgium	496	(4.3)	111	(3.8)	292	(13.5)	346	(10.2)	424	(6.6)	577	(3.5)	630	(2.6)	656	(3.0)
	Canada	529	(1.6)	89	(1.1)	380	(3.7)	412	(3.4)	469	(2.2)	592	(1.8)	641	(2.2)	670	(3.0)
	Czech Republic	511	(2.4)	94	(1.5)	355	(5.6)	389	(4.0)	449	(3.6)	577	(3.8)	632	(4.1)	663	(4.9)
	Denmark	481	(2.8)	103	(2.0)	310	(6.0)	347	(5.3)	410	(4.8)	554	(3.5)	613	(4.4)	645	(4.7)
	Finland	538	(2.5)	86	(1.2)	391	(5.2)	425	(4.2)	481	(3.5)	598	(3.0)	645	(4.3)	674	(4.3)
	France	500	(3.2)	102	(2.0)	329	(6.1)	363	(5.4)	429	(5.3)	575	(4.0)	631	(4.2)	663	(4.9)
	Germany	487	(2.4)	102	(2.0)	314	(9.5)	350	(6.0)	417	(4.9)	560	(3.3)	618	(3.5)	649	(4.7)
	Greece	461	(4.9)	97	(2.6)	300	(9.3)	334	(8.3)	393	(7.0)	530	(5.3)	585	(5.3)	616	(5.8)
	Hungary	496	(4.2)	103	(2.3)	328	(7.5)	361	(4.9)	423	(5.5)	570	(4.8)	629	(5.1)	659	(8.5)
	Iceland	496	(2.2)	88	(1.6)	351	(7.0)	381	(4.3)	436	(3.7)	558	(3.1)	607	(4.1)	635	(4.8)
	Ireland	513	(3.2)	92	(1.7)	361	(6.5)	394	(4.6)	450	(4.4)	578	(3.4)	630	(4.6)	661	(5.4)
	Italy	478	(3.1)	98	(2.6)	315	(7.1)	349	(6.2)	411	(4.4)	547	(3.5)	602	(4.0)	633	(4.4)
	Japan	550	(5.5)	90	(3.0)	391	(11.3)	430	(9.9)	495	(7.2)	612	(5.0)	659	(4.7)	688	(5.7)
	Korea	552	(2.7)	81	(1.8)	411	(5.3)	442	(5.3)	499	(4.0)	610	(3.4)	652	(3.9)	674	(5.7)
	Luxembourg	443	(2.3)	96	(2.0)	278	(7.2)	320	(6.8)	382	(3.4)	510	(2.8)	563	(4.4)	593	(4.0)
	Mexico	422	(3.2)	77	(2.1)	303	(4.8)	325	(4.6)	368	(3.1)	472	(4.7)	525	(5.5)	554	(7.0)
	New Zealand	528	(2.4)	101	(2.3)	357	(5.6)	392	(5.2)	459	(3.8)	600	(3.4)	653	(5.0)	683	(5.1)
	Norway	500	(2.8)	96	(2.0)	338	(7.3)	377	(6.6)	437	(4.0)	569	(3.5)	619	(3.9)	649	(6.2)
	Poland	483	(5.1)	97	(2.7)	326	(9.2)	359	(5.8)	415	(5.5)	553	(7.3)	610	(7.6)	639	(7.5)
	Portugal	459	(4.0)	89	(1.6)	317	(5.0)	343	(5.1)	397	(5.2)	521	(4.7)	575	(5.0)	604	(5.3)
	Spain	491	(3.0)	95	(1.8)	333	(5.1)	367	(4.3)	425	(4.4)	558	(3.5)	613	(3.9)	643	(5.5)
	Sweden	512	(2.5)	93	(1.4)	357	(5.7)	390	(4.6)	446	(4.1)	578	(3.0)	630	(3.4)	660	(4.5)
	Switzerland	496	(4.4)	100	(2.4)	332	(5.8)	366	(5.4)	427	(5.1)	567	(6.4)	626	(6.4)	656	(9.0)
	United Kingdom	532	(2.7)	98	(2.0)	366	(6.8)	401	(6.0)	466	(3.8)	602	(3.9)	656	(4.7)	687	(5.0)
	United States	499	(7.3)	101	(2.9)	330	(11.7)	368	(10.0)	430	(9.6)	571	(8.0)	628	(7.0)	658	(8.4)
	OECD total	*502*	*(2.0)*	*102*	*(0.9)*	*332*	*(3.3)*	*368*	*(3.1)*	*431*	*(2.8)*	*576*	*(2.1)*	*631*	*(1.9)*	*662*	*(2.3)*
	OECD average	*500*	*(0.7)*	*100*	*(0.5)*	*332*	*(1.5)*	*368*	*(1.0)*	*431*	*(1.0)*	*572*	*(0.8)*	*627*	*(0.8)*	*657*	*(1.2)*
NON-OECD COUNTRIES	Brazil	375	(3.3)	90	(2.3)	230	(5.5)	262	(5.9)	315	(3.7)	432	(4.9)	492	(7.8)	531	(8.2)
	Latvia	460	(5.6)	98	(3.0)	299	(10.1)	334	(8.8)	393	(7.7)	528	(5.7)	585	(7.2)	620	(8.0)
	Liechtenstein	476	(7.1)	94	(5.4)	314	(23.5)	357	(20.0)	409	(12.3)	543	(12.7)	595	(12.4)	629	(24.0)
	Russian Federation	460	(4.7)	99	(2.0)	298	(6.5)	333	(5.4)	392	(6.2)	529	(5.8)	591	(5.9)	625	(5.7)

Table 3.4
School's or classroom teacher's pass/fail threshold and performance on the scientific literacy scale

		Below school's or classroom teacher's pass/fail threshold				At or above school's or classroom teacher's pass/fail threshold			
		Percentage of students		Performance on the scientific literacy scale		Percentage of students		Performance on the scientific literacy scale	
		%	S.E.	Mean score	S.E.	%	S.E.	Mean score	S.E
OECD COUNTRIES	Australia	13.4	(0.9)	476	(6.3)	86.6	(0.9)	539	(4.0)
	Austria	3.4	(0.5)	517	(13.9)	96.6	(0.5)	528	(2.7)
	Belgium	m	m	m	m	m	m	m	m
	Canada	11.8	(0.4)	494	(3.2)	88.2	(0.4)	537	(1.5)
	Czech Republic	0.6	(0.2)	c	c	99.4	(0.2)	520	(2.4)
	Denmark	2.2	(0.3)	393	(18.9)	97.8	(0.3)	492	(2.6)
	Finland	0.2	(0.1)	c	c	99.8	(0.1)	539	(2.5)
	France	25.8	(1.1)	480	(4.4)	74.2	(1.1)	531	(3.1)
	Germany	m	m	m	m	m	m	m	m
	Greece	2.5	(0.6)	369	(14.7)	97.5	(0.6)	469	(5.4)
	Hungary	a	a	a	a	100.0	(0.0)	500	(3.9)
	Iceland	11.2	(0.8)	450	(6.2)	88.8	(0.8)	512	(2.5)
	Ireland	m	m	m	m	m	m	m	m
	Italy	19.8	(1.2)	440	(5.5)	80.2	(1.2)	489	(3.5)
	Japan	m	m	m	m	m	m	m	m
	Korea	m	m	m	m	m	m	m	m
	Luxembourg	m	m	m	m	m	m	m	m
	Mexico	5.8	(0.6)	402	(8.2)	94.2	(0.6)	421	(3.4)
	New Zealand	22.2	(1.1)	471	(4.6)	77.8	(1.1)	553	(2.8)
	Norway	1.7	(0.3)	383	(18.7)	98.3	(0.3)	507	(2.6)
	Poland	1.5	(0.3)	460	(20.5)	98.5	(0.3)	491	(5.1)
	Portugal	m	m	m	m	m	m	m	m
	Spain	26.1	(1.1)	440	(4.0)	73.9	(1.1)	514	(3.1)
	Sweden	4.5	(0.6)	417	(8.5)	95.5	(0.6)	517	(2.5)
	Switzerland	4.9	(0.6)	470	(12.1)	95.1	(0.6)	513	(4.6)
	United Kingdom	3.4	(0.5)	423	(10.5)	96.6	(0.5)	543	(3.6)
	United States	m	m	m	m	m	m	m	m
	OECD total	*11.2*	*(0.3)*	*455*	*(2.2)*	*88.8*	*(0.3)*	*496*	*(1.3)*
	OECD average	*8.4*	*(0.2)*	*457*	*(1.7)*	*91.6*	*(0.2)*	*511*	*(0.9)*
NON-OECD COUNTRIES	Brazil	m	m	m	m	m	m	m	m
	Latvia	m	m	m	m	m	m	m	m
	Liechtenstein	9.3	(2.3)	c	c	90.7	(2.3)	488	(7.3)
	Russian Federation	m	m	m	m	m	m	m	m
	Netherlands[1]	8.4	(0.9)	520	(9.6)	91.6	(0.9)	537	(4.0)

1. Response rate is too low to ensure comparability (see Annex A3).

Table 3.5

Between-school and within-school variation in student performance on the mathematical and scientific literacy scales

	Total variation in SP[1]	Total variation in SP expressed as a percentage of the average variation in SP across OECD countries	Total variation in SP between schools	Total variation in SP within schools	Variation explained by the international socio-economic index of occupational status of students		Variation explained by the international socio-economic index of occupational status of students AND schools		Total variation between schools expressed as a percentage of the total variation within the country[2]
					Between-school variation	Within-school variation	Between-school variation	Within-school variation	
MATHEMATICAL LITERACY									
OECD COUNTRIES									
Australia	8 107	93.9	16.2	76.3	7.4	6.0	10.4	6.4	17.5
Austria	8 545	99.0	58.6	53.4	8.4	0.2	29.4	0.3	52.3
Belgium	11 268	130.5	71.6	59.4	13.7	2.7	38.5	2.7	54.7
Canada	7 152	82.9	14.3	68.2	2.9	3.7	4.5	3.8	17.3
Czech Republic	9 276	107.5	45.9	59.2	9.3	2.1	25.8	2.1	43.7
Denmark	7 500	86.9	15.4	70.8	7.9	5.5	8.9	5.7	17.8
Finland	6 451	74.7	6.1	68.5	1.0	5.7	1.0	5.7	8.1
France	m	m	m	m	m	m	m	m	m
Germany	10 512	121.8	65.5	53.1	10.9	1.7	40.1	1.8	55.2
Greece	11 731	135.9	65.4	74.0	9.9	0.9	29.5	0.9	46.9
Hungary	9 592	111.1	60.1	53.6	14.2	0.5	45.2	0.5	52.9
Iceland	7 159	82.9	4.5	78.0	1.1	4.2	1.1	4.1	5.4
Ireland	6 982	80.9	9.4	73.1	3.9	4.3	6.1	4.5	11.4
Italy	8 174	94.7	40.5	55.1	3.3	0.2	15.0	0.2	42.4
Japan[3]	7 559	87.6	43.7	44.3	m	m	m	m	49.7
Korea	7 110	82.4	32.1	50.9	2.7	0.7	13.6	0.7	38.7
Luxembourg	8 566	99.2	24.9	73.4	9.5	6.9	21.0	6.8	25.3
Mexico	6 834	79.2	41.1	39.3	6.1	0.4	23.4	0.4	51.1
New Zealand	9 748	112.9	19.8	93.7	7.8	10.1	11.7	10.2	17.5
Norway	8 383	97.1	7.8	89.1	1.5	6.2	1.6	6.2	8.1
Poland	10 510	121.8	63.3	53.5	7.5	0.3	38.8	0.2	54.2
Portugal	8 341	96.6	30.1	64.0	10.5	4.8	18.2	5.0	32.0
Spain	8 192	94.9	17.1	76.1	5.9	2.5	9.0	2.6	18.3
Sweden	8 724	101.1	8.3	92.7	5.3	8.7	6.0	8.7	8.3
Switzerland	9 922	115.0	47.5	68.2	9.6	3.2	21.1	3.0	41.1
United Kingdom	8 402	97.3	21.2	72.0	8.5	6.0	14.8	6.5	22.7
United States	9 671	112.0	35.0	74.5	12.4	6.3	24.2	6.5	32.0
OECD average	*8 631*								
NON-OECD COUNTRIES									
Brazil	9 493	110.0	40.0	71.5	26.8	71.8	15.5	71.0	35.9
Latvia	10 654	123.4	33.1	90.8	30.9	88.1	24.4	88.0	26.7
Liechtenstein	9 162	106.2	m	m	m	m	m	m	m
Russian Federation	10 837	125.6	45.5	79.9	39.6	77.2	31.8	77.2	36.3
SCIENTIFIC LITERACY									
OECD COUNTRIES									
Australia	8 879	98.4	17.2	81.0	5.7	4.5	9.6	4.8	17.5
Austria	8 327	92.3	58.7	46.5	10.5	0.6	33.4	0.5	55.8
Belgium	12 314	136.5	77.4	62.3	14.4	2.2	46.0	2.3	55.4
Canada	7 893	87.5	13.9	71.9	3.4	4.5	4.9	4.6	16.2
Czech Republic	8 821	97.8	39.2	58.0	9.9	2.0	26.1	2.1	40.3
Denmark	10 652	118.1	19.4	101.6	8.7	10.2	9.7	10.5	16.0
Finland	7 446	82.6	5.5	78.1	0.9	3.8	1.0	3.8	6.6
France	m	m	m	m	m	m	m	m	m
Germany	10 394	115.2	58.5	59.8	11.7	2.3	40.4	2.4	49.5
Greece	9 390	104.1	42.0	62.9	5.5	0.4	18.6	0.3	40.0
Hungary	10 510	116.5	65.9	58.9	11.8	0.7	49.0	0.4	52.8
Iceland	7 705	85.4	6.4	78.3	1.0	1.4	0.8	1.5	7.6
Ireland	8 416	93.3	13.3	81.2	4.7	5.4	7.5	5.4	14.1
Italy	9 612	106.6	46.9	64.2	3.1	0.5	14.1	0.4	42.2
Japan[3]	8 185	90.7	40.6	50.9	m	m	m	m	44.4
Korea	6 508	72.2	27.6	44.5	1.6	0.3	10.0	0.2	38.3
Luxembourg	9 281	102.9	28.0	73.4	6.9	4.6	21.6	4.5	27.6
Mexico	5 940	65.9	26.8	38.8	5.0	0.0	15.5	0.0	40.9
New Zealand	10 149	112.5	18.9	92.6	7.7	10.0	11.4	10.0	16.9
Norway	9 128	101.2	10.2	92.5	2.9	6.7	3.3	6.7	10.0
Poland	9 378	104.0	53.3	50.5	7.0	0.4	33.1	0.4	51.4
Portugal	7 923	87.8	27.4	60.3	8.0	3.9	16.3	3.9	31.3
Spain	9 097	100.9	18.2	82.5	8.1	3.5	11.1	3.6	18.0
Sweden	8 688	96.3	8.0	90.0	3.5	6.0	4.0	6.0	8.2
Switzerland	10 012	111.0	45.4	63.9	8.7	3.7	19.5	3.6	41.6
United Kingdom	9 639	106.9	24.6	76.7	9.0	7.1	16.0	7.6	24.3
United States	10 217	113.3	40.3	73.0	14.1	6.7	26.1	7.1	35.6
OECD average	*9 019*								
NON-OECD COUNTRIES									
Brazil	8 181	90.7	25.5	65.2	7.7	0.2	14.6	0.8	28.1
Latvia	9 543	105.8	29.8	74.5	4.0	3.0	12.2	3.0	28.6
Liechtenstein	8 896	98.6	m	m	m	m	m	m	m
Russian Federation	9 825	108.9	33.2	75.3	4.0	2.0	10.9	1.9	30.6

Variation expressed as a percentage of the average variation in student performance (SP) across OECD countries

1. The total variation in student performance is obtained as the square of the standard deviation shown in Table 3.1 for mathematical literacy and Table 3.3 for scientific literacy. The statistical variance and not the standard deviation is used for this comparison to allow for the decomposition of the components of variation in student performance. For reasons explained in the *PISA 2000 Technical Report*, the sum of the between-school and within-school variance components may, for some countries, differ slightly from the square of the standard deviation shown in Tables 3.1 and 3.3.
2. This index is often referred to as the intra-class correlation (rho).
3. Due to the sampling methods used in Japan, the between-school variance in Japan includes variation between classes within schools.

Table 3.6
Student performance on the combined reading, scientific and mathematical literacy scales and national income

	Performance on the combined reading literacy scale		Performance on the scientific literacy scale		Performance on the mathematical literacy scale		GDP per capita (US dollars[1]) (1999)	Cumulative expenditure on educational institutions per student (US dollars[1]) (1998)
	Mean score	S.E.	Mean score	S.E.	Mean score	S.E.		
Australia	528	(3.5)	528	(3.5)	533	(3.5)	24 400	44 623
Austria	507	(2.4)	519	(2.6)	515	(2.5)	24 600	71 387
Belgium	507	(3.6)	496	(4.3)	520	(3.9)	24 300	46 338
Czech Republic	492	(2.4)	511	(2.4)	498	(2.8)	13 100	21 384
Denmark	497	(2.4)	481	(2.8)	514	(2.4)	26 300	65 794
Finland	546	(2.6)	538	(2.5)	536	(2.2)	22 800	45 363
France	505	(2.7)	500	(3.2)	517	(2.7)	21 900	50 481
Germany	484	(2.5)	487	(2.4)	490	(2.5)	23 600	41 978
Greece	474	(5.0)	461	(4.9)	447	(5.6)	14 800	27 356
Hungary	480	(4.0)	496	(4.2)	488	(4.0)	10 900	20 277
Ireland	527	(3.2)	513	(3.2)	503	(2.7)	25 200	31 015
Italy	487	(2.9)	478	(3.1)	457	(2.9)	21 800	60 824
Japan	522	(5.2)	550	(5.5)	557	(5.5)	24 500	53 255
Korea	525	(2.4)	552	(2.7)	547	(2.8)	15 900	30 844
Mexico	422	(3.3)	422	(3.2)	387	(3.4)	8 100	11 239
Norway	505	(2.8)	500	(2.8)	499	(2.8)	27 600	61 677
Poland	479	(4.5)	483	(5.1)	470	(5.5)	8 100	16 154
Portugal	470	(4.5)	459	(4.0)	454	(4.1)	16 500	36 521
Spain	493	(2.7)	491	(3.0)	476	(3.1)	18 100	36 699
Sweden	516	(2.2)	512	(2.5)	510	(2.5)	23 000	53 386
Switzerland	494	(4.3)	496	(4.4)	529	(4.4)	27 500	64 266
United Kingdom	523	(2.6)	532	(2.7)	529	(2.5)	22 300	42 793
United States	504	(7.1)	499	(7.3)	493	(7.6)	33 900	67 313
OECD total	*499*	*(2.0)*	*502*	*(2.0)*	*498*	*(2.1)*		
OECD average	*500*	*(0.6)*	*500*	*(0.7)*	*500*	*(0.7)*		
Brazil	396	(3.1)	375	(3.3)	334	(3.7)	6 840	9231
Latvia	458	(5.3)	460	(5.6)	463	(4.5)	6 164	m
Liechtenstein	483	(4.1)	476	(7.1)	514	(7.0)	22 235	m
Russian Federation	462	(4.2)	460	(4.7)	478	(5.5)	6 930	m

OECD COUNTRIES
NON-OECD COUNTRIES

1. US dollars converted using PPPs.

Table 4.1
Index of interest in reading and performance on the combined reading literacy scale, by national quarters of the index
Results based on students' self-reports

| | | Index of interest in reading[1] | | | | | | | | | | | | | |
| | | All students | | Males | | Females | | Bottom quarter | | Second quarter | | Third quarter | | Top quarter | |
		Mean index	S.E.	Mean index	S.E.	Mean index	S.E.	Mean index	S.E.	Mean index	S.E.	Mean index	S.E.	Mean index	S.E.
OECD COUNTRIES	Australia	−0.02	(0.02)	−0.16	(0.02)	0.13	(0.03)	−1.03	(0.02)	−0.25	(0.01)	0.21	(0.01)	1.00	(0.02)
	Austria	−0.09	(0.03)	−0.41	(0.02)	0.20	(0.03)	−1.44	(0.01)	−0.44	(0.01)	0.20	(0.01)	1.31	(0.02)
	Belgium (Fl.)	−0.32	(0.02)	−0.54	(0.03)	−0.07	(0.03)	−1.60	(0.01)	−0.55	(0.01)	0.01	(0.01)	0.86	(0.02)
	Czech Republic	0.11	(0.02)	−0.31	(0.03)	0.48	(0.03)	−1.29	(0.02)	−0.27	(0.01)	0.43	(0.01)	1.58	(0.01)
	Denmark	0.19	(0.02)	−0.07	(0.02)	0.45	(0.03)	−1.13	(0.02)	−0.19	(0.01)	0.50	(0.01)	1.58	(0.01)
	Finland	0.19	(0.02)	−0.26	(0.02)	0.61	(0.02)	−1.12	(0.01)	−0.18	(0.01)	0.48	(0.01)	1.58	(0.01)
	Germany	−0.06	(0.02)	−0.38	(0.03)	0.25	(0.02)	−1.44	(0.01)	−0.43	(0.01)	0.24	(0.01)	1.38	(0.02)
	Hungary	−0.06	(0.02)	−0.32	(0.03)	0.20	(0.03)	−1.43	(0.02)	−0.43	(0.01)	0.22	(0.01)	1.40	(0.01)
	Iceland	−0.06	(0.02)	−0.26	(0.02)	0.14	(0.02)	−1.20	(0.02)	−0.35	(0.01)	0.17	(0.01)	1.14	(0.02)
	Ireland	0.04	(0.03)	−0.24	(0.03)	0.32	(0.03)	−1.40	(0.01)	−0.33	(0.01)	0.37	(0.01)	1.54	(0.01)
	Italy	−0.11	(0.03)	−0.39	(0.03)	0.18	(0.03)	−1.43	(0.01)	−0.44	(0.01)	0.22	(0.01)	1.22	(0.01)
	Korea	−0.31	(0.02)	−0.32	(0.03)	−0.29	(0.04)	−1.47	(0.01)	−0.62	(0.00)	−0.11	(0.01)	0.95	(0.02)
	Luxembourg	−0.07	(0.02)	−0.28	(0.03)	0.14	(0.03)	−1.35	(0.02)	−0.39	(0.01)	0.20	(0.01)	1.25	(0.02)
	Mexico	0.15	(0.01)	0.04	(0.02)	0.25	(0.02)	−0.64	(0.02)	−0.05	(0.00)	0.28	(0.00)	0.99	(0.01)
	New Zealand	0.07	(0.02)	−0.10	(0.03)	0.25	(0.02)	−1.16	(0.02)	−0.25	(0.01)	0.33	(0.01)	1.38	(0.02)
	Norway	0.01	(0.02)	−0.30	(0.03)	0.33	(0.03)	−1.38	(0.01)	−0.36	(0.01)	0.32	(0.01)	1.46	(0.01)
	Portugal	0.23	(0.02)	−0.14	(0.02)	0.57	(0.02)	−1.00	(0.01)	−0.05	(0.01)	0.49	(0.01)	1.46	(0.01)
	Sweden	0.09	(0.01)	−0.08	(0.02)	0.26	(0.02)	−0.85	(0.02)	−0.10	(0.00)	0.26	(0.00)	1.07	(0.02)
	Switzerland	0.04	(0.02)	−0.29	(0.03)	0.36	(0.03)	−1.24	(0.02)	−0.28	(0.01)	0.30	(0.01)	1.39	(0.02)
	United States	0.02	(0.03)	−0.16	(0.04)	0.19	(0.03)	−1.22	(0.02)	−0.29	(0.01)	0.27	(0.01)	1.34	(0.02)
	OECD total	*−0.01*	*(0.01)*	*−0.20*	*(0.02)*	*0.19*	*(0.02)*	*−1.20*	*(0.01)*	*−0.31*	*(0.00)*	*0.24*	*(0.00)*	*1.25*	*(0.01)*
	OECD average	*0.00*	*(0.00)*	*−0.24*	*(0.01)*	*0.26*	*(0.01)*	*−1.23*	*(0.00)*	*−0.31*	*(0.00)*	*0.28*	*(0.00)*	*1.30*	*(0.00)*
NON-OECD COUNTRIES	Brazil	0.31	(0.02)	0.12	(0.02)	0.46	(0.02)	−0.70	(0.02)	0.06	(0.01)	0.48	(0.01)	1.39	(0.02)
	Latvia	0.23	(0.02)	−0.04	(0.02)	0.50	(0.03)	−0.91	(0.02)	−0.12	(0.01)	0.49	(0.01)	1.48	(0.01)
	Liechtenstein	−0.07	(0.05)	−0.28	(0.07)	0.15	(0.08)	−1.33	(0.04)	−0.38	(0.02)	0.18	(0.02)	1.23	(0.06)
	Russian Federation	0.15	(0.02)	−0.07	(0.02)	0.35	(0.03)	−1.15	(0.02)	−0.21	(0.01)	0.44	(0.01)	1.51	(0.01)
	Netherlands[3]	−0.17	(0.04)	−0.52	(0.04)	0.18	(0.04)	−1.53	(0.02)	−0.54	(0.01)	0.13	(0.01)	1.27	(0.02)

| | | Performance on the combined reading literacy scale, by national quarters of the index of interest in reading[2] | | | | | | | | Change in the combined reading literacy score per unit of the index of interest in reading[2] | |
| | | Bottom quarter | | Second quarter | | Third quarter | | Top quarter | | | |
		Mean score	S.E.	Mean score	S.E.	Mean score	S.E.	Mean score	S.E.	Change	S.E.
OECD COUNTRIES	Australia	495	(4.0)	505	(4.3)	540	(4.7)	588	(4.6)	41.1	(2.37)
	Austria	481	(3.1)	485	(3.5)	514	(3.4)	557	(3.5)	28.5	(1.48)
	Belgium (Fl.)	515	(4.5)	516	(6.1)	544	(5.3)	570	(6.0)	22.6	(2.05)
	Czech Republic	471	(2.6)	484	(3.0)	512	(3.2)	548	(3.1)	26.7	(1.29)
	Denmark	472	(3.3)	479	(3.4)	503	(3.6)	551	(3.5)	29.6	(1.58)
	Finland	502	(2.7)	527	(4.6)	564	(2.8)	599	(3.2)	36.1	(1.18)
	Germany	468	(3.7)	471	(3.7)	500	(4.2)	552	(3.8)	30.0	(1.65)
	Hungary	451	(3.8)	466	(5.4)	489	(5.2)	529	(4.4)	27.8	(1.55)
	Iceland	475	(3.2)	493	(3.1)	514	(3.4)	560	(3.3)	35.3	(1.85)
	Ireland	495	(3.8)	503	(4.0)	536	(4.1)	580	(3.7)	30.0	(1.46)
	Italy	463	(4.2)	474	(4.2)	490	(3.5)	524	(3.3)	22.5	(1.51)
	Korea	493	(2.8)	519	(3.2)	536	(3.5)	551	(2.6)	22.6	(1.27)
	Luxembourg	444	(3.0)	438	(3.5)	451	(3.0)	490	(3.4)	17.0	(1.77)
	Mexico	422	(4.1)	420	(3.9)	418	(3.7)	433	(5.0)	8.8	(2.61)
	New Zealand	506	(3.5)	509	(4.5)	534	(4.8)	593	(4.0)	34.5	(1.70)
	Norway	473	(5.0)	487	(4.0)	516	(3.7)	569	(3.2)	34.5	(1.85)
	Portugal	442	(4.7)	454	(6.1)	473	(4.7)	513	(4.7)	26.7	(1.61)
	Sweden	479	(3.1)	501	(3.2)	524	(3.3)	568	(2.8)	43.8	(2.01)
	Switzerland	464	(4.2)	479	(4.6)	499	(5.7)	548	(5.1)	31.5	(1.94)
	United States	488	(8.1)	495	(6.5)	507	(7.9)	558	(6.9)	27.0	(2.37)
	OECD total	*474*	*(3.2)*	*482*	*(3.0)*	*497*	*(3.4)*	*537*	*(3.3)*	*23.6*	*(1.16)*
	OECD average	*474*	*(0.8)*	*485*	*(1.1)*	*508*	*(1.1)*	*549*	*(0.9)*	*27.9*	*(0.41)*
NON-OECD COUNTRIES	Brazil	397	(4.3)	395	(3.5)	399	(4.5)	419	(4.3)	10.0	(2.11)
	Latvia	429	(6.6)	440	(6.5)	464	(5.3)	512	(5.6)	32.5	(2.21)
	Liechtenstein	454	(10.0)	463	(9.6)	494	(10.2)	528	(10.8)	29.5	(5.13)
	Russian Federation	440	(5.1)	453	(3.5)	468	(4.8)	498	(5.3)	20.4	(1.16)
	Netherlands[3]	510	(4.8)	516	(4.9)	534	(4.7)	572	(4.6)	22.8	(1.93)

1. For the definition of the index see Annex A1.
2. For explained variation see Annex A2. Unit changes marked in bold are statistically significant. Where bottom and top quarters are marked in bold this indicates that their difference is statistically significant.
3. Response rate is too low to ensure comparability (see Annex A3).

Table 4.2
Index of interest in mathematics and performance on the mathematical literacy scale, by national quarters of the index
Results based on students' self-reports

	Index of interest in mathematics[1]													
	All students		Males		Females		Bottom quarter		Second quarter		Third quarter		Top quarter	
	Mean index	S.E.	Mean index	S.E.	Mean index	S.E.	Mean index	S.E.	Mean index	S.E.	Mean index	S.E.	Mean index	S.E.
OECD COUNTRIES														
Australia	0.04	(0.02)	0.14	(0.02)	−0.08	(0.03)	−0.94	(0.03)	−0.17	(0.01)	0.28	(0.01)	0.99	(0.03)
Austria	−0.23	(0.03)	−0.03	(0.03)	−0.42	(0.03)	−1.35	(0.02)	−0.48	(0.01)	0.02	(0.01)	0.89	(0.03)
Belgium (Fl.)	−0.11	(0.03)	−0.06	(0.04)	−0.16	(0.03)	−1.21	(0.03)	−0.32	(0.01)	0.11	(0.01)	1.00	(0.03)
Czech Republic	−0.07	(0.02)	0.05	(0.03)	−0.17	(0.02)	−1.24	(0.02)	−0.30	(0.01)	0.18	(0.01)	1.09	(0.02)
Denmark	0.47	(0.03)	0.62	(0.04)	0.31	(0.04)	−0.98	(0.03)	0.17	(0.01)	0.76	(0.01)	1.92	(0.02)
Finland	−0.07	(0.02)	0.06	(0.03)	−0.19	(0.03)	−1.28	(0.02)	−0.35	(0.01)	0.18	(0.01)	1.17	(0.03)
Germany	−0.07	(0.03)	0.11	(0.04)	−0.23	(0.03)	−1.32	(0.03)	−0.34	(0.01)	0.19	(0.01)	1.22	(0.03)
Hungary	−0.04	(0.03)	−0.03	(0.04)	−0.06	(0.03)	−1.25	(0.02)	−0.36	(0.01)	0.15	(0.01)	1.28	(0.03)
Iceland	0.11	(0.02)	0.09	(0.03)	0.12	(0.03)	−1.00	(0.03)	−0.17	(0.01)	0.32	(0.01)	1.27	(0.03)
Ireland	−0.01	(0.02)	0.06	(0.03)	−0.08	(0.04)	−1.31	(0.02)	−0.31	(0.01)	0.29	(0.01)	1.28	(0.03)
Italy	0.00	(0.03)	0.03	(0.04)	−0.03	(0.04)	−1.29	(0.03)	−0.29	(0.01)	0.29	(0.01)	1.31	(0.03)
Korea	−0.27	(0.03)	−0.25	(0.05)	−0.29	(0.05)	−1.66	(0.01)	−0.66	(0.01)	−0.01	(0.01)	1.27	(0.03)
Luxembourg	−0.18	(0.03)	−0.05	(0.03)	−0.30	(0.04)	−1.43	(0.02)	−0.48	(0.01)	0.08	(0.01)	1.11	(0.03)
Mexico	0.39	(0.02)	0.38	(0.03)	0.40	(0.03)	−0.47	(0.02)	0.18	(0.01)	0.53	(0.00)	1.32	(0.02)
New Zealand	0.09	(0.03)	0.20	(0.04)	−0.01	(0.03)	−1.15	(0.03)	−0.17	(0.01)	0.37	(0.01)	1.31	(0.02)
Norway	−0.28	(0.03)	−0.04	(0.04)	−0.51	(0.04)	−1.74	(0.02)	−0.60	(0.01)	0.09	(0.01)	1.13	(0.03)
Portugal	0.26	(0.02)	0.20	(0.03)	0.31	(0.03)	−0.96	(0.02)	0.01	(0.01)	0.52	(0.01)	1.48	(0.02)
Sweden	−0.21	(0.02)	−0.08	(0.03)	−0.34	(0.03)	−1.34	(0.02)	−0.37	(0.01)	0.04	(0.01)	0.85	(0.03)
Switzerland	−0.03	(0.03)	0.20	(0.03)	−0.26	(0.03)	−1.21	(0.02)	−0.30	(0.01)	0.24	(0.01)	1.17	(0.02)
United States	0.08	(0.03)	0.10	(0.05)	0.05	(0.03)	−1.18	(0.04)	−0.19	(0.01)	0.36	(0.01)	1.32	(0.03)
OECD total	*0.05*	*(0.01)*	*0.10*	*(0.02)*	*0.01*	*(0.02)*	*−1.15*	*(0.02)*	*−0.22*	*(0.01)*	*0.30*	*(0.01)*	*1.28*	*(0.01)*
OECD average	*0.00*	*(0.00)*	*0.09*	*(0.01)*	*−0.09*	*(0.01)*	*−1.22*	*(0.01)*	*−0.27*	*(0.00)*	*0.25*	*(0.00)*	*1.22*	*(0.01)*
NON-OECD COUNTRIES														
Brazil	0.69	(0.02)	0.75	(0.03)	0.65	(0.03)	−0.38	(0.02)	0.38	(0.01)	0.87	(0.01)	1.91	(0.02)
Latvia	0.40	(0.04)	0.42	(0.04)	0.39	(0.04)	−0.76	(0.03)	0.10	(0.01)	0.68	(0.01)	1.61	(0.03)
Liechtenstein	−0.03	(0.07)	0.22	(0.08)	−0.26	(0.09)	−0.96	(0.09)	−0.24	(0.02)	0.17	(0.01)	0.96	(0.09)
Russian Federation	0.13	(0.03)	0.11	(0.03)	0.14	(0.03)	−1.05	(0.02)	−0.20	(0.01)	0.38	(0.01)	1.37	(0.02)
Netherlands[3]	−0.03	(0.03)	0.26	(0.05)	−0.32	(0.04)	−1.38	(0.03)	−0.31	(0.01)	0.34	(0.01)	1.28	(0.03)

	Performance on the mathematical literacy scale, by national quarters of the index of interest in mathematics[2]								Change in the mathematical literacy score per unit of the index of interest in mathematics[2]	
	Bottom quarter		Second quarter		Third quarter		Top quarter			
	Mean score	S.E.	Mean score	S.E.	Mean score	S.E.	Mean score	S.E.	Change	S.E.
OECD COUNTRIES										
Australia	529	(6.1)	525	(4.8)	530	(4.8)	560	(5.3)	**15.0**	(3.10)
Austria	510	(4.3)	519	(4.4)	510	(5.0)	526	(4.8)	**7.8**	(2.37)
Belgium (Fl.)	533	(5.1)	546	(5.9)	545	(6.6)	564	(7.5)	**12.5**	(3.12)
Czech Republic	497	(4.4)	495	(4.5)	509	(4.3)	527	(4.7)	**13.5**	(2.13)
Denmark	496	(3.9)	507	(3.8)	521	(4.6)	548	(4.4)	**17.1**	(1.80)
Finland	508	(3.5)	527	(3.8)	541	(3.7)	575	(3.4)	**25.0**	(1.75)
Germany	497	(4.4)	487	(4.0)	494	(5.0)	514	(4.7)	**8.9**	(1.97)
Hungary	477	(5.6)	483	(4.7)	492	(5.5)	513	(5.9)	**14.0**	(2.33)
Iceland	499	(4.1)	502	(4.1)	520	(4.1)	549	(4.3)	**22.9**	(2.16)
Ireland	501	(3.9)	500	(4.4)	499	(5.1)	519	(4.6)	**7.8**	(2.08)
Italy	447	(4.1)	455	(5.4)	454	(4.5)	475	(5.1)	**9.3**	(2.29)
Korea	503	(4.0)	537	(3.6)	564	(4.6)	584	(4.1)	**26.7**	(1.74)
Luxembourg	465	(3.9)	454	(4.5)	451	(4.5)	465	(4.5)	0.5	(2.15)
Mexico	385	(5.3)	386	(4.2)	387	(4.5)	396	(5.6)	**9.5**	(3.05)
New Zealand	532	(5.0)	539	(5.0)	534	(5.1)	566	(6.1)	**13.5**	(2.78)
Norway	475	(4.1)	492	(4.5)	502	(4.7)	544	(4.3)	**22.6**	(1.67)
Portugal	433	(4.8)	451	(5.3)	459	(5.3)	474	(5.7)	**15.5**	(2.16)
Sweden	495	(3.3)	509	(4.2)	508	(4.4)	534	(4.6)	**16.0**	(2.10)
Switzerland	525	(6.5)	533	(6.0)	531	(5.5)	541	(5.6)	**6.9**	(2.54)
United States	491	(9.5)	493	(6.2)	489	(10.8)	525	(9.8)	**12.0**	(3.09)
OECD total	*476*	*(3.9)*	*481*	*(3.0)*	*484*	*(4.3)*	*509*	*(4.5)*	***6.1***	*(1.55)*
OECD average	*489*	*(1.2)*	*496*	*(1.2)*	*501*	*(1.1)*	*524*	*(1.3)*	***10.7***	*(0.63)*
NON-OECD COUNTRIES										
Brazil	328	(4.9)	334	(5.4)	340	(5.8)	359	(7.0)	**13.4**	(2.95)
Latvia	442	(6.0)	463	(7.9)	465	(6.4)	492	(6.1)	**18.3**	(3.16)
Liechtenstein	511	(13.9)	511	(16.9)	506	(15.0)	532	(15.3)	7.6	(10.26)
Russian Federation	460	(6.8)	466	(5.8)	482	(7.2)	513	(5.3)	**20.3**	(2.75)
Netherlands[3]	555	(6.1)	555	(6.5)	569	(6.4)	580	(5.8)	9.6	(3.28)

1. For the definition of the index see Annex A1.
2. For explained variation see Annex A2. Unit changes marked in bold are statistically significant. Where bottom and top quarters are marked in bold this indicates that their difference is statistically significant.
3. Response rate is too low to ensure comparability (see Annex A3).

Table 4.3
Index of engagement in reading and performance on the combined reading literacy scale, by national quarters of the index
Results based on students' self-reports

Index of engagement in reading[1]

	All students		Males		Females		Bottom quarter		Second quarter		Third quarter		Top quarter	
	Mean index	S.E.	Mean index	S.E.	Mean index	S.E.	Mean index	S.E.	Mean index	S.E.	Mean index	S.E.	Mean index	S.E.
OECD COUNTRIES														
Australia	−0.07	(0.03)	−0.29	(0.03)	0.16	(0.03)	−1.26	(0.02)	−0.39	(0.01)	0.15	(0.01)	1.21	(0.02)
Austria	−0.04	(0.03)	−0.47	(0.03)	0.35	(0.03)	−1.46	(0.02)	−0.55	(0.01)	0.27	(0.01)	1.57	(0.03)
Belgium	−0.25	(0.02)	−0.52	(0.02)	0.04	(0.02)	−1.43	(0.01)	−0.61	(0.01)	−0.01	(0.00)	1.07	(0.02)
Canada	0.00	(0.01)	−0.31	(0.01)	0.30	(0.02)	−1.31	(0.01)	−0.37	(0.00)	0.26	(0.00)	1.40	(0.01)
Czech Republic	0.17	(0.02)	−0.24	(0.03)	0.54	(0.03)	−1.03	(0.02)	−0.19	(0.01)	0.44	(0.01)	1.47	(0.02)
Denmark	0.00	(0.02)	−0.31	(0.02)	0.32	(0.03)	−1.18	(0.01)	−0.35	(0.01)	0.25	(0.01)	1.30	(0.02)
Finland	0.20	(0.02)	−0.28	(0.02)	0.64	(0.02)	−1.07	(0.02)	−0.16	(0.01)	0.46	(0.01)	1.56	(0.02)
France	−0.06	(0.02)	−0.34	(0.02)	0.19	(0.02)	−1.26	(0.01)	−0.39	(0.01)	0.17	(0.01)	1.24	(0.02)
Germany	−0.08	(0.03)	−0.50	(0.03)	0.32	(0.03)	−1.51	(0.01)	−0.58	(0.01)	0.24	(0.01)	1.50	(0.02)
Greece	−0.01	(0.02)	−0.22	(0.02)	0.19	(0.02)	−0.87	(0.02)	−0.26	(0.00)	0.15	(0.01)	0.92	(0.02)
Hungary	0.07	(0.02)	−0.15	(0.03)	0.29	(0.03)	−0.91	(0.01)	−0.25	(0.00)	0.23	(0.01)	1.20	(0.02)
Iceland	0.02	(0.02)	−0.24	(0.02)	0.27	(0.02)	−1.09	(0.02)	−0.29	(0.01)	0.22	(0.01)	1.23	(0.02)
Ireland	−0.07	(0.02)	−0.36	(0.03)	0.21	(0.03)	−1.26	(0.01)	−0.41	(0.01)	0.18	(0.01)	1.21	(0.02)
Italy	0.00	(0.03)	−0.28	(0.02)	0.29	(0.03)	−1.14	(0.02)	−0.34	(0.01)	0.23	(0.01)	1.25	(0.02)
Japan	0.09	(0.03)	−0.07	(0.03)	0.24	(0.04)	−1.16	(0.01)	−0.33	(0.01)	0.29	(0.01)	1.54	(0.02)
Korea	0.02	(0.02)	−0.08	(0.02)	0.14	(0.04)	−0.97	(0.01)	−0.31	(0.00)	0.18	(0.01)	1.16	(0.02)
Luxembourg	−0.10	(0.02)	−0.43	(0.02)	0.23	(0.02)	−1.38	(0.02)	−0.45	(0.01)	0.16	(0.01)	1.29	(0.02)
Mexico	0.29	(0.02)	0.12	(0.02)	0.46	(0.02)	−0.58	(0.02)	0.02	(0.00)	0.44	(0.01)	1.29	(0.02)
New Zealand	0.01	(0.02)	−0.21	(0.02)	0.22	(0.02)	−1.10	(0.02)	−0.30	(0.01)	0.21	(0.01)	1.23	(0.02)
Norway	−0.22	(0.02)	−0.54	(0.02)	0.12	(0.03)	−1.38	(0.02)	−0.56	(0.01)	0.02	(0.01)	1.07	(0.02)
Poland	−0.01	(0.03)	−0.23	(0.04)	0.22	(0.03)	−0.97	(0.02)	−0.31	(0.01)	0.13	(0.01)	1.13	(0.03)
Portugal	0.31	(0.02)	−0.02	(0.02)	0.63	(0.02)	−0.75	(0.02)	0.01	(0.01)	0.51	(0.01)	1.49	(0.02)
Spain	−0.04	(0.02)	−0.30	(0.02)	0.20	(0.03)	−1.17	(0.01)	−0.38	(0.00)	0.16	(0.01)	1.22	(0.02)
Sweden	−0.06	(0.02)	−0.35	(0.03)	0.24	(0.03)	−1.27	(0.01)	−0.45	(0.01)	0.19	(0.01)	1.28	(0.02)
Switzerland	0.06	(0.03)	−0.39	(0.03)	0.51	(0.03)	−1.38	(0.02)	−0.37	(0.01)	0.38	(0.01)	1.60	(0.02)
United Kingdom	−0.10	(0.02)	−0.32	(0.02)	0.12	(0.03)	−1.22	(0.02)	−0.39	(0.00)	0.12	(0.01)	1.10	(0.02)
United States	−0.13	(0.03)	−0.34	(0.04)	0.06	(0.04)	−1.30	(0.02)	−0.43	(0.01)	0.05	(0.01)	1.16	(0.03)
OECD total	*−0.01*	*(0.01)*	*−0.24*	*(0.01)*	*0.21*	*(0.01)*	*−1.17*	*(0.01)*	*−0.36*	*(0.00)*	*0.19*	*(0.00)*	*1.27*	*(0.01)*
OECD average	*0.00*	*(0.00)*	*−0.28*	*(0.01)*	*0.28*	*(0.01)*	*−1.16*	*(0.00)*	*−0.35*	*(0.00)*	*0.23*	*(0.00)*	*1.29*	*(0.00)*
NON-OECD COUNTRIES														
Brazil	0.15	(0.02)	−0.12	(0.02)	0.38	(0.02)	−0.83	(0.01)	−0.19	(0.01)	0.31	(0.01)	1.30	(0.03)
Latvia	−0.04	(0.02)	−0.29	(0.03)	0.19	(0.03)	−0.94	(0.01)	−0.33	(0.00)	0.12	(0.01)	0.97	(0.02)
Liechtenstein	−0.08	(0.06)	−0.46	(0.07)	0.31	(0.09)	−1.37	(0.04)	−0.51	(0.02)	0.18	(0.02)	1.39	(0.08)
Russian Federation	0.05	(0.01)	−0.12	(0.02)	0.22	(0.02)	−0.82	(0.01)	−0.25	(0.00)	0.18	(0.00)	1.08	(0.01)
Netherlands[3]	−0.27	(0.03)	−0.55	(0.04)	0.02	(0.04)	−1.36	(0.02)	−0.60	(0.01)	−0.04	(0.01)	0.95	(0.03)

Performance on the combined reading literacy scale, by national quarters of the index of engagement in reading[2]

	Bottom quarter		Second quarter		Third quarter		Top quarter		Change in the combined reading literacy score per unit of the index of engagement in reading[2]	
	Mean score	S.E.	Mean score	S.E.	Mean score	S.E.	Mean score	S.E.	Change	S.E.
OECD COUNTRIES										
Australia	479	(3.8)	496	(4.4)	551	(3.8)	591	(4.2)	41.8	(2.06)
Austria	468	(3.3)	483	(3.3)	519	(3.2)	560	(3.1)	29.3	(1.35)
Belgium	483	(3.8)	489	(4.2)	513	(4.7)	562	(5.3)	30.8	(1.71)
Canada	486	(1.9)	514	(2.1)	552	(2.0)	590	(1.6)	36.2	(0.70)
Czech Republic	459	(3.0)	476	(2.8)	518	(3.0)	550	(3.0)	33.8	(1.48)
Denmark	452	(3.7)	476	(3.4)	511	(3.4)	555	(3.5)	40.0	(1.69)
Finland	493	(3.2)	526	(4.5)	566	(3.6)	604	(2.5)	40.0	(1.13)
France	479	(3.2)	489	(3.9)	518	(4.1)	552	(2.9)	27.5	(1.29)
Germany	453	(4.1)	466	(3.2)	505	(4.7)	555	(3.5)	33.3	(1.59)
Greece	452	(6.3)	454	(5.7)	478	(5.4)	520	(5.2)	35.7	(3.51)
Hungary	440	(4.0)	453	(5.3)	493	(5.1)	539	(4.1)	43.0	(2.10)
Iceland	456	(2.9)	488	(2.5)	526	(2.6)	566	(2.9)	43.7	(1.59)
Ireland	482	(3.9)	505	(4.0)	536	(4.1)	588	(3.2)	40.1	(1.63)
Italy	463	(4.0)	468	(3.3)	491	(4.2)	532	(3.0)	28.0	(1.75)
Japan	499	(5.2)	509	(5.9)	526	(5.9)	562	(4.4)	23.8	(1.55)
Korea	494	(2.9)	513	(3.1)	535	(2.7)	558	(2.6)	25.9	(1.26)
Luxembourg	436	(2.8)	434	(3.0)	436	(3.7)	494	(3.4)	19.4	(1.66)
Mexico	413	(5.3)	408	(3.8)	420	(4.1)	445	(4.5)	14.6	(2.59)
New Zealand	487	(3.1)	501	(4.5)	548	(4.4)	591	(4.2)	43.7	(1.95)
Norway	461	(5.1)	484	(3.9)	514	(3.9)	570	(3.1)	42.5	(2.12)
Poland	460	(5.7)	454	(5.2)	483	(4.9)	537	(5.9)	34.1	(3.09)
Portugal	436	(4.6)	449	(5.9)	483	(4.7)	521	(4.5)	33.5	(1.72)
Spain	460	(3.5)	476	(3.4)	501	(3.4)	539	(2.9)	31.3	(1.42)
Sweden	469	(2.8)	496	(3.3)	527	(3.5)	576	(3.2)	39.5	(1.55)
Switzerland	447	(4.2)	470	(4.7)	509	(4.9)	556	(5.1)	34.8	(1.74)
United Kingdom	481	(2.7)	503	(3.3)	536	(3.3)	583	(3.8)	40.4	(1.55)
United States	474	(6.2)	481	(9.8)	514	(8.6)	566	(6.2)	33.0	(2.22)
OECD total	*470*	*(1.7)*	*480*	*(2.6)*	*508*	*(2.4)*	*550*	*(2.0)*	*28.1*	*(0.84)*
OECD average	*465*	*(0.8)*	*480*	*(0.8)*	*512*	*(0.9)*	*554*	*(0.8)*	*32.4*	*(0.39)*
NON-OECD COUNTRIES										
Brazil	386	(4.3)	379	(4.1)	396	(3.9)	431	(4.5)	20.6	(2.24)
Latvia	422	(6.8)	439	(5.5)	467	(5.8)	511	(6.4)	42.3	(3.33)
Liechtenstein	441	(8.7)	446	(10.5)	503	(10.4)	543	(7.4)	35.7	(4.01)
Russian Federation	431	(4.9)	446	(4.0)	470	(4.2)	504	(5.8)	34.9	(1.71)
Netherlands[3]	507	(3.7)	512	(6.0)	538	(5.2)	572	(4.3)	27.6	(2.13)

1. For the definition of the index see Annex A1.
2. For explained variation see Annex A2. Unit changes marked in bold are statistically significant. Where bottom and top quarters are marked in bold this indicates that their difference is statistically significant.
3. Response rate is too low to ensure comparability (see Annex A3).

Table 4.4
Time students usually spend each day reading for enjoyment and performance on the combined reading literacy scale
Results based on student's self-reports

		Students report not reading for enjoyment				Students report reading 30 min. or less each day				Students report reading betweeen 30 and 60 min. each day				Students report reading between 1 and 2 hours each day				Students report reading more than 2 hours each day			
		%	S.E.	Mean score	S.E.	%	S.E.	Mean score	S.E.	%	S.E.	Mean score	S.E.	%	S.E.	Mean score	S.E.	%	S.E.	Mean score	S.E.
OECD COUNTRIES	Australia	33.1	(1.2)	484	(3.9)	30.5	(0.9)	537	(3.9)	20.5	(0.9)	564	(4.7)	11.8	(0.5)	575	(5.5)	4.1	(0.3)	558	(9.8)
	Austria	41.1	(1.1)	477	(2.5)	28.7	(0.8)	528	(3.0)	18.1	(0.7)	539	(4.2)	9.0	(0.5)	540	(5.6)	3.1	(0.4)	532	(7.9)
	Belgium	42.2	(0.9)	487	(3.4)	24.7	(0.7)	534	(4.1)	21.4	(0.6)	541	(4.1)	9.1	(0.4)	546	(6.5)	2.6	(0.3)	511	(12.1)
	Canada	32.7	(0.4)	498	(1.6)	33.7	(0.4)	544	(1.8)	20.4	(0.4)	564	(2.1)	9.6	(0.3)	575	(3.4)	3.6	(0.2)	550	(4.9)
	Czech Republic	26.2	(0.8)	458	(3.0)	29.7	(0.8)	509	(2.9)	25.7	(0.7)	524	(2.8)	12.9	(0.6)	521	(4.3)	5.5	(0.5)	518	(6.2)
	Denmark	26.8	(0.8)	464	(3.3)	36.1	(1.0)	512	(3.3)	23.3	(0.6)	519	(3.5)	9.4	(0.5)	520	(5.7)	4.4	(0.4)	487	(8.5)
	Finland	22.4	(0.7)	498	(3.4)	29.1	(0.7)	542	(3.2)	26.3	(0.7)	568	(3.2)	18.2	(0.6)	577	(4.1)	4.1	(0.3)	584	(6.0)
	France	30.0	(0.9)	472	(3.4)	27.5	(0.7)	519	(2.9)	28.6	(0.8)	533	(3.1)	10.6	(0.5)	539	(4.3)	3.4	(0.3)	514	(10.0)
	Germany	41.6	(0.9)	459	(3.0)	27.0	(0.8)	518	(3.6)	18.0	(0.6)	532	(3.9)	8.8	(0.4)	543	(4.4)	4.6	(0.3)	501	(7.4)
	Greece	22.0	(0.8)	459	(5.9)	26.6	(0.7)	486	(5.8)	22.7	(0.7)	501	(6.3)	20.0	(0.7)	478	(4.7)	8.7	(0.5)	454	(8.0)
	Hungary	26.0	(0.9)	448	(4.3)	28.3	(0.7)	494	(4.2)	24.2	(0.8)	504	(5.1)	13.4	(0.6)	501	(6.3)	8.1	(0.5)	468	(6.9)
	Iceland	29.8	(0.7)	466	(2.9)	38.0	(0.8)	519	(2.2)	22.5	(0.7)	543	(3.5)	6.9	(0.4)	539	(6.1)	2.9	(0.3)	528	(10.7)
	Ireland	33.4	(0.9)	491	(4.1)	30.9	(0.7)	536	(3.8)	20.4	(0.7)	558	(3.9)	11.6	(0.5)	556	(5.2)	3.8	(0.4)	541	(11.4)
	Italy	30.7	(1.1)	461	(3.7)	30.2	(0.6)	498	(3.3)	22.5	(0.7)	509	(3.6)	13.0	(0.7)	502	(4.7)	3.7	(0.3)	509	(9.6)
	Japan	55.0	(1.2)	514	(5.2)	17.8	(0.8)	539	(5.5)	15.4	(0.7)	537	(6.4)	8.2	(0.4)	541	(6.4)	3.5	(0.3)	530	(8.8)
	Korea	30.6	(0.8)	503	(2.7)	29.6	(0.7)	529	(3.1)	21.9	(0.7)	536	(3.2)	12.0	(0.5)	544	(3.5)	6.0	(0.4)	539	(5.2)
	Luxembourg	38.4	(0.8)	437	(2.2)	25.6	(0.7)	460	(3.7)	19.6	(0.7)	463	(3.6)	11.9	(0.6)	462	(6.1)	4.5	(0.4)	465	(9.0)
	Mexico	13.6	(0.7)	420	(6.0)	43.7	(1.1)	423	(3.6)	27.2	(0.7)	439	(3.9)	11.5	(0.6)	426	(5.4)	4.0	(0.4)	406	(7.6)
	New Zealand	29.9	(0.9)	494	(4.1)	36.6	(0.7)	544	(3.4)	19.4	(0.7)	563	(4.4)	10.4	(0.6)	570	(6.5)	3.7	(0.3)	553	(8.0)
	Norway	35.3	(0.8)	471	(3.9)	34.7	(0.8)	528	(3.3)	20.1	(0.7)	538	(4.3)	7.7	(0.4)	536	(5.7)	2.2	(0.3)	506	(11.8)
	Poland	24.2	(1.1)	449	(4.9)	22.7	(0.9)	488	(5.4)	28.7	(0.8)	502	(5.1)	16.5	(0.7)	498	(6.3)	8.0	(0.7)	497	(10.0)
	Portugal	18.4	(0.8)	432	(5.1)	39.1	(0.8)	474	(4.3)	26.5	(0.9)	495	(5.3)	12.4	(0.6)	494	(6.0)	3.7	(0.4)	468	(10.7)
	Spain	31.8	(0.9)	460	(3.3)	32.9	(0.8)	505	(3.1)	24.2	(0.8)	519	(3.0)	8.8	(0.4)	514	(5.1)	2.4	(0.2)	499	(10.1)
	Sweden	36.0	(1.0)	483	(2.8)	30.8	(0.8)	527	(3.6)	21.0	(0.6)	547	(3.1)	8.8	(0.5)	556	(4.9)	3.4	(0.3)	529	(8.8)
	Switzerland	35.2	(1.2)	450	(4.1)	33.0	(0.8)	515	(4.8)	20.5	(0.6)	533	(4.7)	8.3	(0.5)	533	(7.8)	3.0	(0.3)	499	(12.8)
	United Kingdom	29.1	(0.7)	485	(3.0)	35.7	(0.8)	533	(3.1)	22.9	(0.7)	559	(3.5)	9.4	(0.5)	556	(5.6)	2.9	(0.3)	528	(9.8)
	United States	40.7	(1.3)	479	(7.0)	31.2	(1.1)	530	(7.3)	16.2	(0.8)	531	(8.4)	8.1	(0.6)	539	(12.2)	3.9	(0.5)	511	(10.8)
	OECD total	*35.4*	*(0.5)*	*481*	*(2.2)*	*29.8*	*(0.3)*	*511*	*(2.3)*	*20.6*	*(0.3)*	*522*	*(2.0)*	*10.0*	*(0.2)*	*524*	*(2.7)*	*4.1*	*(0.1)*	*505*	*(3.9)*
	OECD average	*31.7*	*(0.2)*	*474*	*(0.8)*	*30.9*	*(0.1)*	*513*	*(0.8)*	*22.2*	*(0.2)*	*527*	*(0.9)*	*11.1*	*(0.1)*	*526*	*(1.0)*	*4.2*	*(0.1)*	*506*	*(2.0)*
NON-OECD COUNTRIES	Brazil	19.3	(1.0)	385	(3.8)	21.3	(0.8)	393	(4.5)	31.4	(1.1)	409	(4.2)	16.8	(0.7)	410	(5.8)	11.2	(0.6)	410	(5.3)
	Latvia	18.0	(1.1)	409	(8.6)	25.7	(1.1)	462	(6.2)	29.5	(1.2)	482	(5.9)	19.7	(0.9)	476	(5.7)	7.3	(0.5)	470	(7.6)
	Liechtenstein	40.0	(2.8)	447	(6.4)	34.2	(2.7)	504	(9.5)	16.6	(2.2)	536	(11.4)	5.2	(1.2)	c	c	4.0	(1.1)	c	c
	Russian Federation	19.4	(0.7)	434	(5.9)	24.6	(0.7)	455	(5.2)	25.8	(0.6)	474	(4.2)	17.4	(0.6)	483	(3.6)	12.7	(0.5)	481	(5.4)
	Netherlands[1]	43.3	(1.5)	508	(3.7)	31.4	(1.1)	554	(4.5)	16.7	(0.9)	562	(5.3)	5.8	(0.7)	549	(9.6)	2.9	(0.4)	530	(12.6)

1. Response rate is too low to ensure comparability (see Annex A3).

Table 4.5
Index of control strategies and performance on the combined reading literacy scale, by national quarters of the index
Results based on students' self-reports

	Index of control strategies[1]															
	All students		Males		Females		Bottom quarter		Second quarter		Third quarter		Top quarter			
	Mean index	S.E.	Mean index	S.E.	Mean index	S.E.	Mean index	S.E.	Mean index	S.E.	Mean index	S.E.	Mean index	S.E.		
OECD COUNTRIES																
Australia	0.02	(0.02)	−0.05	(0.02)	0.10	(0.03)	−1.20	(0.02)	−0.26	(0.01)	0.30	(0.01)	1.24	(0.02)		
Austria	0.40	(0.02)	0.31	(0.03)	0.48	(0.02)	−0.72	(0.02)	0.12	(0.01)	0.64	(0.01)	1.54	(0.02)		
Belgium (Fl.)	0.14	(0.02)	0.07	(0.02)	0.21	(0.03)	−0.96	(0.02)	−0.11	(0.01)	0.37	(0.01)	1.25	(0.02)		
Czech Republic	0.27	(0.02)	0.11	(0.03)	0.42	(0.02)	−0.84	(0.01)	−0.02	(0.00)	0.50	(0.01)	1.45	(0.02)		
Denmark	−0.23	(0.01)	−0.24	(0.02)	−0.22	(0.02)	−1.25	(0.02)	−0.48	(0.01)	0.00	(0.01)	0.81	(0.02)		
Finland	−0.47	(0.02)	−0.52	(0.02)	−0.42	(0.02)	−1.54	(0.02)	−0.71	(0.01)	−0.21	(0.01)	0.58	(0.02)		
Germany	0.24	(0.02)	0.14	(0.04)	0.33	(0.02)	−0.94	(0.02)	−0.05	(0.01)	0.48	(0.00)	1.45	(0.03)		
Hungary	0.21	(0.02)	0.09	(0.03)	0.33	(0.03)	−0.91	(0.02)	−0.05	(0.01)	0.45	(0.01)	1.34	(0.02)		
Iceland	−0.35	(0.02)	−0.36	(0.03)	−0.34	(0.02)	−1.53	(0.02)	−0.60	(0.01)	−0.08	(0.01)	0.79	(0.02)		
Ireland	0.07	(0.02)	−0.10	(0.04)	0.23	(0.03)	−1.28	(0.03)	−0.22	(0.01)	0.37	(0.01)	1.39	(0.02)		
Italy	0.23	(0.02)	0.05	(0.04)	0.41	(0.02)	−0.94	(0.03)	−0.04	(0.01)	0.48	(0.00)	1.41	(0.01)		
Korea	−0.44	(0.02)	−0.47	(0.03)	−0.41	(0.03)	−1.74	(0.02)	−0.70	(0.01)	−0.12	(0.01)	0.79	(0.02)		
Luxembourg	0.05	(0.02)	−0.10	(0.03)	0.19	(0.03)	−1.26	(0.03)	−0.23	(0.01)	0.33	(0.01)	1.34	(0.03)		
Mexico	0.16	(0.02)	0.06	(0.03)	0.25	(0.02)	−0.98	(0.01)	−0.18	(0.01)	0.39	(0.01)	1.41	(0.02)		
New Zealand	0.07	(0.03)	−0.03	(0.03)	0.17	(0.03)	−1.12	(0.02)	−0.23	(0.01)	0.30	(0.01)	1.32	(0.02)		
Norway	−0.58	(0.02)	−0.50	(0.03)	−0.66	(0.02)	−1.76	(0.02)	−0.81	(0.01)	−0.28	(0.01)	0.54	(0.02)		
Portugal	0.19	(0.02)	0.03	(0.02)	0.34	(0.02)	−0.90	(0.02)	−0.13	(0.01)	0.39	(0.01)	1.41	(0.02)		
Sweden	0.03	(0.02)	0.04	(0.03)	0.02	(0.02)	−1.09	(0.02)	−0.22	(0.01)	0.29	(0.01)	1.17	(0.02)		
Switzerland	0.11	(0.02)	0.00	(0.03)	0.22	(0.03)	−1.00	(0.02)	−0.15	(0.00)	0.35	(0.01)	1.26	(0.03)		
United States	−0.08	(0.03)	−0.26	(0.04)	0.09	(0.04)	−1.44	(0.03)	−0.40	(0.01)	0.24	(0.01)	1.30	(0.03)		
OECD total	*0.01*	*(0.02)*	*−0.12*	*(0.02)*	*0.14*	*(0.02)*	*−1.24*	*(0.02)*	*−0.29*	*(0.01)*	*0.29*	*(0.00)*	*1.28*	*(0.01)*		
OECD average	*0.00*	*(0.01)*	*−0.09*	*(0.01)*	*0.09*	*(0.01)*	*−1.17*	*(0.01)*	*−0.28*	*(0.00)*	*0.26*	*(0.00)*	*1.19*	*(0.01)*		
NON-OECD COUNTRIES																
Brazil	0.22	(0.03)	0.12	(0.04)	0.30	(0.03)	−1.15	(0.03)	−0.02	(0.01)	0.51	(0.01)	1.53	(0.02)		
Latvia	−0.12	(0.02)	−0.22	(0.03)	−0.03	(0.02)	−1.10	(0.02)	−0.34	(0.01)	0.12	(0.01)	0.85	(0.01)		
Liechtenstein	0.15	(0.05)	0.10	(0.08)	0.21	(0.08)	−1.06	(0.07)	−0.17	(0.02)	0.41	(0.02)	1.39	(0.07)		
Russian Federation	0.08	(0.02)	0.00	(0.02)	0.17	(0.02)	−1.00	(0.02)	−0.18	(0.01)	0.32	(0.00)	1.19	(0.02)		
Netherlands[3]	−0.07	(0.02)	−0.09	(0.03)	−0.05	(0.03)	−1.09	(0.03)	−0.29	(0.01)	0.19	(0.01)	0.90	(0.03)		

	Performance on the combined reading literacy scale, by national quarters of the index of control strategies[2]								Change in the combined reading literacy score per unit of the index of control strategies[2]	
	Bottom quarter		Second quarter		Third quarter		Top quarter			
	Mean score	S.E.	Mean score	S.E.	Mean score	S.E.	Mean score	S.E.	Change	S.E.
OECD COUNTRIES										
Australia	494	(4.5)	525	(4.6)	540	(4.3)	564	(5.8)	23.8	(2.06)
Austria	485	(4.3)	502	(3.1)	517	(3.9)	531	(3.5)	18.2	(1.95)
Belgium (Fl.)	512	(7.2)	543	(4.2)	542	(5.3)	545	(5.0)	13.4	(3.15)
Czech Republic	464	(3.1)	497	(3.0)	518	(3.3)	532	(2.9)	26.6	(1.36)
Denmark	481	(3.8)	497	(3.6)	507	(3.3)	514	(3.3)	14.9	(1.73)
Finland	527	(3.8)	546	(2.9)	556	(3.6)	562	(3.6)	15.8	(1.64)
Germany	459	(4.3)	495	(4.0)	508	(3.6)	519	(3.3)	22.4	(1.80)
Hungary	456	(5.8)	483	(4.4)	495	(4.3)	496	(5.6)	17.9	(2.79)
Iceland	490	(3.2)	509	(3.2)	513	(3.1)	526	(3.6)	13.6	(2.03)
Ireland	499	(4.3)	525	(5.1)	537	(4.0)	553	(3.8)	18.6	(1.65)
Italy	461	(5.1)	485	(3.8)	499	(3.4)	505	(3.2)	17.5	(1.88)
Korea	496	(3.4)	521	(2.9)	534	(3.1)	548	(3.0)	20.2	(1.54)
Luxembourg	424	(3.3)	453	(3.0)	456	(3.3)	475	(3.3)	16.6	(1.75)
Mexico	394	(3.4)	415	(3.9)	432	(4.3)	449	(4.7)	21.4	(1.80)
New Zealand	494	(4.2)	531	(3.7)	540	(3.6)	572	(5.0)	27.7	(2.15)
Norway	494	(5.2)	505	(3.5)	521	(4.4)	518	(4.1)	13.7	(2.05)
Portugal	419	(5.6)	464	(5.0)	483	(4.4)	515	(4.4)	35.5	(2.30)
Sweden	491	(3.2)	515	(3.2)	527	(3.9)	539	(3.0)	19.3	(1.51)
Switzerland	469	(4.9)	492	(4.9)	503	(4.8)	522	(6.1)	20.6	(2.63)
United States	477	(7.4)	505	(8.3)	528	(5.7)	534	(8.3)	18.3	(2.51)
OECD total	*465*	*(3.2)*	*492*	*(3.5)*	*510*	*(2.6)*	*520*	*(3.6)*	*15.8*	*(1.31)*
OECD average	*474*	*(1.0)*	*500*	*(1.0)*	*512*	*(0.8)*	*526*	*(1.0)*	*15.6*	*(0.43)*
NON-OECD COUNTRIES										
Brazil	368	(4.4)	395	(4.0)	414	(4.0)	425	(4.3)	20.6	(1.67)
Latvia	430	(6.4)	465	(6.3)	463	(6.7)	482	(5.6)	23.2	(2.74)
Liechtenstein	462	(9.9)	479	(10.9)	477	(9.7)	520	(9.7)	20.6	(5.90)
Russian Federation	431	(5.0)	462	(4.9)	476	(4.7)	485	(4.7)	23.7	(1.83)
Netherlands[3]	511	(5.6)	542	(4.2)	541	(3.7)	536	(4.9)	9.4	(2.61)

1. For the definition of the index see Annex A1.
2. For explained variation see Annex A2. Unit changes marked in bold are statistically significant. Where bottom and top quarters are marked in bold this indicates that their difference is statistically significant.
3. Response rate is too low to ensure comparability (see Annex A3).

Table 4.6
Index of memorisation strategies and performance on the combined reading literacy scale, by national quarters of the index
Results based on students' self-reports

	Index of memorisation strategies[1]													
	All students		Males		Females		Bottom quarter		Second quarter		Third quarter		Top quarter	
	Mean index	S.E.	Mean index	S.E.	Mean index	S.E.	Mean index	S.E.	Mean index	S.E.	Mean index	S.E.	Mean index	S.E.
Australia	0.14	(0.02)	0.11	(0.03)	0.18	(0.03)	−0.96	(0.02)	−0.10	(0.01)	0.39	(0.01)	1.25	(0.02)
Austria	−0.03	(0.02)	−0.18	(0.03)	0.11	(0.03)	−1.30	(0.02)	−0.28	(0.01)	0.26	(0.01)	1.22	(0.02)
Belgium (Fl.)	0.06	(0.02)	−0.01	(0.03)	0.14	(0.03)	−1.20	(0.02)	−0.26	(0.01)	0.32	(0.01)	1.38	(0.02)
Czech Republic	−0.06	(0.02)	−0.22	(0.03)	0.09	(0.03)	−1.21	(0.02)	−0.37	(0.01)	0.19	(0.01)	1.17	(0.02)
Denmark	0.05	(0.01)	0.08	(0.02)	0.01	(0.02)	−0.89	(0.02)	−0.14	(0.01)	0.24	(0.01)	0.98	(0.01)
Finland	−0.10	(0.01)	−0.15	(0.02)	−0.07	(0.02)	−1.07	(0.01)	−0.33	(0.00)	0.16	(0.00)	0.83	(0.02)
Germany	0.03	(0.02)	−0.11	(0.02)	0.17	(0.02)	−1.21	(0.02)	−0.26	(0.01)	0.30	(0.01)	1.28	(0.02)
Hungary	0.89	(0.02)	0.75	(0.03)	1.03	(0.03)	−0.12	(0.02)	0.57	(0.00)	1.08	(0.01)	2.04	(0.02)
Iceland	−0.27	(0.02)	−0.27	(0.02)	−0.27	(0.02)	−1.39	(0.02)	−0.50	(0.01)	0.01	(0.01)	0.79	(0.02)
Ireland	0.27	(0.02)	0.14	(0.03)	0.40	(0.02)	−0.96	(0.02)	0.00	(0.01)	0.54	(0.01)	1.50	(0.02)
Italy	−0.69	(0.02)	−0.69	(0.03)	−0.69	(0.02)	−1.79	(0.02)	−1.01	(0.01)	−0.42	(0.01)	0.48	(0.01)
Korea	−0.15	(0.02)	−0.18	(0.02)	−0.11	(0.02)	−1.29	(0.02)	−0.40	(0.01)	0.11	(0.01)	0.97	(0.02)
Luxembourg	−0.09	(0.02)	−0.29	(0.03)	0.11	(0.03)	−1.50	(0.03)	−0.39	(0.01)	0.23	(0.01)	1.30	(0.02)
Mexico	0.06	(0.02)	0.08	(0.03)	0.04	(0.03)	−1.07	(0.02)	−0.26	(0.01)	0.29	(0.01)	1.30	(0.02)
New Zealand	0.24	(0.02)	0.18	(0.03)	0.30	(0.03)	−0.83	(0.02)	−0.05	(0.01)	0.46	(0.01)	1.38	(0.02)
Norway	−0.60	(0.02)	−0.47	(0.03)	−0.73	(0.03)	−1.96	(0.02)	−0.77	(0.01)	−0.25	(0.01)	0.59	(0.02)
Portugal	0.03	(0.02)	0.02	(0.02)	0.05	(0.02)	−1.03	(0.02)	−0.27	(0.01)	0.25	(0.01)	1.19	(0.02)
Sweden	0.17	(0.02)	0.21	(0.03)	0.12	(0.03)	−0.94	(0.02)	−0.09	(0.00)	0.42	(0.01)	1.28	(0.02)
Switzerland	−0.02	(0.02)	−0.10	(0.03)	0.06	(0.02)	−1.09	(0.02)	−0.27	(0.01)	0.22	(0.00)	1.07	(0.02)
United States	0.09	(0.02)	−0.02	(0.04)	0.19	(0.03)	−1.15	(0.03)	−0.23	(0.01)	0.36	(0.01)	1.36	(0.02)
OECD total	*0.00*	*(0.01)*	*−0.07*	*(0.02)*	*0.08*	*(0.02)*	*−1.18*	*(0.01)*	*−0.29*	*(0.01)*	*0.26*	*(0.00)*	*1.23*	*(0.01)*
OECD average	*0.00*	*(0.00)*	*−0.05*	*(0.01)*	*0.06*	*(0.01)*	*−1.14*	*(0.01)*	*−0.27*	*(0.00)*	*0.26*	*(0.00)*	*1.16*	*(0.01)*
Brazil	0.22	(0.02)	0.17	(0.03)	0.27	(0.03)	−1.02	(0.03)	0.00	(0.01)	0.52	(0.01)	1.39	(0.02)
Latvia	0.17	(0.01)	0.10	(0.02)	0.23	(0.02)	−0.71	(0.02)	−0.04	(0.01)	0.39	(0.01)	1.03	(0.02)
Liechtenstein	−0.08	(0.05)	−0.16	(0.07)	−0.01	(0.06)	−1.14	(0.06)	−0.37	(0.02)	0.10	(0.02)	1.07	(0.08)
Russian Federation	0.36	(0.02)	0.29	(0.02)	0.44	(0.02)	−0.60	(0.01)	0.13	(0.01)	0.55	(0.00)	1.38	(0.02)
Netherlands[3]	−0.03	(0.02)	−0.04	(0.03)	−0.01	(0.02)	−1.01	(0.02)	−0.22	(0.01)	0.20	(0.01)	0.94	(0.02)

(OECD COUNTRIES for Australia through United States; NON-OECD COUNTRIES for Brazil through Russian Federation)

	Performance on the combined reading literacy scale, by national quarters of the index of memorisation strategies[2]								Change in the combined reading literacy score per unit of the index of memorisation strategies[2]	
	Bottom quarter		Second quarter		Third quarter		Top quarter			
	Mean score	S.E.	Mean score	S.E.	Mean score	S.E.	Mean score	S.E.	Change	S.E.
Australia	515	(4.7)	528	(4.4)	535	(4.9)	545	(4.9)	10.1	(2.27)
Austria	529	(3.8)	510	(3.7)	502	(3.0)	494	(2.9)	−11.8	(1.53)
Belgium (Fl.)	547	(7.1)	538	(4.9)	536	(4.8)	519	(5.3)	−8.4	(2.49)
Czech Republic	522	(3.8)	500	(3.4)	497	(2.9)	492	(3.1)	−11.1	(1.46)
Denmark	488	(3.8)	507	(3.0)	500	(3.9)	502	(3.3)	5.7	(2.41)
Finland	539	(3.7)	544	(3.7)	553	(2.9)	554	(4.0)	7.7	(2.24)
Germany	496	(4.0)	499	(3.4)	495	(3.5)	492	(3.3)	−1.4	(1.57)
Hungary	460	(6.1)	480	(5.1)	498	(4.6)	490	(4.9)	15.5	(3.48)
Iceland	516	(3.5)	506	(3.3)	513	(3.0)	502	(3.1)	−2.2	(2.40)
Ireland	524	(5.0)	526	(3.9)	529	(3.8)	535	(3.8)	6.0	(1.86)
Italy	505	(4.2)	498	(3.2)	481	(3.8)	466	(4.9)	−15.4	(1.99)
Korea	512	(3.5)	528	(3.4)	529	(2.8)	530	(2.6)	6.5	(1.20)
Luxembourg	456	(3.1)	450	(3.2)	452	(3.5)	448	(3.3)	−2.6	(1.55)
Mexico	428	(5.0)	415	(3.9)	419	(3.5)	427	(4.7)	−1.0	(1.98)
New Zealand	516	(4.5)	532	(4.3)	540	(3.6)	549	(4.3)	12.9	(2.26)
Norway	515	(4.0)	513	(4.2)	510	(3.8)	501	(4.5)	−2.6	(2.00)
Portugal	475	(6.4)	468	(5.3)	463	(5.0)	476	(4.8)	−1.2	(2.08)
Sweden	505	(3.4)	517	(3.2)	524	(3.4)	526	(3.2)	8.1	(1.49)
Switzerland	496	(5.9)	489	(5.4)	501	(4.6)	501	(4.9)	2.5	(2.22)
United States	503	(9.2)	513	(7.4)	514	(7.0)	510	(7.2)	1.9	(2.62)
OECD total	*494*	*(3.9)*	*498*	*(3.2)*	*498*	*(3.2)*	*496*	*(3.1)*	*0.5*	*(1.21)*
OECD average	*501*	*(1.1)*	*503*	*(1.0)*	*504*	*(1.0)*	*503*	*(1.0)*	*0.5*	*(0.47)*
Brazil	380	(3.8)	400	(4.3)	408	(4.0)	414	(4.2)	12.8	(1.72)
Latvia	443	(7.5)	466	(7.2)	464	(4.9)	466	(5.7)	11.8	(3.22)
Liechtenstein	490	(10.6)	490	(10.8)	476	(10.2)	481	(10.8)	−2.5	(6.23)
Russian Federation	442	(5.6)	464	(4.7)	475	(4.4)	472	(4.5)	14.5	(2.04)
Netherlands[3]	535	(5.0)	536	(4.7)	540	(4.6)	518	(5.4)	−6.0	(2.49)

1. For the definition of the index see Annex A1.
2. For explained variation see Annex A2. Unit changes marked in bold are statistically significant. Where bottom and top quarters are marked in bold this indicates that their difference is statistically significant.
3. Response rate is too low to ensure comparability (see Annex A3).

Table 4.7
Index of elaboration strategies and performance on the combined reading literacy scale, by national quarters of the index
Results based on students' self-reports

| | Index of elaboration strategies[1] | | | | | | | | | | | | | |
| | All students | | Males | | Females | | Bottom quarter | | Second quarter | | Third quarter | | Top quarter | |
	Mean index	S.E.	Mean index	S.E.	Mean index	S.E.	Mean index	S.E.	Mean index	S.E.	Mean index	S.E.	Mean index	S.E.
OECD COUNTRIES														
Australia	0.07	(0.02)	0.12	(0.02)	0.02	(0.03)	-1.12	(0.03)	-0.19	(0.01)	0.39	(0.01)	1.21	(0.02)
Austria	0.16	(0.02)	0.23	(0.03)	0.09	(0.03)	-1.16	(0.02)	-0.12	(0.01)	0.49	(0.01)	1.44	(0.02)
Belgium (Fl.)	-0.16	(0.02)	-0.07	(0.03)	-0.26	(0.03)	-1.44	(0.02)	-0.48	(0.01)	0.18	(0.01)	1.10	(0.02)
Czech Republic	0.10	(0.02)	0.12	(0.03)	0.08	(0.02)	-1.09	(0.02)	-0.20	(0.01)	0.39	(0.01)	1.30	(0.02)
Denmark	-0.12	(0.02)	-0.06	(0.02)	-0.18	(0.02)	-1.24	(0.02)	-0.44	(0.01)	0.18	(0.01)	1.02	(0.02)
Finland	-0.15	(0.02)	-0.09	(0.02)	-0.21	(0.02)	-1.24	(0.02)	-0.47	(0.01)	0.16	(0.00)	0.94	(0.02)
Germany	0.05	(0.02)	0.09	(0.03)	0.01	(0.02)	-1.19	(0.02)	-0.22	(0.01)	0.38	(0.01)	1.24	(0.02)
Hungary	0.15	(0.02)	0.20	(0.03)	0.10	(0.03)	-1.04	(0.02)	-0.11	(0.01)	0.49	(0.01)	1.26	(0.02)
Iceland	-0.24	(0.02)	-0.19	(0.02)	-0.29	(0.03)	-1.54	(0.02)	-0.54	(0.01)	0.10	(0.01)	1.02	(0.02)
Ireland	-0.09	(0.02)	-0.12	(0.03)	-0.07	(0.03)	-1.48	(0.02)	-0.39	(0.01)	0.28	(0.01)	1.24	(0.02)
Italy	-0.11	(0.02)	-0.09	(0.03)	-0.13	(0.03)	-1.49	(0.03)	-0.41	(0.01)	0.29	(0.01)	1.18	(0.02)
Korea	-0.03	(0.03)	-0.02	(0.04)	-0.04	(0.04)	-1.38	(0.02)	-0.28	(0.01)	0.30	(0.01)	1.25	(0.02)
Luxembourg	-0.12	(0.02)	-0.15	(0.03)	-0.09	(0.03)	-1.40	(0.03)	-0.44	(0.01)	0.21	(0.01)	1.14	(0.02)
Mexico	0.33	(0.02)	0.29	(0.02)	0.36	(0.02)	-0.85	(0.02)	0.01	(0.01)	0.58	(0.01)	1.58	(0.02)
New Zealand	0.10	(0.02)	0.11	(0.02)	0.09	(0.03)	-1.05	(0.02)	-0.16	(0.01)	0.39	(0.01)	1.22	(0.02)
Norway	-0.22	(0.02)	-0.12	(0.03)	-0.32	(0.03)	-1.44	(0.03)	-0.49	(0.01)	0.13	(0.01)	0.94	(0.02)
Portugal	0.17	(0.02)	0.15	(0.03)	0.18	(0.02)	-0.88	(0.02)	-0.14	(0.01)	0.41	(0.01)	1.27	(0.02)
Sweden	0.01	(0.02)	0.15	(0.02)	-0.13	(0.03)	-1.19	(0.02)	-0.30	(0.01)	0.34	(0.01)	1.20	(0.02)
Switzerland	0.09	(0.02)	0.10	(0.03)	0.08	(0.02)	-1.07	(0.02)	-0.15	(0.01)	0.41	(0.01)	1.18	(0.02)
United States	0.01	(0.03)	-0.04	(0.04)	0.06	(0.03)	-1.28	(0.02)	-0.32	(0.01)	0.34	(0.01)	1.32	(0.03)
OECD total	*0.05*	*(0.01)*	*0.04*	*(0.02)*	*0.06*	*(0.02)*	*-1.21*	*(0.01)*	*-0.25*	*(0.00)*	*0.37*	*(0.00)*	*1.31*	*(0.01)*
OECD average	*0.00*	*(0.00)*	*0.04*	*(0.01)*	*-0.02*	*(0.01)*	*-1.22*	*(0.01)*	*-0.29*	*(0.00)*	*0.33*	*(0.00)*	*1.20*	*(0.00)*
NON-OECD COUNTRIES														
Brazil	0.47	(0.02)	0.41	(0.03)	0.52	(0.03)	-0.85	(0.02)	0.25	(0.01)	0.80	(0.01)	1.69	(0.02)
Latvia	0.04	(0.02)	0.06	(0.02)	0.03	(0.02)	-0.97	(0.02)	-0.16	(0.01)	0.28	(0.01)	1.04	(0.02)
Liechtenstein	0.00	(0.06)	0.11	(0.07)	-0.10	(0.09)	-1.26	(0.08)	-0.28	(0.03)	0.32	(0.03)	1.20	(0.06)
Russian Federation	0.14	(0.02)	0.19	(0.02)	0.10	(0.02)	-1.08	(0.01)	-0.14	(0.01)	0.45	(0.01)	1.34	(0.01)
Netherlands[3]	-0.19	(0.02)	-0.11	(0.03)	-0.28	(0.03)	-1.32	(0.02)	-0.47	(0.01)	0.13	(0.01)	0.90	(0.02)

| | Performance on the combined reading literacy scale, by national quarters of the index of elaboration strategies[2] | | | | | | | | Change in the combined reading literacy score per unit of the index of elaboration strategies[2] | |
| | Bottom quarter | | Second quarter | | Third quarter | | Top quarter | | | |
	Mean score	S.E.	Mean score	S.E.	Mean score	S.E.	Mean score	S.E.	Change	S.E.
OECD COUNTRIES										
Australia	517	(4.4)	523	(4.2)	533	(4.6)	551	(5.3)	13.0	(1.96)
Austria	501	(3.6)	500	(3.3)	509	(3.2)	526	(2.7)	9.8	(1.44)
Belgium (Fl.)	532	(6.6)	536	(4.7)	540	(4.5)	534	(6.1)	0.4	(2.23)
Czech Republic	485	(3.4)	491	(3.0)	506	(3.0)	529	(3.2)	18.2	(1.42)
Denmark	482	(3.9)	492	(4.1)	514	(3.1)	514	(3.3)	13.6	(1.66)
Finland	535	(3.9)	537	(3.2)	553	(3.0)	566	(4.6)	15.4	(1.81)
Germany	474	(4.4)	486	(3.4)	499	(4.4)	525	(3.1)	20.1	(1.77)
Hungary	466	(5.7)	484	(5.8)	490	(5.4)	490	(5.0)	10.7	(2.96)
Iceland	498	(3.5)	501	(2.7)	507	(3.4)	533	(3.6)	12.4	(1.95)
Ireland	521	(4.5)	527	(4.4)	528	(3.8)	539	(4.1)	6.0	(1.62)
Italy	483	(4.1)	480	(4.2)	487	(3.9)	501	(3.6)	6.4	(1.71)
Korea	492	(3.1)	518	(3.1)	537	(2.5)	552	(3.1)	22.4	(1.29)
Luxembourg	441	(3.2)	449	(3.3)	456	(3.2)	467	(3.2)	8.8	(1.69)
Mexico	414	(3.8)	413	(3.9)	425	(4.4)	439	(4.8)	10.9	(1.76)
New Zealand	525	(4.7)	533	(4.4)	538	(3.8)	544	(5.3)	8.7	(2.48)
Norway	490	(4.6)	504	(3.5)	517	(4.2)	529	(4.3)	16.9	(1.77)
Portugal	441	(5.5)	463	(4.8)	476	(5.0)	502	(5.1)	25.2	(2.37)
Sweden	504	(3.0)	513	(3.3)	518	(2.9)	536	(3.1)	12.4	(1.39)
Switzerland	477	(4.7)	493	(4.4)	506	(5.4)	513	(6.1)	15.2	(2.19)
United States	500	(7.6)	505	(8.5)	520	(6.8)	521	(8.1)	7.7	(2.59)
OECD total	*482*	*(3.2)*	*490*	*(3.7)*	*503*	*(3.1)*	*513*	*(3.4)*	*8.1*	*(1.24)*
OECD average	*488*	*(1.1)*	*497*	*(0.9)*	*508*	*(0.9)*	*521*	*(1.1)*	*10.5*	*(0.46)*
NON-OECD COUNTRIES										
Brazil	382	(4.3)	394	(3.4)	410	(4.1)	418	(3.9)	15.9	(1.70)
Latvia	447	(6.3)	459	(6.2)	463	(6.8)	473	(6.0)	11.8	(2.81)
Liechtenstein	473	(9.6)	485	(11.0)	476	(11.0)	505	(10.3)	12.3	(4.84)
Russian Federation	450	(4.7)	459	(5.1)	468	(5.2)	478	(4.3)	10.6	(1.49)
Netherlands[3]	531	(4.3)	528	(4.9)	539	(4.2)	533	(5.3)	1.6	(2.00)

1. For the definition of the index see Annex A1.
2. For explained variation see Annex A2. Unit changes marked in bold are statistically significant. Where bottom and top quarters are marked in bold this indicates that their difference is statistically significant.
3. Response rate is too low to ensure comparability (see Annex A3).

Table 4.8
Index of co-operative learning and performance on the combined reading literacy scale, by national quarters of the index
Results based on students' self-reports

	Index of co-operative learning[1]													
	All students		Males		Females		Bottom quarter		Second quarter		Third quarter		Top quarter	
	Mean index	S.E.	Mean index	S.E.	Mean index	S.E.	Mean index	S.E.	Mean index	S.E.	Mean index	S.E.	Mean index	S.E.
Australia	0.04	(0.01)	−0.03	(0.02)	0.11	(0.02)	−0.76	(0.01)	−0.16	(0.01)	0.09	(0.01)	0.97	(0.02)
Austria	−0.10	(0.02)	−0.26	(0.03)	0.04	(0.02)	−1.14	(0.01)	−0.45	(0.01)	0.11	(0.01)	1.07	(0.02)
Belgium (Fl.)	−0.15	(0.02)	−0.25	(0.02)	−0.03	(0.02)	−0.98	(0.01)	−0.37	(0.00)	−0.05	(0.00)	0.81	(0.02)
Czech Republic	−0.06	(0.02)	−0.23	(0.03)	0.10	(0.02)	−1.09	(0.02)	−0.35	(0.01)	0.13	(0.01)	1.09	(0.02)
Denmark	0.50	(0.02)	0.45	(0.02)	0.56	(0.03)	−0.62	(0.01)	0.19	(0.01)	0.74	(0.01)	1.70	(0.02)
Finland	0.04	(0.02)	−0.11	(0.02)	0.18	(0.02)	−1.00	(0.01)	−0.23	(0.01)	0.22	(0.01)	1.19	(0.02)
Germany	−0.21	(0.02)	−0.33	(0.03)	−0.09	(0.02)	−1.33	(0.02)	−0.52	(0.01)	−0.03	(0.01)	1.05	(0.03)
Hungary	−0.34	(0.02)	−0.45	(0.03)	−0.22	(0.02)	−1.36	(0.02)	−0.70	(0.01)	−0.18	(0.01)	0.88	(0.03)
Iceland	−0.29	(0.02)	−0.38	(0.03)	−0.20	(0.02)	−1.38	(0.02)	−0.53	(0.01)	−0.10	(0.01)	0.85	(0.02)
Ireland	0.22	(0.02)	0.01	(0.03)	0.43	(0.03)	−1.09	(0.02)	−0.17	(0.01)	0.50	(0.01)	1.65	(0.02)
Italy	0.20	(0.03)	−0.04	(0.04)	0.45	(0.03)	−1.07	(0.03)	−0.15	(0.01)	0.51	(0.01)	1.52	(0.02)
Korea	−0.85	(0.01)	−0.81	(0.02)	−0.90	(0.02)	−1.87	(0.02)	−1.15	(0.00)	−0.69	(0.01)	0.31	(0.03)
Luxembourg	−0.40	(0.02)	−0.58	(0.03)	−0.22	(0.03)	−1.66	(0.02)	−0.75	(0.01)	−0.18	(0.01)	0.97	(0.03)
Mexico	0.22	(0.02)	0.12	(0.02)	0.32	(0.03)	−0.79	(0.01)	−0.11	(0.01)	0.30	(0.01)	1.47	(0.02)
New Zealand	0.29	(0.02)	0.17	(0.03)	0.40	(0.03)	−0.85	(0.01)	−0.09	(0.01)	0.53	(0.01)	1.57	(0.02)
Norway	0.17	(0.03)	0.00	(0.03)	0.34	(0.03)	−1.16	(0.02)	−0.17	(0.01)	0.47	(0.01)	1.54	(0.02)
Portugal	0.59	(0.03)	0.41	(0.03)	0.76	(0.02)	−0.61	(0.02)	0.23	(0.01)	0.86	(0.01)	1.88	(0.02)
Sweden	−0.21	(0.01)	−0.23	(0.02)	−0.18	(0.02)	−1.06	(0.02)	−0.42	(0.00)	−0.06	(0.00)	0.72	(0.02)
Switzerland	−0.01	(0.02)	−0.15	(0.02)	0.13	(0.02)	−1.02	(0.02)	−0.29	(0.01)	0.17	(0.01)	1.12	(0.02)
United States	0.35	(0.03)	0.13	(0.05)	0.55	(0.03)	−1.07	(0.04)	−0.07	(0.01)	0.64	(0.01)	1.89	(0.02)
OECD total	*0.10*	*(0.02)*	*−0.07*	*(0.02)*	*0.26*	*(0.02)*	*−1.11*	*(0.02)*	*−0.26*	*(0.01)*	*0.32*	*(0.01)*	*1.45*	*(0.02)*
OECD average	*0.00*	*(0.00)*	*−0.13*	*(0.01)*	*0.14*	*(0.01)*	*−1.09*	*(0.01)*	*−0.31*	*(0.00)*	*0.20*	*(0.00)*	*1.22*	*(0.01)*
Brazil	0.47	(0.02)	0.34	(0.02)	0.58	(0.03)	−0.72	(0.02)	0.08	(0.01)	0.67	(0.01)	1.86	(0.02)
Latvia	0.24	(0.04)	0.08	(0.04)	0.39	(0.05)	−1.00	(0.02)	−0.14	(0.01)	0.51	(0.01)	1.60	(0.03)
Liechtenstein	−0.01	(0.05)	−0.09	(0.07)	0.08	(0.07)	−0.95	(0.07)	−0.26	(0.02)	0.12	(0.02)	1.01	(0.09)
Russian Federation	−0.23	(0.02)	−0.33	(0.02)	−0.13	(0.02)	−1.41	(0.02)	−0.55	(0.01)	0.03	(0.01)	1.02	(0.01)
Netherlands[3]	0.14	(0.03)	−0.02	(0.03)	0.31	(0.03)	−1.00	(0.02)	−0.18	(0.01)	0.39	(0.01)	1.36	(0.02)

(Left margin labels: OECD COUNTRIES; NON-OECD COUNTRIES)

	Performance on the combined reading literacy scale, by national quarters of the index of co-operative learning[2]								Change in the combined reading literacy score per unit of the index of co-operative learning[2]	
	Bottom quarter		Second quarter		Third quarter		Top quarter			
	Mean score	S.E.	Mean score	S.E.	Mean score	S.E.	Mean score	S.E.	Change	S.E.
Australia	527	(5.5)	528	(4.5)	529	(4.9)	543	(4.3)	6.4	(2.75)
Austria	486	(4.5)	511	(3.3)	518	(3.0)	521	(3.5)	12.2	(2.19)
Belgium (Fl.)	524	(5.9)	545	(4.2)	536	(6.3)	538	(6.1)	3.6	(3.15)
Czech Republic	482	(3.7)	505	(2.9)	512	(3.0)	517	(3.3)	12.9	(1.74)
Denmark	488	(5.0)	505	(3.3)	511	(3.3)	501	(3.5)	5.4	(2.52)
Finland	531	(3.2)	546	(3.5)	555	(2.8)	561	(4.7)	11.6	(1.97)
Germany	477	(3.9)	501	(3.6)	502	(3.5)	508	(3.5)	9.0	(1.88)
Hungary	475	(4.6)	488	(5.1)	490	(5.8)	481	(5.1)	1.3	(2.63)
Iceland	493	(3.3)	510	(2.7)	517	(3.3)	521	(2.6)	11.3	(1.63)
Ireland	521	(5.1)	536	(3.7)	532	(4.3)	525	(4.1)	1.1	(1.61)
Italy	478	(5.9)	488	(4.1)	493	(3.0)	492	(3.3)	3.9	(2.22)
Korea	509	(3.4)	525	(3.0)	534	(3.2)	532	(2.5)	9.5	(1.34)
Luxembourg	445	(3.3)	450	(3.1)	468	(3.2)	456	(3.6)	2.2	(1.54)
Mexico	410	(4.4)	424	(4.0)	427	(3.9)	431	(4.8)	8.3	(1.80)
New Zealand	522	(4.5)	536	(3.3)	546	(4.9)	538	(4.8)	6.1	(2.31)
Norway	479	(5.3)	513	(4.3)	525	(3.5)	527	(3.5)	17.6	(2.06)
Portugal	447	(6.9)	471	(5.5)	484	(4.5)	480	(4.7)	13.7	(2.52)
Sweden	515	(3.1)	522	(2.9)	518	(3.5)	517	(3.4)	2.2	(1.93)
Switzerland	473	(5.7)	506	(5.2)	504	(4.8)	506	(4.4)	12.8	(1.96)
United States	483	(9.6)	509	(7.8)	528	(5.5)	528	(6.1)	13.7	(1.79)
OECD total	*477*	*(3.9)*	*497*	*(3.3)*	*507*	*(2.7)*	*508*	*(2.7)*	*7.8*	*(0.85)*
OECD average	*488*	*(1.1)*	*505*	*(1.0)*	*511*	*(1.0)*	*511*	*(1.0)*	*6.5*	*(0.52)*
Brazil	390	(4.6)	399	(4.1)	414	(3.6)	406	(4.3)	6.7	(1.59)
Latvia	432	(6.3)	462	(6.2)	469	(5.9)	483	(6.4)	17.0	(2.05)
Liechtenstein	478	(10.9)	486	(11.4)	479	(10.7)	492	(9.9)	3.1	(6.76)
Russian Federation	447	(4.4)	458	(4.6)	473	(5.0)	479	(5.1)	12.4	(1.30)
Netherlands[3]	516	(6.6)	538	(6.0)	536	(3.6)	541	(3.8)	8.0	(2.90)

1. For the definition of the index see Annex A1.
2. For explained variation see Annex A2. Unit changes marked in bold are statistically significant. Where bottom and top quarters are marked in bold this indicates that their difference is statistically significant.
3. Response rate is too low to ensure comparability (see Annex A3).

Table 4.9
Index of competitive learning and performance on the combined reading literacy scale, by national quarters of the index
Results based on students' self-reports

	Index of competitive learning[1]													
	All students		Males		Females		Bottom quarter		Second quarter		Third quarter		Top quarter	
	Mean index	S.E.	Mean index	S.E.	Mean index	S.E.	Mean index	S.E.	Mean index	S.E.	Mean index	S.E.	Mean index	S.E.
OECD COUNTRIES														
Australia	0.10	(0.02)	0.20	(0.02)	0.00	(0.03)	−0.83	(0.01)	−0.20	(0.01)	0.27	(0.01)	1.17	(0.03)
Austria	−0.19	(0.02)	−0.13	(0.02)	−0.25	(0.03)	−1.32	(0.02)	−0.51	(0.01)	0.04	(0.01)	1.02	(0.02)
Belgium (Fl.)	−0.38	(0.02)	−0.29	(0.02)	−0.48	(0.02)	−1.34	(0.02)	−0.65	(0.01)	−0.18	(0.01)	0.66	(0.02)
Czech Republic	0.14	(0.02)	0.14	(0.02)	0.14	(0.02)	−0.94	(0.01)	−0.17	(0.01)	0.35	(0.01)	1.33	(0.02)
Denmark	0.19	(0.02)	0.33	(0.03)	0.04	(0.03)	−1.09	(0.02)	−0.15	(0.01)	0.42	(0.01)	1.57	(0.02)
Finland	−0.25	(0.02)	−0.13	(0.02)	−0.35	(0.02)	−1.35	(0.02)	−0.55	(0.00)	−0.01	(0.01)	0.92	(0.02)
Germany	−0.07	(0.02)	−0.01	(0.03)	−0.14	(0.02)	−1.14	(0.02)	−0.38	(0.01)	0.13	(0.01)	1.11	(0.02)
Hungary	0.10	(0.02)	0.07	(0.03)	0.13	(0.02)	−1.05	(0.02)	−0.23	(0.00)	0.34	(0.01)	1.32	(0.02)
Iceland	0.01	(0.02)	0.13	(0.03)	−0.09	(0.03)	−1.20	(0.02)	−0.34	(0.01)	0.26	(0.01)	1.34	(0.02)
Ireland	0.15	(0.02)	0.35	(0.03)	−0.06	(0.03)	−1.25	(0.02)	−0.28	(0.01)	0.47	(0.01)	1.66	(0.02)
Italy	−0.01	(0.02)	0.06	(0.03)	−0.07	(0.03)	−1.33	(0.02)	−0.36	(0.01)	0.31	(0.01)	1.37	(0.02)
Korea	−0.14	(0.02)	−0.10	(0.03)	−0.19	(0.03)	−1.31	(0.02)	−0.51	(0.01)	0.07	(0.01)	1.19	(0.02)
Luxembourg	−0.18	(0.02)	−0.16	(0.03)	−0.20	(0.03)	−1.38	(0.02)	−0.49	(0.01)	0.07	(0.01)	1.07	(0.02)
Mexico	0.54	(0.02)	0.59	(0.02)	0.49	(0.02)	−0.46	(0.01)	0.23	(0.00)	0.70	(0.01)	1.70	(0.02)
New Zealand	0.29	(0.02)	0.40	(0.03)	0.17	(0.03)	−0.94	(0.02)	−0.07	(0.01)	0.53	(0.01)	1.63	(0.02)
Norway	−0.03	(0.02)	0.12	(0.03)	−0.19	(0.03)	−1.38	(0.02)	−0.40	(0.01)	0.24	(0.01)	1.41	(0.02)
Portugal	−0.22	(0.02)	−0.04	(0.03)	−0.39	(0.03)	−1.48	(0.02)	−0.58	(0.01)	0.07	(0.01)	1.10	(0.02)
Sweden	−0.01	(0.02)	0.09	(0.02)	−0.12	(0.02)	−1.02	(0.02)	−0.34	(0.01)	0.20	(0.01)	1.10	(0.02)
Switzerland	−0.26	(0.02)	−0.14	(0.02)	−0.38	(0.02)	−1.34	(0.02)	−0.53	(0.01)	−0.02	(0.00)	0.86	(0.02)
United States	0.27	(0.03)	0.30	(0.04)	0.25	(0.03)	−1.02	(0.02)	−0.08	(0.01)	0.52	(0.01)	1.68	(0.02)
OECD total	*0.16*	*(0.01)*	*0.21*	*(0.02)*	*0.12*	*(0.01)*	*−1.02*	*(0.01)*	*−0.18*	*(0.01)*	*0.39*	*(0.00)*	*1.47*	*(0.01)*
OECD average	*0.00*	*(0.00)*	*0.10*	*(0.01)*	*−0.08*	*(0.01)*	*−1.16*	*(0.00)*	*−0.32*	*(0.00)*	*0.25*	*(0.00)*	*1.27*	*(0.01)*
NON-OECD COUNTRIES														
Brazil	−0.03	(0.02)	0.09	(0.03)	−0.12	(0.03)	−1.23	(0.02)	−0.37	(0.01)	0.22	(0.01)	1.29	(0.03)
Latvia	0.22	(0.02)	0.16	(0.03)	0.27	(0.03)	−0.89	(0.02)	−0.07	(0.01)	0.44	(0.01)	1.38	(0.02)
Liechtenstein	−0.20	(0.05)	−0.07	(0.08)	−0.34	(0.06)	−1.18	(0.06)	−0.48	(0.02)	0.02	(0.02)	0.81	(0.07)
Russian Federation	0.13	(0.02)	0.06	(0.02)	0.21	(0.02)	−1.05	(0.02)	−0.20	(0.01)	0.40	(0.01)	1.38	(0.02)
Netherlands[3]	−0.25	(0.03)	−0.07	(0.04)	−0.43	(0.04)	−1.55	(0.03)	−0.60	(0.01)	0.05	(0.01)	1.10	(0.03)

	Performance on the combined reading literacy scale, by national quarters of the index of competitive learning[2]								Change in the combined reading literacy score per unit of the index of competitive learning[2]	
	Bottom quarter		Second quarter		Third quarter		Top quarter			
	Mean score	S.E.	Mean score	S.E.	Mean score	S.E.	Mean score	S.E.	Change	S.E.
OECD COUNTRIES										
Australia	515	(4.8)	522	(4.5)	530	(4.3)	559	(5.6)	21.7	(2.37)
Austria	502	(3.5)	501	(4.1)	510	(3.8)	522	(3.0)	9.5	(1.64)
Belgium (Fl.)	537	(6.0)	542	(4.1)	539	(5.0)	526	(6.7)	−2.9	(2.22)
Czech Republic	483	(3.2)	498	(3.1)	513	(3.5)	521	(3.2)	16.7	(1.58)
Denmark	481	(3.5)	493	(3.6)	502	(3.4)	527	(4.1)	15.9	(1.65)
Finland	530	(4.4)	539	(3.8)	549	(3.3)	574	(3.0)	18.1	(1.85)
Germany	476	(3.9)	498	(3.5)	502	(4.1)	514	(3.3)	15.5	(1.71)
Hungary	460	(5.1)	479	(5.2)	497	(5.2)	498	(4.5)	18.5	(1.86)
Iceland	489	(2.9)	500	(3.6)	514	(3.6)	538	(3.5)	19.5	(1.78)
Ireland	511	(4.7)	520	(4.4)	537	(3.9)	547	(4.3)	13.5	(1.63)
Italy	485	(4.5)	481	(4.0)	488	(3.7)	497	(3.7)	4.3	(1.57)
Korea	495	(3.6)	525	(2.6)	532	(2.9)	547	(2.6)	18.5	(1.16)
Luxembourg	448	(3.3)	456	(3.5)	456	(3.1)	461	(3.4)	3.0	(2.00)
Mexico	409	(4.5)	416	(4.0)	430	(4.5)	437	(4.7)	12.7	(1.97)
New Zealand	512	(4.2)	528	(3.6)	540	(4.0)	560	(5.1)	18.9	(2.09)
Norway	477	(4.6)	496	(3.9)	520	(4.2)	551	(3.7)	24.5	(1.70)
Portugal	481	(5.0)	466	(5.3)	468	(5.5)	467	(5.3)	−5.5	(1.60)
Sweden	507	(3.6)	511	(2.8)	518	(3.5)	535	(3.4)	12.9	(1.83)
Switzerland	503	(5.4)	496	(5.7)	495	(5.2)	496	(5.1)	−3.1	(1.98)
United States	478	(9.4)	505	(6.6)	519	(6.3)	547	(6.2)	24.7	(2.42)
OECD total	*474*	*(4.0)*	*492*	*(2.9)*	*503*	*(2.8)*	*521*	*(2.7)*	*13.2*	*(1.05)*
OECD average	*488*	*(1.0)*	*498*	*(0.9)*	*507*	*(1.0)*	*521*	*(1.0)*	*11.1*	*(0.45)*
NON-OECD COUNTRIES										
Brazil	405	(4.5)	401	(3.7)	397	(4.2)	405	(4.6)	−1.0	(1.35)
Latvia	429	(6.7)	454	(6.3)	467	(5.2)	495	(5.7)	27.8	(2.28)
Liechtenstein	485	(9.3)	477	(11.8)	498	(9.7)	478	(11.4)	−0.5	(6.85)
Russian Federation	442	(4.7)	454	(4.3)	471	(5.3)	490	(4.6)	19.0	(1.50)
Netherlands[3]	538	(5.5)	527	(4.8)	532	(5.1)	534	(4.6)	−0.8	(2.15)

1. For the definition of the index see Annex A1.
2. For explained variation see Annex A2. Unit changes marked in bold are statistically significant. Where bottom and top quarters are marked in bold this indicates that their difference is statistically significant.
3. Response rate is too low to ensure comparability (see Annex A3).

Table 4.10
Index of interest in computers and performance on the combined reading literacy scale, by national quarters of the index
Results based on students' self-reports

| | Index of interest in computers[1] | | | | | | | | | | | | | |
| | All students | | Males | | Females | | Bottom quarter | | Second quarter | | Third quarter | | Top quarter | |
	Mean index	S.E.	Mean index	S.E.	Mean index	S.E.	Mean index	S.E.	Mean index	S.E.	Mean index	S.E.	Mean index	S.E.
OECD COUNTRIES														
Australia	−0.21	(0.02)	−0.04	(0.03)	−0.41	(0.03)	−1.70	(0.02)	−0.40	(0.01)	0.35	(0.02)	Max	
Belgium	0.00	(0.02)	0.18	(0.02)	−0.22	(0.02)	−1.34	(0.02)	−0.21	(0.01)	0.64	(0.01)	Max	
Canada	−0.09	(0.01)	0.07	(0.01)	−0.24	(0.01)	−1.54	(0.01)	−0.28	(0.01)	0.57	(0.01)	Max	
Czech Republic	−0.03	(0.02)	0.14	(0.03)	−0.21	(0.03)	−1.33	(0.02)	−0.22	(0.01)	0.52	(0.01)	Max	
Denmark	−0.23	(0.02)	0.18	(0.02)	−0.66	(0.03)	−1.78	(0.02)	−0.47	(0.01)	0.41	(0.01)	Max	
Finland	−0.15	(0.02)	0.10	(0.02)	−0.39	(0.03)	−1.58	(0.02)	−0.33	(0.01)	0.41	(0.01)	Max	
Germany	0.24	(0.02)	0.43	(0.02)	0.04	(0.03)	−1.09	(0.03)	0.27	(0.02)	0.90	(0.00)	Max	
Hungary	−0.02	(0.02)	0.14	(0.03)	−0.21	(0.04)	−1.46	(0.02)	−0.19	(0.01)	0.66	(0.02)	Max	
Ireland	0.00	(0.02)	0.02	(0.03)	−0.02	(0.02)	−1.17	(0.02)	−0.22	(0.01)	0.51	(0.02)	Max	
Luxembourg	0.29	(0.02)	0.45	(0.02)	0.12	(0.03)	−1.04	(0.03)	0.39	(0.02)	0.90	(0.00)	Max	
Mexico	0.28	(0.02)	0.27	(0.03)	0.29	(0.03)	−0.99	(0.04)	0.30	(0.02)	0.90	(0.00)	Max	
New Zealand	−0.28	(0.02)	−0.15	(0.03)	−0.41	(0.03)	−1.75	(0.02)	−0.48	(0.01)	0.23	(0.02)	Max	
Norway	a	a	a	a	a	a	a	a	a	a	a	a	a	
Sweden	0.06	(0.02)	0.29	(0.02)	−0.18	(0.03)	−1.31	(0.02)	−0.10	(0.00)	0.77	(0.01)	Max	
Switzerland	0.06	(0.02)	0.24	(0.02)	−0.12	(0.03)	−1.43	(0.02)	−0.10	(0.01)	0.89	(0.00)	Max	
United States	0.31	(0.02)	0.29	(0.04)	0.33	(0.02)	−0.92	(0.04)	0.37	(0.02)	0.90	(0.00)	Max	
OECD total	*0.19*	*(0.01)*	*0.26*	*(0.02)*	*0.13*	*(0.01)*	*−1.11*	*(0.02)*	*0.18*	*(0.01)*	*0.81*	*(0.00)*	*0.90*	*(0.00)*
OECD average	*0.00*	*(0.00)*	*0.17*	*(0.01)*	*−0.17*	*(0.01)*	*−1.39*	*(0.01)*	*−0.13*	*(0.00)*	*0.62*	*(0.00)*	*0.90*	*(0.00)*
NON-OECD COUNTRIES														
Brazil	0.36	(0.02)	0.39	(0.03)	0.34	(0.03)	−0.66	(0.04)	0.32	(0.03)	0.90	(0.00)	Max	
Latvia	0.31	(0.02)	0.34	(0.03)	0.28	(0.03)	−0.92	(0.04)	0.37	(0.02)	0.90	(0.00)	Max	
Liechtenstein	0.17	(0.05)	0.35	(0.06)	−0.02	(0.08)	−1.28	(0.08)	0.20	(0.05)	0.90	(0.00)	Max	
Russian Federation	0.18	(0.03)	0.18	(0.04)	0.18	(0.04)	−1.44	(0.04)	0.36	(0.02)	0.90	(0.00)	Max	

| | Performance on the combined reading literacy scale, by national quarters of the index of interest in computers[2] | | | | | | | | Change in the combined reading literacy score per unit of the index of interest in computers[2] | |
| | Bottom quarter | | Second quarter | | Third quarter | | Top quarter | | | |
	Mean score	S.E.	Mean score	S.E.	Mean score	S.E.	Mean score	S.E.	Change	S.E.
OECD COUNTRIES										
Australia	534	(5.0)	538	(4.1)	532	(4.1)	525	(5.0)	−3.4	(1.76)
Belgium	527	(3.9)	518	(4.8)	523	(3.7)	524	(3.9)	−0.1	(1.70)
Canada	534	(2.2)	535	(1.9)	536	(2.2)	536	(2.0)	1.3	(0.81)
Czech Republic	503	(3.9)	503	(3.2)	507	(3.5)	507	(2.9)	0.7	(1.55)
Denmark	507	(3.3)	502	(3.6)	501	(3.9)	501	(3.5)	−2.4	(1.41)
Finland	**560**	(4.8)	553	(3.8)	548	(3.0)	**540**	(3.5)	**−8.4**	(1.36)
Germany	505	(4.0)	500	(4.0)	496	(3.7)	497	(4.3)	**−4.1**	(2.06)
Hungary	498	(6.2)	490	(5.0)	484	(4.5)	489	(4.7)	−4.4	(2.32)
Ireland	535	(4.3)	534	(4.6)	533	(4.1)	545	(4.2)	3.1	(1.93)
Luxembourg	**447**	(3.5)	455	(3.9)	461	(3.7)	**461**	(3.9)	2.7	(2.06)
Mexico	**404**	(4.7)	422	(5.5)	450	(5.3)	446	(4.8)	**20.6**	(2.20)
New Zealand	**547**	(4.3)	536	(5.0)	536	(4.3)	**531**	(4.7)	**−5.7**	(2.06)
Norway	a	a	a	a	a	a	a	a	a	a
Sweden	525	(3.5)	521	(3.4)	511	(3.5)	518	(3.2)	**−4.4**	(1.59)
Switzerland	503	(6.0)	508	(5.6)	495	(4.9)	496	(4.7)	−2.6	(2.02)
United States	**492**	(10.5)	526	(7.3)	528	(6.5)	**533**	(5.8)	**23.7**	(3.67)
OECD total	*491*	*(4.9)*	*508*	*(3.60)*	*511*	*(3.28)*	*513*	*(2.9)*	*8.8*	*(1.45)*
OECD average	*511*	*(1.3)*	*512*	*(1.2)*	*511*	*(1.1)*	*512*	*(1.1)*	*−3.8*	*(0.49)*
NON-OECD COUNTRIES										
Brazil	**400**	(5.8)	410	(5.5)	419	(5.2)	**418**	(5.5)	**13.7**	(2.84)
Latvia	454	(9.2)	472	(7.4)	467	(6.4)	475	(8.2)	**9.7**	(3.29)
Liechtenstein	481	(10.8)	493	(12.2)	492	(10.2)	474	(11.2)	−1.6	(5.72)
Russian Federation	**433**	(5.8)	472	(4.2)	482	(4.6)	**478**	(4.6)	**20.9**	(1.72)

1. For the definition of the index see Annex A1. "Max" is used to represent countries which have more than 25 per cent of students at the highest value of this index, which is 0.90.
2. For explained variation see Annex A2. Unit changes marked in bold are statistically significant. Where bottom and top quarters are marked in bold this indicates that their difference is statistically significant.

Table 4.11
Index of comfort with and perceived ability to use computers and performance on the combined reading literacy scale, by national quarters of the index
Results based on students' self-reports

Index of comfort with and perceived ability to use computers[1]

	All students		Males		Females		Bottom quarter		Second quarter		Third quarter		Top quarter	
	Mean index	S.E.	Mean index	S.E.	Mean index	S.E.	Mean index	S.E.	Mean index	S.E.	Mean index	S.E.	Mean index	S.E.
OECD COUNTRIES														
Australia	0.44	(0.02)	0.56	(0.02)	0.30	(0.03)	−0.75	(0.02)	0.08	(0.01)	0.81	(0.01)	1.61	(0.01)
Belgium	0.15	(0.02)	0.35	(0.02)	−0.07	(0.02)	−1.11	(0.02)	−0.20	(0.01)	0.49	(0.01)	1.40	(0.01)
Canada	0.49	(0.01)	0.67	(0.01)	0.32	(0.01)	−0.71	(0.01)	0.17	(0.00)	0.86	(0.00)	1.66	(0.01)
Czech Republic	−0.31	(0.02)	−0.07	(0.02)	−0.53	(0.02)	−1.39	(0.02)	−0.55	(0.01)	−0.11	(0.01)	0.82	(0.01)
Denmark	−0.05	(0.02)	0.31	(0.03)	−0.41	(0.02)	−1.20	(0.02)	−0.43	(0.01)	0.19	(0.01)	1.24	(0.01)
Finland	−0.12	(0.02)	0.19	(0.02)	−0.42	(0.02)	−1.29	(0.02)	−0.45	(0.01)	0.10	(0.01)	1.15	(0.01)
Germany	−0.31	(0.02)	−0.07	(0.02)	−0.53	(0.02)	−1.36	(0.02)	−0.59	(0.01)	−0.13	(0.00)	0.86	(0.02)
Hungary	−0.34	(0.02)	−0.20	(0.02)	−0.48	(0.02)	−1.37	(0.02)	−0.60	(0.01)	−0.12	(0.01)	0.72	(0.02)
Ireland	−0.13	(0.03)	−0.08	(0.04)	−0.19	(0.03)	−1.47	(0.02)	−0.49	(0.01)	0.15	(0.01)	1.27	(0.02)
Luxembourg	−0.09	(0.02)	0.11	(0.03)	−0.29	(0.03)	−1.28	(0.02)	−0.45	(0.01)	0.11	(0.01)	1.27	(0.02)
Mexico	−0.19	(0.03)	−0.14	(0.04)	−0.23	(0.04)	−1.44	(0.02)	−0.44	(0.01)	0.12	(0.01)	1.01	(0.02)
New Zealand	0.24	(0.02)	0.27	(0.03)	0.21	(0.02)	−0.95	(0.02)	−0.13	(0.01)	0.59	(0.01)	1.45	(0.01)
Norway	−0.01	(0.02)	0.35	(0.03)	−0.37	(0.02)	−1.31	(0.02)	−0.54	(0.02)	0.36	(0.00)	1.46	(0.02)
Sweden	−0.09	(0.02)	0.22	(0.02)	−0.41	(0.02)	−1.14	(0.02)	−0.40	(0.01)	0.08	(0.01)	1.10	(0.02)
Switzerland	−0.26	(0.02)	−0.03	(0.02)	−0.48	(0.02)	−1.28	(0.01)	−0.55	(0.00)	−0.11	(0.00)	0.92	(0.02)
United States	0.62	(0.02)	0.70	(0.03)	0.54	(0.03)	−0.53	(0.03)	0.30	(0.01)	0.95	(0.01)	1.76	(0.01)
OECD total	*0.25*	*(0.02)*	*0.37*	*(0.02)*	*0.14*	*(0.02)*	*−0.91*	*(0.02)*	*−0.06*	*(0.01)*	*0.55*	*(0.01)*	*1.41*	*(0.01)*
OECD average	*0.00*	*(0.00)*	*0.2*	*(0.01)*	*−0.19*	*(0.01)*	*−1.16*	*(0.00)*	*−0.33*	*(0.00)*	*0.27*	*(0.00)*	*1.23*	*(0.01)*
NON-OECD COUNTRIES														
Brazil	−0.50	(0.03)	−0.35	(0.04)	−0.62	(0.04)	−2.06	(0.02)	−0.80	(0.01)	−0.08	(0.01)	0.96	(0.02)
Latvia	−0.22	(0.02)	−0.07	(0.03)	−0.35	(0.03)	−1.26	(0.02)	−0.48	(0.01)	−0.03	(0.01)	0.90	(0.02)
Liechtenstein	−0.27	(0.05)	−0.02	(0.08)	−0.52	(0.05)	−1.16	(0.05)	−0.52	(0.02)	−0.13	(0.01)	0.79	(0.07)
Russian Federation	−0.31	(0.02)	−0.24	(0.03)	−0.39	(0.02)	−1.45	(0.02)	−0.56	(0.00)	−0.10	(0.01)	0.84	(0.02)

Performance on the combined reading literacy scale, by national quarters of the index of comfort with and perceived ability to use computers[2] / Change in the combined reading literacy score per unit of the index of comfort with and perceived ability to use computers[2]

	Bottom quarter		Second quarter		Third quarter		Top quarter		Change	S.E.
	Mean score	S.E.	Mean score	S.E.	Mean score	S.E.	Mean score	S.E.		
OECD COUNTRIES										
Australia	**505**	(5.1)	525	(4.3)	543	(5.0)	**546**	(4.2)	**18.0**	(1.87)
Belgium	**508**	(4.4)	518	(4.3)	515	(3.6)	**527**	(4.0)	**7.8**	(1.74)
Canada	**515**	(2.4)	535	(2.1)	542	(1.8)	**549**	(2.1)	**14.7**	(0.91)
Czech Republic	**482**	(3.2)	503	(3.1)	506	(3.2)	**519**	(3.8)	**16.3**	(1.69)
Denmark	**486**	(4.1)	503	(3.5)	504	(3.8)	**510**	(4.0)	**10.6**	(2.21)
Finland	**541**	(3.8)	548	(3.7)	551	(3.3)	**553**	(3.7)	4.5	(1.55)
Germany	**496**	(4.1)	501	(3.1)	495	(3.3)	**497**	(4.6)	**12.3**	(1.99)
Hungary	**471**	(4.5)	471	(5.3)	489	(3.8)	**498**	(4.8)	**12.3**	(1.48)
Ireland	**516**	(3.8)	519	(4.2)	531	(4.5)	**548**	(4.0)	**12.0**	(2.05)
Luxembourg	458	(3.7)	459	(3.5)	458	(3.3)	449	(3.6)	−3.4	(2.01)
Mexico	**400**	(3.5)	419	(4.3)	427	(4.3)	**454**	(5.4)	**19.2**	(2.07)
New Zealand	**511**	(5.0)	528	(4.1)	541	(4.1)	**552**	(3.8)	**16.5**	(2.05)
Norway	505	(4.6)	517	(3.7)	513	(3.8)	506	(4.0)	0.5	(1.60)
Sweden	510	(4.0)	517	(3.3)	524	(2.7)	518	(3.4)	4.9	(2.00)
Switzerland	**477**	(5.5)	497	(4.8)	500	(4.9)	**510**	(4.7)	**12.9**	(1.83)
United States	**480**	(7.3)	511	(7.6)	529	(6.3)	**532**	(7.9)	**24.2**	(2.37)
OECD total	*475*	*(3.5)*	*497*	*(3.7)*	*508*	*(3.3)*	*515*	*(3.8)*	*22.4*	*(1.40)*
OECD average	*492*	*(1.3)*	*505*	*(1.1)*	*511*	*(1.0)*	*518*	*(1.1)*	*13.4*	*(0.50)*
NON-OECD COUNTRIES										
Brazil	**382**	(3.9)	389	(4.1)	402	(5.6)	**432**	(4.9)	**15.3**	(1.97)
Latvia	456	(6.8)	463	(6.7)	460	(6.8)	468	(6.2)	**7.2**	(2.50)
Liechtenstein	469	(11.2)	486	(10.5)	490	(10.0)	490	(9.4)	11.4	(6.35)
Russian Federation	**449**	(5.6)	466	(4.1)	469	(4.2)	**478**	(4.5)	−0.5	(2.35)

1. For the definition of the index see Annex A1.
2. For explained variation see Annex A2. Unit changes marked in bold are statistically significant. Where bottom and top quarters are marked in bold this indicates that their difference is statistically significant.

Table 5.1a

Student performance on the combined reading, mathematical and scientific literacy scales, by gender

	Combined reading literacy						Mathematical literacy						Scientific literacy					
	Males		Females		Difference[1]		Males		Females		Difference[1]		Males		Females		Difference[1]	
	Mean score	S.E.	Mean score	S.E.	Score dif.	S.E.	Mean score	S.E.	Mean score	S.E.	Score dif.	S.E.	Mean score	S.E.	Mean score	S.E.	Score dif.	S.E.
OECD COUNTRIES																		
Australia	513	(4.0)	546	(4.7)	−34	(5.4)	539	(4.1)	527	(5.1)	12	(6.2)	526	(3.9)	529	(4.8)	−3	(5.3)
Austria	495	(3.2)	520	(3.6)	−26	(5.2)	530	(4.0)	503	(3.7)	**27**	(5.9)	526	(3.8)	514	(4.3)	**12**	(6.3)
Belgium	492	(4.2)	525	(4.9)	−33	(6.0)	524	(4.6)	518	(5.2)	6	(6.1)	496	(5.2)	498	(5.6)	−2	(6.7)
Canada	519	(1.8)	551	(1.7)	−32	(1.6)	539	(1.8)	529	(1.6)	10	(1.9)	529	(1.9)	531	(1.7)	−2	(1.9)
Czech Republic	473	(4.1)	510	(2.5)	−37	(4.7)	504	(4.4)	492	(3.0)	12	(5.2)	512	(3.8)	511	(3.2)	1	(5.1)
Denmark	485	(3.0)	510	(2.9)	−25	(3.3)	522	(3.1)	507	(3.0)	**15**	(3.7)	488	(3.9)	476	(3.5)	**12**	(4.8)
Finland	520	(3.0)	571	(2.8)	−51	(2.6)	537	(2.8)	536	(2.6)	1	(3.3)	534	(3.5)	541	(2.7)	−6	(3.8)
France	490	(3.5)	519	(2.7)	−29	(3.4)	525	(4.1)	511	(2.8)	**14**	(4.2)	504	(4.2)	498	(3.8)	6	(4.8)
Germany	468	(3.2)	502	(3.9)	−35	(5.2)	498	(3.1)	483	(4.0)	15	(5.1)	489	(3.4)	487	(3.4)	3	(4.7)
Greece	456	(6.1)	493	(4.6)	−37	(5.0)	451	(7.7)	444	(5.4)	7	(7.4)	457	(6.1)	464	(5.2)	−7	(5.7)
Hungary	465	(5.3)	496	(4.3)	−32	(5.7)	492	(5.2)	485	(4.9)	7	(6.2)	496	(5.8)	497	(5.0)	−2	(6.9)
Iceland	488	(2.1)	528	(2.1)	−40	(3.1)	513	(3.1)	518	(2.9)	−5	(4.0)	495	(3.4)	499	(3.0)	−5	(4.7)
Ireland	513	(4.2)	542	(3.6)	−29	(4.6)	510	(4.0)	497	(3.4)	**13**	(5.1)	511	(4.2)	517	(4.2)	−6	(5.5)
Italy	469	(5.1)	507	(3.6)	−38	(7.0)	462	(5.3)	454	(3.8)	8	(7.3)	474	(5.6)	483	(3.9)	−9	(7.7)
Japan	507	(6.7)	537	(5.4)	−30	(6.4)	561	(7.3)	553	(5.9)	8	(7.4)	547	(7.2)	554	(5.9)	−7	(7.2)
Korea	519	(3.8)	533	(3.7)	−14	(6.0)	559	(4.6)	532	(5.1)	**27**	(7.8)	561	(4.3)	541	(5.1)	**19**	(7.6)
Luxembourg	429	(2.6)	456	(2.3)	−27	(3.8)	454	(3.0)	439	(3.2)	**15**	(4.7)	441	(3.6)	448	(3.2)	−7	(5.0)
Mexico	411	(4.2)	432	(3.8)	−20	(4.3)	393	(4.5)	382	(3.8)	11	(4.9)	423	(4.2)	419	(3.9)	4	(4.8)
New Zealand	507	(4.2)	553	(3.8)	−46	(6.3)	536	(5.0)	539	(4.1)	−3	(6.7)	523	(4.6)	535	(3.8)	−12	(7.0)
Norway	486	(3.8)	529	(2.9)	−43	(4.0)	506	(3.8)	495	(2.9)	**11**	(4.0)	499	(4.1)	505	(3.3)	−7	(5.0)
Poland	461	(6.0)	498	(5.5)	−36	(7.0)	472	(7.5)	468	(6.3)	5	(8.5)	486	(6.1)	480	(6.5)	6	(7.4)
Portugal	458	(5.0)	482	(4.6)	−25	(4.6)	464	(4.7)	446	(4.7)	**19**	(4.9)	456	(4.8)	462	(4.2)	−6	(4.3)
Spain	481	(3.4)	505	(2.8)	−24	(3.2)	487	(4.3)	469	(3.3)	**18**	(4.5)	492	(3.5)	491	(3.6)	1	(4.0)
Sweden	499	(2.6)	536	(2.5)	−37	(2.7)	514	(3.2)	507	(3.0)	7	(4.0)	512	(3.5)	513	(2.9)	0	(3.9)
Switzerland	480	(4.9)	510	(4.5)	−30	(4.2)	537	(5.3)	523	(4.8)	**14**	(5.0)	500	(5.7)	493	(4.7)	7	(5.4)
United Kingdom	512	(3.0)	537	(3.4)	−26	(4.3)	534	(3.5)	526	(3.7)	8	(5.0)	535	(3.4)	531	(4.0)	4	(5.2)
United States	490	(8.4)	518	(6.2)	−29	(4.1)	497	(8.9)	490	(7.3)	7	(5.4)	497	(8.9)	502	(6.5)	−5	(5.3)
OECD total	*485*	*(2.3)*	*514*	*(2.0)*	*−29*	*(1.6)*	*504*	*(2.6)*	*493*	*(2.3)*	*11*	*(2.3)*	*502*	*(2.5)*	*503*	*(2.0)*	*0*	*(2.0)*
OECD average	*485*	*(0.8)*	*517*	*(0.7)*	*−32*	*(0.9)*	*506*	*(1.0)*	*495*	*(0.9)*	*11*	*(1.2)*	*501*	*(0.9)*	*501*	*(0.8)*	*0*	*(1.0)*
NON-OECD COUNTRIES																		
Brazil	388	(3.9)	404	(3.4)	−17	(4.0)	349	(4.7)	322	(4.7)	**27**	(5.6)	376	(4.8)	376	(3.8)	0	(5.6)
Latvia	432	(5.5)	485	(5.4)	−53	(4.2)	467	(5.3)	460	(5.6)	6	(5.8)	449	(6.4)	472	(5.8)	−23	(5.4)
Liechtenstein	468	(7.3)	500	(6.8)	−31	(11.5)	521	(11.5)	510	(11.1)	12	(17.7)	484	(10.9)	468	(9.3)	16	(4.7)
Russian Federation	443	(4.5)	481	(4.1)	−38	(2.9)	478	(5.7)	479	(6.2)	−2	(4.8)	453	(5.4)	467	(5.2)	**−14**	(4.5)
Netherlands[2]	517	(4.8)	547	(3.8)	−30	(5.7)	569	(4.9)	558	(4.6)	11	(6.2)	529	(6.3)	529	(5.1)	1	(8.1)

1. Positive differences indicate that males perform better than females, negative differences indicate that females perform better than males. Differences that are statistically significant are indicated in bold.
2. Response rate is too low to ensure comparability (see Annex A3).

Table 5.1*b*

Student performance on the retrieving information, interpreting texts, and reflection and evaluation scales, by gender

	Retrieving information						Interpreting texts						Reflection and evaluation					
	Males		Females		Difference[1]		Males		Females		Difference[1]		Males		Females		Difference[1]	
	Mean score	S.E.	Mean score	S.E.	Score dif.	S.E.	Mean score	S.E.	Mean score	S.E.	Score dif.	S.E.	Mean score	S.E.	Mean score	S.E.	Score dif.	S.E.
Australia	523	(4.3)	551	(5.0)	**−28**	(5.7)	511	(4.1)	545	(4.9)	**−34**	(5.7)	507	(4.0)	548	(4.7)	**−42**	(5.5)
Austria	495	(3.3)	510	(3.6)	**−16**	(5.4)	497	(3.1)	520	(3.8)	**−23**	(5.3)	493	(3.5)	532	(3.8)	**−39**	(5.5)
Belgium	504	(4.7)	529	(5.4)	**−25**	(6.6)	498	(3.9)	529	(4.7)	**−31**	(6.1)	475	(5.2)	522	(5.3)	**−47**	(6.4)
Canada	519	(1.9)	543	(1.8)	**−25**	(1.8)	518	(1.8)	547	(1.7)	**−29**	(1.6)	521	(1.8)	566	(1.7)	**−45**	(1.7)
Czech Republic	467	(4.7)	495	(2.8)	**−27**	(5.4)	483	(4.1)	517	(2.6)	**−34**	(4.6)	457	(4.3)	511	(2.6)	**−54**	(4.7)
Denmark	491	(3.4)	506	(3.2)	**−14**	(3.5)	485	(3.1)	506	(2.9)	**−21**	(3.4)	480	(3.2)	523	(3.3)	**−43**	(3.6)
Finland	534	(3.4)	578	(3.1)	**−44**	(3.4)	529	(3.3)	579	(3.2)	**−51**	(3.1)	501	(3.0)	564	(3.1)	**−63**	(2.8)
France	503	(3.8)	527	(3.0)	**−23**	(3.6)	492	(3.5)	519	(2.7)	**−27**	(3.3)	477	(3.7)	515	(2.9)	**−39**	(3.9)
Germany	471	(3.0)	497	(4.0)	**−26**	(5.2)	472	(2.9)	505	(3.8)	**−33**	(4.8)	455	(3.5)	503	(4.2)	**−48**	(5.5)
Greece	435	(6.7)	466	(5.0)	**−32**	(5.6)	459	(5.5)	492	(4.2)	**−33**	(4.6)	468	(6.8)	522	(5.4)	**−54**	(6.1)
Hungary	465	(6.0)	491	(4.8)	**−25**	(6.3)	466	(5.1)	494	(4.1)	**−28**	(5.4)	460	(5.7)	503	(4.5)	**−43**	(5.8)
Iceland	485	(2.4)	517	(2.2)	**−32**	(3.3)	497	(2.1)	535	(2.1)	**−38**	(3.0)	476	(2.0)	529	(1.9)	**−54**	(2.8)
Ireland	514	(4.2)	536	(3.6)	**−22**	(4.7)	513	(4.3)	541	(3.6)	**−27**	(4.7)	515	(4.0)	552	(3.3)	**−37**	(4.3)
Italy	474	(5.7)	504	(4.0)	**−31**	(7.8)	470	(4.6)	509	(3.3)	**−39**	(6.4)	460	(5.5)	507	(3.8)	**−47**	(7.6)
Japan	512	(7.0)	539	(5.8)	**−27**	(6.8)	505	(6.3)	530	(5.3)	**−25**	(6.1)	508	(7.2)	551	(5.5)	**−42**	(7.0)
Korea	527	(4.1)	533	(4.3)	−6	(6.9)	521	(3.7)	530	(3.6)	−9	(5.9)	514	(3.7)	541	(3.5)	**−27**	(5.8)
Luxembourg	424	(2.6)	444	(2.5)	**−20**	(4.0)	433	(2.6)	460	(2.3)	**−27**	(3.9)	423	(3.0)	464	(2.8)	**−40**	(4.5)
Mexico	396	(5.0)	408	(4.4)	−12	(5.1)	410	(3.8)	427	(3.3)	**−17**	(3.9)	428	(4.9)	463	(4.5)	**−35**	(5.6)
New Zealand	516	(4.7)	555	(4.1)	**−39**	(7.1)	506	(4.3)	549	(3.9)	**−43**	(6.6)	502	(4.2)	559	(3.9)	**−57**	(6.4)
Norway	490	(3.9)	523	(2.9)	**−32**	(4.0)	487	(3.7)	527	(2.7)	**−40**	(3.8)	479	(4.0)	539	(2.9)	**−60**	(4.1)
Poland	461	(6.6)	489	(6.2)	**−28**	(7.8)	465	(5.5)	500	(5.5)	**−35**	(6.6)	451	(6.4)	504	(5.8)	**−53**	(7.4)
Portugal	447	(5.5)	464	(5.0)	**−16**	(4.2)	461	(4.7)	485	(4.3)	**−24**	(3.5)	461	(5.1)	497	(4.5)	**−36**	(3.8)
Spain	477	(3.7)	493	(3.1)	**−16**	(3.8)	481	(3.3)	502	(2.8)	**−21**	(3.4)	487	(3.5)	526	(2.9)	**−39**	(3.5)
Sweden	501	(2.7)	532	(2.9)	**−30**	(3.2)	505	(2.5)	540	(2.5)	**−34**	(2.8)	486	(2.7)	536	(2.5)	**−51**	(2.6)
Switzerland	487	(5.2)	510	(4.7)	**−22**	(4.7)	484	(4.8)	510	(4.4)	**−26**	(4.2)	465	(5.4)	511	(5.1)	**−46**	(4.5)
United Kingdom	515	(3.1)	534	(3.4)	**−19**	(4.4)	503	(2.9)	527	(3.5)	**−24**	(4.3)	522	(3.0)	557	(3.4)	**−35**	(4.4)
United States	486	(8.8)	512	(6.5)	**−26**	(4.5)	491	(8.4)	518	(6.4)	**−27**	(4.2)	488	(8.4)	524	(6.3)	**−36**	(4.5)
OECD total	*485*	*(2.4)*	*508*	*(2.1)*	***−23***	*(1.8)*	*485*	*(2.3)*	*512*	*(2.0)*	***−26***	*(1.6)*	*483*	*(2.3)*	*523*	*(2.0)*	***−40***	*(1.8)*
OECD average	*486*	*(0.9)*	*510*	*(0.8)*	***−24***	*(1.1)*	*487*	*(0.8)*	*516*	*(0.7)*	***−29***	*(0.9)*	*480*	*(0.8)*	*525*	*(0.8)*	***−45***	*(1.0)*
Brazil	360	(4.3)	370	(4.0)	−10	(4.5)	393	(3.8)	408	(3.5)	**−14**	(4.1)	404	(4.2)	429	(3.7)	**−25**	(4.3)
Latvia	428	(6.1)	474	(6.0)	**−46**	(4.9)	434	(5.0)	485	(5.0)	**−51**	(3.8)	423	(5.7)	493	(6.1)	**−71**	(4.7)
Liechtenstein	484	(8.2)	504	(7.7)	−20	(12.3)	474	(7.8)	497	(6.9)	−23	(11.6)	447	(8.9)	492	(8.6)	−45	(13.3)
Russian Federation	434	(5.5)	468	(4.8)	**−34**	(3.7)	450	(4.4)	486	(3.9)	**−36**	(3.1)	431	(4.2)	480	(4.0)	**−49**	(2.8)
Netherlands[2]	537	(5.4)	559	(4.4)	−22	(6.6)	519	(5.0)	551	(4.1)	−32	(6.1)	508	(4.3)	543	(3.5)	−35	(5.4)

OECD COUNTRIES / NON-OECD COUNTRIES

1. Positive differences indicate that males perform better than females, negative differences indicate that females perform better than males. Differences that are statistically significant are indicated in bold.
2. Response rate is too low to ensure comparability (see Annex A3).

Table 5.2a
Percentage of students at each level of proficiency on the combined reading literacy scale, by gender

	Below Level 1 (less than 335 score points)		Level 1 (from 335 to 407 score points)		Level 2 (from 408 to 480 score points)		Level 3 (from 481 to 552 score points)		Level 4 (from 553 to 625 score points)		Level 5 (above 625 score points)		Increased likelihood of males performing at Level 1 or below[1]	
Males	%	S.E.	%	S.E.	%	S.E.	%	S.E.	%	S.E.	%	S.E.	Ratio	S.E.
Australia	4.7	(0.7)	11.3	(1.0)	21.3	(1.8)	26.0	(1.8)	22.5	(1.2)	14.2	(1.1)	1.75	(0.20)
Austria	5.9	(0.8)	11.9	(1.0)	23.3	(1.4)	30.3	(1.6)	21.9	(1.6)	6.7	(0.9)	1.65	(0.18)
Belgium	9.7	(1.3)	13.1	(1.0)	18.7	(1.1)	25.7	(1.2)	23.0	(1.1)	9.9	(0.9)	1.63	(0.19)
Canada	3.3	(0.3)	9.4	(0.4)	20.4	(0.6)	28.8	(0.7)	25.3	(0.7)	12.9	(0.6)	2.06	(0.13)
Czech Republic	9.0	(1.2)	14.6	(1.1)	26.9	(1.5)	28.6	(1.8)	15.6	(1.2)	5.3	(0.7)	2.10	(0.21)
Denmark	7.6	(0.8)	14.2	(1.1)	23.5	(1.1)	28.5	(1.3)	19.5	(1.1)	6.8	(0.7)	1.69	(0.13)
Finland	2.5	(0.6)	8.5	(0.7)	19.7	(1.0)	31.8	(1.1)	26.5	(1.2)	11.0	(0.9)	3.19	(0.59)
France	6.0	(0.9)	13.9	(1.2)	22.9	(1.3)	29.8	(1.3)	21.0	(1.3)	6.4	(0.7)	1.78	(0.14)
Germany	12.6	(0.9)	13.9	(0.9)	24.3	(1.3)	26.9	(1.6)	15.6	(1.4)	6.7	(0.8)	1.45	(0.12)
Greece	12.7	(1.7)	18.2	(1.6)	26.6	(1.5)	25.2	(2.1)	13.7	(1.4)	3.6	(0.7)	1.82	(0.16)
Hungary	9.4	(1.2)	17.9	(1.6)	27.2	(1.7)	27.2	(1.6)	14.9	(1.4)	3.5	(0.8)	1.64	(0.16)
Iceland	5.7	(0.6)	14.4	(0.9)	24.4	(1.3)	29.9	(1.3)	19.2	(1.5)	6.4	(1.0)	2.40	(0.23)
Ireland	4.0	(0.6)	9.5	(1.1)	21.4	(1.5)	29.9	(1.5)	24.1	(1.5)	11.2	(1.1)	1.62	(0.19)
Italy	8.0	(1.4)	16.6	(1.5)	28.3	(1.7)	28.1	(1.6)	15.2	(1.4)	3.7	(0.6)	1.97	(0.31)
Japan	4.4	(1.1)	9.9	(1.6)	20.2	(1.5)	32.6	(1.7)	25.4	(2.1)	7.5	(1.3)	2.51	(0.43)
Korea	1.3	(0.3)	6.1	(0.9)	19.4	(1.4)	39.3	(1.4)	29.6	(1.9)	4.4	(0.7)	1.98	(0.41)
Luxembourg	17.6	(1.1)	22.5	(1.2)	26.6	(1.5)	22.9	(1.3)	9.2	(0.8)	1.2	(0.5)	1.36	(0.07)
Mexico	20.0	(1.6)	29.9	(1.9)	27.8	(1.4)	16.5	(1.4)	5.0	(0.9)	0.8	(0.3)	1.28	(0.06)
New Zealand	7.3	(0.9)	11.1	(0.9)	19.1	(1.5)	26.1	(1.8)	22.6	(1.3)	13.7	(1.2)	2.34	(0.28)
Norway	8.8	(1.0)	14.4	(1.4)	21.0	(1.4)	27.6	(1.2)	20.2	(1.2)	8.1	(0.8)	2.17	(0.19)
Poland	12.2	(1.5)	18.1	(1.9)	23.4	(1.7)	26.1	(1.9)	16.0	(1.7)	4.1	(0.8)	1.80	(0.23)
Portugal	12.3	(1.4)	19.1	(1.4)	25.9	(1.5)	24.7	(1.6)	14.3	(1.2)	3.8	(0.6)	1.47	(0.09)
Spain	5.8	(0.7)	14.6	(1.3)	27.2	(1.2)	30.1	(1.2)	18.7	(1.5)	3.6	(0.7)	1.77	(0.14)
Sweden	4.6	(0.6)	12.2	(1.0)	23.3	(1.0)	29.8	(1.2)	22.7	(1.6)	7.4	(0.8)	2.13	(0.21)
Switzerland	8.3	(0.9)	16.4	(1.2)	23.7	(1.4)	26.3	(1.4)	18.1	(1.2)	7.3	(0.9)	1.57	(0.13)
United Kingdom	5.0	(0.6)	10.4	(0.7)	21.8	(1.2)	27.4	(1.3)	22.2	(1.1)	13.2	(1.1)	1.58	(0.16)
United States	9.3	(1.8)	13.7	(1.6)	21.8	(1.2)	25.5	(1.6)	18.8	(1.6)	11.0	(1.6)	1.80	(0.13)
OECD total	*8.5*	*(0.5)*	*14.2*	*(0.5)*	*22.9*	*(0.5)*	*27.5*	*(0.5)*	*19.2*	*(0.5)*	*7.7*	*(0.4)*	*1.67*	*(0.05)*
OECD average	*8.0*	*(0.2)*	*14.2*	*(0.2)*	*23.3*	*(0.3)*	*27.9*	*(0.3)*	*19.4*	*(0.2)*	*7.2*	*(0.2)*	*1.71*	*(0.03)*
Brazil	27.4	(1.9)	32.1	(1.5)	25.5	(1.6)	11.9	(1.4)	2.8	(0.7)	0.4	(0.2)	1.14	(0.04)
Latvia	18.4	(2.1)	22.3	(1.8)	25.8	(1.6)	21.7	(1.8)	9.3	(1.1)	2.5	(0.5)	2.09	(0.15)
Liechtenstein	9.9	(2.6)	17.2	(4.1)	23.4	(3.7)	27.6	(4.1)	18.0	(3.7)	3.9	(1.9)	1.54	(0.35)
Russian Federation	12.9	(1.6)	22.2	(1.2)	29.9	(1.0)	22.8	(1.2)	10.0	(0.8)	2.3	(0.5)	1.87	(0.09)
Netherlands[2]	3.0	(0.9)	10.2	(1.5)	18.8	(2.1)	29.9	(2.1)	27.5	(2.0)	10.6	(1.4)	2.17	(0.50)
Females														
Australia	1.7	(0.4)	6.7	(0.9)	16.5	(1.2)	25.3	(1.5)	28.3	(1.4)	21.6	(2.0)		
Austria	2.8	(0.5)	8.3	(0.7)	20.2	(1.3)	29.8	(1.5)	28.0	(1.4)	10.9	(1.1)		
Belgium	5.3	(1.0)	8.9	(1.0)	14.6	(1.0)	26.3	(1.1)	30.4	(1.4)	14.5	(1.0)		
Canada	1.3	(0.3)	4.7	(0.4)	15.3	(0.6)	27.3	(0.6)	30.5	(0.7)	21.0	(0.7)		
Czech Republic	3.2	(0.4)	8.3	(0.7)	22.9	(1.3)	33.2	(1.2)	23.8	(1.0)	8.6	(0.8)		
Denmark	3.8	(0.6)	9.6	(0.9)	21.6	(1.3)	30.6	(1.5)	24.8	(1.3)	9.6	(0.9)		
Finland	1.0	(0.6)	2.2	(0.4)	9.1	(0.8)	25.8	(1.3)	36.4	(1.5)	25.5	(1.4)		
France	2.3	(0.5)	8.2	(0.8)	21.1	(1.2)	31.4	(1.3)	26.5	(1.2)	10.5	(0.8)		
Germany	6.8	(1.1)	11.3	(0.9)	20.2	(1.2)	26.9	(1.2)	23.5	(1.2)	11.1	(0.8)		
Greece	4.7	(1.0)	13.0	(1.6)	25.0	(2.0)	31.1	(1.8)	19.8	(1.7)	6.4	(0.9)		
Hungary	4.5	(0.7)	13.4	(1.6)	22.7	(1.8)	30.5	(1.6)	22.2	(1.6)	6.7	(1.0)		
Iceland	1.8	(0.5)	6.2	(0.7)	19.6	(1.0)	32.1	(1.2)	28.4	(1.4)	11.9	(0.9)		
Ireland	2.0	(0.5)	6.2	(0.9)	14.3	(1.0)	29.6	(1.3)	30.4	(1.4)	17.4	(1.2)		
Italy	2.5	(0.6)	10.1	(1.1)	22.9	(1.3)	33.5	(1.4)	24.0	(1.7)	7.0	(0.7)		
Japan	1.1	(0.4)	4.9	(0.9)	15.8	(1.6)	34.1	(1.6)	32.1	(2.0)	12.1	(1.5)		
Korea	0.5	(0.2)	3.3	(0.6)	17.6	(1.6)	38.1	(1.6)	33.1	(2.0)	7.4	(1.0)		
Luxembourg	10.5	(0.8)	18.5	(1.0)	28.2	(1.7)	27.0	(1.5)	13.5	(0.8)	2.2	(0.4)		
Mexico	12.5	(1.4)	26.4	(1.5)	32.4	(1.6)	20.8	(1.5)	6.9	(0.9)	0.9	(0.3)		
New Zealand	2.0	(0.4)	6.3	(0.6)	15.3	(1.1)	23.2	(1.2)	29.2	(1.6)	24.0	(1.6)		
Norway	3.1	(0.6)	7.3	(0.8)	18.0	(1.0)	29.1	(1.4)	27.7	(1.2)	14.7	(1.0)		
Poland	5.0	(1.2)	10.9	(1.3)	24.8	(2.0)	30.4	(1.8)	21.2	(1.8)	7.7	(1.3)		
Portugal	6.9	(1.0)	14.3	(1.6)	24.8	(1.3)	30.2	(1.4)	19.1	(1.4)	4.7	(0.7)		
Spain	2.2	(0.5)	9.3	(1.0)	24.1	(1.2)	35.8	(1.7)	23.8	(1.3)	4.9	(0.5)		
Sweden	1.8	(0.4)	6.0	(0.6)	17.1	(1.1)	31.2	(1.4)	28.7	(1.2)	15.1	(1.1)		
Switzerland	5.5	(0.8)	10.2	(1.0)	19.0	(1.2)	29.9	(1.3)	24.1	(1.3)	11.3	(1.4)		
United Kingdom	2.2	(0.4)	7.6	(0.8)	17.2	(1.0)	27.8	(1.3)	26.8	(1.2)	18.3	(1.3)		
United States	3.7	(0.8)	9.5	(1.1)	20.2	(1.9)	29.2	(1.9)	24.0	(1.6)	13.4	(1.6)		
OECD total	*3.9*	*(0.3)*	*9.8*	*(0.4)*	*20.6*	*(0.6)*	*29.8*	*(0.6)*	*24.6*	*(0.6)*	*11.3*	*(0.5)*		
OECD average	*3.7*	*(0.1)*	*9.3*	*(0.2)*	*20.0*	*(0.2)*	*29.6*	*(0.3)*	*25.4*	*(0.3)*	*11.9*	*(0.2)*		
Brazil	19.3	(1.4)	32.8	(1.7)	29.9	(1.8)	13.9	(1.5)	3.4	(0.7)	0.7	(0.3)		
Latvia	6.7	(1.1)	13.5	(1.2)	26.8	(1.5)	28.9	(1.4)	18.2	(1.6)	5.8	(1.0)		
Liechtenstein	5.0	(2.2)	10.8	(3.2)	23.0	(4.9)	33.4	(4.8)	21.5	(3.3)	6.4	(2.6)		
Russian Federation	5.0	(0.7)	14.7	(1.4)	28.6	(1.2)	31.1	(1.4)	16.6	(1.4)	4.1	(0.6)		
Netherlands[2]	1.4	(0.6)	4.4	(1.2)	14.7	(1.3)	29.2	(2.2)	32.3	(2.2)	18.1	(1.5)		

1. Values that are statistically significant are indicated in bold.
2. Response rate is too low to ensure comparability (see Annex A3).

Table 5.2*b*

Percentage of students scoring below 400 points and above 600 points on the mathematical literacy scale

	Percentage of students scoring below 400 points on the mathematical literacy scale						Relative likelihood of males scoring below 400 points on the mathematical literacy scale[1]	
	All students		Males		Females			
	%	S.E.	%	S.E.	%	S.E.	Ratio	S.E.
Australia	7	(0.8)	7	(1.0)	8	(1.3)	0.89	(0.16)
Austria	11	(0.7)	9	(1.1)	13	(1.1)	**0.76**	(0.11)
Belgium	14	(1.3)	15	(1.4)	13	(1.7)	1.18	(0.14)
Canada	6	(0.4)	6	(0.6)	6	(0.4)	0.96	(0.08)
Czech Republic	16	(0.9)	15	(1.5)	16	(1.2)	0.87	(0.11)
Denmark	10	(0.9)	9	(1.1)	10	(1.2)	0.82	(0.10)
Finland	5	(0.7)	5	(1.0)	4	(0.8)	1.14	(0.24)
France	10	(0.9)	10	(1.1)	11	(1.1)	0.90	(0.12)
Germany	19	(1.1)	18	(1.2)	21	(1.9)	**0.86**	(0.07)
Greece	32	(2.2)	32	(2.9)	32	(2.3)	1.04	(0.09)
Hungary	19	(1.4)	19	(1.8)	20	(1.9)	0.88	(0.10)
Iceland	8	(0.7)	9	(0.9)	8	(1.1)	1.09	(0.17)
Ireland	11	(0.9)	10	(1.2)	12	(1.3)	0.84	(0.13)
Italy	26	(1.2)	25	(2.1)	26	(1.9)	1.00	(0.12)
Japan	5	(1.0)	6	(1.6)	4	(1.0)	1.46	(0.50)
Korea	5	(0.6)	4	(0.9)	6	(1.1)	0.69	(0.16)
Luxembourg	28	(1.1)	26	(1.5)	30	(1.6)	**0.85**	(0.06)
Mexico	56	(1.9)	54	(2.5)	59	(2.4)	0.94	(0.04)
New Zealand	9	(0.8)	10	(1.3)	8	(1.0)	1.41	(0.28)
Norway	14	(1.1)	14	(1.4)	13	(1.2)	1.05	(0.11)
Poland	24	(1.8)	26	(2.6)	23	(2.5)	1.15	(0.16)
Portugal	28	(1.8)	25	(2.0)	30	(2.3)	**0.85**	(0.07)
Spain	20	(1.3)	18	(1.6)	21	(1.9)	0.95	(0.09)
Sweden	12	(0.9)	12	(1.2)	13	(1.1)	0.87	(0.09)
Switzerland	10	(0.9)	9	(1.0)	11	(1.2)	0.91	(0.11)
United Kingdom	8	(0.7)	8	(0.8)	8	(1.0)	1.07	(0.16)
United States	18	(2.4)	18	(2.9)	17	(2.4)	1.07	(0.12)
OECD total	*18*	*(0.7)*	*18*	*(0.9)*	*18*	*(0.8)*	*0.99*	*(0.04)*
OECD average	*16*	*(0.3)*	*15*	*(0.3)*	*16*	*(0.4)*	*0.95*	*(0.02)*
Brazil	75	(1.6)	70	(2.4)	79	(2.1)	**0.86**	(0.02)
Latvia	27	(1.9)	26	(2.4)	27	(2.2)	0.97	(0.08)
Liechtenstein	13	(3.0)	11	(4.2)	14	(3.8)	0.88	(0.31)
Russian Federation	23	(1.8)	24	(2.1)	22	(1.9)	1.03	(0.06)
Netherlands[2]	4	(1.0)	4	(1.3)	4	(1.2)	1.03	(0.28)

	Percentage of students scoring above 600 points on the mathematical literacy scale						Relative likelihood of males scoring above 600 points on the mathematical literacy scale[1]	
	All students		Males		Females			
	%	S.E.	%	S.E.	%	S.E.	Ratio	S.E.
Australia	23	(1.6)	25	(1.9)	21	(2.3)	1.17	(0.13)
Austria	18	(1.2)	23	(1.8)	13	(1.6)	**1.73**	(0.24)
Belgium	24	(1.1)	27	(1.6)	21	(1.6)	**1.34**	(0.12)
Canada	22	(0.6)	25	(0.9)	19	(0.7)	**1.28**	(0.05)
Czech Republic	15	(1.2)	18	(1.7)	12	(1.3)	**1.55**	(0.16)
Denmark	16	(0.9)	19	(1.2)	12	(1.2)	**1.65**	(0.17)
Finland	22	(1.0)	22	(1.2)	21	(1.3)	1.06	(0.07)
France	18	(1.1)	21	(1.4)	15	(1.3)	**1.36**	(0.12)
Germany	14	(0.8)	16	(1.4)	12	(0.9)	1.28	(0.15)
Greece	7	(1.2)	9	(1.8)	6	(1.1)	1.48	(0.37)
Hungary	13	(1.4)	14	(1.9)	12	(1.6)	1.33	(0.17)
Iceland	16	(0.9)	16	(1.3)	16	(1.3)	1.09	(0.12)
Ireland	12	(1.2)	14	(1.8)	9	(1.2)	**1.63**	(0.20)
Italy	5	(0.8)	6	(1.1)	4	(0.7)	**2.06**	(0.41)
Japan	32	(2.4)	36	(3.4)	28	(2.6)	1.24	(0.12)
Korea	27	(1.5)	32	(2.4)	21	(2.2)	**1.46**	(0.19)
Luxembourg	4	(0.5)	5	(0.7)	2	(0.6)	**2.26**	(0.60)
Mexico	0	(0.2)	0	(0.2)	0	(0.2)	1.82	(1.27)
New Zealand	28	(1.6)	28	(1.9)	27	(2.3)	0.97	(0.08)
Norway	14	(1.1)	16	(1.7)	11	(1.1)	**1.54**	(0.17)
Poland	10	(1.6)	12	(2.2)	8	(1.4)	**1.66**	(0.30)
Portugal	4	(0.6)	6	(1.1)	3	(0.7)	**2.07**	(0.48)
Spain	9	(0.8)	12	(1.5)	5	(0.8)	**2.62**	(0.39)
Sweden	16	(0.9)	18	(1.2)	15	(1.2)	1.09	(0.10)
Switzerland	25	(1.8)	28	(2.1)	22	(2.1)	**1.21**	(0.10)
United Kingdom	23	(1.2)	25	(1.8)	20	(1.7)	1.20	(0.12)
United States	14	(1.7)	16	(2.1)	12	(1.7)	1.27	(0.15)
OECD total	*17*	*(0.5)*	*19*	*(0.7)*	*14*	*(0.6)*	*1.33*	*(0.06)*
OECD average	*16*	*(0.2)*	*18*	*(0.3)*	*14*	*(0.3)*	*1.34*	*(0.03)*
Brazil	0	(0.2)	1	(0.3)	0	(0.2)	6.85	(6.61)
Latvia	9	(0.9)	10	(1.3)	8	(1.3)	**1.47**	(0.19)
Liechtenstein	18	(3.1)	21	(4.6)	15	(4.6)	1.64	(0.56)
Russian Federation	13	(1.4)	13	(1.4)	12	(1.7)	1.18	(0.12)
Netherlands[2]	37	(2.1)	40	(2.6)	34	(2.7)	1.09	(0.08)

OECD COUNTRIES / *NON-OECD COUNTRIES*

1. Values that are statistically significant are indicated in bold.
2. Response rate is too low to ensure comparability (see Annex A3).

Table 5.3
Time students usually spend each day reading for enjoyment

		Students report not reading for enjoyment				Students report reading 30 minutes or less each day				Students report reading between 30 and 60 minutes each day			
		Females		Males		Females		Males		Females		Males	
		%	S.E.	%	S.E.	%	S.E.	%	S.E.	%	S.E.	%	S.E.
OECD COUNTRIES	Australia	25.4	(1.5)	40.1	(1.7)	31.4	(1.3)	29.7	(1.3)	24.3	(1.1)	17.1	(1.3)
	Austria	30.3	(1.0)	52.9	(1.4)	30.5	(1.0)	26.8	(1.2)	22.3	(1.0)	13.5	(0.8)
	Belgium	30.6	(0.7)	53.1	(1.4)	28.0	(0.9)	21.7	(1.0)	25.7	(0.9)	17.4	(0.8)
	Canada	23.0	(0.5)	42.6	(0.7)	36.7	(0.6)	30.7	(0.5)	24.6	(0.6)	16.1	(0.5)
	Czech Republic	15.1	(0.7)	38.7	(1.4)	29.1	(1.0)	30.4	(1.2)	31.3	(1.0)	19.5	(0.9)
	Denmark	17.4	(1.0)	35.8	(1.3)	37.5	(1.2)	34.7	(1.3)	27.9	(1.0)	18.8	(0.7)
	Finland	10.3	(0.6)	35.3	(1.1)	27.3	(1.0)	31.0	(0.9)	32.0	(1.2)	20.1	(0.8)
	France	21.2	(0.9)	39.5	(1.1)	28.0	(1.0)	27.0	(0.9)	33.4	(1.3)	23.3	(1.0)
	Germany	29.1	(0.9)	54.5	(1.2)	30.3	(1.1)	23.7	(0.9)	23.0	(0.9)	12.7	(0.7)
	Greece	19.4	(0.9)	24.6	(1.4)	26.7	(1.0)	26.6	(1.2)	23.7	(1.0)	21.7	(1.1)
	Hungary	18.8	(1.0)	33.3	(1.2)	29.0	(1.2)	27.6	(0.9)	27.3	(1.1)	21.1	(1.1)
	Iceland	22.7	(1.0)	37.0	(1.0)	38.4	(1.1)	37.5	(1.1)	27.3	(1.1)	17.6	(1.0)
	Ireland	24.5	(1.0)	42.4	(1.4)	32.0	(1.0)	29.7	(0.9)	23.8	(1.1)	17.0	(0.9)
	Italy	23.3	(1.1)	38.0	(1.3)	28.4	(0.8)	31.8	(1.0)	25.5	(1.0)	19.5	(0.9)
	Japan	54.9	(1.5)	55.2	(1.6)	17.8	(0.9)	17.9	(1.1)	15.4	(1.1)	15.5	(0.9)
	Korea	29.7	(1.4)	31.2	(1.2)	32.7	(1.2)	27.1	(0.7)	22.5	(0.9)	21.5	(0.9)
	Luxembourg	28.5	(1.1)	48.7	(1.2)	26.5	(1.0)	24.6	(1.0)	24.4	(1.2)	14.6	(0.9)
	Mexico	8.9	(0.8)	18.4	(1.1)	41.8	(1.3)	45.7	(1.4)	29.2	(1.0)	25.1	(1.0)
	New Zealand	23.1	(1.0)	36.8	(1.3)	36.8	(1.1)	36.5	(0.9)	23.3	(1.1)	15.3	(0.8)
	Norway	24.7	(1.1)	45.6	(1.3)	38.9	(1.1)	30.5	(1.1)	23.6	(1.1)	16.8	(1.0)
	Poland	16.1	(1.0)	32.2	(1.8)	21.6	(1.3)	23.8	(1.2)	31.0	(1.2)	26.4	(1.2)
	Portugal	8.3	(0.6)	29.4	(1.3)	36.1	(1.0)	42.4	(1.2)	32.2	(1.2)	20.1	(1.0)
	Spain	22.4	(1.1)	41.5	(1.2)	33.0	(0.9)	32.8	(1.1)	30.5	(1.0)	17.6	(0.8)
	Sweden	27.0	(1.3)	44.9	(1.2)	33.9	(1.1)	27.7	(1.1)	25.1	(0.9)	17.1	(0.7)
	Switzerland	21.5	(1.1)	48.9	(1.6)	35.4	(0.9)	30.6	(1.2)	27.7	(1.0)	13.2	(0.8)
	United Kingdom	22.6	(0.9)	35.8	(1.0)	36.4	(1.1)	34.8	(1.0)	26.2	(1.0)	19.5	(0.8)
	United States	32.0	(1.5)	50.1	(1.8)	35.2	(1.6)	26.8	(1.2)	18.7	(0.9)	13.6	(1.1)
	OECD total	*28.5*	*(0.5)*	*42.6*	*(0.6)*	*31.2*	*(0.5)*	*28.3*	*(0.4)*	*23.4*	*(0.4)*	*17.8*	*(0.3)*
	OECD average	*23.3*	*(0.2)*	*40.2*	*(0.3)*	*31.8*	*(0.2)*	*30.0*	*(0.2)*	*26.1*	*(0.2)*	*18.2*	*(0.2)*
NON-OECD COUNTRIES	Brazil	12.8	(0.9)	27.1	(1.4)	17.9	(1.2)	25.4	(0.9)	32.4	(1.2)	30.1	(1.4)
	Latvia	9.5	(0.9)	26.8	(1.6)	23.4	(1.3)	28.0	(1.3)	34.7	(1.3)	24.1	(1.8)
	Liechtenstein	31.5	(3.9)	48.5	(3.9)	33.4	(3.6)	35.0	(3.9)	22.7	(3.5)	10.6	(2.5)
	Russian Federation	13.9	(0.7)	25.0	(0.9)	21.7	(1.0)	27.6	(0.8)	27.7	(0.9)	23.9	(1.0)
	Netherlands[1]	29.3	(1.8)	57.1	(2.2)	36.9	(1.7)	25.9	(1.6)	22.3	(1.4)	11.1	(1.0)

		Students report reading between 1 and 2 hours each day				Students report reading more than 2 hours each day			
		Females		Males		Females		Males	
		%	S.E.	%	S.E.	%	S.E.	%	S.E.
OECD COUNTRIES	Australia	13.9	(0.9)	9.9	(0.6)	5.1	(0.5)	3.2	(0.4)
	Austria	12.4	(0.8)	5.3	(0.6)	4.5	(0.6)	1.5	(0.3)
	Belgium	12.4	(0.6)	5.9	(0.4)	3.4	(0.4)	1.9	(0.3)
	Canada	11.4	(0.3)	7.8	(0.4)	4.3	(0.3)	2.8	(0.2)
	Czech Republic	16.9	(1.0)	8.4	(0.6)	7.6	(0.7)	3.1	(0.4)
	Denmark	11.8	(0.8)	7.2	(0.8)	5.4	(0.6)	3.4	(0.4)
	Finland	24.9	(0.9)	11.0	(0.7)	5.5	(0.5)	2.6	(0.3)
	France	13.3	(0.7)	7.6	(0.7)	4.2	(0.5)	2.5	(0.3)
	Germany	11.6	(0.7)	5.8	(0.6)	5.9	(0.4)	3.3	(0.4)
	Greece	20.7	(1.1)	19.2	(1.0)	9.5	(0.7)	7.9	(0.6)
	Hungary	16.5	(0.9)	10.2	(0.7)	8.4	(0.7)	7.8	(0.7)
	Iceland	8.0	(0.6)	5.8	(0.5)	3.6	(0.5)	2.0	(0.4)
	Ireland	14.6	(0.8)	8.5	(0.7)	5.1	(0.6)	2.4	(0.4)
	Italy	18.1	(0.9)	7.9	(0.6)	4.6	(0.4)	2.8	(0.4)
	Japan	8.5	(0.6)	7.8	(0.7)	3.4	(0.4)	3.7	(0.4)
	Korea	10.7	(0.8)	13.0	(0.7)	4.5	(0.5)	7.1	(0.6)
	Luxembourg	15.1	(1.0)	8.7	(0.8)	5.6	(0.6)	3.4	(0.5)
	Mexico	15.0	(0.9)	7.9	(0.7)	5.1	(0.7)	2.8	(0.4)
	New Zealand	12.4	(0.9)	8.4	(0.7)	4.3	(0.4)	3.0	(0.4)
	Norway	10.1	(0.8)	5.4	(0.5)	2.7	(0.4)	1.6	(0.3)
	Poland	21.2	(0.9)	11.6	(0.8)	9.9	(0.9)	6.0	(0.7)
	Portugal	17.9	(1.0)	6.3	(0.7)	5.5	(0.6)	1.8	(0.3)
	Spain	11.5	(0.6)	5.9	(0.4)	2.6	(0.3)	2.2	(0.3)
	Sweden	10.2	(0.7)	7.4	(0.6)	3.8	(0.5)	3.0	(0.4)
	Switzerland	11.6	(0.7)	5.1	(0.5)	3.7	(0.4)	2.2	(0.3)
	United Kingdom	11.2	(0.7)	7.6	(0.6)	3.5	(0.4)	2.3	(0.4)
	United States	9.6	(0.8)	6.4	(0.7)	4.5	(0.6)	3.2	(0.5)
	OECD total	*12.2*	*(0.3)*	*7.9*	*(0.2)*	*4.8*	*(0.2)*	*3.5*	*(0.2)*
	OECD average	*13.8*	*(0.2)*	*8.3*	*(0.1)*	*5.1*	*(0.1)*	*3.4*	*(0.1)*
NON-OECD COUNTRIES	Brazil	21.1	(0.9)	11.6	(1.0)	15.8	(0.9)	5.7	(0.6)
	Latvia	23.9	(1.1)	15.2	(1.2)	8.5	(0.8)	6.0	(0.8)
	Liechtenstein	8.4	(2.0)	1.9	(1.1)	4.0	(1.6)	4.0	(1.6)
	Russian Federation	21.3	(1.0)	13.4	(0.5)	15.4	(0.6)	10.0	(0.7)
	Netherlands[1]	7.7	(0.9)	3.9	(0.8)	3.8	(0.7)	2.0	(0.4)

1. Response rate is too low to ensure comparability (see Annex A3).

Table 5.4a
Index of self-concept in reading, by gender and performance on the combined reading literacy scale, by national quarters of the index
Results based on students' self-reports

		Index of self-concept in reading[1]												
		Males		Females		Difference[2]		Bottom quarter		Second quarter		Third quarter		Top quarter	
		Mean index	S.E.	Mean index	S.E.	Index dif.	S.E.	Mean index	S.E.	Mean index	S.E.	Mean index	S.E.	Mean index	S.E.
OECD COUNTRIES	Australia	-0.11	(0.02)	0.06	(0.03)	**-0.17**	(0.03)	-0.94	(0.02)	-0.24	(0.01)	0.00	(0.01)	1.06	(0.02)
	Austria	-0.15	(0.03)	0.21	(0.03)	**-0.35**	(0.05)	-1.23	(0.02)	-0.37	(0.01)	0.25	(0.01)	1.50	(0.01)
	Belgium	-0.24	(0.02)	-0.11	(0.02)	**-0.13**	(0.03)	-1.12	(0.02)	-0.38	(0.01)	-0.06	(0.00)	0.83	(0.02)
	Czech Republic	-0.45	(0.03)	-0.09	(0.02)	**-0.36**	(0.04)	-1.43	(0.02)	-0.61	(0.01)	-0.04	(0.01)	1.04	(0.02)
	Denmark	0.20	(0.03)	0.52	(0.03)	**-0.32**	(0.04)	-0.91	(0.02)	-0.01	(0.01)	0.66	(0.01)	1.70	(0.01)
	Finland	-0.28	(0.02)	0.14	(0.03)	**-0.42**	(0.03)	-1.19	(0.01)	-0.40	(0.01)	0.15	(0.01)	1.19	(0.02)
	Germany	-0.34	(0.02)	0.11	(0.03)	**-0.45**	(0.03)	-1.35	(0.02)	-0.50	(0.01)	0.13	(0.01)	1.28	(0.02)
	Hungary	-0.30	(0.03)	0.02	(0.03)	**-0.32**	(0.04)	-1.24	(0.02)	-0.56	(0.01)	0.10	(0.01)	1.14	(0.02)
	Iceland	-0.15	(0.02)	0.05	(0.02)	**-0.20**	(0.03)	-1.26	(0.02)	-0.39	(0.01)	0.16	(0.01)	1.29	(0.02)
	Ireland	0.20	(0.04)	0.35	(0.04)	**-0.15**	(0.05)	-1.12	(0.02)	-0.16	(0.01)	0.66	(0.01)	1.71	(0.01)
	Italy	0.08	(0.03)	0.52	(0.03)	**-0.44**	(0.04)	-1.12	(0.02)	-0.10	(0.01)	0.67	(0.01)	1.73	(0.01)
	Korea	-0.34	(0.02)	-0.36	(0.03)	0.02	(0.05)	-1.33	(0.01)	-0.63	(0.01)	-0.22	(0.01)	0.81	(0.02)
	Luxembourg	0.06	(0.03)	0.26	(0.03)	**-0.21**	(0.04)	-1.16	(0.02)	-0.27	(0.01)	0.43	(0.01)	1.65	(0.01)
	Mexico	-0.10	(0.02)	0.11	(0.02)	**-0.21**	(0.03)	-0.88	(0.02)	-0.27	(0.01)	0.11	(0.01)	1.06	(0.02)
	New Zealand	-0.26	(0.02)	0.03	(0.03)	**-0.29**	(0.04)	-1.39	(0.02)	-0.49	(0.01)	0.08	(0.01)	1.35	(0.02)
	Norway	-0.23	(0.03)	0.15	(0.03)	**-0.38**	(0.04)	-1.27	(0.02)	-0.44	(0.01)	0.19	(0.01)	1.35	(0.02)
	Portugal	-0.23	(0.03)	0.08	(0.03)	**-0.31**	(0.03)	-1.21	(0.02)	-0.42	(0.01)	0.17	(0.01)	1.20	(0.02)
	Sweden	-0.11	(0.02)	0.19	(0.03)	**-0.30**	(0.03)	-0.94	(0.02)	-0.22	(0.01)	0.21	(0.01)	1.10	(0.02)
	Switzerland	-0.20	(0.02)	0.11	(0.03)	**-0.31**	(0.03)	-1.12	(0.01)	-0.37	(0.01)	0.13	(0.01)	1.18	(0.02)
	United States	0.05	(0.04)	0.44	(0.04)	**-0.39**	(0.04)	-1.11	(0.02)	-0.23	(0.01)	0.64	(0.01)	1.73	(0.01)
	OECD total	*-0.09*	*(0.02)*	*0.24*	*(0.02)*	*-0.33*	*(0.02)*	*-1.13*	*(0.01)*	*-0.31*	*(0.00)*	*0.35*	*(0.01)*	*1.41*	*(0.01)*
	OECD average	*-0.14*	*(0.01)*	*0.15*	*(0.01)*	*-0.29*	*(0.01)*	*-1.17*	*(0.00)*	*-0.35*	*(0.00)*	*0.23*	*(0.00)*	*1.30*	*(0.01)*
NON-OECD COUNTRIES	Brazil	0.11	(0.03)	-0.17	(0.03)	**-0.28**	(0.03)	-1.12	(0.02)	-0.35	(0.01)	0.17	(0.01)	1.22	(0.02)
	Latvia	0.36	(0.04)	-0.15	(0.02)	**-0.51**	(0.04)	-1.07	(0.02)	-0.31	(0.01)	0.34	(0.01)	1.49	(0.02)
	Liechtenstein	0.08	(0.07)	-0.29	(0.06)	**-0.37**	(0.10)	-1.15	(0.04)	-0.40	(0.02)	0.05	(0.02)	1.07	(0.08)
	Russian Federation	0.37	(0.03)	-0.15	(0.02)	**-0.52**	(0.03)	-1.14	(0.01)	-0.32	(0.01)	0.39	(0.01)	1.52	(0.01)
	Netherlands[1]	0.13	(0.04)	-0.11	(0.04)	**-0.25**	(0.05)	-1.11	(0.02)	-0.33	(0.01)	0.19	(0.01)	1.30	(0.02)

Performance on the combined reading literacy scale, by national quarters of the index of self-concept in reading

		Bottom quarter		Second quarter		Third quarter		Top quarter	
		Mean score	S.E.	Mean score	S.E.	Mean score	S.E.	Mean score	S.E.
OECD COUNTRIES	Australia	499	(4.6)	519	(4.9)	538	(4.4)	572	(4.5)
	Austria	484	(3.8)	492	(4.1)	513	(3.6)	547	(3.3)
	Belgium	514	(6.6)	529	(5.2)	553	(4.4)	548	(5.1)
	Czech Republic	478	(3.8)	490	(3.2)	511	(3.1)	536	(3.1)
	Denmark	456	(3.9)	491	(3.5)	510	(3.2)	548	(3.4)
	Finland	509	(3.1)	531	(3.9)	560	(3.2)	593	(3.6)
	Germany	477	(3.8)	476	(4.0)	503	(3.6)	534	(3.8)
	Hungary	458	(4.1)	464	(5.4)	491	(4.8)	521	(5.0)
	Iceland	474	(3.2)	495	(3.4)	522	(3.2)	551	(3.3)
	Ireland	513	(4.4)	527	(3.8)	533	(4.3)	542	(4.8)
	Italy	452	(5.4)	484	(3.6)	501	(3.1)	514	(3.7)
	Korea	498	(3.1)	518	(2.9)	531	(3.3)	552	(2.4)
	Luxembourg	417	(3.3)	442	(3.6)	471	(2.9)	492	(3.2)
	Mexico	410	(4.9)	415	(4.7)	425	(4.0)	441	(4.2)
	New Zealand	514	(3.9)	510	(4.1)	544	(4.8)	573	(4.4)
	Norway	470	(4.8)	490	(4.5)	523	(3.4)	561	(3.9)
	Portugal	433	(5.9)	454	(5.2)	483	(4.5)	512	(5.0)
	Sweden	481	(3.0)	503	(2.8)	528	(3.2)	559	(3.5)
	Switzerland	473	(4.9)	482	(5.6)	511	(4.6)	524	(5.2)
	United States	469	(9.0)	496	(6.3)	526	(7.0)	558	(6.2)
	OECD total	*465*	*(3.6)*	*484*	*(2.9)*	*507*	*(3.1)*	*533*	*(3.0)*
	OECD average	*473*	*(1.0)*	*490*	*(1.1)*	*513*	*(1.0)*	*539*	*(1.0)*
NON-OECD COUNTRIES	Brazil	391	(4.3)	392	(3.8)	401	(3.4)	424	(5.1)
	Latvia	425	(6.8)	441	(6.8)	467	(5.6)	513	(5.4)
	Liechtenstein	458	(10.6)	472	(9.8)	494	(11.1)	515	(8.6)
	Russian Federation	435	(5.3)	447	(4.0)	471	(4.3)	505	(5.1)
	Netherlands[3]	515	(6.8)	529	(5.0)	538	(4.6)	549	(4.2)

1. For a definition of the index, see Annex A1.
2. Positive differences indicate that males perform better than females, negative differences indicate that females perform better than males. Differences that are statistically significant are indicated in bold.
3. Response rate is too low to ensure comparability (see Annex A3).

Table 5.4b

Index of self-concept in mathematics, by gender and performance on the mathematical literacy scale, by national quarters of the index

Results based on students' self-reports

| | Index of self-concept in mathematics[1] | | | | | | | | | | | | | |
| | Males | | Females | | Difference[2] | | Bottom quarter | | Second quarter | | Third quarter | | Top quarter | |
	Mean index	S.E.	Mean index	S.E.	Index dif.	S.E.	Mean index	S.E.	Mean index	S.E.	Mean index	S.E.	Mean index	S.E.
OECD COUNTRIES														
Australia	0.27	(0.02)	0.04	(0.03)	**0.23**	(0.04)	−0.84	(0.02)	−0.07	(0.01)	0.39	(0.01)	1.19	(0.02)
Austria	0.09	(0.03)	−0.20	(0.03)	**0.29**	(0.04)	−1.29	(0.02)	−0.38	(0.01)	0.22	(0.01)	1.21	(0.02)
Belgium	0.09	(0.03)	−0.09	(0.03)	**0.18**	(0.04)	−1.04	(0.02)	−0.26	(0.01)	0.32	(0.01)	1.02	(0.02)
Czech Republic	0.02	(0.03)	−0.24	(0.03)	**0.26**	(0.04)	−1.29	(0.01)	−0.41	(0.01)	0.16	(0.01)	1.08	(0.02)
Denmark	0.68	(0.03)	0.29	(0.03)	**0.39**	(0.04)	−0.88	(0.02)	0.26	(0.01)	0.91	(0.01)	1.67	(0.01)
Finland	0.15	(0.03)	−0.20	(0.03)	**0.35**	(0.04)	−1.41	(0.01)	−0.41	(0.01)	0.31	(0.01)	1.39	(0.02)
Germany	0.24	(0.03)	−0.18	(0.03)	**0.42**	(0.04)	−1.29	(0.02)	−0.32	(0.01)	0.34	(0.01)	1.35	(0.02)
Hungary	−0.25	(0.04)	−0.37	(0.03)	**0.12**	(0.05)	−1.49	(0.01)	−0.68	(0.01)	−0.09	(0.01)	1.03	(0.02)
Iceland	0.11	(0.04)	−0.09	(0.03)	**0.20**	(0.05)	−1.36	(0.01)	−0.39	(0.01)	0.38	(0.01)	1.41	(0.02)
Ireland	−0.02	(0.02)	−0.11	(0.04)	0.09	(0.04)	−1.40	(0.01)	−0.40	(0.01)	0.26	(0.01)	1.27	(0.02)
Italy	0.14	(0.04)	−0.04	(0.03)	**0.17**	(0.05)	−1.36	(0.01)	−0.30	(0.01)	0.43	(0.01)	1.45	(0.02)
Korea	−0.42	(0.04)	−0.57	(0.04)	**0.15**	(0.06)	−1.62	(0.00)	−1.06	(0.01)	−0.24	(0.01)	0.97	(0.03)
Luxembourg	0.11	(0.03)	−0.17	(0.04)	**0.28**	(0.05)	−1.33	(0.02)	−0.34	(0.01)	0.30	(0.01)	1.25	(0.02)
Mexico	0.17	(0.03)	0.12	(0.03)	0.05	(0.03)	−0.81	(0.02)	−0.15	(0.01)	0.38	(0.01)	1.15	(0.02)
New Zealand	0.30	(0.04)	0.04	(0.04)	**0.26**	(0.04)	−1.21	(0.02)	−0.18	(0.01)	0.53	(0.01)	1.53	(0.01)
Norway	0.17	(0.04)	−0.33	(0.04)	**0.50**	(0.06)	−1.49	(0.01)	−0.49	(0.01)	0.27	(0.01)	1.36	(0.02)
Portugal	−0.14	(0.03)	−0.28	(0.03)	**0.13**	(0.04)	−1.50	(0.01)	−0.64	(0.01)	0.17	(0.01)	1.11	(0.02)
Sweden	0.13	(0.02)	−0.23	(0.03)	**0.36**	(0.04)	−1.16	(0.02)	−0.33	(0.01)	0.20	(0.01)	1.11	(0.02)
Switzerland	0.32	(0.03)	−0.18	(0.03)	**0.50**	(0.04)	−1.13	(0.02)	−0.23	(0.01)	0.39	(0.01)	1.26	(0.02)
United States	0.38	(0.05)	0.29	(0.04)	0.09	(0.06)	−0.98	(0.04)	0.08	(0.01)	0.67	(0.01)	1.58	(0.01)
OECD total	*0.19*	*(0.02)*	*0.04*	*(0.02)*	*0.15*	*(0.03)*	*−1.12*	*(0.01)*	*−0.20*	*(0.01)*	*0.43*	*(0.01)*	*1.36*	*(0.01)*
OECD average	*0.12*	*(0.01)*	*−0.13*	*(0.01)*	*0.25*	*(0.01)*	*−1.25*	*(0.01)*	*−0.34*	*(0.00)*	*0.31*	*(0.00)*	*1.27*	*(0.01)*
NON-OECD COUNTRIES														
Brazil	0.29	(0.04)	0.04	(0.04)	**0.25**	(0.05)	−1.06	(0.03)	−0.15	(0.01)	0.45	(0.01)	1.37	(0.02)
Latvia	0.14	(0.03)	−0.04	(0.04)	**0.18**	(0.05)	−1.20	(0.02)	−0.18	(0.02)	0.42	(0.01)	1.17	(0.02)
Liechtenstein	0.28	(0.09)	−0.11	(0.09)	**0.39**	(0.12)	−0.92	(0.07)	−0.22	(0.03)	0.35	(0.03)	1.16	(0.08)
Russian Federation	0.04	(0.03)	0.02	(0.04)	0.01	(0.04)	−1.32	(0.02)	−0.32	(0.01)	0.43	(0.01)	1.34	(0.01)
Netherlands[3]	0.29	(0.05)	−0.36	(0.05)	**0.65**	(0.07)	−1.40	(0.02)	−0.42	(0.01)	0.34	(0.01)	1.39	(0.03)

Performance on the mathematical literacy scale, by national quarters of the index of self-concept in mathematics

| | Bottom quarter | | Second quarter | | Third quarter | | Top quarter | |
	Mean score	S.E.	Mean score	S.E.	Mean score	S.E.	Mean score	S.E.
OECD COUNTRIES								
Australia	507	(4.8)	521	(5.0)	544	(5.2)	572	(4.9)
Austria	496	(3.9)	507	(4.4)	513	(4.5)	550	(4.5)
Belgium	530	(6.6)	545	(5.0)	555	(5.8)	560	(7.6)
Czech Republic	477	(4.1)	495	(5.2)	514	(4.4)	542	(4.5)
Denmark	476	(3.6)	512	(4.3)	529	(3.7)	557	(5.0)
Finland	497	(3.4)	515	(3.7)	547	(2.9)	593	(3.0)
Germany	482	(4.7)	486	(5.1)	498	(5.7)	529	(3.9)
Hungary	465	(4.4)	482	(5.5)	497	(5.0)	524	(6.9)
Iceland	478	(4.3)	498	(3.6)	521	(3.8)	573	(4.0)
Ireland	484	(3.4)	495	(4.0)	509	(4.6)	533	(5.0)
Italy	434	(3.8)	445	(5.4)	464	(4.3)	488	(4.8)
Korea	512	(3.9)	535	(4.4)	556	(4.3)	584	(4.0)
Luxembourg	455	(4.0)	457	(4.5)	455	(3.9)	474	(5.1)
Mexico	382	(4.8)	384	(3.9)	389	(5.1)	401	(5.3)
New Zealand	506	(4.3)	525	(4.5)	543	(5.0)	598	(4.9)
Norway	456	(4.7)	488	(4.1)	507	(5.0)	563	(4.2)
Portugal	424	(4.1)	453	(5.6)	460	(6.2)	480	(5.6)
Sweden	475	(3.6)	489	(4.0)	521	(4.4)	562	(4.6)
Switzerland	514	(6.0)	527	(7.0)	532	(5.1)	559	(5.4)
United States	473	(7.0)	488	(9.1)	496	(10.1)	545	(8.0)
OECD total	*464*	*(3.0)*	*477*	*(3.9)*	*489*	*(4.2)*	*523*	*(3.7)*
OECD average	*475*	*(1.2)*	*492*	*(1.1)*	*507*	*(1.2)*	*539*	*(1.5)*
NON-OECD COUNTRIES								
Brazil	326	(5.9)	335	(6.5)	342	(6.5)	361	(6.4)
Latvia	439	(6.2)	455	(6.6)	466	(6.1)	504	(6.8)
Liechtenstein	488	(15.8)	519	(12.9)	503	(16.1)	554	(14.8)
Russian Federation	453	(7.6)	459	(6.4)	488	(6.0)	523	(5.9)
Netherlands[3]	556	(7.1)	552	(6.0)	564	(6.3)	588	(5.2)

1. For a definition of the index, see Annex A1.
2. Positive differences indicate that males perform better than females, negative differences indicate that females perform better than males. Differences that are statistically significant are indicated in bold.
3. Response rate is too low to ensure comparability (see Annex A3).

Table 6.1a
International socio-economic index of occupational status (ISEI) and performance on the combined reading literacy scale, by national quarters of the index
Results based on students' self-reports

	International socio-economic index of occupational status[1]									
	All students		Bottom quarter		Second quarter		Third quarter		Top quarter	
	Mean index	S.E.	Mean index	S.E.	Mean index	S.E.	Mean index	S.E.	Mean index	S.E.
OECD COUNTRIES										
Australia	52.3	(0.5)	31.1	(0.2)	46.3	(0.1)	58.4	(0.2)	73.2	(0.3)
Austria	49.7	(0.3)	32.9	(0.2)	44.7	(0.1)	52.2	(0.1)	69.1	(0.3)
Belgium	49.0	(0.4)	28.4	(0.1)	42.1	(0.1)	53.5	(0.1)	71.8	(0.2)
Canada	52.8	(0.2)	31.3	(0.1)	48.1	(0.1)	58.9	(0.1)	72.9	(0.1)
Czech Republic	48.3	(0.3)	31.2	(0.2)	44.4	(0.1)	51.5	(0.0)	66.1	(0.3)
Denmark	49.7	(0.4)	29.0	(0.2)	44.0	(0.1)	54.9	(0.2)	71.1	(0.3)
Finland	50.0	(0.4)	29.7	(0.2)	43.4	(0.1)	55.1	(0.1)	71.8	(0.2)
France	48.3	(0.4)	27.7	(0.2)	41.1	(0.2)	53.1	(0.1)	71.2	(0.3)
Germany	48.9	(0.3)	30.0	(0.2)	42.6	(0.1)	52.5	(0.1)	70.2	(0.2)
Greece	47.8	(0.6)	25.6	(0.3)	40.2	(0.2)	53.0	(0.1)	72.3	(0.4)
Hungary	49.5	(0.5)	30.4	(0.2)	42.6	(0.1)	53.7	(0.1)	71.5	(0.2)
Iceland	52.7	(0.3)	31.4	(0.2)	47.3	(0.1)	58.6	(0.2)	73.8	(0.2)
Ireland	48.4	(0.5)	28.5	(0.2)	42.7	(0.2)	53.2	(0.1)	69.4	(0.2)
Italy	47.1	(0.3)	28.5	(0.1)	40.6	(0.1)	50.3	(0.1)	68.9	(0.4)
Japan[2]	m	m	m	m	m	m	m	m	m	m
Korea	42.8	(0.4)	26.5	(0.1)	35.9	(0.1)	46.0	(0.1)	62.9	(0.5)
Luxembourg	44.8	(0.3)	25.1	(0.1)	37.5	(0.1)	50.6	(0.1)	66.1	(0.4)
Mexico	42.5	(0.7)	24.4	(0.1)	32.3	(0.1)	46.8	(0.2)	66.5	(0.5)
New Zealand	52.2	(0.4)	30.5	(0.3)	47.1	(0.1)	57.7	(0.2)	73.6	(0.2)
Norway	53.9	(0.4)	35.6	(0.2)	47.1	(0.1)	59.0	(0.2)	73.9	(0.2)
Poland	46.0	(0.5)	27.3	(0.2)	40.0	(0.1)	49.8	(0.1)	67.0	(0.4)
Portugal	43.9	(0.6)	26.8	(0.2)	34.5	(0.1)	48.4	(0.1)	65.7	(0.5)
Spain	45.0	(0.6)	26.8	(0.1)	36.2	(0.1)	49.6	(0.1)	67.3	(0.5)
Sweden	50.6	(0.4)	30.4	(0.2)	44.1	(0.1)	55.7	(0.1)	72.1	(0.2)
Switzerland	49.2	(0.5)	29.3	(0.2)	42.5	(0.1)	53.2	(0.1)	71.9	(0.3)
United Kingdom	51.3	(0.3)	30.7	(0.2)	45.7	(0.1)	56.9	(0.2)	71.8	(0.2)
United States	52.4	(0.8)	30.3	(0.2)	47.4	(0.2)	59.5	(0.2)	72.5	(0.3)
OECD total	*49.0*	*(0.2)*	*29.1*	*(0.1)*	*42.5*	*(0.1)*	*54.0*	*(0.1)*	*70.3*	*(0.1)*
OECD average	*48.9*	*(0.1)*	*29.3*	*(0.0)*	*42.4*	*(0.0)*	*53.6*	*(0.0)*	*70.2*	*(0.1)*
NON-OECD COUNTRIES										
Brazil	43.9	(0.6)	24.6	(0.2)	34.5	(0.2)	49.6	(0.2)	67.1	(0.4)
Latvia	50.2	(0.5)	27.7	(0.1)	40.4	(0.2)	58.5	(0.3)	74.1	(0.3)
Liechtenstein	47.5	(0.9)	28.0	(0.6)	41.8	(0.4)	52.1	(0.2)	68.2	(0.9)
Russian Federation	49.4	(0.5)	30.0	(0.2)	40.3	(0.1)	53.4	(0.2)	73.9	(0.2)
Netherlands[3]	50.9	(0.5)	29.5	(0.2)	45.3	(0.2)	57.3	(0.3)	71.3	(0.2)

	Performance on the combined reading literacy scale, by national quarters of the international socio-economic index of occupational status[4]								Change in the combined reading literacy score per 16.3 units of the international socio-economic index of occupational status[4]		Increased likelihood of students in the bottom quarter of the ISEI distribution scoring in the bottom quarter of the national reading literacy performance distribution[5]	
	Bottom quarter		Second quarter		Third quarter		Top quarter					
	Mean score	S.E.	Mean score	S.E.	Mean score	S.E.	Mean score	S.E.	Change	S.E.	Ratio	S.E.
OECD COUNTRIES												
Australia	490	(3.8)	523	(4.5)	538	(4.2)	576	(5.4)	31.7	(2.10)	1.9	(0.14)
Austria	467	(3.9)	500	(3.3)	522	(3.4)	547	(3.5)	35.2	(2.07)	2.1	(0.10)
Belgium	457	(6.2)	497	(4.5)	537	(3.2)	560	(3.4)	38.2	(2.23)	2.4	(0.14)
Canada	503	(2.2)	529	(1.9)	545	(1.9)	570	(2.0)	25.7	(0.98)	1.9	(0.06)
Czech Republic	445	(3.1)	487	(2.8)	499	(3.5)	543	(2.9)	43.2	(1.68)	2.3	(0.13)
Denmark	465	(3.3)	490	(3.3)	511	(3.2)	543	(3.6)	29.1	(1.89)	1.8	(0.11)
Finland	524	(4.5)	535	(3.3)	555	(3.1)	576	(3.3)	20.8	(1.76)	1.5	(0.08)
France	469	(4.3)	496	(3.2)	520	(3.1)	552	(3.6)	30.8	(1.91)	2.2	(0.13)
Germany	427	(5.4)	471	(4.0)	513	(3.4)	541	(3.5)	45.3	(2.10)	2.6	(0.19)
Greece	440	(5.6)	460	(7.2)	486	(5.5)	519	(5.5)	28.1	(2.51)	1.8	(0.16)
Hungary	435	(4.9)	461	(4.5)	504	(3.8)	531	(5.9)	39.2	(2.38)	2.2	(0.16)
Iceland	487	(3.1)	496	(3.2)	513	(3.2)	540	(2.6)	19.3	(1.45)	1.5	(0.09)
Ireland	491	(4.3)	520	(4.3)	535	(3.7)	570	(3.7)	30.3	(1.79)	1.9	(0.10)
Italy	457	(4.3)	481	(3.3)	494	(3.6)	525	(3.9)	26.4	(1.84)	1.8	(0.13)
Japan[2]	m	m	m	m	m	m	m	m	m	m	m	m
Korea	509	(4.5)	524	(2.9)	531	(2.8)	542	(3.4)	14.6	(2.12)	1.5	(0.11)
Luxembourg	394	(4.1)	428	(3.4)	473	(3.3)	497	(2.8)	39.2	(2.02)	2.5	(0.15)
Mexico	385	(4.1)	408	(3.7)	435	(4.0)	471	(5.9)	31.8	(2.28)	1.9	(0.18)
New Zealand	489	(4.3)	523	(3.8)	549	(3.4)	574	(4.5)	31.9	(2.14)	2.0	(0.12)
Norway	477	(4.1)	494	(3.8)	514	(3.8)	547	(4.2)	29.7	(2.02)	1.6	(0.09)
Poland	445	(5.6)	472	(4.8)	493	(5.3)	534	(6.4)	35.4	(2.72)	2.0	(0.16)
Portugal	431	(4.9)	452	(4.9)	485	(4.3)	527	(5.0)	38.4	(2.14)	2.0	(0.13)
Spain	461	(3.5)	482	(3.6)	507	(2.7)	529	(3.0)	26.5	(1.61)	1.9	(0.11)
Sweden	485	(2.9)	509	(3.2)	522	(3.1)	558	(3.3)	27.1	(1.50)	1.8	(0.10)
Switzerland	434	(4.3)	492	(4.6)	513	(4.3)	549	(5.3)	40.2	(2.17)	2.7	(0.17)
United Kingdom	481	(3.1)	513	(3.1)	543	(3.5)	579	(3.6)	38.4	(1.60)	2.1	(0.11)
United States	466	(7.5)	507	(5.9)	528	(6.1)	556	(5.9)	33.5	(2.71)	2.1	(0.20)
OECD total	*462*	*(2.3)*	*492*	*(1.7)*	*515*	*(1.9)*	*543*	*(2.1)*	*34.0*	*(0.90)*	*2.0*	*(0.06)*
OECD average	*463*	*(0.9)*	*491*	*(0.8)*	*515*	*(0.7)*	*545*	*(0.9)*	*33.6*	*(0.44)*	*2.0*	*(0.02)*
NON-OECD COUNTRIES												
Brazil	368	(3.9)	387	(3.8)	413	(4.0)	435	(4.5)	26.1	(1.94)	1.9	(0.13)
Latvia	428	(6.4)	449	(5.0)	479	(6.7)	492	(6.6)	21.3	(2.22)	1.8	(0.12)
Liechtenstein	437	(11.0)	491	(11.9)	495	(9.1)	523	(9.3)	32.6	(5.15)	2.1	(0.40)
Russian Federation	429	(5.5)	450	(3.8)	472	(4.7)	502	(3.9)	26.5	(1.86)	1.8	(0.09)
Netherlands[3]	495	(5.6)	525	(5.2)	555	(3.6)	566	(4.4)	29.9	(2.45)	2.2	(0.20)

1. For the definition of the index see Annex A1.
2. Japan was excluded from this comparison because of a high proportion of missing data.
3. Response rate is too low to ensure comparability (see Annex A3).
4. For explained variation see Annex A2. Unit changes marked in bold are statistically significant. Where bottom and top quarters are marked in bold this indicates that their difference is statistically significant. 16.3 units on the index corresponds to one international standard deviation.
5. Ratios statistically significantly greater than 1 are marked in bold.

Table 6.1b
International socio-economic index of occupational status (ISEI) and performance on the mathematical literacy scale, by national quarters of the index
Results based on students' self-reports

	International socio-economic index of occupational status[1]									
	All students		Bottom quarter		Second quarter		Third quarter		Top quarter	
	Mean index	S.E.	Mean index	S.E.	Mean index	S.E.	Mean index	S.E.	Mean index	S.E.
OECD COUNTRIES										
Australia	52.32	(0.64)	30.65	(0.31)	46.19	(0.15)	58.66	(0.22)	73.83	(0.33)
Austria	49.83	(0.35)	33.17	(0.24)	44.86	(0.10)	52.26	(0.08)	69.11	(0.38)
Belgium	49.07	(0.44)	28.26	(0.18)	42.50	(0.16)	53.59	(0.12)	71.95	(0.25)
Canada	52.94	(0.25)	31.44	(0.12)	48.21	(0.09)	59.07	(0.10)	73.03	(0.16)
Czech Republic	48.24	(0.31)	31.29	(0.22)	44.45	(0.17)	51.52	(0.04)	65.74	(0.38)
Denmark	49.80	(0.48)	29.24	(0.21)	44.01	(0.17)	54.96	(0.18)	70.99	(0.36)
Finland	49.99	(0.47)	29.48	(0.22)	43.14	(0.17)	55.40	(0.18)	71.97	(0.26)
France	48.39	(0.50)	27.72	(0.20)	41.37	(0.24)	53.18	(0.07)	71.32	(0.31)
Germany	49.11	(0.34)	29.99	(0.20)	42.67	(0.15)	52.80	(0.08)	70.99	(0.27)
Greece	48.29	(0.63)	25.58	(0.30)	40.94	(0.20)	53.78	(0.15)	72.91	(0.39)
Hungary	49.80	(0.49)	30.50	(0.25)	42.97	(0.13)	53.99	(0.17)	71.78	(0.36)
Iceland	52.44	(0.38)	31.43	(0.35)	47.06	(0.18)	57.92	(0.27)	73.39	(0.35)
Ireland	48.00	(0.51)	28.53	(0.20)	42.48	(0.20)	52.74	(0.09)	68.29	(0.34)
Italy	46.94	(0.39)	28.22	(0.17)	40.41	(0.19)	50.34	(0.07)	68.81	(0.44)
Japan[2]	m	m	m	m	m	m	m	m	m	m
Korea	42.98	(0.51)	26.65	(0.15)	36.21	(0.12)	46.14	(0.19)	62.96	(0.45)
Luxembourg	44.37	(0.35)	24.99	(0.19)	36.92	(0.20)	50.11	(0.17)	65.50	(0.46)
Mexico	42.72	(0.71)	24.71	(0.17)	32.74	(0.15)	47.13	(0.21)	66.32	(0.54)
New Zealand	52.40	(0.45)	30.62	(0.36)	46.90	(0.15)	58.02	(0.28)	74.12	(0.28)
Norway	53.71	(0.42)	35.65	(0.26)	47.01	(0.16)	58.51	(0.27)	73.71	(0.31)
Poland	45.88	(0.46)	27.15	(0.20)	40.07	(0.17)	49.88	(0.13)	66.52	(0.54)
Portugal	44.20	(0.68)	27.00	(0.18)	34.81	(0.16)	48.65	(0.13)	66.38	(0.57)
Spain	44.87	(0.66)	26.78	(0.17)	35.96	(0.15)	49.48	(0.15)	67.32	(0.63)
Sweden	50.30	(0.48)	29.93	(0.18)	43.76	(0.16)	55.64	(0.20)	71.89	(0.28)
Switzerland	48.96	(0.63)	29.04	(0.23)	41.92	(0.10)	52.85	(0.10)	72.05	(0.51)
United Kingdom	51.22	(0.35)	30.57	(0.21)	45.66	(0.18)	56.89	(0.22)	71.75	(0.25)
United States	52.33	(0.81)	30.47	(0.32)	47.26	(0.26)	59.22	(0.27)	72.47	(0.39)
OECD total	*48.97*	*(0.24)*	*29.15*	*(0.10)*	*42.56*	*(0.13)*	*53.94*	*(0.15)*	*70.30*	*(0.15)*
OECD average	*48.86*	*(0.10)*	*29.28*	*(0.06)*	*42.38*	*(0.05)*	*53.56*	*(0.05)*	*70.26*	*(0.07)*
NON-OECD COUNTRIES										
Brazil	44.00	(0.70)	24.64	(0.24)	34.33	(0.25)	49.72	(0.30)	67.37	(0.53)
Latvia	49.89	(0.61)	27.76	(0.19)	39.93	(0.20)	57.67	(0.38)	74.26	(0.35)
Liechtenstein	46.69	(1.30)	28.41	(0.70)	40.21	(0.54)	51.29	(0.52)	67.39	(1.33)
Russian Federation	49.80	(0.54)	30.02	(0.29)	40.71	(0.12)	54.25	(0.22)	74.26	(0.22)
Netherlands[3]	50.91	(0.54)	29.45	(0.27)	45.46	(0.26)	57.14	(0.35)	71.68	(0.31)

	Performance on the mathematical literacy scale, by national quarters of the international socio-economic index of occupational status[4]								Change in the mathematical literacy score per 16.3 units of the international socio-economic index of occupational status[4]		Increased likelihood of students in the bottom quarter of the ISEI distribution scoring in the bottom quarter of the national math. literacy performance distribution[5]	
	Bottom quarter		Second quarter		Third quarter		Top quarter					
	Mean score	S.E.	Mean score	S.E.	Mean score	S.E.	Mean score	S.E.	Change	S.E.	Ratio	S.E.
OECD COUNTRIES												
Australia	495	(4.3)	527	(4.7)	545	(4.6)	578	(6.1)	29.2	(2.25)	2.1	(0.22)
Austria	479	(5.0)	509	(4.1)	528	(4.8)	549	(4.3)	31.1	(2.66)	1.8	(0.15)
Belgium	473	(6.7)	507	(4.8)	547	(4.0)	574	(4.4)	38.1	(2.71)	2.3	(0.17)
Canada	509	(2.1)	527	(2.2)	541	(2.3)	563	(2.3)	21.2	(1.03)	1.8	(0.06)
Czech Republic	454	(4.3)	491	(3.6)	507	(4.0)	545	(4.3)	41.8	(2.36)	2.1	(0.15)
Denmark	489	(3.8)	505	(3.9)	531	(4.2)	553	(4.5)	24.8	(2.04)	2.0	(0.17)
Finland	513	(3.6)	528	(3.3)	543	(3.1)	565	(3.7)	19.3	(1.61)	1.6	(0.10)
France	486	(4.8)	512	(3.9)	530	(3.6)	560	(3.8)	26.9	(2.18)	2.0	(0.16)
Germany	438	(5.3)	481	(5.5)	513	(4.0)	541	(4.3)	39.9	(2.46)	2.6	(0.22)
Greece	411	(6.5)	430	(7.9)	456	(6.6)	499	(7.7)	30.5	(3.24)	1.7	(0.19)
Hungary	439	(4.7)	468	(5.2)	513	(4.5)	543	(6.9)	41.6	(2.95)	2.2	(0.16)
Iceland	496	(4.7)	511	(4.3)	518	(4.3)	540	(3.8)	16.5	(2.10)	1.5	(0.12)
Ireland	472	(4.1)	498	(4.4)	513	(4.1)	536	(4.4)	25.9	(2.22)	1.8	(0.12)
Italy	433	(5.1)	449	(4.4)	467	(4.5)	486	(5.0)	21.3	(2.49)	1.6	(0.13)
Japan[2]	m	m	m	m	m	m	m	m	m	m	m	m
Korea	523	(4.2)	549	(3.6)	553	(4.1)	573	(4.2)	21.9	(2.30)	1.8	(0.14)
Luxembourg	408	(5.2)	434	(4.4)	470	(4.1)	494	(3.7)	33.2	(2.04)	2.1	(0.17)
Mexico	354	(4.8)	375	(4.7)	398	(5.0)	433	(5.9)	30.0	(2.58)	1.8	(0.19)
New Zealand	500	(5.9)	529	(4.5)	555	(4.2)	584	(4.7)	31.0	(2.56)	1.9	(0.13)
Norway	476	(5.0)	485	(4.5)	506	(4.4)	537	(4.4)	25.9	(2.41)	1.5	(0.13)
Poland	438	(7.0)	459	(6.5)	488	(6.9)	525	(6.4)	35.3	(2.97)	1.8	(0.17)
Portugal	420	(5.3)	441	(4.9)	464	(4.8)	507	(4.9)	33.9	(2.40)	1.9	(0.17)
Spain	443	(4.8)	465	(4.3)	493	(3.5)	513	(4.8)	27.6	(2.35)	1.9	(0.13)
Sweden	474	(4.2)	499	(4.5)	518	(3.5)	555	(3.9)	30.6	(2.00)	2.0	(0.15)
Switzerland	478	(4.7)	531	(5.3)	541	(5.9)	578	(5.3)	34.0	(2.00)	2.3	(0.18)
United Kingdom	488	(3.3)	524	(3.5)	547	(4.1)	578	(4.0)	34.5	(1.94)	2.3	(0.14)
United States	452	(7.6)	495	(8.0)	513	(6.8)	551	(6.9)	35.9	(3.19)	2.3	(0.21)
OECD total	*458*	*(2.7)*	*489*	*(2.3)*	*509*	*(2.1)*	*539*	*(2.5)*	*34.2*	*(1.17)*	*2.0*	*(0.06)*
OECD average	*465*	*(1.2)*	*491*	*(0.9)*	*513*	*(1.0)*	*542*	*(1.2)*	*32.6*	*(0.55)*	*1.7*	*(0.18)*
NON-OECD COUNTRIES												
Brazil	299	(5.1)	315	(4.7)	353	(6.0)	385	(7.6)	33.1	(3.19)	2.0	(0.17)
Latvia	438	(6.9)	459	(5.2)	486	(8.1)	481	(6.5)	14.2	(2.38)	1.5	(0.14)
Liechtenstein	486	(14.2)	514	(17.0)	532	(13.5)	546	(15.0)	23.3	(8.17)	c	c
Russian Federation	451	(7.4)	466	(6.4)	488	(6.6)	515	(5.0)	23.7	(2.33)	1.7	(0.14)
Netherlands[3]	531	(5.7)	558	(6.4)	582	(4.6)	597	(4.4)	27.2	(2.62)	1.8	(0.23)

1. For the definition of the index see Annex A1.
2. Japan was excluded from this comparison because of a high proportion of missing data.
3. Response rate is too low to ensure comparability (see Annex A3).
4. For explained variation see Annex A2. Unit changes marked in bold are statistically significant. Where bottom and top quarters are marked in bold this indicates that their difference is statistically significant. 16.3 units on the index corresponds to one international standard deviation.
5. Ratios statistically significantly greater than 1 are marked in bold.

Table 6.1c

International socio-economic index of occupational status (ISEI) and performance on the scientific literacy scale, by national quarters of the index

Results based on students' self-reports

	International socio-economic index of occupational status[1]									
	All students		Bottom quarter		Second quarter		Third quarter		Top quarter	
	Mean index	S.E.	Mean index	S.E.	Mean index	S.E.	Mean index	S.E.	Mean index	S.E.
OECD COUNTRIES										
Australia	51.97	(0.56)	31.07	(0.20)	46.33	(0.13)	58.38	(0.17)	73.23	(0.27)
Austria	49.52	(0.37)	32.94	(0.22)	44.69	(0.08)	52.24	(0.06)	69.06	(0.28)
Belgium	48.94	(0.41)	28.38	(0.13)	42.08	(0.13)	53.52	(0.08)	71.83	(0.20)
Canada	52.74	(0.25)	31.32	(0.08)	48.14	(0.07)	58.94	(0.08)	72.94	(0.13)
Czech Republic	48.46	(0.28)	31.19	(0.20)	44.40	(0.12)	51.53	(0.02)	66.14	(0.28)
Denmark	49.56	(0.49)	29.01	(0.19)	44.03	(0.13)	54.85	(0.15)	71.08	(0.28)
Finland	50.05	(0.43)	29.65	(0.18)	43.40	(0.12)	55.14	(0.13)	71.84	(0.20)
France	48.50	(0.46)	27.69	(0.17)	41.09	(0.16)	53.07	(0.06)	71.21	(0.28)
Germany	48.86	(0.36)	30.04	(0.20)	42.64	(0.13)	52.52	(0.06)	70.21	(0.23)
Greece	46.72	(0.70)	25.55	(0.26)	40.22	(0.21)	52.99	(0.10)	72.33	(0.37)
Hungary	49.39	(0.56)	30.39	(0.19)	42.62	(0.10)	53.67	(0.12)	71.45	(0.24)
Iceland	52.88	(0.41)	31.36	(0.24)	47.26	(0.12)	58.57	(0.21)	73.76	(0.25)
Ireland	48.47	(0.50)	28.45	(0.18)	42.72	(0.15)	53.22	(0.08)	69.36	(0.25)
Italy	47.24	(0.40)	28.47	(0.15)	40.64	(0.13)	50.30	(0.06)	68.91	(0.37)
Japan[2]	m	m	m	m	m	m	m	m	m	m
Korea	43.00	(0.45)	26.50	(0.14)	35.89	(0.10)	45.97	(0.14)	62.87	(0.45)
Luxembourg	45.07	(0.39)	25.09	(0.14)	37.46	(0.14)	50.55	(0.12)	66.06	(0.37)
Mexico	42.40	(0.75)	24.36	(0.13)	32.33	(0.11)	46.79	(0.16)	66.46	(0.48)
New Zealand	52.10	(0.46)	30.53	(0.27)	47.05	(0.12)	57.66	(0.20)	73.56	(0.20)
Norway	53.90	(0.46)	35.59	(0.25)	47.14	(0.13)	58.97	(0.18)	73.94	(0.22)
Poland	46.18	(0.59)	27.32	(0.17)	39.97	(0.12)	49.82	(0.09)	67.02	(0.43)
Portugal	43.38	(0.60)	26.80	(0.16)	34.47	(0.10)	48.40	(0.11)	65.74	(0.55)
Spain	45.10	(0.67)	26.82	(0.11)	36.23	(0.14)	49.63	(0.12)	67.30	(0.49)
Sweden	50.38	(0.46)	30.40	(0.16)	44.08	(0.12)	55.71	(0.13)	72.10	(0.20)
Switzerland	49.15	(0.54)	29.26	(0.19)	42.49	(0.09)	53.21	(0.06)	71.94	(0.30)
United Kingdom	51.13	(0.37)	30.66	(0.17)	45.68	(0.14)	56.92	(0.19)	71.82	(0.19)
United States	52.56	(0.91)	30.29	(0.22)	47.36	(0.19)	59.50	(0.22)	72.48	(0.30)
OECD total	*49.02*	*(0.27)*	*29.09*	*(0.10)*	*42.55*	*(0.12)*	*54.15*	*(0.13)*	*70.36*	*(0.16)*
OECD average	*48.81*	*(0.10)*	*29.24*	*(0.06)*	*42.32*	*(0.06)*	*53.51*	*(0.05)*	*70.21*	*(0.08)*
NON-OECD COUNTRIES										
Brazil	44.04	(0.66)	24.56	(0.23)	34.50	(0.19)	49.60	(0.18)	67.12	(0.37)
Latvia	50.01	(0.70)	27.68	(0.15)	40.41	(0.19)	58.46	(0.31)	74.07	(0.27)
Liechtenstein	48.77	(1.18)	28.01	(0.63)	41.82	(0.38)	52.11	(0.24)	68.22	(0.92)
Russian Federation	49.22	(0.45)	30.03	(0.18)	40.27	(0.08)	53.39	(0.17)	73.85	(0.18)
Netherlands[3]	50.26	(0.56)	29.52	(0.21)	45.34	(0.16)	57.29	(0.28)	71.27	(0.22)

	Performance on the scientific literacy scale, by national quarters of the international socio-economic index of occupational status[4]								Change in the combined scientific literacy score per 16.3 units of the international socio-economic index of occupational status[4]		Increased likelihood of students in the bottom quarter of the ISEI distribution scoring in the bottom quarter of the national scientific literacy performance distribution[5]	
	Bottom quarter		Second quarter		Third quarter		Top quarter					
	Mean score	S.E.	Mean score	S.E.	Mean score	S.E.	Mean score	S.E.	Change	S.E.	Ratio	S.E.
OECD COUNTRIES												
Australia	498	(4.9)	522	(4.7)	531	(4.6)	571	(6.2)	26.2	(2.41)	2.0	(0.16)
Austria	479	(4.7)	511	(3.5)	534	(3.7)	556	(4.1)	34.1	(2.59)	2.3	(0.14)
Belgium	444	(9.0)	486	(4.6)	524	(3.6)	552	(4.1)	40.2	(2.87)	2.4	(0.18)
Canada	501	(2.7)	524	(2.2)	538	(2.1)	563	(2.4)	23.3	(1.27)	1.8	(0.07)
Czech Republic	468	(4.1)	504	(3.8)	519	(4.0)	561	(3.9)	41.7	(2.41)	2.2	(0.14)
Denmark	445	(4.5)	473	(5.1)	493	(4.1)	532	(5.3)	32.1	(2.56)	1.8	(0.14)
Finland	517	(4.2)	526	(3.8)	546	(4.4)	565	(4.3)	18.4	(2.17)	1.3	(0.11)
France	460	(4.5)	488	(5.0)	518	(4.5)	556	(4.5)	33.9	(2.20)	2.0	(0.15)
Germany	437	(5.4)	473	(5.9)	512	(3.8)	539	(3.9)	40.7	(2.51)	2.3	(0.19)
Greece	429	(6.0)	443	(7.7)	477	(5.6)	498	(7.0)	25.9	(3.02)	1.7	(0.18)
Hungary	444	(6.6)	478	(5.2)	519	(4.5)	554	(5.9)	43.3	(3.24)	2.2	(0.16)
Iceland	487	(4.4)	484	(4.3)	497	(3.9)	519	(4.2)	13.5	(2.27)	1.2	(0.10)
Ireland	482	(4.8)	504	(4.9)	523	(4.5)	553	(4.5)	28.9	(2.15)	1.7	(0.13)
Italy	451	(5.0)	471	(4.5)	480	(5.1)	514	(4.2)	24.4	(2.18)	1.5	(0.13)
Japan[2]	m	m	m	m	m	m	m	m	m	m	m	m
Korea	534	(5.1)	549	(4.5)	559	(3.8)	575	(4.7)	18.8	(2.74)	1.5	(0.14)
Luxembourg	403	(5.3)	434	(4.8)	466	(4.2)	490	(5.4)	33.3	(3.00)	2.2	(0.19)
Mexico	392	(4.1)	410	(3.8)	430	(4.5)	461	(6.4)	25.8	(2.49)	1.7	(0.14)
New Zealand	490	(5.5)	518	(3.6)	546	(3.9)	575	(4.1)	31.7	(2.45)	2.2	(0.18)
Norway	473	(4.5)	498	(4.7)	507	(4.3)	536	(4.4)	25.7	(2.46)	1.6	(0.11)
Poland	452	(6.0)	475	(6.7)	493	(6.3)	535	(7.9)	32.8	(2.90)	1.7	(0.18)
Portugal	426	(4.5)	445	(5.2)	475	(3.9)	504	(5.3)	32.4	(2.30)	1.9	(0.17)
Spain	455	(4.4)	477	(4.9)	506	(3.8)	533	(4.7)	30.3	(2.25)	1.9	(0.14)
Sweden	485	(3.7)	498	(4.3)	519	(4.1)	552	(3.8)	25.2	(1.83)	1.5	(0.12)
Switzerland	442	(4.8)	485	(5.8)	510	(5.0)	554	(5.9)	40.2	(2.45)	2.5	(0.16)
United Kingdom	492	(4.1)	522	(3.2)	548	(4.5)	588	(3.9)	37.5	(2.28)	2.2	(0.14)
United States	464	(8.4)	497	(6.5)	521	(6.9)	555	(7.8)	33.4	(3.33)	2.2	(0.19)
OECD total	*465*	*(2.6)*	*492*	*(1.9)*	*514*	*(2.2)*	*545*	*(2.5)*	*32.6*	*(1.06)*	*1.9*	*(0.03)*
OECD average	*465*	*(0.9)*	*490*	*(0.9)*	*512*	*(0.9)*	*543*	*(1.1)*	*31.9*	*(0.49)*	*1.9*	*(0.03)*
NON-OECD COUNTRIES												
Brazil	346	(5.6)	363	(5.1)	391	(5.1)	414	(6.7)	25.7	(3.21)	1.8	(0.14)
Latvia	433	(7.1)	451	(5.9)	483	(7.7)	490	(8.2)	19.3	(2.90)	1.6	(0.17)
Liechtenstein	437	(14.7)	472	(12.8)	495	(12.3)	523	(15.4)	35.7	(7.69)	c	c
Russian Federation	431	(5.6)	448	(5.6)	469	(5.4)	499	(5.4)	24.0	(2.20)	1.6	(0.12)
Netherlands[3]	496	(8.3)	519	(5.9)	554	(5.2)	564	(5.8)	29.2	(3.57)	2.1	(0.20)

1. For the definition of the index see Annex A1.
2. Japan was excluded from this comparison because of a high proportion of missing data.
3. Response rate is too low to ensure comparability (see Annex A3).
4. For explained variation see Annex A2. Unit changes marked in bold are statistically significant. Where bottom and top quarters are marked in bold this indicates that their difference is statistically significant. 16.3 units on the index corresponds to one international standard deviation.
5. Ratios statistically significantly greater than 1 are marked in bold.

Table 6.2
Index of family wealth and performance on the combined reading literacy scale, by national quarters of the index
Results based on students' self-reports

| | | Index of family wealth[1] | | | | | | | | |
| | | All students | | Bottom quarter | | Second quarter | | Third quarter | | Top quarter | |
		Mean index	S.E.	Mean index	S.E.	Mean index	S.E.	Mean index	S.E.	Mean index	S.E.
OECD COUNTRIES	Australia	0.42	(0.02)	−0.64	(0.02)	0.15	(0.01)	0.66	(0.01)	1.53	(0.02)
	Austria	0.25	(0.02)	−0.70	(0.02)	0.00	(0.00)	0.45	(0.01)	1.24	(0.02)
	Belgium	−0.09	(0.02)	−1.03	(0.01)	−0.35	(0.00)	0.11	(0.00)	0.90	(0.02)
	Canada	0.41	(0.01)	−0.67	(0.01)	0.15	(0.00)	0.66	(0.00)	1.51	(0.01)
	Czech Republic	−0.86	(0.02)	−1.92	(0.01)	−1.12	(0.01)	−0.61	(0.01)	0.20	(0.02)
	Denmark	0.49	(0.02)	−0.46	(0.02)	0.26	(0.01)	0.72	(0.00)	1.46	(0.01)
	Finland	0.22	(0.02)	−0.71	(0.02)	0.03	(0.00)	0.47	(0.00)	1.10	(0.01)
	France	−0.15	(0.02)	−1.08	(0.01)	−0.38	(0.01)	0.08	(0.00)	0.77	(0.01)
	Germany	0.20	(0.02)	−0.85	(0.02)	−0.07	(0.01)	0.43	(0.01)	1.30	(0.02)
	Greece	−0.45	(0.03)	−1.49	(0.02)	−0.73	(0.01)	−0.22	(0.01)	0.63	(0.04)
	Hungary	−0.87	(0.03)	−1.96	(0.02)	−1.16	(0.01)	−0.59	(0.01)	0.25	(0.01)
	Iceland	0.53	(0.01)	−0.45	(0.02)	0.30	(0.01)	0.78	(0.01)	1.52	(0.01)
	Ireland	0.05	(0.03)	−1.03	(0.01)	−0.21	(0.01)	0.31	(0.01)	1.11	(0.02)
	Italy	0.12	(0.02)	−0.85	(0.02)	−0.13	(0.01)	0.34	(0.01)	1.13	(0.02)
	Japan	−0.14	(0.02)	−0.99	(0.01)	−0.31	(0.00)	0.08	(0.01)	0.67	(0.01)
	Korea	−0.27	(0.02)	−1.14	(0.02)	−0.42	(0.01)	−0.02	(0.00)	0.49	(0.01)
	Luxembourg	0.32	(0.02)	−0.80	(0.02)	0.05	(0.01)	0.58	(0.01)	1.45	(0.02)
	Mexico	−1.44	(0.06)	−2.81	(0.02)	−1.90	(0.01)	−1.14	(0.01)	0.10	(0.06)
	New Zealand	0.22	(0.02)	−0.88	(0.02)	−0.06	(0.01)	0.50	(0.01)	1.34	(0.02)
	Norway	0.56	(0.02)	−0.37	(0.02)	0.34	(0.01)	0.77	(0.01)	1.50	(0.01)
	Poland	−1.00	(0.03)	−2.23	(0.02)	−1.30	(0.01)	−0.72	(0.01)	0.24	(0.03)
	Portugal	−0.13	(0.03)	−1.37	(0.02)	−0.45	(0.01)	0.19	(0.01)	1.12	(0.02)
	Spain	−0.14	(0.03)	−1.16	(0.01)	−0.43	(0.01)	0.09	(0.01)	0.93	(0.02)
	Sweden	0.65	(0.02)	−0.37	(0.02)	0.43	(0.00)	0.93	(0.01)	1.63	(0.02)
	Switzerland	0.05	(0.03)	−0.98	(0.01)	−0.23	(0.01)	0.28	(0.01)	1.14	(0.04)
	United Kingdom	0.42	(0.02)	−0.61	(0.02)	0.15	(0.01)	0.66	(0.00)	1.51	(0.02)
	United States	0.61	(0.06)	−0.60	(0.02)	0.35	(0.01)	0.91	(0.01)	1.80	(0.02)
	OECD total	*0.00*	*(0.02)*	*−1.08*	*(0.02)*	*−0.26*	*(0.01)*	*0.26*	*(0.02)*	*1.09*	*(0.02)*
	OECD average	*0.00*	*(0.00)*	*−1.04*	*(0.01)*	*−0.26*	*(0.01)*	*0.25*	*(0.01)*	*1.06*	*(0.01)*
NON-OECD COUNTRIES	Brazil	−1.39	(0.04)	−2.69	(0.01)	−1.79	(0.01)	−1.13	(0.01)	0.05	(0.03)
	Latvia	−1.46	(0.03)	−2.63	(0.03)	−1.71	(0.01)	−1.18	(0.01)	−0.31	(0.02)
	Liechtenstein	0.26	(0.05)	−0.73	(0.05)	0.02	(0.01)	0.52	(0.02)	1.27	(0.05)
	Russian Federation	−1.79	(0.03)	−2.87	(0.02)	−2.04	(0.01)	−1.54	(0.01)	−0.70	(0.02)
	Netherlands[2]	0.18	(0.03)	−0.69	(0.02)	−0.01	(0.01)	0.40	(0.01)	1.03	(0.02)

| | | Performance on the combined reading literacy scale, by national quarters of the index of family wealth[3] | | | | | | | | Change in the combined reading literacy score per unit of the index of family wealth[3] | | Increased likelihood of students in the bottom quarter of the wealth distribution scoring in the bottom quarter of the national reading literacy performance distribution[4] | |
| | | Bottom quarter | | Second quarter | | Third quarter | | Top quarter | | | | | |
		Mean score	S.E.	Mean score	S.E.	Mean score	S.E.	Mean score	S.E.	Change	S.E.	Ratio	S.E.
OECD COUNTRIES	Australia	510	(4.3)	523	(4.6)	538	(4.7)	544	(5.0)	16.6	(2.64)	1.4	(0.11)
	Austria	495	(3.9)	508	(3.4)	514	(3.7)	514	(3.8)	10.8	(2.37)	1.3	(0.07)
	Belgium	494	(5.9)	509	(4.6)	516	(3.1)	515	(3.7)	9.6	(2.98)	1.3	(0.08)
	Canada	514	(2.4)	538	(2.0)	543	(1.9)	546	(2.2)	13.8	(1.19)	1.4	(0.05)
	Czech Republic	475	(2.9)	491	(3.8)	499	(3.0)	502	(4.0)	11.6	(2.03)	1.3	(0.07)
	Denmark	485	(3.8)	492	(3.8)	511	(3.6)	506	(3.8)	12.1	(2.42)	1.3	(0.08)
	Finland	535	(5.6)	544	(2.9)	551	(3.2)	556	(3.8)	12.2	(4.20)	1.2	(0.08)
	France	478	(4.5)	501	(3.8)	514	(3.3)	528	(3.3)	26.2	(2.56)	1.6	(0.10)
	Germany	451	(5.3)	484	(3.5)	497	(4.0)	506	(4.1)	25.2	(3.96)	1.7	(0.14)
	Greece	459	(7.0)	469	(5.6)	474	(5.8)	495	(6.6)	15.1	(3.45)	1.3	(0.11)
	Hungary	456	(5.9)	469	(4.7)	494	(5.0)	502	(5.1)	22.2	(3.05)	1.6	(0.13)
	Iceland	515	(3.1)	508	(3.3)	508	(3.1)	501	(3.1)	−5.6	(2.33)	0.9	(0.06)
	Ireland	513	(4.1)	523	(4.2)	531	(4.2)	543	(4.8)	11.9	(2.47)	1.3	(0.08)
	Italy	476	(4.0)	487	(3.6)	488	(4.8)	500	(3.5)	9.9	(2.02)	1.2	(0.08)
	Japan	521	(6.7)	526	(5.5)	526	(5.1)	527	(5.6)	3.9	(3.14)	1.1	(0.07)
	Korea	509	(4.0)	525	(3.0)	531	(2.9)	534	(3.2)	15.3	(2.90)	1.6	(0.10)
	Luxembourg	405	(3.7)	447	(3.8)	455	(3.2)	464	(3.5)	25.0	(1.76)	1.9	(0.13)
	Mexico	392	(4.1)	408	(4.2)	424	(3.5)	464	(6.9)	24.4	(2.37)	1.6	(0.15)
	New Zealand	497	(4.6)	529	(4.3)	540	(4.1)	552	(4.2)	21.8	(2.39)	1.8	(0.09)
	Norway	496	(4.1)	515	(4.2)	511	(5.5)	504	(4.0)	4.2	(2.96)	1.2	(0.08)
	Poland	464	(4.7)	483	(5.8)	490	(5.8)	488	(6.3)	8.8	(2.62)	1.3	(0.09)
	Portugal	432	(4.9)	457	(5.1)	486	(4.9)	507	(5.2)	29.8	(2.39)	1.8	(0.12)
	Spain	472	(3.8)	491	(4.2)	499	(2.9)	512	(3.1)	17.2	(1.98)	1.5	(0.10)
	Sweden	508	(3.7)	518	(3.3)	520	(3.2)	522	(3.4)	8.2	(2.10)	1.3	(0.07)
	Switzerland	476	(5.5)	497	(4.2)	502	(4.6)	504	(6.7)	13.5	(2.52)	1.5	(0.10)
	United Kingdom	508	(3.8)	520	(3.7)	531	(3.4)	541	(3.7)	14.9	(1.93)	1.3	(0.08)
	United States	455	(8.4)	503	(6.3)	525	(6.6)	540	(6.9)	32.0	(3.06)	2.3	(0.14)
	OECD total	*472*	*(2.7)*	*497*	*(1.8)*	*509*	*(1.9)*	*520*	*(2.2)*	*25.1*	*(0.89)*	*1.6*	*(0.03)*
	OECD average	*481*	*(0.9)*	*499*	*(0.9)*	*508*	*(0.8)*	*515*	*(0.8)*	*19.8*	*(0.54)*	*1.4*	*(0.02)*
NON-OECD COUNTRIES	Brazil	370	(3.6)	385	(3.7)	396	(4.5)	437	(5.7)	25.2	(2.15)	1.6	(0.12)
	Latvia	449	(5.7)	455	(5.4)	468	(7.2)	465	(7.8)	7.5	(3.27)	1.2	(0.11)
	Liechtenstein	468	(11.9)	478	(11.0)	495	(11.6)	490	(11.1)	14.9	(7.17)	c	c
	Russian Federation	449	(6.1)	460	(4.4)	464	(4.9)	477	(3.7)	12.1	(2.64)	1.4	(0.08)
	Netherlands[2]	532	(5.6)	539	(4.6)	532	(5.1)	525	(4.6)	−3.9	(4.27)	1.0	(0.11)

1. For the definition of the index see Annex A1.
2. Response rate is too low to ensure comparability (see Annex A3).
3. For explained variation see Annex A2. Unit changes marked in bold are statistically significant. Where bottom and top quarters are marked in bold this indicates that their difference is statistically significant.
4. Ratios statistically significantly greater than 1 are marked in bold.

Table 6.3
Index of possessions in the family home related to "classical" culture and performance on the combined reading literacy scale, by national quarters of the index
Results based on students' self-reports

| | Index of cultural possessions in the family home[1] | | | | | | | | | |
| | All students | | Bottom quarter | | Second quarter | | Third quarter | | Top quarter | |
	Mean index	S.E.	Mean index	S.E.	Mean index	S.E.	Mean index	S.E.	Mean index	S.E.
OECD COUNTRIES										
Australia	−0.09	(0.03)	−1.38	(0.02)	−0.50	(0.01)	0.38	(0.02)	Max	
Austria	0.01	(0.02)	−1.24	(0.02)	−0.30	(0.01)	0.41	(0.02)	Max	
Belgium	−0.41	(0.02)	−1.65	(0.00)	−0.76	(0.01)	−0.15	(0.01)	0.93	(0.01)
Canada	−0.12	(0.01)	−1.39	(0.01)	−0.56	(0.00)	0.33	(0.01)	Max	
Czech Republic	0.18	(0.02)	−1.06	(0.02)	−0.08	(0.01)	0.72	(0.02)	Max	
Denmark	−0.11	(0.02)	−1.31	(0.02)	−0.55	(0.01)	0.28	(0.01)	Max	
Finland	0.12	(0.02)	−1.18	(0.02)	−0.25	(0.01)	0.75	(0.02)	Max	
France	−0.30	(0.02)	−1.65	(0.00)	−0.65	(0.01)	0.12	(0.00)	1.00	(0.01)
Germany	−0.02	(0.02)	−1.30	(0.02)	−0.33	(0.01)	0.39	(0.01)	Max	
Greece	0.20	(0.03)	−0.96	(0.02)	−0.02	(0.01)	0.63	(0.02)	Max	
Hungary	0.33	(0.02)	−0.84	(0.03)	0.12	(0.00)	0.90	(0.01)	Max	
Iceland	0.67	(0.01)	−0.44	(0.02)	0.83	(0.02)	1.15	(0.00)	Max	
Ireland	−0.08	(0.03)	−1.39	(0.02)	−0.43	(0.01)	0.36	(0.01)	Max	
Italy	0.34	(0.02)	−0.98	(0.02)	0.12	(0.00)	1.07	(0.01)	Max	
Japan	−0.27	(0.03)	−1.63	(0.00)	−0.62	(0.00)	0.09	(0.00)	1.09	(0.01)
Korea	0.24	(0.02)	−1.02	(0.02)	0.06	(0.01)	0.75	(0.02)	Max	
Luxembourg	−0.11	(0.02)	−1.50	(0.01)	−0.48	(0.01)	0.38	(0.01)	Max	
Mexico	−0.58	(0.03)	−1.65	(0.00)	−1.15	(0.01)	−0.29	(0.01)	0.77	(0.02)
New Zealand	−0.22	(0.02)	−1.51	(0.01)	−0.62	(0.00)	0.10	(0.01)	Max	
Norway	0.14	(0.02)	−1.21	(0.02)	−0.25	(0.01)	0.86	(0.02)	Max	
Poland	0.18	(0.02)	−1.03	(0.02)	0.00	(0.01)	0.60	(0.02)	Max	
Portugal	−0.10	(0.03)	−1.44	(0.01)	−0.38	(0.01)	0.25	(0.01)	Max	
Spain	0.17	(0.03)	−1.16	(0.02)	−0.04	(0.01)	0.73	(0.02)	Max	
Sweden	0.05	(0.02)	−1.18	(0.02)	−0.34	(0.01)	0.57	(0.02)	Max	
Switzerland	−0.08	(0.03)	−1.37	(0.01)	−0.42	(0.01)	0.31	(0.01)	Max	
United Kingdom	−0.07	(0.02)	−1.50	(0.01)	−0.43	(0.01)	0.48	(0.02)	Max	
United States	−0.12	(0.04)	−1.49	(0.02)	−0.51	(0.01)	0.35	(0.02)	Max	
OECD total	*−0.10*	*(0.01)*	*−1.40*	*(0.01)*	*−0.45*	*(0.01)*	*0.35*	*(0.01)*	*1.10*	*(0.00)*
OECD average	*0.00*	*(0.00)*	*−1.27*	*(0.00)*	*−0.31*	*(0.00)*	*0.47*	*(0.00)*	*1.12*	*(0.00)*
NON-OECD COUNTRIES										
Brazil	−0.41	(0.02)	−1.65	(0.00)	−0.68	(0.01)	−0.06	(0.01)	0.77	(0.02)
Latvia	0.55	(0.02)	−0.53	(0.03)	0.44	(0.02)	1.15	(0.00)	Max	
Liechtenstein	−0.03	(0.05)	−1.24	(0.05)	−0.28	(0.04)	0.27	(0.04)	Max	
Russian Federation	0.44	(0.03)	−0.44	(0.03)	0.12	(0.00)	0.95	(0.01)	Max	
Netherlands[2]	−0.45	(0.02)	−1.65	(0.00)	−0.68	(0.01)	−0.21	(0.02)	0.77	(0.03)

| | Performance on the combined reading literacy scale, by national quarters of the index of cultural possessions in the family home[3] | | | | | | | | Change in the combined reading literacy score per unit of the index of cultural possessions[3] | |
| | Bottom quarter | | Second quarter | | Third quarter | | Top quarter | | | |
	Mean score	S.E.	Mean score	S.E.	Mean score	S.E.	Mean score	S.E.	Change	S.E.
OECD COUNTRIES										
Australia	492	(3.8)	511	(4.9)	541	(4.2)	572	(4.5)	32.30	(2.09)
Austria	485	(4.0)	492	(3.4)	512	(3.8)	542	(3.7)	22.92	(2.08)
Belgium	466	(5.2)	504	(4.3)	517	(3.8)	549	(3.3)	31.61	(1.81)
Canada	508	(2.2)	524	(2.0)	543	(2.2)	567	(1.8)	22.84	(0.94)
Czech Republic	453	(3.8)	489	(3.6)	509	(3.3)	522	(3.5)	30.89	(2.68)
Denmark	466	(4.1)	490	(2.9)	506	(3.7)	534	(3.3)	25.98	(1.78)
Finland	516	(4.4)	543	(3.1)	563	(3.3)	565	(3.3)	21.57	(1.62)
France	456	(4.2)	498	(3.5)	530	(3.0)	538	(3.2)	31.94	(1.76)
Germany	448	(6.8)	467	(6.1)	491	(4.6)	532	(4.1)	33.94	(3.32)
Greece	435	(6.7)	470	(4.6)	489	(5.6)	505	(5.5)	32.08	(2.99)
Hungary	426	(4.7)	477	(5.7)	506	(4.5)	513	(4.2)	42.08	(2.58)
Iceland	484	(3.7)	511	(3.3)	520	(3.4)	518	(3.2)	22.23	(2.42)
Ireland	502	(4.4)	517	(4.6)	536	(3.9)	556	(4.0)	22.02	(2.17)
Italy	456	(4.0)	486	(4.0)	506	(3.7)	503	(3.2)	23.26	(2.02)
Japan	493	(6.8)	525	(4.9)	538	(5.0)	544	(5.2)	18.86	(2.00)
Korea	502	(3.5)	524	(2.9)	534	(3.1)	541	(2.9)	16.73	(1.68)
Luxembourg	395	(3.8)	429	(3.6)	456	(3.5)	495	(2.9)	36.71	(1.75)
Mexico	400	(3.3)	405	(3.2)	422	(4.0)	464	(5.6)	27.28	(2.31)
New Zealand	505	(3.8)	519	(4.1)	525	(3.9)	572	(4.9)	24.26	(2.27)
Norway	464	(4.2)	501	(4.0)	524	(4.4)	539	(3.9)	29.70	(2.01)
Poland	437	(5.5)	490	(5.5)	494	(5.4)	506	(6.7)	30.28	(3.02)
Portugal	426	(5.2)	454	(5.0)	495	(4.4)	508	(5.0)	33.68	(2.02)
Spain	455	(3.7)	493	(3.3)	510	(2.6)	516	(3.2)	25.60	(1.58)
Sweden	484	(3.0)	509	(2.9)	530	(3.7)	545	(3.2)	26.21	(1.47)
Switzerland	465	(4.2)	485	(4.2)	496	(5.7)	536	(5.7)	26.65	(2.22)
United Kingdom	489	(2.9)	505	(3.1)	540	(4.3)	566	(4.8)	29.07	(1.95)
United States	465	(6.3)	488	(10.2)	519	(7.7)	552	(6.8)	32.79	(2.59)
OECD total	*464*	*(1.9)*	*490*	*(2.8)*	*512*	*(2.3)*	*535*	*(2.0)*	*28.94*	*(0.87)*
OECD average	*466*	*(0.9)*	*493*	*(0.9)*	*513*	*(0.8)*	*534*	*(0.8)*	*27.02*	*(0.44)*
NON-OECD COUNTRIES										
Brazil	380	(3.7)	386	(4.1)	405	(4.1)	423	(5.1)	19.94	(2.33)
Latvia	421	(6.6)	462	(6.0)	483	(7.0)	474	(5.9)	34.31	(3.40)
Liechtenstein	450	(10.8)	472	(10.2)	493	(9.8)	520	(10.7)	27.34	(6.10)
Russian Federation	440	(4.8)	466	(5.4)	473	(4.7)	476	(3.6)	24.06	(2.35)
Netherlands[2]	509	(5.2)	526	(4.6)	535	(4.3)	560	(4.2)	20.61	(1.91)

1. For the definition of the index see Annex A1. "Max" is used for countries with more than 25 per cent of students at the highest value of this index, which is 1.15.
2. Response rate is too low to ensure comparability (see Annex A3).
3. For explained variation see Annex A2. Unit changes marked in bold are statistically significant. Where bottom and top quarters are marked in bold this indicates that their difference is statistically significant.

Table 6.4
Index of activities related to "classical" culture and performance on the combined reading literacy scale, by national quarters of the index
Results based on students' self-reports

| | Index of cultural activities[1] | | | | | | | | | |
| | All students | | Bottom quarter | | Second quarter | | Third quarter | | Top quarter | |
	Mean index	S.E.	Mean index	S.E.	Mean index	S.E.	Mean index	S.E.	Mean index	S.E.
OECD COUNTRIES										
Australia	−0.34	(0.03)	Min		−0.99	(0.02)	−0.05	(0.01)	0.94	(0.02)
Austria	0.16	(0.03)	−1.26	(0.00)	−0.15	(0.00)	0.65	(0.01)	1.41	(0.02)
Belgium	−0.10	(0.03)	Min		−0.50	(0.02)	0.26	(0.01)	1.14	(0.02)
Canada	0.12	(0.01)	−1.21	(0.01)	−0.15	(0.00)	0.57	(0.00)	1.27	(0.01)
Czech Republic	0.60	(0.02)	−0.59	(0.02)	0.46	(0.01)	0.92	(0.01)	1.62	(0.01)
Denmark	0.31	(0.02)	−0.86	(0.02)	0.09	(0.01)	0.64	(0.01)	1.35	(0.02)
Finland	−0.16	(0.03)	Min		−0.58	(0.02)	0.23	(0.01)	0.99	(0.02)
France	−0.36	(0.02)	Min		−1.03	(0.02)	−0.06	(0.01)	0.94	(0.02)
Germany	0.01	(0.02)	Min		−0.25	(0.01)	0.37	(0.01)	1.21	(0.02)
Greece	0.34	(0.03)	−0.82	(0.02)	0.18	(0.01)	0.67	(0.01)	1.34	(0.02)
Hungary	0.71	(0.03)	−0.59	(0.02)	0.56	(0.00)	1.10	(0.01)	1.78	(0.01)
Iceland	0.21	(0.02)	−0.99	(0.02)	−0.11	(0.01)	0.62	(0.01)	1.34	(0.01)
Ireland	−0.03	(0.02)	Min		−0.18	(0.00)	0.28	(0.01)	1.07	(0.02)
Italy	−0.02	(0.03)	Min		−0.34	(0.01)	0.33	(0.01)	1.21	(0.01)
Japan	−0.72	(0.02)	Min		−1.28	(0.00)	−0.71	(0.02)	0.39	(0.02)
Korea	−0.70	(0.02)	Min		−1.28	(0.00)	−0.79	(0.02)	0.54	(0.02)
Luxembourg	−0.16	(0.02)	Min		−0.74	(0.02)	0.18	(0.01)	1.21	(0.02)
Mexico	−0.08	(0.04)	Min		−0.54	(0.02)	0.28	(0.01)	1.21	(0.02)
New Zealand	−0.08	(0.02)	Min		−0.40	(0.02)	0.23	(0.01)	1.14	(0.02)
Norway	−0.21	(0.03)	Min		−0.69	(0.02)	0.10	(0.01)	1.01	(0.02)
Poland	0.27	(0.03)	−1.12	(0.01)	0.01	(0.01)	0.69	(0.01)	1.52	(0.02)
Portugal	0.09	(0.03)	−1.21	(0.01)	−0.16	(0.00)	0.48	(0.01)	1.25	(0.02)
Spain	0.03	(0.03)	Min		−0.27	(0.01)	0.40	(0.01)	1.25	(0.02)
Sweden	−0.13	(0.03)	Min		−0.56	(0.02)	0.23	(0.01)	1.11	(0.02)
Switzerland	0.07	(0.03)	Min		−0.22	(0.01)	0.48	(0.01)	1.31	(0.02)
United Kingdom	−0.04	(0.03)	Min		−0.43	(0.01)	0.33	(0.01)	1.22	(0.02)
United States	0.20	(0.04)	−1.11	(0.02)	−0.08	(0.01)	0.64	(0.01)	1.36	(0.02)
OECD total	*−0.08*	*(0.01)*	*−1.20*	*(0.00)*	*−0.46*	*(0.01)*	*0.24*	*(0.01)*	*1.12*	*(0.01)*
OECD average	*0.00*	*(0.00)*	*−1.17*	*(0.00)*	*−0.36*	*(0.00)*	*0.34*	*(0.00)*	*1.19*	*(0.00)*
NON-OECD COUNTRIES										
Brazil	−0.25	(0.03)	Min		−0.78	(0.02)	0.09	(0.02)	0.98	(0.02)
Latvia	0.55	(0.03)	−0.79	(0.02)	0.40	(0.01)	0.96	(0.01)	1.64	(0.01)
Liechtenstein	0.05	(0.05)	−1.12	(0.04)	−0.16	(0.00)	0.30	(0.04)	1.19	(0.06)
Russian Federation	0.11	(0.05)	Min		−0.31	(0.01)	0.55	(0.01)	1.47	(0.02)
Netherlands[2]	−0.26	(0.03)	Min		−0.84	(0.02)	0.07	(0.01)	1.00	(0.02)

| | Performance on the combined reading literacy scale, by national quarters of the index of cultural activities[3] | | | | | | | | Change in the combined reading literacy score per unit of the index of cultural activities[3] | |
| | Bottom quarter | | Second quarter | | Third quarter | | Top quarter | | | |
	Mean score	S.E.	Mean score	S.E.	Mean score	S.E.	Mean score	S.E.	Change	S.E.
OECD COUNTRIES										
Australia	507	(4.3)	507	(4.3)	534	(4.4)	570	(5.3)	28.78	(2.64)
Austria	475	(3.4)	504	(3.4)	515	(3.3)	540	(3.9)	23.77	(1.76)
Belgium	465	(5.5)	494	(3.9)	528	(3.6)	554	(4.9)	37.36	(2.29)
Canada	502	(1.9)	525	(1.9)	547	(2.0)	567	(2.1)	26.26	(0.83)
Czech Republic	472	(3.5)	494	(3.4)	504	(2.9)	535	(3.2)	26.49	(1.85)
Denmark	473	(3.6)	491	(3.3)	509	(4.0)	526	(4.2)	24.87	(1.73)
Finland	530	(4.5)	540	(3.1)	555	(2.7)	564	(4.6)	16.22	(1.73)
France	479	(3.8)	491	(3.8)	515	(3.4)	539	(3.5)	26.09	(1.90)
Germany	460	(4.2)	486	(3.3)	498	(3.2)	536	(3.9)	31.08	(2.03)
Greece	463	(6.3)	478	(5.6)	479	(6.0)	483	(6.5)	9.75	(2.90)
Hungary	454	(4.9)	465	(5.4)	486	(4.2)	518	(5.4)	25.71	(2.32)
Iceland	483	(3.4)	499	(2.9)	518	(3.2)	534	(3.6)	22.24	(1.85)
Ireland	509	(4.5)	525	(3.5)	533	(3.7)	547	(4.9)	16.51	(2.11)
Italy	466	(4.2)	480	(3.8)	495	(3.5)	511	(4.2)	18.22	(1.77)
Japan	511	(5.4)	513	(6.5)	525	(5.6)	547	(5.1)	21.41	(2.66)
Korea	521	(2.8)	519	(3.1)	524	(2.9)	537	(3.2)	8.47	(1.60)
Luxembourg	420	(3.2)	431	(3.4)	454	(3.5)	475	(4.1)	22.69	(1.98)
Mexico	394	(3.5)	412	(3.7)	433	(3.9)	458	(6.2)	26.15	(2.32)
New Zealand	513	(4.2)	523	(4.2)	539	(4.3)	547	(5.7)	16.02	(2.54)
Norway	482	(4.2)	498	(3.7)	517	(3.7)	533	(3.9)	20.44	(1.95)
Poland	447	(5.9)	479	(4.2)	498	(5.9)	508	(7.3)	22.00	(3.07)
Portugal	447	(5.2)	460	(5.0)	474	(5.4)	504	(6.2)	23.14	(2.61)
Spain	457	(3.8)	488	(3.0)	502	(3.2)	529	(2.8)	28.02	(1.56)
Sweden	498	(3.1)	512	(2.8)	522	(3.3)	538	(3.7)	15.22	(1.74)
Switzerland	469	(4.5)	486	(4.1)	494	(4.8)	536	(6.5)	24.46	(2.64)
United Kingdom	494	(2.9)	509	(2.7)	537	(3.4)	564	(5.0)	29.54	(2.04)
United States	468	(7.7)	496	(5.9)	523	(7.6)	538	(8.7)	28.65	(2.84)
OECD total	*473*	*(2.2)*	*491*	*(1.7)*	*510*	*(2.3)*	*532*	*(2.6)*	*19.31*	*(1.23)*
OECD average	*477*	*(0.8)*	*493*	*(0.8)*	*510*	*(0.9)*	*531*	*(1.0)*	*18.23*	*(0.45)*
NON-OECD COUNTRIES										
Brazil	400	(4.4)	394	(3.3)	402	(4.1)	407	(5.0)	3.83	(2.16)
Latvia	442	(6.0)	463	(7.1)	464	(7.4)	472	(6.9)	**13.56**	(2.95)
Liechtenstein	455	(10.0)	480	(10.9)	482	(11.5)	522	(10.8)	**28.08**	(5.53)
Russian Federation	447	(6.2)	456	(4.3)	469	(4.1)	490	(4.7)	**16.18**	(1.93)
Netherlands[2]	505	(3.7)	511	(5.6)	545	(4.2)	570	(4.6)	28.98	(2.13)

1. For the definition of the index see Annex A1. "Min" is used for countries with more than 25 per cent of students at the lowest value of this index, which is −1.28.
2. Response rate is too low to ensure comparability (see Annex A3).
3. For explained variation see Annex A2. Unit changes marked in bold are statistically significant. Where bottom and top quarters are marked in bold this indicates that their difference is statistically significant.

ANNEX B1

Table 6.5

Index of social communication with parents and performance on the combined reading literacy scale, by national quarters of the index

Results based on students' self-reports

	Index of social communication[1]									
	All students		Bottom quarter		Second quarter		Third quarter		Top quarter	
	Mean index	S.E.	Mean index	S.E.	Mean index	S.E.	Mean index	S.E.	Mean index	S.E.
OECD COUNTRIES										
Australia	−0.31	(0.02)	−1.49	(0.02)	−0.68	(0.01)	−0.12	(0.01)	1.05	(0.01)
Austria	−0.27	(0.01)	−1.37	(0.02)	−0.64	(0.01)	−0.09	(0.01)	1.03	(0.01)
Belgium	−0.12	(0.02)	−1.28	(0.02)	−0.54	(0.00)	0.16	(0.01)	Max	
Canada	−0.20	(0.01)	−1.34	(0.01)	−0.58	(0.00)	−0.05	(0.00)	1.16	(0.00)
Czech Republic	0.28	(0.02)	−0.99	(0.02)	−0.09	(0.01)	0.99	(0.02)	Max	
Denmark	0.20	(0.02)	−0.92	(0.02)	−0.11	(0.01)	0.63	(0.02)	Max	
Finland	−0.20	(0.01)	−1.10	(0.01)	−0.51	(0.00)	−0.05	(0.01)	0.86	(0.02)
France	0.16	(0.02)	−1.03	(0.02)	−0.20	(0.01)	0.67	(0.02)	Max	
Germany	−0.24	(0.02)	−1.27	(0.01)	−0.58	(0.01)	−0.09	(0.01)	0.99	(0.01)
Greece	0.10	(0.02)	−1.12	(0.02)	−0.22	(0.01)	0.53	(0.02)	Max	
Hungary	0.54	(0.02)	−0.69	(0.02)	0.46	(0.02)	1.20	(0.00)	Max	
Iceland	−0.09	(0.02)	−1.20	(0.02)	−0.51	(0.01)	0.15	(0.01)	Max	
Ireland	−0.05	(0.02)	−1.25	(0.02)	−0.44	(0.01)	0.30	(0.02)	Max	
Italy	0.77	(0.02)	−0.42	(0.02)	1.09	(0.01)	1.20	(0.00)	Max	
Japan	−0.19	(0.03)	−1.47	(0.02)	−0.65	(0.01)	0.14	(0.01)	Max	
Korea	−0.18	(0.03)	−1.61	(0.02)	−0.65	(0.01)	0.34	(0.02)	Max	
Luxembourg	−0.19	(0.02)	−1.37	(0.02)	−0.58	(0.01)	−0.02	(0.01)	1.19	(0.00)
Mexico	−0.05	(0.02)	−1.45	(0.02)	−0.47	(0.01)	0.54	(0.02)	Max	
New Zealand	−0.28	(0.02)	−1.48	(0.02)	−0.69	(0.01)	−0.09	(0.01)	1.13	(0.01)
Norway	−0.01	(0.02)	−1.18	(0.02)	−0.36	(0.01)	0.30	(0.02)	Max	
Poland	0.04	(0.02)	−1.26	(0.02)	−0.32	(0.01)	0.54	(0.02)	Max	
Portugal	0.38	(0.02)	−0.92	(0.02)	0.04	(0.01)	1.20	(0.00)	Max	
Spain	0.19	(0.02)	−1.12	(0.01)	−0.18	(0.01)	0.86	(0.01)	Max	
Sweden	−0.04	(0.02)	−1.14	(0.01)	−0.47	(0.01)	0.27	(0.02)	Max	
Switzerland	−0.25	(0.02)	−1.25	(0.01)	−0.60	(0.01)	−0.11	(0.01)	0.95	(0.01)
United Kingdom	0.01	(0.02)	−1.27	(0.02)	−0.36	(0.01)	0.46	(0.02)	Max	
United States	0.06	(0.03)	−1.44	(0.02)	−0.36	(0.01)	0.85	(0.02)	Max	
OECD total	*0.01*	*(0.01)*	*−1.30*	*(0.01)*	*−0.36*	*(0.01)*	*0.53*	*(0.01)*	*1.18*	*(0.00)*
OECD average	*0.00*	*(0.00)*	*−1.20*	*(0.00)*	*−0.34*	*(0.00)*	*0.40*	*(0.00)*	*1.15*	*(0.00)*
NON-OECD COUNTRIES										
Brazil	0.10	(0.03)	−1.51	(0.03)	−0.34	(0.01)	1.06	(0.01)	Max	
Latvia	0.10	(0.03)	−1.10	(0.02)	−0.25	(0.01)	0.57	(0.03)	Max	
Liechtenstein	−0.34	(0.05)	−1.28	(0.02)	−0.70	(0.02)	−0.16	(0.02)	0.79	(0.07)
Russian Federation	0.47	(0.02)	−0.90	(0.02)	0.39	(0.02)	1.20	(0.00)	Max	
Netherlands[2]	0.29	(0.03)	−1.07	(0.04)	−0.10	(0.01)	1.14	(0.01)	Max	

Performance on the combined reading literacy scale, by national quarters of the index of social communication[3]

	Bottom quarter		Second quarter		Third quarter		Top quarter		Change in the combined reading literacy score per unit of the index of social communication[3]	
	Mean score	S.E.	Mean score	S.E.	Mean score	S.E.	Mean score	S.E.	Change	S.E.
OECD COUNTRIES										
Australia	502	(4.6)	526	(5.0)	545	(3.9)	545	(4.8)	**17.41**	(1.97)
Austria	493	(4.4)	504	(3.2)	520	(3.4)	514	(2.9)	**10.98**	(1.65)
Belgium	492	(5.4)	516	(3.9)	520	(3.7)	513	(3.9)	**10.49**	(1.99)
Canada	515	(2.4)	536	(2.1)	543	(2.2)	548	(1.7)	**13.80**	(0.94)
Czech Republic	487	(3.3)	503	(3.3)	505	(2.8)	509	(3.1)	**9.87**	(1.46)
Denmark	469	(4.4)	505	(3.6)	508	(3.0)	516	(3.3)	**21.28**	(2.23)
Finland	535	(5.1)	551	(3.2)	554	(3.4)	549	(3.4)	**7.42**	(2.72)
France	486	(4.6)	511	(3.0)	516	(3.4)	511	(3.1)	**12.43**	(1.93)
Germany	479	(3.8)	497	(3.7)	504	(3.3)	498	(3.5)	**7.95**	(1.71)
Greece	457	(6.8)	484	(5.4)	477	(4.3)	480	(5.8)	**9.60**	(2.12)
Hungary	465	(5.2)	479	(4.8)	491	(5.5)	488	(4.5)	**13.96**	(2.22)
Iceland	491	(3.4)	509	(3.3)	516	(3.2)	518	(3.3)	**11.96**	(1.85)
Ireland	515	(4.8)	526	(4.2)	535	(4.0)	536	(4.1)	**9.99**	(1.78)
Italy	480	(4.6)	488	(4.7)	493	(3.4)	491	(3.4)	**8.66**	(2.65)
Japan	491	(7.4)	525	(5.4)	534	(5.1)	546	(5.0)	**20.05**	(2.24)
Korea	492	(3.4)	524	(2.8)	540	(2.3)	545	(3.4)	**18.26**	(1.55)
Luxembourg	424	(4.0)	451	(3.6)	459	(3.4)	446	(3.1)	**11.64**	(2.02)
Mexico	397	(3.7)	422	(3.9)	429	(4.7)	440	(4.6)	**14.54**	(1.78)
New Zealand	511	(4.3)	525	(3.5)	545	(4.4)	541	(4.3)	**13.79**	(1.89)
Norway	480	(4.4)	509	(4.1)	526	(4.0)	513	(4.2)	**16.47**	(2.22)
Poland	457	(6.0)	489	(4.5)	494	(5.8)	489	(5.2)	**14.75**	(2.10)
Portugal	442	(5.7)	468	(5.4)	488	(4.7)	485	(5.1)	**22.00**	(1.69)
Spain	475	(3.8)	500	(3.5)	499	(3.4)	500	(3.1)	**11.05**	(1.38)
Sweden	506	(3.1)	520	(3.5)	521	(3.3)	521	(3.6)	**5.43**	(1.83)
Switzerland	473	(6.0)	498	(5.1)	508	(4.7)	504	(5.0)	**14.69**	(2.30)
United Kingdom	503	(3.6)	529	(3.4)	532	(3.5)	538	(3.9)	**13.70**	(1.55)
United States	480	(8.1)	515	(7.6)	516	(6.8)	515	(8.4)	**12.43**	(2.16)
OECD total	*477*	*(2.4)*	*505*	*(2.1)*	*510*	*(1.9)*	*512*	*(2.4)*	*11.93*	*(0.79)*
OECD average	*481*	*(0.9)*	*504*	*(0.8)*	*512*	*(0.7)*	*511*	*(0.9)*	*10.01*	*(0.38)*
NON-OECD COUNTRIES										
Brazil	372	(4.1)	402	(3.9)	405	(4.7)	413	(3.7)	**12.33**	(1.51)
Latvia	444	(9.0)	464	(6.5)	463	(5.3)	467	(6.5)	**9.62**	(2.49)
Liechtenstein	462	(11.1)	488	(10.5)	491	(10.0)	494	(10.4)	14.42	(7.13)
Russian Federation	444	(5.4)	466	(4.7)	471	(4.5)	472	(3.6)	**13.04**	(1.58)
Netherlands[2]	493	(6.2)	547	(4.2)	545	(4.1)	546	(5.0)	**23.25**	(2.68)

1. For the definition of the index see Annex A1. "Max" is used to represent countries which have more than 25 per cent of students at the highest value of this index, which is 1.20.
2. Response rate is too low to ensure comparability (see Annex A3).
3. For explained variation see Annex A2. Unit changes marked in bold are statistically significant. Where bottom and top quarters are marked in bold this indicates that their difference is statistically significant.

289

Table 6.6
Index of communication with parents related to aspects of culture and performance on the combined reading literacy scale, by national quarters of the index
Results based on students' self-reports

Index of cultural communication[1]

	All students		Bottom quarter		Second quarter		Third quarter		Top quarter	
	Mean index	S.E.	Mean index	S.E.	Mean index	S.E.	Mean index	S.E.	Mean index	S.E.
OECD COUNTRIES										
Australia	-0.13	(0.03)	-1.47	(0.03)	-0.39	(0.01)	0.27	(0.01)	1.09	(0.02)
Austria	-0.15	(0.02)	-1.42	(0.02)	-0.39	(0.01)	0.21	(0.01)	1.01	(0.01)
Belgium	-0.24	(0.02)	-1.67	(0.01)	-0.49	(0.01)	0.15	(0.01)	1.03	(0.01)
Canada	0.08	(0.01)	-1.17	(0.01)	-0.14	(0.00)	0.42	(0.00)	1.21	(0.01)
Czech Republic	-0.15	(0.02)	-1.35	(0.02)	-0.37	(0.01)	0.19	(0.01)	0.95	(0.01)
Denmark	0.11	(0.02)	-1.22	(0.02)	-0.10	(0.01)	0.55	(0.01)	1.21	(0.01)
Finland	-0.01	(0.02)	-1.11	(0.02)	-0.17	(0.00)	0.27	(0.01)	0.96	(0.01)
France	0.27	(0.02)	-0.94	(0.02)	0.08	(0.01)	0.65	(0.01)	1.30	(0.01)
Germany	-0.14	(0.02)	-1.42	(0.02)	-0.35	(0.01)	0.23	(0.01)	0.98	(0.01)
Greece	0.19	(0.02)	-0.92	(0.02)	0.00	(0.01)	0.52	(0.01)	1.18	(0.01)
Hungary	0.33	(0.02)	-0.82	(0.02)	0.15	(0.01)	0.65	(0.01)	1.35	(0.01)
Iceland	0.08	(0.02)	-1.26	(0.02)	-0.14	(0.01)	0.44	(0.01)	1.28	(0.02)
Ireland	-0.09	(0.02)	-1.35	(0.02)	-0.30	(0.01)	0.24	(0.01)	1.05	(0.01)
Italy	0.41	(0.02)	-0.84	(0.02)	0.23	(0.01)	0.84	(0.00)	1.41	(0.01)
Japan	0.09	(0.03)	-1.48	(0.03)	-0.08	(0.01)	0.56	(0.01)	1.34	(0.02)
Korea	-0.59	(0.03)	-2.20	(0.00)	-1.08	(0.02)	-0.05	(0.01)	0.99	(0.02)
Luxembourg	-0.20	(0.02)	-1.55	(0.02)	-0.44	(0.01)	0.17	(0.01)	1.03	(0.02)
Mexico	0.00	(0.02)	-1.29	(0.02)	-0.28	(0.01)	0.33	(0.01)	1.23	(0.01)
New Zealand	0.07	(0.02)	-1.23	(0.02)	-0.15	(0.01)	0.44	(0.01)	1.22	(0.02)
Norway	-0.22	(0.02)	-1.51	(0.02)	-0.47	(0.01)	0.13	(0.01)	0.99	(0.02)
Poland	-0.03	(0.02)	-1.35	(0.03)	-0.24	(0.01)	0.33	(0.01)	1.15	(0.02)
Portugal	-0.02	(0.03)	-1.32	(0.02)	-0.23	(0.01)	0.36	(0.01)	1.13	(0.01)
Spain	0.17	(0.02)	-0.97	(0.02)	-0.02	(0.01)	0.49	(0.01)	1.18	(0.01)
Sweden	-0.14	(0.02)	-1.38	(0.02)	-0.36	(0.01)	0.18	(0.01)	0.99	(0.01)
Switzerland	-0.01	(0.02)	-1.29	(0.02)	-0.24	(0.01)	0.35	(0.01)	1.14	(0.02)
United Kingdom	0.06	(0.02)	-1.10	(0.02)	-0.12	(0.00)	0.35	(0.01)	1.11	(0.02)
United States	0.22	(0.04)	-1.23	(0.03)	-0.01	(0.01)	0.65	(0.01)	1.48	(0.02)
OECD total	*0.07*	*(0.01)*	*-1.29*	*(0.01)*	*-0.15*	*(0.00)*	*0.47*	*(0.00)*	*1.26*	*(0.01)*
OECD average	*0.00*	*(0.00)*	*-1.29*	*(0.01)*	*-0.23*	*(0.00)*	*0.37*	*(0.00)*	*1.15*	*(0.00)*
NON-OECD COUNTRIES										
Brazil	0.17	(0.03)	-1.31	(0.02)	-0.09	(0.01)	0.63	(0.01)	1.48	(0.02)
Latvia	0.25	(0.02)	-1.01	(0.02)	0.02	(0.01)	0.64	(0.01)	1.36	(0.02)
Liechtenstein	-0.20	(0.05)	-1.43	(0.07)	-0.46	(0.02)	0.14	(0.02)	0.96	(0.05)
Russian Federation	0.19	(0.02)	-1.22	(0.02)	-0.06	(0.01)	0.62	(0.01)	1.43	(0.01)
Netherlands[2]	-0.35	(0.03)	-1.85	(0.02)	-0.61	(0.01)	0.11	(0.01)	0.95	(0.02)

Performance on the combined reading literacy scale, by national quarters of the index of cultural communication[3]

	Bottom quarter		Second quarter		Third quarter		Top quarter		Change in the combined reading literacy score per unit of the index of cultural communication[3]	
	Mean score	S.E.	Mean score	S.E.	Mean score	S.E.	Mean score	S.E.	Change	S.E.
OECD COUNTRIES										
Australia	488	(4.1)	515	(4.7)	543	(4.1)	573	(4.8)	30.84	(1.77)
Austria	474	(3.3)	503	(3.6)	520	(3.7)	535	(3.2)	24.44	(1.82)
Belgium	490	(4.1)	508	(3.5)	514	(4.5)	531	(4.2)	13.63	(1.41)
Canada	507	(1.9)	528	(2.0)	542	(2.0)	564	(2.1)	22.06	(0.88)
Czech Republic	474	(3.2)	494	(3.3)	507	(2.9)	530	(2.9)	21.76	(1.56)
Denmark	459	(3.8)	488	(3.2)	511	(3.6)	540	(3.3)	33.11	(1.77)
Finland	514	(4.7)	544	(2.8)	558	(3.0)	573	(3.1)	26.20	(2.49)
France	474	(4.4)	500	(3.3)	519	(3.3)	532	(3.2)	22.93	(1.99)
Germany	460	(3.3)	492	(4.2)	504	(2.7)	522	(5.3)	23.70	(1.82)
Greece	448	(5.6)	468	(5.7)	487	(5.1)	498	(6.3)	22.81	(2.47)
Hungary	457	(4.5)	480	(4.6)	489	(4.2)	497	(6.1)	18.21	(2.66)
Iceland	480	(3.2)	505	(3.2)	516	(3.2)	533	(3.5)	19.14	(1.78)
Ireland	502	(4.2)	522	(3.7)	535	(4.3)	554	(4.1)	18.68	(1.98)
Italy	459	(3.9)	486	(3.7)	505	(4.1)	503	(4.3)	18.85	(1.68)
Japan	493	(7.5)	519	(5.3)	539	(4.8)	545	(4.9)	18.40	(2.08)
Korea	509	(3.2)	521	(3.2)	529	(2.7)	544	(3.5)	10.52	(1.14)
Luxembourg	414	(3.7)	450	(3.6)	451	(3.3)	466	(3.6)	16.90	(1.89)
Mexico	395	(3.4)	416	(4.1)	433	(4.2)	450	(5.1)	22.02	(1.95)
New Zealand	508	(3.8)	522	(4.3)	540	(3.8)	552	(5.3)	16.97	(2.31)
Norway	467	(4.4)	499	(4.2)	516	(3.9)	545	(4.1)	29.68	(1.69)
Poland	455	(5.1)	479	(5.2)	495	(4.9)	501	(6.4)	16.17	(2.24)
Portugal	423	(4.9)	463	(4.7)	486	(4.3)	513	(5.1)	34.97	(1.97)
Spain	454	(3.8)	487	(3.6)	507	(3.0)	528	(2.8)	31.79	(1.48)
Sweden	483	(2.8)	512	(3.4)	528	(2.8)	546	(3.6)	23.93	(1.50)
Switzerland	457	(4.9)	489	(4.4)	507	(5.0)	531	(5.5)	27.53	(2.04)
United Kingdom	493	(2.8)	520	(3.3)	531	(3.4)	561	(4.6)	28.24	(2.03)
United States	471	(7.4)	499	(7.6)	526	(6.7)	529	(8.7)	20.66	(1.96)
OECD total	*470*	*(2.2)*	*495*	*(2.0)*	*515*	*(2.0)*	*526*	*(2.5)*	*19.56*	*(0.79)*
OECD average	*471*	*(0.9)*	*497*	*(0.8)*	*513*	*(0.8)*	*530*	*(0.9)*	*20.50*	*(0.38)*
NON-OECD COUNTRIES										
Brazil	371	(3.7)	384	(4.1)	411	(4.1)	435	(4.7)	19.87	(1.64)
Latvia	437	(7.4)	448	(5.7)	475	(5.8)	479	(7.0)	16.78	(2.37)
Liechtenstein	465	(10.6)	471	(10.3)	475	(10.9)	528	(11.7)	21.63	(6.13)
Russian Federation	440	(5.6)	461	(4.4)	475	(4.4)	483	(3.9)	14.30	(1.30)
Netherlands[2]	500	(4.4)	525	(4.2)	541	(4.4)	568	(4.3)	22.00	(1.88)

1. For the definition of the index see Annex A1.
2. Response rate is too low to ensure comparability (see Annex A3).
3. For explained variation see Annex A2. Unit changes marked in bold are statistically significant. Where bottom and top quarters are marked in bold this indicates that their difference is statistically significant.

Table 6.7
Percentage of students and performance on the combined reading, mathematical and scientific literacy scales, by level of mothers' education
Results based on students' self-reports

	Mothers with completed primary or lower secondary education (ISCED Levels 1 or 2)[1]								Mothers with completed upper secondary education (ISCED Level 3)[1]							
			Performance								Performance					
			Combined reading literacy scale		Mathematical literacy scale		Scientific literacy scale				Combined reading literacy scale		Mathematical literacy scale		Scientific literacy scale	
	% of students[2]	S.E.	Mean score	S.E.	Mean score	S.E.	Mean score	S.E.	% of students[2]	S.E.	Mean score	S.E.	Mean score	S.E.	Mean score	S.E.
Australia	29.0	(1.2)	502	(4.0)	508	(4.5)	505	(4.2)	40.0	(0.9)	530	(3.7)	531	(4.5)	529	(3.5)
Austria	28.1	(0.8)	482	(3.8)	491	(4.6)	497	(4.8)	53.7	(0.9)	517	(2.9)	520	(3.3)	526	(3.3)
Belgium	24.3	(1.0)	463	(5.3)	474	(5.6)	452	(5.9)	43.0	(0.8)	536	(3.2)	547	(3.7)	523	(3.4)
Canada	14.9	(0.4)	496	(2.4)	502	(2.6)	493	(2.9)	35.6	(0.4)	531	(1.9)	529	(1.8)	527	(2.0)
Czech Republic	6.6	(0.5)	421	(12.2)	444	(10.8)	461	(10.9)	79.4	(0.8)	492	(2.3)	494	(2.8)	509	(2.4)
Denmark	22.9	(0.9)	447	(4.5)	476	(5.2)	430	(6.4)	32.6	(0.9)	498	(2.7)	517	(3.5)	480	(4.0)
Finland	31.0	(0.9)	529	(2.8)	520	(3.2)	523	(3.4)	42.2	(0.9)	553	(3.3)	540	(2.9)	539	(3.4)
France	32.0	(0.9)	480	(4.5)	495	(4.2)	470	(5.0)	35.8	(0.7)	518	(2.9)	532	(3.4)	512	(3.9)
Germany	20.0	(0.8)	408	(5.5)	420	(5.9)	432	(6.0)	60.1	(0.9)	507	(2.5)	509	(2.7)	504	(3.0)
Greece	42.1	(1.2)	446	(5.6)	414	(6.0)	436	(5.6)	32.5	(1.1)	490	(4.9)	464	(6.3)	470	(5.5)
Hungary	16.8	(1.1)	424	(5.7)	426	(5.7)	435	(7.9)	62.1	(1.1)	481	(3.6)	486	(3.6)	496	(4.0)
Iceland	46.7	(0.8)	495	(2.2)	502	(3.1)	485	(3.1)	30.7	(0.9)	516	(2.8)	525	(3.7)	499	(4.2)
Ireland	40.7	(1.3)	511	(3.5)	486	(3.1)	493	(3.8)	31.8	(1.0)	536	(3.7)	516	(3.7)	522	(4.3)
Italy	45.5	(1.0)	468	(3.8)	442	(4.1)	457	(4.6)	40.6	(0.9)	504	(3.2)	471	(3.7)	493	(4.3)
Japan[3]	m	m	m	m	m	m	m	m	m	m	m	m	m	m	m	m
Korea	41.9	(1.3)	509	(3.1)	527	(3.2)	536	(3.2)	45.1	(1.0)	535	(2.5)	557	(3.3)	559	(3.4)
Luxembourg	52.3	(1.0)	424	(2.5)	434	(3.2)	429	(3.3)	31.4	(0.9)	467	(3.2)	470	(4.3)	463	(3.7)
Mexico	73.6	(1.8)	404	(2.9)	371	(3.0)	407	(2.7)	14.0	(0.8)	479	(5.0)	436	(6.6)	463	(5.8)
New Zealand	17.3	(0.7)	499	(5.0)	508	(6.5)	491	(6.0)	37.5	(1.0)	539	(3.3)	542	(4.3)	535	(3.8)
Norway	19.1	(0.8)	485	(4.5)	482	(6.7)	478	(5.5)	39.0	(0.9)	509	(3.0)	504	(3.0)	504	(4.3)
Poland	8.1	(0.5)	447	(5.8)	454	(9.5)	452	(9.4)	73.6	(0.9)	478	(4.1)	467	(5.3)	481	(5.1)
Portugal	72.3	(1.5)	460	(4.2)	445	(3.7)	450	(3.7)	13.5	(0.7)	488	(7.1)	460	(8.7)	484	(7.4)
Spain	62.1	(1.5)	478	(3.0)	461	(3.3)	472	(3.4)	21.3	(0.8)	516	(2.8)	501	(5.3)	516	(4.4)
Sweden	15.9	(0.7)	490	(3.8)	486	(5.7)	490	(5.4)	36.8	(0.8)	523	(2.6)	518	(3.8)	514	(3.6)
Switzerland	43.1	(1.3)	458	(4.2)	497	(4.9)	456	(4.5)	39.5	(1.0)	532	(4.0)	563	(4.7)	532	(5.0)
United Kingdom	17.4	(0.7)	490	(5.0)	497	(5.7)	494	(6.3)	44.1	(1.1)	527	(2.8)	534	(3.1)	538	(3.3)
United States	12.1	(1.9)	449	(6.4)	432	(7.2)	446	(9.6)	54.3	(1.4)	508	(5.1)	496	(6.0)	500	(6.1)
OECD total	*28.7*	*(0.7)*	*453*	*(1.4)*	*443*	*(1.5)*	*455*	*(1.7)*	*44.8*	*(0.5)*	*509*	*(1.9)*	*503*	*(2.2)*	*507*	*(2.3)*
OECD average	*32.3*	*(0.3)*	*467*	*(0.9)*	*464*	*(0.9)*	*465*	*(0.9)*	*41.1*	*(0.2)*	*511*	*(0.8)*	*510*	*(0.9)*	*510*	*(0.9)*
Brazil	65.8	(1.5)	379	(3.0)	316	(3.4)	358	(3.6)	21.9	(0.9)	431	(4.2)	372	(6.9)	403	(5.9)
Latvia	8.2	(0.6)	401	(8.5)	413	(13.4)	395	(9.8)	55.9	(1.4)	457	(5.1)	462	(4.3)	458	(5.2)
Liechtenstein	56.6	(2.7)	468	(6.2)	503	(8.6)	462	(7.8)	35.9	(2.4)	520	(7.9)	545	(11.8)	514	(10.8)
Russian Federation	6.3	(0.4)	413	(6.3)	445	(10.1)	417	(9.3)	57.6	(1.1)	461	(4.1)	477	(6.0)	456	(4.7)
Netherlands[4]	54.5	(1.5)	522	(3.6)	555	(4.7)	515	(4.5)	26.1	(1.2)	553	(6.0)	586	(5.9)	552	(6.8)

	Mothers with tertiary education (ISCED Levels 5 or 6)									
			Performance						Increased likelihood of students whose mothers have not completed upper secondary education scoring in the bottom quarter of the national reading literacy performance distribution[5]	
			Combined reading literacy scale		Mathematical literacy scale		Scientific literacy scale			
	% of students[2]	S.E.	Mean score	S.E.	Mean score	S.E.	Mean score	S.E.	Ratio	S.E.
Australia	31.0	(1.1)	560	(5.0)	565	(4.6)	554	(5.6)	1.6	(0.11)
Austria	18.2	(0.8)	539	(3.9)	551	(5.1)	547	(4.8)	1.7	(0.09)
Belgium	32.8	(0.9)	525	(4.5)	540	(4.6)	515	(5.4)	2.3	(0.15)
Canada	49.5	(0.5)	553	(1.8)	549	(1.9)	547	(1.8)	1.7	(0.06)
Czech Republic	14.0	(0.7)	540	(6.2)	553	(6.7)	563	(6.7)	2.1	(0.18)
Denmark	44.5	(1.1)	531	(2.8)	540	(3.2)	516	(3.7)	2.4	(0.14)
Finland	26.8	(1.0)	563	(3.7)	553	(3.4)	557	(4.4)	1.4	(0.07)
France	32.3	(1.0)	528	(3.4)	535	(4.1)	530	(4.3)	1.9	(0.13)
Germany	20.0	(0.7)	534	(3.8)	535	(5.0)	537	(5.2)	3.0	(0.22)
Greece	25.3	(1.2)	503	(6.9)	483	(9.1)	492	(7.8)	1.9	(0.14)
Hungary	21.1	(1.1)	533	(5.8)	550	(6.7)	557	(6.5)	2.4	(0.19)
Iceland	22.6	(0.8)	539	(3.3)	544	(4.6)	528	(5.0)	1.5	(0.08)
Ireland	27.5	(1.0)	545	(5.0)	517	(4.6)	539	(5.4)	1.4	(0.10)
Italy	13.9	(0.8)	514	(5.2)	482	(5.6)	511	(5.9)	1.6	(0.12)
Japan[3]	m	m	m	m	m	m	m	m	m	m
Korea	13.0	(1.0)	540	(5.0)	576	(6.9)	579	(7.5)	1.6	(0.11)
Luxembourg	16.3	(0.7)	485	(4.9)	477	(6.9)	490	(6.8)	2.1	(0.14)
Mexico	12.4	(1.2)	474	(7.5)	436	(6.8)	469	(8.0)	3.7	(0.57)
New Zealand	45.2	(1.0)	553	(4.0)	564	(3.7)	552	(3.8)	1.6	(0.10)
Norway	41.9	(1.0)	522	(4.1)	511	(4.0)	516	(3.9)	1.5	(0.09)
Poland	18.3	(0.9)	535	(8.1)	530	(9.2)	530	(8.7)	1.4	(0.14)
Portugal	14.2	(1.1)	520	(7.9)	501	(7.7)	495	(8.6)	1.6	(0.16)
Spain	16.5	(1.2)	535	(3.3)	517	(4.8)	540	(5.0)	2.2	(0.16)
Sweden	47.4	(1.1)	527	(2.8)	518	(3.5)	522	(3.4)	1.5	(0.08)
Switzerland	17.3	(0.9)	518	(7.5)	553	(7.3)	524	(7.6)	2.5	(0.17)
United Kingdom	38.5	(1.0)	551	(3.8)	555	(4.0)	557	(3.8)	1.7	(0.12)
United States	33.5	(2.2)	537	(7.4)	528	(8.3)	536	(8.5)	2.1	(0.20)
OECD total	*26.5*	*(0.7)*	*534*	*(2.9)*	*530*	*(3.3)*	*535*	*(3.2)*	*1.7*	*(0.07)*
OECD average	*26.6*	*(0.2)*	*534*	*(0.9)*	*533*	*(1.0)*	*532*	*(1.1)*	*1.7*	*(0.03)*
Brazil	12.3	(0.9)	440	(6.3)	378	(10.2)	428	(8.1)	2.4	(0.22)
Latvia	35.9	(1.4)	479	(7.0)	482	(6.5)	486	(8.1)	2.1	(0.19)
Liechtenstein	7.6	(1.6)	c	c	580	(30.5)	c	c	c	c
Russian Federation	36.2	(1.1)	477	(4.8)	494	(6.0)	478	(6.3)	2.0	(0.11)
Netherlands[4]	19.4	(1.0)	554	(5.5)	582	(7.6)	561	(7.3)	1.7	(0.17)

1. Mean scores marked in bold indicate that the difference in performance between students whose mothers have completed upper secondary education and those whose mothers have not is statistically significant.
2. Percentage of students participating in the assessment of reading literacy with the respective level of mothers' education.
3. Japan was excluded from this comparison because of a high proportion of missing data.
4. Response rate is too low to ensure comparability (see Annex A3).
5. Ratios statistically significantly greater than 1 are marked in bold.

Table 6.8
Percentage of the adult population who have completed tertiary education and the probability of obtaining a tertiary qualification, by parents' level of education

	Percentage of the population 16 to 65 years of age who have completed tertiary education, by level of educational attainment of their parents			Increased likelihood of obtaining a tertiary qualification for individuals whose parents have also completed tertiary education compared with individuals whose parents have not completed secondary education		
	Below upper secondary education	Upper secondary education	Tertiary education	Total (16-65 years)	26-35 years-old	46-55 years-old
Australia	20.0	25.7	39.2	2.0	2.4	1.9
Belgium (Fl.)	15.3	32.8	49.7	3.3	2.6	4.4
Canada	23.7	41.5	57.2	2.4	2.9	2.2
Germany	16.0	23.3	38.4	2.3	2.9	2.4
Ireland	12.0	36.1	57.4	4.8	m	m
Netherlands	12.8	22.5	42.6	3.3	3.3	4.3
New Zealand	21.4	28.8	45.3	2.1	2.8	2.0
Poland	9.2	26.0	53.8	5.8	6.6	m
Sweden	18.7	29.5	40.2	2.2	2.8	2.6
Switzerland	8.8	19.6	37.8	4.3	4.3	5.6
United Kingdom	16.5	38.2	47.0	2.9	3.3	3.1
United States	19.7	35.7	64.2	3.3	3.6	4.6

Source: OECD and Statistics Canada (1995).

Table 6.9
Percentage of students and performance on the combined reading literacy scale, by type of family structure
Results based on students' self-reports

	Students from single-parent families[1]				Students from other types of families[1]				Increased likelihood of students from single-parent families scoring in the bottom quarter of the national reading literacy performance distribution[2]	
	% of students	S.E.	Mean score	S.E.	% of students	S.E.	Mean score	S.E.	Ratio	S.E.
Australia	16.2	(0.7)	521	(4.7)	83.8	(0.7)	530	(3.8)	1.1	(0.09)
Austria	12.6	(0.5)	508	(5.2)	87.4	(0.5)	507	(2.5)	0.9	(0.07)
Belgium	12.8	(0.5)	487	(5.5)	87.2	(0.5)	512	(3.6)	1.3	(0.08)
Canada	15.6	(0.3)	527	(2.5)	84.4	(0.3)	537	(1.6)	1.1	(0.05)
Czech Republic	11.0	(0.5)	494	(6.4)	89.0	(0.5)	492	(2.3)	1.0	(0.09)
Denmark	16.9	(0.7)	484	(5.8)	83.1	(0.7)	501	(2.4)	1.3	(0.11)
Finland	18.7	(0.7)	529	(6.8)	81.4	(0.7)	551	(2.2)	1.4	(0.09)
France	15.0	(0.6)	488	(4.7)	85.0	(0.6)	508	(2.7)	1.3	(0.08)
Germany	15.3	(0.7)	478	(5.4)	84.8	(0.7)	485	(2.6)	1.1	(0.09)
Greece	8.7	(0.5)	473	(8.3)	91.3	(0.5)	475	(4.9)	1.1	(0.12)
Hungary	17.2	(0.6)	474	(4.6)	82.8	(0.6)	482	(4.2)	1.1	(0.09)
Iceland	13.2	(0.6)	507	(4.5)	86.8	(0.6)	508	(1.7)	1.0	(0.09)
Ireland	12.3	(0.6)	508	(6.2)	87.7	(0.6)	530	(3.2)	1.3	(0.12)
Italy	19.7	(0.6)	481	(4.5)	80.3	(0.6)	490	(2.7)	1.2	(0.08)
Japan	10.8	(0.7)	510	(8.6)	89.2	(0.7)	527	(5.0)	1.2	(0.15)
Korea	7.8	(0.4)	510	(5.6)	92.2	(0.4)	526	(2.4)	1.4	(0.11)
Luxembourg	10.8	(0.6)	432	(5.5)	89.2	(0.6)	444	(1.7)	1.2	(0.12)
Mexico	17.4	(0.7)	420	(4.4)	82.6	(0.7)	423	(3.6)	1.1	(0.09)
New Zealand	20.5	(0.7)	513	(4.9)	79.5	(0.7)	535	(2.8)	1.3	(0.08)
Norway	16.0	(0.6)	489	(5.5)	84.0	(0.6)	510	(2.9)	1.3	(0.10)
Poland	9.6	(0.6)	479	(6.2)	90.4	(0.6)	482	(4.7)	1.1	(0.11)
Portugal	11.2	(0.4)	468	(5.7)	88.8	(0.4)	472	(4.5)	1.1	(0.08)
Spain	16.9	(0.6)	486	(3.6)	83.1	(0.6)	495	(2.8)	1.1	(0.09)
Sweden	16.8	(0.6)	501	(4.0)	83.2	(0.6)	521	(2.1)	1.3	(0.09)
Switzerland	13.0	(0.5)	496	(6.0)	87.0	(0.5)	495	(4.4)	1.0	(0.08)
United Kingdom	20.5	(0.6)	502	(3.2)	79.6	(0.6)	531	(2.9)	1.4	(0.08)
United States	21.0	(0.9)	484	(8.6)	79.0	(0.9)	512	(7.4)	1.4	(0.11)
OECD total	16.2	(0.3)	485	(3.0)	83.8	(0.3)	503	(1.9)	1.3	(0.04)
OECD average	14.7	(0.1)	491	(1.0)	85.3	(0.1)	503	(0.6)	1.2	(0.02)
Brazil	18.1	(0.7)	396	(5.4)	81.9	(0.7)	398	(3.0)	0.9	(0.09)
Latvia	20.6	(0.9)	451	(8.7)	79.4	(0.9)	461	(4.9)	1.2	(0.09)
Liechtenstein	12.6	(1.5)	468	(16.5)	87.4	(1.5)	485	(4.4)	1.4	(0.40)
Russian Federation	19.5	(0.6)	462	(4.8)	80.5	(0.6)	462	(4.1)	1.0	(0.06)
Netherlands[3]	10.3	(0.8)	503	(8.4)	89.7	(0.8)	535	(3.3)	1.5	(0.17)

OECD COUNTRIES / NON-OECD COUNTRIES

1. For the definition of family type, see Annex A1. Scores marked in bold represent statistically significant differences on the combined reading literacy scale between students from single-parent families and those from other types of families.
2. Ratios statistically significantly greater than 1 are marked in bold.
3. Response rate is too low to ensure comparability (see Annex A3).

Table 6.10
Percentage of students and performance on the combined reading, mathematical and scientific literacy scales, by students' nationality and the nationality of their parents
Results based on students' self-reports

		Native students (students who were born in the country of assessment with at least one of their parents born in the same country)							First-generation students (students who were born in the country of assessment but whose parents were foreign-born)						
			Performance[1]							Performance[1]					
		% of students[2]	S.E.	Combined reading literacy scale		Mathematical literacy scale		Scientific literacy scale		% of students[2]	S.E.	Combined reading literacy scale		Mathematical literacy scale		Scientific literacy scale	
				Mean score	S.E.	Mean score	S.E.	Mean score	S.E.			Mean score	S.E.	Mean score	S.E.	Mean score	S.E.
OECD COUNTRIES	Australia	77.4	(1.8)	532	(3.6)	536	(3.6)	531	(3.5)	10.7	(1.1)	528	(7.1)	535	(7.3)	523	(9.0)
	Austria	90.4	(0.9)	515	(2.4)	523	(2.6)	528	(2.5)	3.7	(0.4)	453	(9.4)	462	(12.9)	447	(13.6)
	Belgium	88.0	(1.1)	522	(3.8)	536	(4.0)	511	(4.6)	8.6	(0.9)	411	(8.7)	418	(10.3)	401	(9.0)
	Canada	79.5	(1.0)	538	(1.5)	536	(1.4)	535	(1.6)	10.8	(0.5)	539	(3.1)	530	(3.6)	521	(4.1)
	Czech Republic	98.9	(0.2)	501	(2.1)	504	(2.7)	518	(2.4)	0.6	(0.1)	c	c	c	c	c	c
	Denmark	93.8	(0.6)	504	(2.2)	520	(2.3)	488	(2.7)	2.4	(0.4)	409	(13.9)	448	(15.9)	395	(17.4)
	Finland	98.7	(0.2)	548	(2.6)	537	(2.1)	539	(2.5)	0.2	(0.1)	c	c	c	c	c	c
	France	88.0	(0.9)	512	(2.8)	523	(2.8)	510	(3.3)	9.8	(0.7)	471	(6.2)	487	(7.0)	451	(7.4)
	Germany	84.8	(0.8)	507	(2.3)	510	(2.5)	507	(2.5)	5.1	(0.5)	432	(9.0)	437	(7.7)	423	(12.0)
	Greece	95.2	(0.9)	478	(4.7)	452	(5.6)	464	(4.8)	0.5	(0.1)	c	c	c	c	c	c
	Hungary	98.3	(0.2)	482	(4.0)	489	(4.0)	498	(4.2)	0.1	(0.0)	c	c	c	c	a	a
	Iceland	99.2	(0.2)	509	(1.5)	516	(2.2)	497	(2.2)	0.2	(0.1)	c	c	c	c	c	c
	Ireland	97.7	(0.3)	528	(3.2)	503	(2.7)	514	(3.2)	0.9	(0.2)	519	(20.2)	c	c	c	c
	Italy	99.1	(0.2)	489	(2.9)	459	(2.9)	479	(2.9)	0.2	(0.1)	c	c	c	c	c	c
	Japan[3]	99.9	(0.1)	525	(5.1)	559	(5.5)	553	(5.5)	0.0	(0.0)	c	c	c	c	c	c
	Korea[3]	a	a	a	a	a	a	a	a	a	a	a	a	a	a	a	a
	Luxembourg	65.8	(0.7)	474	(1.7)	472	(2.3)	473	(2.5)	17.8	(0.7)	399	(4.6)	422	(5.4)	407	(5.3)
	Mexico	96.4	(0.4)	427	(3.3)	391	(3.4)	425	(3.2)	1.1	(0.2)	378	(15.3)	c	c	380	(14.5)
	New Zealand	80.4	(1.1)	538	(2.7)	543	(3.2)	536	(2.4)	6.4	(0.5)	507	(10.3)	503	(12.0)	506	(11.2)
	Norway	95.4	(0.4)	510	(2.7)	503	(2.7)	506	(2.7)	1.5	(0.3)	464	(10.6)	481	(15.9)	437	(13.0)
	Poland	99.7	(0.1)	482	(4.4)	474	(5.1)	485	(5.1)	0.0	(0.0)	c	c	c	c	c	c
	Portugal	96.9	(0.3)	472	(4.5)	456	(4.0)	461	(4.1)	1.8	(0.2)	463	(14.3)	434	(20.3)	438	(14.1)
	Spain	98.0	(0.4)	494	(2.6)	478	(3.0)	493	(2.9)	0.6	(0.1)	450	(15.9)	c	c	c	c
	Sweden	89.5	(0.9)	523	(2.1)	517	(2.3)	518	(2.6)	4.7	(0.6)	485	(7.3)	466	(9.0)	486	(10.7)
	Switzerland	79.3	(0.9)	514	(4.0)	548	(4.2)	514	(4.4)	9.3	(0.6)	460	(6.8)	489	(8.8)	454	(8.5)
	United Kingdom	90.4	(1.2)	528	(2.6)	534	(2.5)	537	(2.7)	7.0	(0.9)	510	(9.4)	505	(11.1)	519	(10.2)
	United States	86.4	(2.1)	511	(6.5)	500	(7.2)	506	(6.7)	7.4	(1.4)	478	(19.4)	467	(20.2)	462	(22.6)
	OECD total	*91.3*	*(0.6)*	*503*	*(1.9)*	*500*	*(2.0)*	*505*	*(1.9)*	*4.6*	*(0.4)*	*479*	*(9.1)*	*476*	*(10.0)*	*467*	*(11.1)*
	OECD average	*91.0*	*(0.2)*	*506*	*(0.6)*	*504*	*(0.7)*	*504*	*(0.7)*	*4.3*	*(0.1)*	*467*	*(2.8)*	*474*	*(2.9)*	*462*	*(3.4)*
NON-OECD COUNTRIES	Brazil	99.6	(0.1)	398	(3.0)	337	(3.7)	377	(3.2)	0.3	(0.1)	c	c	c	c	c	c
	Latvia	77.9	(2.4)	462	(6.0)	466	(5.4)	466	(6.0)	1.5	(0.3)	423	(15.1)	c	c	433	(20.9)
	Liechtenstein	79.4	(2.1)	500	(5.0)	528	(7.9)	492	(7.4)	10.2	(1.8)	446	(14.8)	c	c	c	c
	Russian Federation	95.4	(0.6)	463	(4.3)	480	(5.6)	461	(4.9)	1.8	(0.3)	452	(9.9)	473	(11.7)	452	(12.7)
	Netherlands[4]	88.1	(1.8)	542	(3.0)	575	(3.2)	541	(3.7)	7.4	(1.2)	470	(14.2)	494	(16.0)	441	(17.4)

Non-native students (students who were foreign-born and whose parents were also foreign-born)

			Performance					
		% of students[2]	S.E.	Combined reading literacy scale		Mathematical literacy scale		Scientific literacy scale	
				Mean score	S.E.	Mean score	S.E.	Mean score	S.E.
OECD COUNTRIES	Australia	11.9	(1.2)	513	(9.3)	526	(9.5)	514	(10.5)
	Austria	5.9	(0.6)	422	(8.2)	429	(9.9)	434	(9.8)
	Belgium	3.4	(0.4)	431	(9.5)	432	(11.1)	419	(10.7)
	Canada	9.8	(0.6)	511	(4.9)	522	(5.1)	503	(5.4)
	Czech Republic	0.5	(0.1)	c	c	c	c	c	c
	Denmark	3.8	(0.4)	433	(7.6)	447	(9.1)	413	(11.6)
	Finland	1.0	(0.2)	468	(12.9)	c	c	459	(17.0)
	France	2.2	(0.3)	434	(11.5)	441	(13.9)	408	(16.8)
	Germany	10.1	(0.6)	419	(7.5)	423	(9.7)	410	(7.9)
	Greece	4.3	(0.9)	403	(17.5)	351	(17.5)	386	(18.5)
	Hungary	1.6	(0.2)	486	(11.6)	491	(18.2)	472	(14.8)
	Iceland	0.6	(0.1)	c	c	c	c	c	c
	Ireland	1.4	(0.3)	573	(9.2)	c	c	572	(14.9)
	Italy	0.8	(0.2)	445	(15.1)	c	c	c	c
	Japan	0.1	(0.1)	c	c	c	c	c	c
	Korea[3]	a	a	a	a	a	a	a	a
	Luxembourg	16.4	(0.6)	370	(4.7)	385	(5.7)	374	(6.5)
	Mexico	2.5	(0.3)	329	(8.2)	309	(13.9)	355	(11.0)
	New Zealand	13.2	(0.8)	507	(7.6)	538	(8.4)	510	(7.9)
	Norway	3.1	(0.3)	449	(8.5)	436	(12.4)	443	(9.6)
	Poland	0.2	(0.1)	c	c	c	c	c	c
	Portugal	1.4	(0.2)	450	(15.8)	c	c	420	(16.1)
	Spain	1.4	(0.3)	460	(17.8)	459	(25.0)	434	(23.6)
	Sweden	5.9	(0.6)	450	(7.2)	446	(12.1)	439	(9.1)
	Switzerland	11.4	(0.7)	402	(6.1)	443	(7.1)	407	(6.6)
	United Kingdom	2.6	(0.4)	456	(15.1)	483	(18.0)	457	(16.5)
	United States	6.1	(0.9)	466	(10.0)	451	(10.7)	473	(14.2)
	OECD total	*4.1*	*(0.3)*	*452*	*(4.9)*	*450*	*(5.6)*	*453*	*(6.5)*
	OECD average	*4.7*	*(0.1)*	*446*	*(2.5)*	*456*	*(3.0)*	*444*	*(3.0)*
NON-OECD COUNTRIES	Brazil	0.1	(0.1)	c	c	c	c	c	c
	Latvia	20.6	(2.4)	454	(7.3)	464	(8.2)	451	(8.4)
	Liechtenstein	10.4	(1.6)	392	(21.4)	c	c	c	c
	Russian Federation	2.8	(0.4)	458	(9.6)	461	(15.3)	467	(12.7)
	Netherlands[4]	4.5	(0.8)	453	(15.6)	470	(19.9)	437	(15.4)

1. Mean scores marked in bold indicate that the difference in performance between native and first-generation students is statistically significant.
2. Percentage of students participating in the assessment of reading literacy in their respective category.
3. This question was not asked in Korea.
4. Response rate is too low to ensure comparability (see Annex A3).

Table 6.11

Students performance on the combined reading, mathematical and scientific literacy scales, by language spoken at home
Results based on students' self-reports

	Language spoken at home most of the time IS DIFFERENT from the language of assessment, from other official languages or from other national dialects								Language spoken at home most of the time IS THE SAME as the language of assessment, other official languages or another national dialects							
			Performance[1]								Performance[1]					
			Combined reading literacy scale		Mathematical literacy scale		Scientific literacy scale				Combined reading literacy scale		Mathematical literacy scale		Scientific literacy scale	
	% of students[2]	S.E.	Mean score	S.E.	Mean score	S.E.	Mean score	S.E.	% of students[2]	S.E.	Mean score	S.E.	Mean score	S.E.	Mean score	S.E.
OECD COUNTRIES																
Australia	17.0	(1.6)	**504**	(7.6)	**522**	(6.8)	**496**	(9.4)	83.0	(1.6)	534	(3.6)	537	(3.6)	534	(3.2)
Austria	6.7	(0.7)	**434**	(7.2)	**443**	(9.2)	**439**	(9.7)	93.3	(0.7)	515	(2.4)	523	(2.5)	527	(2.4)
Belgium	4.9	(0.6)	**403**	(8.6)	**420**	(10.6)	**381**	(9.4)	95.2	(0.6)	518	(3.7)	531	(3.9)	507	(4.5)
Canada	9.4	(0.6)	**506**	(3.8)	**522**	(4.3)	**498**	(4.5)	90.6	(0.6)	540	(1.5)	536	(1.4)	534	(1.6)
Czech Republic	0.8	(0.2)	c	c	c	c	c	c	99.2	(0.2)	494	(2.2)	499	(2.7)	513	(2.4)
Denmark	6.7	(0.4)	**425**	(8.1)	**446**	(8.7)	**405**	(11.5)	93.3	(0.4)	503	(2.2)	520	(2.4)	488	(2.7)
Finland	1.3	(0.2)	**470**	(12.5)	**469**	(19.2)	**472**	(19.1)	98.7	(0.2)	548	(2.6)	537	(2.1)	539	(2.4)
France	4.0	(0.5)	**442**	(7.7)	**463**	(8.8)	**431**	(9.8)	96.0	(0.5)	510	(2.6)	521	(2.7)	506	(3.1)
Germany	7.9	(0.8)	**386**	(13.9)	**395**	(11.4)	**390**	(10.3)	92.1	(0.8)	500	(2.9)	505	(2.6)	504	(2.6)
Greece	2.8	(0.6)	**407**	(18.3)	**371**	(17.4)	**379**	(20.8)	97.2	(0.6)	477	(4.8)	451	(5.6)	464	(4.6)
Hungary	m	m	m	m	m	m	m	m	m	m	m	m	m	m	m	m
Iceland	1.9	(0.3)	**463**	(13.4)	c	c	471	(21.5)	98.1	(0.3)	509	(1.5)	516	(2.2)	497	(2.2)
Ireland	0.9	(0.2)	c	c	c	c	c	c	99.1	(0.2)	527	(3.2)	503	(2.7)	514	(3.1)
Italy	0.7	(0.2)	c	c	c	c	c	c	99.3	(0.2)	491	(3.0)	460	(3.1)	481	(3.1)
Japan	0.3	(0.1)	c	c	c	c	c	c	99.7	(0.1)	525	(5.2)	559	(5.5)	553	(5.5)
Korea[3]	a	a	a	a	a	a	a	a	a	a	a	a	a	a	a	a
Luxembourg	18.3	(0.7)	**367**	(4.1)	**389**	(5.6)	**377**	(5.3)	81.7	(0.7)	460	(1.6)	462	(2.2)	459	(2.4)
Mexico	0.2	(0.1)	c	c	c	c	c	c	99.8	(0.1)	422	(3.4)	388	(3.4)	422	(3.3)
New Zealand	9.6	(0.6)	**469**	(9.6)	**511**	(10.2)	**474**	(9.6)	90.4	(0.6)	541	(2.6)	545	(3.2)	540	(2.4)
Norway	5.3	(0.4)	**459**	(8.4)	**456**	(11.1)	**449**	(9.4)	94.7	(0.4)	510	(2.8)	504	(2.9)	506	(2.9)
Poland	0.5	(0.2)	c	c	c	c	c	c	99.5	(0.2)	482	(4.4)	474	(5.1)	486	(5.2)
Portugal	1.5	(0.2)	**416**	(13.8)	**424**	(21.1)	**385**	(15.4)	98.5	(0.2)	471	(4.6)	455	(4.0)	461	(4.0)
Spain	1.2	(0.2)	**456**	(16.0)	**437**	(25.5)	**442**	(23.2)	98.8	(0.2)	495	(2.6)	478	(3.0)	493	(2.8)
Sweden	6.7	(0.6)	**456**	(7.1)	**448**	(10.9)	**450**	(9.3)	93.3	(0.6)	523	(2.0)	517	(2.3)	519	(2.5)
Switzerland	13.6	(0.6)	**414**	(6.1)	**455**	(7.3)	**419**	(6.4)	86.4	(0.6)	509	(4.1)	543	(4.3)	508	(4.5)
United Kingdom	4.1	(0.7)	**470**	(12.8)	**476**	(14.1)	**481**	(16.4)	95.9	(0.7)	528	(2.5)	534	(2.5)	536	(2.6)
United States	10.8	(2.4)	**438**	(13.1)	**430**	(11.3)	**440**	(16.0)	89.2	(2.4)	514	(5.8)	503	(6.7)	509	(6.2)
OECD total	*5.5*	*(0.7)*	*443*	*(8.2)*	*443*	*(8.5)*	*443*	*(9.6)*	*94.5*	*(0.7)*	*503*	*(1.8)*	*500*	*(1.9)*	*505*	*(1.8)*
OECD average	*5.5*	*(0.2)*	*440*	*(2.6)*	*454*	*(3.0)*	*438*	*(2.8)*	*94.5*	*(0.2)*	*506*	*(0.6)*	*503*	*(0.7)*	*504*	*(0.7)*
NON-OECD COUNTRIES																
Brazil	0.8	(0.2)	c	c	c	c	c	c	99.2	(0.2)	397	(3.0)	335	(3.7)	376	(3.3)
Latvia	0.0	(0.0)	a	a	a	a	a	a	100.0	(0.0)	460	(5.2)	464	(4.4)	462	(5.5)
Liechtenstein	20.7	(2.2)	**441**	(14.3)	**490**	(18.6)	**432**	(18.6)	79.3	(2.2)	494	(5.1)	520	(8.3)	488	(7.4)
Russian Federation	7.3	(2.1)	**432**	(9.3)	**465**	(14.9)	**437**	(10.2)	92.7	(2.1)	465	(4.3)	480	(5.8)	462	(5.1)
Netherlands[4]	6.3	(1.1)	466	(13.1)	496	(14.9)	457	(13.9)	93.7	(1.1)	539	(2.7)	571	(3.0)	538	(3.3)

Increased likelihood of students who do not speak the language of assessment at home scoring in the bottom quarter of the national reading literacy performance distribution[5]

	Ratio	S.E.
OECD COUNTRIES		
Australia	1.6	(0.12)
Austria	2.3	(0.18)
Belgium	2.8	(0.23)
Canada	1.6	(0.07)
Czech Republic	c	c
Denmark	2.5	(0.17)
Finland	c	c
France	2.3	(0.21)
Germany	2.9	(0.29)
Greece	2.3	(0.41)
Hungary	m	m
Iceland	c	c
Ireland	c	c
Italy	c	c
Japan	c	c
Korea[3]		
Luxembourg	2.8	(0.13)
Mexico	c	c
New Zealand	2.1	(0.15)
Norway	1.8	(0.15)
Poland	c	c
Portugal	c	c
Spain	c	c
Sweden	2.1	(0.19)
Switzerland	2.8	(0.15)
United Kingdom	1.9	(0.24)
United States	2.1	(0.22)
OECD total	*2.0*	*(0.12)*
OECD average	*2.1*	*(0.05)*
NON-OECD COUNTRIES		
Brazil	c	c
Latvia	a	a
Liechtenstein	c	c
Russian Federation	1.5	(0.22)
Netherlands[4]	2.2	(0.29)

1. Mean scores marked in bold indicate that the difference between students who do not speak the language of assessment at home and those who do is statistically significant.
2. Percentage of students participating in the assessment of reading literacy in their respective category.
3. This question was not asked in Korea.
4. Response rate is too low to ensure comparability (see Annex A3).
5. Ratios statistically significantly greater than 1 are marked in bold.

Table 7.1
Index of teacher support and performance on the combined reading literacy scale, by national quarters of the index
Results based on students' self-reports

	Index of teacher support[1]							
	All students		Bottom quarter		Middle half		Top quarter	
	Mean index	S.E.	Mean index	S.E.	Mean index	S.E.	Mean index	S.E.
Australia	0.41	(0.02)	0.07	(0.03)	0.41	(0.01)	0.78	(0.02)
Austria	−0.25	(0.03)	−0.75	(0.04)	−0.24	(0.02)	0.22	(0.03)
Belgium	−0.28	(0.02)	−0.67	(0.02)	−0.29	(0.01)	0.11	(0.02)
Canada	0.31	(0.01)	−0.08	(0.02)	0.31	(0.01)	0.69	(0.01)
Czech Republic	−0.50	(0.02)	−0.88	(0.03)	−0.49	(0.01)	−0.13	(0.03)
Denmark	0.17	(0.02)	−0.20	(0.03)	0.18	(0.01)	0.54	(0.02)
Finland	0.02	(0.02)	−0.33	(0.03)	0.04	(0.01)	0.36	(0.02)
France	−0.20	(0.03)	−0.62	(0.03)	−0.18	(0.01)	0.17	(0.02)
Germany	−0.34	(0.02)	−0.78	(0.02)	−0.34	(0.01)	0.11	(0.02)
Greece	0.14	(0.02)	−0.24	(0.02)	0.16	(0.01)	0.48	(0.03)
Hungary	0.05	(0.02)	−0.32	(0.03)	0.06	(0.01)	0.43	(0.04)
Iceland	0.13	(0.01)	−0.27	(0.03)	0.13	(0.02)	0.55	(0.03)
Ireland	0.13	(0.03)	−0.27	(0.02)	0.13	(0.02)	0.52	(0.02)
Italy	−0.28	(0.02)	−0.65	(0.02)	−0.29	(0.01)	0.13	(0.02)
Japan	−0.17	(0.04)	−0.72	(0.05)	−0.15	(0.02)	0.34	(0.04)
Korea	−0.67	(0.03)	−1.03	(0.02)	−0.68	(0.01)	−0.31	(0.03)
Luxembourg	−0.34	(0.02)	−0.64	(0.03)	−0.33	(0.03)	−0.03	(0.04)
Mexico	0.07	(0.03)	−0.30	(0.03)	0.08	(0.01)	0.45	(0.02)
New Zealand	0.34	(0.02)	0.00	(0.03)	0.34	(0.02)	0.67	(0.03)
Norway	−0.03	(0.03)	−0.42	(0.04)	−0.01	(0.01)	0.34	(0.02)
Poland	−0.39	(0.03)	−0.73	(0.03)	−0.39	(0.01)	−0.04	(0.04)
Portugal	0.47	(0.02)	0.12	(0.03)	0.48	(0.01)	0.79	(0.02)
Spain	0.09	(0.03)	−0.38	(0.03)	0.09	(0.02)	0.58	(0.03)
Sweden	0.21	(0.02)	−0.13	(0.03)	0.23	(0.01)	0.53	(0.02)
Switzerland	0.01	(0.03)	−0.47	(0.03)	0.03	(0.01)	0.46	(0.03)
United Kingdom	0.50	(0.02)	0.14	(0.02)	0.52	(0.01)	0.83	(0.01)
United States	0.34	(0.04)	−0.13	(0.05)	0.36	(0.02)	0.81	(0.04)
OECD total	*0.02*	*(0.01)*	*−0.41*	*(0.02)*	*0.04*	*(0.01)*	*0.44*	*(0.02)*
OECD average	*0.00*	*(0.01)*	*−0.40*	*(0.01)*	*0.01*	*(0.01)*	*0.39*	*(0.01)*
Brazil	0.38	(0.03)	−0.07	(0.04)	0.38	(0.02)	0.81	(0.02)
Latvia	−0.20	(0.03)	−0.52	(0.03)	−0.22	(0.01)	0.16	(0.03)
Liechtenstein	0.09	(0.05)	−0.33	(0.09)	0.07	(0.06)	0.47	(0.10)
Russian Federation	0.16	(0.02)	−0.20	(0.02)	0.16	(0.01)	0.51	(0.02)
Netherlands[2]	−0.21	(0.03)	−0.52	(0.04)	−0.19	(0.01)	0.07	(0.02)

Performance on the combined reading literacy scale, by national quarters of the index of teacher support[3]

	Bottom quarter		Middle half		Top quarter		Change in the combined reading literacy score per unit of the index of teacher support[3]	
	Mean score	S.E.	Mean score	S.E.	Mean score	S.E.	Change	S.E.
Australia	524	(8.1)	533	(5.0)	529	(7.9)	7.37	(2.24)
Austria	528	(9.1)	498	(5.3)	510	(9.1)	−0.62	(2.34)
Belgium	526	(8.8)	514	(5.9)	485	(14.0)	−4.83	(2.38)
Canada	536	(2.3)	536	(2.5)	534	(3.4)	4.42	(0.97)
Czech Republic	514	(8.1)	498	(4.9)	494	(6.5)	0.77	(2.32)
Denmark	490	(6.4)	500	(3.0)	507	(4.1)	11.65	(2.34)
Finland	543	(5.0)	551	(2.7)	543	(7.0)	5.48	(2.03)
France	**524**	(8.2)	501	(5.7)	**499**	(9.4)	−2.53	(1.77)
Germany	532	(7.2)	500	(5.1)	443	(9.6)	**−12.55**	(2.12)
Greece	466	(12.5)	489	(9.2)	459	(9.0)	2.20	(2.42)
Hungary	490	(11.3)	491	(7.6)	453	(12.9)	−2.43	(2.76)
Iceland	507	(3.0)	506	(2.0)	514	(2.8)	**8.87**	(1.92)
Ireland	530	(6.1)	530	(5.1)	521	(6.9)	−0.13	(1.90)
Italy	523	(7.1)	492	(6.0)	444	(8.6)	**−11.46**	(2.21)
Japan	517	(12.2)	522	(8.3)	537	(7.5)	**6.23**	(2.28)
Korea	516	(6.3)	526	(4.9)	532	(7.6)	**5.56**	(1.61)
Luxembourg	493	(2.4)	426	(2.3)	430	(2.9)	**−5.13**	(1.48)
Mexico	435	(10.1)	422	(6.3)	410	(8.5)	−2.60	(2.29)
New Zealand	524	(6.5)	534	(4.1)	530	(8.3)	**5.26**	(2.45)
Norway	502	(5.1)	511	(4.3)	504	(6.0)	**14.95**	(2.26)
Poland	**444**	(12.5)	493	(8.7)	**499**	(12.1)	**9.20**	(2.96)
Portugal	483	(12.5)	469	(6.3)	462	(9.9)	−1.33	(2.78)
Spain	487	(6.0)	497	(4.0)	494	(6.4)	2.53	(1.89)
Sweden	516	(5.0)	514	(3.5)	524	(3.9)	**6.20**	(1.82)
Switzerland	546	(9.2)	489	(5.7)	458	(7.6)	**−13.40**	(2.24)
United Kingdom	522	(6.6)	525	(6.4)	529	(7.6)	**6.66**	(1.45)
United States	502	(12.8)	508	(8.3)	507	(12.3)	**6.87**	(2.61)
OECD total	*503*	*(3.7)*	*502*	*(2.8)*	*496*	*(4.4)*	*2.96*	*(0.90)*
OECD average	*508*	*(1.8)*	*503*	*(1.3)*	*495*	*(2.0)*	*2.82*	*(0.45)*
Brazil	390	(8.1)	394	(4.7)	410	(6.6)	**4.60**	(1.79)
Latvia	456	(11.9)	451	(6.0)	481	(9.7)	**15.56**	(2.42)
Liechtenstein	**584**	(7.3)	480	(4.8)	**408**	(10.3)	**−14.19**	(5.19)
Russian Federation	465	(5.8)	462	(7.3)	463	(8.0)	**6.40**	(1.41)
Netherlands[2]	**563**	(11.5)	528	(7.3)	**510**	(13.3)	−5.54	(3.55)

1. For the definition of the index see Annex A1.
2. Response rate is too low to ensure comparability (see Annex A3).
3. For explained variation see Annex A2. Unit changes marked in bold are statistically significant. Where bottom and top quarters are marked in bold this indicates that their difference is statistically significant.

Table 7.2
Index of student-related factors affecting school climate and performance on the combined reading literacy scale, by national quarters of the index

Results based on reports from school principals and reported proportionate to the number of 15-year-olds enrolled in the school

	Index of student-related factors affecting school climate[1]							
	All students		Bottom quarter		Middle half		Top quarter	
	Mean index	S.E.	Mean index	S.E.	Mean index	S.E.	Mean index	S.E.
OECD COUNTRIES								
Australia	0.06	(0.06)	−1.12	(0.05)	0.01	(0.04)	1.32	(0.09)
Austria	−0.16	(0.06)	−1.16	(0.05)	−0.14	(0.03)	0.80	(0.06)
Belgium	0.26	(0.07)	−1.32	(0.10)	0.30	(0.04)	1.75	(0.07)
Canada	−0.27	(0.03)	−1.24	(0.04)	−0.30	(0.02)	0.77	(0.04)
Czech Republic	0.56	(0.06)	−0.57	(0.06)	0.51	(0.04)	1.76	(0.06)
Denmark	0.73	(0.06)	−0.34	(0.08)	0.70	(0.04)	1.85	(0.07)
Finland	−0.42	(0.05)	−1.10	(0.04)	−0.46	(0.02)	0.35	(0.07)
France	m	m	m	m	m	m	m	m
Germany	−0.10	(0.05)	−1.04	(0.08)	−0.11	(0.02)	0.85	(0.08)
Greece	−1.05	(0.10)	−2.45	(0.07)	−1.22	(0.07)	0.65	(0.11)
Hungary	0.15	(0.09)	−1.45	(0.08)	0.23	(0.06)	1.52	(0.07)
Iceland	−0.22	(0.00)	−1.06	(0.00)	−0.31	(0.00)	0.77	(0.01)
Ireland	−0.22	(0.06)	−1.23	(0.06)	−0.22	(0.04)	0.73	(0.07)
Italy	0.18	(0.07)	−1.06	(0.07)	0.13	(0.04)	1.47	(0.08)
Japan	0.69	(0.09)	−0.61	(0.08)	0.73	(0.06)	1.88	(0.08)
Korea	0.92	(0.08)	−0.61	(0.13)	0.98	(0.05)	2.27	(0.07)
Luxembourg	−0.41	(0.00)	−1.27	(0.00)	−0.43	(0.00)	0.35	(0.00)
Mexico	−0.05	(0.09)	−1.62	(0.14)	0.06	(0.04)	1.27	(0.05)
New Zealand	−0.19	(0.05)	−1.16	(0.08)	−0.16	(0.02)	0.72	(0.06)
Norway	−0.21	(0.05)	−1.12	(0.07)	−0.23	(0.03)	0.71	(0.06)
Poland	0.03	(0.11)	−1.27	(0.08)	−0.02	(0.06)	1.36	(0.11)
Portugal	−0.33	(0.07)	−1.35	(0.07)	−0.39	(0.04)	0.79	(0.09)
Spain	0.00	(0.07)	−1.33	(0.09)	−0.01	(0.04)	1.30	(0.07)
Sweden	−0.05	(0.06)	−0.89	(0.05)	−0.08	(0.03)	0.82	(0.07)
Switzerland	−0.01	(0.06)	−1.01	(0.06)	−0.06	(0.03)	1.07	(0.06)
United Kingdom	0.04	(0.05)	−1.01	(0.05)	−0.07	(0.03)	1.30	(0.09)
United States	−0.23	(0.07)	−1.19	(0.08)	−0.21	(0.05)	0.65	(0.05)
OECD total	*0.09*	*(0.02)*	*−1.09*	*(0.03)*	*0.09*	*(0.02)*	*1.22*	*(0.04)*
OECD average	*0.00*	*(0.01)*	*−1.13*	*(0.02)*	*−0.02*	*(0.01)*	*1.13*	*(0.02)*
NON-OECD COUNTRIES								
Brazil	−0.35	(0.08)	−1.83	(0.11)	−0.37	(0.04)	1.14	(0.08)
Latvia	0.00	(0.07)	−1.01	(0.06)	−0.04	(0.04)	1.05	(0.14)
Liechtenstein	m	m	m	m	m	m	m	m
Russian Federation	−0.96	(0.08)	−2.46	(0.09)	−1.01	(0.06)	0.60	(0.11)
Netherlands[2]	−0.11	(0.08)	−1.19	(0.09)	−0.07	(0.04)	0.87	(0.06)

	Performance on the combined reading literacy scale, by national quarters of the index of student-related factors affecting school climate[3]						Change in the combined reading literacy score per unit of the index of student-related factors affecting school climate[3]	
	Bottom quarter		Middle half		Top quarter			
	Mean score	S.E.	Mean score	S.E.	Mean score	S.E.	Change	S.E.
OECD COUNTRIES								
Australia	503	(7.1)	524	(3.7)	562	(8.4)	23.35	(3.08)
Austria	488	(9.1)	513	(5.9)	517	(7.5)	16.37	(5.67)
Belgium	443	(11.5)	517	(5.6)	554	(9.5)	37.91	(4.02)
Canada	519	(3.7)	539	(2.0)	543	(2.3)	12.41	(1.97)
Czech Republic	458	(10.4)	495	(4.9)	519	(7.7)	31.03	(4.84)
Denmark	480	(6.9)	499	(4.0)	505	(5.3)	14.48	(4.70)
Finland	545	(4.1)	544	(4.3)	554	(5.1)	4.30	(3.67)
France	m	m	m	m	m	m	m	m
Germany	412	(11.1)	506	(8.0)	519	(8.5)	50.74	(7.09)
Greece	474	(14.1)	472	(8.1)	478	(12.2)	1.49	(4.98)
Hungary	429	(8.7)	480	(7.2)	527	(8.6)	29.41	(3.80)
Iceland	502	(3.1)	505	(2.1)	517	(3.2)	8.29	(1.93)
Ireland	502	(8.2)	528	(3.8)	548	(6.3)	21.87	(3.92)
Italy	445	(12.0)	489	(5.5)	526	(7.3)	33.98	(4.93)
Japan	471	(11.1)	532	(6.5)	553	(7.9)	34.74	(4.85)
Korea	489	(7.1)	531	(3.9)	547	(3.7)	19.55	(2.59)
Luxembourg	453	(2.5)	419	(2.6)	481	(2.9)	11.44	(2.09)
Mexico	407	(9.1)	430	(6.7)	423	(9.5)	4.31	(4.00)
New Zealand	504	(6.5)	536	(4.6)	546	(5.9)	26.17	(4.03)
Norway	503	(5.6)	505	(4.4)	509	(5.3)	5.25	(3.45)
Poland	421	(12.2)	481	(9.4)	530	(8.5)	38.90	(6.53)
Portugal	451	(9.5)	473	(6.2)	484	(11.0)	13.28	(5.50)
Spain	471	(5.8)	490	(4.1)	519	(5.9)	18.15	(2.53)
Sweden	498	(5.7)	520	(3.2)	526	(4.9)	15.70	(3.74)
Switzerland	463	(8.3)	502	(7.0)	508	(8.1)	19.05	(5.15)
United Kingdom	487	(5.9)	521	(3.8)	567	(7.6)	36.69	(3.12)
United States	489	(13.1)	505	(7.7)	520	(10.0)	15.92	(9.23)
OECD total	*466*	*(3.9)*	*503*	*(2.2)*	*522*	*(3.2)*	*23.59*	*(1.78)*
OECD average	*473*	*(1.8)*	*502*	*(1.0)*	*522*	*(1.5)*	*20.11*	*(0.85)*
NON-OECD COUNTRIES								
Brazil	383	(6.2)	389	(5.4)	422	(6.2)	12.21	(2.70)
Latvia	452	(10.5)	450	(6.3)	484	(14.6)	9.52	(7.99)
Liechtenstein	m	m	m	m	m	m	m	m
Russian Federation	450	(6.7)	463	(6.5)	471	(8.4)	7.83	(3.20)
Netherlands[2]	458	(13.2)	545	(8.1)	572	(7.6)	52.09	(6.24)

1. For the definition of the index see Annex A1. *The scale was inverted so that positive and high values represent a positive school climate with regard to student-related factors*.
2. Response rate is too low to ensure comparability (see Annex A3).
3. For explained variation see Annex A2. Unit changes marked in bold are statistically significant. Where bottom and top quarters are marked in bold this indicates that their difference is statistically significant.

Table 7.3
Index of disciplinary climate and performance on the combined reading literacy scale, by national quarters of the index
Results based on students' self-reports

	Index of disciplinary climate[1]							
	All students		Bottom quarter		Middle half		Top quarter	
	Mean index	S.E.	Mean index	S.E.	Mean index	S.E.	Mean index	S.E.
OECD COUNTRIES								
Australia	−0.09	(0.03)	−0.51	(0.03)	−0.10	(0.02)	0.33	(0.02)
Austria	0.19	(0.04)	−0.37	(0.03)	0.18	(0.02)	0.76	(0.04)
Belgium	−0.12	(0.02)	−0.57	(0.02)	−0.12	(0.01)	0.33	(0.02)
Canada	−0.14	(0.01)	−0.52	(0.01)	−0.15	(0.01)	0.27	(0.01)
Czech Republic	0.14	(0.03)	−0.43	(0.04)	0.11	(0.02)	0.77	(0.03)
Denmark	−0.20	(0.02)	−0.57	(0.02)	−0.20	(0.01)	0.18	(0.02)
Finland	−0.16	(0.03)	−0.55	(0.03)	−0.18	(0.01)	0.27	(0.04)
France	−0.05	(0.03)	−0.49	(0.02)	−0.07	(0.01)	0.42	(0.03)
Germany	0.10	(0.02)	−0.39	(0.04)	0.10	(0.02)	0.55	(0.02)
Greece	−0.42	(0.02)	−0.78	(0.02)	−0.42	(0.02)	−0.06	(0.03)
Hungary	0.23	(0.04)	−0.38	(0.05)	0.23	(0.02)	0.80	(0.03)
Iceland	−0.08	(0.01)	−0.62	(0.03)	−0.07	(0.02)	0.44	(0.03)
Ireland	0.09	(0.03)	−0.37	(0.03)	0.08	(0.02)	0.54	(0.04)
Italy	−0.24	(0.03)	−0.74	(0.03)	−0.25	(0.02)	0.28	(0.03)
Japan	0.49	(0.05)	−0.22	(0.05)	0.51	(0.03)	1.14	(0.05)
Korea	0.20	(0.03)	−0.26	(0.03)	0.20	(0.02)	0.63	(0.04)
Luxembourg	0.12	(0.02)	−0.10	(0.04)	0.09	(0.02)	0.37	(0.04)
Mexico	0.17	(0.03)	−0.24	(0.03)	0.15	(0.01)	0.61	(0.03)
New Zealand	−0.15	(0.02)	−0.48	(0.03)	−0.16	(0.02)	0.21	(0.03)
Norway	−0.36	(0.03)	−0.72	(0.03)	−0.38	(0.01)	0.02	(0.03)
Poland	0.37	(0.04)	−0.24	(0.04)	0.39	(0.02)	0.91	(0.04)
Portugal	−0.05	(0.02)	−0.32	(0.02)	−0.05	(0.01)	0.20	(0.02)
Spain	−0.17	(0.03)	−0.65	(0.04)	−0.16	(0.01)	0.27	(0.02)
Sweden	−0.19	(0.02)	−0.57	(0.03)	−0.19	(0.01)	0.17	(0.02)
Switzerland	0.30	(0.03)	−0.23	(0.03)	0.30	(0.02)	0.83	(0.03)
United Kingdom	0.02	(0.03)	−0.44	(0.02)	0.01	(0.02)	0.49	(0.04)
United States	0.03	(0.03)	−0.40	(0.02)	0.01	(0.01)	0.47	(0.04)
OECD total	*0.09*	*(0.01)*	*−0.40*	*(0.01)*	*0.08*	*(0.01)*	*0.57*	*(0.02)*
OECD average	*0.00*	*(0.01)*	*−0.45*	*(0.01)*	*−0.01*	*(0.01)*	*0.45*	*(0.01)*
NON-OECD COUNTRIES								
Brazil	−0.34	(0.02)	−0.72	(0.02)	−0.35	(0.01)	0.06	(0.04)
Latvia	0.38	(0.03)	−0.07	(0.04)	0.40	(0.01)	0.79	(0.02)
Liechtenstein	0.35	(0.05)	0.05	(0.10)	0.36	(0.08)	0.52	(0.06)
Russian Federation	0.45	(0.03)	0.01	(0.02)	0.42	(0.02)	0.92	(0.03)
Netherlands[2]	−0.33	(0.03)	−0.73	(0.05)	−0.31	(0.02)	0.02	(0.03)

Performance on the combined reading literacy scale, by national quarters
of the index of disciplinary climate[3]

	Bottom quarter		Middle half		Top quarter		Change in the combined reading literacy score per unit of the index of disciplinary climate[3]	
	Mean score	S.E.	Mean score	S.E.	Mean score	S.E.	Change	S.E.
OECD COUNTRIES								
Australia	**506**	(5.3)	528	(5.5)	**553**	(7.9)	**16.69**	(2.26)
Austria	**483**	(8.3)	513	(5.3)	**524**	(8.2)	**4.98**	(1.99)
Belgium	511	(9.2)	504	(7.1)	521	(14.9)	3.15	(2.48)
Canada	**522**	(3.9)	536	(2.0)	**547**	(2.7)	**13.28**	(0.95)
Czech Republic	**468**	(6.0)	506	(4.6)	**523**	(6.7)	**12.37**	(1.78)
Denmark	**483**	(5.4)	501	(4.0)	**510**	(5.1)	**9.71**	(2.41)
Finland	545	(4.9)	545	(3.8)	554	(4.5)	**9.56**	(1.76)
France	507	(8.4)	497	(5.5)	523	(10.2)	1.53	(1.72)
Germany	**467**	(7.6)	496	(5.9)	**515**	(8.0)	**10.13**	(1.64)
Greece	461	(11.4)	470	(7.4)	500	(11.1)	2.96	(2.74)
Hungary	**432**	(8.9)	483	(7.5)	**525**	(8.0)	**16.05**	(3.62)
Iceland	**493**	(3.2)	513	(2.2)	**515**	(2.8)	**8.90**	(1.80)
Ireland	**509**	(7.2)	532	(4.7)	**537**	(6.6)	**15.41**	(1.67)
Italy	**442**	(9.9)	493	(5.2)	**521**	(7.7)	**14.11**	(2.13)
Japan	**475**	(10.5)	527	(6.1)	**567**	(5.9)	**17.15**	(2.98)
Korea	**501**	(8.2)	525	(4.1)	**548**	(5.6)	**6.88**	(1.41)
Luxembourg	458	(4.0)	436	(2.0)	449	(2.4)	2.41	(1.82)
Mexico	425	(9.1)	417	(6.6)	429	(9.0)	2.03	(2.89)
New Zealand	**517**	(7.1)	532	(3.6)	**541**	(7.9)	**12.47**	(2.58)
Norway	492	(6.0)	513	(3.4)	510	(6.8)	7.79	(2.66)
Poland	**418**	(10.1)	486	(8.2)	**532**	(9.3)	**20.88**	(2.41)
Portugal	452	(12.5)	470	(6.3)	491	(8.0)	**10.57**	(2.15)
Spain	**480**	(6.4)	492	(4.5)	**510**	(5.3)	**12.18**	(1.83)
Sweden	**502**	(4.0)	514	(3.1)	**537**	(4.0)	**12.44**	(1.81)
Switzerland	483	(10.5)	493	(6.9)	511	(10.2)	**9.81**	(2.42)
United Kingdom	**503**	(6.1)	524	(3.7)	**548**	(9.3)	**20.10**	(2.01)
United States	505	(9.8)	491	(9.9)	536	(9.6)	**13.17**	(2.33)
OECD total	*482*	*(3.2)*	*497*	*(2.7)*	*527*	*(3.3)*	*11.99*	*(0.79)*
OECD average	*483*	*(1.6)*	*501*	*(1.1)*	*522*	*(1.7)*	*9.45*	*(0.45)*
NON-OECD COUNTRIES								
Brazil	416	(7.9)	387	(4.9)	398	(6.2)	**−5.95**	(2.34)
Latvia	445	(7.3)	462	(7.9)	470	(14.0)	**9.04**	(2.47)
Liechtenstein	**512**	(7.1)	527	(5.8)	**414**	(7.2)	−2.59	(6.04)
Russian Federation	442	(6.8)	463	(6.8)	482	(7.6)	**10.06**	(1.84)
Netherlands[2]	532	(12.2)	520	(6.8)	555	(12.7)	2.63	(3.86)

1. For the definition of the index see Annex A1. *The scale was inverted so that positive and high values represent a positive student perception of disciplinary climate.*
2. Response rate is too low to ensure comparability (see Annex A3).
3. For explained variation see Annex A2. Unit changes marked in bold are statistically significant. Where bottom and top quarters are marked in bold this indicates that their difference is statistically significant.

Table 7.4
Index of teacher-related factors affecting school climate and performance on the combined reading literacy scale, by national quarters of the index

Results based on reports from school principals and reported proportionate to the number of 15-year-olds enrolled in the school

	Index of teacher-related factors affecting school climate[1]							
	All students		Bottom quarter		Middle half		Top quarter	
	Mean index	S.E.	Mean index	S.E.	Mean index	S.E.	Mean index	S.E.
OECD COUNTRIES								
Australia	−0.11	(0.07)	−1.13	(0.04)	−0.30	(0.05)	1.26	(0.13)
Austria	0.11	(0.05)	−0.79	(0.05)	0.03	(0.03)	1.17	(0.10)
Belgium	0.07	(0.06)	−1.17	(0.07)	0.05	(0.04)	1.34	(0.08)
Canada	0.12	(0.03)	−0.91	(0.03)	0.02	(0.02)	1.34	(0.05)
Czech Republic	0.53	(0.05)	−0.55	(0.04)	0.47	(0.04)	1.71	(0.08)
Denmark	0.81	(0.07)	−0.23	(0.05)	0.70	(0.03)	2.05	(0.06)
Finland	−0.08	(0.06)	−0.89	(0.05)	−0.10	(0.04)	0.77	(0.05)
France	m	m	m	m	m	m	m	m
Germany	−0.16	(0.05)	−1.10	(0.04)	−0.14	(0.03)	0.72	(0.05)
Greece	−1.18	(0.13)	−2.99	(0.13)	−1.38	(0.08)	0.93	(0.17)
Hungary	0.42	(0.08)	−1.01	(0.09)	0.46	(0.05)	1.69	(0.07)
Iceland	0.33	(0.00)	−0.73	(0.00)	0.27	(0.00)	1.47	(0.00)
Ireland	−0.02	(0.08)	−1.15	(0.09)	−0.17	(0.04)	1.35	(0.10)
Italy	0.05	(0.10)	−1.36	(0.07)	0.01	(0.05)	1.50	(0.10)
Japan	0.12	(0.09)	−0.99	(0.07)	−0.03	(0.03)	1.50	(0.11)
Korea	0.38	(0.08)	−0.69	(0.07)	0.37	(0.05)	1.45	(0.09)
Luxembourg	−0.47	(0.00)	−1.40	(0.00)	−0.53	(0.00)	0.20	(0.00)
Mexico	−0.65	(0.08)	−1.94	(0.09)	−0.62	(0.04)	0.56	(0.10)
New Zealand	−0.05	(0.06)	−1.07	(0.09)	−0.14	(0.03)	1.13	(0.08)
Norway	−0.29	(0.06)	−1.06	(0.05)	−0.38	(0.03)	0.62	(0.07)
Poland	0.10	(0.10)	−0.94	(0.14)	0.02	(0.05)	1.23	(0.11)
Portugal	−0.29	(0.08)	−1.31	(0.07)	−0.33	(0.04)	0.82	(0.11)
Spain	0.20	(0.07)	−1.05	(0.07)	0.13	(0.06)	1.55	(0.11)
Sweden	0.00	(0.07)	−1.00	(0.05)	−0.14	(0.03)	1.25	(0.10)
Switzerland	0.13	(0.05)	−0.74	(0.04)	0.08	(0.03)	1.09	(0.08)
United Kingdom	−0.08	(0.07)	−1.18	(0.06)	−0.22	(0.03)	1.28	(0.09)
United States	−0.07	(0.10)	−1.00	(0.05)	−0.17	(0.04)	1.01	(0.13)
OECD total	*−0.04*	*(0.03)*	*−1.12*	*(0.02)*	*−0.12*	*(0.02)*	*1.15*	*(0.04)*
OECD average	*0.00*	*(0.01)*	*−1.09*	*(0.02)*	*−0.08*	*(0.01)*	*1.18*	*(0.02)*
NON-OECD COUNTRIES								
Brazil	0.23	(0.08)	−1.31	(0.08)	0.15	(0.05)	1.88	(0.08)
Latvia	0.55	(0.08)	−0.51	(0.06)	0.53	(0.05)	1.63	(0.11)
Liechtenstein	m	m	m	m	m	m	m	m
Russian Federation	−0.75	(0.09)	−2.19	(0.06)	−0.83	(0.04)	0.81	(0.12)
Netherlands[2]	−0.63	(0.07)	−1.47	(0.05)	−0.71	(0.04)	0.33	(0.06)

Performance on the combined reading literacy scale, by national quarters of the index of teacher-related factors affecting school climate[3]

	Bottom quarter		Middle half		Top quarter		Change in the combined reading literacy score per unit of the index of teacher-related factors affecting school climate[3]	
	Mean score	S.E.	Mean score	S.E.	Mean score	S.E.	Change	S.E.
OECD COUNTRIES								
Australia	**503**	(7.2)	532	(5.1)	**546**	(7.3)	**15.16**	(3.17)
Austria	**525**	(6.5)	511	(5.2)	**484**	(7.8)	**−14.26**	(5.54)
Belgium	**467**	(8.9)	511	(7.5)	**543**	(9.4)	**24.33**	(5.79)
Canada	**529**	(3.9)	534	(2.2)	**542**	(2.6)	**4.62**	(1.85)
Czech Republic	490	(12.1)	494	(6.6)	490	(7.6)	1.64	(4.65)
Denmark	484	(6.9)	498	(3.5)	503	(5.7)	**6.46**	(3.53)
Finland	549	(4.3)	548	(2.5)	541	(7.3)	−4.96	(4.46)
France	m	m	m	m	m	m	m	m
Germany	456	(12.0)	505	(6.9)	478	(13.2)	17.09	(9.49)
Greece	492	(11.7)	465	(8.4)	475	(11.4)	−2.13	(4.05)
Hungary	464	(9.1)	483	(7.0)	487	(9.9)	**10.25**	(4.39)
Iceland	**499**	(3.2)	509	(2.1)	**512**	(2.9)	**6.69**	(1.69)
Ireland	525	(6.5)	529	(4.8)	523	(7.7)	1.82	(3.58)
Italy	472	(10.0)	488	(6.0)	503	(10.0)	7.19	(4.57)
Japan	**485**	(10.9)	531	(7.2)	**541**	(9.0)	**17.38**	(5.92)
Korea	519	(6.6)	523	(5.2)	534	(6.1)	**9.25**	(3.41)
Luxembourg	**449**	(3.4)	456	(2.6)	**422**	(2.8)	**−10.68**	(2.18)
Mexico	416	(8.7)	426	(6.3)	420	(8.1)	−0.89	(4.57)
New Zealand	**512**	(7.5)	532	(4.3)	**547**	(5.2)	**16.40**	(4.00)
Norway	499	(6.5)	505	(3.5)	512	(6.6)	6.20	(4.52)
Poland	459	(15.2)	474	(8.5)	509	(12.0)	12.54	(9.82)
Portugal	462	(9.2)	473	(8.0)	472	(10.1)	7.12	(6.26)
Spain	**484**	(5.3)	492	(4.0)	**503**	(7.6)	**9.41**	(3.15)
Sweden	508	(6.0)	519	(3.9)	520	(4.2)	3.50	(2.87)
Switzerland	483	(10.1)	504	(6.6)	483	(8.3)	−4.55	(5.76)
United Kingdom	**506**	(6.5)	515	(4.1)	**560**	(7.8)	**22.81**	(3.68)
United States	**479**	(8.5)	514	(9.3)	**514**	(11.0)	**13.08**	(5.99)
OECD total	*479*	*(3.0)*	*504*	*(2.6)*	*509*	*(3.8)*	***15.67***	*(1.53)*
OECD average	*489*	*(1.9)*	*503*	*(1.1)*	*505*	*(1.9)*	***9.95***	*(1.05)*
NON-OECD COUNTRIES								
Brazil	**385**	(7.1)	394	(4.7)	**410**	(7.4)	**6.31**	(2.99)
Latvia	472	(8.8)	455	(8.3)	454	(14.9)	−7.92	(9.12)
Liechtenstein	m	m	m	m	m	m	m	m
Russian Federation	445	(12.2)	469	(4.7)	465	(5.9)	5.46	(3.42)
Netherlands[2]	486	(14.6)	540	(6.6)	554	(8.2)	**33.53**	(8.93)

1. For the definition of the index see Annex A1. *The scale was inverted so that positive and high values represent a positive school climate with regard to teacher-related factors.*
2. Response rate is too low to ensure comparability (see Annex A3).
3. For explained variation see Annex A2. Unit changes marked in bold are statistically significant. Where bottom and top quarters are marked in bold this indicates that their difference is statistically significant.

Table 7.5
Index of principals' perception of teachers' morale and commitment and performance on the combined reading literacy scale, by national quarters of the index
Results based on reports from school principals and reported proportionate to the number of 15-year-olds enrolled in the school

| | Index of school principals' perception of teachers' morale and commitment[1] | | | | | | | |
| | All students | | Bottom quarter | | Middle half | | Top quarter | |
	Mean index	S.E.	Mean index	S.E.	Mean index	S.E.	Mean index	S.E.
Australia	0.04	(0.08)	−0.96	(0.07)	−0.08	(0.05)	1.29	(0.07)
Austria	0.63	(0.07)	−0.46	(0.06)	0.63	(0.04)	1.73	(0.03)
Belgium	−0.20	(0.06)	−1.12	(0.06)	−0.29	(0.03)	0.95	(0.06)
Canada	0.08	(0.04)	−1.04	(0.04)	0.02	(0.03)	1.34	(0.04)
Czech Republic	−0.29	(0.05)	−1.14	(0.07)	−0.31	(0.04)	0.62	(0.06)
Denmark	0.02	(0.06)	−0.85	(0.08)	−0.10	(0.05)	1.15	(0.07)
Finland	0.02	(0.06)	−0.90	(0.07)	−0.04	(0.05)	1.08	(0.09)
France	m	m	m	m	m	m	m	m
Germany	−0.01	(0.06)	−1.04	(0.07)	−0.01	(0.04)	1.02	(0.07)
Greece	0.37	(0.11)	−0.98	(0.10)	0.35	(0.08)	1.78	(0.00)
Hungary	0.27	(0.07)	−1.09	(0.09)	0.41	(0.04)	1.38	(0.07)
Iceland	0.28	(0.00)	−0.98	(0.01)	0.27	(0.00)	1.67	(0.00)
Ireland	0.19	(0.08)	−0.89	(0.10)	0.07	(0.06)	1.57	(0.05)
Italy	−0.69	(0.07)	−1.68	(0.04)	−0.77	(0.05)	0.46	(0.08)
Japan	0.14	(0.11)	−1.35	(0.11)	0.14	(0.07)	1.64	(0.05)
Korea	−0.72	(0.08)	−1.79	(0.05)	−0.77	(0.04)	0.47	(0.10)
Luxembourg	−0.02	(0.01)	−0.98	(0.00)	−0.09	(0.00)	1.22	(0.01)
Mexico	0.39	(0.09)	−1.02	(0.09)	0.42	(0.06)	1.77	(0.01)
New Zealand	0.22	(0.07)	−0.92	(0.09)	0.12	(0.06)	1.59	(0.04)
Norway	−0.09	(0.07)	−0.95	(0.08)	−0.15	(0.04)	0.91	(0.08)
Poland	−0.53	(0.09)	−1.47	(0.07)	−0.55	(0.07)	0.53	(0.10)
Portugal	−0.57	(0.07)	−1.66	(0.05)	−0.59	(0.04)	0.60	(0.07)
Spain	−0.31	(0.06)	−1.46	(0.03)	−0.33	(0.05)	0.91	(0.09)
Sweden	0.34	(0.08)	−0.83	(0.10)	0.36	(0.03)	1.51	(0.06)
Switzerland	0.43	(0.07)	−0.85	(0.05)	0.43	(0.06)	1.73	(0.03)
United Kingdom	0.02	(0.07)	−1.06	(0.08)	−0.03	(0.05)	1.27	(0.08)
United States	−0.04	(0.11)	−1.07	(0.22)	−0.17	(0.08)	1.30	(0.13)
OECD total	*−0.05*	*(0.03)*	*−1.20*	*(0.06)*	*−0.09*	*(0.02)*	*1.22*	*(0.04)*
OECD average	*0.00*	*(0.01)*	*−1.10*	*(0.02)*	*−0.04*	*(0.01)*	*1.21*	*(0.02)*
Brazil	−0.42	(0.07)	−1.58	(0.04)	−0.50	(0.04)	0.95	(0.09)
Latvia	−0.47	(0.08)	−1.49	(0.07)	−0.50	(0.04)	0.69	(0.12)
Liechtenstein	m	m	m	m	m	m	m	m
Russian Federation	−0.15	(0.07)	−1.21	(0.06)	−0.22	(0.04)	1.08	(0.07)
Netherlands[2]	−0.19	(0.09)	−0.93	(0.10)	−0.28	(0.06)	0.75	(0.11)

Performance on the combined reading literacy scale, by national quarters of the index of school principals' perception of teachers' morale and commitment[3]

| | Bottom quarter | | Middle half | | Top quarter | | Change in the combined reading literacy score per unit of the index of school principals' perception of teachers' morale and commitment[3] | |
	Mean score	S.E.	Mean score	S.E.	Mean score	S.E.	Change	S.E.
Australia	**512**	(6.9)	526	(5.4)	**550**	(6.0)	**18.24**	(3.53)
Austria	518	(8.8)	508	(5.8)	496	(8.2)	−7.83	(6.05)
Belgium	**457**	(8.8)	513	(8.0)	**553**	(8.3)	**35.77**	(6.28)
Canada	**525**	(4.1)	536	(2.0)	**539**	(2.8)	**5.57**	(1.96)
Czech Republic	493	(10.1)	481	(7.2)	511	(8.0)	5.31	(5.66)
Denmark	490	(6.8)	498	(3.6)	503	(5.7)	**8.96**	(4.12)
Finland	543	(3.6)	546	(4.4)	551	(4.7)	**5.96**	(2.75)
France	m	m	m	m	m	m	m	m
Germany	474	(11.7)	491	(6.8)	488	(13.7)	14.25	(7.60)
Greece	464	(12.7)	476	(8.4)	480	(9.4)	8.19	(5.13)
Hungary	**463**	(8.8)	476	(8.3)	**508**	(10.6)	**16.09**	(5.80)
Iceland	506	(3.4)	506	(2.3)	511	(3.2)	2.47	(1.68)
Ireland	525	(6.2)	523	(4.9)	538	(7.0)	**7.48**	(3.46)
Italy	484	(8.9)	490	(5.6)	488	(9.3)	3.89	(5.44)
Japan	**482**	(11.7)	529	(6.7)	**550**	(9.1)	**19.99**	(4.93)
Korea	**497**	(6.2)	537	(3.7)	**530**	(8.2)	**12.00**	(4.57)
Luxembourg	**414**	(3.0)	446	(2.1)	**470**	(2.8)	**22.66**	(1.71)
Mexico	409	(8.6)	426	(6.2)	428	(10.6)	5.45	(4.83)
New Zealand	**502**	(6.5)	538	(4.6)	**544**	(5.5)	**11.17**	(4.11)
Norway	505	(5.3)	506	(4.0)	505	(7.5)	1.94	(5.06)
Poland	**456**	(15.4)	468	(9.4)	**527**	(10.6)	**30.43**	(8.74)
Portugal	460	(10.4)	470	(6.3)	484	(10.6)	9.89	(5.70)
Spain	**466**	(5.4)	499	(3.9)	**506**	(5.8)	**15.69**	(3.02)
Sweden	509	(7.0)	518	(3.5)	522	(4.3)	6.27	(3.84)
Switzerland	488	(10.0)	489	(6.3)	510	(10.0)	4.04	(5.30)
United Kingdom	**507**	(5.9)	526	(4.3)	**542**	(9.9)	**17.50**	(4.31)
United States	494	(8.5)	494	(8.9)	540	(9.7)	11.85	(6.23)
OECD total	*481*	*(3.6)*	*498*	*(2.7)*	*519*	*(3.6)*	*10.37*	*(1.92)*
OECD average	*486*	*(1.8)*	*501*	*(1.1)*	*515*	*(1.7)*	*10.20*	*(0.83)*
Brazil	397	(9.2)	391	(4.7)	405	(8.0)	6.91	(4.48)
Latvia	462	(12.7)	462	(8.1)	452	(11.4)	−6.14	(7.89)
Liechtenstein	m	m	m	m	m	m	m	m
Russian Federation	**433**	(9.9)	465	(4.7)	**486**	(10.1)	**18.55**	(6.61)
Netherlands[2]	522	(12.6)	534	(9.9)	533	(12.8)	11.44	(11.18)

1. For the definition of the index see Annex A1.
2. Response rate is too low to ensure comparability (see Annex A3).
3. For explained variation see Annex A2. Unit changes marked in bold are statistically significant. Where bottom and top quarters are marked in bold this indicates that their difference is statistically significant.

Table 7.6
Index of time spent on homework per week in the language of assessment, mathematics and science courses and performance on the combined reading literacy scale, by national quarters of the index
Results based on students' self-reports

	Index of time spent on homework in the language of assessment, mathematics and science courses[1]										Performance on the combined reading literacy scale, by national quarters of the index of time spent on homework in the language of assessment, mathematics and science courses[2]							
	All students		Bottom quarter		Second quarter		Third quarter		Top quarter		Bottom quarter		Second quarter		Third quarter		Top quarter	
	Mean index	S.E.	Mean index	S.E.	Mean index	S.E.	Mean index	S.E.	Mean index	S.E.	Mean score	S.E.	Mean score	S.E.	Mean score	S.E.	Mean score	S.E.
OECD COUNTRIES																		
Australia	0.05	(0.03)	−1.12	(0.02)	−0.30	(0.01)	0.39	(0.01)	1.23	(0.02)	491	(4.8)	524	(4.1)	542	(4.3)	562	(4.9)
Austria	−0.42	(0.03)	−1.54	(0.02)	−0.66	(0.00)	−0.13	(0.01)	0.65	(0.02)	508	(4.5)	511	(3.6)	516	(3.4)	499	(3.4)
Belgium	−0.10	(0.02)	−1.27	(0.03)	−0.38	(0.01)	0.26	(0.01)	0.97	(0.01)	458	(4.9)	517	(5.8)	536	(3.0)	535	(3.1)
Canada	0.09	(0.01)	−1.22	(0.01)	−0.22	(0.00)	0.42	(0.00)	1.38	(0.01)	504	(2.5)	534	(2.0)	547	(2.0)	557	(1.9)
Czech Republic	−0.34	(0.02)	−1.58	(0.02)	−0.58	(0.01)	−0.05	(0.01)	0.83	(0.01)	483	(3.8)	496	(2.8)	514	(3.1)	512	(3.1)
Denmark	0.04	(0.02)	−0.97	(0.03)	−0.16	(0.01)	0.24	(0.01)	1.04	(0.02)	484	(5.6)	508	(3.6)	510	(3.5)	495	(3.8)
Finland	−0.28	(0.02)	−1.23	(0.02)	−0.59	(0.01)	−0.03	(0.01)	0.75	(0.01)	532	(3.6)	542	(4.5)	562	(2.9)	552	(3.3)
France	0.11	(0.02)	−0.98	(0.02)	−0.08	(0.01)	0.39	(0.01)	1.13	(0.01)	466	(4.8)	510	(3.5)	521	(3.1)	538	(2.9)
Germany	−0.01	(0.02)	−1.05	(0.02)	−0.25	(0.01)	0.27	(0.01)	1.00	(0.02)	474	(3.8)	498	(4.3)	502	(4.2)	503	(3.5)
Greece	0.65	(0.04)	−0.81	(0.03)	0.41	(0.01)	1.10	(0.01)	1.91	(0.01)	419	(6.5)	475	(6.0)	491	(4.3)	516	(4.1)
Hungary	0.35	(0.03)	−0.60	(0.02)	0.07	(0.01)	0.61	(0.01)	1.30	(0.01)	444	(5.7)	476	(5.3)	493	(4.0)	512	(4.9)
Iceland	0.02	(0.01)	−1.05	(0.02)	−0.21	(0.01)	0.26	(0.01)	1.07	(0.02)	494	(3.1)	523	(3.1)	514	(3.4)	507	(2.8)
Ireland	0.20	(0.02)	−1.15	(0.03)	−0.11	(0.01)	0.55	(0.01)	1.52	(0.02)	501	(5.0)	533	(4.3)	537	(3.7)	541	(3.9)
Italy	0.21	(0.03)	−0.89	(0.02)	−0.05	(0.01)	0.46	(0.00)	1.33	(0.02)	457	(5.8)	482	(3.1)	498	(3.3)	519	(4.3)
Japan	−0.77	(0.05)	−2.35	(0.00)	−1.17	(0.01)	−0.38	(0.01)	0.83	(0.01)	490	(7.7)	522	(4.8)	535	(5.2)	550	(5.0)
Korea	−0.16	(0.03)	−1.84	(0.01)	−0.59	(0.01)	0.30	(0.01)	1.48	(0.02)	501	(3.2)	520	(3.5)	534	(3.1)	546	(2.9)
Luxembourg	−0.20	(0.01)	−1.27	(0.02)	−0.49	(0.01)	0.04	(0.01)	0.93	(0.02)	444	(3.5)	449	(3.4)	453	(3.7)	449	(3.3)
Mexico	0.23	(0.02)	−0.89	(0.01)	−0.09	(0.01)	0.47	(0.00)	1.42	(0.02)	407	(3.9)	419	(4.6)	428	(4.1)	434	(3.9)
New Zealand	0.06	(0.02)	−1.07	(0.02)	−0.29	(0.01)	0.39	(0.01)	1.22	(0.02)	495	(4.2)	533	(4.2)	547	(3.9)	551	(4.6)
Norway	−0.08	(0.02)	−1.18	(0.02)	−0.42	(0.01)	0.29	(0.01)	1.01	(0.02)	481	(5.2)	512	(4.1)	527	(3.3)	511	(3.8)
Poland	0.24	(0.03)	−0.96	(0.02)	−0.06	(0.01)	0.54	(0.00)	1.43	(0.02)	437	(5.6)	485	(4.7)	490	(5.5)	519	(5.8)
Portugal	0.15	(0.02)	−1.04	(0.02)	−0.24	(0.01)	0.47	(0.00)	1.42	(0.02)	452	(5.6)	468	(4.9)	478	(4.9)	488	(5.5)
Spain	0.24	(0.02)	−1.05	(0.02)	−0.01	(0.01)	0.54	(0.00)	1.48	(0.02)	453	(4.3)	496	(3.0)	509	(2.9)	518	(2.5)
Sweden	−0.37	(0.02)	−1.43	(0.02)	−0.64	(0.00)	−0.14	(0.01)	0.72	(0.02)	513	(3.3)	523	(3.4)	525	(3.1)	507	(3.6)
Switzerland	−0.18	(0.02)	−1.14	(0.02)	−0.47	(0.01)	0.06	(0.01)	0.84	(0.02)	478	(4.9)	508	(4.3)	508	(5.3)	492	(5.9)
United Kingdom	0.28	(0.02)	−0.82	(0.02)	0.13	(0.01)	0.52	(0.00)	1.30	(0.02)	479	(3.1)	529	(3.4)	541	(3.7)	555	(3.7)
United States	−0.04	(0.05)	−1.34	(0.05)	−0.43	(0.01)	0.33	(0.01)	1.28	(0.03)	468	(6.4)	497	(6.0)	528	(7.3)	542	(7.6)
OECD total	*−0.04*	*(0.01)*	*−1.31*	*(0.01)*	*−0.36*	*(0.01)*	*0.29*	*(0.00)*	*1.22*	*(0.01)*	*468*	*(1.9)*	*498*	*(1.8)*	*515*	*(2.1)*	*527*	*(2.3)*
OECD average	*0.00*	*(0.00)*	*−1.18*	*(0.00)*	*−0.29*	*(0.00)*	*0.30*	*(0.00)*	*1.17*	*(0.00)*	*475*	*(1.0)*	*503*	*(0.8)*	*514*	*(0.8)*	*519*	*(0.8)*
NON-OECD COUNTRIES																		
Brazil	−0.05	(0.03)	−1.17	(0.04)	−0.44	(0.01)	0.27	(0.01)	1.15	(0.02)	386	(4.1)	387	(4.3)	401	(3.8)	419	(4.0)
Latvia	0.28	(0.02)	−0.89	(0.02)	−0.03	(0.01)	0.58	(0.01)	1.45	(0.02)	431	(7.0)	464	(6.9)	471	(5.2)	476	(6.9)
Liechtenstein	−0.25	(0.04)	−1.14	(0.06)	−0.54	(0.02)	−0.04	(0.02)	0.72	(0.06)	474	(10.8)	488	(10.7)	500	(10.8)	471	(12.1)
Russian Federation	0.60	(0.02)	−0.89	(0.03)	0.33	(0.01)	1.06	(0.01)	1.90	(0.01)	419	(5.2)	458	(4.1)	486	(4.1)	491	(4.9)
Netherlands[3]	−0.12	(0.02)	−1.12	(0.03)	−0.45	(0.01)	0.18	(0.01)	0.92	(0.03)	518	(5.3)	527	(4.7)	549	(4.0)	538	(5.4)

	Change in the combined reading literacy score per unit of the index of time spent on homework[2]		Estimated mean number of hours spent on homework in the language assessment, mathematics and science courses		Correlation between the index of time spent on homework and the international socio-economic index of occupational status
	Change	S.E.	Mean	S.E.	
OECD COUNTRIES					
Australia	27.31	(1.99)	4.7	(0.11)	0.14
Austria	−2.85	(2.14)	3.5	(0.08)	0.00
Belgium	32.94	(1.83)	4.3	(0.06)	0.17
Canada	18.99	(1.03)	5.0	(0.04)	0.13
Czech Republic	12.58	(1.72)	3.6	(0.07)	0.05
Denmark	7.55	(3.79)	4.7	(0.06)	0.04
Finland	12.97	(1.95)	3.5	(0.06)	0.02
France	31.58	(1.94)	4.9	(0.07)	0.14
Germany	11.57	(2.07)	4.5	(0.06)	0.00
Greece	34.28	(2.05)	7.0	(0.15)	0.18
Hungary	32.67	(3.19)	5.8	(0.09)	0.16
Iceland	4.17	(1.80)	4.7	(0.05)	0.03
Ireland	13.05	(1.76)	5.4	(0.08)	0.07
Italy	26.61	(2.97)	5.2	(0.09)	0.09
Japan	17.70	(2.14)	2.9	(0.13)	0.07
Korea	13.24	(1.07)	4.4	(0.10)	0.17
Luxembourg	2.58	(1.96)	4.0	(0.04)	0.00
Mexico	11.27	(1.58)	5.2	(0.07)	0.01
New Zealand	20.07	(2.05)	4.7	(0.07)	0.11
Norway	15.05	(2.18)	4.3	(0.06)	0.04
Poland	30.28	(2.40)	5.3	(0.09)	0.10
Portugal	12.28	(1.67)	5.0	(0.07)	0.09
Spain	24.65	(1.65)	5.4	(0.08)	0.14
Sweden	−1.01	(1.91)	3.3	(0.06)	0.02
Switzerland	3.38	(2.39)	3.9	(0.07)	−0.01
United Kingdom	31.92	(2.13)	5.4	(0.06)	0.16
United States	26.53	(1.97)	4.6	(0.15)	0.14
OECD total	*15.97*	*(0.87)*	*4.6*	*(0.05)*	*0.18*
OECD average	*13.87*	*(0.44)*	*4.6*	*(0.02)*	*0.17*
NON-OECD COUNTRIES					
Brazil	14.13	(1.83)	4.4	(0.09)	0.11
Latvia	16.91	(2.67)	m	m	m
Liechtenstein	−4.94	(9.92)	m	m	0.05
Russian Federation	25.93	(1.45)	m	m	m
Netherlands[3]	10.38	(3.28)	4.1	(0.08)	0.03

1. For the definition of the index see Annex A1.
2. For explained variation see Annex A2. Unit changes marked in bold are statistically significant. Where bottom and top quarters are marked in bold this indicates that their difference is statistically significant.
3. Response rate is too low to ensure comparability (see Annex A3).

Table 7.7
Student participation in educational courses outside school
Results based on-students' self-reports

		Percentage of students who have sometimes or regularly attended courses in the language of assessment, courses in other subjects, or extension or additional courses in the last three years		Percentage of students who have sometimes or regularly attended remedial courses in the language of assessment, remedial courses in other subjects, training to improve study skills or private tutoring in the last three years	
		Percentage	S.E.	Percentage	S.E.
OECD COUNTRIES	Australia	22.9	(1.1)	31.8	(1.3)
	Austria	11.0	(0.6)	35.4	(1.1)
	Belgium	21.9	(0.7)	17.3	(0.6)
	Canada	14.4	(0.4)	31.6	(0.6)
	Czech Republic	18.7	(0.7)	20.2	(0.8)
	Denmark	15.2	(0.7)	14.1	(0.7)
	Finland	4.6	(0.4)	9.1	(0.5)
	France	m	m	m	m
	Germany	10.4	(0.4)	36.2	(0.9)
	Greece	m	m	24.8	(1.0)
	Hungary	46.6	(1.1)	47.2	(0.9)
	Iceland	18.3	(0.5)	26.6	(0.7)
	Ireland	30.5	(1.0)	40.5	(1.2)
	Italy	5.6	(0.4)	48.0	(0.9)
	Japan	70.7	(1.5)	17.3	(0.9)
	Korea	63.6	(1.0)	57.5	(1.0)
	Luxembourg	22.3	(0.7)	36.6	(0.9)
	Mexico	51.4	(1.0)	47.1	(1.0)
	New Zealand	18.1	(0.7)	40.3	(1.0)
	Norway	5.8	(0.4)	10.7	(0.6)
	Poland	51.4	(1.2)	53.4	(1.1)
	Portugal	21.1	(0.8)	44.9	(1.1)
	Spain	30.8	(0.7)	54.5	(0.8)
	Sweden	7.8	(0.5)	7.8	(0.5)
	Switzerland	7.2	(0.4)	30.4	(0.9)
	United Kingdom	20.1	(0.7)	24.4	(0.8)
	United States	24.7	(1.3)	28.8	(1.3)
	OECD total	*33.9*	*(0.5)*	*34.0*	*(0.4)*
	OECD average	*24.9*	*(0.2)*	*32.3*	*(0.2)*
NON-OECD COUNTRIES	Brazil	14.5	(0.9)	50.9	(1.2)
	Latvia	54.9	(1.3)	56.0	(1.3)
	Liechtenstein	9.8	(1.7)	28.7	(2.6)
	Russian Federation	45.2	(0.9)	20.5	(0.7)
	Netherlands[1]	m	m	18.7	(0.9)

1. Response rate is too low to ensure comparability (see Annex A3).

Table 7.8
Index of teacher shortage and performance on the combined reading literacy scale, by national quarters of the index
Results based on reports from school principals and reported proportionate to the number of 15-year-olds enrolled in the school

		Index of teacher shortage[1]							
		All students		Bottom quarter		Middle half		Top quarter	
		Mean index	S.E.	Mean index	S.E.	Mean index	S.E.	Mean index	S.E.
OECD COUNTRIES	Australia	−0.18	(0.08)	−1.39	(0.04)	−0.16	(0.08)	Max	
	Austria	0.53	(0.05)	−0.43	(0.08)	0.79	(0.04)	Max	
	Belgium	0.25	(0.07)	−0.89	(0.08)	0.47	(0.07)	Max	
	Canada	−0.01	(0.04)	−1.41	(0.03)	0.20	(0.04)	Max	
	Czech Republic	0.51	(0.04)	−0.36	(0.06)	0.71	(0.04)	Max	
	Denmark	0.31	(0.05)	−0.71	(0.04)	0.50	(0.05)	Max	
	Finland	0.09	(0.06)	−0.88	(0.03)	0.13	(0.04)	Max	
	France	m	m	m	m	m	m	m	m
	Germany	−0.23	(0.06)	−1.47	(0.04)	−0.23	(0.04)	Max	
	Greece	−0.73	(0.14)	−2.97	(0.15)	−0.52	(0.10)	Max	
	Hungary	0.29	(0.08)	−1.04	(0.12)	0.61	(0.05)	Max	
	Iceland	−0.39	(0.00)	−1.59	(0.00)	−0.47	(0.00)	Max	
	Ireland	−0.06	(0.08)	−1.35	(0.11)	0.07	(0.07)	Max	
	Italy	−0.28	(0.09)	−1.53	(0.07)	−0.30	(0.08)	Max	
	Japan	−0.23	(0.07)	−1.51	(0.07)	−0.19	(0.09)	Max	
	Korea	0.32	(0.06)	−0.90	(0.09)	0.62	(0.06)	Max	
	Luxembourg	−0.10	(0.01)	−1.66	(0.00)	−0.14	(0.01)	c	c
	Mexico	−0.53	(0.09)	−1.88	(0.08)	−0.60	(0.05)	0.94	(0.01)
	New Zealand	−0.18	(0.07)	−1.42	(0.06)	−0.15	(0.07)	Max	
	Norway	−0.32	(0.07)	−1.42	(0.07)	−0.41	(0.05)	0.92	(0.03)
	Poland	0.30	(0.10)	−1.05	(0.20)	0.64	(0.05)	Max	
	Portugal	0.03	(0.08)	−0.97	(0.03)	0.05	(0.10)	Max	
	Spain	0.52	(0.06)	−0.59	(0.11)	0.85	(0.03)	Max	
	Sweden	−0.25	(0.07)	−1.54	(0.06)	−0.21	(0.06)	Max	
	Switzerland	0.35	(0.06)	−0.78	(0.07)	0.61	(0.05)	Max	
	United Kingdom	−0.40	(0.07)	−1.71	(0.06)	−0.42	(0.06)	Max	
	United States	0.20	(0.08)	−1.18	(0.09)	0.48	(0.07)	Max	
	OECD total	*−0.01*	*(0.03)*	*−1.32*	*(0.03)*	*0.14*	*(0.02)*	*Max*	
	OECD average	*0.00*	*(0.01)*	*−1.24*	*(0.03)*	*0.12*	*(0.01)*	*Max*	
NON-OECD COUNTRIES	Brazil	−0.07	(0.07)	−1.32	(0.06)	0.03	(0.07)	Max	
	Latvia	−0.05	(0.10)	−1.18	(0.12)	0.00	(0.04)	Max	
	Liechtenstein	m	m	m	m	m	m	m	m
	Russian Federation	−0.75	(0.10)	−2.52	(0.10)	−0.70	(0.06)	0.90	(0.03)
	Netherlands[2]	−0.37	(0.09)	−1.37	(0.06)	−0.41	(0.06)	0.67	(0.08)

Performance on the combined reading literacy scale, by national quarters of the index of teacher shortage[3]

		Bottom quarter		Middle half		Top quarter		Change in the combined reading literacy score per unit of the index of teacher shortage[3]	
		Mean score	S.E.	Mean score	S.E.	Mean score	S.E.	Change	S.E.
OECD COUNTRIES	Australia	510	(5.8)	534	(5.3)	534	(6.9)	13.95	(3.23)
	Austria	478	(10.2)	514	(4.4)	523	(7.4)	27.15	(7.81)
	Belgium	501	(11.6)	543	(7.2)	542	(14.6)	23.01	(8.05)
	Canada	531	(2.6)	536	(2.3)	535	(3.3)	2.11	(1.42)
	Czech Republic	459	(11.2)	502	(4.4)	502	(10.5)	42.06	(11.26)
	Denmark	485	(5.5)	497	(3.8)	505	(6.0)	9.29	(4.28)
	Finland	544	(4.0)	548	(2.8)	546	(7.4)	1.23	(4.09)
	France	m	m	m	m	m	m	m	m
	Germany	424	(11.5)	498	(6.1)	522	(8.3)	42.31	(5.68)
	Greece	476	(13.7)	458	(7.7)	504	(10.1)	2.61	(3.84)
	Hungary	460	(10.5)	490	(6.2)	477	(11.7)	12.25	(5.77)
	Iceland	504	(3.3)	503	(2.2)	517	(3.2)	5.25	(1.49)
	Ireland	519	(7.9)	528	(4.6)	532	(7.2)	2.83	(3.65)
	Italy	477	(9.3)	494	(6.4)	487	(8.8)	2.62	(5.05)
	Japan	501	(10.7)	525	(8.0)	538	(8.9)	12.04	(4.47)
	Korea	515	(7.8)	531	(4.6)	522	(6.0)	8.09	(4.33)
	Luxembourg	467	(3.7)	422	(2.5)	473	(3.0)	−4.22	(1.45)
	Mexico	411	(8.1)	430	(6.9)	419	(10.6)	3.90	(4.43)
	New Zealand	512	(6.8)	529	(4.3)	550	(7.1)	12.66	(3.82)
	Norway	501	(6.6)	506	(3.8)	506	(6.9)	4.47	(3.66)
	Poland	447	(14.2)	487	(9.7)	496	(13.5)	7.75	(8.93)
	Portugal	470	(9.0)	472	(6.7)	470	(11.7)	0.68	(6.11)
	Spain	485	(5.3)	496	(4.4)	492	(6.1)	2.90	(3.41)
	Sweden	511	(6.8)	513	(3.2)	527	(3.9)	7.88	(2.53)
	Switzerland	479	(10.4)	497	(8.1)	503	(11.2)	18.74	(6.30)
	United Kingdom	507	(7.3)	519	(5.4)	556	(7.5)	18.47	(3.49)
	United States	488	(10.3)	510	(7.7)	513	(11.5)	13.54	(4.21)
	OECD total	*481*	*(3.2)*	*503*	*(2.3)*	*509*	*(3.6)*	*13.65*	*(1.39)*
	OECD average	*488*	*(1.9)*	*502*	*(1.1)*	*510*	*(1.7)*	*9.36*	*(0.96)*
NON-OECD COUNTRIES	Brazil	384	(6.9)	397	(5.9)	404	(9.0)	6.16	(3.99)
	Latvia	465	(12.4)	454	(7.4)	463	(12.2)	−6.96	(8.63)
	Liechtenstein	m	m	m	m	m	m	m	m
	Russian Federation	459	(9.2)	462	(8.3)	460	(7.1)	0.41	(3.52)
	Netherlands[2]	508	(13.8)	543	(7.0)	529	(11.6)	18.48	(7.84)

1. For the definition of the index see Annex A1. *The scale was inverted so that positive and high values indicate that teacher shortage is perceived as less of a problem, compared to the OECD average.* "Max" is used in cases where more than 25 per cent of students are enrolled in schools in which the responses from school principals correspond to the highest value on the index, which is 0.95.
2. Response rate is too low to ensure comparability (see Annex A3).
3. For explained variation see Annex A2. Unit changes marked in bold are statistically significant. Where bottom and top quarters are marked in bold this indicates that their difference is statistically significant.

Table 7.9
Index of the quality of the schools' physical infrastructure and performance on the combined reading literacy scale, by national quarters of the index

Results based on reports from school principals and reported proportionate to the number of 15-year-olds enrolled in the school

| | Index of the quality of the schools' physical infrastructure[1] | | | | | | | |
| | All students | | Bottom quarter | | Middle half | | Top quarter | |
	Mean index	S.E.	Mean index	S.E.	Mean index	S.E.	Mean index	S.E.
Australia	0.05	(0.08)	−1.11	(0.06)	0.08	(0.06)	Max	
Austria	−0.07	(0.09)	−1.52	(0.14)	0.05	(0.05)	Max	
Belgium	0.33	(0.06)	−0.79	(0.06)	0.48	(0.05)	Max	
Canada	0.35	(0.03)	−0.80	(0.05)	0.54	(0.03)	Max	
Czech Republic	0.66	(0.05)	−0.32	(0.05)	0.89	(0.03)	Max	
Denmark	−0.07	(0.08)	−1.29	(0.08)	−0.05	(0.03)	1.07	(0.04)
Finland	−0.22	(0.08)	−1.41	(0.08)	−0.24	(0.04)	0.97	(0.05)
France	m	m	m	m	m	m	m	m
Germany	0.14	(0.06)	−1.00	(0.10)	0.22	(0.05)	Max	
Greece	−1.17	(0.12)	−2.78	(0.10)	−1.35	(0.06)	0.68	(0.09)
Hungary	0.42	(0.07)	−0.61	(0.15)	0.57	(0.05)	Max	
Iceland	0.31	(0.00)	−0.85	(0.00)	0.46	(0.00)	Max	
Ireland	0.19	(0.09)	−1.10	(0.11)	0.35	(0.07)	Max	
Italy	−0.20	(0.09)	−1.67	(0.11)	−0.14	(0.06)	Max	
Japan	−0.21	(0.08)	−1.26	(0.06)	−0.26	(0.04)	0.88	(0.06)
Korea	−0.36	(0.08)	−1.65	(0.12)	−0.34	(0.05)	0.83	(0.06)
Luxembourg	−0.28	(0.00)	−1.32	(0.00)	−0.35	(0.00)	0.50	(0.00)
Mexico	−0.39	(0.09)	−1.95	(0.09)	−0.35	(0.06)	0.99	(0.05)
New Zealand	0.10	(0.06)	−0.96	(0.08)	0.11	(0.04)	Max	
Norway	−0.59	(0.07)	−1.77	(0.11)	−0.58	(0.03)	0.53	(0.06)
Poland	−0.15	(0.10)	−1.50	(0.19)	−0.03	(0.05)	0.91	(0.06)
Portugal	0.14	(0.07)	−1.14	(0.11)	0.29	(0.06)	Max	
Spain	0.13	(0.07)	−1.27	(0.11)	0.33	(0.06)	Max	
Sweden	0.01	(0.08)	−1.20	(0.08)	0.02	(0.05)	Max	
Switzerland	0.49	(0.06)	−0.62	(0.08)	0.73	(0.05)	Max	
United Kingdom	−0.41	(0.08)	−1.65	(0.07)	−0.49	(0.04)	0.95	(0.05)
United States	0.20	(0.08)	−0.77	(0.06)	0.20	(0.05)	Max	
OECD total	*−0.01*	*(0.02)*	*−1.19*	*(0.03)*	*0.04*	*(0.02)*	*1.03*	*(0.01)*
OECD average	*0.00*	*(0.01)*	*−1.22*	*(0.02)*	*0.08*	*(0.01)*	*1.01*	*(0.01)*
Brazil	0.30	(0.07)	−1.14	(0.12)	0.59	(0.05)	Max	
Latvia	−0.07	(0.10)	−1.25	(0.13)	−0.09	(0.07)	Max	
Liechtenstein	m	m	m	m	m	m	m	m
Russian Federation	−0.52	(0.09)	−2.07	(0.08)	−0.51	(0.05)	0.98	(0.03)
Netherlands[2]	0.09	(0.13)	−1.28	(0.20)	0.21	(0.08)	Max	

Performance on the combined reading literacy scale, by national quarters of the index of the quality of the schools' physical infrastructure[3]

| | Bottom quarter | | Middle half | | Top quarter | | Change in the combined reading literacy score per unit of the index of the quality of the schools' physical infrastructure[3] | |
	Mean score	S.E.	Mean score	S.E.	Mean score	S.E.	Change	S.E.
Australia	527	(9.1)	530	(4.6)	527	(7.6)	1.39	(4.82)
Austria	510	(9.5)	507	(5.4)	505	(8.9)	−3.07	(4.41)
Belgium	490	(11.4)	516	(5.8)	510	(10.4)	**15.25**	(7.39)
Canada	536	(3.3)	534	(2.3)	535	(3.0)	−1.30	(2.13)
Czech Republic	508	(8.0)	478	(3.9)	502	(8.1)	−6.09	(6.55)
Denmark	498	(5.7)	492	(4.2)	500	(6.0)	−2.66	(3.27)
Finland	550	(4.6)	549	(3.1)	538	(6.6)	−2.88	(3.49)
France	m	m	m	m	m	m	m	m
Germany	468	(13.9)	489	(7.8)	497	(9.7)	14.06	(9.22)
Greece	468	(10.4)	465	(9.1)	492	(10.5)	8.01	(4.69)
Hungary	462	(11.1)	492	(8.4)	471	(11.1)	11.68	(9.02)
Iceland	512	(3.4)	505	(2.1)	506	(2.7)	−2.18	(1.76)
Ireland	517	(7.4)	533	(4.8)	524	(7.3)	4.34	(4.17)
Italy	470	(11.2)	493	(6.5)	493	(7.2)	5.92	(4.37)
Japan	519	(11.4)	520	(7.6)	529	(7.9)	4.81	(5.61)
Korea	518	(7.3)	525	(5.1)	526	(8.2)	2.93	(4.54)
Luxembourg	**435**	(3.6)	416	(2.3)	**499**	(2.3)	**34.98**	(1.99)
Mexico	399	(8.5)	417	(6.2)	454	(9.4)	**16.88**	(3.91)
New Zealand	525	(8.5)	536	(4.4)	525	(6.8)	2.99	(4.86)
Norway	504	(6.1)	504	(4.3)	505	(6.9)	0.49	(3.42)
Poland	**502**	(13.7)	480	(9.0)	**454**	(14.1)	**−16.87**	(6.72)
Portugal	**498**	(8.2)	464	(7.9)	**455**	(7.6)	**−16.16**	(4.50)
Spain	484	(6.1)	494	(4.2)	496	(6.3)	9.18	(3.14)
Sweden	**506**	(6.4)	519	(3.5)	**521**	(4.5)	6.01	(3.08)
Switzerland	487	(11.6)	491	(7.0)	507	(10.9)	11.11	(6.33)
United Kingdom	514	(8.4)	521	(3.6)	540	(9.6)	8.92	(4.83)
United States	507	(11.1)	508	(6.9)	499	(13.9)	−2.16	(6.10)
OECD total	*495*	*(3.8)*	*499*	*(2.6)*	*502*	*(3.8)*	*6.09*	*(1.64)*
OECD average	*498*	*(1.8)*	*499*	*(1.1)*	*504*	*(1.6)*	*5.08*	*(0.98)*
Brazil	386	(7.4)	398	(4.2)	403	(9.1)	**9.32**	(4.38)
Latvia	462	(14.8)	460	(8.3)	457	(9.0)	1.89	(6.60)
Liechtenstein	m	m	m	m	m	m	m	m
Russian Federation	**445**	(7.9)	461	(5.9)	**482**	(9.4)	12.22	(3.94)
Netherlands[2]	519	(15.9)	531	(7.8)	542	(12.2)	3.10	(6.40)

1. For the definition of the index see Annex A1. *The scale was inverted so that positive and high values indicate that the school's physical infrastructure is perceived as less of a problem, compared to the OECD average.* "Max" is used in cases where more than 25 per cent of students are enrolled in schools in which the responses from school principals correspond to the highest value on the index, which is 1.12.
2. Response rate is too low to ensure comparability (see Annex A3).
3. For explained variation see Annex A2. Unit changes marked in bold are statistically significant. Where bottom and top quarters are marked in bold this indicates that their difference is statistically significant.

Table 7.10
Index of the quality of the schools' educational resources and performance on the combined reading literacy scale, by national quarters of the index
Results based on reports from school principals and reported proportionate to the number of 15-year-olds enrolled in the school

	Index of the quality of the schools' educational resources[1]							
	All students		Bottom quarter		Middle half		Top quarter	
	Mean index	S.E.	Mean index	S.E.	Mean index	S.E.	Mean index	S.E.
Australia	0.28	(0.08)	−0.82	(0.06)	0.10	(0.05)	1.63	(0.09)
Austria	0.02	(0.08)	−1.09	(0.10)	0.05	(0.04)	1.02	(0.10)
Belgium	0.45	(0.06)	−0.77	(0.08)	0.44	(0.04)	1.69	(0.04)
Canada	0.24	(0.04)	−0.98	(0.05)	0.15	(0.02)	1.61	(0.03)
Czech Republic	0.22	(0.09)	−0.92	(0.05)	0.05	(0.04)	1.68	(0.06)
Denmark	0.25	(0.06)	−0.77	(0.07)	0.28	(0.03)	1.18	(0.07)
Finland	−0.22	(0.06)	−1.17	(0.07)	−0.28	(0.03)	0.79	(0.08)
France	m	m	m	m	m	m	m	m
Germany	−0.20	(0.07)	−1.31	(0.09)	−0.24	(0.04)	0.99	(0.07)
Greece	−0.93	(0.09)	−2.09	(0.09)	−0.99	(0.04)	0.33	(0.12)
Hungary	0.50	(0.08)	−0.63	(0.07)	0.44	(0.05)	1.71	(0.06)
Iceland	−0.19	(0.00)	−1.11	(0.00)	−0.29	(0.00)	0.91	(0.00)
Ireland	−0.19	(0.10)	−1.45	(0.09)	−0.25	(0.05)	1.15	(0.11)
Italy	0.07	(0.08)	−1.17	(0.07)	0.01	(0.05)	1.40	(0.09)
Japan	0.00	(0.07)	−0.96	(0.07)	−0.11	(0.04)	1.18	(0.09)
Korea	0.00	(0.08)	−1.00	(0.05)	−0.09	(0.04)	1.13	(0.11)
Luxembourg	0.11	(0.00)	−0.65	(0.00)	0.01	(0.00)	0.95	(0.00)
Mexico	−0.95	(0.10)	−2.28	(0.08)	−1.13	(0.05)	0.70	(0.13)
New Zealand	0.11	(0.06)	−0.83	(0.06)	−0.06	(0.03)	1.35	(0.07)
Norway	−0.55	(0.06)	−1.34	(0.08)	−0.63	(0.03)	0.37	(0.09)
Poland	−0.17	(0.09)	−1.35	(0.08)	−0.18	(0.06)	0.98	(0.08)
Portugal	0.14	(0.08)	−1.06	(0.08)	0.09	(0.04)	1.42	(0.09)
Spain	0.15	(0.09)	−1.12	(0.09)	0.05	(0.05)	1.58	(0.07)
Sweden	0.00	(0.07)	−0.99	(0.06)	−0.13	(0.04)	1.22	(0.10)
Switzerland	0.51	(0.07)	−0.56	(0.05)	0.38	(0.05)	1.78	(0.03)
United Kingdom	−0.44	(0.07)	−1.62	(0.08)	−0.52	(0.04)	0.85	(0.11)
United States	0.40	(0.08)	−0.60	(0.07)	0.30	(0.05)	1.55	(0.10)
OECD total	*0.01*	*(0.03)*	*−1.09*	*(0.04)*	*−0.08*	*(0.02)*	*1.27*	*(0.03)*
OECD average	*0.00*	*(0.02)*	*−1.09*	*(0.02)*	*−0.08*	*(0.01)*	*1.22*	*(0.02)*
Brazil	−0.36	(0.10)	−1.82	(0.10)	−0.44	(0.05)	1.21	(0.10)
Latvia	−0.67	(0.09)	−1.85	(0.13)	−0.65	(0.05)	0.41	(0.09)
Liechtenstein	m	m	m	m	m	m	m	m
Russian Federation	−1.27	(0.08)	−2.53	(0.06)	−1.31	(0.03)	0.04	(0.09)
Netherlands[2]	0.10	(0.12)	−1.18	(0.18)	0.03	(0.05)	1.45	(0.13)

Performance on the combined reading literacy scale, by national quarters of the index of the quality of the schools' educational resources[3]

	Bottom quarter		Middle half		Top quarter		Change in the combined reading literacy score per unit of the index of the quality of the schools' educational resources[3]	
	Mean score	S.E.	Mean score	S.E.	Mean score	S.E.	Change	S.E.
Australia	515	(6.3)	528	(5.5)	542	(6.7)	9.76	(3.33)
Austria	503	(9.0)	512	(5.7)	503	(8.0)	2.96	(5.74)
Belgium	491	(11.8)	514	(5.6)	516	(11.4)	9.21	(5.84)
Canada	530	(3.2)	535	(2.0)	539	(3.7)	4.50	(1.49)
Czech Republic	489	(7.3)	495	(6.7)	487	(12.2)	0.23	(5.44)
Denmark	485	(6.4)	498	(3.7)	503	(6.0)	6.21	(3.42)
Finland	551	(5.2)	547	(3.0)	541	(6.7)	−4.39	(4.02)
France	m	m	m	m	m	m	m	m
Germany	447	(16.2)	497	(9.0)	502	(10.0)	24.99	(9.01)
Greece	486	(13.7)	459	(8.3)	488	(10.8)	7.92	(7.62)
Hungary	462	(13.4)	485	(8.0)	486	(10.6)	10.06	(7.00)
Iceland	509	(2.9)	500	(2.1)	519	(3.1)	6.48	(1.75)
Ireland	519	(7.1)	533	(5.4)	522	(6.7)	1.78	(3.73)
Italy	469	(11.9)	489	(6.0)	502	(10.2)	11.43	(5.81)
Japan	511	(10.5)	517	(7.7)	544	(7.1)	13.65	(4.99)
Korea	526	(6.0)	518	(5.0)	534	(6.9)	1.63	(4.41)
Luxembourg	407	(4.2)	445	(2.1)	470	(2.5)	22.98	(2.28)
Mexico	391	(8.7)	413	(5.1)	472	(9.7)	26.01	(3.86)
New Zealand	516	(7.4)	530	(3.9)	545	(7.8)	12.78	(4.03)
Norway	490	(5.7)	508	(4.0)	514	(5.9)	9.09	(4.22)
Poland	464	(16.4)	476	(9.0)	498	(12.6)	8.59	(9.19)
Portugal	458	(10.5)	474	(7.1)	474	(12.1)	5.31	(5.12)
Spain	480	(5.8)	490	(3.6)	509	(7.0)	10.12	(2.97)
Sweden	509	(5.8)	513	(3.4)	530	(4.6)	6.89	(2.78)
Switzerland	484	(13.0)	494	(6.0)	504	(7.6)	8.35	(5.04)
United Kingdom	507	(6.0)	522	(4.7)	546	(7.0)	16.86	(3.19)
United States	481	(7.0)	521	(9.6)	498	(12.8)	0.66	(6.56)
OECD total	*480*	*(3.2)*	*502*	*(2.9)*	*511*	*(3.2)*	*16.88*	*(1.68)*
OECD average	*488*	*(2.1)*	*501*	*(1.2)*	*511*	*(1.6)*	*10.85*	*(1.00)*
Brazil	380	(7.0)	392	(4.9)	421	(9.5)	12.70	(3.44)
Latvia	453	(14.0)	467	(8.7)	452	(11.2)	9.45	(5.09)
Liechtenstein	m	m	m	m	m	m	m	m
Russian Federation	455	(7.1)	459	(6.0)	473	(8.0)	9.09	(3.36)
Netherlands[2]	513	(12.7)	541	(8.9)	527	(13.7)	11.39	(7.30)

1. For the definition of the index see Annex A1. *The scale was inverted so that positive and high values indicate that the school's educational resources are not perceived as an important problem.*
2. Response rate is too low to ensure comparability (see Annex A3).
3. For explained variation see Annex A2. Unit changes marked in bold are statistically significant. Where bottom and top quarters are marked in bold this indicates that their difference is statistically significant.

Table 7.11
Percentage of students enrolled in schools which have at least some responsibility for the following aspects of school policy and management
Results based on reports from school principals and reported proportionate to the number of 15-year-olds enrolled in the school

		Appointing teachers	S.E.	Dismissing teachers	S.E.	Establishing teachers' starting salaries	S.E.	Determining teachers' salary increases	S.E.	Formulating the school budget	S.E.	Deciding on budget allocations within the school	S.E.
OECD COUNTRIES	Australia	60	(2.2)	47	(3.1)	18	(2.2)	19	(2.6)	96	(1.5)	100	(0.2)
	Austria	15	(2.9)	5	(1.7)	1	(0.5)	1	(0.5)	14	(2.7)	93	(2.0)
	Belgium	96	(1.3)	95	(1.4)	7	(1.7)	7	(1.8)	98	(1.0)	99	(0.6)
	Canada	82	(1.2)	61	(1.7)	34	(1.8)	34	(1.7)	77	(1.4)	99	(0.3)
	Czech Republic	96	(1.2)	95	(1.3)	70	(3.1)	73	(3.1)	83	(2.6)	99	(0.6)
	Denmark	97	(1.3)	57	(3.2)	13	(2.5)	15	(2.7)	89	(2.2)	98	(1.0)
	Finland	35	(3.8)	21	(3.3)	1	(0.8)	2	(1.0)	56	(3.9)	99	(0.9)
	France	m	m	m	m	m	m	m	m	m	m	m	m
	Germany	10	(2.3)	4	(1.3)	2	(0.9)	11	(2.2)	13	(2.0)	96	(1.3)
	Greece	65	(4.7)	70	(4.4)	73	(4.3)	77	(3.9)	87	(3.4)	95	(2.1)
	Hungary	100	(0.0)	99	(1.0)	41	(4.3)	50	(4.3)	61	(4.1)	92	(2.3)
	Iceland	99	(0.0)	99	(0.1)	4	(0.1)	7	(0.1)	76	(0.2)	87	(0.1)
	Ireland	88	(2.5)	73	(3.0)	4	(1.7)	5	(2.2)	79	(3.1)	100	(0.0)
	Italy	10	(2.1)	11	(2.6)	1	(0.8)	1	(0.8)	94	(2.4)	57	(5.0)
	Japan	33	(1.9)	32	(2.0)	32	(2.0)	32	(2.0)	50	(3.3)	91	(2.9)
	Korea	32	(4.1)	22	(4.0)	15	(3.1)	7	(2.4)	88	(2.5)	95	(1.7)
	Luxembourg	m	m	m	m	m	m	m	m	100	(0.0)	100	(0.0)
	Mexico	57	(3.4)	48	(3.8)	26	(3.1)	28	(3.1)	68	(4.2)	77	(3.7)
	New Zealand	100	(0.0)	99	(0.8)	17	(2.4)	41	(3.3)	98	(1.1)	100	(0.0)
	Norway	m	m	m	m	m	m	m	m	m	m	m	m
	Poland	m	m	m	m	m	m	m	m	m	m	m	m
	Portugal	13	(2.1)	9	(1.2)	1	(0.7)	1	(0.7)	89	(2.9)	95	(2.0)
	Spain	38	(2.5)	39	(2.6)	9	(2.2)	9	(2.2)	90	(2.5)	98	(1.3)
	Sweden	99	(0.8)	83	(3.2)	62	(3.6)	74	(3.6)	85	(3.1)	99	(0.6)
	Switzerland	93	(1.7)	82	(2.3)	13	(2.7)	15	(3.0)	54	(3.3)	87	(2.9)
	United Kingdom	99	(0.3)	89	(1.3)	72	(3.0)	70	(3.1)	92	(0.8)	100	(0.1)
	United States	97	(0.9)	98	(1.2)	76	(4.9)	74	(5.1)	96	(1.9)	99	(1.0)
	OECD average	*61*	*(0.4)*	*54*	*(0.5)*	*23*	*(0.5)*	*26*	*(0.5)*	*76*	*(0.6)*	*94*	*(0.3)*
NON-OECD COUNTRIES	Brazil	39	(2.7)	33	(2.9)	10	(1.7)	10	(1.7)	55	(3.4)	75	(2.8)
	Latvia	100	(0.0)	99	(0.9)	25	(4.2)	35	(5.2)	33	(4.5)	89	(3.8)
	Liechtenstein	m	m	m	m	m	m	m	m	m	m	m	m
	Russian Federation	100	(0.4)	98	(0.7)	41	(3.2)	47	(3.3)	47	(4.0)	70	(3.8)
	Cross-country correlation between country's average achievement on the combined reading literacy scale and the percentage indicated by the respective column header[1]	0.16		0.10		−0.05		−0.06		0.00		0.37	
	Netherlands[2]	100	(0.0)	100	(0.0)	71	(5.0)	45	(5.6)	100	(0.0)	100	(0.0)

		Establishing student disciplinary policies	S.E.	Establishing student assessment policies	S.E.	Approving students for admittance to school	S.E.	Choosing which textbooks are used	S.E.	Determining course content	S.E.	Deciding which courses are offered	S.E.
OECD COUNTRIES	Australia	100	(0.2)	99	(0.6)	94	(1.6)	100	(0.2)	84	(3.2)	96	(1.8)
	Austria	96	(1.6)	69	(3.5)	75	(2.9)	99	(0.7)	54	(3.6)	57	(3.7)
	Belgium	99	(0.9)	100	(0.4)	95	(1.7)	99	(0.6)	59	(3.7)	61	(3.6)
	Canada	98	(0.5)	94	(1.0)	89	(1.0)	89	(0.9)	49	(1.8)	90	(1.1)
	Czech Republic	100	(0.5)	100	(0.3)	89	(1.7)	100	(0.0)	82	(2.9)	82	(2.8)
	Denmark	99	(0.8)	87	(2.4)	87	(2.6)	100	(0.0)	90	(1.9)	77	(2.6)
	Finland	96	(1.9)	89	(2.6)	54	(4.0)	100	(0.0)	91	(2.3)	95	(2.0)
	France	m	m	m	m	m	m	m	m	m	m	m	m
	Germany	95	(1.4)	79	(2.8)	79	(3.0)	96	(1.7)	35	(3.3)	35	(3.4)
	Greece	97	(1.5)	94	(2.2)	90	(2.5)	90	(2.9)	92	(2.6)	89	(2.9)
	Hungary	100	(0.0)	98	(1.0)	99	(0.7)	100	(0.4)	97	(1.3)	98	(1.0)
	Iceland	99	(0.0)	98	(0.1)	74	(0.1)	99	(0.0)	79	(0.2)	62	(0.2)
	Ireland	99	(0.6)	99	(0.9)	95	(2.0)	100	(0.0)	37	(4.1)	97	(1.3)
	Italy	100	(0.0)	100	(0.0)	63	(5.1)	100	(0.0)	93	(2.9)	22	(4.0)
	Japan	100	(0.4)	100	(0.0)	100	(0.0)	99	(0.7)	99	(0.7)	98	(1.3)
	Korea	100	(0.0)	99	(0.1)	97	(1.4)	99	(0.6)	99	(0.6)	93	(2.3)
	Luxembourg	m	m	m	m	100	(0.0)	m	m	m	m	m	m
	Mexico	99	(0.7)	92	(2.5)	86	(2.3)	81	(3.0)	59	(4.1)	58	(3.4)
	New Zealand	100	(0.0)	100	(0.0)	94	(1.2)	100	(0.0)	87	(2.7)	100	(0.1)
	Norway	m	m	m	m	m	m	m	m	m	m	m	m
	Poland	m	m	m	m	m	m	m	m	m	m	m	m
	Portugal	92	(2.2)	88	(2.6)	85	(3.1)	100	(0.0)	20	(3.4)	54	(4.5)
	Spain	99	(0.8)	97	(1.5)	89	(2.4)	100	(0.4)	86	(2.9)	54	(3.8)
	Sweden	100	(0.0)	97	(1.5)	54	(4.0)	100	(0.0)	88	(2.8)	76	(3.7)
	Switzerland	98	(1.2)	75	(3.6)	82	(3.0)	51	(4.1)	29	(3.5)	34	(3.4)
	United Kingdom	99	(0.5)	100	(0.2)	66	(3.6)	100	(0.0)	94	(1.5)	100	(0.1)
	United States	99	(0.9)	93	(2.2)	89	(2.6)	92	(3.0)	84	(4.3)	97	(1.3)
	OECD average	*95*	*(0.2)*	*89*	*(0.4)*	*84*	*(0.5)*	*92*	*(0.2)*	*69*	*(0.6)*	*71*	*(0.6)*
NON-OECD COUNTRIES	Brazil	98	(0.7)	91	(1.8)	79	(3.3)	100	(0.3)	90	(2.2)	57	(3.4)
	Latvia	100	(0.1)	77	(4.6)	98	(1.3)	99	(0.6)	76	(4.9)	90	(3.5)
	Liechtenstein	m	m	m	m	m	m	m	m	m	m	m	m
	Russian Federation	100	(0.0)	100	(0.4)	99	(0.6)	97	(1.0)	95	(1.4)	96	(1.3)
	Cross-country correlation between country's average achievement on the combined reading literacy scale and the percentage indicated by the respective column header[1]	0.21		0.20		−0.21		0.30		0.25		0.51	
	Netherlands[2]	100	(0.0)	100	(0.0)	100	(0.0)	100	(0.0)	92	(3.2)	95	(2.4)

1. Correlation values indicated in bold are statistically significant.

2. Response rate is too low to ensure comparability (see Annex A3).

Table 7.12
Percentage of students enrolled in schools in which teachers have at least some responsibility for the following aspects of school policy and management
Results based on reports from school principals and reported proportionate to the number of 15-year-olds enrolled in the school

	Appointing teachers	S.E.	Dismissing teachers	S.E.	Establishing teachers' starting salaries	S.E.	Determining teachers' salary increases	S.E.	Formulating the school budget	S.E.	Deciding on budget allocations within the school	S.E.
OECD COUNTRIES												
Australia	1.4	(1.0)	m	m	0.3	(0.2)	1.2	(0.7)	11.3	(2.5)	12.6	(2.6)
Austria	1.7	(0.9)	1.7	(1.0)	m	m	m	m	3.7	(1.3)	22.6	(3.0)
Belgium	0.6	(0.6)	0.4	(0.4)	m	m	m	m	3.0	(1.3)	8.1	(2.0)
Canada	2.2	(0.4)	m	m	1.0	(0.4)	1.1	(0.4)	7.8	(0.8)	20.4	(1.4)
Czech Republic	m	m	0.6	(0.6)	m	m	m	m	1.3	(0.6)	6.1	(1.8)
Denmark	19.5	(2.6)	1.6	(0.9)	m	m	0.9	(0.6)	12.7	(2.3)	21.7	(3.0)
Finland	1.0	(0.7)	1.7	(0.9)	0.4	(0.4)	m	m	15.8	(2.8)	39.0	(4.2)
France	m	m	m	m	m	m	m	m	m	m	m	m
Germany	0.9	(0.5)	0.5	(0.3)	0.5	(0.3)	0.5	(0.3)	6.8	(1.5)	38.1	(3.6)
Greece	0.4	(0.4)	0.8	(0.6)	m	m	m	m	m	m	0.1	(0.1)
Hungary	m	m	0.5	(0.5)	m	m	0.8	(0.8)	2.9	(1.2)	7.4	(2.2)
Iceland	m	m	m	m	m	m	m	m	3.9	(0.1)	11.6	(0.2)
Ireland	0.9	(1.0)	m	m	m	m	m	m	4.2	(1.8)	7.4	(1.8)
Italy	m	m	m	m	m	m	m	m	m	m	m	m
Japan	0.7	(0.7)	m	m	m	m	m	m	m	m	4.7	(1.8)
Korea	0.8	(0.8)	m	m	0.8	(0.8)	0.8	(0.8)	4.1	(1.9)	2.6	(1.5)
Luxembourg	m	m	m	m	m	m	m	m	m	m	m	m
Mexico	2.2	(1.1)	1.2	(0.9)	m	m	m	m	2.2	(1.0)	3.1	(1.3)
New Zealand	m	m	m	m	m	m	m	m	4.9	(1.8)	6.2	(1.7)
Norway	m	m	m	m	m	m	m	m	m	m	m	m
Poland	m	m	m	m	m	m	m	m	m	m	m	m
Portugal	m	m	m	m	m	m	m	m	1.3	(0.9)	3.6	(1.6)
Spain	0.6	(0.6)	0.6	(0.6)	0.6	(0.6)	0.6	(0.6)	4.5	(1.4)	5.5	(1.7)
Sweden	5.5	(1.6)	m	m	0.6	(0.5)	0.6	(0.5)	2.8	(1.4)	13.9	(2.7)
Switzerland	4.7	(1.8)	1.8	(1.2)	m	m	m	m	11.8	(2.7)	31.5	(3.3)
United Kingdom	3.0	(1.3)	m	m	m	m	m	m	0.9	(0.6)	4.3	(1.6)
United States	9.5	(3.2)	m	m	8.6	(3.1)	12.4	(3.9)	13.5	(4.4)	24.2	(4.9)
OECD average	*2.2*	*(0.2)*	*0.5*	*(0.1)*	*0.4*	*(0.1)*	*0.7*	*(0.1)*	*4.8*	*(0.3)*	*12.0*	*(0.5)*
NON-OECD COUNTRIES												
Brazil	1.4	(1.3)	m	m	m	m	m	m	7.2	(2.2)	15.7	(2.8)
Latvia	m	m	m	m	m	m	2.2	(1.2)	m	m	1.8	(1.0)
Liechtenstein	m	m	m	m	m	m	m	m	m	m	m	m
Russian Federation	m	m	0.4	(0.2)	m	m	1.9	(1.1)	m	m	m	m
Cross-country correlation between country's average achievement on the combined reading literacy scale and the percentage indicated by the respective column header[1]	*-0.09*		*0.25*		*-0.21*		*0.00*		*0.35*		*0.24*	
Netherlands[2]	3.9	(2.3)	2.4	(1.8)	m	m	0.8	(0.7)	m	m	1.8	(1.9)

	Establishing student disciplinary policies	S.E.	Establishing student assessment policies	S.E.	Approving students for admittance to school	S.E.	Choosing which textbooks are used	S.E.	Determining course content	S.E.	Deciding which courses are offered	S.E.
OECD COUNTRIES												
Australia	60.8	(3.7)	57.4	(3.9)	1.2	(0.8)	63.2	(4.4)	63.0	(3.9)	38.6	(4.1)
Austria	67.0	(3.3)	68.1	(2.9)	12.9	(2.5)	90.1	(2.1)	55.1	(3.8)	42.0	(4.0)
Belgium	45.7	(4.6)	52.4	(3.5)	17.6	(2.9)	89.0	(2.2)	59.8	(3.7)	24.5	(3.1)
Canada	58.8	(2.0)	64.1	(1.9)	1.7	(0.5)	65.8	(1.9)	47.1	(1.8)	39.0	(1.9)
Czech Republic	51.0	(3.5)	59.1	(3.5)	5.7	(1.3)	66.6	(3.3)	45.2	(3.7)	11.7	(2.5)
Denmark	59.0	(3.9)	53.4	(4.0)	13.1	(2.0)	85.7	(2.7)	88.9	(2.2)	52.4	(3.5)
Finland	86.7	(2.8)	92.4	(2.2)	5.9	(2.0)	94.2	(1.9)	97.9	(1.2)	82.1	(3.3)
France	m	m	m	m	m	m	m	m	m	m	m	m
Germany	64.7	(3.1)	79.0	(3.0)	3.1	(1.2)	52.3	(3.3)	37.3	(3.7)	22.4	(3.3)
Greece	41.5	(4.6)	25.0	(4.1)	3.3	(1.7)	9.0	(2.4)	2.7	(1.7)	3.4	(2.0)
Hungary	59.2	(4.5)	67.6	(4.2)	16.2	(3.1)	82.7	(3.0)	81.4	(3.2)	32.7	(4.1)
Iceland	76.3	(0.2)	85.3	(0.1)	4.9	(0.1)	96.8	(0.0)	77.9	(0.2)	47.6	(0.2)
Ireland	72.3	(4.0)	74.3	(4.2)	15.9	(3.0)	97.6	(1.8)	47.0	(3.8)	52.1	(4.1)
Italy	16.5	(4.4)	93.3	(2.9)	2.8	(1.7)	89.3	(3.4)	55.2	(6.0)	20.7	(4.0)
Japan	25.3	(3.5)	22.0	(3.6)	6.1	(2.2)	34.5	(4.2)	24.6	(3.6)	26.2	(4.0)
Korea	9.4	(2.5)	19.8	(4.0)	0.6	(0.6)	68.8	(3.9)	87.1	(2.8)	16.5	(3.3)
Luxembourg	m	m	m	m	m	m	m	m	m	m	m	m
Mexico	32.8	(3.5)	49.1	(3.7)	9.7	(2.4)	62.4	(4.0)	32.8	(3.8)	18.7	(3.4)
New Zealand	37.8	(3.8)	39.2	(3.7)	1.7	(0.7)	57.4	(3.8)	49.8	(3.8)	24.1	(3.4)
Norway	m	m	m	m	m	m	m	m	m	m	m	m
Poland	m	m	m	m	m	m	m	m	m	m	m	m
Portugal	61.2	(4.5)	77.9	(3.4)	1.2	(0.9)	87.6	(2.7)	19.5	(3.3)	19.4	(3.4)
Spain	36.7	(3.8)	75.1	(4.3)	0.6	(0.6)	74.2	(3.1)	73.5	(3.3)	12.4	(2.6)
Sweden	40.1	(3.9)	64.2	(3.6)	5.2	(1.8)	83.0	(3.3)	77.8	(3.1)	49.3	(4.3)
Switzerland	82.2	(2.8)	69.7	(3.4)	13.0	(2.7)	56.2	(3.7)	35.8	(4.0)	42.1	(3.5)
United Kingdom	42.3	(4.0)	47.8	(3.9)	3.4	(1.5)	93.2	(1.3)	87.6	(2.0)	50.2	(3.9)
United States	38.2	(6.0)	35.1	(5.0)	3.1	(2.1)	71.6	(5.4)	61.3	(4.8)	47.2	(6.1)
OECD average	*48.8*	*(0.7)*	*56.7*	*(0.8)*	*6.2*	*(0.4)*	*70.2*	*(0.6)*	*54.7*	*(0.7)*	*32.0*	*(0.8)*
NON-OECD COUNTRIES												
Brazil	52.7	(3.8)	62.8	(3.6)	14.3	(3.0)	93.1	(1.5)	83.6	(2.4)	33.3	(4.2)
Latvia	30.5	(5.0)	38.6	(4.3)	2.2	(1.3)	87.5	(3.2)	56.2	(5.7)	21.1	(3.3)
Liechtenstein	m	m	m	m	m	m	m	m	m	m	m	m
Russian Federation	3.0	(1.2)	10.0	(1.8)	1.6	(1.0)	78.6	(2.2)	18.1	(2.2)	33.7	(3.1)
Cross-country correlation between country's average achievement on the combined reading literacy scale and the percentage indicated by the respective column header[1]	*0.16*		*-0.03*		*-0.15*		*0.22*		*0.46*		*0.55*	
Netherlands[2]	19.2	(5.0)	27.2	(5.6)	8.7	(3.5)	75.6	(4.1)	75.0	(4.7)	15.3	(4.3)

1. Correlation values indicated in bold are statistically significant.

2. Response rate is too low to ensure comparability (see Annex A3).

Table 7.13

Percentage of students and performance on the combined reading literacy scale, by type of school

Results based on reports from school principals and reported proportionate to the number of 15-year-olds enrolled in the school

		Government or public schools[1]						Government-dependent private schools[2]						Government-independent private schools[3]					
				Performance on the combined reading lite- racy scale		International socio- economic index of occupational status (ISEI)				Performance on the combined reading lite- racy scale		International socio- economic index of occupational status (ISEI)				Performance on the combined reading lite- racy scale		International socio- economic index of occupational status (ISEI)	
		% of stu- dents	S.E.	Mean score	S.E.	Mean score	S.E.	% of stu- dents	S.E.	Mean score	S.E.	Mean score	S.E.	% of stu- dents	S.E.	Mean score	S.E.	Mean score	S.E.
OECD COUNTRIES	Australia	m	m	m	m	m	m	m	m	m	m	m	m	m	m	m	m	m	m
	Austria	88.8	(2.8)	504	(3.4)	48.9	(0.4)	6.2	(2.0)	531	(15.9)	54.1	(3.2)	5.0	(1.8)	532	(10.8)	59.0	(1.4)
	Belgium	m	m	m	m	m	m	m	m	m	m	m	m	m	m	m	m	m	m
	Canada	93.8	(0.5)	532	(1.6)	52.2	(0.2)	3.8	(0.5)	573	(7.5)	59.2	(1.1)	2.6	(0.4)	568	(7.2)	64.3	(0.8)
	Czech Republic	94.1	(1.6)	491	(2.7)	48.4	(0.3)	5.7	(1.6)	502	(12.6)	47.3	(1.8)	0.2	(0.2)	c	c	c	c
	Denmark	75.5	(2.3)	497	(2.9)	49.6	(0.5)	24.5	(2.3)	496	(5.8)	50.8	(0.9)	a	a	a	a	a	a
	Finland	97.2	(1.3)	546	(2.6)	49.9	(0.4)	2.8	(1.3)	555	(14.7)	55.1	(3.0)	a	a	a	a	a	a
	France	m	m	m	m	m	m	m	m	m	m	m	m	m	m	m	m	m	m
	Germany	95.9	(1.3)	481	(3.7)	48.7	(0.4)	4.1	(1.3)	563	(12.8)	56.9	(1.8)	a	a	a	a	a	a
	Greece	95.9	(2.1)	468	(5.2)	46.3	(0.6)	a	a	a	a	a	a	4.1	(2.1)	549	(26.2)	66.9	(2.9)
	Hungary	95.2	(1.7)	480	(4.3)	49.4	(0.5)	4.4	(1.6)	494	(35.5)	52.6	(3.3)	0.3	(0.3)	394	(4.8)	38.0	(0.0)
	Iceland	99.2	(0.0)	507	(1.5)	52.6	(0.3)	a	a	a	a	a	a	0.8	(0.0)	c	c	c	c
	Ireland	39.5	(2.0)	501	(4.9)	44.6	(0.7)	57.7	(2.4)	541	(3.9)	50.1	(0.5)	2.9	(1.4)	586	(7.6)	62.5	(0.8)
	Italy	94.1	(1.6)	486	(3.3)	46.8	(0.3)	0.8	(0.8)	c	c	c	c	5.1	(1.4)	513	(12.9)	53.6	(2.0)
	Japan	69.6	(1.0)	524	(5.9)	49.2	(0.7)	0.8	(0.8)	c	c	c	c	29.6	(1.1)	518	(11.0)	53.0	(1.2)
	Korea	50.7	(4.5)	519	(5.6)	42.8	(0.8)	15.7	(3.6)	522	(7.9)	40.2	(1.7)	33.6	(3.8)	532	(3.6)	44.1	(0.7)
	Luxembourg	87.9	(0.0)	444	(1.8)	45.5	(0.3)	12.1	(0.0)	440	(3.6)	41.5	(0.8)	a	a	a	a	a	a
	Mexico	85.1	(3.1)	413	(3.6)	39.7	(0.5)	a	a	a	a	a	a	14.9	(3.1)	492	(7.5)	58.3	(1.5)
	New Zealand	95.1	(0.6)	528	(2.8)	51.7	(0.4)	0.1	(0.1)	c	c	c	c	4.8	(0.6)	599	(24.1)	64.0	(1.3)
	Norway	98.6	(0.9)	505	(2.9)	53.8	(0.4)	1.4	(0.9)	519	(12.9)	54.0	(5.6)	a	a	a	a	a	a
	Poland	97.1	(1.3)	478	(5.0)	45.6	(0.5)	a	a	a	a	a	a	2.9	(1.3)	500	(25.2)	57.9	(3.9)
	Portugal	92.6	(0.8)	469	(4.9)	43.8	(0.6)	5.9	(0.9)	482	(16.7)	41.7	(2.1)	1.5	(0.7)	508	(47.0)	56.1	(7.0)
	Spain	62.0	(2.0)	478	(3.7)	41.3	(0.6)	28.9	(3.3)	503	(7.0)	46.5	(1.3)	9.2	(2.5)	543	(6.2)	62.8	(1.4)
	Sweden	96.6	(0.7)	516	(2.2)	50.4	(0.4)	3.4	(0.7)	520	(16.0)	54.8	(2.2)	a	a	a	a	a	a
	Switzerland	94.1	(1.6)	492	(4.6)	48.2	(0.4)	1.2	(0.6)	530	(20.6)	51.7	(2.7)	4.7	(1.5)	523	(28.8)	63.3	(2.2)
	United Kingdom	90.8	(1.2)	515	(2.5)	50.1	(0.4)	a	a	a	a	a	a	9.2	(1.2)	614	(9.4)	64.8	(0.9)
	United States	94.6	(2.3)	502	(5.6)	51.7	(0.6)	1.1	(1.2)	523	(3.2)	47.9	(0.0)	4.3	(2.1)	545	(24.2)	55.3	(3.8)
NON-OECD COUNTRIES	Brazil	89.5	(2.2)	386	(3.9)	41.5	(0.7)	a	a	a	a	a	a	10.5	(2.2)	459	(15.7)	57.0	(1.9)
	Latvia	99.2	(0.8)	463	(6.4)	50.7	(0.7)	0.8	(0.8)	c	c	c	c	a	a	a	a	a	a
	Liechtenstein	m	m	m	m	m	m	m	m	m	m	m	m	m	m	m	m	m	m
	Russian Federation	100.0	(0.0)	461	(4.2)	49.3	(0.4)	a	a	a	a	a	a	a	a	a	a	a	a
	Netherlands[4]	26.2	(5.2)	514	(13.2)	49.3	(1.3)	73.9	(5.2)	538	(7.0)	51.6	(0.8)	a	a	a	a	a	a

		Difference in performance on the combined reading literacy scale				Difference on the international socio-economic index of occupational status			
		Government- dependent private schools and public schools[5]		Government- independent private schools and public schools[6]		Government- dependent private schools and public schools[5]		Government- independent private schools and public schools[6]	
		Difference	S.E.	Difference	S.E.	Difference	S.E.	Difference	S.E.
OECD COUNTRIES	Australia	m	m	m	m	m	m	m	m
	Austria	26	(16.5)	28	(11.8)	5.2	(3.3)	10.1	(1.5)
	Belgium	m	m	m	m	m	m	m	m
	Canada	41	(7.6)	36	(7.3)	7.0	(1.1)	12.1	(0.8)
	Czech Republic	11	(13.5)	c	c	-1.1	(1.9)	c	c
	Denmark	-2	(6.7)	a	a	1.2	(1.1)	a	a
	Finland	9	(15.0)	a	a	5.3	(3.1)	a	a
	France	m	m	m	m	m	m	m	m
	Germany	83	(13.8)	a	a	8.2	(1.9)	a	a
	Greece	a	a	81	(26.7)	a	a	20.6	(3.0)
	Hungary	14	(36.2)	-85	(6.3)	3.2	(3.4)	-11.4	(0.5)
	Iceland	a	a	c	c	a	a	c	c
	Ireland	41	(6.3)	86	(9.0)	5.5	(0.9)	18.0	(1.1)
	Italy	c	c	27	(13.3)	c	c	6.8	(2.1)
	Japan	c	c	-6	(12.5)	c	c	3.8	(1.4)
	Korea	3	(11.4)	13	(7.1)	-2.6	(2.1)	1.3	(1.1)
	Luxembourg	-4	(3.8)	a	a	-4.0	(0.9)	a	a
	Mexico	a	a	79	(8.9)	a	a	18.5	(1.7)
	New Zealand	c	c	71	(24.4)	c	c	12.3	(1.4)
	Norway	14	(13.3)	a	a	0.2	(5.7)	a	a
	Poland	a	a	22	(26.2)	a	a	12.3	(4.0)
	Portugal	13	(17.5)	39	(47.3)	-2.1	(2.2)	12.3	(7.1)
	Spain	25	(7.9)	65	(7.1)	5.2	(1.4)	21.5	(1.5)
	Sweden	3	(16.3)	a	a	4.3	(2.3)	a	a
	Switzerland	38	(22.6)	31	(29.4)	3.5	(2.8)	15.1	(2.3)
	United Kingdom	a	a	98	(9.8)	a	a	14.7	(1.0)
	United States	22	(6.1)	43	(26.2)	-3.9	(0.6)	3.5	(4.0)
NON-OECD COUNTRIES	Brazil	a	a	74	(16.4)	a	a	15.4	(2.1)
	Latvia	c	c	a	a	c	c	a	a
	Liechtenstein	m	m	m	m	m	m	m	m
	Russian Federation	a	a	a	a	a	a	a	a
	Netherlands[4]	24	(18.5)	a	a	2.3	(1.7)	a	a

1. Government or public: Schools which are directly controlled or managed by: i) a public education authority or agency, or ii) by a government agency directly or by a governing body, most of whose members are either appointed by a public authority or elected by public franchise.
2. Private, government-dependent: Schools which receive more than 50 per cent of their core funding (funding that support the basic educational services of the institution) from government agencies.
3. Private, government-independent: Schools which receive less than 50 per cent of their core funding (funding that support the basic educational services of the institution) from government agencies.
4. Response rate is too low to ensure comparability (see Annex A3).
5. Positive differences favour government-dependent private schools while negative differences favour public schools. Bold values are statistically significant.
6. Positive differences favour government-independent private schools while negative differences favour public schools. Bold values are statistically significant.

Table 8.1
Relationship between student performance and socio-economic background
*Estimated level, slope and strength of the relationship between student performance on the combined reading literacy scale
and the PISA index of economic, social and cultural status (ESCS)*

		(1) Unadjusted mean score	(2) Mean score if ESCS was equal to the OECD average		(3) Slope of socio-economic gradient[1]		(4) Strength of relationship	(5) Length of projection of gradient line	(6) Missing data for the ESCS
		Mean score	Mean score	S.E.	Score point difference associated with one unit on the ESCS	S.E.	Percentage of explained variance	Difference between 95th and 5th percentile of the ESCS	Percentage of students
OECD COUNTRIES	Australia	528	513	(3.10)	46	(2.36)	17	2.9	1.2
	Austria	507	507	(2.62)	41	(2.26)	14	2.7	0.6
	Belgium	507	520	(2.84)	48	(2.35)	21	3.1	1.9
	Canada	534	527	(1.52)	37	(1.31)	11	2.8	3.4
	Czech Republic	492	500	(2.42)	50	(2.22)	20	2.7	1.1
	Denmark	497	498	(2.32)	42	(2.07)	15	2.8	1.7
	Finland	546	546	(2.22)	30	(2.40)	9	2.9	0.5
	France	505	512	(2.48)	47	(2.17)	22	2.9	1.1
	Germany	484	476	(3.80)	60	(3.44)	22	2.8	1.7
	Greece	474	484	(4.12)	38	(3.05)	15	3.3	1.7
	Hungary	480	488	(3.46)	53	(2.89)	26	2.9	0.6
	Iceland	507	492	(2.13)	24	(2.05)	5	2.8	1.2
	Ireland	527	526	(2.89)	38	(2.22)	13	2.9	1.1
	Italy	487	487	(3.11)	32	(2.35)	11	3.1	0.5
	Japan	522	533	(4.62)	21	(2.87)	6	2.6	6.1
	Korea	525	534	(2.22)	21	(2.37)	9	2.9	0.3
	Luxembourg	441	447	(2.10)	46	(1.69)	24	3.4	2.4
	Mexico	422	459	(3.04)	35	(2.47)	23	4.4	3.8
	New Zealand	529	524	(2.52)	45	(2.27)	16	3.1	1.2
	Norway	505	487	(3.03)	41	(1.83)	13	2.9	1.7
	Poland	479	496	(4.36)	36	(3.40)	14	3.2	2.1
	Portugal	470	488	(3.76)	40	(2.09)	20	3.6	0.9
	Spain	493	504	(2.23)	32	(1.52)	16	3.3	1.2
	Sweden	516	504	(1.97)	36	(1.86)	11	2.7	1.0
	Switzerland	494	499	(3.55)	49	(2.24)	19	3.0	1.1
	United Kingdom	523	519	(2.31)	49	(1.87)	19	2.9	1.8
	United States	504	497	(4.79)	48	(2.75)	22	3.3	5.9
	OECD average	*500*	*505*	*(1.31)*	*41*	*(0.97)*	*20*	*3.0*	*1.7*
NON-OECD COUNTRIES	Brazil	396	434	(3.28)	38	(2.60)	19	4.0	3.4
	Liechtenstein	483	478	(5.31)	49	(6.30)	18	2.5	0.7
	Russian Federation	462	480	(3.20)	31	(2.79)	11	3.0	2.1
	Netherlands[2]	m	m		38	(2.61)	15	2.8	0.6

1. Slopes marked in bold are statistically significantly different from the OECD average slope.
2. Response rate is too low to ensure comparability (see Annex A3).

Table 8.2
Effects of selected family background and demographic factors on student performance on the combined reading literacy scale

		(1)	(2)		(3)		(4)		(5)	
		Unadjusted mean score	Mean score adjusted by the background factors shown in this table		Student from single-parent family[1]		Number of siblings[1] (1 sibling increase)		Student is foreign-born[1]	
		Mean score	Mean score	S.E.	Effect	S.E.	Effect	S.E.	Effect	S.E.
OECD COUNTRIES	Australia	528	518	(3.01)	3.5	(4.46)	**−5.2**	(1.28)	**−22.1**	(5.60)
	Austria	507	499	(2.26)	1.7	(4.68)	**−3.8**	(1.18)	**−56.8**	(6.78)
	Belgium	507	505	(2.92)	−8.2	(5.26)	**−11.2**	(1.38)	**−32.7**	(6.15)
	Canada	534	523	(1.57)	−2.2	(2.08)	**−4.6**	(0.87)	**−27.8**	(3.71)
	Czech Republic	492	471	(2.71)	7.7	(5.50)	**−8.9**	(1.19)	−2.5	(11.90)
	Denmark	497	496	(1.76)	−5.1	(4.37)	**−3.3**	(1.11)	**−32.6**	(6.08)
	Finland	546	543	(2.42)	**−13.9**	(5.63)	**−3.3**	(0.89)	**−33.2**	(10.40)
	France	505	505	(2.05)	**−11.2**	(3.45)	**−6.4**	(1.10)	**−28.0**	(8.65)
	Germany	484	470	(2.40)	1.2	(3.55)	**−7.0**	(1.26)	**−20.2**	(5.82)
	Greece	474	471	(3.69)	0.5	(6.22)	**−7.7**	(1.57)	**−44.0**	(10.14)
	Hungary	480	459	(3.04)	0.3	(3.38)	**−7.5**	(1.37)	−12.2	(9.56)
	Iceland	507	484	(2.54)	6.7	(5.08)	−0.2	(0.96)	−12.5	(6.45)
	Ireland	527	529	(2.85)	**−11.4**	(5.23)	**−6.1**	(1.13)	15.5	(6.77)
	Italy	487	474	(3.15)	**−7.7**	(3.56)	**−14.5**	(1.65)	−16.1	(9.48)
	Japan	522	534	(5.95)	−9.5	(5.41)	−4.2	(1.92)	−37.0	(27.50)
	Korea	525	525	(2.49)	**−11.6**	(4.78)	**−5.6**	(1.68)		
	Luxembourg	441	453	(1.98)	−3.3	(5.42)	**−6.3**	(1.22)	**−41.2**	(3.94)
	Mexico	422	450	(3.12)	0.5	(3.08)	**−7.1**	(0.77)	**−50.9**	(7.12)
	New Zealand	529	531	(2.01)	−6.3	(4.78)	**−9.0**	(1.29)	**−32.9**	(4.82)
	Norway	505	493	(2.65)	−7.7	(4.98)	**−4.9**	(1.98)	**−24.5**	(6.60)
	Poland	479	483	(3.65)	3.8	(5.62)	−2.8	(1.16)	−33.6	(18.45)
	Portugal	470	471	(3.37)	8.0	(4.26)	**−12.6**	(1.27)	−9.4	(5.94)
	Spain	493	494	(2.17)	−3.4	(3.28)	**−7.7**	(1.34)	−16.0	(9.12)
	Sweden	516	511	(2.05)	**−11.8**	(3.54)	**−5.0**	(0.84)	**−42.8**	(7.00)
	Switzerland	494	495	(3.42)	−1.6	(4.22)	−4.2	(1.63)	**−60.3**	(4.88)
	United Kingdom	523	523	(1.94)	**−17.2**	(2.82)	**−5.7**	(0.93)	**−17.5**	(7.70)
	United States	504	512	(4.00)	**−14.6**	(4.76)	**−6.7**	(1.01)	−4.8	(6.93)
	OECD average	*500*	*505*	*(1.08)*	*−10.7*	*(1.97)*	*−7.9*	*(0.49)*	*−26.2*	*(2.89)*
NON-OECD COUNTRIES	Brazil	396	424	(3.25)	−1.1	(3.62)	**−6.9**	(0.84)	−43.0	(23.63)
	Liechtenstein	483	488	(5.13)	−5.4	(16.41)	−3.3	(3.99)	**−62.5**	(19.71)
	Russian Federation	462	463	(3.55)	**6.3**	(2.78)	**−4.7**	(0.64)	7.3	(5.42)
	Netherlands[3]	m	m		−9.4	(5.96)	−3.7	(1.98)	−41.6	(8.58)

		(6)		(7)		(8)		(9)	
		International socio-economic index of occupational status (ISEI)[2] (1 international standard deviation increase)		Parental years of schooling[1] (1 year increase)		Index of home educational resources[2] (1 unit increase)		Index of cultural possessions in the family home[2] (1 unit increase)	
		Effect	S.E.	Effect	S.E.	Effect	S.E.	Effect	S.E.
OECD COUNTRIES	Australia	**20.3**	(9.70)	**4.8**	(0.82)	**11.5**	(1.67)	**18.8**	(1.85)
	Austria	**50.8**	(8.72)	**4.3**	(0.61)	**13.8**	(2.14)	**8.2**	(1.90)
	Belgium	**51.6**	(10.27)	**2.6**	(0.51)	**22.3**	(2.87)	**13.3**	(1.43)
	Canada	**19.2**	(4.74)	**4.6**	(0.43)	**7.9**	(0.97)	**11.8**	(0.87)
	Czech Republic	**33.1**	(11.08)	**7.6**	(1.32)	**15.9**	(2.49)	**13.8**	(1.88)
	Denmark	11.4	(9.73)	**9.4**	(0.67)	**8.3**	(1.65)	**10.4**	(1.68)
	Finland	12.4	(10.71)	**3.7**	(0.49)	3.8	(1.67)	**12.3**	(1.55)
	France	**22.5**	(6.44)	**2.7**	(0.51)	**16.1**	(1.69)	**17.2**	(1.45)
	Germany	**66.7**	(13.19)	**5.4**	(0.93)	**22.3**	(4.42)	**14.8**	(2.77)
	Greece	8.5	(8.31)	**3.2**	(0.64)	**12.2**	(1.82)	**15.0**	(1.98)
	Hungary	19.4	(10.74)	**12.1**	(1.16)	**10.3**	(1.69)	**20.3**	(2.07)
	Iceland	−9.4	(8.95)	**3.6**	(0.60)	2.1	(1.70)	**12.7**	(2.38)
	Ireland	7.6	(8.17)	**2.2**	(0.83)	**13.7**	(1.62)	**10.2**	(1.96)
	Italy	**26.1**	(8.93)	**2.6**	(0.60)	**9.5**	(2.24)	**10.5**	(1.98)
	Japan	**33.1**	(14.65)	−1.1	(2.37)	**11.7**	(2.06)	**13.4**	(1.47)
	Korea	13.6	(9.03)	**3.3**	(0.37)	**5.8**	(1.24)	**9.8**	(1.23)
	Luxembourg	**24.0**	(7.66)	**2.5**	(0.48)	**18.2**	(2.03)	**18.2**	(1.69)
	Mexico	**17.4**	(6.86)	**2.6**	(0.49)	**10.9**	(1.09)	**8.3**	(1.59)
	New Zealand	**29.0**	(8.57)	**2.5**	(0.73)	**18.9**	(1.71)	**7.1**	(1.83)
	Norway	6.8	(9.58)	**2.0**	(0.78)	**19.5**	(1.78)	**12.8**	(1.91)
	Poland	18.1	(9.86)	**6.0**	(1.31)	**12.2**	(1.94)	**11.4**	(2.30)
	Portugal	**23.4**	(8.12)	1.1	(0.60)	**14.5**	(1.61)	**14.9**	(1.39)
	Spain	**18.6**	(5.26)	**3.6**	(0.39)	**10.6**	(1.39)	**12.5**	(1.40)
	Sweden	5.5	(8.08)	1.1	(0.86)	3.6	(1.35)	**15.1**	(1.49)
	Switzerland	**41.8**	(6.21)	**6.1**	(0.69)	**15.2**	(1.91)	**8.3**	(1.56)
	United Kingdom	16.8	(8.95)	**5.5**	(0.66)	**11.5**	(1.33)	**12.7**	(1.50)
	United States	19.2	(10.79)	**4.7**	(1.11)	**10.3**	(1.69)	**15.8**	(2.38)
	OECD average	*28.1*	*(3.60)*	*4.7*	*(0.30)*	*12.0*	*(0.70)*	*13.4*	*(0.81)*
NON-OECD COUNTRIES	Brazil	0.1	(6.85)	**2.6**	(0.51)	**12.7**	(1.25)	**4.2**	(2.01)
	Liechtenstein	35.0	(30.87)	**6.0**	(2.06)	10.6	(6.92)	10.1	(7.05)
	Russian Federation	**39.8**	(8.23)	0.5	(0.59)	**12.5**	(1.11)	**8.9**	(1.83)
	Netherlands[3]	**26.1**	(12.34)	**2.4**	(0.68)	**21.6**	(2.91)	**4.7**	(1.73)

Effects marked in bold are statistically significant.
1. For the definitions of the measures, see Annex A1.
2. For the definitions of the indices, see Annex A1.
3. Response rate is too low to ensure comparability (see Annex A3).

Table 8.3
Variation in performance on the combined reading literacy scale explained by socio-economic background

	Percentage of BETWEEN-school variance that is explained by the socio-economic background factors shown in Table 8.2	Percentage of WITHIN-school variance that is explained by the socio-economic background factors shown in Table 8.2
Australia	64	16
Austria	28	5
Belgium	31	9
Canada	42	14
Czech Republic	43	11
Denmark	58	18
Finland	18	20
France	m	m
Germany	27	12
Greece	25	8
Hungary	25	4
Iceland	31	12
Ireland	59	12
Italy	19	3
Japan	11	3
Korea	17	3
Luxembourg	54	21
Mexico	31	4
New Zealand	70	19
Norway	48	20
Poland	10	2
Portugal	43	14
Spain	59	12
Sweden	73	17
Switzerland	35	18
United Kingdom	61	18
United States	61	17
OECD average	*34*	*14*
Brazil	35	6
Liechtenstein	20	15
Russian Federation	27	10
Netherlands[1]	31	10

1. Response rate is too low to ensure comparability (see Annex A3).

OECD COUNTRIES / NON-OECD COUNTRIES

ANNEX B1

Table 8.4
Effects of the students' and schools' socio-economic background on performance on the combined reading literacy scale
Effect of an increase of half a student-level standard deviation of the index of economic, social and cultural status

		Interquartile range of school mean index of economic, social and cultural status[1]	Effect of the students' economic, social and cultural status on performance[1]	Effect of the schools' mean economic, social and cultural status on performance[1]
OECD COUNTRIES	Australia	0.73	17	21
	Austria	0.83	4	59
	Belgium	0.97	7	56
	Canada	0.60	14	22
	Czech Republic	0.52	10	52
	Denmark	0.54	17	22
	Finland	0.44	13	8
	France	m	m	m
	Germany	0.63	8	66
	Greece	0.75	7	39
	Hungary	0.86	4	47
	Iceland	0.50	11	5
	Ireland	0.55	13	23
	Italy	1.04	3	44
	Japan[2]	m	m	m
	Korea	0.85	3	30
	Luxembourg	0.96	12	40
	Mexico	1.20	3	22
	New Zealand	0.64	16	22
	Norway	0.57	17	12
	Poland	0.92	2	49
	Portugal	0.66	11	29
	Spain	0.77	10	16
	Sweden	0.50	14	16
	Switzerland	0.50	12	32
	United Kingdom	0.93	15	29
	United States	0.61	13	28
	OECD average	*0.72*	*10*	*32*
NON-OECD COUNTRIES	Brazil	1.16	6	22
	Liechtenstein	0.49	5	64
	Russian Federation	0.79	8	27
	Netherlands[3]	0.66	7	57

1. For the definition of the index, see Annex A1.
2. Data for Japan are not included in this table due to a high percentage of missing data on parental education and parental occupation.
3. Response rate is too low to ensure comparability (see Annex A3).

Table 8.5
Effects of student-level and school-level factors on performance on the combined reading, mathematical and scientific literacy scales, for all OECD countries combined

READING LITERACY SCALE	Increase	Model 1: Impact of school factors		Model 2: Impact of family background		Model 3: Joint impact of school factors and family background	
		Effect	S.E.	Effect	S.E.	Effect	S.E.
Family background and student characteristics							
Student-level index of economic, social and cultural status[1]	1 unit			**20.1**	(2.07)	**20.1**	(2.07)
— Student-level index of economic, social and cultural status squared				**−1.7**	(0.34)	**−1.7**	(0.35)
School mean index of economic, social and cultural status[1]	1 student-level unit			**67.5**	(6.48)	**56.6**	(5.41)
Student is female				**25.5**	(1.97)	**25.0**	(2.03)
Student is foreign-born[2]				**−23.2**	(2.87)	**−23.1**	(2.88)
School resources							
Student-teaching staff ratio (1 student less for each FTE teacher)[2]	−1 student	3.0	(1.58)			1.1	(0.64)
— Student-teaching staff ratio squared		**−0.1**	(0.03)			0.0	(0.01)
— Student-teaching staff ratio is greater than 50		**−27.8**	(14.98)			**−18.6**	(11.60)
School size	100 students	**4.8**	(1.21)			**1.5**	(0.51)
School size squared		**−0.1**	(0.05)			0.0	(0.02)
Percentage of computers at school available to 15-year-olds[2]	1 percentage point	−0.1	(0.19)			0.0	(0.13)
Percentage of teachers in school with a university tertiary-level qualification with a major in the respective subject domain	1 percentage point	**0.4**	(0.08)			**0.2**	(0.04)
Percentage of teachers in school participating in professional development programmes[2]	1 percentage point	**−0.1**	(0.03)			**−0 1**	(0.01)
Index of the quality of the schools' physical infrastructure[1] *	1 unit	1.2	(1.16)			0.9	(0.65)
Index of students' use of school resources[1] *	1 unit	**18.3**	(3.30)			**9.1**	(1.84)
School policy and practice							
Index of the use of formal student assessments[1] *	1 unit	−0.1	(0.90)			0.9	(0.83)
Index of teacher-related factors affecting school climate[1] *	1 unit	**6.3**	(1.92)			1.6	(0.96)
Index of the principals' perceptions of teachers' morale and commitment[1] *	1 unit	**2.2**	(0.95)			−0.4	(0.55)
Index of teacher autonomy[1] *	1 unit	−1.3	(1.30)			−0.1	(0.82)
Index of school autonomy[1] *	1 unit	**4.9**	(1.48)			−0.1	(0.76)
Classroom practice							
Index of the use of informal student assessments[1] *	1 unit	−1.6	(1.00)			**−1.1**	(0.55)
Index of teacher-student relations[1] *	1 unit	**18.0**	(1.73)			**10.1**	(1.07)
Index of disciplinary climate[1] *	1 unit	**10.5**	(1.79)			**7.0**	(1.16)
Index of achievement press[1] *	1 unit	3.8	(2.50)			2.1	(1.31)
Percentage of variance explained							
Students within schools		0.0		12.4		12.4	
Schools within countries		31.0		66.1		71.9	
Between countries		20.8		34.3		43.4	

MATHEMATICAL LITERACY SCALE	Increase	Model 1: Impact of school factors		Model 2: Impact of family background		Model 3: Joint impact of school factors and family background	
		Effect	S.E.	Effect	S.E.	Effect	S.E.
Family background and student characteristics							
Student-level index of economic, social and cultural status[1]	1 unit			**19.3**	(1.76)	**19.3**	(1.76)
— Student-level index of economic, social and cultural status squared				**−1.2**	(0.45)	**−1.2**	(0.44)
School mean index of economic, social and cultural status[1]	1 student-level unit			**62.8**	(6.97)	**52.7**	(5.76)
Student is female				**−16.2**	(1.56)	**−16.8**	(1.60)
Student is foreign-born[2]				**−21.1**	(3.78)	**−21.5**	(3.85)
School resources							
Student-teaching staff ratio (1 student less for each FTE teacher)[2]	−1 student	2.3	(1.43)			0.8	(0.59)
— Student-teaching staff ratio squared		**−0.1**	(0.03)			0.0	(0.01)
— Student-teaching staff ratio is greater than 50		**−26.0**	(11.20)			−16.9	(10.35)
School size	100 students	**4.1**	(1.28)			**1.3**	(0.63)
School size squared		**−0.1**	(0.05)			0.0	(0.03)
Percentage of computers at school available to 15-year-olds[2]	1 percentage point	−0.3	(0.20)			−0.2	(0.14)
Percentage of teachers in school with a university tertiary-level qualification with a major in the respective subject domain	1 percentage point	**0.3**	(0.05)			**0.1**	(0.03)
Percentage of teachers in school participating in professional development programmes[2]	1 percentage point	**−0.1**	(0.03)			**−0.1**	(0.02)
Index of the quality of the schools' physical infrastructure[1] *	1 unit	1.7	(1.10)			**1.3**	(0.62)
Index of students' use of school resources[1] *	1 unit	**20.0**	(3.38)			**10.7**	(2.02)
School policy and practice							
Index of the use of formal student assessments[1] *	1 unit	1.5	(1.12)			1.9	(1.33)
Index of teacher-related factors affecting school climate[1] *	1 unit	**5.6**	(2.02)			1.4	(1.19)
Index of the principals' perceptions of teachers' morale and commitment[1] *	1 unit	**2 1**	(0.82)			−0.4	(0.57)
Index of teacher autonomy[1] *	1 unit	−1.5	(1.27)			−0.3	(0.88)
Index of school autonomy[1] *	1 unit	**4.2**	(1.35)			−0.1	(0.81)
Classroom practice							
Index of the use of informal student assessments[1] *	1 unit	−1.2	(0.93)			−0.9	(0.63)
Index of teacher-student relations[1] *	1 unit	**14.7**	(1.96)			**8.9**	(1.09)
Index of disciplinary climate[1] *	1 unit	**9.2**	(1.66)			**6.4**	(1.08)
Index of achievement press[1] *	1 unit	3.2	(2.71)			1.3	(1.54)
Percentage of variance explained							
Students within schools		0.0		11.0		11.2	
Schools within countries		28.3		62.0		67.8	
Between countries		21.8		26.0		32.2	

* These indices were standardised to have a mean of 0 and a standard deviation of 1 for schools in OECD countries.
Effects marked in bold are statistically significant.
1. For the definitions of the indices, see Annex A1.
2. For the definitions of the measures, see Annex A1.

Table 8.5 *(continued)*

Effects of student-level and school-level factors on performance on the combined reading, mathematical and scientific literacy scales, for all OECD countries combined

SCIENTIFIC LITERACY SCALE	Increase	Model 1: Impact of school factors		Model 2: Impact of family background		Model 3: Joint impact of school factors and family background	
		Effect	S.E.	Effect	S.E.	Effect	S.E.
Family background and student characteristics							
Student-level index of economic, social and cultural status[1]	1 unit			**19.3**	(1.94)	**19.3**	(1.95)
— Student-level index of economic, social and cultural status squared				**−0.8**	(0.42)	**−0.8**	(0.42)
School mean index of economic, social and cultural status[1]	1 student-level unit			**65.4**	(6.78)	**54.9**	(5.62)
Student is female				**−5.2**	(1.67)	**−6.0**	(1.76)
Student is foreign-born[2]				**−25.6**	(3.87)	**−25.9**	(3.90)
School resources							
Student-teaching staff ratio (1 student less for each FTE teacher)[2]	−1 student	2.8	(1.59)			1.2	(0.70)
— Student-teaching staff ratio squared		**−0.1**	(0.03)			0.0	(0.02)
— Student-teaching staff ratio is greater than 50		**−35.0**	(13.71)			**−26.9**	(10.54)
School size	100 students	**4.0**	(1.25)			1.0	(0.61)
School size squared		−0.1	(0.05)			0.0	(0.03)
Percentage of computers at school available to 15-year-olds[2]	1 percentage point	−0.2	(0.19)			−0.1	(0.12)
Percentage of teachers in school with a university tertiary-level qualification with a major in the respective subject domain	1 percentage point	**0.3**	(0.07)			**0.1**	(0.04)
Percentage of teachers in school participating in professional development programmes[2]	1 percentage point	**−0.1**	(0.03)			**−0.1**	(0.01)
Index of the quality of the schools' physical infrastructure[1] *	1 unit	1.4	(0.99)			1.2	(0.65)
Index of students' use of school resources[1] *	1 unit	**18.6**	(3.23)			**9.9**	(1.86)
School policy and practice							
Index of the use of formal student assessment[1] *	1 unit	0.5	(1.00)			1.4	(1.04)
Index of teacher-related factors affecting school climate[1] *	1 unit	**5.1**	(1.79)			0.5	(0.94)
Index of the principals' perceptions of teachers' morale and commitment[1] *	1 unit	**3.1**	(1.01)			0.3	(0.57)
Index of teacher autonomy[1] *	1 unit	−1.0	(1.14)			0.2	(0.68)
Index of school autonomy[1] *	1 unit	**4.8**	(1.30)			0.4	(0.80)
Classroom practice							
Index of the use of informal student assessments[1] *	1 unit	−1.2	(0.97)			−0.9	(0.65)
Index of teacher-student relations[1] *	1 unit	**16.5**	(1.96)			**10.1**	(1.12)
Index of disciplinary climate[1] *	1 unit	**10.5**	(1.73)			**7.0**	(1.22)
Index of achievement press[1] *	1 unit	2.2	(2.50)			1.2	(1.40)
Percentage of variance explained							
Students within schools		0.0		10.7		10.7	
Schools within countries		29.4		62.6		69.0	
Between countries		20.2		8.3		15.6	

* These indices were standardised to have a mean of 0 and a standard deviation of 1 for schools in OECD countries.
Effects marked in bold are statistically significant.
1. For the definitions of the indices, see Annex A1.
2. For the definitions of the measures, see Annex A1.

Table 8.5a
Effects of student-level and school-level factors on performance on the combined reading literacy scale

		Difference in average school performance for schools with a student-teaching staff ratio between 20 and 25 and those with a ratio below 20[1]		Difference in average school performance for schools with a student-teaching staff ratio between 25 and 30 and those with a ratio below 20[1]		Difference in average school performance for schools with a student-teaching staff ratio greater than 30 and those with a ratio below 20[1]		Percentage of computers at school available to 15-years olds[1] (1 percentage point increase)		Percentage of teachers in school with a university tertiary-level qualification with a major in the respective subject domain (1 percentage point increase)	
		Effect	S.E.	Effect	S.E.	Effect	S.E.	Effect	S.E.	Effect	S.E.
OECD COUNTRIES	Australia	−48.22	(9.84)	a	a	−65.10	(10.84)	−0.36	(0.45)	0.37	(0.12)
	Austria	−38.95	(19.93)	−14.10	(19.24)	−8.31	(17.09)	0.51	(0.46)	0.41	(0.20)
	Belgium	26.84	(16.73)	a	a	−93.31	(44.11)	−2.51	(0.76)	0.98	(0.20)
	Canada	22.86	(4.77)	−7.70	(20.20)	−40.71	(14.40)	−0.51	(0.16)	0.39	(0.05)
	Czech Republic	−12.42	(8.52)	−12.19	(19.84)	−0.02	(11.64)	0.39	(0.27)	0.32	(0.19)
	Denmark	a	a	a	a	a	a	−1.12	(0.47)	0.37	(0.14)
	Finland	a	a	a	a	a	a	−0.84	(1.03)	−0.19	(0.12)
	France	m	m	m	m	m	m	m	m	m	m
	Germany	−8.77	(10.74)	−28.17	(14.12)	−22.46	(25.04)	−2.31	(1.22)	1.03	(0.14)
	Greece	23.29	(17.50)	a	a	a	a	−1.35	(0.41)	a	a
	Hungary	a	a	a	a	−39.12	(28.24)	0.25	(0.40)	0.50	(0.49)
	Iceland	a	a	−22.72	(8.50)	a	a	−0.36	(0.54)	0.02	(0.10)
	Ireland	a	a	a	a	a	a	−1.43	(1.17)	0.07	(0.32)
	Italy	a	a	a	a	a	a	−2.04	(0.99)	0.75	(0.29)
	Japan	27.45	(19.70)	a	a	a	a	−1.65	(0.43)	−0.17	(0.29)
	Korea	15.97	(5.71)	27.52	(8.92)	−17.14	(10.31)	−0.86	(0.26)	0.01	(0.10)
	Luxembourg	a	a	a	a	a	a	1.28	(2.06)	3.09	(0.62)
	Mexico	11.96	(6.85)	−19.69	(12.00)	−1.13	(7.25)	1.02	(0.56)	−0.12	(0.13)
	New Zealand	a	a	a	a	a	a	−0.73	(0.87)	0.03	(0.17)
	Norway	a	a	a	a	a	a	−1.09	(0.49)	0.15	(0.12)
	Poland	−2.23	(15.24)	−49.39	(23.38)	50.14	(25.86)	−0.69	(0.28)	0.87	(0.73)
	Portugal	43.03	(32.13)	a	a	a	a	−0.11	(0.33)	−0.13	(0.42)
	Spain	18.82	(7.67)	−11.87	(12.17)	a	a	−2.54	(0.77)	0.03	(0.10)
	Sweden	a	a	a	a	−26.74	(10.83)	−0.22	(0.60)	0.16	(0.08)
	Switzerland	−41.26	(54.87)	a	a	−13.34	(11.78)	−0.68	(0.36)	0.62	(0.10)
	United Kingdom	44.42	(20.25)	−11.42	(13.54)	−49.51	(17.20)	−0.74	(0.37)	0.13	(0.12)
	United States	−14.62	(15.62)	9.28	(10.27)	a	a	−1.41	(0.40)	0.39	(0.15)
	Meta effect	*−0.73*	*(8.47)*	*−10.03*	*(6.41)*	*−22.48*	*(7.61)*	*−0.69*	*(0.16)*	*0.30*	*(0.07)*
NON-OECD COUNTRIES	Brazil	20.89	(12.71)	−12.22	(7.02)	−5.09	(7.08)	1.19	(0.15)	0.22	(0.10)
	Liechtenstein[3]	m	m	m	m	m	m	m	m	m	m
	Russian Federation	−4.27	(10.68)	−4.35	(15.95)	−3.92	(21.75)	−1.41	(1.15)	0.09	(0.19)
	Netherlands[4]	9.51	(9.63)	14.15	(18.82)	a	a	−0.18	(0.44)	0.08	(0.22)

		Percentage of teachers in school participating in professional development programmes[1] (1 percentage point increase)		Index of the quality of the schools' physical infrastructure[2] (1 unit increase)		Index of students' use of school resources[2] (1 unit increase)		Index of the use of formal student assessments[2] (1 unit increase)	
		Effect	S.E.	Effect	S.E.	Effect	S.E.	Effect	S.E.
OECD COUNTRIES	Australia	−0.01	(0.07)	−0.79	(3.50)	11.98	(3.77)	2.40	(2.98)
	Austria	0.14	(0.20)	−4.12	(5.62)	28.06	(9.89)	−7.04	(4.95)
	Belgium	0.00	(0.20)	−1.64	(4.39)	49.50	(7.33)	−7.05	(4.18)
	Canada	−0.02	(0.04)	2.41	(1.24)	8.44	(2.50)	−0.62	(1.34)
	Czech Republic	−0.21	(0.14)	−7.25	(3.38)	34.30	(4.20)	4.86	(4.34)
	Denmark	0.01	(0.08)	2.72	(3.22)	10.35	(4.27)	6.85	(4.22)
	Finland	−0.21	(0.10)	0.30	(3.40)	3.75	(10.01)	6.26	(3.50)
	France	m	m	m	m	m	m	m	m
	Germany	−0.25	(0.14)	13.36	(4.85)	−0.94	(11.71)	3.32	(5.56)
	Greece	−0.17	(0.32)	2.67	(5.86)	−14.67	(14.76)	11.80	(6.50)
	Hungary	−0.64	(0.30)	−5.12	(5.45)	31.51	(10.32)	8.53	(8.37)
	Iceland	0.00	(0.08)	3.96	(3.83)	2.95	(6.31)	−5.05	(6.50)
	Ireland	−0.16	(0.13)	−1.07	(3.69)	16.24	(8.05)	−3.04	(5.00)
	Italy	−0.05	(0.19)	17.13	(5.36)	7.48	(7.23)	1.09	(5.87)
	Japan	−0.19	(0.15)	2.71	(4.56)	12.43	(5.28)	−1.57	(3.42)
	Korea	0.08	(0.10)	−2.94	(2.95)	−2.80	(3.75)	0.78	(2.33)
	Luxembourg	−1.08	(0.62)	45.85	(8.94)	−65.96	(28.74)	a	a
	Mexico	−0.08	(0.10)	8.81	(3.51)	33.89	(4.55)	3.29	(3.84)
	New Zealand	0.02	(0.11)	3.75	(4.06)	14.53	(7.79)	−7.13	(6.44)
	Norway	0.01	(0.07)	4.39	(4.28)	5.52	(3.76)	−1.19	(2.93)
	Poland	−0.08	(0.15)	4.06	(6.05)	53.20	(6.55)	6.47	(9.10)
	Portugal	−0.36	(0.20)	0.96	(4.73)	−3.57	(8.54)	1.15	(6.19)
	Spain	−0.27	(0.09)	5.04	(2.42)	9.46	(4.15)	0.78	(2.84)
	Sweden	−0.04	(0.06)	3.71	(2.46)	3.60	(3.32)	2.99	(5.84)
	Switzerland	−0.13	(0.10)	4.21	(4.11)	22.42	(7.46)	−2.96	(3.86)
	United Kingdom	−0.18	(0.07)	−2.40	(3.38)	14.04	(4.56)	−10.64	(4.60)
	United States	0.05	(0.12)	−5.59	(5.88)	39.74	(5.77)	−7.20	(6.50)
	Meta effect	*−0.07*	*(0.02)*	*2.26*	*(1.14)*	*16.18*	*(3.39)*	*−0.18*	*(0.73)*
NON-OECD COUNTRIES	Brazil	−0.26	(0.09)	9.68	(2.94)	20.00	(4.27)	−0.78	(3.29)
	Liechtenstein[3]	m	m	m	m	m	m	m	m
	Russian Federation	−0.11	(0.16)	8.48	(3.45)	34.20	(8.28)	3.67	(4.98)
	Netherlands[4]	−0.15	(0.14)	−6.76	(4.29)	52.39	(6.47)	−9.01	(6.61)

Effects marked in bold are statistically significant.
1. For the definitions of the measures, see Annex A1.
2. For the definitions of the indices, see Annex A1.
3. Calculations for Liechtenstein was not possible due to the small number of schools.
4. Response rate is too low to ensure comparability (see Annex A3).

Table 8.5a (continued)
Effects of student-level and school-level factors on performance on the combined reading literacy scale

	Index of teacher-related factors affecting school climate[1] (1 unit increase)		Index of principals' perceptions of teachers' morale and commitment[1] (1 unit increase)		Index of teacher autonomy[1] (1 unit increase)		Index of school autonomy[1] (1 unit increase)	
	Effect	S.E.	Effect	S.E.	Effect	S.E.	Effect	S.E.
Australia	8.31	(3.17)	7.00	(3.39)	−5.61	(2.12)	14.32	(4.60)
Austria	−8.02	(6.66)	−8.41	(5.93)	−32.81	(6.59)	38.47	(7.65)
Belgium	17.17	(4.76)	5.61	(4.87)	−3.11	(4.12)	11.15	(6.97)
Canada	3.77	(1.82)	−0.36	(1.50)	1.99	(1.38)	8.21	(2.38)
Czech Republic	5.91	(3.54)	0.49	(3.80)	−5.63	(3.98)	2.04	(4.45)
Denmark	0.36	(3.12)	9.62	(3.57)	−3.82	(2.71)	−0.65	(3.03)
Finland	−2.89	(4.31)	7.73	(3.86)	5.50	(3.57)	−3.69	(3.62)
France	m	m	m	m	m	m	m	m
Germany	4.32	(7.48)	0.83	(6.13)	−10.95	(4.49)	−7.52	(6.43)
Greece	1.79	(3.13)	−2.32	(4.56)	8.06	(8.95)	5.78	(10.00)
Hungary	7.25	(5.26)	−0.10	(5.59)	3.83	(5.49)	−9.11	(8.05)
Iceland	5.68	(3.89)	−2.70	(3.79)	−2.00	(3.86)	6.51	(6.51)
Ireland	2.60	(5.33)	4.12	(3.94)	0.88	(4.51)	15.37	(6.40)
Italy	12.51	(5.06)	−1.29	(5.68)	−5.50	(5.98)	9.00	(8.46)
Japan	−0.40	(4.65)	9.05	(3.70)	3.39	(3.03)	−8.59	(5.26)
Korea	3.59	(2.92)	−0.86	(3.68)	1.11	(4.29)	0.02	(4.13)
Luxembourg	−41.32	(12.28)	−6.04	(12.43)	a	a	a	a
Mexico	−1.46	(3.29)	0.35	(3.15)	−2.50	(3.91)	8.29	(4.44)
New Zealand	11.90	(5.24)	3.51	(3.51)	−5.37	(4.50)	7.72	(9.11)
Norway	6.07	(4.44)	1.69	(4.65)	a	a	a	a
Poland	0.59	(7.72)	13.89	(5.99)	a	a	a	a
Portugal	11.81	(7.93)	2.41	(6.32)	−1.41	(8.74)	−13.29	(7.39)
Spain	6.85	(2.63)	6.35	(3.13)	1.73	(2.90)	9.39	(2.27)
Sweden	−0.87	(3.08)	3.72	(3.37)	2.75	(2.47)	−1.07	(4.57)
Switzerland	−7.95	(4.59)	3.62	(4.08)	−1.51	(4.19)	8.58	(3.67)
United Kingdom	16.87	(2.55)	4.52	(2.55)	−1.61	(2.69)	0.91	(3.03)
United States	8.71	(7.89)	7.36	(4.66)	−1.07	(4.67)	9.11	(5.76)
Meta effect	*4.24*	*(1.34)*	*3.03*	*(0.84)*	*−2.28*	*(1.26)*	*4.30*	*(1.84)*
Brazil	0.97	(2.55)	0.35	(3.38)	−10.78	(4.03)	13.58	(3.68)
Liechtenstein[2]	m	m	m	m	m	m	m	m
Russian Federation	1.22	(2.77)	14.16	(3.59)	−1.53	(5.64)	4.03	(6.10)
Netherlands[3]	20.09	(7.10)	−1.38	(6.98)	−2.00	(5.57)	−2.21	(7.04)

	Index of the use of formal student assessments[1] (1 unit increase)		Index of teacher-student relations[1] (1 unit increase)		Index of disciplinary climate[1] (1 unit increase)		Index of achievement press[1] (1 unit increase)	
	Effect	S.E.	Effect	S.E.	Effect	S.E.	Effect	S.E.
Australia	−6.97	(2.76)	7.90	(6.12)	19.33	(4.92)	−6.22	(5.06)
Austria	−3.81	(5.24)	13.20	(4.62)	9.32	(5.94)	5.94	(5.38)
Belgium	−1.93	(3.37)	24.82	(5.78)	1.05	(5.24)	16.90	(5.78)
Canada	−0.21	(1.74)	18.09	(2.55)	9.72	(2.08)	−3.46	(3.18)
Czech Republic	−1.90	(3.15)	7.76	(3.73)	6.66	(3.79)	1.15	(3.46)
Denmark	−1.85	(3.32)	28.50	(5.26)	1.50	(5.52)	4.82	(6.61)
Finland	−0.29	(3.85)	10.66	(5.68)	6.01	(3.71)	−12.75	(6.29)
France	m	m	28.49	(3.75)	−9.04	(4.84)	−7.02	(6.09)
Germany	−8.25	(4.69)	31.91	(5.24)	1.05	(6.10)	−0.47	(7.33)
Greece	0.89	(6.60)	11.36	(7.85)	1.67	(11.46)	37.20	(6.38)
Hungary	4.04	(7.47)	10.11	(7.23)	26.86	(6.69)	−1.53	(9.33)
Iceland	0.62	(2.17)	10.44	(4.08)	3.82	(2.79)	−8.47	(5.33)
Ireland	3.84	(5.09)	4.24	(7.14)	11.27	(5.13)	11.79	(11.30)
Italy	−8.02	(4.44)	13.43	(6.83)	26.80	(6.24)	6.08	(10.85)
Japan	−1.97	(2.35)	25.45	(5.15)	13.56	(3.89)	0.33	(3.17)
Korea	−1.60	(2.33)	5.62	(4.40)	10.25	(3.68)	23.84	(3.70)
Luxembourg	a	a	10.33	(18.33)	0.11	(20.73)	−12.86	(21.85)
Mexico	−3.89	(3.31)	26.92	(5.63)	0.46	(4.83)	10.83	(5.17)
New Zealand	0.09	(4.91)	29.09	(8.11)	3.41	(7.68)	−26.51	(11.94)
Norway	a	a	13.66	(4.10)	7.11	(6.05)	−0.59	(4.84)
Poland	2.68	(6.23)	9.08	(4.99)	22.93	(5.38)	26.71	(10.55)
Portugal	−5.81	(5.71)	33.01	(13.60)	29.03	(10.86)	22.32	(11.14)
Spain	3.34	(1.55)	0.51	(3.14)	8.98	(3.15)	1.63	(3.89)
Sweden	−0.52	(3.83)	12.77	(5.73)	18.94	(4.14)	−6.81	(4.95)
Switzerland	−3.78	(5.39)	11.32	(4.43)	10.00	(3.75)	−11.15	(5.23)
United Kingdom	2.61	(2.74)	19.08	(6.00)	14.63	(4.15)	−7.41	(7.20)
United States	−1.44	(7.76)	20.00	(8.98)	3.99	(6.58)	9.42	(9.06)
Meta effect	*−0.81*	*(0.78)*	*15.73*	*(1.81)*	*9.56*	*(1.61)*	*2.86*	*(2.54)*
Brazil	0.75	(3.10)	17.49	(4.98)	−14.70	(4.65)	9.76	(5.74)
Liechtenstein[2]	m	m	m	m	m	m	m	m
Russian Federation	a	a	−6.00	(5.94)	16.04	(4.32)	25.08	(6.92)
Netherlands[3]	1.40	(6.06)	38.34	(8.82)	−2.18	(6.33)	−8.58	(8.13)

Effects marked in bold are statistically significant.
1. For the definitions of the indices, see Annex A1.
2. Calculations for Liechtenstein was not possible due to the small number of schools.
3. Response rate is too low to ensure comparability (see Annex A3).

Table 8.6
Country means of selected school-level indices and their correlation with the school mean economic, social and cultural status (ESCS)

	Index of student-teaching staff ratio[1]			Index of school size[1]			Percentage of teachers in school with a university tertiary-level qualification with a major in the respective subject domain			Index of students' use of school resources[1] (rescaled)			Index of teacher-related factors affecting school climate[1] (rescaled)		
	Mean index	S.E.	Correlation with ESCS	Mean index	S.E.	Correlation with ESCS	Mean index	S.E.	Correlation with ESCS	Mean index	S.E.	Correlation with ESCS	Mean index	S.E.	Correlation with ESCS
OECD COUNTRIES															
Australia	9.9	(0.04)	−0.08	5.6	(0.21)	0.47	7.5	(0.17)	0.17	7.5	(0.08)	0.08	4.9	(0.13)	0.31
Austria	9.8	(0.07)	0.07	3.6	(0.20)	0.42	9.0	(0.18)	0.21	5.3	(0.09)	0.15	4.9	(0.10)	−0.03
Belgium	9.8	(0.10)	−0.09	4.5	(0.18)	0.40	3.1	(0.16)	0.49	3.9	(0.08)	0.56	4.8	(0.13)	0.30
Canada	9.7	(0.04)	0.03	5.2	(0.10)	0.28	6.8	(0.09)	0.18	6.5	(0.04)	0.18	4.9	(0.05)	0.27
Czech Republic	10.0	(0.02)	0.01	3.3	(0.15)	0.27	8.7	(0.16)	0.37	3.5	(0.11)	0.39	6.2	(0.11)	0.15
Denmark	10.0	(0.00)	m	2.8	(0.13)	0.31	6.0	(0.14)	0.22	7.9	(0.09)	0.21	6.5	(0.10)	0.16
Finland	10.0	(0.00)	m	2.4	(0.14)	0.38	8.3	(0.20)	−0.15	5.0	(0.09)	−0.13	4.6	(0.11)	0.22
France	m	m	m	m	m	m	m	m	m	m	m	m	m	m	m
Germany	9.9	(0.05)	0.00	4.2	(0.17)	0.44	6.3	(0.22)	0.48	4.4	(0.07)	−0.26	4.4	(0.10)	0.26
Greece	10.0	(0.00)	m	2.0	(0.10)	0.29	7.0	(0.00)		3.0	(0.09)	−0.18	2.9	(0.23)	−0.19
Hungary	10.0	(0.00)	m	3.5	(0.15)	0.19	9.7	(0.11)	0.01	4.4	(0.11)	0.38	6.2	(0.15)	0.01
Iceland	10.0	(0.01)	0.02	2.0	(0.18)	0.45	2.3	(0.24)	−0.02	6.1	(0.09)	−0.04	5.3	(0.16)	−0.02
Ireland	9.9	(0.09)	−0.27	4.1	(0.17)	0.31	9.5	(0.10)	0.09	4.2	(0.08)	0.21	4.8	(0.15)	0.17
Italy	10.0	(0.00)	m	3.9	(0.21)	0.05	8.6	(0.13)	0.33	3.5	(0.10)	0.03	5.6	(0.15)	0.17
Japan	10.0	(0.00)	m	7.3	(0.24)	0.30	9.8	(0.09)	−0.16	2.7	(0.15)	0.14	5.3	(0.16)	0.31
Korea	9.9	(0.03)	−0.08	7.3	(0.28)	0.56	7.7	(0.25)	−0.10	3.5	(0.12)	−0.06	5.7	(0.16)	0.41
Luxembourg	10.0	(0.00)	m	8.5	(0.49)	0.30	7.8	(0.29)	0.58	4.2	(0.14)	−0.44	3.7	(0.25)	−0.04
Mexico	8.1	(0.26)	−0.08	3.1	(0.25)	0.38	2.5	(0.22)	0.17	3.9	(0.12)	0.53	4.4	(0.17)	0.12
New Zealand	10.0	(0.00)	m	5.5	(0.26)	0.58	7.1	(0.17)	0.14	6.5	(0.11)	0.20	4.6	(0.13)	−0.09
Norway	10.0	(0.00)	m	1.0	(0.08)	0.41	4.4	(0.21)	0.22	6.7	(0.12)	0.08	4.6	(0.11)	−0.24
Poland	10.0	(0.02)	0.07	3.1	(0.30)	0.01	9.8	(0.06)	−0.01	4.7	(0.11)	0.37	5.2	(0.15)	0.30
Portugal	10.0	(0.00)	m	5.7	(0.25)	0.34	9.8	(0.09)	−0.06	4.8	(0.11)	−0.18	4.3	(0.12)	0.22
Spain	9.9	(0.03)	0.22	5.1	(0.19)	0.15	7.4	(0.15)	−0.02	3.9	(0.10)	0.35	5.4	(0.14)	0.47
Sweden	10.0	(0.02)	0.09	4.0	(0.20)	0.25	6.2	(0.27)	0.20	7.8	(0.11)	0.08	4.7	(0.12)	0.10
Switzerland	10.0	(0.03)	0.03	2.3	(0.14)	0.16	3.2	(0.20)	0.36	4.7	(0.08)	−0.02	5.3	(0.10)	0.14
United Kingdom	10.0	(0.03)	0.09	6.8	(0.16)	−0.28	8.0	(0.12)	−0.18	6.4	(0.06)	0.34	5.3	(0.12)	0.58
United States	10.0	(0.00)	−0.02	3.6	(0.24)	0.16	7.5	(0.26)	0.30	5.8	(0.10)	0.33	5.2	(0.11)	0.09
OECD average	*9.9*	*(0.01)*	*0.13*	*4.3*	*(0.02)*	*0.18*	*7.1*	*(0.02)*	*0.08*	*5.0*	*(0.01)*	*0.34*	*5.0*	*(0.01)*	*0.15*
NON-OECD COUNTRIES															
Brazil	6.8	(0.19)	0.23	5.6	(0.19)	−0.07	8.0	(0.16)	0.21	2.5	(0.08)	0.43	5.5	(0.13)	0.26
Liechtenstein	10.0	(0.00)	m	1.3	(0.51)	0.42	3.9	(1.16)	0.15	5.8	(0.27)	−0.24	4.3	(0.61)	0.03
Russian Federation	9.9	(0.05)	0.01	3.4	(0.21)	0.63	9.1	(0.12)	0.13	4.7	(0.06)	0.46	3.4	(0.14)	0.04
Netherlands[2]	10.0	(0.01)	−0.05	6.3	(0.31)	0.23	8.2	(0.30)	0.14	4.3	(0.13)	0.56	3.7	(0.14)	0.52

	Index of principals' perceptions of teachers' morale and commitment[1] (rescaled)			Index of school autonomy[1] (rescaled)			Index of teacher-student relations[1] (rescaled)			Index of disciplinary climate[1] (rescaled)			Index of achievement press[1] (rescaled)		
	Mean index	S.E.	Correlation with ESCS	Mean index	S.E.	Correlation with ESCS	Mean index	S.E.	Correlation with ESCS	Mean index	S.E.	Correlation with ESCS	Mean index	S.E.	Correlation with ESCS
OECD COUNTRIES															
Australia	5.1	(0.11)	0.23	5.9	(0.09)	0.39	6.1	(0.08)	0.21	4.8	(0.09)	0.21	5.7	(0.07)	0.14
Austria	6.4	(0.12)	−0.02	4.4	(0.09)	0.16	4.1	(0.14)	0.06	5.8	(0.14)	0.18	4.3	(0.13)	0.04
Belgium	4.5	(0.12)	0.28	5.8	(0.08)	−0.06	5.2	(0.11)	0.41	4.5	(0.10)	−0.13	4.3	(0.13)	0.52
Canada	5.2	(0.06)	0.10	5.7	(0.04)	0.13	5.8	(0.04)	0.24	4.3	(0.05)	0.18	5.9	(0.04)	0.07
Czech Republic	4.4	(0.09)	−0.04	7.8	(0.11)	−0.14	4.6	(0.13)	0.04	5.7	(0.14)	0.11	4.4	(0.13)	−0.10
Denmark	5.0	(0.11)	0.18	6.2	(0.11)	−0.10	5.8	(0.11)	0.37	4.2	(0.09)	0.15	5.2	(0.10)	−0.04
Finland	4.9	(0.12)	0.42	5.3	(0.12)	−0.29	5.7	(0.10)	−0.05	4.4	(0.11)	−0.04	5.7	(0.09)	−0.24
France	m	m	m	m	m	m	m	m	m	m	m	m	m	m	m
Germany	4.9	(0.12)	0.11	3.9	(0.09)	0.22	4.0	(0.12)	0.37	5.3	(0.12)	0.15	5.0	(0.09)	−0.12
Greece	5.7	(0.17)	0.16	3.1	(0.08)	0.07	4.3	(0.15)	−0.07	3.4	(0.11)	0.07	4.3	(0.14)	0.19
Hungary	5.9	(0.13)	−0.07	6.9	(0.11)	−0.14	5.4	(0.15)	−0.03	5.6	(0.17)	−0.08	5.7	(0.14)	−0.04
Iceland	5.3	(0.17)	0.27	6.5	(0.09)	−0.09	5.0	(0.14)	−0.06	5.0	(0.19)	−0.07	6.4	(0.11)	−0.01
Ireland	5.2	(0.17)	0.14	4.9	(0.10)	0.24	5.3	(0.11)	0.17	5.3	(0.11)	0.17	6.1	(0.06)	−0.03
Italy	3.7	(0.15)	0.07	2.4	(0.10)	0.13	4.5	(0.17)	0.36	3.5	(0.16)	0.43	5.9	(0.10)	0.04
Japan	4.7	(0.21)	0.36	5.4	(0.10)	0.14	3.6	(0.17)	0.52	6.3	(0.18)	0.58	0.9	(0.12)	0.04
Korea	4.1	(0.18)	0.17	4.6	(0.09)	0.15	5.2	(0.15)	−0.03	5.2	(0.12)	0.12	4.0	(0.15)	0.76
Luxembourg	5.0	(0.33)	0.26	3.7	(0.00)	−0.01	3.4	(0.26)	−0.02	5.5	(0.19)	−0.14	3.4	(0.22)	−0.20
Mexico	5.9	(0.17)	0.16	4.3	(0.14)	0.41	5.3	(0.12)	0.30	5.9	(0.12)	−0.33	4.7	(0.11)	0.27
New Zealand	5.0	(0.16)	0.24	6.7	(0.10)	−0.42	6.0	(0.08)	0.50	4.7	(0.14)	−0.36	6.0	(0.11)	0.51
Norway	5.1	(0.13)	−0.19	5.1	(0.00)		4.4	(0.15)	0.17	4.0	(0.15)	−0.22	5.1	(0.14)	0.06
Poland	3.8	(0.15)	0.51	5.1	(0.00)		2.9	(0.17)	0.03	6.1	(0.16)	0.12	5.7	(0.11)	0.51
Portugal	4.0	(0.16)	0.20	1.5	(0.11)	0.07	6.2	(0.09)	0.00	4.5	(0.07)	0.23	5.1	(0.09)	−0.05
Spain	4.5	(0.13)	0.39	3.8	(0.18)	0.31	5.0	(0.11)	0.22	4.3	(0.12)	0.43	5.0	(0.09)	0.14
Sweden	5.6	(0.13)	0.12	6.1	(0.10)	0.17	5.9	(0.09)	0.02	4.2	(0.13)	0.25	5.4	(0.11)	0.15
Switzerland	6.2	(0.11)	0.05	3.9	(0.13)	0.31	5.6	(0.11)	−0.06	6.2	(0.12)	0.09	4.9	(0.11)	−0.33
United Kingdom	5.4	(0.10)	0.45	6.5	(0.10)	0.20	6.1	(0.05)	0.35	5.3	(0.09)	0.49	6.3	(0.04)	0.07
United States	4.6	(0.13)	−0.09	5.6	(0.14)	0.34	5.8	(0.13)	0.42	5.4	(0.13)	0.42	6.0	(0.10)	0.20
OECD average	*5.0*	*(0.01)*	*0.13*	*5.0*	*(0.01)*	*0.21*	*5.0*	*(0.01)*	*0.14*	*5.0*	*(0.01)*	*0.01*	*5.1*	*(0.01)*	*0.18*
NON-OECD COUNTRIES															
Brazil	4.4	(0.10)	0.23	4.5	(0.12)	0.33	6.1	(0.06)	0.23	3.9	(0.08)	−0.05	5.0	(0.08)	0.23
Liechtenstein	5.1	(0.46)	0.27	3.2	(0.65)	0.29	5.3	(0.38)	0.02	6.6	(0.39)	0.08	4.8	(0.47)	−0.30
Russian Federation	4.3	(0.11)	0.35	3.6	(0.06)	−0.01	5.6	(0.09)	−0.18	6.7	(0.11)	0.21	5.9	(0.07)	−0.01
Netherlands[2]	4.6	(0.13)	0.19	6.7	(0.11)	−0.11	5.8	(0.18)	0.38	3.5	(0.14)	0.00	4.0	(0.14)	−0.17

Units marked in bold are statistically significant.
1. For the definitions of the indices, see Annex A1. For the methods used to rescale these indices, for the purpose of this table, see Box 8.3.
2. Response rate is too low to ensure comparability (see Annex A3).

Annex B2: Performance differences between the Flemish and French Communities of Belgium and the linguistic communities in Switzerland

In the case of Belgium and Switzerland, the sample design allows the results of PISA to be shown separately for sub-national entities. These are shown in Table B2.1.

Table B2.1
Performance differences between the Flemish and French Communities of Belgium and the linguistic communities in Switzerland

| | Mean | | Standard deviation | | Percentiles | | | | | | | | | | | |
| | | | | | 5th | | 10th | | 25th | | 75th | | 90th | | 95th | |
	Mean score	S.E.	S.D.	S.E.	Score	S.E.	Score	S.E.	Score	S.E.	Score	S.E.	Score	S.E.	Score	S.E.
Combined reading literacy scale																
Belgium (Fr.)	476	(7.2)	111	(3.6)	283	(12.3)	321	(11.8)	395	(10.4)	561	(5.6)	614	(4.6)	642	(5.8)
Belgium (Fl.)	532	(4.3)	96	(3.6)	348	(15.8)	396	(9.5)	476	(7.5)	601	(3.1)	644	(3.0)	668	(3.2)
Switzerland (German)	489	(5.2)	105	(2.2)	308	(6.8)	346	(6.2)	417	(7.1)	565	(5.6)	622	(6.6)	653	(6.2)
Switzerland (French)	512	(6.0)	89	(3.8)	353	(10.2)	391	(11.3)	452	(8.0)	576	(8.2)	622	(8.3)	647	(7.4)
Switzerland (Italian)	498	(16.4)	83	(8.7)	351	(16.9)	389	(16.0)	446	(19.6)	552	(24.4)	600	(28.6)	630	(36.0)
Combined reading / retrieving information scale																
Belgium (Fr.)	476	(7.9)	124	(3.7)	260	(13.9)	305	(12.4)	388	(11.1)	572	(5.7)	630	(6.0)	660	(5.5)
Belgium (Fl.)	545	(4.7)	107	(3.8)	340	(14.3)	397	(11.6)	483	(7.4)	621	(3.2)	671	(3.3)	698	(3.2)
Switzerland (German)	492	(5.4)	116	(2.4)	287	(7.6)	335	(6.9)	415	(6.8)	575	(5.4)	635	(5.8)	668	(7.1)
Switzerland (French)	518	(6.4)	101	(3.9)	337	(12.4)	381	(11.3)	452	(9.4)	589	(6.9)	641	(10.0)	670	(9.1)
Switzerland (Italian)	500	(17.4)	103	(9.3)	321	(30.2)	371	(21.7)	437	(12.2)	567	(25.8)	629	(32.4)	660	(32.9)
Combined reading / interpreting scale																
Belgium (Fr.)	482	(5.8)	107	(2.6)	300	(8.0)	337	(9.0)	403	(8.9)	563	(5.5)	617	(4.8)	646	(5.3)
Belgium (Fl.)	536	(4.3)	97	(3.6)	356	(13.5)	400	(10.0)	476	(6.6)	606	(2.9)	650	(3.2)	676	(2.8)
Switzerland (German)	491	(5.0)	103	(2.2)	314	(5.4)	350	(5.8)	420	(6.6)	565	(5.6)	621	(6.4)	652	(6.5)
Switzerland (French)	516	(6.2)	92	(3.8)	351	(14.4)	390	(10.7)	456	(7.9)	582	(8.6)	627	(7.8)	658	(10.3)
Switzerland (Italian)	496	(16.6)	85	(9.1)	348	(21.4)	391	(20.5)	444	(13.6)	552	(22.9)	603	(33.0)	629	(31.8)
Combined reading / reflection and evaluation scale																
Belgium (Fr.)	466	(9.1)	120	(6.8)	247	(27.6)	302	(18.6)	386	(13.2)	556	(6.2)	610	(5.5)	640	(6.5)
Belgium (Fl.)	521	(4.4)	103	(3.9)	324	(13.0)	379	(11.1)	465	(7.2)	593	(2.9)	639	(3.1)	666	(3.3)
Switzerland (German)	484	(5.8)	118	(2.5)	279	(9.3)	326	(7.2)	404	(7.9)	569	(6.8)	631	(6.9)	667	(6.8)
Switzerland (French)	500	(6.1)	95	(3.9)	333	(14.3)	377	(11.7)	439	(7.7)	566	(8.0)	618	(8.8)	651	(8.4)
Switzerland (Italian)	503	(20.4)	99	(5.1)	345	(26.6)	383	(19.9)	441	(20.6)	573	(21.8)	624	(23.5)	661	(33.7)
Combined mathematical literacy scale																
Belgium (Fr.)	491	(7.2)	109	(3.8)	301	(13.0)	340	(11.0)	415	(11.8)	572	(6.4)	626	(5.5)	653	(7.5)
Belgium (Fl.)	543	(4.6)	98	(4.0)	356	(18.8)	408	(13.8)	487	(6.8)	612	(3.9)	658	(4.6)	684	(4.2)
Switzerland (German)	525	(5.3)	102	(2.3)	344	(10.8)	386	(7.9)	459	(6.0)	599	(6.4)	651	(6.7)	681	(5.8)
Switzerland (French)	547	(7.1)	90	(4.8)	400	(14.4)	431	(9.9)	489	(9.0)	609	(10.6)	663	(10.5)	686	(12.6)
Switzerland (Italian)	525	(13.8)	91	(10.2)	371	(33.0)	422	(20.7)	481	(15.4)	584	(21.4)	628	(27.9)	658	(34.4)
Combined scientific literacy scale																
Belgium (Fr.)	467	(8.7)	122	(5.8)	253	(24.8)	299	(19.0)	383	(11.4)	560	(6.2)	620	(7.7)	652	(5.7)
Belgium (Fl.)	519	(4.2)	95	(3.4)	352	(12.0)	392	(9.2)	457	(6.9)	588	(3.6)	634	(3.2)	659	(3.6)
Switzerland (German)	492	(5.3)	99	(2.7)	329	(6.2)	362	(6.2)	423	(6.8)	562	(8.2)	619	(7.3)	649	(6.6)
Switzerland (French)	514	(7.3)	103	(4.8)	344	(15.9)	383	(11.5)	441	(11.3)	587	(10.9)	648	(12.6)	685	(16.0)
Switzerland (Italian)	483	(16.7)	94	(11.5)	316	(36.9)	368	(32.2)	428	(17.7)	539	(27.4)	605	(24.9)	632	(29.4)

ANNEX

THE DEVELOPMENT AND IMPLEMENTATION OF PISA: A COLLABORATIVE EFFORT

Annex C: The development and implementation of PISA – A collaborative effort

Introduction

PISA is a collaborative effort, bringing together scientific expertise from the participating countries, steered jointly by their governments on the basis of shared, policy-driven interests.

A Board of Participating Countries on which each country is represented determines, in the context of OECD objectives, the policy priorities for PISA and oversees adherence to these priorities during the implementation of the programme. This includes the setting of priorities for the development of indicators, for the establishment of the assessment instruments and for the reporting of the results.

Experts from participating countries also serve on working groups that are charged with linking policy objectives with the best internationally available technical expertise. By participating in these expert groups, countries ensure that: the instruments are internationally valid and take into account the cultural and educational contexts in OECD Member countries; the assessment materials have strong measurement properties; and the instruments place an emphasis on authenticity and educational validity.

Through National Project Managers, participating countries implement PISA at the national level subject to the agreed administration procedures. National Project Managers play a vital role in ensuring that the implementation of the survey is of high quality, and verify and evaluate the survey results, analyses, reports and publications.

The design and implementation of the surveys, within the framework established by the Board of Participating Countries, is the responsibility of the PISA consortium, referred to as the PISA Consortium, led by the Australian Council for Educational Research (ACER). Other partners in this consortium include the Netherlands National Institute for Educational Measurement (Citogroep), The National Institute for Educational Research in Japan (NIER), the Educational Testing Service in the United States (ETS), and WESTAT in the United States.

The OECD Secretariat has overall managerial responsibility for the programme, monitors its implementation on a day-to-day basis, acts as the secretariat for the Board of Participating Countries, builds consensus among countries and serves as the interlocutor between the Board of Participating Countries and the international consortium charged with the implementation of the activities. The OECD Secretariat also produces the indicators and analyses and prepares the international reports and publications in co-operation with the PISA consortium and in close consultation with Member countries both at the policy level (Board of Participating Countries) and at the level of implementation (National Project Managers).

The following lists the members of the various PISA bodies and the individual experts and consultants who have contributed to PISA.

Members of the PISA Board of Participating Countries

Chair: Eugene Owen

Australia: Wendy Whitham

Austria: Friedrich Plank

Belgium: Dominique Barthélémy, Christiane Blondin, Dominique Lafontaine, Liselotte van de Perre

Brazil: Maria Helena Guimarães de Castro

Canada: Satya Brink, Patrick Bussière, Dianne Pennock,

Czech Republic: Jan Koucky, Jana Strakova

Denmark: Birgitte Bovin

Finland: Ritva Jakku-Sihvonen

France: Gérard Bonnet

Germany: Jochen Schweitzer, Helga Hinke, Gudrun Stoltenberg

Greece: Vassilis Koulaidis

Hungary: Péter Vári

Iceland: Einar Gudmundsson

Ireland: Gerry Shiel

Italy: Chiara Croce, Elisabetta Midena, Benedetto Vertecchi

Japan: Ryo Watanabe

Korea: Kooghyang Ro

Luxembourg: Jean-Paul Reeff

Mexico: Fernando Córdova Calderón

Netherlands: Arnold Spee

New Zealand: Lynne Whitney

Norway: Alette Schreiner

Poland: Kazimierz Korab

Portugal: Glória Ramalho

Spain: Guillermo Gil

Sweden: Anders Auer, Birgitta Fredander, Anita Wester

Switzerland: Heinz Gilomen

United Kingdom: Lorna Bertrand, Brian Semple

United States: Mariann Lemke

PISA National Project Managers

Australia: Jan Lokan

Austria: Günter Haider

Belgium: Dominique Lafontaine, Luc van de Poele

Brazil: Tereza Cristina Cotta, Maria Lucia Guardia, Maria Inês Pestana

Canada: Marc Lachance, Dianne Pennock

Czech Republic: Jana Straková

Denmark: Vita Bering Pruzan

Finland: Jouni Välijärvi

France: Jean-Pierre Jeantheau

Germany: Juergen Baumert, Petra Stanat

Greece: Katerina Kassotakis

Hungary: Peter Vari

Iceland: Julius Bjornsson, Ragna Benedikta Garðarsdóttir

Ireland: Judith Cosgrove

Italy: Emma Nardi

Japan: Ryo Watanabe

Korea: Kooghyang Ro

Latvia: Andris Kangro

Luxembourg: Iris Blanke, Jean-Paul Reeff

Mexico: Fernando Córdova Calderón

Netherlands: Johan Wijnstra

New Zealand: Steve May

Norway: Svein Lie

Poland: Michal Federowicz

Portugal: Glória Ramalho

Spain: Guillermo Gil

Sweden: Bengt-Olov Molander, Astrid Pettersson, Karin Taube

Switzerland: Huguette McCluskey

United Kingdom: Baljit Gill, Graham Thorpe

United States: Ghedam Bairu, Marilyn Binkley

OECD Secretariat

Andreas Schleicher (overall co-ordination of PISA and Member country relations)

Claudia Tamassia (project management)

Eric Charbonnier (statistical support)

Hannah Cocks (statistical support)

Juliet Evans (administrative support)

PISA Expert Groups

Mathematics Functional Expert Group

Jan de Lange (Chair) (Utrecht University, The Netherlands)

Raimondo Bolletta (Istituto Nazionale di Valutazione, Italy)

Sean Close (St Patrick's College, Ireland)

Maria Luisa Moreno (IES "Lope de Vega", Spain)

Mogens Niss (IMFUFA, Roskilde University, Denmark)

Kyungmee Park (Hongik University, Korea)

Thomas A. Romberg (United States)

Peter Schüller (Federal Ministry of Education and Cultural Affairs, Austria)

Reading Functional Expert Group

Irwin Kirsch (Chair) (Educational Testing Service, United States)

Marilyn Binkley (National Center for Educational Statistics, United States)

Alan Davies (University of Edinburgh, United Kingdom)

Stan Jones (Statistics Canada, Canada)

John de Jong (Language Testing Services, The Netherlands)

Dominique Lafontaine (Université de Liège Sart Tilman, Belgium)

Pirjo Linnakylä (University of Jyväskylä, Finland)

Martine Rémond (Institut National de Recherche Pédagogique, France)

Wolfgang Schneider (University of Würzburg, Germany)

Ryo Watanabe (National Institute for Educational Research, Japan)

Science Functional Expert Group

Wynne Harlen (Chair) (University of Bristol, United Kingdom)

Peter Fensham (Monash University, Australia)

Raul Gagliardi (University of Geneva, Switzerland)

Svein Lie (University of Oslo, Norway)

Manfred Prenzel (Universität Kiel, Germany)

Senta A. Raizen (National Center for Improving Science Education (NCISE), United States)

Donghee Shin (DankooK University, Korea)

Elizabeth Stage (University of California, United States)

PISA Technical Advisory Group

Ray Adams (ACER, Australia)

Pierre Foy (Statistics Canada, Canada)

Aletta Grisay (Belgium)

Larry Hedges (The University of Chicago, United States)

Eugene Johnson (American Institutes for Research, United States)

John de Jong (Language Testing Services, The Netherlands)

Geoff Masters (ACER, Australia)

Keith Rust (WESTAT, United States)

Norman Verhelst (Citogroep, The Netherlands)

J. Douglas Willms (University of New Brunswick, Canada)

PISA Consortium

Australian Council for Educational Research

Ray Adams (Project Director of the PISA Consortium)

Alla Berezner (data processing, data analysis)

Claus Carstensen (data analysis)

Lynne Darkin (reading test development)

Brian Doig (mathematics test development)

Adrian Harvey-Beavis (quality monitoring, questionnaire development)

Kathryn Hill (reading test development)

John Lindsey (mathematics test development)

Jan Lokan (quality monitoring, field procedures development)

Le Tu Luc (data processing)

Greg Macaskill (data processing)

Joy McQueen (reading test development and reporting)

Gary Marks (questionnaire development)

Juliette Mendelovits (reading test development and reporting)

Christian Monseur (Director of the PISA Consortium for data processing, data analysis, quality monitoring)

Gayl O'Connor (science test development)

Alla Routitsky (data processing)

Wolfram Schulz (data analysis)

Ross Turner (test analysis and reporting co-ordination)

Nikolai Volodin (data processing)

Craig Williams (data processing, data analysis)

Margaret Wu (Deputy Project Director of the PISA Consortium)

Westat

Nancy Caldwell (Director of the PISA Consortium for field operations and quality monitoring)

Ming Chen (sampling and weighting)

Fran Cohen (sampling and weighting)

Susan Fuss (sampling and weighting)

Brice Hart (sampling and weighting)

Sharon Hirabayashi (sampling and weighting)

Sheila Krawchuk (sampling and weighting)

Dward Moore (field operations and quality monitoring)

Phu Nguyen (sampling and weighting)

Monika Peters (field operations and quality monitoring)

Merl Robinson (field operations and quality monitoring)

Keith Rust (Director of the PISA Consortium for sampling and weighting)

Leslie Wallace (sampling and weighting)

Dianne Walsh (field operations and quality monitoring)

Trevor Williams (questionnaire development)

Citogroep

Steven Bakker (science test development)

Bart Bossers (reading test development)

Truus Decker (mathematics test development)

Erna van Hest (reading test development and quality monitoring)

Kees Lagerwaard (mathematics test development)

Gerben van Lent (mathematics test development)

Ico de Roo (science test development)

Maria van Toor (office support and quality monitoring)

Norman Verhelst (technical advice, data analysis)

Educational Testing Service

Irwin Kirsch (reading test development)

Other experts

Cordula Artelt (questionnaire development)

Marc Demeuse (quality monitoring)

Harry Ganzeboom (questionnaire development)

Aletta Grisay (technical advice, data analysis, translation, questionnaire development)

Donald Hirsch (editorial review)

Jules Peschar (questionnaire development)

Erich Ramseier (questionnaire development)

Gundula Schumel (questionnaire development)

Marie-Andrée Somers (data analysis and reporting)

Peter Sutton (editorial review)

Rich Tobin (questionnaire development and reporting)

J. Douglas Willms (questionnaire development, data analysis and reporting)

OECD PUBLICATIONS, 2, rue André-Pascal, 75775 PARIS CEDEX 16
PRINTED IN FRANCE
(96 2001 14 1 P) ISBN 92-64-19671-4 – No. 52233 2001

ERRATUM

1. Page 154, Figure 6.5 Correction of label:

Latvia should not be included in the lower part of this figure. The corrected section is shown below:

Percentage of students who speak a language at home most of the time that is different from the language of assessment, from other official languages or from other national dialects (left scale) and performance of students on the combined reading literacy scale by language group (right scale)

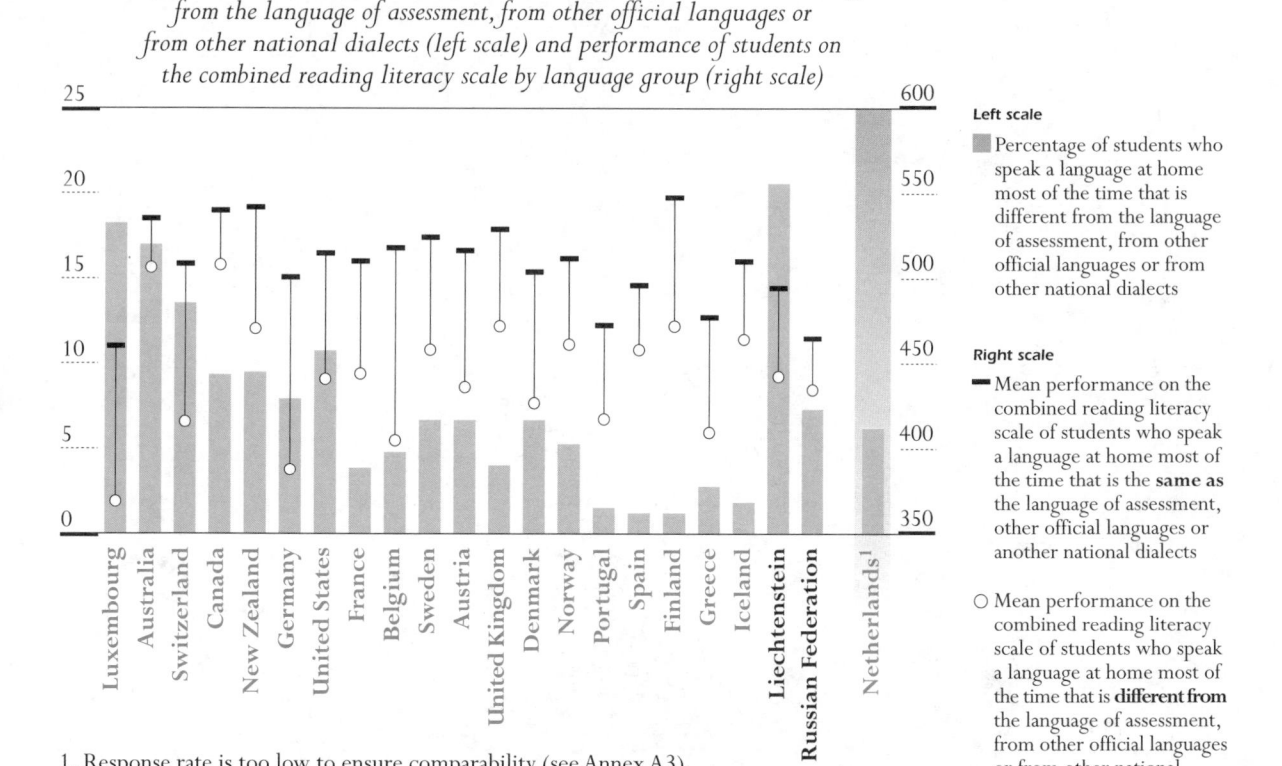

Left scale

■ Percentage of students who speak a language at home most of the time that is different from the language of assessment, from other official languages or from other national dialects

Right scale

▬ Mean performance on the combined reading literacy scale of students who speak a language at home most of the time that is the **same as** the language of assessment, other official languages or another national dialects

○ Mean performance on the combined reading literacy scale of students who speak a language at home most of the time that is **different from** the language of assessment, from other official languages or from other national dialects

1. Response rate is too low to ensure comparability (see Annex A3).
Source: OECD PISA database, 2001. Table 6.10.

2. Page 306, Table 7.12 Correction of title (marked in bold):

Percentage of students enrolled in schools in which teachers have **the main** responsibility for the following aspects of school policy and management.